Therapeutic Activities for Children and Teens Coping with Health Issues

Robyn Hart and Judy Rollins

JOHN WILEY & SONS, INC

Library of Congress Cataloging-in-Publication Data:
Hart, Robyn, author.
  Therapeutic activities for children and teens coping with health issues / Robyn Hart and Judy Rollins.
    p. ; cm.
  Includes bibliographical references and index.
  ISBN 978-0-470-55500-2 (paper : alkaline paper); 978-0-470-93352-7 (ePDF); 978-0-470-93353-4; (eMobi); 978-0-470-93354-1; (ePub)
  1. Play therapy. 2. Child psychotherapy. 3. Adolescent psychotherapy. 4. Patients—Psychology. I. Rollins, Judy, 1943– author. II. Title.
  [DNLM: 1. Child Psychology. 2. Play Therapy—methods. 3. Adolescent Psychology. 4. Mental Disorders—therapy.
5. Patients—psychology. WS 350.4]
  RJ505.P6.H37 2011
  618.92′891653—dc22   2010045669

Printed in the United States of America
10 9 8 7 6 5 4 3 2

To our husbands, Steve Koress and Mike Rollins, who fortunately for us,
had the both the artistic and technical skills and willingness to contribute so enormously to this book.

CONTENTS

3   Self-Esteem   45

4   Body Image   69

Note: Asterisk (*) denotes that the activity is available on the CD that accompanies this book.

FOREWORD

As a parent you wish the best for your children—good health, happiness, love, prosperity. But life is often a roller-coaster ride, with unexpected turns and dips. It has a way of throwing us curve balls, and when it comes to our children's health, sometimes the outcome can be traumatic for the child, the parent, or both.

Even when children visit a doctor for wellness checkups, they may become anxious and stressed by the visit. Many aspects of the visit with the doctor can be threatening or uncomfortable, from being held by unfamiliar people and having their movement restricted to receiving shots. Such routine visits can have long-term effects of anxiety and stress on the child. Depending on the developmental stage of the child, his or her understanding and reaction to the everyday experience of a doctor's visit may become confusing and difficult to understand.

When children have to be hospitalized, undergo surgery, or cope with a chronic congenital medical problem, the stress and anxiety associated with their treatment, coupled with separation from their parents, homes, schools, and familiar surroundings are magnified exponentially. The long-term impact can be substantial, not only on the children but on the parents as well. Children, and even teens, may have difficulty understanding the complex medical procedures and events that are occurring or that they will be experiencing. Their ability to communicate their pain and hurt can be significantly limited, and their conceptualization of why such things are happening to them may become distorted and confused.

I am reminded of my earliest memory as a child of 5, being left overnight in a hospital, along with my brother, to have our tonsils out. Alone, without our parents, we were placed in a ward of screaming and crying children, all of us scared and confused as to why we were there. The next day I woke up in a strange bed, unable to talk, unable to make my needs known or to express my fear. All I could do was cry. The trauma of the separation, the strangeness of the people, and the intrusive medical procedures happening to me remain fixed in my memory to this day. In contrast, the hospital experience of my youngest son, Seth, was light years better. At age 2 years, he needed to go into the hospital to have same-day surgery for bilateral myringotomies (incisions in the eardrums) and tubes put into his ears to stop his chronic ear infections. He and I met the anesthesiologist a day before the surgery. The doctor explained what would happen, showed my son the stethoscope, mask, and monitor he would use, and allowed him time to play with them. The day of the surgery, my son chose his teddy bear to accompany him. Both his father and I were allowed to accompany him down to the surgical door—but only Teddy could go with him into the surgery. We were notified once the surgery was over, and were permitted to come down to the recovery area to be there when Seth awoke. The nurse had put cotton on both of Teddy's ears, and taped them, to show Seth that Teddy had also had his own "surgery." We were allowed to remain with our son for the few hours he needed to stay in the hospital before coming home to sleep off the anesthesia. Today, the experience is hardly a memory for our son, who was able to play out his experience afterwards, and felt comforted throughout the medical experience by caring and supportive staff and the presence of his parents.

No one wants to see a child in pain or upset or feeling helpless in the face of medical procedures. We want to be able to offer support and emotional comfort. We want to have the tools necessary to use in our therapeutic work as play therapists, child life specialists, nurses, teachers, and parents. *Therapeutic Activities for Children and Teens Coping with Health Issues* is one of those tools—really, an entire toolkit of resources.

It has long been recognized that play is the work of children, the means through which they process difficult experiences. Allowing a child to play is one of the most powerful and effective ways to lower children's stress and increase empowerment. More specifically, play is a means through which children act out and process unpleasant experiences and minimize the resulting negative psychological impact. We know from research and the abundance of available writings that play has therapeutic and healing properties. We also can gain valuable insight into children's emotional states through their play. When a child feels safe enough to express and play out a variety of feelings, the negative feelings brought on by past and/or current unpleasant medical experiences can be processed. Most children need very little encouragement to participate in dramatic medical play and play-based activities. Children are readily drawn into play situations, because play is their most natural and major means of communication. Through play, trained child play therapists and child life specialists are able to encourage children and teens with medical issues to talk, interact, and process their feelings and concerns, along with helping them to sort out their perceptions, understanding, and knowledge of what is going on. Medical dramatic play opens for the play therapist a window into the child's feelings, through which he or she can help provide and reinforce correct information about medical care.

The power of play through planned medical play activities is that it allows children to participate actively in a learning process that helps them better understand what has happened, or is happening, to them, and/or become familiar with impending procedures. Dramatic medical play gives children the chance to handle various pieces of medical equipment and provides opportunities for rehearsing, becoming desensitized to, and expressing feelings related to the medical experience. In this way, play can become an empowering experience, one that helps build self-esteem and allow self-expression for children.

Robyn Hart and Judy Rollins deeply understand the power of play and humor in helping children and teens to heal. They offer the reader hundreds of evidence-based and age-appropriate therapeutic activities that have been designed specifically for use with children who are hospitalized or are in the healthcare system. They cover every angle of the myriad issues facing children, teens, and their parents who are dealing with medical issues. *Therapeutic Activities for Children and Teens Coping with Health Issues* is useful not only for hospitalized children, but also for those in residential treatment and victims of sexual and physical abuse. Topics such as dealing with separation anxiety, self-esteem, body image, death, isolation, pain, aggression, physical handicaps, immobilization, and desensitization to medical procedures are tackled in an easy-to-read manner. The authors have a solid grasp on key issues, such as the benefits and usefulness of humor, the importance that culture has on understanding medical procedures, and how to relate and modify therapy approaches to accommodate group settings as well as the individual child's developmental level. They also explain the rationale behind each of the practical play-based therapeutic activities. A rich compendium of therapeutic activities are offered, along with the age range each is appropriate to, the materials needed, special precautions and limitations to their application, and easy-to-follow directions for their implementation. With approximately 15 to 20 activities per chapter, therapists, child life specialists, and nurses, as well as parents and teachers, have at their fingertips hundreds of therapeutic activities to choose from, for both individual and group work.

Oh, how I wish the doctors and nurses had this book when I was little. How glad I am that such a volume is available today to help the thousands of children and teens coping with health issues, who can benefit from the therapeutic activities!

So, dear reader, sit back and enjoy. This will become a much-used book in your professional library!

Athena A. Drewes, PsyD, RPT-S
Director of Clinical Training and APA-Accredited Internship
Astor Services for Children & Families
Poughkeepsie, New York

PREFACE

As the science and technology of pediatric medical care continue to advance, so too has awareness of the integral connection between children's physical health and mental well-being. We know that children who receive psychosocial interventions in managing hospitalization and other stressful, potentially traumatic healthcare experiences do better in both short-term coping and long-term psychological adjustment. Research tells us that these interventions can improve physical outcomes, as well. Evidence exists that appropriate and timely psychosocial care may help contain costs by reducing hospital length of stay, decrease the need for analgesics, and promote cooperation during procedures—important considerations in today's financially driven healthcare environment.

Around the globe, those who care for children increasingly acknowledge the growing need to address psychosocial issues. Enormous changes have occurred in our understanding of the range of children's psychosocial needs, the implications of culture in how healthcare is provided and received, treatment techniques, and where care is provided. These complex psychosocial issues have amplified the need for child life specialists, play specialists, and mental health professionals in children's medical settings, and challenged nurses and other healthcare professionals to apply the same high standards they use when providing physical care, to the emotional care they deliver to children.

Theoretically sound, evidenced-based resources are urgently needed to address this developing movement. *Therapeutic Activities for Children and Teens Coping with Health Issues* builds and expands on the first author's book, *Therapeutic Play Activities for Hospitalized Children* (1992). We have revised chapters from the earlier book and added five new chapters incorporating different approaches, such as humor, and expanded topics, including grief, separation, and culture. In response to the increasing challenge of transitioning pediatric patients to adult care, we have included a chapter on teaching activities, as well. With today's emphasis on evidence-based practice, we also have expanded the chapter introductions to include more theory and research, to meet the needs of students who are bridging theory to practice, and the needs of experienced practitioners who wish to keep abreast of current research on psychosocial care.

More than 200 practical, evidence-based, age-appropriate activities and useful ideas for interventions that promote coping are logically organized around therapeutic goals that target specific issues children face, whether as a result of their own health issues or those of a loved one. The activities can be quickly read, easily understood, and readily implemented in a variety of settings.

Our goal for this practical reference is to assist mental health practitioners, students, and members of the pediatric healthcare team—including parents—in understanding and, more importantly, implementing culturally sensitive, evidence-based, inexpensive activities within the context and challenges of today's dynamic healthcare environment. We hope, too, that the activities will inspire others to develop additional exciting activities to help in the important work of humanizing healthcare experiences for children and their families.

Robyn Hart
Judy Rollins

ACKNOWLEDGMENTS

We gratefully acknowledge the coauthors of this book's predecessor, *Therapeutic Play Activities for Hospitalized Children*: Marcia Powell, Patricia Mather, and, sadly, the late Jeanne M. Slack. They helped lay the foundation for our continued work in this area.

We sincerely thank Alison Spicer, Maggie Leininger, Abby Csanda, Paul Sznewajs, and others from Snow City Arts, who inspire us and have enhanced this book by sharing their knowledge, talents, and incredibly innovative approaches to working with sick children. We acknowledge the influence of the late Donna Wong, whose firm commitment to evidence-based practice provided the motivation to seek a sound research foundation to support this book's activities and recommendations.

Credits for photography go to Steven Koress, Michael Rollins, and Abby Csanda. We sincerely appreciate their contributions and their helping to bring our book to life.

We also express our appreciation to the many child life specialists, nurses, other healthcare professionals, and students who have generously shared their wisdom and creative ideas through conference presentations, list-serve postings, and personal communications.

We are especially indebted to the people at John Wiley & Sons, who provided us with this opportunity. A special thank-you to Isabel Pratt, editor, who first believed in our idea and offered encouragement and patience throughout the writing process.

INTRODUCTION

Hospitalization and other healthcare experiences can be difficult for children, both physically and emotionally. Fortunately, accompanying these changes is a growing body of knowledge of therapeutic interventions that caring adults can use to help children cope more effectively with these experiences.

The purpose of this introduction is not to review children's healthcare literature in depth, but to describe the major issues that form the theoretical framework for the activities in this book. Tips for working with special populations also are included, to assist the reader in using the activities in a variety of settings. Please note that throughout the book the term *children* is used to include children and adolescents, unless otherwise specified.

Today, a child's encounter with the healthcare system can take many forms. Some experiences, such as a scheduled well-child visit to the doctor's office for immunizations, are planned; others, such as an unexpected trip to the emergency department for an injury incurred on the football field, are not. Encounters may be short and time-limited, such as those required to deal with the acute demands of a case of the flu or appendicitis; others, such as those associated with heart disease, diabetes, cystic fibrosis, or cerebral palsy, typically demand a lifetime of frequent and often lengthy contact with the healthcare system.

Some children who are ill or injured are likely to experience several phases of care, which vary from child to child depending on diagnosis and individual needs. The progression through these phases is called the *continuum of care* (Olson, 1999). Children may enter the continuum at different points, and will not necessarily experience all phases of care. Each phase has its own set of stressors and psychosocial considerations (see Table I.1). Also, considerations within the phases themselves influence children's responses. For example, a child's admission to an acute care setting could be emergent or planned; family members may be accommodated (e.g., a bed for a parent at child's bedside) or not.

These situational factors need to be considered when predicting the specific stressors and the impact of the healthcare experience on each child. However, other considerations play an equally important role.

Children's Understanding of Illness

The meaning children assign to being ill will influence the impact their healthcare experiences have on them. Meaning varies by age, and depends on the child's cognitive ability and level of knowledge (Hockenberry & Wilson, 2007). Young children 2 to 7 years perceive an external, unrelated, concrete phenomenon as the cause of their illness or that illness occurred by "magic." Children 7 to 10-plus years perceive the cause as a person, an object, or an action external to them that is "bad" or "harmful" to the body. Children 13 years and older perceive the cause as a malfunctioning or nonfunctioning organ or process, and understand that illness may occur from several causes. For detailed information about developmental aspects of children's understanding of illness, see Chapter 14, "Teaching."

Although previous experience of illness can influence the impact of a healthcare encounter, some research indicates that medical experience variables (i.e., duration of medical condition, total hospitalization days, higher life-threat medical conditions) are not significant predictors of children's illness concepts (Kury & Rodrigue, 1995). Thus, care should be taken to guard against overestimating the illness concepts of children with prior medical experience. However, others claim that children's understanding of illness can relate to previous experiences and the severity of the illness. For example, Yoos and McMullen (1996) reported that children with asthma can understand their illness as a fatal disease, with risk of dying from lack of air. Further, children can understand far more about their illness experience when they are given proper explanations.

Table I.1 Phases of Care and Selected Considerations

Phase	Selected Considerations
1. Identification of illness or injury	Sudden or prolonged Part of routine health examination, or trauma treatment Required immediate attention, or during scheduled appointment Chronic or life-threatening or acute and treatable
2. Urgent care	Familiar care provider in familiar surroundings, or unfamiliar care provider in strange surroundings
3. Emergent care	Transported in familiar mode (family car) by family member, or unfamiliar mode (ambulance, helicopter) by unknown healthcare providers Family available or not Retained at original facility, or transferred to another facility with required specialty or pediatric expertise Trauma or illness
4. Acute care setting within a hospital	Emergent or planned admission Pediatric or adult hospital Placed with age mates or by diagnosis Family members accommodated (e.g., cot for parent at bedside) or not
5. Intensive care	Transfer planned or unplanned Sedated, versus alert/aware Familiar primary care provider continues involvement, or total transfer to pediatric specialty Family members welcomed or not
6. Intermediate care	Transferred from higher level of care (intensive care, with family accustomed to close monitoring of child), or from lower level of care (outpatient facility) Transfer decision accommodated family's readiness, or dictated by the facility
7. Rehabilitation	Transferred to unit within present facility or to a different facility Rehabilitation included in medical insurance benefits, or not covered Purpose to gain limited skills or strength, or to return to previous level of function
8. Outpatient specialty care	Occurred as part of diagnostic workup, or as part of recovery and follow-up care Involved surgical/invasive procedures, or noninvasive monitoring Involved preparation at home before arrival, or no preparation Involved follow-up instructions for home care, or follow-up home care not required
9. Home care	Initiated with previous hospitalization or not Included multiple care providers or a limited number of familiar care providers
10. Transition from acute to chronic illness	Expected or unexpected (e.g., occurred over time due to recurrence of health problem or natural course of disease, or as a complication of illness or injury) Response of child and family to diagnosis and treatment focus similar to response to acute illness, or different

Note. Adapted from Nehring, W. (1999). Chronic conditions: The continuum of care. In M. Broome & J. Rollins (Eds.), *Core curriculum for the nursing care of children and their families* (pp. 331–341). Pitman, NJ: Jannetti Publications, Inc. Reprinted with permission.

Hospitalization

Children who are hospitalized must confront hospitalization stressors, as well as those related to their illness or injury. In recent years, with the average hospital stay for children at 3–1/2 days (Owen, Thompson, Elixhauser, & Ryan, 2003), lengthy hospitalizations are rare. However, with increasingly sophisticated transplant technology and other advances in treatment for certain chronic or life-threatening conditions, we see some children hospitalized for many months, often with a good portion of that stay in isolation, to protect their fragile immune systems. Thus, for many children, the experience is not only lengthy but also very intense. Although necessary for adequate medical care, prolonged hospitalizations change the physical and emotional environment, disciplinary context, schooling, and family life (Pao, Ballard, & Rosenstein, 2007).

Hospitalization is difficult for anyone but is especially so for the developing child (Pearson, 2005). Rarely are children permitted to refuse treatments, medications, and procedures, and "things" are constantly being "done" to them. They are asked to "hold still" for painful procedures that they may not understand, and often are left feeling powerless and confused. Being placed in passive roles with limited opportunities to make meaningful choices, children's emotions are often intense and confusing (Rollins, 2005a).

The hospital environment seethes with the unfamiliar. An older study reveals that children see many strangers, typically more than 50 in their first 24 hours of hospitalization (Johnson, 1975). This figure likely remains fairly accurate today. There are other strange sights, sounds, smells, and tastes—any of which can be frightening if the child does not know what they are. Being touched in the hospital, while often comforting, also can be a source of discomfort and confusion, especially when children are examined in areas of their bodies they have been told never to let strangers touch (Rollins, 2008).

A recent study of 4- to 6-year-old children revealed that more than 90% of the children were afraid of at least one aspect of being in a hospital (Salmela, Salanterä, & Aronen, 2009). Most involved fears of nursing interventions, fears of being a patient, and fears related to the developmental age of the child. Also mentioned were fears caused by the unfamiliar environment or lack of information; child-staff relations; and the physical, social, and symbolic environment. In a study with hospitalized school-agers, children ages 7 to 14 years identified a range of fears and concerns, which included separation from parents and family, unfamiliar environment, investigations and treatments, and loss of self-determination (Coyne, 2006).

The dignity of hospitalized children has become a topic of discussion in recent years, even though a clear definition of the term is lacking (Reed, Smith, Fletcher, & Bradding, 2003, p. 67): "Dignity is a slippery concept most easily understood when it has been lost." However, research confirms that children's privacy and dignity are not always respected in hospitals (Rylance, 1999), which for some children might be the most difficult stressor of all.

The most practical guide to understanding the ways children respond to the stressors of illness and hospitalization is knowledge of the child's developmental stage. For a summary of developmental stage-related issues of concern and possible responses, see Table I.2. Due to their rapid development, infants and toddlers are two of the age groups at highest risk for the negative effects of hospitalization.

Child Variables

In addition to developmental stage, the ways a child responds to healthcare experiences are influenced by individual characteristics of the child, such as cognitive ability, age, gender, and temperament. Other factors that may have an impact include the child's previous experience with illness, separation, or hospitalization; innate or acquired coping skills; seriousness of the diagnosis; and available support systems.

Cognitive Ability and Age

How children respond to the stress of hospitalization and illness may be in part determined by their determination of the seriousness of the stress and what is at stake. An individual's response to a stressor is a function of two sequentially linked cognitive processes: *primary appraisal* and *secondary appraisal* (Lazarus & Folkman, 1984). In primary appraisal the stressor is interpreted as a threat, as harmful, or as a challenge. Next, a secondary appraisal is made in which the individual decides whether he or she has the coping resources to deal effectively with the stressor. Studies suggest that negative appraisals (i.e., threat, harmful) are associated with negative psychological and physical adjustment, whereas positive appraisals (i.e., challenges) are associated with positive psychological and physical adjustment (Roesch, Weiner, & Vaughn, 2002).

One can assume that a child's cognitive ability plays a role in these appraisals. Perhaps the most significant determination that applies to *all* children's cognitive ability was mentioned earlier: their developmental level, which may or may not match the child's chronological age. Research findings are inconclusive, with some studies finding no association between a child's age and response to hospitalization, postbehavioral upset, anxiety, or fear; and others indicating

Table I.2 Under-standing Children Who Are Hospitalized: A Developmental Perspective

Hospitalization Issues	Possible Troublesome Responses
Infant (0–1 Year)	
Separation Lack of stimulation Pain	Failure to bond Distrust Anxiety Delayed skills development
Toddler (1–3 years)	
Separation Fear of bodily injury and pain Frightening fantasies Immobility or restriction Forced regression Loss of routine and rituals	Regression (including loss of newly learned skills) Uncooperativeness Protest (verbal and physical) Despair Negativism Temper tantrums Resistance
Preschooler (3–6 years)	
Separation Fear of loss of control; sense of own power Fear of bodily mutilation or penetration by surgery or injections; castration	Regression Anger toward primary caregiver Acting out Protest (less aggressive than toddler) Despair and detachment Physical and verbal aggression Dependency Withdrawal
School-ager (6–12 years)	
Separation Fear of loss of control Fear of loss of mastery Fear of bodily mutilation Fear of bodily injury and pain, especially intrusive procedures in genital area Fear of illness itself, disability, and death	Regression Inability to complete some tasks Uncooperativeness Withdrawal Depression Displaced anger and hostility Frustration
Adolescent (12–18 years)	
Dependence on adults Separation from family and peers Fear of bodily injury and pain Fear of loss of identity Body image and sexuality Concern about peer group status after hospitalization	Uncooperativeness Withdrawal Anxiety Depression

Note. Adapted from Rollins, J., & Mahan, C. (2010). *From artist to artist-in-residence: Preparing artists to work in pediatric healthcare settings* (2nd ed.). Washington, DC: Rollins & Associates. Reprinted with permission.

that younger children are more likely to be anxious and fearful compared to older children, and less likely to feel in control of their health (Koller, 2008a).

Gender

It is uncertain whether or not gender has an effect on a child's response to hospitalization. An older study (Tiedeman & Clatworthy, 1990) reported that boys tended to be more anxious than girls at admission, discharge, and postdischarge; more recent studies found that girls were more anxious than boys (Rennick, Johnston, Dougherty, Platt, & Ritchie, 2002; Small & Melnyck, 2006).

Temperament

Temperament is an individual's consistent and stable pattern of behavior or reaction, one that persists across time, activity, and context. A child's temperament accounts for as much as 50% of the variance in his or her behavioral responses prior to and up to one month after hospitalization (McClowry, 1990). Children who tend to be more positive in mood, more predictable, easier to distract, more approachable, and adaptable while being less reactive to stimuli seem to respond better to healthcare experiences than children who are more passive (Helgadottir & Wilson, 2004).

Whether or not a child's previous experience with hospitalization increases his or her ability to cope is unclear. Some studies have found no association between the number of previous hospitalizations and behavior problems (McClowry, 1991), or level of anxiety or coping experienced by the child (Lowery Thompson, 1994). However, Tiedeman and Clatworthy (1990) reported that children with no previous hospital experience were more anxious than those who had been hospitalized before, which suggests the potential benefits of being familiar with the hospital setting. Kyle (2008) points out that the defining factor may be whether previous experiences were positive or negative.

Previous Experience with Hospitalization

Coping style is the individual's cognitive, affective, or behavioral responses to stress. Individuals tend to be either blunters (information avoidant) or monitors (information seeking) (Miller, 1991). Blunters restrict their thoughts about an upcoming event, deny their worries, and detach from stressful stimuli. Monitors seek out detailed information and are alert to stressful stimuli. Optimal coping appears to occur when there is a match between level of information provided and the patient's preferred style. Monitors tend to fare better when provided with detailed information and enhanced self-efficacy expectations; blunters, in contrast, tend to fare better when provided with minimal information (Miller, Fang, Diefenbach, & Bales, 2001).

Coping Style and Strategies

Spirito, Stark, and Tyc (1994) found that acutely ill/injured children were more likely to use avoidant-coping strategies than chronically ill children. LaMontagne, Hepworth, Johnson, and Cohen (1996) report an association between the monitor's vigilant coping style and a timely return to normal activities over the course of recovery.

Children have a vast array of coping strategies. Ryan-Wenger's (1992) synthesis of research of coping strategies used by primarily healthy children led to the development of a taxonomy of 15 mutually exclusive categories, ranging from aggressive activities to stressor modification. A child's repertoire of coping strategies is the same during health and illness, but the frequency or effectiveness of some of the strategies is often quite different (Ryan-Wenger, 1996).

Parental anxiety is strongly related to children's adverse responses during hospitalization. Maternal anxiety can be used to predict both children's emotional distress and children's distress during invasive procedures. Small and Melnyk (2006) found that high levels of maternal state anxiety significantly increased a child's likelihood to engage in negative behaviors such as hyperactivity and aggression. A mother's anxiety also has been found to mediate the positive effect of an intervention on hospitalized children's posthospital behavior (Mazurek Melnyk & Feinstein, 2001).

Family Response and Support

It seems reasonable to assume that having a supportive parent present could have a significant influence on a child's ability to cope with healthcare experiences, especially for younger children where the issue of separation is paramount. Yet, in an early study, Shaw and Routh (1982) rated the behavior of children receiving an injection with their mothers present as more negative than that of children whose mothers were absent. For many years, findings from this study, along with anecdotal evidence, resulted in healthcare providers banishing parents from treatment rooms. However, in discussing the findings of the study, the researchers concluded that children might feel more comfortable protesting during a procedure when a parent is present. In a later, randomized controlled study of children undergoing venipuncture, both children and parents exhibited less distress when the parent was present (Wolfram, Turner, & Philput, 1997).

Because of findings from studies such as Wofram and colleagues', along with general agreement regarding Shaw and Routh's interpretation of children simply feeling more comfortable protesting when a parent is present, parental presence has become more the norm for children undergoing procedures. However, an evidence-based review of studies about parental presence during anesthesia induction and parent/child anxiety concluded that, in most cases parental presence does not appear to alleviate parents' or children's anxiety (Chundamala, Wright,

& Kemp, 2009). The authors cited several limitations in the studies reviewed, but their concerns about these findings have led to revisiting their hospital's guidelines on parental presence.

The determining factor regarding benefits of parental presence appears to be the parent's level of anxiety. Kain et al. (2003) found that anxious children are less anxious when a calm parent is present, and calm children are more anxious when an anxious parent is present. Thus, it would be interesting to see if more substantive preparation programs designed specifically to reduce parents' anxiety would led to better outcomes. More rigorous research is needed in this area.

In part in response to the family-centered care movement, parental presence even during medical resuscitation of children has become a common practice (Meeks, 2009). Parents and other family members have the opportunity to stroke the child, hold the child's hand, and, in the event that resuscitation is unsuccessful, say goodbye, and begin the initial stage of grief. However, in the case of pediatric trauma resuscitation, family presence is rarely permitted, though Meeks notes that with appropriate support, family presence during trauma resuscitation can be successful and beneficial, and calls for more research to examine this option.

Research supports parental presence on pediatric intensive care unit (PICU) rounds. Cameron, Schleien, and Morris (2009) found that 81% of parents who chose to join rounds said it improved their overall satisfaction with their child's care; and in 57% of rounding events, one or more of the healthcare providers said they had learned relevant new details from the parents. Conversely, some healthcare providers believed having parents involved limited the discussion, and some parents suggested that participation might increase their anxiety. In another study on family-centered rounds (FCR), resident physicians cited improved relationships among providers, increased parent/family satisfaction, decreased need for plan clarification, and improved "nondidactic" teaching (Rappaport, Cellucci, & Leffler, 2010).

Illness Variables

Illness variables influence the length of a child's hospitalization and where in the hospital the child receives care, factors that within themselves may have an impact on a child's adjustment to hospitalization and effects after discharge. Although Rennick and colleagues (2002) reported that length of stay has minimal effects, Tiedeman and Clatworthy (1990) found that shorter hospital stays were associated with higher levels of anxiety in children at discharge. Thompson and Vernon (1993) reported that children hospitalized for periods of two to three days exhibited more behavioral distress after discharge than did those hospitalized for either shorter or longer periods. Regarding the impact of the hospital unit where the child is located, research suggests that PICU hospitalization can result in negative psychological sequelae in children, which can manifest up to one year postdischarge (Rennick & Rashotte, 2009).

Illness variables also help determine, in part, the child's exposure to invasive procedures, which in turn have an impact on the child's level of stress, anxiety, and fear experienced during and following hospitalization. About a third of the children who have a diagnostic or surgical procedure that includes anesthesia will develop some negative behavior when returning home (Karling, Stenlund, & Hagglof, 2007). Invasive procedures can be a strong predictor of children's psychological distress, manifested in symptoms of depression, anxiety, fear, and posttraumatic stress. Rennick et al. (2004) reported that school-aged children who were exposed to high numbers of invasive procedures experienced the most psychological sequelae postdischarge. However, Mabe, Treiber, and Riley (1991) did not find this association with their sample of school-aged children, and suggested that because their study participants had experienced frequent hospitalizations, the children may have learned effective coping strategies.

Results of studies comparing responses of children with chronic conditions to those of children with acute conditions cite both similarities and differences. For example, Hart and Bossert (1994) found no association between the degree of children's fears and whether they had a chronic or acute illness. That said, Bossert (1994a) found that acutely ill children were more likely to perceive their coping as effective than were chronically ill children. Bossert (1994b) reported that chronically ill children perceived more intrusive events as stressful, whereas acutely ill children identified more physical symptoms that way.

Studies using children's self-reports have consistently reported surprisingly low levels of distress in children with cancer, even significantly lower levels of depression than in their healthy peers (Canning, Canning, & Boyce, 1992; Phipps & Srivastava, 1997). This phenomenon has also been found with measures of anxiety, self-esteem, behavioral problems, general psychopathology, and even somatic distress (Canning et al., 1992; Elkin, Phipps, Mulhern, & Fairclough, 1997; Phipps et al., 1995; Phipps & Srivastava, 1997). Possibly the positive self-reports of children with cancer may be a valid reflection of their exceptionally high level of functioning, but Phipps and Steele (2002) believe that these self-reports may be biased in some way toward minimization of distress. They found that an increased prevalence of repressive adaption was not unique to children with cancer, but may be generally characteristic of children with serious chronic illness, and question whether repression in the context of serious illness is adaptive. Disattention to threat that is characteristic of a repressive adaptive style may lead to poor outcomes. A child may be reluctant to seek social support, unable to engage effectively in psychotherapy, and experience a lack of attention to internal signals of distress, including physical symptoms that could delay or interfere with effective medical treatment.

In recent years, research has begun to focus on the role of benefit finding in adaptation to highly stressful experiences (Helgeson, Reynolds, & Tomich, 2006). Although often precipitating a number of debilitating psychological symptoms, serious illness also can serve as a catalyst for personal growth (Tedeschi & Calhoun, 2004). The "silver lining" in the personal or social consequences of illness that many adults with cancer report has also been experienced by children with cancer (Currier, Hermes, & Phipps, 2009).

Other Stressors

The literature reveals two categories of stressors in children: normative and nonnormative (Berk, 1997). Normative stressors are the common, developmental stressors of daily life (e.g., being left out of the group, parents fighting, getting bad grades), while nonnormative stressors arise from unusual or traumatic experiences (e.g., serious illness of the child or parent, child abuse, community disasters).

When a child is ill, it often is understandable to focus on the features of the illness and healthcare experience that are causing stress for the child. However, children who are ill are subject as well to nondisease-related stressors common to contemporary childhood, such as parental divorce and remarriage, unavailable parents, geographic mobility, maternal employment and alternative sources of child care, competitive pressure, and peer pressure. Rollins (1990) found that some children with cancer reported experiencing a higher level of stress from such nondisease-related stressors than from those related to their disease and treatment. Brenner (1984) argues that when several stresses are combined, the effects are more likely to increase geometrically than to be simply additive. Therefore, a comprehensive approach to supporting the child must consider nonhealthcare-related stressors as well.

Assessment

Knowledge of various elements of psychosocial assessment can help when planning activities for individual children, monitoring the children's responses and progress, and making adaptations and recommendations. Basic components of psychosocial assessment include the child's affect, temperament, ability to communicate and interact with peers, personal or family stressors, coping style, number and type of defense mechanisms used, self-concept, and level of self-esteem (Brantly, 1991).

The Child Life Council Evidence-Based Practice Statement on *Child Life Assessment: Variables Associated with a Child's Ability to Cope with Hospitalization* (www.childlife.org) provides an excellent guideline for psychosocial assessment for the hospitalized child (Koller, 2008a). It considers as key factors the child's temperament and coping style, the parental level of anxiety, and the number of invasive medical procedures. The statement stresses that although child life specialists have a primary role in psychosocial care, evidence-based practice models support interprofessional collaboration (e.g., child life, social work, nursing, occupational therapy, art therapy, pediatric psychology) as a means of addressing complex issues associated with child and family adaptation to hospitalization.

The Family

A child's sickness can be a major source of stress and anxiety for the whole family. Children are part of a family system, thus, whatever happens in one part of the system—such as a child's illness—is experienced in some way by all family members. The ways in which family members deal with the stress can have a significant impact on the child's own coping and adjustment.

Parents, siblings, and grandparents (nuclear and extended family) are the individuals we traditionally think of when we hear the word "family," yet others who are not actually blood-related to the child may be considered as family members. Because the support these individuals receive will help determine the support they will be able to give to the child, identifying them and understanding what the experience of the child's illness is like for them are very important first steps.

In recent years, family composition has assumed new configurations, with the single-parent family and blended family becoming prominent forms. Today nearly 70% of children live with two parents (who may or may not be married), 22.7% with their mother only, 3.5% with their father only, and 3.8% with neither parent. Of those who live with neither parent, 2% live with grandparents (U.S. Census Bureau, 2008). Although the single-parent family is not a new phenomenon, the contemporary single-parent family has emerged partially as a consequence of the women's rights movement whereby some single women have chosen to have children and not get married, and more women (and men) have established separate households because of divorce, death, or desertion. In conjunction, a more liberal attitude in the courts has made it possible for single persons, both males and females, as well as gay or lesbian couples, to adopt children.

Parents

Nearly all parents react to a child's illness and hospitalization in a similar manner (Hockenberry & Wilson, 2007). The initial response is disbelief, especially when illness is sudden and serious. After acknowledging the illness, parents tend to react with anger, guilt, or both. Parents often search for reasons for the child's illness, sometimes blaming themselves; other parents project their anger at other people for some wrongdoing. Regardless of the severity of the illness, parents typically question their adequacy as caregivers and review any actions they could have taken or omissions they might have made that could have prevented, or caused, the illness. Hospitalization intensifies parental guilt because they feel helpless in alleviating the child's physical and emotional pain. They feel fear, anxiety, and frustration, and ultimately may react with some degree of depression. A number of studies have reported posttraumatic stress disorder (PSTD) in parents of children with a variety of conditions, such as post heart transplantation (Farley et al., 2007) and cancer (Kazak et al., 2004; Kazak, Boeving, Alderfer, Hwang, & Reilly, 2005).

It is not surprising that a child's admission to a pediatric intensive care unit (PICU) can be extremely stressful for both mothers and fathers. Criteria for admission alone are frightening and can realistically prompt fear that the child could die or become severely disabled. Worry about ongoing procedures and medical treatment, coupled with distressing sights and sounds, all contribute to parental distress. Diaz-Caneja, Gledhill, Weaver, Nadel, and Garralds (2005) found that sources of stress differed according to the following stages:

1. *Onset*—mainly related to the child's illness

2. *Admission*—focused on child's appearance

3. *Discharge*—possible relapse; impact of the admission on the child and family, and the lack of clear follow-up

Research confirms that mothers of children hospitalized on the PICU experience more anxiety, depression, anger, and confusion than mothers of children hospitalized on the general pediatric unit or mothers of ill children who are not hospitalized (Youngblut, Brooten, & Kuluz, 2005), and Board (2004) found similar results for fathers. The extent of negative emotions varies with the nature of the child's illness and the conditions of hospitalization (e.g., emergency admission versus nonemergency admission). Berenbaum and Hatcher (1992) found that maternal age, family stress, number of prior hospitalizations of the ill child, and the mother's rating of the severity of her child's illness were predictive of emotional distress for mothers. Fathers' responses were related to the sights and sounds of the unit and procedures their child underwent. However, even when mothers and fathers rate the severity of their child's condition similarly, mothers may experience greater stress than fathers (Younblut et al., 2005). Moreover, in Youngblut and colleagues' study, social support decreased the stress for mothers but not for fathers.

Hospitalization of children with long-term disabilities requires parents to make changes in their usual parenting role. Some parents report this alteration in the caretaking role to be the most stressful factor resulting from their child's hospitalization (Nizam & Norzila, 2001). Parents describe the need to (a) understand the illness experience, (b) become familiar with the hospital environment, (c) adapt to their changing relationship with the child and other family members, and (d) negotiate with health professionals about their child's care. Much parental stress can be attributed to differences in parental perception of their role in the care of their hospitalized child and that of the healthcare professional.

Grandparents

The literature documents the unique contribution grandparents can make when a child is ill, hospitalized, or disabled. Findler (2000) reported that mothers of children with and without disabilities ranked grandparents as a more important source of support than friends, neighbors, other family members, or even professionals. Grandparents provide both emotional and instrumental support. For example, today, with the number of mothers in the workforce, it is often a grandparent taking a shift at a child's bedside during hospitalization.

Often, little thought is given to the fact that a child's healthcare experience may be a difficult time for the grandparents themselves. Most studies on the impact on grandparents have reported on families of children with disabilities or chronic illness, and focus on the concept of "double grief" (Simons, 1987). For example, after the birth of a child with a disability, both parents and grandparents experience similar feelings of consternation, shock, and grief. However, the grandparents' reaction is double, as they suffer not only for the newborn but for their own child's pain as well. Woodbridge, Buys, and Miller (2009) documented the three key themes that characterize the grandparent's emotional journey: (a) adjusting, the transition from anger to acceptance; (b) the "double grief," sadness about what might have been for both their child and grandchild; and (c) pride in family, in the family's ability to adjust to the challenges of the situation.

A more comprehensive view of family-centered care in recent years has led to studies of grandparents coping with grandchildren with acute illness or short-term hospitalization. Hall's research (2004a, 2004b) with grandmothers and grandfathers of critically ill grandchildren revealed a similar "double concern." Grandmothers were concerned about how their own children—the parents—were managing the situation, and also were scared, worried, and frustrated while waiting for the parents to contact them and keep them apprised of their grandchild's status. Grandfathers, too, worried for both their children (the parents) and their ill grandchildren (Hall, 2004b). They reported feeling scared and helpless, unable to concentrate on work.

Finally, today, approximately 1 in 12 children are living in households headed by grandparents (4.5 million children) or other relatives (U.S. Census Bureau, 2003). In many of these homes, grandparents are taking on primary responsibility for the children's needs. Often, they assume this responsibility without either of the child's parents present in the home. Thus, a number of grandparents are struggling to maintain the role of grandparent while assuming the additional acting role of parent.

Siblings

A brother's or sister's illness or hospitalization can have a significant impact on siblings. Much of the research to date, which focuses on sibling response to a child with chronic illness or disability, presents an ambivalent picture. Some studies suggest that sibling risk for dysfunction is increased, and that the manifestations of poor adjustment are seen in problems with self-esteem, peer relationships, and adjustment; other studies focus on the impressive resilience siblings exhibit to family stress, their personal growth, maturation, and heightened sensitivity (Fleitas, 2000). A landmark study on adjustment for siblings of children with cancer found that, emotionally, siblings fared the same as or worse than their brother or sister with cancer (Spinetta, 1981).

When a child is hospitalized, healthy siblings face changes in family and daily functioning, including alterations in the well sibling's relationship with other family members; feelings of displacement, loneliness, confusion, and isolation; lack of communication; and the healthy siblings' concerns for their own health. When Fleitas (2000) asked children to share their feelings about having a sister or brother with medical problems (some hospitalized, some not), they wrote of responsibility and loneliness, fear, jealousy, resentment, and guilt. They admitted to feeling sad, embarrassed, and sometimes overwhelmingly confused.

As bone marrow and other transplantation has become standard therapy for many life-threatening conditions, siblings have assumed a more prominent role in the lives of their ill brothers or sisters, as donors. In a qualitative study of the psychosocial impact of pediatric hematopoietic stem cell transplants, siblings reported that informed consent involved "no choice" and that the psychological aspects of the procedure outweighed the physical aspects (MacLeod, Whitsett, Mash, & Pelletier, 2003). Major themes siblings identify include feelings of isolation, anger, depression, anxiety, and low self-esteem (Packman, Beck, VanZutphen, Long, & Spengler, 2003). Such research findings reinforce the importance of providing sibling donors with developmentally accurate information and long-term psychological support.

Cultural Considerations

A family's culture—the shared values, norms, traditions, customs, arts, history, and institutions shared by a group of people—may influence their health, healing, and wellness belief systems; how they perceive illness, disease, and the causes; their behaviors when seeking healthcare, and attitudes toward healthcare providers; and the delivery and quality of services they receive. Sociocultural differences among family, healthcare providers, and the healthcare system may include variations in the family's ability to recognize clinical symptoms of disease and illness, thresholds for seeking care (including the impact of racism and mistrust), expectations of care (including preferences for or against diagnostic and therapeutic procedures), and the ability to understand the prescribed treatment (Betancourt, Green, & Carrillo, 2002).

Families subscribe to culture group norms to varying degrees. The family's health beliefs and practices arise from a combination of normative cultural values, together with personal experience and perception (Flores, 2000). Thus, individuals—even within families—in a cultural group do not think and act in an identical manner.

The following are several components of culture known to affect children's healthcare (Flores, 2000):

- *Normative cultural values*. Differences in beliefs, ideas, and behaviors that a particular cultural group values and expects in interpersonal communication can result in confusion, misunderstanding, and mistrust.
- *Language*. Being unable to speak the same language as the healthcare provider can have a substantial impact on multiple aspects of healthcare, including access, health status, use of health services, and health outcomes.
- *Folk illnesses*. Culturally constructed diagnostic categories commonly recognized by an ethnic group often conflict with biomedical paradigms.
- *Parent/patient beliefs*. Beliefs of parents and children can impede preventive efforts, delay or complicate medical care, and result in the use of neutral or harmful remedies.
- *Provider practices*. Studies suggest that clinicians sometimes provide a lower quality of care to patients of different cultures. Cultural differences may impede effective communication, leading to misunderstandings; subtle or overt bias might be responsible in some instances.

Factors such as the family's socioeconomic background, the degree of acculturation, the country of birth, level of education, and language proficiency of the dominant culture may influence normative cultural values and folk illnesses. It will be important to assess for selected cultural values before conducting some of the activities in this book. For example, several of the activities use photo images and some cultures prohibit the use of photographs. However, as with any interpretation regarding culture, generalizing should be avoided. For additional information about culture, see Chapter 10, "Culture."

Other Family Factors

Just as is the child, family members are faced with other normative and nonnormative stressors. Their perceptions of these stressors, as well as their perceptions of their resources—financial and social—and ability to deal with them, will influence individual family members' responses. Assuming a family-centered approach means considering these factors, as well.

How to Use This Book

This book offers a variety of therapeutic play and other educational and expressive activities for adults to facilitate with children who are coping with healthcare experiences. Play, including initiation of actions by children, and the responsiveness to children by others, is one of the most powerful processes by which children regulate their experiences and environments (Bolig, 2005). Jessee and Gaynard (2009) point out four traditional play paradigms: (a) play as enjoyment, (b) play as development, (c) play as learning, and (d) play as therapy. In addition, they call attention to expanded paradigms of play that can relate specifically to play with children in healthcare settings: (a) play as flow (a state of being totally consumed in play and its joyful feelings), (b) play as comfort, and (c) play as hope. *Therapeutic Activities for Children and Teens Coping with Healthcare Issues* strives to address play in all of these contexts.

In the healthcare context, therapeutic play refers to specialized activities that are developmentally supportive and facilitate the emotional well-being of a pediatric patient (Koller, 2008b). Although the terms *therapeutic play* and *play therapy* are often used interchangeably, the focus of therapeutic play is on the promotion of continuing "normal development" while enabling children to respond more effectively to difficult situations such as medical experiences (Oremland & Oremland, 2000). Play therapy, on the other hand, addresses basic and persistent psychological issues associated with how children may interact with their world. Thus, therapeutic play, in a less structured way, focuses on the process of play as a mechanism for mastering developmental milestones and critical events such as hospitalization (Koller, 2008b). The *Child Life Council Evidence-Based Practice Statement on Therapeutic Play in Pediatric Health Care: The Essence of Child Life Practice* (Koller, 2008b) documents the many psychological, physiological, and educational benefits of therapeutic play. The statement can be accessed on the Child Life Council web site (www.childlife.org).

Overview of Activities

Therapeutic Activities for Children and Teens Coping with Health Issues comprises 16 chapters of therapeutic and educational activities designed to promote understanding, adaptation, and coping for children and adolescents experiencing healthcare encounters, or for children who are affected by those of a family member.

Chapters begin with an introduction that provides (a) a research-based theoretical overview explaining the rationale for the activities, (b) special considerations for conducting the activities, and (c) therapeutic activity goals, followed by (d) the chapter-relevant activities. Each activity identifies the following elements:

1. Therapeutic goal(s)
2. Age group for which it is most appropriate
3. Adult/child ratio (approximate)
4. Required time (approximate)
5. Materials and equipment needed
6. Process

And, when appropriate:

7. Restrictions and precautions: safety information and/or categories of children for whom the activity might not be appropriate
8. Populations for which activities might be especially appropriate as is, or adapted to more specific use, such as for children with traumatic brain injury, blind children, non-English speaking children, or children who cannot play because of certain situations.
9. Hints and variations

Selecting Appropriate Activities

The following steps are helpful to consider when selecting an appropriate activity for a child or group of children (Rollins, 1991; Rollins & Mahan, 2010):

1. *Determine the child's age and developmental level*. This information may help assess the child's understanding of the healthcare issue, which, in turn, will influence the child's behavior. This knowledge also informs safety issues and suggests typical age-appropriate concerns.

2. *Assess child's temperament and coping style*. Knowing the child's temperament and coping style will reveal clues as to which issues may be of greatest concern for the child, and how to best address them.

3. *Review the child's behavior for areas of common concern*. A sampling of issues of common concern in healthcare settings can be found in Table I.3.

4. *Review the child's history and present condition for physical limitations, restrictions, and abilities*. This information will help determine adaptations that might be required.

5. *Consider the child's energy level and attention span*. This knowledge can help determine the child's ability to engage in the activity, the need to break the activity into more than one session, or the need for help in completing all or parts of it.

6. *Determine whether a group or an individual intervention is appropriate*. Group sessions provide an opportunity for socialization and mutual support; individual sessions allow for a more intense intervention, with a focus on the child's unique needs.

General Guidelines for Working with Children

Communication is a primary consideration when facilitating the activities in this book. Thus, a word or two about the process that occurs, or may occur, during these activities needs defining. In some instances, children will merely complete activities. In other cases, the activity can serve as a starting point for unrepresented content that the child wants to communicate. This phenomenon is referred to as the *campfire effect*, the result of an activity or experience that provides a focal point shared by the individuals involved, and serves to increase conversation in both quantity and intensity (Rollins, 2005b). Much like sitting around a campfire, "sitting around the activity," so to speak, allows the activity, and not the child, to serve as an object of focus, for both the child and the adult. This transfer of focus from the child to the activity often seems to relax the child, by relieving the pressure of being the object of direct verbal communication;

Table I.3 Sampling of Issues of Common Concern in Healthcare Settings

Issue	Rationale
Separation	Therapeutic play provides an opportunity for children to learn to cope effectively with separation from significant others, and allows them to establish a nurturing relationship with an adult other than a parent.
Autonomy and mastery	Healthcare experiences place the child in the role of passive recipient of an active treatment, often provided by strangers. Therapeutic play, particularly medical play, helps the child become involved in the treatment (even if only in a very small way) and retain a sense of competence.
Medical information and procedures	Children's fears and anxieties are based on their perceptions, which sometimes differ from reality. Medical play helps identify misconceptions, and can be used to dispel myths and establish trust.
Surgery	Preoperative play interventions are effective in reducing or preventing an increase in presurgical and postsurgical anxiety.
Injections	Along with the uncomfortable experience of receiving an injection, children often are confused about the purpose. Medical play provides an opportunity for desensitizing and clarifying.
Disability or chronic condition	Therapeutic play may be especially helpful for the child with a disability or chronic condition who is dealing with altered body image and low self-esteem.
Grief	Children typically find the difficult feelings of grief easier to express through play.

Note. Adapted from Rollins, J. (1991). Assisting with therapeutic play. In D. Smith (Ed.), *Comprehensive child and family nursing skills* (pp. 70–77). St. Louis, MO: Mosby Year Book.

thus, communication flows more easily. Therefore, much of the content in the guidelines that follow concern guidance on communication for the facilitator:

1. *Define limits, as appropriate to the child and/or the activity.* Knowing what to expect and what is expected helps ensure an effective and safe experience.

   - *Approximate time available for the session.* Children dislike being interrupted in the middle of attempting to master a task.

   - *Behavior to be limited.* This knowledge helps children understand that they may not say hurtful things, hurt others or themselves, or destroy property.

   - *Gentle redirection of behavior.* Medical play, particularly needle play, is often very aggressive at first. Gently redirecting unrealistic play will help children understand that their play is not being criticized.

2. *Offer choices.* Look for every possible opportunity to offer children choices (e.g., in the activities, materials, techniques), to help encourage a sense of control.

3. *Reflect the child's feelings.* Mirroring children's emotions helps them to understand how they feel (e.g., "It sounds like you are very angry.").

4. *Consider using the third-person technique when children seem to be struggling to put their thoughts or feelings into words.* The third-person technique implies permission to share concerns and fears (e.g., "Many children with cancer tell me that they think they did something wrong, and that is why they got sick. I wonder if you have ever felt that way, too.").

5. *Incorporate special considerations listed in activities.* Some activities list restrictions and precautions (e.g., safety information, categories of children for whom the activity would not be appropriate).

6. *Thank the child at the completion of the session.* Expressing gratitude for spending time together strengthens the child's sense of self-worth, as well as the adult/child bond.

7. *Celebrate the child's accomplishments.* When appropriate and with the child's permission, display or present the child's work to family members and healthcare providers. Children feel a sense of "ownership" when their work is on display; sense of ownership is associated with a perception of control over one's environment.

Children, regardless of their diagnoses, are more alike than different when dealing with healthcare experiences. Nevertheless, there are unique considerations when using the activities with special populations. A sampling of considerations for special populations presents a starting point. Understanding the issues involved with the populations described here may help the facilitator when using the activities with other populations with similar considerations.

Considerations and Techniques for Special Populations

Children with Emotional/Behavioral Disorders. Approximately one in five children and adolescents have a mental health disorder (U.S. Department of Health and Human Services, Substance Abuse and Mental Health Services Administration [USDHHS, SAMHSA], 2003). Causes include biology, environment, or a combination of the two. Behavioral problems and psychological disorders occur twice as frequently in children with chronic illness as in those without (Dixon & Stein, 2006).

The National Information Center for Children and Youth with Disabilities (NICHY) (1997) identified the following characteristics and behaviors seen in children who have emotional disorders:

- *Hyperactivity*: Short attention span, impulsiveness

- *Aggression/self-injurious behavior*: Acting out, fighting

- *Withdrawal*: Failure to initiate interaction with others; retreat from exchanges of social interaction; excessive fear or anxiety

- *Immaturity*: Inappropriate crying, temper tantrums, poor coping skills

- *Learning difficulties*: Academically performing below grade level

Children with more serious emotional disorders may exhibit distorted thinking, excessive anxiety, bizarre motor acts, and abnormal mood swings. Although many children who do not have emotional disorders may display some of these same behaviors at various times during their development, when children have serious emotional disorders, these behaviors continue over long periods of time. Thus, their behavior signals that they are not coping well with their environment and/or peers.

Illness and/or hospitalization can further stress a child who is already having difficulty coping in the everyday environment. Many of the activities in this book are designed to help children cope with experiences they may encounter in the healthcare environment; yet, at times, a child's emotional/behavioral issues may prove challenging for implementation. Some tips for using the activities in this book with children with emotional disorders include the following:

1. *Call attention to available choices*. The ability to choose is important for all children so that they may feel a sense of control over what is happening to them. However, children with emotional/behavioral disorders often need to be reminded that they have choices, and may need help in determining specifically what those choices are.

2. *Help children be proactive in managing their behavior*. Talking with children about recognizing signs of escalating tension, and giving them the opportunity to choose when to "take some space," or to follow the adult's suggestion to take some space, is a positive, empowering approach for cooling down, and often avoids adults asking children to take a "time out" later.

3. *Explain expected behavior*. A positive approach is respectful and more likely to be heard and understood than being told what *not* to do.

4. *Set limits*. Limits can be powerful tools for teaching appropriate behavior. The purpose of setting limits is not to show who is "boss," but to give children guidance, respect, and a feeling of security.

5. *Pay attention to behavioral warning signs*. Be alert for signals that may indicate distress or discontent, such as (a) significant changes in "normal" behavior or routines; (b) sudden changes in expression, physical activity, or posture; (c) dramatic increase or change in voice, volume, or tone; (d) expressions that communicate extreme anxiety or distress; (e) communications of despair and hopelessness; (f) body posture that is intimidating or threatening; and (g) verbal or physical threats.

6. *Encourage new beginnings*. Remind children that even when their day has had a bad start, they have within their power the ability to "turn the day around."

When it is anticipated that a child with an emotional/behavioral disorder will be hospitalized for more than a day or two, establishing a team approach to managing behavior is essential. Speaking to the child's parents, and if the child attends school or preschool, speaking with his or her teacher as well, may prove helpful.

Children with Developmental Disabilities. Developmental disabilities affect approximately 17% of children younger than 18 years of age in the United States (National Center on Birth Defects and Developmental Disabilities, 2006). The term *developmental disability* means a severe, chronic disability of an individual that (a) is attributable to a mental or physical impairment or combination of mental and physical impairments; (b) is manifested before the individual attains age 22; (c) is likely to continue indefinitely; (d) results in substantial functional limitations in three or more of areas of major life activity; and (e) reflects the individual's need for a combination and sequence of special, interdisciplinary, or generic services, individualized supports, or other forms of assistance that are of lifelong or extended duration and are individually planned and coordinated (USDHHS, Administration for Children & Families [ACF], 2000).

Developmental disabilities include (a) nervous system disabilities affecting how the brain, spinal cord, and nervous system function, which may result in intellectual disabilities or learning and behavioral disorders; (b) sensory-related disabilities, which can cause vision (the understanding of what is seen), sight (the ability to see something clearly), and hearing problems; (c) metabolic disorders, which affect how the body processes the materials it needs to function;

and (d) degenerative disorders, which might only become apparent when children are older. The developmental disability, autism spectrum disorder (ASD), can cause severe and pervasive impairment in thinking, feeling, language, and the ability to relate to others (see section that follows on Autism Spectrum Disorder).

Children with developmental disabilities may have a short attention span and be easily distracted. They often are afraid to try new things, and have difficulty and become frustrated with change and transitions. Cognitively, they may not remember things well, have difficulty in problem solving, and may be unable to transfer learning to a new situation. They sometimes repeat the same movement over and over, and may stumble and fall because of poor body control. They often prefer to play with younger children, and speak and use the language of a younger child.

The following tips may be helpful in using the activities presented in this book with children who have developmental disabilities:

1. *Determine the child's interests.* Confidence builds when children are successful doing something they enjoy.

2. *Select activities that match the child's developmental age and abilities.* Using the child's developmental age and abilities as criteria, as opposed to chronological age, will more likely result in a successful experience.

3. *Consider activities that include sensory stimulation, unless contraindicated (e.g., seizures).* Some children with developmental disabilities crave sensory stimulation; others are uncomfortable with it.

4. *Break activities into small steps and present information one item at a time.* Children with developmental disabilities may feel overwhelmed if too much instruction is given at once.

5. *Speak slowly and keep verbal instructions simple.* Keeping things short and simple can help ensure comprehension.

6. *Use visuals whenever possible.* Visuals will help to reinforce verbal messages.

7. *Ask for feedback.* Feedback will help to assure comprehension and offer an opportunity for clarification.

8. *Guide the child's hands and body through the motions of an activity.* Showing reinforces telling.

9. *Give the child an opportunity to practice.* Practicing can provide opportunities for clarification and confidence building.

10. *Provide opportunities for the child to be near another child who is doing a similar activity.* Such opportunities can give the child with developmental disabilities some ideas on how to use and explore the same materials.

11. *When using several objects in an activity, make certain that there are obvious differences in sizes, shapes, and colors.* Subtle differences between colors and shapes can be confusing to the child with developmental disabilities.

12. *Limit the number of art materials or toys.* Offering too many choices can overwhelm the child with developmental disabilities.

13. *Give ample warning when an activity is about to change or end.* Transitions and change typically are difficult issues for the child with developmental disabilities.

Childern with Autism Spectrum Disorder. Because of its complex nature and growing prevalence, ASD will be discussed further here. It is estimated that a range of 1 in 80 to 1 in 240, with an average of 1 in 110 children in the United States, have an ASD (Rice, 2009). Although healthcare experiences can be difficult for any child, for children with ASD, the situation may be overwhelming. For a summary of the major characteristics of individuals with ASD, see Table I.4.

Autism is a developmental brain disorder that typically affects a person's ability to communicate, engage in social interactions, and respond appropriately to the environment. Autism spectrum disorders, sometimes called *pervasive developmental disorders* (PDD), represent a range of

**Table I.4 Major
Characteristics of
Individuals with ASD**

Characteristics	Examples
Impaired social skills	Difficulty entering a group Difficulty with reciprocal interactions Lack of understanding of social cues Difficulty understanding nonverbal communication (e.g., gestures, expressions of emotion) Often have preferred, narrow topic of interest Awkward gaze when trying to decipher social interaction May prefer not to interact at all
Communication challenges	Difficulty entering a conversation Literal and concrete thinkers and interpreters Complex vocabularies May be nonverbal—communicating using sign language or pictures May be echolalic—repeating phrases and words Struggle interpreting the meaning of a conversation
Restricted interests and repetitive behaviors	Strong preferences Intense special interests Repeating same routine over and over Easily overwhelmed and anxious Difficulty predicting and interpreting behavior of others Impulsive
Sensory issues	Difficulty organizing, interpreting, and responding to stimuli or sensations Extreme reaction to sensory stimuli (hypo versus hyper) Lack of awareness of self within environment Clumsy posture and gait Sudden or abrupt gestures
Weak executive functioning	Difficulty with overall processing—planning, organizing, and breaking down complex tasks or requests Difficulty interpreting nonverbal communication Highly visual; better at understanding information that is presented visually rather than verbally Difficulty shifting attention or transitioning quickly Often unaware of perspective of others
Tendency to be visual learners	Difficulty orienting to and following verbal directions Preference for specific and organized information Able to refer back to visual information given
Nonverbal communication	Overstimulated when trying to focus on multiple features of communication Often look away or past a person, to listen better Failure to understand full range of emotions—own or of others Difficulty interpreting subtleties of communication such as voice inflection, gestures, and figurative versus literal expression (e.g., ''it's raining cats and dogs'')
Need for routine	Preference for structure and order Ask same questions repeatedly Interactions seem stilted/rehearsed
High levels of stress and anxiety	Trigger easily Climbing mountain of emotion Often do not indicate internal stress and anxiety building until reaching peak

Note. Adapted from Hudson, J. (2006). *Prescription for success: Supporting children with autism spectrum disorders in the medical environment.* Shawnee Mission, KS: Autism Asperger Publishing Company.

neurological disorders that most markedly involve some degree of difficulty with communication and interpersonal relationships, as well as obsessions and repetitive behaviors. There can be a wide range of effects. Children at the lower-functioning end of the spectrum may be unable to break out of their own world, and may be described as having autism. Children at the higher-functioning end, sometimes diagnosed with Asperger's syndrome (AS), may be able to lead independent lives but still be awkward in their social interactions (Mauro, 2009).

Because of the uniqueness of each child's disorder and situation, Hudson (2006) recommends assessing the child's strengths and limitations, developmental level, and the rate at which the child takes in information and sensory stimuli. An intervention assessment is useful in choosing an intervention that best matches the child and the situation. For example, if the child has a special interest, that interest can be used as a motivator. Some tips for using the activities in this book with children with ASD include the following:

1. *Be aware of the stimuli in the environment (e.g., sound, light, crowds, touch).* This includes stimuli that you may provide. Children with ASD often have sensory issues and become overwhelmed easily. An individual approach is necessary; for example, some children find light touch excruciating and so prefer firm touch.

2. *Offer choices.* Children with ASD find it easier to respond when given specific choices rather than being asked open-ended questions.

3. *Present instructions in simple steps.* Limit steps to only three to five at a time. Tell children what they should do, rather than what they should not do, in as few words as possible.

4. *Present instructions in a clear, concise, and concrete manner.* Children with ASD often have difficulty interpreting abstractions.

5. *Use simple images to illustrate the steps.* Children with ASD are typically better at understanding information that is presented visually rather than verbally.

6. *Provide transition cues when moving from one activity or step to the next.* Abrupt transitions can be very stressful for children with ASD. Refer to a storyboard that visually depicts the various steps of an activity to help the child see the beginning, middle, and end. Another technique is to set up picture boards that depict now-then scenarios—"If you paint your flowerpot now, then you can play until it dries."

7. *Offer support for social interactions.* Building on the child's interests, suggest topics the child can talk about with other children (e.g., favorite movies, colors, TV shows, toys).

8. *Help the child develop a cue to give to avoid meltdowns.* With the help of an adult, the child can decide on a sign that indicates he or she is getting overwhelmed and needs a break.

Children with Brain Injuries. Each year approximately 475,000 traumatic brain injuries (TBIs) occur among children ages 0 to 14 years. Falls are the leading cause, with rates highest for children ages 0 to 4 years (Langlois, Rutland-Brown, & Thomas, 2006). Motor vehicle crashes, sports, and abuse/assault are the other most frequent causes.

TBI can cause a wide range of functional changes that affect thinking (e.g., memory, reasoning), sensation (e.g., touch, taste, smell), language (e.g., communication, expressions, understanding), and emotions (e.g., depression, anxiety, personality changes, aggression, acting out, social inappropriateness) (National Institute of Neurologic Disorders and Stroke, 2002). Impairments may be either temporary or permanent, and may cause partial or total functional disability, as well as psychosocial maladjustment.

Children with TBI share many of the same issues as children with congenital disabling conditions, yet, in some respects, the sudden onset of a severe disability resulting from trauma is very different. Children can often remember how they were before the injury, which can cause emotional and psychosocial problems not usually present in children with congenital disabilities. This feature also may have a profound effect on family, friends, and healthcare professionals who remember what the child was like before the injury and now must shift goals and expectations.

In working with children with TBI, it is important to determine what a child may need to relearn. Also, because a child's short-term memory may be impaired, what appears to have been learned may be forgotten by the end of the day. Tips for using the activities in this book with children who have TBI include the following:

1. Gauge whether children with TBI can follow one-step instructions well before challenging them with a sequence of two or more directions.

2. Provide repetition and consistency.

3. Demonstrate new tasks, state instructions, and provide examples to illustrate ideas and concepts.

4. Avoid figurative language.

5. Reinforce lengthening periods of attention to appropriate tasks.

6. Probe skill acquisition frequently and provide repeated practice.

7. Teach compensatory strategies for improving memory.

8. Be prepared for children's reduced stamina and increased fatigue, and provide rest breaks as needed.

9. Keep the environment as distraction-free as possible.

Because attention often is focused on children's disabilities after their injury, their self-esteem suffers. Thus, selecting activities that present opportunities for success, and maximize children's strengths, can make a significant positive contribution to their recovery.

Abused, Maltreated, Neglected Children. Child abuse and neglect is (a) any recent act or failure to act on the part of a parent or caretaker that results in death, serious physical or emotional harm, sexual abuse or exploitation; or (b) an act or failure to act that presents an imminent risk of serious harm. According to the latest figures, an estimated 794,000 children were determined to be victims of abuse or neglect. Of these children, infants had the highest rate of victimization. Neglect was the most common form of child maltreatment, followed by physical abuse, sexual abuse, and psychological maltreatment (U.S. Department of Health and Human Services, Administration on Children, Youth and Families [USDHHS, ACYF], 2009).

The consequences of child abuse or neglect can be profound and may endure long after the maltreatment occurs. Effects may appear in childhood, adolescence, or adulthood, and affect various aspects of an individual's development (e.g., physical, cognitive, psychological, behavioral), and range in consequence from minor physical injuries, low self-esteem, attention disorders, and poor peer relations to severe brain damage, extremely violent behavior, and death (Goldman, Salus, Wolcott, & Kennedy, 2003). Not every child who is maltreated experiences these negative consequences. Protective factors that appear to mediate or serve as a buffer against the effects of the negative experiences include (a) personal characteristics, such as optimism, high self-esteem, high intelligence, or a sense of hopefulness; and (b) social support and relationships with a supportive adult(s).

Children who have been abused and neglected may believe that they are unworthy of attention or that their safety and protection is not important. They may take risks that can be dangerous or life-threatening, not care about the outcome of their behavior, or try to hurt themselves; other children may never have learned to recognize that some actions and behaviors are dangerous or life-threatening. Children separated from their family, or whose family has been disrupted by the discovery of abuse or neglect, need to focus their energy on determining what will happen next and on maintaining emotional equilibrium. Children who have experienced a loss may feel sad, alone, and needy; others may feel strongly hostile toward themselves and others, or have feelings of despair, worthlessness, and defectiveness. Some children enter a state that is much less intense in emotional tone and more energy conserving, which is characterized by withdrawal and vague sensations of numbness, emptiness, and hypochondria.

The following guidelines for working with children who have been abused or neglected can be applied when facilitating the activities in this book (American Humane Association, 2008; Urquiza & Winn, 1994):

1. *Help children feel emotionally safe.* Familiarize them with the new surroundings and situations; remind them of their accomplishments and strengths; teach and practice problem-solving skills; and acknowledge the frustration and challenges of a difficult situation.

2. *Be an approachable, patient, and supportive listener.* Listen without being critical or negative toward children or the children's parents.

3. *Communicate in words and actions that children who have experienced abuse or neglect are worthy of protection.* Help them in and out of the bed or chair; reach for activity materials, toys,

and other objects, that may be out of their reach; and introduce a protector during fantasy play.

4. *Show that you understand and believe what children say, even if it is difficult.* Make sure to avoid saying anything that could be interpreted as blame, punishment, or accusation of children doing anything wrong.

5. *Let children know that you are there for them, to talk to openly, should they wish to do so.* Leaving a line of communication open is much more beneficial to children than pressuring them to disclose or reveal their experiences of abuse or neglect before they are ready to do so.

6. *Validate children's feelings, emotions, and experiences.* Avoid saying anything that children might interpret as belittlement or minimizing their feelings; they have those feelings for a reason.

7. *Affirm children's decision to confide in you.* Tell children that they are doing the right thing by talking to an adult they can trust. Let them know that you are there for them, and want to help keep them safe.

8. *Assure children frequently that they are not to blame.* Child victims may believe that the abuse or neglect is their fault.

9. *Stay calm.* Fear and anger are normal reactions to hearing about child abuse and neglect, but you may frighten children and prevent them from confiding in you in the future if you become agitated.

10. *Avoid talking negatively about the abuser in front of the children.* Child victims of abuse may be very loyal to their abusers, especially if the abuser is a parent. Despite the abuse, many children still love their parents and want to be loved and wanted by them.

11. *Provide positive feedback and reinforcement to help build children's self-esteem.* Tell children how they contribute positively to the lives of others. Talk about their potential and what they have to offer; express sincerely that they are good, smart, and kind.

12. *Help children learn conflict resolution skills by teaching and/or modeling them.* Children who have been abused or neglected may be unfamiliar with nonviolent ways of dealing with conflict.

13. *When children act in ways that seem strange, look for the feelings behind the actions.* Children may try to protect themselves from their negative feelings by pretending those feelings do not exist. Also, they may seek attention through negative behaviors, because they do not know how to gain attention using positive ones.

14. *Foster children's relationships with peers.* Encourage extracurricular and school-related activities.

Disaster Victims. The American Academy of Pediatrics (AAP) defines a disaster as a calamitous event that generally involves injury or loss of life and destruction of property (AAP, 1995). Such events are traumatic and customarily outside the scope of normal human experience; thus, they are likely to involve psychological as well as physical injury.

Children's psychological responses to disasters can range from transient mild stress reactions to the more severe and prolonged consequences of posttraumatic stress disorder (PTSD). Five primary responses are seen in children, resulting from loss, exposure to trauma, and disruption of routine: (a) increased dependency on parents or guardians; (b) nightmares; (c) regression in developmental achievements; (d) specific fears about reminders of the disaster; and (e) demonstration of the disaster via posttraumatic play and reenactments (AAP, 1995). Responses are influenced greatly by the nature of disaster itself, the level of exposure to the disaster, the extent to which the children and those around them are personally affected by the disaster, and the individual characteristics of children, including their age and stage of development (see Table I.5).

Gender also is a factor in response to disasters. Boys tend to be more antisocial than girls, and display violent and aggressive behaviors and other externalizing symptoms more often than girls, and require a longer recovery period than girls. Girls typically display more internalizing

Table I.5 Common Age-Related Responses to Disasters

Age	Possible Responses
Infants	Increased crying and irritability Separation anxiety Exaggerated startle response Difficulty being soothed Withdrawn; seem lethargic and unresponsive
Toddlers and Preschoolers	Sleep terrors and nightmares Behavioral and skill regression, manifesting as helplessness Clinging behavior Increased temper tantrums Decreased appetite Vomiting, constipation, diarrhea Tics, stuttering, muteness Exaggerated startle response Posttraumatic stress disorder Whimpering and trembling Moving aimlessly Becoming immobile
School-aged Children	Fear, anxiety Trauma-related themes in play Aggressive behavior Increased hostility with siblings Sleep disturbances Regressive behaviors (e.g., separation anxiety) Withdrawn or apathetic Physical complaints Behavioral problems Decreased interest in peers, hobbies, school Rebellion (e.g., refusal to do chores) Interpersonal difficulties Posttraumatic stress disorder
Adolescents	Decreased interest in social activities, peers, hobbies, school Anhedonia (an inability to experience pleasure) Decline in responsible behaviors Fatigue Rebellion, behavior problems Physical complaints Sleep disorders Eating disorders Change in physical activities Confusion Lack of concentration Risk-taking behaviors Posttraumatic stress disorder Suicidal thoughts

Note. Adapted from: National Institute of Mental Health. (2008). *Helping children and adolescents cope with violence and disasters: What community members can do.* Bethesda, MD: Author. American Academy of Pediatrics Committee on Psychosocial Aspects of Child and Family Health. (1999). How pediatricians can respond to the psychosocial implications of disasters. *Pediatrics, 103*(2), 521–523. National Center for Children Exposed to Violence. (2005). *Parents' guide in helping children in the wake of disaster.* New Haven, CT: Author. Hagan, J., & Committee on Psychosocial Aspects of Child and Family Health and the Task Force on Terrorism. (2005). Psychosocial implications of disaster or terrorism on children: A guide for the pediatrician. *Pediatrics, 116,* 787–795. American Academy of Pediatrics, Work Group on Disasters. (1995). *Psychological issues for children in disasters: A guide for the primary care physician.* (Publication No. (SMA) 95–3022). Washington, DC: U.S. Department of Health and Human Services.

symptoms such as anxiety and mood disturbances, but they tend to be more expressive about their emotions than boys and have more frequent thoughts about the disaster (Pine & Cohen, 2002).

Children respond to disasters in two distinct stages. During the first stage, immediately after the disaster, children react with fear, disbelief, denial, grief, and relief if loved ones have not been harmed. Occurring a few days to several weeks after the disaster, the second stage is characterized by developmental regression and manifestations of emotional distress, such as anxiety, fear, sadness, and depressive symptoms; hostility and aggressive behavior toward others; apathy; withdrawal; sleep disturbances; somatization; pessimistic thoughts about the future; and play demonstrating themes related to the traumatic event. This is a normal response and can be expected to last for a few weeks. Children with adverse stress reactions and behavior symptoms that last longer than a month may be at risk for posttraumatic stress disorder.

The following tips may be helpful when using the activities in this book with children who have experienced a disaster:

1. Indicate that you are available to listen.
2. Use a calm tone of voice.
3. Get on the child's level—stoop or sit on the floor.
4. Follow the child's lead:
    -   If the child wants to talk, listen.
    -   If the child wants to be held or picked up, do so.
    -   If the child is clingy, be patient.
5. Allow children to show their fears; give support.
6. Help children identify their feelings.
7. Point out that there are many ways other than talking to express feelings, and introduce activities as options.
8. Consider group projects, which often feel safer for some children than individual projects.
9. Use collage, which may feel safer to children because they are allowed to use others' symbols.
10. Use puppets to help children "tell" or "live" a story.
11. Allow children to tell you what they want to draw or what they want to direct you in drawing.
12. Work on projects together, such as writing and illustrating a book.
13. Allow a full range of expression during these activities.
14. Provide reassurance that there is no "right way" to express thoughts and feelings, that their creations will not be judged.
15. Exercise as little control as possible.
16. Exhibit children's creations only if they want to share them with others.
17. After completing activities, allow children to talk about them, if they want to. Discussion can help to bring closure to the experiences and feelings related to the disaster, which is an important step in the process of healing. Other children will gain closure by listening to their peers.

Children with Physical Restrictions. Children dealing with health issues may exhibit a wide range of physical disabilities or restrictions. Some disabilities, such as visual impairment, may be permanent. Others, immobilizing a limb for treatment, for example, are temporary physical restrictions. Lack of mobility, overprotective parental attitudes, preoccupation with treatment, authoritarian treatment climate, limited personal responsibility, and lack of decision-making experiences often result in children with physical disabilities perceiving themselves as less than competent. Unfortunately, children with a physical disability may extend their perceptions of physical limitations beyond those imposed by the disability. With less control over their lives than their physically able peers, they frequently lack self-confidence.

The following tips are designed to help children with physical disabilities successfully participate in creative activities:

1. *Create an accepting environment.* Such an environment serves as an insulator against the rejection that the child may experience.

2. *Avoid assuming a child cannot do something.* Often, some skills, such as the child's method of holding a spoon, can be transferred to holding a paintbrush. Children can be extremely inventive in this process.

3. *Adapt the materials and equipment to meet the child's needs.* Adaptation helps children with physical disabilities to become more independent and confident. Box I.1 provides an example of the process for designing an adaptation. Also see Chapter 2, "Self-Expression" Table 2.1, for selected adaptations.

4. *Consider the use of adaptive equipment.* Special equipment designed to help children with specific tasks of daily living might also prove helpful when participating in the activities.

5. *Find out what the child's strengths are and capitalize on them.* All children have strengths.

6. *Keep your expectations high.* Children will typically rise to realistic expectations set for them, especially if you set them together.

7. *Think ahead which steps of the activity might be challenging for a particular child, and prepare to the greatest extent possible.* For example, a child with spasticity will likely have difficulty drawing on a piece of paper unless it is taped to the table.

8. *Let the child do as much as possible.* Avoid interfering with the process. Children with disabilities often are a bit slower in getting started. If they seem to be struggling, ask if they would like some specific help (e.g., "Would you like me to hold the paper while you cut?")

9. *Be an extension of and for the child who is physically unable to do all or parts of an activity.* Offer children choices at every step of the way, and let them make all the decisions. When children have engaged in the problem-solving process of creating, and have made the important decisions, the final product is truly theirs.

**BOX I.1.
EXAMPLE OF HOW
TO ADAPT
EQUIPMENT:
PLAYING CARDS
ONE-HANDED**

Making adaptive equipment is easy. Start with the task you wish to perform and think carefully about the requirements. Identify all parts of the body normally used to complete the task, then think about how else it might be performed. Break down the task into its component parts and treat each one as a separate stage. (This is called a *task analysis.*) Some children may be independent at some stages of a task and need adaptive equipment only for certain other stages.

In this case, the task is to play a game of cards, which comprises these steps/stages:

1. Shuffle the cards (someone else can do this).

2. Hold a small number of cards in your hands, facing the child.

3. Select one card at a time and place it into a pile in the table.

4. Follow the rules of the game.

5. Participate in a sporting manner.

As you can see, most steps can be done by a child or done in a different way. The tricky part for a child with a physical disability affecting hand function is holding the cards. The solution is to use a fingernail brush. Turn the brush upside down and place it flat on the table. Slot the cards into the brush so that the child can see them. The child can then use his or her hands to select the cards (reducing fatigue) or can gesture to a card and let another helper take it out. This increases independence and promotes direct involvement in the game more readily—all for the price of a simple nail brush.

Note. Adapted from Vize, A. (2010). *Making adaptive equipment the easy way.* Retrieved January 24, 2010, from www.brighthub.com/education/special/articles/61848.aspx. Reprinted with permission.

Activities that may be helpful for children with specific physical restrictions will be noted throughout the book. More about immobilization and special activities designed to address this and related issues can be found in Chapter 11, "Isolation and Immobilization."

Children Who Cannot Play. Certain situations may render a child unable to play. A common intervention in critical care is intubation and assisted ventilation. Some children, although alert, may be unable to verbalize because of the paralyzing effect of required drugs; other children may be fully awake, yet prevented from talking because of a new tracheostomy or dependence on a ventilator. Children who are intubated have a limited repertoire of coping strategies. While intubated, procedures often are imposed on them when they cannot verbally and/or physically resist; thus, loss of control can be a significant issue.

To maintain some semblance of control, it is important to try to find methods for children to have a role in decision making. Communication boards, mechanical speaking aids, computer programs, writing assists, and hand and eye signals may be appropriate methods to help children actively participate in making choices. Pearson (2009) points out that often the creative work of the child life specialist can help motivate the child to learn to use these devices and techniques through developmentally appropriate play or preparation.

Children may be unable to play for other reasons, such a paralysis due to an automobile accident or sports injury. Many of the tips for working with children with physical disabilities (see Chapter 2, "Self-Expression") apply here as well. Also important to remember is that although children may be physically inactive, their imaginations are likely active and intact and can be used as an entrée into activities to provide a sense of control. For example, devising a method for children to communicate can allow them, through participating in and contributing to a story, to take a journey in their imagination and make critical decisions along the way. This journey may also have a physiological benefit (Daboo, 2007). For example, Robertson (1999) described a case wherein people imagined they were running on a treadmill that was going at different speeds: "Even though they were not physically moving, their heart rate and breathing increased in direct proportion to the speed of the mental treadmill" (p. 40).

Children are naturally curious and learn from their senses of touch, taste, sight, hearing, and smell; therefore, a safe but stimulating environment with appropriate limits and supervision must be provided. The primary areas to consider are the child's age and developmental level, materials, techniques/activity, and the child's condition.

Safety Considerations for Implementing Activities

Child's Age and Developmental Level. The child's developmental level should be evaluated to ensure that no discrepancy exists between developmental skill level and the child's ability to manipulate materials for the therapeutic activities. For example, children under the age of 12 may not understand the need for precautions, or carry them out consistently and effectively. Infants and toddlers use mouthing behaviors to explore, which can lead to the ingestion of unsafe materials or injury from sharp objects. Toddlers often run with small toys or objects in their mouths, so caution should be taken with any materials that could lead to choking. Preschool-aged children will sometimes deliberately put things into their mouths and/or swallow them. Habits such as nail-biting or thumb-sucking increase the risk of choking on or ingesting substances that could be harmful.

Materials. Toxic materials should never be used. Toxic substances can be inhaled, ingested, or absorbed through the skin; and exposure to these substances can cause acute or chronic illness, an allergic reaction, or skin damage. Many safe alternatives exist (see Appendix A, "Art Materials and Projects for Children and Other High-Risk Individuals").

Additionally, materials considered safe for children may not be safe for a *particular* child. For example, children with cancer are susceptible to overwhelming, life-threatening infection at the time of diagnosis and/or relapse, during immunosuppressive therapy, and after prolonged antibiotic therapy. Certain seemingly innocent items such as fruits and vegetables used for printmaking may carry harmful organisms that can be devastating for these children. Also, children with compromised immune systems should always be offered new, unopened supplies (e.g., paint sets, clay, crayons) to avoid transmitting potentially harmful organisms from other children.

Although only nontoxic supplies should be used, some nontoxic supplies, such as colored felt tip markers, may emit strong odors. These odors, even if considered pleasant (e.g., mint, strawberry, bubblegum) can provoke nausea in certain sensitive individuals, such as postoperative patients or patients receiving chemotherapy. On the other hand, some children (e.g., children in isolation, children with visual impairments) may benefit from the sensory stimulation scented materials provide. Thus, having both types available is advisable.

Using recycled materials for projects is recommended as being both economical and environmentally friendly. Many excellent examples of their use can be found throughout this book. Moreover, children delight in transforming something intended for one purpose into something new. The source of these materials should always be determined to address safety concerns.

Glitter should be used only with children old enough to follow directions consistently. It should not be used with children who may put their fingers in their mouths or rub their eyes while working with glitter, because it may be transferred from fingers to mouth or eyes. In short, children using glitter require supervision.

Some of the activities in this book require the use of sharp tools or materials. In any activities requiring the use of scissors, the child should be taught how to use them properly. Blunt-edge scissors should be provided to children less than 7 years of age. Although some activities would not be considered safe with a group of children, many can be facilitated safely with one-on-one supervision.

For safety reasons, most hospitals prohibit the use of latex balloons. Children, particularly those under the age of 3, tend to put objects in their mouths. If a balloon pops in the child's mouth, a piece may be aspirated into the airway when the child inhales suddenly, as a reflex to the unexpected event. The piece of balloon can block air passageways, causing hypoxia, and even death. Further, certain types of latex balloons have extremely high levels of allergens, so some children may be at risk of an allergic reaction. Children who are more likely to become latex-sensitive are those who have frequent exposure to latex during medical procedures, including children with spina bifida; complex genitourinary disease; chronic indwelling medical devices made of latex; or hay fever, eczema, or asthma; and children who have had many surgeries or who have allergies to certain foods (Brehler & Kutting, 2001). Fortunately, Mylar balloons do not pose either of these risks and can often be substituted for latex balloons in activities.

Toys. Certain principles apply when selecting toys to use in therapeutic activities.

1. Follow all age recommendations and information concerning the safe use of the toy. Adapt as necessary for children who are developmentally delayed.
2. Do not use toys with sharp edges or points and small loose parts.
3. Provide close supervision when using any objects that can be propelled.
4. Be alert for toys with flexible joints that can catch a child's finger.
5. Use only toys made with nontoxic materials.

Techniques/Activity. Physical agents, such as noise, vibration, repetitive motion, heat, or electrical equipment, can cause injury and illness. For example, loud music may further decrease what hearing remains for a child with a hearing impairment. Also, a noisy activity could disturb children nearby who may need rest or sleep, thereby compromising the recovery of others. Therapeutic activities involving the use of heating elements and other electrical devices should be used only with children 8 years of age and older. Only low-temperature glue guns should be used.

Another consideration is the area where the activity will take place. Is the intended space sufficient? In a child's room, for example, available flat surface area may be minimal (e.g., due to an array of medical supplies and equipment; small hospital bedside tables). Rolling carts or tables or bed easels can be brought into the child's room to provide extra space and to prevent overcrowding existing space. Such measures will reduce the likelihood of accidents (e.g., tipping over paint containers) and the resulting discomfort the child would likely experience during an extensive cleanup.

Child's Condition. Exposure to materials or processes, or participation in activities that exceed an individual child's physical limitations, may place the child at high risk of further illness or injury. Many of the hazards can be eliminated or reduced with one-to-one supervision or other appropriate measures.

Therapeutic Activities for Children and Teens Coping with Healthcare Issues concludes with two appendices that contain valuable resources: Appendix A offers an extensive list of safety considerations, along with substitutions and adaptations for activity materials and methods; Appendix B lists helpful web sites. **Appendixes**

The CD bound to the back of this book contains all of the activities found in the book, as well as those marked with an asterisk in the table of contents. This allows the reader electronic access to facilitate reproduction of templates for use with activities. **CD**

CHAPTER 1

SEPARATION AND STRANGER ANXIETY

Young humans, perhaps more than any species, are exquisitely dependent organisms. The child needs reliable, loving attachment figures for normal social, emotional, behavioral, linguistic, and cognitive development. As such, children's separation distress, as well as their attachment behaviors (e.g., proximity seeking and displays of emotional distress in response to separation), are not only understandable but seen as necessary for survival.

Children may be separated from their parents for a variety of reasons, including parental separation or divorce; a parent's or child's illness, treatment, or hospitalization; child welfare involvement, such as foster or kinship care; disaster; incarceration of a parent; or military deployment; among others. Factors associated with parental separation, such as maternal depression, intimate partner violence, and parental substance abuse, have been shown to affect children's development and cognitive functioning (Black et al., 2002; Kernic et al., 2002). Jee and colleagues (2008) report that urban children who have experienced separation from a parent may have more learning difficulties at entrance to kindergarten. Separation from parents, regardless of the circumstances, can prove extremely stressful for the developing child.

Courtesy of Steven Koress Photography

LIST OF ACTIVITIES

Note: Asterisk (*) denotes that the activity is available on the CD that accompanies this book.

Separation Anxiety

Separation anxiety is a developmental stage during which children experience anxiety when separated from the primary caregiver, usually the mother. Separation anxiety is a normal occurrence between about 8 and 14 months of age. Some degree of separation anxiety is a good thing; it indicates that the child has developed healthy attachments to parents.

However, during the last half of the 20th century, a large body of literature developed that describes the difficulties hospitalized children, separated from their parents, experience (Bowlby, 1960; Quinton & Rutter, 1976; Robertson, 1958; Vernon, Schulman, & Foley, 1966). The research denotes the seriousness of separation anxiety for hospitalized children, including those beyond the age of 14 months, when "normal" children are placed in an "abnormal" situation in a strange environment without the presence and support of their parents. A recent study at a pediatric hospital during a two-week period found that about one third of children were sometimes unaccompanied (Roberts, 2010).

Unlike being separated from parents while at school or summer camp, children in the hospital face a variety of experiences that are truly scary and often painful or uncomfortable. Just the number of strangers children see can be overwhelming for any child. Strangers may be especially difficult for the child in the age group where separation anxiety and stranger anxiety coincide with a new intellectual skill, called *object permanence* (approximately 8 to 15 months), when the child now remembers objects and people that are not present. However, because in the hospital strangers often come to "do" something unpleasant or painful, even older children become very anxious when they see another unfamiliar face.

Separation anxiety is considered the primary source of stress for middle infancy through preschool-age children (ages 6 months through 3 years) who are hospitalized (Pearson, 2005). Although preschoolers can tolerate brief periods of separation, they still may display some separation anxiety behaviors. However, considering the disruption of familiar routines, differences between the hospital environment and home, and the regression that typically occurs when children are hospitalized, separation may be the primary source of stress for children up to 5 years of age and older.

As a result of the stress associated with illness, injury, and hospitalization, separation concerns may resurface for older children. School-age children cope better than younger children, but separation from family members remains high on the list of stressors. In many circumstances, for adolescents who are gaining independence, separation from their peers tends to be more intimidating than separation from family members when hospitalized.

Stages of Separation Anxiety

Young children separated from their parents respond to the separation in three stages: protest, despair, and detachment (Bowlby, 1960; Robertson; 1958).

1. *Protest*. The protest stage is an active and aggressive response to the absence of the parent, characterized by crying, screaming, or kicking. The child seems inconsolable and constantly watches for signs of the parent's return. This stage may last for several hours to a week.

2. *Despair*. The second stage is a time of increasing hopelessness. Crying basically stops and the child appears depressed. Although the child may continue to cry intermittently, more often he or she appears withdrawn and quiet. When the parent returns, the child will once again cry vigorously. This response often was misinterpreted as re-upsetting the child who had finally adjusted to the parent's absence, and thus provided the rationale for keeping parents away during hospitalization and procedures.

3. *Detachment*. After a long period of parental absence, detachment occurs. This stage is characterized by the child's reinvestment in his or her surroundings and normal activity. The child forms superficial attachments to others, becoming increasingly self-centered and more interested in material objects (Bowlby, 1960). If the parent returns, he or she is met with apathy and the child's inability to reattach. The adverse effects are less likely to be reversed once the child has reached the stage of detachment.

Dramatic changes in hospital visiting policies over the last four decades, with parents now welcomed around the clock, and with beds provided for them to room-in with their children, have been key strategies in decreasing the occurrence of the third stage of separation anxiety for hospitalized children. Protest and despair, however, continue to be observed, even with brief separations from either parent.

Homesickness

Although separation anxiety is an issue of special concern for younger children, children of all ages can experience homesickness. Homesickness is "the distress and functional impairment caused by an actual or anticipated separation from home and attachment objects such as parents" (Thurber, Walton, & Council on School Health, 2007, p. 192). Characteristics of homesickness include acute longing and preoccupying thoughts of home. Apart from familiar people and environments, almost all children, adolescents, and adults experience some degree of homesickness.

Homesickness may be one of the most prevalent types of distress experienced by hospitalized children. In a study of homesickness in hospitalized children, 88% of the children reported some homesick feelings (Thurber, Patterson et al., 2007). Half of the children had moderate to severe levels of homesickness, and at least 20% had associated symptoms of acute depression and anxiety, with anxiety a more reliable covariate of homesickness than depression. Researchers have found no gender differences in the prevalence or intensity of homesickness (Thurber, 1999; Thurber, Patterson et al., 2007; Thurber, Sigman, Weisz, & Schmidt, 1999); nor are there cultural differences in the way individuals and researchers define the term "homesickness" (Thurber, 1995; Verschuur, Eurelings-Bontekoe, Spinhoven, & Duijsens, 2003).

Although little previous experience away from home is a risk factor for homesickness at camp or school, research indicates that previous experience away from home does not function as a protective factor against homesickness for hospitalized children (Thurber, 2005). The types of previous separation experiences shape expectations of future separation. Thus, if an earlier separation through hospitalization has been a negative experience then expectations of future separations may be negative, which, in turn, can cause homesickness. Thurber, Walton et al. (2007) conclude that experience is probably most valuable when it refines coping strategies.

The child's belief that homesickness will be strong, and a negative first impression of, and low expectations for, the new environment are powerful predictors of homesickness (Thurber & Sigman, 1998). The child's attitude about hospitalization is strong predictor of homesickness intensity. However, an insecure attachment relationship with primary caregivers is the most common risk factor associated with homesickness (Thurber, Patterson et al., 2007; Thurber & Sigman, 1998). Children and adolescents with an anxious-ambivalent attachment style are particularly likely to experience significant distress on separation from home. Further, Thurber, Patterson et al. found that frequent visitation has a strong positive correlation with positive emotion; and, unfortunately, mothers who rate themselves as insecurely attached to their children are less likely to visit them in the hospital (Robinson, Rankin, & Drotar, 1996). Unsure about how reliably or positively primary caregivers will respond to their displays of distress, these children may have mixed feelings about how worthy they are of other people's love and attention. However, Thurber, Patterson et al. point out that although these children's moods are clearly affected by insecure attachment and low perceived control, the same children in their study did not necessarily miss home or primary caregivers: "For some children, inpatient hospitalization represented a significant upgrade from their home environment. In the hospital, they received three square meals a day, positive attention from adults, clear boundaries, and supervised play with peers" (p. 19).

Special Considerations

Interventions to help children cope with separation anxiety center around increasing children's sense of control and enhancing their ability to understand and effectively cope with their healthcare experience (Gaynard et al., 1990). Suggested general strategies for hospital staff can be found in Table 1.1.

Separation activities assist the healthcare professional in making contact and establishing rapport with a child and family in a supportive and nonthreatening way. The activities can

Table 1.1 Hospital Staff Strategies and Rationale for Helping Children Cope with Separation Anxiety

Strategy	Rationale
1. Encourage parents to bring in reminders of home. • For infants and very young children, ask parents to bring an article of clothing they have worn or blanket they have slept with, which has their scent on it, to put in the child's bed. • If parents wear cologne, suggest they dab some on a stuffed animal that the child can cuddle. • Tell parents to bring transitional objects, such as the child's blanket.	Familiar objects or sensations are comforting for children away from home.
2. Establish a routine. • Ask parents to complete a questionnaire that identifies feeding, bath, and bedtime rituals for young children so that they can be incorporated into hospital routines. • Post a daily schedule listing such information as meal times, rest periods, and personal care.	A routine offers children a sense of structure and predictability.
3. Provide information by using concepts the child will understand. • Help children who can't tell time anticipate when their family will return by connecting the time to a familiar event, such as breakfast or when a favorite show is on TV. • Suggest parents use concepts such as ''I'll be back when you are having your lunch.''	The provision of age-appropriate information reduces children's fear of the unknown and thus enhances children's sense of control.
4. Assign a consistent volunteer to spend time with the child whose family is unable to visit often.	Consistency fosters trust and bonding with a surrogate caregiver.
5. Encourage parents to be thoughtful and honest when communicating with the child. • Remind parents to call if an emergency delays their return to the hospital. • Discourage parents from ''sneaking away'' when the child is distracted or asleep.	Predictability and honesty build trust.
6. Encourage parents to try to schedule departures after naps and mealtimes.	Children are more susceptible to separation anxiety when tired, hungry, or sick.
7. Establish innovative protocols to help children cope with predictably difficult separations. • Equip the child and parent with walkie-talkies to enable voice communication until the child is anesthetized or sedated for surgery or other procedures.*	Hearing a parent talk or sing comforts children and eases the stress of separation.

*Cardinal Glennon Children's Hospital in Saint Louis, MO, has been using walkie-talkies for children having surgery since 2002. See Mossman, B. (2004). How I do it: Using walkie-talkies to overcome the fear of separation in children having surgery. *ORL — Head and Neck Nursing, 22*(2), 21–22.

promote a smooth transition into the healthcare system. For children who were prepared before their admission, the activities will reinforce what they were told and therefore promote trust.

During hospitalization, children seek information and express concerns in a variety of ways. Healthcare professionals should be sure to observe both the child's nonverbal and verbal communication. While engaging in the activities, the professional will be able to discern a variety of factors about the child: age appropriateness of behavior, emotional maturity, disabling conditions, ability to comprehend directions or information, and acquired skills. Psychological indicators to be considered during these observations include the number of hospital admissions, family support system, stress factors in the home at the time of admission, reason for admission, the anticipated length of stay, and the ability of parents or other significant people in the child's life to room-in with or visit the child. These observations can help the professional select additional activities found in this and other chapters.

An accurate understanding of homesickness is needed when working with hospitalized children. For example, severe homesickness does not remit spontaneously; it does, however, get better with positive coping efforts. Thus, children should be encouraged to seek support from surrogate caregivers in the new environment. Talking about homesickness will not cause homesickness; rather, it provides a way to educate and encourage a homesick child. Not all children are homesick for their parents; what some children most miss is home cooking or the family pet. Instead of assuming, it is important to always ask, "What do you miss most about home?" Because homesickness does not always feel like sadness or nervousness, homesick children are sometimes difficult to identify. Some homesick children feel angry, irritable, or disoriented.

A variety of strategies exist for healthcare providers to use to prevent homesickness in hospitalized children (see Table 1.2). These strategies form the rationale for many of the activities

Table 1.2 Hospital Staff Homesickness Prevention Strategies and Rationales

Strategy	Rationale
1. Prior to admission, encourage parents to be honest with their child about the purpose and timing of hospitalization.	Coping with reality prior to admission prevents uncomfortable surprises once admitted. Dishonesty can cause children to lose confidence in the reliability of their caregivers, which can increase homesickness and lessen trust.
2. Orient the child to the unit. • Tour the unit. • Point out labeled photographs of staff members, calendars, and the unit's daily schedule. • Introduce the child to other children.	Children who feel they have some control over the novel hospital environment may experience less fear and homesickness.
3. Convey a consistent message about the length of the hospital stay.	Conflicting messages reduce children's confidence in caregivers. Unpredictability leads to anxiety.
4. Help the child make contact, by telephone or in person, when other family members are hospitalized as a result of a traumatic event.	When family members are in different parts of the hospital, or even different hospitals, this can induce homesickness and separation anxiety.
5. Continue efforts to orient the child to time and place. • Hang photographs of family members, large clocks, and calendars in the child's room. • Turn lights on in the child's room during the day. • Provide frequent reminders regarding caregivers' presence.	Even within the course of a day, children's mental status can change dramatically. Changes often involve a distorted sense of time and a fluctuating awareness of the caregivers' presence, which can cause homesickness.
6. Apprise caregivers of the importance of frequent, reliable contact with the child, and encourage them to call and give ample warning if they are unable to make a scheduled visit.	Uncertainties and changes in caregiver visitations can cause disappointment and homesickness, and reduce trust.
7. Keep the child apprised of the day's schedule, and give ample warning if there are going to be times when the child will be left alone, however briefly.	Homesickness can result when children feel left alone, especially early in a hospital stay before they know the staff and routine.
8. Forewarn parents if and when their child will be moved to a different room, and assure the child that this information has been shared with his or her parents.	Finding the room empty or occupied by a stranger is unsettling for parents. Children may fear that their parents will be unable to find them.
9. Minimize discharge uncertainty, whenever possible. • Avoid changing the date, if possible. • Tell children and parents that discharge dates are difficult to predict and give them a range of possible dates.	When an exact date is spoken out loud, children (and parents) tend to fixate on it. Homesickness can be provoked by a change in the promised date.

Note. Adapted from Thurber, C., Walton, E., & Council on School Health. (2007). Preventing and treating homesickness. *Pediatrics, 119*, 192–201.

in this chapter. For unplanned hospitalizations, the focus is on the treatment of homesickness by providing information, positive modeling, and coping skills training as soon as the child is stable. The first step is to normalize the experience for the child; children need to know that almost all children feel a bit sad and nervous when they are separated from home and loved ones.

An important component of these activities is the opportunity they provide for the healthcare professional to address the needs of the child and family. Information from the activities can be shared with other professionals when appropriate. Ancillary professionals can be brought into the treatment process when warranted. Most importantly, the activities provide the healthcare professional with information to develop an individualized intervention program for a child and produce the ways and means for follow-up.

Activity Goals

Early research documented the value of therapeutic play in helping children to cope with separation and to ease homesickness (Hyde, 1971; Latimer, 1978). Later research emphasizes the importance of the relationship between the adult and the child (Carroll, 2002). The activities in this chapter incorporate both concepts and can be grouped into four major intervention strategies: providing information, personalizing space, using familial and other support systems, and identifying coping techniques.

Providing Information

The coping behavior most often used by children who are confronted with a new healthcare experience is orienting, for example, attempts to learn about the new environment. Orienting behaviors can help the child ease the physical unfamiliarity of the hospital, as well as the procedural unfamiliarity of what happens there. Staff Mix-Up and Scavenger Hunt are activities that support the orienting responses of children, which enable them to learn information about their surroundings. Gaining this knowledge is an important way that children can attempt to gain control over the stressful situation.

Personalizing Space

Children usually are in the hospital for only a short time before personal objects start to accumulate at their bedside, to personalize their space. These "bedside displays" can play an important role in developing, deepening, and enriching relationships between children, families, and hospital staff (Lewis, Kerridge, & Jorden, 2009), and therefore help reduce the negative impact of separation. The boundaries between the hospital environment and home appear blurred when observing hospital bedside displays (HBDs). Such displays are not simply an aesthetic device; children and families who create them are conscious that others can view the display, thus serving as a source of communication. Objects may serve as talismans, symbols of hope, substitutes for personal vigilance, and markers of the illness trajectory (Lewis, 2007). Some objects can facilitate memories of special events, such as rites of passage; plus the displays make those memories accessible to others present in the hospital, including staff, other patients, and families. Research suggests that displays have many important functions: providing reassurance and familiarity, strengthening identify, creating possibilities for communication, and maintaining important connections with people, places, and social networks (Lewis et al., 2009).

Doorknob Signs, Bulletin Board, and No-Sew Pillow are activities designed to help children personalize their space. The creations resulting from these activities can serve as important objects that convey information about the child, as well as provide an excellent resource for communication.

Using Familial and Other Support Systems

Hospitalized children usually express concern over family separation, and view the presence of parents as important for minimizing discomfort. Activities that promote discussion of the family (or other support network if a traditional family is not present) and friends can help reinforce the important emotional connection between the child and significant others, as well as give the healthcare professional an understanding of issues that may need to be addressed. All About Me, CD Postcards, Funny Family Fotos, People Important to Me Tree, Pop Art Photo Tints, Special People Chain, The People I Live With, Rubber-Stamped Stationery, No Tick-Tock Clock, ABCD News via Skype, and Warm Wishes Tree can accomplish this.

Activities elsewhere in the book that involve interactions among patients can encourage supportive relationships between patients. These relationships can be particularly helpful for adolescents.

Hospitalized children have greater difficulty than healthy children in identifying coping techniques that they can use to deal with a hospital experience. They face many new experiences, in most cases with some level of anxiety, which interferes with their ability to problem-solve. Healthcare professionals can help children recognize coping strategies and understand their meanings. Activities such as The Key to Making the Best of the Situation and Steps to Staying Connected encourage discussion of coping techniques. They also indicate to the child that he or she will be discharged from the hospital, an underlying concern of many children.

Identifying Coping Techniques

ACTIVITY 1.1.   ABCD NEWS VIA SKYPE

Skyping is a wonderful tool to help children who are homebound, hospitalized, or in hospice stay connected with family, friends, and classmates. Older children will have little trouble sustaining meaningful conversations, whereas younger children with less social experience may experience some challenges in doing so. This project allows children to interact, but in a more structured manner, guided by an adult.

Therapeutic Goal: To reduce feelings of home-sickness by promoting communication with classmates.	**Materials:**
	☐ Computers
Age Group: Primary/school-age	☐ Skype software
Adult/Child Ratio: 1:1	☐ Short cardboard tube
Required Time: Varies—can be a longer project	☐ Styrofoam ball
Restrictions and Precautions: Take glue precautions.	☐ Glue

Process

1. Contact the child's teacher to invite participation in a Skype project between the child and his or her classmates. One format is to have the children pretend to be TV journalists or "talking heads" in a news broadcast. Provide examples of various approaches the child can use, such as doing interviews, reading a news report, giving an editorial, providing entertainment (e.g., sing a song or do a magic trick); or presenting an experience they have documented, using photographs or drawings (i.e., photojournalism). The topic can be connected to a subject being studied in the classroom or something in which the child has a special interest.

2. Once the topic has been decided, help the child (while the teacher works with classmates) formulate and put together what he or she would like to do. Take age and energy level into consideration.

3. If desired, the child can make a microphone by gluing a Styrofoam ball to one end of the cardboard tube.

4. Coordinate the time with the teacher and set up communication via Skype (www.skype.com).

5. Allow the child to present his or her portions of the "show."

6. When the show is completed, encourage the child to discuss the experience.

ACTIVITY 1.2.   ALL ABOUT ME

The information obtained by having children complete All About Me sheets can help staff to learn about each child's unique personality and, thereby, tailor their approach, choice of conversation topic, and delivery of care accordingly.

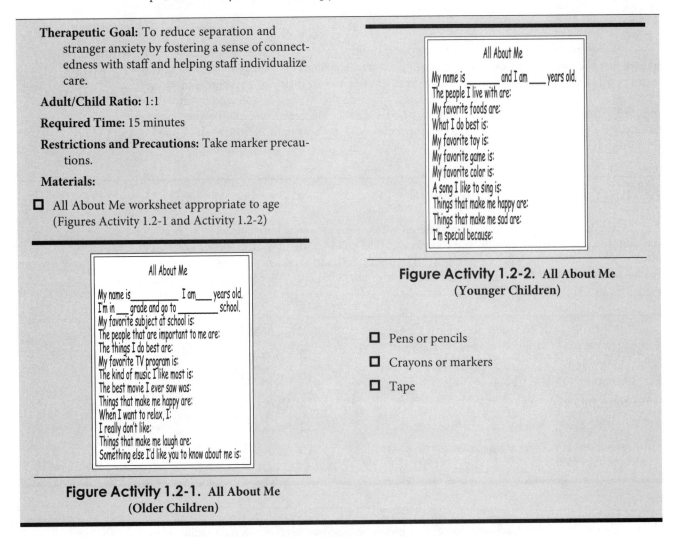

Therapeutic Goal: To reduce separation and stranger anxiety by fostering a sense of connectedness with staff and helping staff individualize care.

Adult/Child Ratio: 1:1

Required Time: 15 minutes

Restrictions and Precautions: Take marker precautions.

Materials:

☐ All About Me worksheet appropriate to age (Figures Activity 1.2-1 and Activity 1.2-2)

> All About Me
>
> My name is _____ I am ___ years old.
> I'm in ___ grade and go to _____ school.
> My favorite subject at school is:
> The people that are important to me are:
> The things I do best are:
> My favorite TV program is:
> The kind of music I like most is:
> The best movie I ever saw was:
> Things that make me happy are:
> When I want to relax, I:
> I really don't like:
> Things that make me laugh are:
> Something else I'd like you to know about me is:

Figure Activity 1.2-1. All About Me
(Older Children)

> All About Me
>
> My name is _____ and I am ___ years old.
> The people I live with are:
> My favorite foods are:
> What I do best is:
> My favorite toy is:
> My favorite game is:
> My favorite color is:
> A song I like to sing is:
> Things that make me happy are:
> Things that make me sad are:
> I'm special because:

Figure Activity 1.2-2. All About Me
(Younger Children)

☐ Pens or pencils

☐ Crayons or markers

☐ Tape

Process

1. Have the child fill in the worksheet, providing assistance if needed.

2. Invite the child to use crayons or markers to color in and decorate the worksheet.

3. Encourage the child to select a place in his or her room or just outside it to display the completed worksheet, so staff can read it.

ACTIVITY 1.3.   BULLETIN BOARD

Unlike typical bulletin boards, these can be used even by preschoolers because they don't require the use of thumbtacks. The little ones can participate by choosing the fabric and ribbon, and you can easily and quickly finish the project for them.

Therapeutic Goal: To reduce feelings of homesickness by personalizing the children's space.

Age Group: Preschool/primary/school-age/adolescent

Adult/Child Ratio: 1:6 (lower with small children)

Required Time: 30 minutes

Restrictions and Precautions: Take scissors and glue gun precautions.

Materials:

☐ Pieces of Styrofoam (3/4-inch thick), 1 foot × 2 foot or larger (1 per child)

☐ Fabric, cut 2 inches wider on all sides from the Styrofoam pieces (try to provide an assortment of fabrics for children to choose from, including traditional fabrics of other cultures)

☐ Glue gun

☐ Ruler

☐ Scissors

☐ Ribbons

☐ Buttons (optional)

☐ Removable picture hangers

Process

1. Allow the children to select the fabric and ribbons that they wish to use.

2. Instruct the children to lay their piece of fabric face down on a hard surface.

3. Ask the children to center their piece of Styrofoam atop the fabric and glue the fabric to one of the long sides of the Styrofoam.

4. Allow the glue to cool completely and then show the children how to glue the fabric on the opposing side, pulling it taut so that it is smooth on the front side.

5. Demonstrate how to fold up the two shorter ends as if wrapping a gift (i.e., fold in the sides, fold down the flap, and glue it in place), then have the children do the same.

6. Show the children how to arrange the ribbon in a grid pattern on the front side of the bulletin board (diagonally or vertically), spacing them about 2 inches apart; glue the ends to the back side of the bulletin board.

7. Let the children glue on buttons or other decorative trims to make a border, if they wish.

8. Hang the bulletin board with removable picture hangers.

9. To use, simply tuck messages, cards, and photos between the board and the ribbons.

ACTIVITY 1.4.   CD POSTCARDS

Texting is the method of communication preferred by most teens these days. Even so, many of them will still find it fun to make and send these clever "postcards" in spite of the seeming obsolescence of "putting pen to paper."

Therapeutic Goal: To reduce feelings of separation by promoting communication with family and friends.

Age Group: School-age/adolescent

Adult/Child Ratio: 1:10

Required Time: 15–20 minutes

Restrictions and Precautions: Take marker precautions.

Materials:

☐ Recycled CDs (e.g., damaged, dated, or from junk mail)

☐ Permanent markers

☐ Stickers (tiny)

☐ Postage stamp (check for current rate)

Process

1. Tell the children to write their message on the side of the CD with the label. They can write their message in traditional line format or write it in a spiral fashion.

2. Let the children decorate around the message using stickers and/or permanent markers.

3. Ask the children to write the mailing address on the shiny side of the CD, using a permanent marker.

4. Help the children to place postage stamps of the correct denomination on the shiny side, above and to the right of the address.

Variation   Paper plates also can be used as postcards.

ACTIVITY 1.5. DOORKNOB SIGNS

Taking ownership of their small room in a hospital can be a first step toward positive coping for children. Doorknob signs can help them define their personal space. Children should be supported in the use of other methods for identifying their personal space, as well, such as bringing their own pillows or sheets from home, or hanging artwork they have created or chosen on the wall.

Therapeutic Goal: To reduce feelings of separation by allowing children to personalize their space.	**Materials:**
Age Group: Preteen/adolescent	☐ Lightweight cardboard, cut into 8-inch × 4-inch pieces
Adult/Child Ratio: 1:10	☐ Pencil
Required Time: 30 minutes	☐ Compass
Restrictions and Precautions: Take scissors and marker precautions.	☐ Scissors
	☐ Markers

Process

1. Explain how privacy signs are used in hotels to let guests communicate their wishes to staff, such as "Do not disturb" or "Please clean room."

2. Ask the children what message they would like people to read before entering their room; for example:

   • Privacy Please

   • Danger Ahead

   • Do Not Disturb

   • Please Knock

   • No Grumpy People Allowed

   • Poke-free Zone

   • No Trespassing

   • Beware of Kid

   • Enter at Your Own Risk

   • Friendly Faces Welcome

3. Show the children how to use the compass to draw a 3-inch circle, 1 inch below the top of the cardboard.

4. When they have finished drawing the circle, instruct them to make a cut from the center of the top edge to the circle, and then cut out the circle.

5. Pass around markers to the children to write their message on the cardboard, using bold lettering and creating a colorful design on the background.

6. Encourage the children to display their signs on their doors, reminding them that staff may not always be able to comply with their wishes.

ACTIVITY 1.6.   NO-SEW PILLOW

Fleece is wonderfully soft and comforting. These pretty pillows will help make hospitalized children's rooms more homelike. If possible, provide a variety of colors and patterns from which children can choose. Teens may enjoy drawing and cutting the pattern themselves.

Therapeutic Goal: To facilitate coping with home-sickness by personalizing the environment.

Age Group: School-age/adolescent

Adult/Child Ratio: 1:8

Required Time: 40 minutes, plus advance preparation

Restrictions and Precautions: Take scissors and paint precautions.

Materials:

☐ Two 14-inch × 14-inch squares of fleece per pillow

☐ Scissors with sharp blades

☐ Ruler

☐ Crayon or pen

☐ Polyester stuffing

☐ Fabric paint or markers

Process

1. On the wrong side (the side without the pattern) of one of the fabric pieces, use the ruler and crayon or pen to draw an 11-inch square in the center of the fabric, each side of the square equidistant from the fabric edge.

2. Lay the two pieces of fabric together, with the piece with the square drawn on it facing up.

3. Cut strips from the edges of the fabric toward the center, 1 inch apart and 3 inches in length (to the crayon lines), around the perimeter of the fabric.

4. Demonstrate for the children how to place the wrong sides of the two squares together and match up the top and bottom fringe pieces.

5. Show them how to tie an overhand knot close to the base of the fringe, and tug gently. Let the children continue tying knots for each pair of fringe pieces on three sides of the pillow cover, leaving the last side open for stuffing.

6. Ask the children to insert the stuffing into the pillow cover, and then finish tying knots across the last side of the pillow.

7. Invite the children to decorate the pillow with fabric markers, if desired.

ACTIVITY 1.7.   FUNNY FAMILY FOTOS

Family photographs are always helpful for children to look at when they are missing their loved ones. Funny Family Fotos can be especially beneficial for sad children, because most can't help but smile when they look at them.

Therapeutic Goal: To reduce separation anxiety by creating a family keepsake.

Age Group: School-age/adolescent

Adult/Child Ratio: 1:8

Required Time: 30 minutes

Restrictions and Precaution: Take glue and scissor precautions.

Materials:

☐ Photographs of family

☐ Magazine, postcards, or downloaded pictures of a group of people, cartoon characters, or animals. Examples include:

  • *The Simpsons* or other well-known cartoon family

  • A pride of lions

  • Addams Family or the Munsters

  • A rock band

  • Robots

  • Formally dressed musicians or people dressed in clothing from another era

  Note: The group picture should have as many people or more as those in each child's family, with heads that are approximately the same size or slightly smaller than those in the photo.

☐ Glue

☐ Colored cardstock or cardboard

☐ Clear self-adhesive paper

Process

1. Have the children carefully cut out the heads from the family snapshot.

2. Glue the heads from the snapshot over the heads of the people or characters in the group photo.

3. Mount the picture on cardstock or cardboard.

4. Cover with self-adhesive paper.

Variation

Use the Lights, Camera, Color! program found on Crayola.com to turn a family photo, which has been downloaded into a computer, into a coloring page for young children. Don't forget pets!

ACTIVITY 1.8.   NO TICK-TOCK CLOCK

This activity allows children who are unable to tell time to anticipate when their family will return. If the child is capable, allow him or her to assist in making the clock.

Therapeutic Goal: To reduce separation anxiety by helping the child to understand when his or her family will visit next.

Age Group: Preschool/primary

Adult/Child Ratio: 1:1

Required Time: 10 minutes

Restrictions and Precautions: Take scissor precautions if the child is helping to make clock.

Materials:

☐ Paper plate

☐ Scissors

☐ Poster board scraps or cardstock

☐ Paper fasteners

☐ Markers

☐ Real clock

Process

1. Draw numbers on the paper plate, as they would appear on the face of a clock.

2. Cut two strips of cardboard, one 2 – 1/2 inches in length, and the other 1 – 1/2 inches in length.

3. Cut one end of each cardboard strip to a point.

4. Attach the squared end of the two strips to the center of the plate with the paper fastener.

5. Set the clock to the time of an anticipated family visit.

6. Provide the child with a real clock and explain what will happen when the real clock hands are in the same position as those on the No Tick-Tock Clock. The child can then watch the real clock and compare it with the No Tick-Tock Clock to see when they coincide.

ACTIVITY 1.9.   PEOPLE IMPORTANT TO ME TREE

This activity is best suited for long-term patients.

Therapeutic Goal: To reduce separation anxiety by identifying familial and social support systems and provide comfort during times of separation.

Age Group: School-age/adolescent

Adult/Child Ratio: 1: 1

Required Time: 30 minutes advance preparation at least one day prior to the activity; 1 hour or more for activity

Restrictions and Precautions: Mix the plaster of paris in a well-ventilated area. Take scissors and glue precautions. Not recommended for children with short attention spans.

Materials:

☐ Bare tree branch

☐ Paint (optional)

☐ Paintbrush (optional)

☐ 5-pound coffee can or similar-size container (or smaller if using a small branch)

☐ Plaster of paris

☐ Paint stirrer or other utensil for mixing

☐ Photographs or drawings the child has made of family and friends (ask family members to bring from home)

☐ Wooden or plastic shower curtain loops

☐ Pencils

☐ Heavy wrapping paper or colored cardstock

☐ Glue

☐ Scissors

☐ Ribbon

Process

1. Paint the branch, if desired.

2. Mix the plaster of paris according to package directions and pour it into the can or container.

3. As the plaster begins to harden, insert the branch and hold it in place for several minutes until it stands without support. Allow to dry overnight.

4. Show the child how to use the curtain loop as a template and trace the shape onto the back of each photo; then cut them out along the traced lines.

5. To back the photos, tell the child to glue them to the wrong side of the wrapping paper or colored paper and cut out the circle again.

6. Have the child glue each photo to a curtain loop.

7. Help the child to string a small piece of ribbon through the small hangers at the top of the loops and tie them to the tree branches.

8. Invite the child to identify each of the people on the tree and tell why they are important to him or her.

9. Help the child think of things he or she can do while in the hospital to stay in touch with the people he or she cares about.

Variation

Seasonal or holiday decorations, such as shamrocks, candy canes, stars, pumpkins, turkeys, watermelons, eggs, or valentine hearts may be hung on the tree, as well.

ACTIVITY 1.10.   THE PEOPLE MATCH GAME

The People Match Game is located on the CD that accompanies this book.

ACTIVITY 1.11.   POP ART PHOTO TINTS

This activity is based on pop artist Andy Warhol's unique style of silk-screening, using repeated images. Children can be shown a picture of a Warhol creation in this style to stimulate the creative use of color and help them visualize the project outcome.

Therapeutic Goal: To reduce separation anxiety by creating a family keepsake and providing comfort during times of separation.

Age Group: Primary/school-age/adolescent

Adult/Child Ratio: 1:10

Required Time: 45 minutes

Restrictions and Precautions: Take glue, marker, and/or paint precautions.

Materials:

☐ Family photos, on disc or scanned into a computer (1 per child)

☐ Colored pencils, light-colored watercolor markers, or crayons

☐ Poster board

☐ Glue

Process

1. Make three or more copies of each child's photo, printing it in high-contrast black and white.

2. Provide the children with three or more copies of their family photos.

3. Encourage the children to paint or color each of the photos, using a different color combination for each. Encourage the imaginative use of color.

4. Help the children mount the pictures on the poster board in a square, vertical, or horizontal formation (depending on artistic preference or the piece of poster board being used).

5. Invite the children to display the finished creation in their room (Figure Activity 1.11-1).

Figure Activity 1.11-1. Pop Art Photo Tints

Variation

Open a photograph using photo-editing software. Manipulate the colors in the photos using paint tools or color modes. Use the software collage tool or print out four or more images, each with variations of color, and mount them together.

ACTIVITY 1.12. RUBBER-STAMPED STATIONERY

Stamping projects are good for children with low energy or poor coordination, or who enjoy repetition, such as those with autism. There are a many creative possibilities for using rubber stamps. As such, it is worth investing in a wide variety so children have many to choose from as a means to express their individuality.

Therapeutic Goal: To reduce feelings of separation by promoting communication with family and friends.

Age Group: Primary/school-age, adolescent

Adult/Child Ratio: 1:10 (lower with young children)

Required Time: 20 minutes

Restrictions and Precautions: Take scissor precautions.

Materials:

- ☐ Scrap paper or large Post-it Notes
- ☐ Stationery paper and envelopes

- ☐ Ruler
- ☐ Pencils
- ☐ Scissors
- ☐ Assorted rubber stamps
- ☐ Ink stamp pads, assorted colors
- ☐ Fine-line markers (optional)

Process

1. Help the children measure and cut a piece of scrap paper or Post-it Note to create a "mask" that covers the center area of the stationery, leaving a 1 to 1–1/2-inch border on all sides. (Note: Young children will need more assistance.)

2. Encourage the children to experiment on scrap paper using different stamps, colors, and techniques (e.g., random or structured).

3. When the children determine the approach they wish to take, have them center the "mask" on a piece of stationery, leaving a uniform border on all four sides.

4. Have the children ink the rubber stamp and, while holding the mask in place, stamp around the border.

5. Instruct the children to remove the mask and allow the ink to dry. Repeat steps 3 to 5 for additional sheets of paper.

6. If a more finished look is desired, give the children the ruler and a fine-line marker to frame the inside edge.

7. For envelopes, have the children place a single stamp in the lower left quadrant on the front of the envelope and stamp the flap with a single image, or many if desired.

8. Encourage children to write letters to family and friends.

ACTIVITY 1.13. SCAVENGER HUNT

This activity appeals to most age groups. Vary the number and type of items for children to retrieve in accordance with their age and your goals for the activity (e.g., acquainting children with staff, orienting them to the environment, and/or familiarizing patients with medical equipment).

Therapeutic Goal: To promote coping with stranger anxiety by familiarizing children with staff and orienting them to the environment.

Age Group: Primary/school-age/adolescent

Adult/Child Ratio: Varies with ages of the children

Required Time: However long you wish to make it

Restrictions and Precautions: Provide explicit instructions on where the children can and cannot go, such as off the unit or into other people's rooms.

Materials:

☐ List of items to be found

☐ Rules of the game

☐ Labeled map of unit

☐ Small bags

Process

1. Create a list of items for the children to collect. Place some of the items in common areas such as an activity room, kitchen, and waiting areas. Locating some of the items should require that the children interact with staff, such as getting a signature from a nurse or obtaining an item to which only a staff member has access. Some ideas include:

   • Drinking straw

   • Cotton swab

   • Hospital bracelet

   • Bandage

   • Piece of chewing gum

   • Penny

   • Signature of a nurse who likes broccoli

   • Red pen

   • Large paper clip

   • Business card

2. Explain the object of the game to the children: to obtain as many objects from the list as they can in a specified period of time.

3. Discuss the rules of the game—for example, not leaving the unit, not going into other children's rooms. Provide each child with a list of the rules.

4. Provide each child with a list of items to be located and a small bag in which to carry them. Let the children know when and where to meet when the game is over.

Variation

For toddlers and preschoolers, simply place toys in different areas and ask staff who are not familiar to the children to point them out.

ACTIVITY 1.14.   SPECIAL-PEOPLE CHAIN

The image of people holding hands is symbolic of strength, unity, and friendship. This activity can help remind children of their connectedness with family and friends, or be used to foster a greater sense of connectedness with those involved in their care.

Therapeutic Goal: To reduce separation anxiety by identifying familial and social support systems and creating a symbolic representation of support systems.

Age Group: Preschool/primary/school-age

Adult/Child Ratio: 1:1

Required Time: 30 minutes

Restrictions and Precautions: Take scissors, glue, and marker precautions.

Materials:

☐ Colored paper

☐ Gingerbread man cookie cutter

☐ Pencil

☐ Colored paper

☐ Scissors

☐ Markers

☐ Crayons

☐ Decorative trims (e.g., yarn, sequins, fabric scraps, glitter)

☐ Glue

1. Measure the height and width of the cookie cutter.

2. Cut a long strip of paper to the same height as the cookie cutter.

3. Give the children the cookie cutter to use as a stencil, and trace the gingerbread man onto the far left side of the paper.

4. Leaving the gingerbread man on top, demonstrate how to fold the paper back and forth accordion style, so that there are four or five same-size squares.

5. Have the children cut around the tracing, leaving the outstretched hands uncut, to create a chain of people holding hands.

6. Ask the children to write the name of one of their family members or friends on each of the figures. If needed, make an additional chain of people.

7. Encourage the children to color and/or decorate the figures with crayons, yarn, sequins, and/or fabric, and to include characteristics that match their friends' or family member's features, such as eye color, hair color, and clothing style.

8. Invite the children to talk about each of the people in the chain.

9. Encourage the children to display their chain in a prominent place.

Variation

To promote enhanced patient/staff relations, suggest that the children make a chain of people representing the healthcare team that is caring for them.

ACTIVITY 1.15.   STAFF MIX-UP

Incorporating humor while introducing the healthcare team is a good way to relax children and make the staff seem less threatening. Making the Staff Mix-Up book can be time-consuming, but laminating it allows you to disinfect it and use it over and over again. This is a good project to give to a student or volunteer.

Therapeutic Goal: To reduce stranger anxiety by familiarizing children with staff.	☐ Glue stick
Age Group: Preschool/primary	☐ Paper cutter (for best results)
Adult/Child Ratio: 1:1	☐ Laminator
Required Time: 1–1–1/2-hour advance preparation; 15–20 minutes to implement	☐ Notebook (9–1/2-inch × 6-inch), with rings
Restrictions and Precautions: None	☐ Heavy paper for notebook
Materials:	☐ Ruler
☐ Digital camera	☐ Pencil
☐ Printer	☐ Scissors

Process

1. Take close-up photos of the faces of six or more staff members. When taking the photos, stand the same distance away from each person, so that the images will be of uniform size.

2. Enlarge the images to 5-inches × 7-inches and print.

3. Center each photo on a page of notebook paper and glue it in place. The nose and the bottom of the person's ears should fall into the middle segment of the page.

4. Laminate each page.

5. Use the paper cutter to divide each photo into three equal horizontal segments, placing each picture in the notebook as it is completed.

6. With the child, look at each staff member's photo and tell the child the staff member's name and role, and say something nice about him or her.

7. After "introducing" each of the staff members, let the child flip the page segments and combine different photos to create funny new faces.

For more ideas, see Bright Ideas for Coping with a Strange Environment (Box Activity 1.15-1).

BOX ACTIVITY 1.15-1. BRIGHT IDEAS FOR COPING WITH A STRANGE ENVIRONMENT

- Ask parents of young children to complete a questionnaire that identifies feeding, bath, and bedtime rituals so that they can be incorporated into hospital routines.

- Post a daily schedule listing information such as meal times, rest periods, and personal care times, so that children can have a sense of structure and predictability.

- Assign a consistent volunteer to spend time with children whose family cannot visit often.

- Create a bulletin board and post on it current pictures of each staff member, along with pictures of them as an infant or child. Make a game of challenging the child to match current staff photos to pictures of them when they were young.

- Arrange for a "Welcome Wagon" committee to visit the child as soon after admission as possible; after they introduce themselves, ask them to tell the child some positive things about the hospital. To add to the warm welcome, suggest to visitors that they bring a small gift or activity packet for the newly admitted child.

- Compile a mobile library of interchangeable art for the wall in children's rooms, to enable them to personalize their space.

ACTIVITY 1.16.   STEPS TO STAYING CONNECTED

Steps to Staying Connected can be easily adapted to help children identify goals or positive coping strategies for just about any stressor they may encounter.

Therapeutic Goal: To reduce separation anxiety or homesickness by identifying coping techniques.

Age Group: Primary/school-age

Adult/Child Ratio: 1:8

Required Time: 30–40 minutes

Restrictions and Precautions: Take paint precautions.

Materials:

☐ Writing paper (1 sheet per child)

☐ Pencil (1 per child)

☐ Cushioned insoles, preferably child-size (1 per child)

☐ Brayers (a hand roller used to spread ink)

☐ Printing ink

☐ Butcher paper (one 4-foot × 3-foot sheet per child)

☐ Markers

Process

1. Provide each child with writing paper, butcher paper, and a pencil.

2. Engage the children in a discussion about what it feels like to be away from family and friends.

3. Ask the children to generate a list of "steps they can take" to feel connected with those they miss. If needed, give examples, such as calling on the telephone, sending an email, Skyping, writing a letter, drawing a picture, or looking at photographs. Have them write down the ideas they like.

4. Using the insole as a stamp, show the children how to apply ink to the latex side of the insole and make at least one footprint on their butcher paper for each idea they have written down. They can make a walking pattern, abstract designs, or totally random placements.

5. When the paint has dried, give the children markers to write a "step to take" in each footprint.

6. Encourage the children to hang their paintings where they can see them frequently and be reminded of the coping strategies they have identified.

For more ideas, see Bright Ideas for Staying Connected (Box Activity 1.16-1).

- Ask parents to bring photo albums or family pictures for children to look at.
- Ask parents to tape-record themselves reading their child's favorite stories or singing their child's favorite songs.
- Give teens a video camera to use as a way to communicate with friends, school, and extended family.
- Encourage parents to bring favorite family foods from home (if compatible with children's hospital diets).
- Help children who cannot tell time anticipate when their family will return by connecting the time to a familiar event, such as breakfast or when a favorite show comes on TV.

ACTIVITY 1.17. THE KEY TO MAKING THE BEST OF THE SITUATION

The Key to Making the Best of the Situation is located on the CD that accompanies this book.

ACTIVITY 1.18. THE PEOPLE I LIVE WITH

This activity produces a colorful collage of family photos that the child can personalize.

Therapeutic Goal: To reduce separation anxiety by identifying familial and social support systems.

Age Group: Preschool/primary

Adult/Child Ratio: 1:1

Required Time: 20 – 30 minutes

Restrictions and Precautions: Take marker, scissors, and glue precautions

Materials:

☐ Two sheets of construction paper or lightweight poster board of contrasting colors

☐ Pencil

☐ Scissors or craft knife

☐ Markers or crayons

☐ Photos of people who live with the child (Note: Head shots work best.)

Process

1. Stack one sheet of construction paper or poster board on top of the other.
2. Draw the shape of a house on the top sheet of paper or poster board and cut it out from both sheets of paper. Use the full width and height of the paper. (Note: Omit this step if the child lives in an apartment.)
3. Out of the top sheet of paper or board, cut a window for each person living in the house or apartment.
4. Cut out a flap for the front door and fold it open.

5. Glue the two pieces of paper or poster board together.

6. Cut the background off each photo (optional).

7. Have the child glue one family member's photo in each window and the door; or, if photos are not available, encourage the child to draw pictures of his or her family members.

8. Assist the child as needed in writing the street number of the house where he or she lives, along with the names of each family member.

9. Give the child markers or crayons to add details to the house (Figure Activity 1.18-1).

Figure Activity 1.18-1. The People I Live With

10. Encourage the child to talk about the people he or she lives with and how it feels to be away from them.

11. Remind the child that family members are all waiting eagerly for him or her to come home, and help identify ways for the child to keep in touch with them.

12. Hang the picture of the house where the child can see it.

ACTIVITY 1.19.   UNIT SCRAPBOOK

Though time-consuming to make, unit scrapbooks are extremely beneficial, especially for those children who come to the unit disoriented or in an emergent situation. Because the books are laminated, they can be used many times over.

Therapeutic Goal: To facilitate coping with separation and homesickness by orienting children to their surroundings.	**Required Time:** 1–2 hours to make
	Precautions and Restrictions: None
Age Group: Primary/school-age/adolescent	**Materials:**
Adult/child Ratio: 1:1	☐ Digital camera

- ☐ Decorative scrapbooking materials
- ☐ Scissors
- ☐ Adhesive
- ☐ Plastic-covered photo album with plastic-covered pages or plastic-covered scrapbook

(pages will need to be laminated when completed for infection control)
- ☐ Crayons or markers
- ☐ Paper
- ☐ Pencil

Process

1. Compile photographs of staff, equipment, and/or various areas of interest on the unit.

2. Arrange the photographs decoratively in the album, using colorful papers and lettering to make it look visually appealing and less institutional.

3. Laminate.

4. Look at the scrapbook with the child and talk about each picture, inviting the child to ask questions about them.

5. Encourage the child to draw a picture of his or her room to add to the scrapbook.

ACTIVITY 1.20.   WARM WISHES TREE

This activity is adapted from the Japanese New Year's celebration custom of placing fortunes on bare-limbed trees.

Therapeutic Goal: To reduce separation anxiety by facilitating communication with family and friends and providing comfort during times of separation.

Age Group: Preschool/primary/school-age

Adult/Child Ratio: 1:1

Required Time: 30 minutes

Restrictions and Precautions: None

Materials:

- ☐ Heavy brown paper bag or package wrap
- ☐ Scissors
- ☐ Spray bottle filled with water
- ☐ 12-ounce or 1-liter plastic beverage bottle
- ☐ Small stones or other weights
- ☐ Cupcake liners
- ☐ Fine-line markers or pens
- ☐ Hole punch
- ☐ Green curling ribbon, yarn, thread, or string

Process

1. Cut off and discard the bottom of a large, brown paper bag, and cut open one side to create a rectangle; or cut a sheet of brown paper into a rectangle, approximately 3-feet × 2-feet square or larger.

2. Spray the paper lightly with water.

3. Gather the paper around the beverage bottle and twist it around the bottle neck (Figure Activity 1.20-1, step 1).

4. Cut down from the top of the paper to create four or five strips that will become the limbs of the tree (Figure Activity 1.20-1, steps 2 and 3).

5. Cut the untwisted ends into two or three strips and twist them to create smaller branches (Figure Activity 1.20-1, step 4).

Step 1   Step 2   Step 3

Step 4

Figure Activity 1.20-1. Warm Wishes Tree

6. Remove the bottle and fill the trunk with small stones or other weights.

7. Each time they visit, ask family and friends to write personal messages or affirmations around the perimeters of the cupcake liners.

8. Fold the liners in fourths and punch a hole in the narrow part of the folded paper.

9. Make buds on the tree by threading a piece of ribbon through the hole in each message then tie them to the tree.

10. Invite the child to pick a message off the tree whenever he or she is feeling lonely, or as part of his or her bedtime ritual. Read the message together with the child.

11. Leave the cupcake liners and pens in the child's room, along with a sign to remind loved ones to write new messages each time they come.

CHAPTER 2

SELF-EXPRESSION

Self-expression is the manifestation of one's individuality—displaying one's personal characteristics, showing one's internal beliefs or character by means of external actions or changes. Expression can occur with or without self-awareness. Children express themselves in a variety of ways, depending on their age, communication abilities, health status, and personality, to name just a few variables. The creative process allows children to escape from their situation and return to the world they know (Greaves, 1996). Sensitively selected play and other expressive opportunities can promote children's self-expression, an important adaptive technique for coping with stress.

Courtesy of Snow City Arts

There is a rich and growing body of research connecting expressive arts in healthcare programs to improved quality of care for patients, their families, and even medical staff, which is documented in the *State of the Field Report: Arts in Healthcare* 2009 (State of the Field Committee, 2009). This report can be accessed on the Society for the Arts in Healthcare web site (www.thesah.org).

LIST OF ACTIVITIES

Activity 2.1 Bridge to the Future	Activity 2.11 I Want to Scream
Activity 2.2 Emotion Ocean	Activity 2.12 Inside-Outside Boxes
Activity 2.3 Feeling Faces	Activity 2.13 Personalized T-Shirts
Activity 2.4 Feelings Collage	Activity 2.14 Sense-itivity Poems
Activity 2.5 Inner Vision/Outer View Masks	Activity 2.15 Interactive Storytelling
Activity 2.6 Felt Puppets	Activity 2.16 Temper-Rate
Activity 2.7 Get a-Head	Activity 2.17 The Complaint Department Is In
Activity 2.8 Graffiti Wall	Activity 2.18 Wishing Wells
Activity 2.9 Grand Designs	Activity 2.19 Wound Care for Feelings
Activity 2.10 Hospital Road Signs*	Activity 2.20 Zen-ga

Note: Asterisk (*) denotes that the activity is available on the CD that accompanies this book.

Developmental Aspects of Self-Expression

The recognition of the utility of emotional expression dates back to Charles Darwin, who emphasized its contribution to survival (Darwin, 1872; Oatley, 1992). Somewhere between the ages of about 4 and 8 months, infants mimic the emotional facial expressions of their caregivers. Because they are unable to differentiate themselves from their environment, they are imitating what they perceive. By the age of 4 years, children finally internalize their understanding of emotional expressions. However, there is an ongoing debate about whether expressed emotions are equivalent to a feeling state, when no cognition occurs. Feeling states often are difficult to access, especially in younger children.

We know that a typical 2-year-old displays a full range of emotions, and expresses them freely. In the toddler and preschool years, expressed emotions become increasingly complex and elaborate (Hyson, 1994). By the age of 5 years, children have developed more poise and control. By 7 years, children begin to become more introverted and thoughtful and, thus, they develop greater self-control and emotional stability. At around 8 years of age, children begin to openly express their feelings. In the next year or two, children learn to manage their emotional expressiveness in different situations, according to cultural expectations and for self-preservative purposes (Denham, 1998).

As children, we think first in images. Next we learn the words for these images. Then we often hide behind these words. Self-expressive activities can provide a nonthreatening and often nonverbal method to release thoughts and feelings. After engaging in such activities, children are typically less reluctant to say what is on their minds.

Self-Expression and Coping

Much of what we know about stress and coping stems from the literature about adults. However, Ryan-Wenger (1992) provides some rationale for the efficacy of the use of self-expression for children coping with healthcare issues: "Emotional expression," defined as behavior other than aggressive motor and verbal activities that expresses feelings or emotions, is among the 15 categories of strategies children use to cope with stress. Although the frequency or effectiveness of some of the strategies is often different, children's repertoire of coping strategies is the same during health and illness (Ryan-Wenger, 1996).

When feelings are not released, they are given the ability to fester and grow. Actively holding back or inhibiting thoughts and feelings can be hard work, and over time, the work of inhibition gradually undermines the body's defenses (Pennebaker, 1997). As with other stressors, inhibition can affect immune function, the action of the heart and vascular system, and even the biochemical workings of the brain and nervous system. Excessive holding back of thoughts, feelings, and behaviors can place individuals at risk for both major and minor diseases. Suppressing emotions also can reduce rapport and inhibit the formation of relationships between individuals (Butler et al., 2003).

Self-expressive activities help children cope by providing an opportunity for them to work through, reflect, and find meaning in their experiences (Rollins, 2008, 2009). When difficult feelings are dealt with openly and honestly, they lose some of their strength. For example, programs intended to promote expression of feelings have demonstrated positive results with respect to a variety of psychosocial measures in grieving children (Heiney, Dunaway, & Webster, 1995), children whose parent or grandparent has cancer (Heiney & Lesesne, 1996), children who have been witnesses to violence (Rollins, 1997), children with leukemia and undergoing painful procedures (Favara-Scacco, Smirne, Schilirò, & DiCataldo, 2001), and school-aged children of alcoholics (Emshoff & Anyan, 1991). Bolig (1990) reports that self-expression seems to lessen the negative impact of hospitalization for children.

Research shows that offering opportunities for self-expression via verbal, written, or other behavioral forms helps adolescents cope with hospitalization (Denholm, 1990). Posthospital interviews with adolescents indicate that opportunities for self-expression contributed to more positive memories about the hospitalization experience, as well as personal growth and insight gained from the experience. Ventilation of feelings was cited as the fourth most often used method of coping cited by adolescents with cystic fibrosis (Patton, Ventura, & Savedra, 1986).

Wistrom (2005) investigated what takes place during play therapy when hospitalized children were given the opportunity to use expressive art materials such as clay, paint, and/or textile, and the meaning children assign to their art objects. Through their activities, the children expressed fear, powerlessness, and longing. Wistrom argues that through these expressive activities, the children mastered and reduced these negative feelings. This assumption is supported by Erikson's (1950) and Prugh's (1995) research, reporting that play facilitates emotional release, meaning the joyful activities lead into a self-adjusting system.

Special Considerations

Sufficient rapport should be established before conducting self-expression activities with children. Children will be more likely to reveal thoughts and feelings to someone who is known and trusted. Activities should occur in a safe place, and children should choose whether they wish to participate in the activity. The adult should be nonjudgmental and supportive.

Children have different temperaments and communication styles that reflect individual differences. These preferences and styles should be considered when selecting a self-expression activity. For example, more indirect forms of communication are better for the shy, less open participant. The age of the child also helps determine the type of activity most appropriate, especially when it involves being able to identify feelings, write, or draw.

Promoting Creative Self-Expression

Throughout their lifetimes, spontaneous and creative self-expression can increase children's sense of competence and well-being. Children can express themselves through a variety of means, including visual art, music, dance, poetry, story, and drama. The main ingredient of creativity is play.

We commonly associate art materials (e.g., paint, brushes) with creative expression, but natural objects, fabrics, dramatic play props, musical instruments and materials to create musical instruments, and so on, should be made available, as well. Also, appreciating and striving to understand creative expression in others can be an important prompt in encouraging self-expression. Opportunities for children to be exposed to a wide variety of creative expressions, including the masters as well as the work of other children, can be very helpful in getting children started.

Children need to be supported in their eagerness to explore materials without fear or disapproval from adults or peers. They need adults who are prepared to find the resources they need to satisfy their creative thirsts; often, they also need time and space to express themselves. Thus, sometimes in a group activity, a child may want to break away and pursue his or her own discovery, which may not be a part of the group plan. Flexibility in planning is key to capturing these expressive moments.

Adaptations for Children with Physical Disabilities. Promoting self-expression in children with physical disabilities may require specific strategies or adaptations. Table 2.1 outlines adaptations for a sampling of physical limitations, whether permanent or temporary.

Talking with Children About Their Expressions

The ways adults speak with children about their creative endeavors can reinforce or undermine the joy of the experience. It is important to ask children if they would like to tell you about their art (e.g., "Would you like to tell me about your painting?"), rather than commanding them. Regarding praise, focus on the effort, not the product (e.g., "You were really concentrating." "What an interesting way you are using your crayons."). Comment on specifics that you notice (e.g., "I like the way you have combined the colors in the sky."). Provide encouragement when a child seems to be struggling (e.g., "I like that you are not afraid to try new things."). Remember, too, to ask children whether or not they would like their work displayed for others to see.

Green (2007) reminds us that, as with many actions under our voluntary control, some individuals might attempt to express their thoughts or feelings, but fail to do so: "It is not just that some self-expressions are more successful than others; it is also that some attempts at self-expression simply do not succeed" (p. 38). Again, it is important for the adult facilitating the activity to be nonjudgmental and supportive of the child's efforts.

Activity Goals

Carroll (2002) points out that when engaging in expressive activities, children distinguish between talking and playing, with both having a role. For some children, having fun is the most significant aspect of the therapeutic process. Other children are able to reflect more deeply and recognize the value of thinking about and understanding difficult feelings.

Table 2.1 Selected Adaptations

Grasping Difficulties	• Slip foam hair rollers over brush handles, pencils, and the like. • Wrap pieces of foam around handles, and secure with rubber bands. • Wrap handles in Model Magic; air-dry, and seal with a glaze. • Shape Model Magic around pens, pencils, and other writing implements to customize a grip. • Use flexible rubber tubing to build up handle thickness. • Cut down brushes and tape a short dowel across the end in a T-shape using electrical duct tape. • Apply Velcro dots or strips to brush handles. • Glue a Velcro strap or band to a cut-down cotton glove and slip it over the child's working hand to prevent brushes from slipping. • Use shaving brushes. • Tape paintbrushes to a child's hands or elbows. • Give a child round items to use that have been dipped in paint (e.g., plastic or rubber balls). • Introduce wide-handled brushes, small paint rollers, or sponge-wedge brushes from paint stores. • Show the child how to blow through straw to spread paint. • Fill deodorant roll-on applicators, sponge-tipped bingo markers, empty plastic shampoo bottles, or ketchup or mustard squeeze bottles with paint. • Use rigid plastic chalk holders, available at educational supply stores, to cover pastels. • Purchase special-shaped tools such as flat, wide markers, wide-handle brushes, or triangular crayons. • Give the child a switch-activated fan to use to spread paint; or roll straws through paint. • Show the child how to use a flour sifter for spreading glitter, with sifter placed directly on the paper. • Use large pieces of paper to give the child greater freedom.
Unable to Use Arms	• Using only water-soluble and fume-free paints, demonstrate to the child how to hold markers and brushes in his or her mouth; apply tape to the end of paintbrushes to avoid chipping paint from the brush handle. • Create an accessible work surface using easels, reading stands, or papers tacked to the wall. • Make a headband from foam with a Velcro closure, and add a chin strap to secure it; attach the drawing tool to the center front with foam pipe insulating tubing. • Show the child how to hold drawing or painting tools with his or her feet. • Dip or paint the child's feet with a roller and demonstrate how to use the feet themselves as printing tools.
Aids for Organization	• Use foil baking pans and plastic bins to store materials; label contents. • Give the child shallow trays (e.g., cookie sheets) to work with to create a boundary and prevent materials from falling off the table or bed; arrange pencils, markers, and crayons on a solid-color cloth or in an easy-access container so they will stay in place. • Attach projects to tables with C-clamps. • Use reading stands for sketchbooks and other drawing activities. • Clip paper to a Masonite board or cardboard; it can be used as an easel and leaned against the over-bed table for the child in the hospital. • Use revolving trays or containers (lazy Susans or desk caddies) to make reaching objects easier. • Tape paper to table using masking tape. • Use nonslip tub strips or mats to keep objects in place. • To avoid spills from water when painting, use a plastic container (such as those used in delicatessens); cut a hole in the lid that is big enough for a paintbrush, fill the container with water, and replace the lid. • Use Styrofoam blocks, florist blocks, or rubber silverware storage trays to store pencils and brushes. • To store yarn, use a coffee can or other container with a lid; punch a hole in the lid, put yarn inside, bring the end up through hole, and replace lid.
Visual Disabilities	• Use a screen board—a piece of cardboard with a section of window screen taped to it—and place paper on screen; when the child marks the paper with crayons (or similar material) the screen texture will emerge to become raised lines that the child can feel. • Give the child a tracing wheel to use (for tracing patterns when sewing) on paper that has been placed on a rubber mat or newspaper; the wheel will produce embossed lines that the child can touch. • Use other embossing techniques, such as metal repoussé. • Assist the child's vision with devices such as screen readers, screen enlargers, magnifiers, large-type books, taped books, Braillers, light boxes, high-contrast materials, thermoform graphics, synthesizers, and scanners. • Let the child ''draw'' by gluing yarn on board or paper; once dry, the child can embellish the areas within the yarn lines with crayons, paints, fabric, etc. • Help the child learn to associate color through scented markers or paints (e.g., orange essence = orange; banana or lemon = yellow; cinnamon = brown). • Add sand or vermiculite to paint to create texture. • Add soap flakes to paint for finger painting. • Show the child how to draw directly on sandpaper with crayons, to produce raised lines the child can feel.

Table 2.1 (*continued*)

	• Use visually stimulating materials such as florescent crayons, pastels, paper, paint, clay, or stickers; foil paper; glitter; metallic-looking paints; colored acetate and cellophane; and reflective tapes and strips. • Use high contrast for materials and methods (e.g., bright pastels on dark paper; light paper on a dark table). • Present materials in a clocklike manner.
Hearing Disabilities	• Install good lighting to make it easier for the child to read lips and facial expressions. • Use visual aids to help the child understand instructions. • Demonstrate the use of tools and equipment. • Limit background noise.
Sensitivity to Touch	• Offer gloves or tools for finger painting or modeling. • Provide toy vehicles to roll through paint; or provide small feathers, cotton swabs, or sticks for brushing paint.

Note. Some adaptations are from: Rodriguez, S. (1992). *The special artist's handbook: Art activities and adaptive aids for handicapped students.* Palo Alto, CA: Dale Seymour Publications. Davalos, S. (1999). *Making sense of art: Sensory-based art activities for children with autism, Asperger syndrome, and other pervasive developmental disorders.* Shawnee Mission, KS: Autism Asperger Publishing Company.

The activities in this chapter can be grouped according to three major goals, based on how directly the child is expressing feelings.

Indirect or Symbolic Communication

Some children may be reluctant or unable to communicate verbally. Activities like Graffiti Wall, Hospital Road Signs, Inside-Outside Boxes, Bridge to the Future, I Want to Scream, Personalized T-shirts, Wishing Well, and Felt Puppets are helpful with these children.

Identification and Discussion of Feelings

The next level of expression involves identifying and discussing feelings in a more direct ways. Feeling Faces, Inner Vision/Outer View Masks, Interactive Storytelling, and Temper-Rate can accomplish this goal.

Constructive Expression of Feelings

Children may be ready to move beyond expression of feelings to coping with them. Activities such as Emotion Ocean, Feelings Collage, and Zen-ga can encourage these children to move to new and more advanced levels of coping.

Self-expression activities can provide an acceptable and safe outlet for anger, frustration, and aggression. Children do not always have the verbal skills to express feelings and thoughts. Often, they do not have words to describe how they feel; or sometimes things are too difficult or painful to put into words. Once children are given an acceptable means to express their emotions they are better equipped to handle stresses associated with hospitalization, illnesses, or other health issues.

ACTIVITY 2.1.   BRIDGE TO THE FUTURE

Bridge to the Future encourages children to look toward a future that holds positive possibilities and outcomes for them. Use this activity as a springboard to help children identify and discuss strategies to help them meet their goals.

Therapeutic Goal: To promote self-expression by identifying and discussing goals.	**Required Time:** Allow ample time for children to conduct and process the activity.
Age Group: Preteen/adolescent	**Restrictions and Precautions:** Establish ground rules for sharing feelings within a group. Take glue and marker precautions.
Adult/Child Ratio: 1:8	

Materials:

- [ ] Large sheets of drawing paper
- [ ] Pencil
- [ ] Ruler
- [ ] Markers, thick-nib and fine-point
- [ ] Infant tongue depressors
- [ ] Glue

Process

1. Have the children place their paper horizontally on the table and use a pencil and ruler to draw two vertical lines on their paper, dividing it in thirds.

2. On the left third of the paper, ask the children to create an image of where they are in their lives now.

3. On the right third of the paper, ask the children to create an image of where they would like to be in the future.

4. Encourage the children to think about what they believe they need to do to achieve their goals for the future.

5. Tell them to write each idea they have on a tongue depressor.

6. Demonstrate for the children how to use these tongue depressors to build a bridge or staircase from the image of where they are now to the image of where they would like to be, then glue them in place.

7. Invite the children to share their goals and the steps they have identified to achieve them.

Note. Adapted from a drawing task designed to promote self-expression through the use of metaphor, developed by Hays, R., & Lyons, S. (1981). The bridge drawing: A projective technique for assessment in art therapy. *Arts in Psychotherapy, 8,* 207–217.

ACTIVITY 2.2.   EMOTION OCEAN

This activity is equally beneficial for sick children or their siblings.

Therapeutic Goal: To promote self-expression by identifying negative emotions and positive coping strategies.

Age Group: School-age

Adult/Child Ratio: 1:8

Required Time: 1 hour

Restrictions and Precautions: Take marker and glue precautions.

Materials:

- [ ] Wrapping paper with a sea motif; or a blue disposable tablecloth (to represent the ocean)
- [ ] Post-it Notes
- [ ] Markers with thin tips
- [ ] Tongue depressors
- [ ] White glue
- [ ] Glue dots

Process

1. Tape the representation of the ocean to a wall.

2. Engage the children in a discussion about negative emotions such as anger, anxiety, jealousy, stress, guilt, and fear.

3. Encourage the children to share examples of times they experienced these emotions since they or their loved ones have been sick.

4. Have the children write or draw each feeling onto a Post-it Note.

5. Ask the children to place these feeling-notes somewhere in the "ocean."

6. Help the children identify and discuss the activities and people that make them feel better, such as talking to their friends, having a special dinner with their family, writing in a journal, or pounding clay.

7. Ask the children to write each of the coping strategies and supportive people they have identified on a tongue depressor.

8. Show the children how to glue the tongue depressors together to make a "raft" (Figure Activity 2.2-1). Talk about how these supports and activities keep them "afloat" and help them cope with the turbulent emotions they have. Encourage the children to let the other people in their lives know which supports are helpful to them.

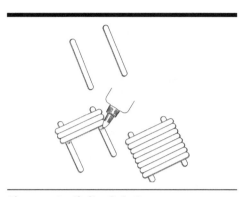

Figure Activity 2.2-1. **Emotion Ocean**

9. Put glue dots on the rafts and have the children place their rafts where they wish in the "ocean."

Note. Emotion Ocean was adapted with permission from SuperSibs!, a national program working to support the brothers and sisters of children with cancer.

ACTIVITY 2.3.   FEELING FACES

This simple activity is very effective with young children.

Therapeutic Goal: To promote self-expression by helping children identify and discuss different emotions.	**Materials:**
	☐ Paper plates
Age Group: Preschool/primary	☐ Crayons or markers
Adult/Child Ratio: 1:6	☐ Tape
Required Time: 30 minutes	☐ Paste
Restrictions and Precautions: Take marker precautions.	☐ Tongue depressors

Process

1. Give each child two paper plates.

2. Have the children use crayons or markers to draw a happy face on one plate and a sad face on the other plate.

3. Help the children position one end of a tongue depressor to the center point of one of their "feeling faces," with the other end extending below the mouth; tape it in place.

4. Show the children how to paste or tape the two faces together, back to back. The children now have flip-faces to express the two different emotions.

5. If desired, repeat the process to make another flip-face, with two different emotions, such as fear, loneliness, or anger.

6. Describe different scenarios that children may experience that evoke these emotions, such as parents leaving, getting a shot, successfully coping with a procedure, or talking on the phone with a friend.

7. Encourage the children to use their "faces" to indicate how they would feel in these situations. Invite the children to talk about a time when they felt different emotions.

8. Read a story to the children and encourage them to use their "feeling faces" to identify the emotions of the characters as the story progresses.

ACTIVITY 2.4. FEELINGS COLLAGE

This activity is a good choice for children who have difficulty expressing themselves, as it provides an opportunity to graphically illustrate their feelings.

Therapeutic Goal: To foster self-expression by identifying negative emotions and positive coping strategies.

Age Group: School-age, adolescent

Adult/Child Ratio: 1:7

Required Time: 1 hour

Restrictions and Precautions: Take scissors, markers, and/or paint precautions.

Materials:

☐ Construction paper: large sheets, white

☐ Markers or paint and paintbrushes

☐ Scissors

☐ Index cards

Process

1. Engage the children in a discussion about negative emotions, such as anger, stress, frustration, anxiety, loneliness, and sadness.

2. Let the children each choose an emotion that they find especially difficult to cope with, or one that is currently dominating all others.

3. Ask the children to write on a strip of paper the emotion they chose, in large letters, using color and a style of lettering that best conveys the emotion. Then have the children cut the word out.

4. Give the children markers or paint to create a design on a piece of construction paper, one that uses lines and colors to show what that emotion looks like.

5. Ask the children to fold two strips of paper accordion style and glue one end to the word cutout and the other end to the center of the paper.

6. Give each child four or five index cards and ask them to draw pictures of experiences or situations that make them feel that emotion. Children who are reluctant to draw can write words instead.

7. Have the children arrange the pictures around the word in the center of the piece and glue them in place.

8. Ask the children to talk about their emotional challenges and describe how they cope with them. Assist the children in identifying more positive coping strategies, if necessary.

ACTIVITY 2.5. INNER VISION/OUTER VIEW MASKS

This activity may elicit emotionally charged feelings in some children. Therefore, the activity should be conducted when ample time is available to create the masks and process the experience. The activity should be conducted individually or in a small group only, with children who are comfortable with one another and only after firm ground rules for discussion have been established.

Therapeutic Goal: To foster self expression by encouraging the identification and verbalization of feelings.

Age Group: Adolescent

Adult/Child Ratio: 1:5

Required Time: 45 minutes

Restrictions and Precautions: None

Materials:

- ☐ Cardboard masks (available at craft stores)
- ☐ Acrylic paints
- ☐ Paintbrushes
- ☐ Water
- ☐ Pictures and words cut from magazines
- ☐ Glue

Process

1. Show the children how to divide their masks vertically, with one side symbolizing how they feel or where in their lives they are now, and the other side symbolizing how or where they want to be in the future. This should be intentionally vague so that children may interpret the instruction as they wish. Note, however, that some children may need assistance.

2. Have the children paint each side a different color, then use design, words, and/or images to express themselves. If necessary, provide verbal prompts to help children who are experiencing difficulty.

3. Use the masks as a basis of discussion to encourage children to explore their feelings and aspirations.

Note. Adapted from Breiner, S. (2003). An evidence-based eating disorder program. *Journal of Pediatric Nursing, 18*(1), 75–80.

ACTIVITY 2.6.   FELT PUPPETS

Puppets have an almost universal appeal to children. Children will often express feelings that they are reluctant to share with adults while speaking through a puppet or by having a direct conversation with a puppet.

Therapeutic Goal: To promote self-expression by providing a vehicle for communication.

Age Group: Primary/school-age

Adult/Child Ratio: 1:6

Required Time: 30 minutes, plus drying time to make puppets; varies for using the puppets.

Restrictions and Precautions: Take glue and scissors precautions.

Materials:

- ☐ Puppet template (Figure Activity 2.6-1)
- ☐ Felt (two 6-inch squares per child)
- ☐ Pencil
- ☐ Scissors
- ☐ Fabric crayons
- ☐ Felt scraps, yarn, buttons, and other decorative trims

Figure Activity 2.6-1. Felt Puppets

Process

1. Using the template, trace and cut out two puppet forms per child.

2. Give each child the forms and ask them to spread glue around the perimeter of one, excluding the base where the child's hand will be inserted.

3. Have the children press the two pieces together, matching the edges carefully.

4. Give the children fabric crayons, fabric scraps, and decorative trims to make the puppet's facial features, clothing, hair, and other embellishments.

5. Allow the puppets to dry completely.

6. Encourage the children to use their puppets to tell a story about what it is like to be sick or in the hospital, or other relevant topics. Ask open-ended questions that will promote expression of the puppet's feelings, fears, and concerns.

Variation

Have premade (preferably sewn) puppet forms on hand so that low-energy children or those with physical limitations can participate in the activity without having to construct the puppet body.

ACTIVITY 2.7.   GET A-HEAD

When completed, these heads often look like elegant sculpture. Children who wear wigs can use their finished project as a wig stand.

Therapeutic Goal: To promote self-expression by creating a symbolic representation of self.

Age Group: Preteen/adolescent

Adult/Child Ratio: 1:5

Required Time: 1 hour

Restrictions and Precautions: Take glue, scissors, and marker precautions.

Materials:

☐ Styrofoam wig forms, available from most beauty supply stores (1 per child)

☐ Assorted art and craft materials, such as:

- Paint markers
- Glitter
- Mosaic tiles
- Sequins
- Beads
- Buttons
- Yarn
- Old costume jewelry

☐ Craft glue

☐ Scissors

☐ EEG leads (optional)

☐ Fabric for scarves (optional)

☐ Grout (optional)

Process

1. Provide each child with a wig form.

2. Invite the children to use the materials provided to create a three-dimensional symbolic representation of themselves (Figure Activity 2.7-1). Note: Children who would prefer to create a representation of someone else should be supported in doing so.

3. Encourage the children to talk about their sculptures and explain the significance of the colors, materials, and design they used in depicting themselves. Ask the children what, if their heads could talk, they would say.

Figure Activity 2.7-1. Get a-Head

ACTIVITY 2.8. GRAFFITI WALL

This activity is good to use in hospitals or clinics. It is important to create an atmosphere that is supportive and allows for freedom of expression.

Therapeutic Goal: To promote self-expression by providing a vehicle for children to express their thoughts, feelings, and concerns.

Age Group: School-age/adolescent

Adult/Child Ratio: Not applicable

Required Time: Ongoing

Restrictions and Precautions: Set ground rules, which should include a prohibition against foul language.

Materials:

☐ Large sheet of butcher paper (or a dry-erase board for a permanent graffiti wall)

☐ Markers

☐ String

☐ Tape

Process

1. Tape the paper to a wall horizontally, at a level that is within reach of all children.

2. Draw a vertical line to divide the paper in half.

3. Label one side of the paper with a positive statement, such as "Things I like Here" or "Things That Give Me Strength."

4. Use different-colors markers to label the other side of the paper with a negative statement, such as "Things I Dislike Here" or "Things That Bring Me Down."

5. Tie one end of the string around the marker and tape the loose end to the wall next to the butcher paper.

6. Encourage the children to contribute their feelings by writing or drawing them on the appropriate side of the sheet of paper.

ACTIVITY 2.9. GRAND DESIGNS

This activity stimulates creative thinking and problem solving. Although the solutions children formulate to remedy the things they don't like may be more imaginative than practical, the discussion leading into the project encourages children to articulate their feelings.

Therapeutic Goal: To foster self-expression by providing an outlet for the constructive expression of feelings.

Age Group: School-age

Adult/Child Ratio: 1:6

Required Time: 30 minutes

Restrictions and Precautions: Take marker precautions.

Materials:

☐ Pens or pencils

☐ Construction paper

☐ Markers

☐ Room template (optional) (Figure Activity 2.9-1)

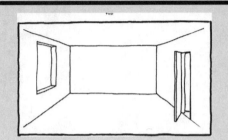

Figure Activity 2.9-1. **Room Template for Grand Designs**

Process

1. Engage the children in a discussion about things they don't like about where they receive care (e.g., their hospital room, infusion room, dialysis unit) and/or their treatment (e.g. getting injections, taking medication, receiving an enema).

2. Brainstorm different ways these things could be improved upon, real or imagined.

3. Provide each child with a room template and/or a piece of construction paper.

4. Encourage the children to design a better room and/or a machine that will address one or more of the concerns they identified (e.g., a machine to improve the taste of medicine, or a painless syringe).

5. Ask the children to draw their ideas on the room template or construction paper. If they design a machine, ask them to give it a name (Figure Activity 2.9-2).

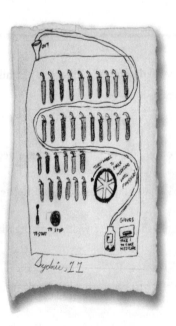 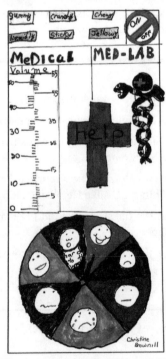

Figure Activity 2.9-2. **Machines Designed by Children to Make Medicine Taste Better**
Courtesy of Snow City Arts

6. Invite the children to share their creations and explain how they work and the improvements they will provide.

ACTIVITY 2.10.   HOSPITAL ROAD SIGNS

Hospital Road Signs is located on the CD that accompanies this book.

ACTIVITY 2.11.   I WANT TO SCREAM

Many children will recognize the image of the man in Edvard Munch's famous painting "The Scream" as the same image used on the mask in the Hollywood film *Scream*. Likewise, the scream made famous by Macaulay Culkin in the movie *Home Alone* also appears to have been modeled after Munch's painting. Use these examples from popular culture as a platform to build a discussion about coping with one's fears.

Therapeutic Goal: To promote self-expression by providing a vehicle that children can use to express their fears symbolically.

Age Group: Preteen/adolescent

Adult/Child Ratio: 1:8

Required Time: 30–40 minutes

Restrictions and Precautions: Take marker precautions.

Materials:

☐ Poster or computer printout of Munch's painting, "The Scream"

☐ Sharpie markers (black and other colors)

☐ Thick drawing paper

Process

1. Show the children the painting.

2. Ask the children to identify and discuss the feelings conveyed in the painting, such as tension, stress, and fear. Point out how the artist used line and color to depict these emotions.

3. Ask the children to give examples of times they have felt like the person in the picture.

4. Give each child a sheet of drawing paper and a black marker and invite them to draw an outline of the "screamer."

5. Encourage the children to use color and symbols to draw things that they fear *around* the image, and the feelings they evoke *inside* the image.

6. Invite the children to share their pictures and discuss what they illustrate. Encourage them to explain how they cope with these feelings. If indicated, help the children identify more positive coping strategies they might use when they feel fearful, for example deep breathing or talking to an adult.

ACTIVITY 2.12.   INSIDE-OUTSIDE BOXES

This activity may elicit powerful emotions from children coping with a serious illness of their own or that of a loved one. The adult conducting the activity should have well-developed relationships with the participants. Ample time should be available for the children to express their feelings and receive emotional support.

Therapeutic Goal: To promote self-expression by providing a vehicle for children to express their self-perceptions symbolically.

Age Group: Preteen/adolescent

Adult/Child Ratio: 1:8

Required Time: 1 hour

Restrictions and Precautions: Take scissors and glue precautions.

Materials:

☐ Cigar boxes or similarly sized sturdy box with top (1 per child)

☐ Teen/youth magazines

☐ Scissors   ☐ Mod Podge

☐ Glue sticks   ☐ Paintbrushes

☐ Permanent markers

Process

1. Explain to the children that they will be making collages that represent themselves on their boxes. The outside of the box should be symbolic of those aspects of themselves or their illness that others (e.g., staff, family, friends) see. The inside of the box should symbolize how they view themselves; their own internal thoughts, feelings, qualities, and aspirations.

2. Have the children go through the magazines and cut out images, poems, and words that reflect their internal and external selves.

3. When the children are satisfied with the words and images they have cut out, have them arrange them on their boxes and glue them in place. Note: Some children may want privacy when working on the inside of their boxes.

4. Provide the children with markers to add any details they wish.

5. Optionally, let the children brush Mod Podge on their boxes, per package instructions (Figure Activity 2.12-1).

Figure Activity 2.12-1. **Inside-Outside Box**

6. Ask reflective questions to encourage the children to explore the difference between the feelings depicted inside their boxes and what they allow others to see or that others perceive them to have.

ACTIVITY 2.13. PERSONALIZED T-SHIRTS

An adolescent boy who was given a grim prognosis 10 years earlier made a T-shirt that was both poignant and humorous. It read: "Still Not Dead." He wore it to every clinic and hospital visit.

Therapeutic Goal: To promote self-expression by providing a vehicle for communication.

Age Group: School-age/adolescent

Adult/Child Ratio: 1:10

Required Time: 45 minutes

Restrictions and Precautions: Use marker and paint precautions.

Materials:

☐ White or light-colored 50% cotton T-shirts (1 per child)

☐ Pencils

☐ Cardboard, cut into 12-inch × 16-inch rectangles (1 per child)

☐ Masking tape

☐ Fabric marker pens

☐ Stencils

☐ Fabric paint

☐ Paintbrushes

Process

1. Discuss how T-shirts are used by many people as a vehicle for self-expression. Give examples of statements that may be expressed on a T-shirt, such as a person's political views, places he or she has visited, musical preferences, favorite teams, or a message the wearer wishes to convey. Ask the children to share specific examples they have seen.

2. Tell the children that they will be designing their own T-shirts.

3. Ask the children to think of something meaningful to them that they would like to convey on their T-shirts. It may be an inspirational quote, their position on an issue they feel strongly about, a self-affirmation, a statement descriptive of who they are, or something else.

4. Give each of the children a T-shirt and a pencil with which to sketch what they want their T-shirt to say, on both the front and back.

5. Show the children how to insert a piece of cardboard inside the shirt to prevent paint from bleeding through to the other side.

6. Hand out the fabric pens and paints to the children to outline and fill in their designs. Allow to dry.

7. Repeat on the other side of the T-shirt.

Variation

For children who cannot wear T-shirts because of IVs, other medical equipment, or access needed for exams or treatments, simply cut the T-shirt lengthwise in back and hem it. Then, sew on ties or use Velcro closures for easy opening and removal of the "gown."

ACTIVITY 2.14. SENSE-ITIVITY POEMS

This is a very simple, but often powerful activity.

Therapeutic Goal: To promote self-expression by providing a vehicle for children to express their thoughts, feelings, and concerns symbolically.

Age Group: School-age/adolescent

Adult/Child Ratio: 1:6

Required Time: 20 minutes	**Materials:**
Restrictions and Precautions: Take marker precautions.	☐ Paper ☐ Fine-line markers

Process

1. Engage the children in a discussion about different emotions they have experienced.

2. Ask each child to think of the emotion that he or she has felt most strongly as of late.

3. Encourage the children to think about the emotion they have chosen and then experience it using all of their senses: taste, smell, hearing, sight, and touch.

4. Have the children write a sentence that describes the emotion from the perspective of each of their senses. For example,

   - Rage is bright red in color (sight).
   - It tastes like hot peppers (taste).
   - It smells like rotten eggs (smell).
   - It sounds like crackling thunder (hearing).
   - It feels like shattered glass (touch).

5. Allow time for children to illustrate their poems.

6. Invite children to read their poems aloud and talk about them. If a child has chosen a negative emotion, encourage him or her to explore the source of the emotion and help identify coping strategies.

Activity 2.15. Interactive Storytelling

People have engaged in storytelling throughout history and across cultures. Like play, storytelling can be used as a technique to help children create meaning, mediate difficult experiences, and express feelings.

| **Therapeutic Goal:** To promote self-expression by providing a vehicle children can use to express their feelings and concerns symbolically.
Age Group: Preschool/primary
Adult/Child Ratio: 1:1
Required Time: 20 minutes | **Restrictions and Precautions:** None
Materials:
☐ Paper
☐ Pen
☐ Photographs or pictures from magazines |

Process

1. Create a series of prompts to use to elicit a story from the child. Some examples include:

   - Once upon a time, there was a . . .
   - And every single day . . .
   - And then suddenly there was a . . .
   - And because of that . . .
   - Until finally . . .

- And ever since that happened . . .

Or:

- One day a little girl found out that . . .

- This made her feel . . .

- She decided to . . .

- What happened then was . . .

- This caused . . .

- In the end . . .

2. Explain to the child that you will be taking turns making up a story together.

3. Begin with the first prompt and continue until the story has an ending. Write the story down or record it so that you can review it together and/or share it with others (if the child chooses).

4. Let the child give the story a name and create an illustration for it.

Use pictures in place of verbal prompts.   **Variation**

ACTIVITY 2.16.   TEMPER-RATE

This activity is a good choice to adapt for use with sibling support groups.

Therapeutic Goal: To promote self-expression by helping children identify and discuss aspects about their illness that make them angry.

Age Group: School-age

Adult/Child Ratio: 1:10

Required Time: 45 minutes – 1 hour

Restrictions and Precautions: None

Materials:

☐ Flipchart or large piece of paper taped to a wall

☐ Worksheet (Figure Activity 2.16-1)

☐ Fine-point markers

Figure Activity 2.16-1. Temper-Rate Worksheet

1. Introduce the activity by brainstorming with the children to come up with a list of things that   **Process**
make them angry about their illness and treatment. Write down what each child says on the flipchart then ask the others if they ever feel the same way.

2. When the children are satisfied with the list they have generated as a group, ask them to choose the 5 to 10 items on the list that are most difficult for them personally. Then ask them to rank the items according to the degree of anger they evoke.

3. Give the children the Temper-Rate worksheet so they can transcribe their list to the "thermometer."

4. Invite the children to take turns sharing something from their worksheet that makes them angry, and tell how they deal with it. Help the children explore more positive coping strategies, where indicated.

ACTIVITY 2.17.   THE COMPLAINT DEPARTMENT IS IN

This activity requires no preparation, minimal materials, and can be easily adapted to various settings and themes.

Therapeutic Goal: To foster self-expression by providing an outlet for the constructive expression of feelings.

Age Group: School-age

Adult/Child Ratio: 1:6

Required Time: Varies

Restrictions and Precautions: None

Materials:

☐ Pen

☐ Paper

Process

1. Invite the children to imagine they are the president of the hospital, the manager of the clinic, or the director of the complaint department (or, with very hospital-savvy patients, call it the "patient relations or patient satisfaction" department).

2. Have the children generate a list of complaints they might receive in their job. Encourage complaints that are serious, while also allowing those that are outrageously silly.

3. Ask the children to respond in writing to each of the complaints, offering explanations or solutions for each of the concerns listed.

4. Encourage the children to share and discuss what they have written.

ACTIVITY 2.18.   WISHING WELLS

The wishing wells can be made in advance if the activity will involve children who are unable to do so themselves. If time is limited, the children can simply paint them and/or talk about things they wish for, and write them down, or dictate if needed.

Therapeutic Goal: To promote self-expression by asking children to identify their hopes and dreams.

Age Group: School-age/adolescent

Adult/Child Ratio: 1:10

Required Time: 1 hour

Restrictions and Precautions: Take scissors and hot glue precautions. Do not use this activity with children who are still in the "magical thinking" phase of cognitive development.

Materials:

☐ Plastic or glass jar, the height of a tongue depressor half, or slightly shorter, approximately 4 inches wide (1 per child)

☐ Cardboard, cut 2 inches wider than the diameter of the jar

☐ White glue

☐ Tongue depressors or craft sticks, cut in half using a craft knife

☐ Ruler

☐ Construction paper

☐ Scissors

☐ Hot glue gun

☐ Acrylic or tempera paint (optional)

☐ Paintbrushes (optional)

☐ Rubber band

1. Introduce the activity by discussing what is meant by a "wishing well."   **Process**

2. Discuss with the children different things people may wish for, such as:

    •   What they wish they could do

    •   What they wish they could say

    •   What they wish they could change

    •   What they wish for a loved one

    •   What they wish for the future

3. Ask the children to think about things they wish for and write each of them down on a tiny piece of paper. Explain that they will be making their own wishing well.

4. To make the roof, crease the cardboard pieces by folding them in half; give one to each child.

5. Show the children how to line up the tongue depressors horizontally across the cardboard, and glue them down, starting at the crease and working out to both ends. Trim any excess cardboard.

6. Help the children measure and cut a piece of construction paper to fit around the jar.

7. Have the children glue the construction paper to the jar.

8. Keeping the bottom side of the jar down on the table, show the children how to glue the tongue depressors around the circumference, making sure that the cut end of the tongue depressors are even on the bottom and touching the table.

9. Demonstrate for the children how to wrap a rubber band around the jar, one third up from the bottom.

10. To make the roof support, help the children hot-glue two uncut tongue depressors to the inside of the wishing well, directly across from one another.

11. Assist the children in gluing half a tongue depressor across the side support of each roof.

12. Help the child glue the roof to the support, and allow to dry (Figure Activity 2.18-1).

Figure Activity 2.18-1. Wishing Well

13. Let the children decorate the wishing wells, if desired.

14. Encourage the children to fold the papers on which they wrote their wishes and place them in their wishing well.

ACTIVITY 2.19.   WOUND CARE FOR FEELINGS

Being engaged in a creative activity helps children feel more relaxed when discussing difficult feelings.

Therapeutic Goal: To promote self-expression by helping children identify and discuss coping strategies.

Age Group: Primary/school-age

Adult/Child Ratio: 1:6

Required Time: 30 minutes

Restrictions and Precautions: Use marker precautions

Materials:

☐ Band-Aid template (Figure Activity 2.19-1)

☐ Heavyweight computer paper, various colors

☐ Scissors

☐ Band-Aid

☐ Fine-line markers

☐ Boxes, large enough to hold several cutout templates

Figure Activity 2.19-1. Band-Aid Templates

Process

1. Enlarge the templates and make enough photocopies so that each child can choose several from a variety of colors and sizes. Cut out the "Band-Aids."

2. Show the children the real Band-Aid and tell them that it is often applied to a place on their body that hurts. Ask the children to tell of a time when a Band-Aid was placed somewhere on their body that was hurt (e.g., injection site, incision site).

3. Explain that because of an illness or injury, we sometimes experience emotional hurts, as well. Give some examples (e.g., missing a special party, loneliness because of isolation, being teased). Then ask the children to tell about some of the "emotional hurts" they have experienced as a result of their illness.

4. Ask the children to share some of the things that have helped their emotional "hurts" feel better (e.g., a hug from mom, talking to a friend on the phone, playing music). Let the children brainstorm to identify additional coping strategies that might help them feel better when they are feeling bad.

5. Invite the children to design special bandages that help make emotional injuries and hurts feel better.

6. Allow the children to select several "Band-Aids" of different sizes and colors.

7. On the underside of the "Band-Aid," invite the children to draw a picture or write words that describe an emotional injury or "hurt" they have to cope with.

8. On the top of the "Band-Aids," ask the children to write things that can help them to feel better.

9. Encourage the children to share with the group the hurts and coping strategies they identified.

Activity 2.20.   Zen-ga

Zen-ga makes a great teaching game. Just change the questions from open-ended to factual questions about illness, nutrition, or whatever educational content you wish to reinforce.

Therapeutic Goal: To promote self-expression by helping children verbalize their feelings and identify positive coping strategies.

Age Group: School-age/adolescent

Adult/Child Ratio: 1:4

Required Time: Varies

Restrictions and Precautions: None

Materials:

☐ Jenga game

☐ Envelope labels, 2.865 inches × .87 inches

Process

1. On a computer, make 27 labels, each printed with one of the questions listed below or one you have crafted.
2. Affix one label to each Jenga block.
3. Explain to the children that the object of the game is to build a tower using the blocks and then to take turns removing blocks, one at a time, and answering the question written on it, without causing the tower to topple.
4. Demonstrate how to build a tower according to the directions of the game, making sure that all of the questions written on the blocks are facing down.
5. Play moves clockwise, with each player taking a turn removing a block and reading the question on the bottom aloud.
6. The player may choose to answer the question or ask another player to do so.
7. The game continues until the tower falls.

Ideas for Zen-ga Questions

1. What is the hardest emotion for you to deal with?
2. Name something that recently made you happy?
3. What is something that recently made you feel sad?
4. What is something that recently made you angry?
5. What is something that scares you now?
6. What is something that makes you feel frustrated?
7. What is something that makes you jealous?
8. How do you let someone know you are mad?
9. How can you deal with your anger when alone?
10. What is the worst thing about your illness?
11. What frustrates you most about doctors (or nurses, hospitals, clinics)?
12. What is the most challenging thing you have to do to take care of yourself?
13. What is the main driving force in your life, and why?
14. What is something you do to help get you out of a bad mood?
15. What is something you could change about yourself to make life easier?
16. Who is the person you like to talk to most, and why?

17. What would you change about the hospital (or another setting) to make it better?

18. What do you do to relax when stressed?

19. How has being sick caused you to change or shaped who you are?

20. How has your illness affected your relationships with other people?

21. If you could be someone else, who would that person be, and why?

22. What makes you laugh?

23. Whom do you admire most, and why?

24. What do most people who don't have your illness not understand about your situation?

25. What has been your favorite time in life so far, and why?

26. What is the most important thing you've learned?

27. What is the most effective coping strategy you use?

For more ideas, see Bright Ideas for Self-Expression (Box Activity 2.20-1).

Box Activity 2.20-1. Bright Ideas for Self-expression	• As a hands-on medium to promote self-expression, provide adolescents with a video recorder to create video diaries, describe their experiences, or communicate with others. If you get several movies that the creators are willing to share, hold a film fest or movie night, replete with popcorn.
	• Play recorded music that evokes different emotions—happiness, sadness, anger, and excitement—and ask the children to describe what it reminds them of.
	• Show the children a picture that depicts another child or family displaying emotion and ask the children to tell you a story about what they think is happening in it.
	• Fashion a crystal ball by wrapping an appropriately sized ball with aluminum foil. Use this to encourage children to articulate their hopes and dreams for the future.
	• Fasten a lightweight ball to an empty paper roll to make a microphone. Hold an "open mike" session where the microphone is passed around and the children can say anything they want, or use it to interview family, friends, or healthcare providers.
	• Give children journals and encourage them to write in it daily about their feelings, reflections, and experiences during their journey through treatment. Also encourage them to decorate the covers creatively to, for example, express something about themselves that not a lot of people know.

Chapter 3

Self-Esteem

A child with a strong sense of self-esteem is more likely to have the confidence to develop new coping mechanisms, make positive adjustments to change, and capably handle stress. Fostering self-esteem is, therefore, an important psychosocial goal for the pediatric healthcare professional. The activities in this chapter are designed to help meet this goal. Supplemental activities addressing self-expression, body image, and group interactions can be found in Chapters 2, 4, and 5, respectively.

LIST OF ACTIVITIES

Activity 3.1 Auto Photography	Activity 3.10 Mini-Me Paper Dolls
Activity 3.2 Business Cards	Activity 3.11 Name Bracelets
Activity 3.3 Casting Bandage Masks	Activity 3.12 Personalized Pennants
Activity 3.4 Crown Me	Activity 3.13 Uno, Dose
Activity 3.5 DNA Necklace: Genes in a Bottle	Activity 3.14 V.I.P (Very Important Patient or Person)
Activity 3.6 Fingerprint Detective	Activity 3.15 Vote for Me!
Activity 3.7 Graffiti Name Signs	Activity 3.16 What's-in-a-Name Poems
Activity 3.8 In Good Hands	Activity 3.17 You're in the Money
Activity 3.9 Magazine Name Collages	

The Concept of Self-Esteem

Self-esteem is the affective or emotional aspect of self, which generally refers to how individuals feel about or how they value themselves (self-worth) (Huitt, 2009). Self-esteem answers the question, "Am I worthy?" This concept includes the individual's overall evaluation of him- or herself, including feelings of general happiness and satisfaction (Harter, 1999). In other words, self-esteem is what individuals feel about their self-concept, primarily a function of being loved and of gaining the respect of others. Children evaluate themselves in four areas: competence, sense of control, moral worth, and worthiness of love and acceptance (see Table 3.1).

One's overall sense of worth is constructed on the basis of competencies in those areas the individual considers important. Discrepancies between perceived competence and the importance to succeed in that particular area, as acknowledged by the individual and by other important people, put the person at risk for impairment in self-esteem. Children's level of self-esteem will influence their ability to master tasks and seek solutions to problems. A child's self-esteem may fluctuate because of developmental considerations (e.g., struggling with task mastery); this is, however, only a temporary modification in the child with a healthy sense of self (Hockenberry & Wilson, 2007).

Table 3.1 Evaluative Dimensions of Self-Esteem

Dimension	Evaluative Concept	Questions
Competence	Adequacy of cognitive, physical, and social skills	How do I compare academically with my classmates? How fast a runner am I? How quickly do I make friends?
Sense of Control	Ability to complete tasks needed to produce desired outcomes Assignation of responsibility for success or failure	Am I able to perform a dance piece well enough to receive a high mark in the competition? Is someone or something else responsible for my success? Was my failure a matter of bad luck?
Moral Worth	How closely actions and behaviors meet moral standards that have been set	How closely do my actions and behaviors meet moral standards that have been set?
Worthiness of Love and Acceptance	Degree of worthiness of love and acceptance from parents, other significant adults, siblings, and peers	Am I worthy of the love and trust my parents show me? Am I good enough for my little brother to look upon me as a role model?

Note. Adapted from Sieving, R., & Zirbel-Donisch, S. (1990). Development and enhancement of self-esteem in children. *Journal of Pediatric Health Care, 4,* 290–296.

Development of Self-Esteem

The development of children's self-esteem involves both developmental issues and environmental influences. Environmental influences include (a) abilities and opportunities available to accomplish age-appropriate developmental tasks, (b) significant others, (c) social roles assumed and the expectations of these roles, and (d) individual temperaments and personalities (Sieving & Zirbel-Donisch, 1990).

Infancy Through Preschool Years

Although the infant, toddler, and preschooler do not yet evaluate themselves, the formation of a sense of self begins during these early years. During infancy (birth to about 18 months), the task is to develop trust without completely eliminating the capacity for mistrust. Infants, with the attainment of developmental milestones and caregiver interactions that typically take place within the first year or so, begin to sense themselves as separate beings, independent of others. They develop a sense that they affect people and objects and learn to view the world as basically responsive or nonresponsive to their needs (Sieving & Zirbel-Donisch, 1990). These accomplishments require a competent infant developing within a responsive, supportive world of adults that recognize and respond to the infant's individual needs, desires, and temperament.

In early childhood (18 months to 3 years), the toddler's task is to achieve a degree of autonomy while minimizing shame and doubt. With the proper, positive balance, the toddler will develop the virtue of willpower (determination). Toddlers, too, require parental interaction, both positive (acceptance, praise) and negative (limit-setting), and parental guidelines to validate the development of self. Newfound motor, cognitive, and language skills, along with parental guidance, allow toddlers to (a) begin to establish independent goals for exploring their worlds; (b) realize that others can be made aware of their needs, desires, and concerns; and (c) learn that even when they take stances contrary to their parents, these adults continue to recognize their "good self" by trying to reestablish harmonious interactions (Sieving & Zirbel-Donisch, 1990). Highly egocentric, toddlers are unaware of any difference between competence and social approval: "They are the center of their world, and to them all positive experiences are evidence of their importance and value" (Hockenberry & Wilson, 2007, p. 129). What are the consequences for a toddler whose movement is restricted or is no longer able to do something for him- or herself (e.g., use the potty) because of illness, injury, or hospitalization? The child may feel ashamed, which may result in a lower self-esteem, shame, and doubt.

Preschoolers (3 to 5 years) have the task of learning initiative without too much guilt. Critical issues regarding self-esteem include (a) references to "I," along with initial descriptions of self activities, thereby signaling the onset of self-awareness; (b) rudimentary internalization of parent demands; and (c) movement from seeing themselves as the center of the universe to seeing themselves as satellites attached to more powerful and competent others (Sieving & Zirbel-Donisch, 1990). Their world of emotionally significant people now includes siblings and peers, yet preschoolers continue to depend heavily on parental guidelines and validation. They attach greater emotional significance to parental demands, and increasingly realize their personal limitations. They are becoming more aware of the discrepancy between their competencies and the abilities of more advanced children, and are expected to evaluate a situation and anticipate the consequences of their behavior before they act (Hockenberry & Wilson, 2007). *Initiative* means responding positively to the world's challenges, taking on responsibilities, learning new skills, feeling purposeful. It is easy to see how health issues, such as fatigue from cancer, could interfere with these activities and lower self-esteem.

The school-age child (6 to 12 years) is tasked with developing a capacity for industry while avoiding an excessive sense of inferiority. At around the age of 4 years, children begin to voice judgments about themselves, and children between the ages of 4 and 7 years frequently confuse wishes with reality (Harter & Pike, 1984). They typically enter school at some time during this period. This presents a new set of challenges, rules, and expectations, adding interactions with new adults and children and, thus, providing additional feedback about themselves (Sieving & Zirbel-Donisch, 1990). Acceptance by these persons becomes more important to them than the acceptance by the family group. These new, valued people in their world are likely not to be as proud of their achievements or as tolerant of their limitation as their families are. Recently acquired capacity for guilt may lead to anxiety over failure for children in this age group, leaving them more vulnerable to feelings of worthlessness and depression. However, as competence increases and meaningful relationships are formed, their self-esteem rises (Hockenberry & Wilson, 2007). Yet, health issues may limit opportunities for children to conceive a plan, carry it out, and experience the feeling of success, whether it is in school or on the playground—academic or social.

School-Aged

For children around 8 years of age, peer comparison becomes more extensive as a means for evaluating their own abilities. School achievement (e.g., reading at higher levels, earning good grades) and skill-building carry more weight than in the past. Health issues may not only interfere with a child's ability to compare favorably with peers, but also draw attention to being "different," and thus a possible target for teasing, which can be devastating to a child's self-esteem.

The 8- to 11-year-old can think in terms of concrete, observable categories. Children this age look at themselves in terms of traits, such as smart, friendly, or athletic (Harter, 1983). Judgments about self become more specific with children factoring in sense of control for successes and failures and applying moral judgment (Sieving & Zirbel-Donisch, 1990). At this point in development, children can verbalize overall feelings of self-esteem (Harter).

Beginning with puberty and ending at around 18 or 20 years of age, adolescence is a time to achieve ego identity and avoid role confusion. Along with the anatomic and physiologic changes of puberty, adolescence typically brings transitions to different school structures, which hold new standards, expectations, and demands; increasingly complex relationships with same- and opposite-sex peers; and a need for variable degrees of autonomy from parents and other family members (Sieving & Zirbel-Donisch, 1990). Also new are abstract thought and introspection, which teenagers begin to use to judge their own worth. Judgment is made on very specific dimensions, such as (a) academic, physical, and social achievements; (b) physical attributes; (c) interpersonal acceptance; (d) moral behaviors as they compare with internal standards; and (e) sense of control over personal accomplishments, relationships, and activities (Sieving & Zirbel-Donisch). Integrating feelings about themselves within each of these categories results in an overall sense of self-esteem.

Adolescence

Health issues can have a profound effect on adolescents. Life becomes more complex as the teenager attempts to find his or her own identity, struggles with social interactions, and grapples with moral issues. With an increased desire for intimacy at this stage, a health-related issue such as a colostomy bag can become a major identity factor, adding another layer of concern about body image that other teens do not have to face.

Risk Factors for Self-Esteem Issues

Certain factors put children more at risk for self-esteem issues. One factor is special healthcare needs, yet there are several others.

Children with Special Healthcare Needs

Research suggests that some children with special healthcare needs may be at increased risk for low self-esteem compared to children without special healthcare needs. Children with special healthcare needs include those with physical disabilities, behavioral or emotional problems, learning difficulties, and chronic medical illness.

Children with Physical Disabilities. To understand the possible impact of physical disability on a child's self-esteem, it may be helpful to look more closely at children's physical development through the lens of self-esteem. *Corporality*, the state or quality of being material or having a body, develops in three stages: discovery, experimentation, and incorporation (Mulderij, 2000). In the *discovery* stage, the infant becomes orientated to time and space, demarking between what has and what has not yet been experienced. Hands and feet are gradually discovered as things that are part of the self. During the *experimentation* stage, the infant works with the discovery. In the process of developing into a toddler, the child grasps things, crawls, experimenting all the way. This does not automatically happen, however, for not everything allows itself to be grasped, not all floors are equally easy to crawl on, and not all adults allow children to climb on them. Children undergo a physical self-education process as they meet the resistance and opportunities that the world has to offer; the body truly functions as representative of personal identity. We see annoyance and frustration with failures and the joy of success. In the *incorporation* stage, children conquer the resistance of the body to incorporate a new physical skill, which then allows them to divert their energies and move on to the next experiment. The body's resistance is accompanied by feelings of being challenged, daring, pride, and competence, or a sense of anxiety, pain, and failure. These feelings can be reinforced or mollified by parents, who give children more or less confidence in their own physical abilities.

Let us look for a moment at the ways in which having a physical disability can interfere with this smooth three-stage process (Mulderij, 2000). During the experimental stage, for babies and toddlers with physical disabilities, the stubbornness of the body and resistance of the world offer little guarantee of success. This may cause children to lose heart and want to cease experimenting. As they experiment less, they experience less incorporation. Forced to be satisfied with fewer victories over their bodies, children with physical disabilities have to fight hard for the victories that they do achieve. Further, whereas incorporation is usually final for children without disabilities, children with disabilities often have to fight to regain it (e.g., posthospitalization). They integrate routine skills, which typically are gained only with difficulty. This integration gives these skills a stable place among the child's other achievements, giving him or her the peace, clarity, focus, and courage to develop further.

What impact does the interference with the development of corporality have on the self-esteem of children with physical disabilities? Some studies have reported an association between physical disability and a lower sense of self-worth, greater anxiety, and a less integrated view of self (Harvey & Greenway, 1984), while later studies have found no differences in global self-esteem when comparing groups of children and adolescents with and without physical disabilities (Shields, Loy, Murdoch, Taylor, & Dodd, 2007).

In a recent study of children and adolescents with mobility impairment, Jemta, Fugl-Meyer, Oberg, and Dahl (2009) found the majority of participants acknowledged a positive self-esteem. Disability characteristics such as acquired disease or injury and experience of pain were the variables responsible for most of the significant relationships to a lower level of self-esteem. Children and adolescents with an acquired disease or injury have expressed regrets of loss of their identity (Jemta, Dahl, Fugl-Neyer, & Stensman, 2005). Pain is common, which is associated with lower self-reported well-being/quality of life (Dickinson et al., 2007; Russo, Miller, Haan, Cameron, & Crotty, 2008).

Minor physical disabilities can have a large negative effect on the self-esteem of physical competence (Jemta et al., 2009; Miyahara & Piek, 2006), yet Antle (2004) found no significant relationships between severity of disability and perceptions of physical appearance or global self-worth. The definitions of severity of disability may in part explain these contradictory findings. Jetma and colleagues hypothesize that young people with minor functional limitations identify with their peers without disabilities and therefore are met with greater demands from themselves as well as the environment. Miyahara and Piek provide another explanation: Children and adolescents with major visible physical disabilities to a relatively greater extent receive other people's empathy and attention and, consequently, get more opportunities to receive social support.

Children with Behavioral or Learning Difficulties. Children with behavioral disorders often receive negative attention due to their behavior. Children with attention deficit hyperactivity disorder (ADHD), for example, typically exhibit difficulties in social situations and lack conversational skills, conflict-management skills, and effective ways of dealing with their anger (Barber, Grubbs, & Cottrell, 2005). Their insufficient social skills translate into less success interacting with peers and developing close friendships. They often are unable to contain inappropriate responses, have difficulty delaying gratification, and cannot stop inappropriate behavior once directed to do so (McKay & Halperin, 2001). Years of negativity and social rejection can accumulate and lead to low self-esteem and a negative self-perception (Gentschel & McLaughlin, 2000). These concepts are supported by the findings of the American Academy of Pediatrics (2000a) on the clinical presentation of ADHD, which is often associated with low self-esteem, poor peer relationships, and school difficulties.

Children with Chronic Conditions. Children living with a chronic condition often find it difficult in their routine environments to feel a sense of empowerment and capability, necessary elements in the development of self-esteem (Thomas & Gaslin, 2001). Their physical symptoms might decrease their ability to participate in sports, attend school, play with peers, and perform task mastery skills. Children may experience many small insults to their sense of self on a daily basis. If they are fortunate, they also experience many positive words and actions that contribute to building and maintaining a healthy sense of self, or self-esteem.

Children progress through complex, developmental changes; a chronic illness can slow, if not halt, further advances. The fewer opportunities children have to perform age-appropriate roles and tasks, the more self-esteem deteriorates. Circumstances often force children into dependent roles in which they must relinquish control and subsequently question their sense of self-worth. A negative attitude toward having a chronic condition is related to increased depression, increased behavioral problems, and subsequent lower self-esteem (Heimlich, Westbrook, Austin, Cramer, & Devinsky, 2000). Other studies suggest that some children develop heightened stress tolerance and subsequent effective coping skills and thus the positive self-esteem that results from successfully handling life's ups and downs (Kellerman, Zeltzer, Ellenberg, Dash, & Rigler, 1980).

Other Risk Factors

Several other factors may increase children's risk for low self-esteem. For example, merely *being unattractive* can put children at risk. Attractiveness is considered a totally subjective judgment, yet research shows that a high degree of agreement exists among naïve judges (both children and adults) as to who is attractive and unattractive within a given culture, with attractiveness stereotypes appearing to be more stringently applied to females than males. Unattractive children often deal with more than exclusion from their peers; they frequently are openly ridiculed and harassed. When children get the message that others do not want to be associated with them, they tend to have less self-confidence and self-acceptance than attractive children. Thus, their self-esteem may plummet.

Evidence exists that *children who are overweight* have lower levels of self-esteem when compared to children of normal weight (O'Dea, 2006). Although some researchers acknowledge that it may be difficult to sort out whether obesity affects self-esteem or whether self-esteem affects obesity, a recent study drawn from Canada's National Longitudinal Survey of Children and Youth concludes that excess body weight precedes the development of low self-esteem, rather than the reverse (Wang, Wild, Kipp, Kuhle, & Veugelers, 2009). This finding remained true even when the effects of a number of variables known to influence self-esteem were taken into account. Teasing from peers and social stigma are believed to be contributors to low self-esteem in children who are obese (Musher-Eizenman, Holub, Miller, Goldstein, & Edwards-Leeper, 2004).

Children who have been abused or neglected also are at greater risk. Low self-esteem is among the many mental health problems children who are maltreated may experience. Many children in these circumstances are removed from their homes and placed in foster care. Research shows that children who have been abused and neglected who were placed and remained in foster care demonstrated better mental health functioning than maltreated children who reunified with their biologic families, or maltreated children who were never removed from their homes (Taussig & Culhane, 2005). Nevertheless, children in foster care are still at significant risk for adverse mental health outcomes as a consequence of the maltreatment, plus the additional trauma of removal and possible isolation from their homes, schools, friends, and families (Shipman & Taussig, 2009). Children who are adopted often come from deprived backgrounds, including abuse and neglect, lack of medical care, and malnutrition in orphanages (Miller, 2005). Because self-esteem has been suggested to be the corollary of a secure attachment, and adoption involves the breaking and making of affectional bonds, secure attachments and related self-esteem may be more difficult to develop than in nonadopted children.

Being bullied or ostracized puts children at greater risk for low self-esteem. Despite a renewed focus on awareness, bullying experiences are becoming increasingly more common for children and can have devastating consequences for their self-esteem (Twyman et al., 2010). Ostracism is a type of social exclusion whereby the individual is completely ignored and made to feel like he or she does not exist. It is believed that the effects of ostracism may potentially be more devastating than bullying because victims of bullying are at least acknowledged for their existence, whereas ostracism makes the individual feel invisible (Williams & Nida, 2009). Twyman and colleagues (2010) report that children with special healthcare needs—including physical disabilities, behavioral or emotional problems, learning difficulties, and chronic medical illness—may be at increased risk for these experiences. Children with ADHD, autism spectrum disorder, and/or learning disabilities often have social difficulties and externalizing behavior that place them at higher risk for both bullying and victimization.

Our concept of self-worth is developed at least in part by how others treat our bodies, thus, *corporal punishment* is a risk factor for low self-esteem. Physical or corporal punishment is "the use of physical force with the intention of causing a child to experience pain but not injury for the purposes of correction or control of the child's behavior" (Straus, 1995, p. 75). Frequent corporal punishment can weaken the parent-child relationship, an important factor in the development of positive self-esteem. The verbal attacks and lack of warmth sometimes displayed by parents and other adults when physically punishing children may only serve to further diminish children's fragile self-esteem.

Special Considerations

A child's level of self-esteem is often apparent by assessing the following factors (Brantly, 1991, p. 45):

- Statements the child makes about him- or herself,
- Ability to be goal oriented,
- Readiness with which the child takes risks,
- Need for approval from adults,
- Ability to delineate strengths and weaknesses, and
- Ability to make independent choices based on likes and dislikes.

Low self-esteem may be attributable to any of the risk factors listed here. Some risk factors, such as physical disability, may be obvious. Others, such as being bullied at school, may need to be brought out through sensitive interviewing techniques, for example, using the "third person" technique described in the Introduction.

The availability of significant others as well as their interaction with the child are important variables affecting self-esteem. Considering the child's psychosocial stage can help predict these significant others. Healthcare providers can become significant others in the life of the sick child and can facilitate patient contact with close family and friends. They also can play a role in coordinating a successful transition from a healthcare environment into the home, school, and community.

Nonverbal communication of significant others provides powerful feedback to the child. Facial expressions, body language, and voice tones can indicate care, concern, and respect for the child and subsequently influence self-esteem.

Enhancing Children's Self-Esteem

A variety of strategies can be used to boost a child or teenager's self-esteem. For general strategies when working with children and families, see Table 3.2.

Interventions designed specifically to promote self-esteem in the hospital setting address five basic attitudes in the child (Reasoner, 1983):

1. *Sense of security.* Hospitalized children gain a sense of security by feeling they can trust and have confidence in the adults responsible for them. The healthcare professional is often a significant other in the life experience of the patient, especially in healthcare settings where there is high contact, such as in intensive or extended care units. Children also gain a sense of security when significant others tell them (in age-appropriate way) what will be happening to them and what is expected of them.

2. *Sense of identity.* To promote a sense of identity children need to have positive feedback and recognition for their strengths. They need encouragement to evaluate their own strengths and weaknesses to better help themselves. All of these interventions must be done while demonstrating love and acceptance.

3. *Sense of belonging.* A sense of belonging is an important step in building self-esteem, especially among adolescents. To accomplish this goal, children and adolescents need experiences that enable them to realize when it is appropriate to be a unique individual and when it is important to identify with and be a part of a group.

4. *Sense of purpose.* A sense of purpose can be promoted by setting reasonable expectations for children while helping them set realistic goals for themselves. Healthcare professionals can then communicate faith and confidence that children will achieve their goals, and encourage them to expand their interests, skills, and talents even while they are ill.

5. *Sense of personal competence.* A sense of personal competence is achieved when children believe that they are able to cope with problems or meet goals. A sense of personal competence evolves with successful experiences. Healthcare professionals can help children choose from options available, provide encouragement and support, and offer feedback regarding their progress. In an environment of positive support and openness, self-esteem is promoted. Children have opportunities to make choices and decisions, and competition is avoided while cooperation is encouraged.

For specific age-related interventions for enhancing self-concept/self-esteem for hospitalized children, see Table 3.3.

Activity Goals

The activities in this chapter are designed to enhance self-esteem by focusing on children's sense of identity and uniqueness or their strengths and accomplishments.

Sense of Identity and Uniqueness

Activities that incorporate the child's name, such as What's-in-a-Name Poems, Graffiti Name Signs, and Magazine Name Collages promote a sense of identity. Fingerprint Detectives and creating a DNA necklace also help children appreciate their uniqueness. Healthcare professionals can encourage children to display their finished products to personalize their space.

Table 3.2 General Strategies for Enhancing Children's Self-Esteem

	Strategies
With Children	1. Determine children's confidence in their own judgment. 2. Reinforce the personal strengths that children identify. 3. Provide experiences that increase children's autonomy. 4. Convey confidence in children's ability to handle situations. 5. Explore previous achievements of success and encourage children to accept new challenges. 6. Reward or praise children's progress toward reaching goals. 7. Facilitate an environment and activities that will increase self-esteem. 8. Discuss impact of peer group on feelings of self-worth.

With Parents	1. Expectations
	  • Assess parents' expectations for their children.
	  • Review anticipated developmental milestones with parents.
	2. Valued Human Being
	  • Encourage parents to communicate their confidence in their children.
	  • Discuss with parents the importance of their interest and support in their children's development of a positive self-concept.
	  • Discuss with parents ways to structure situations to help children experience success.
	  • Review with parents effective ways to praise their children.
	  • Encourage parents to value children's ideas and to recognize all accomplishments and achievements.
	  • Encourage parents to value themselves.
	3. Communication
	  • Encourage parents to communicate their confidence in their children.
	  • Promote and model effective listening skills.
	  • Encourage parents to be open with feelings.
	  • Instruct parents to avoid the use of judgmental statements.
	4. Discipline
	  • Inform parents of effective methods of limit-setting.
	  • Discuss appropriate consequences.
	  • Review problem solving techniques.
	  • Discourage parental use of physical punishment.
	  • Model age-appropriate disciplinary techniques.
	5. Child-Centered Guidance
	  • Encourage parents to talk with their children often
	  • Discuss with parents the importance of knowing their children's activities when away from home.
	  • Inspire parents to be interested in events at their children's school.
	6. Autonomy
	  • Review with parents methods of promoting autonomy in their children.

Note. Adapted from Mott, S. (1999). Reprinted from *Core curriculum for the nursing care of children and their families* (p. 314). Reprinted with permission of the publisher, Jannetti Publications, Inc., East Holly Avenue, Box 56, Pitman, NJ 08071-0056; (856) 256-2300; fax (856) 589-7463; web site: www.pediatricnursing.net; Sieving, R., & Zirbel-Donisch, S. (1990). Development and enhancement of self-esteem in children. *Journal of Pediatric Health Care, 4,* 290–296. Reprinted with permission.

Table 3.3 Age-Related Interventions for Enhancing Self-Concept/Self-Esteem for Hospitalized Children

Age	Intervention
Infancy	Encourage positive, parent-child interaction (e.g., encourage parent to smile directly at child and play games such as peek-a-boo). Encourage touching and talking to the infant. Encourage play according to the infant's developmental level. Support parents (e.g., by enhancing their sense of competency with their ill child, being an empathetic listener, assisting them in building a support network with other parents).
Preschool	Encourage developmentally appropriate play and medical play. Incorporate parents in the plan of care, encouraging rooming in or suggesting appropriate parental substitutes when parents cannot be with the child. Allow child to make age-appropriate decisions about care and activities. Provide positive reinforcement when the child is appropriately cooperative.
School-age	Allow child to make age-appropriate decisions about care and activities. Encourage daily contact with child's teacher. Assist child to complete schoolwork. Encourage school-age friends to visit, call, write, email, text, and Skype. Assign a room with same-aged peer, if multi-occupancy rooms are used. Encourage alternative forms of play. Plan for speedy return to school after discharge, beginning with half-day involvement.
Adolescent	Provide opportunities for self-disclosure in a group or 1:1 setting. Encourage visits by family and friends (including peers), phone calls, letters, texts, emails, Skype, cards, and gifts. Emphasize the attention adolescent is receiving by these significant others. Reassure confidentiality of information shared. Emphasize privacy and avoid situations that may be embarrassing; if such situations must occur, acknowledge feelings of embarrassment. Maintain limits of behavior. Limit number of caregivers. Include adolescent in planning care and give choices when possible. Provide self-monitoring activities (e.g., charts, checklists, calendars, diary). Encourage questions about health status and airing of concerns; clarify misconceptions. Provide explanations/preparation of procedures and routines. Avoid negative criticism and use positive reinforcement. Arrange for the adolescent to have short passes from hospital, if possible. Provide unit activities with other adolescents. Encourage identification of support systems. Emphasize adolescent's abilities and strengths. Role-play situation in which the adolescent may feel uncomfortable (e.g., question from friends about his or her illness or appearance). Provide education to adolescent's class about the illness, with his or her permission.

Note. From Brantly, D. (1991). Conducting a psychosocial assessment of the child. In D. Smith (Ed.), *Comprehensive child and family nursing skills* (pp. 43–47). St. Louis: Mosby Year Book. Reprinted with permission.

Personal Strengths and Accomplishments

The ill child is challenged to find effective means for dealing with stressful experiences. Activities such as In Good Hands and Vote for Me can help children focus on personal strengths and accomplishments.

ACTIVITY 3.1. AUTO PHOTOGRAPHY

Auto photography is particularly beneficial for nonverbal children and children who, because of their physical condition, can only passively engage in activity. It can be done as a cumulative project with long-term patients or patients with anticipated repeat admissions.

Therapeutic Goal: To foster self-esteem by emphasizing uniqueness and self-worth and focusing on personal strengths.

Age Group: School-age, adolescent

Adult/Child Ratio: 1:4

Required Time: Varies

Restrictions and Precautions: Take markers and glue precautions.

Materials:

☐ Digital camera (one per child, or have children take turns)

☐ Computer/printer

☐ Cardboard or foam board (one sheet per child)

☐ Glue stick

☐ Pens or markers

Process

1. Explain to the children that they will be taking, or asking someone else to take, 10 (or more) photographs that describe special interests, personal strengths, people, or things that are important to them, or talents. Some children may require examples to begin.

2. After discussing the instructions, ask the children to compose a list of things they would like to photograph/have someone else photograph.

3. When the children are satisfied with the plan, provide them with a digital camera and, if necessary, instructions on its use.

4. When all of the photographs have been taken, print them out from a computer and have the children number them in order of importance or relevance.

5. Have the children glue the photographs on cardboard or foam board.

6. Ask the children to write or dictate a description of the significance of each photograph. This may be inscribed beneath each picture.

7. Invite children to display their photo collection in a prominent place.

Variation   Instead of mounting the photographs on board, give the child the option to place them in a scrapbook.

Activity 3.2.   Business Cards

Even young adult professionals are proud to distribute their first business cards. Having their own business cards can make children feel grown-up and important.

Therapeutic Goal: To foster self-esteem by emphasizing uniqueness and self-worth.

Age Group: School-age

Adult/Child Ratio: 1:2

Required Time: 20–30 minutes

Restrictions and Precautions: Instruct children not to give cards with their real contact information to people they don't know.

Materials:

☐ Computer

☐ Sheets of business cards for computer printing

☐ Samples of business cards

Process

1. Show the children samples of business cards.

2. Discuss the typical information found on business cards (e.g., name, address, phone number, business name, and business type).

3. Invite the children to design their own business cards. The cards can list the children's real contact information, to be given *only* to friends and family, or, they can be fictional. For example:

```
┌─────────────────────────┐     ╭─────────────────────────╮
│                         │    │  Calvin Washington, President │
│    Ashley Thomas        │    │ Funny Bone Consultants, LTD │
│  Artist Extra ordinaire │    │   Room 222, Bed B        │
│    Room 555, Bed A      │    │     Orthopedics          │
│    Joe's Hospital       │    │  Call 1-800-555-BONE     │
│ "Syringe Squirt Specialist" │  │  Bones are our business! │
└─────────────────────────┘     ╰─────────────────────────╯
```

4. Encourage the children to pass out their cards to new friends and staff.

For sports enthusiasts, make sports cards.   **Variation**

ACTIVITY 3.3.   CASTING BANDAGE MASKS

This activity is somewhat time-consuming and messy. However, the masks are unique and personal and often become cherished mementos for both the child and family.

Therapeutic Goal: To foster self-esteem by empha-sizing uniqueness and individuality.

Age Group: Preteen, adolescent

Adult/Child Ratio: 1:1

Required Time: Two 30–40 minute sessions

Restrictions and Precautions: Carefully assess the child to determine his or her appropriateness for this activity. Some children do not like having their faces covered. This activity should not be used with children whose skin may be sensitive or allergic to the casting material, or who have burns, lacerations, or incisions on their faces. Do not apply casting material directly to the skin.

Materials:

☐ Scissors

☐ Gauze pads (4-inch × 4-inch)

☐ Plaster casting bandage

☐ Petroleum jelly

☐ Basin of water

☐ Towels

☐ Blow dryer

☐ Casting bandage shears (optional)

☐ Paintbrushes

☐ Paint

☐ Acrylic sealer (optional)

1. Demonstrate to the child how to, first, cut two nose-size triangles from the casting bandage   **Process**
    and, then, a large number of strips. This works best if the bandage is twofold.

2. Ask the child to lie down or sit in a chair (whichever preferred) with his or her head tilted back.

3. Cover the child's face with petroleum jelly, avoiding the eyes.

4. Cut two pieces of gauze large enough to cover the child's eyes and place them over the eyes.

5. Dip the two triangles in water and place them over the child's nose.

6. Continue to apply bandage strips to the nose area until the nose and upper lip are completely covered. Take care not to block the nostrils and interfere with breathing. (Drinking straws can be placed in the nostrils as a precaution.)

7. Cover the rest of the face with strips of twofold casting bandage, gently pressing on the facial features so that they are impressed into the casting bandage.

8. Let the mask dry for 10 minutes and remove it from the child's face. Expedite drying time by using a blow dryer.

9. Trim uneven edges with scissors or casting bandage shears.

10. After the mask has dried, let the child paint the mask as desired.

11. When the paint has dried, spray it with acrylic sealer. Allow to dry completely before giving the mask to the child.

ACTIVITY 3.4. CROWN ME

Be it from reading fairytales, watching cartoons, or going to the movies, most children know that kings and queens wear crowns to symbolize their importance.

Therapeutic Goal: To foster self-esteem.

Age Group: Preschool/primary

Adult/Child Ratio: 1:4

Required Time: 30 minutes

Restrictions and Precautions: Take scissors, glue, and marker precautions.

Materials:

- ☐ Crown template (Figure Activity 3.4-1)
- ☐ Thin cardboard pieces, 22 inches × 5 inches
- ☐ Pencil
- ☐ Scissors
- ☐ Markers
- ☐ Craft jewels with adhesive backing
- ☐ Glitter, sequins
- ☐ Cotton balls
- ☐ Glue
- ☐ Tape

Figure Activity 3.4-1. **Crown Me Template**

Process

1. Using the template, trace the crown onto the cardboard and cut it out.

2. Give the crowns to the children to color and decorate with craft jewels and other decorative materials.

3. Wrap the crown around each child's head to determine the size needed then secure with tape.

4. Encourage the children to wear their crowns to remind them that they are important to all those who love and care for them.

ACTIVITY 3.5. DNA NECKLACE: GENES IN A BOTTLE

DNA usually first appears in school curricula during the seventh grade. Although not viable for DNA testing, the DNA used in this activity is real, hence unique. The activity can be used as a follow-up to teaching about genetic disorders or to create a keepsake or gift.

Therapeutic Goal: To foster self-esteem by emphasizing uniqueness and individuality.

Age Group: Older school-age/adolescent

Adult/Child Ratio: 1:10

Required Time: 30–45 minutes

Restrictions and Precautions: None

Materials:

- ☐ Clear dishwashing soap
- ☐ Clear Gatorade or saltwater solution (children, of course, prefer the taste of Gatorade)

- ☐ Two small, clear glass cups, test tubes, or shot glasses (per child)
- ☐ Isopropyl or rubbing alcohol, ice cold (keep in freezer until ready to use)
- ☐ Measuring spoon
- ☐ Wooden toothpick (one per child)
- ☐ Exam gloves
- ☐ Spoon
- ☐ 12–18 inches of string, gimp, or leather cord (per child)
- ☐ Jewelry vials (one per child), which can be purchased from various sites on the Internet
- ☐ Beads, spacers, and a clasp (optional)

Process

1. Instruct the children not to eat or brush their teeth for at least an hour prior to the activity.

2. Ask the children to tell you what they know about DNA. Provide an age-appropriate explanation of DNA to children who do not know what it is. Emphasize that, like a fingerprint, each person's DNA is unique.

3. Have the children pour 1 tablespoon of dishwashing liquid into a cup.

4. Tell the children to pour 1 tablespoon of Gatorade or saltwater solution into a second cup.

5. To obtain sloughed cells from which to extract the DNA, demonstrate for the children how to swish the Gatorade or saltwater solution in their mouths for one minute, while gently biting the inside of their cheeks.

6. Instruct the children to spit the solution into the container with soap.

7. Advise the children to try to avoid creating bubbles while they gently stir the mixture for 2 to 3 minutes.

8. Instruct the children to tilt the container and slowly pour 2 teaspoons of alcohol down the sides, taking care not to cause the liquid to splash.

9. Allow the mixture to sit for 1 to 2 minutes, until white wisps of DNA begin to form. Explain that, normally, DNA is not visible to the naked eye. However, combining it with the soap, electrolytes, and alcohol causes the cell wall to break down and produce puffy double-helix strands.

10. Show the children how to use their toothpicks to gather the wisps and push them into their vials.

11. Tell the children to spoon a small amount of the remaining liquid from the cup into their vial.

12. Seal the vials according to the instructions accompanying them. Some vials may require the use of Super Glue or another type of sealant.

13. Have the children rinse off their vials and thread them onto a piece of ribbon, cord, or gimp.

14. Invite the children to string beads and add a clasp, if they wish. If not, tell the children to knot the two ends securely so they can wear their necklaces.

ACTIVITY 3.6. FINGERPRINT DETECTIVE

Children who watch crime shows on TV will enjoy this opportunity to play detective.

Therapeutic Goal: To foster self-esteem by emphasizing uniqueness and individuality.

Age Group: School-age

Adult/Child Ratio: Any

Required Time: 30 minutes

Restrictions and Precautions: None

Materials:

- ☐ Stamp pad

☐ White paper	☐ Baby powder
☐ Magnifying glass	☐ Clear tape, at least 1 inch wide
☐ Glass object (e.g., drinking glass or hand mirror)	☐ Black paper

Process

1. Give the child a stamp pad and white paper to collect the fingerprints of staff, friends, and/or family members.

2. Help the child take his or her own fingerprint, as well.

3. Encourage the child to study each fingerprint using the magnifying glass.

4. Discuss how each person's fingerprint is different and unique.

5. Next, without letting the child see, ask one of the family members, friends, or staff whose fingerprint is "on file" to grasp the glass object and move it.

6. Instruct the child to sprinkle the surface of the object with baby powder and gently blow off any excess. Fingerprints should be visible.

7. Demonstrate for the child how to hold a strip of tape tautly above the clearest fingerprint, lower it gently to the glass, then smooth out the tape to release any air bubbles, taking care not to smear the fingerprints.

8. Have the child lift up the strip of tape and press it down on the black paper.

9. Challenge the child to compare this fingerprint to those "on file" and to try to identify to whom it belongs.

10. Reinforce how each person's fingerprints have different patterns and are unique, just like people have different personalities and strengths that make them unique.

ACTIVITY 3.7.   GRAFFITI NAME SIGNS

Children like seeing their names written; it makes them feel important. Even in years gone by, naughty children would write their names in wet concrete, scratch it into trees and wooden desks, and draw it on bathroom or public walls. Although graffiti is commonly regarded as a form of vandalism, one only has to look at the work of Keith Haring and other contemporary artists to see that it has become a style of art as well.

Therapeutic Goal: To promote positive self-esteem by emphasizing uniqueness and individuality and identifying personal space.

Age Group: School-age/adolescent

Adult/Child Ratio: 1:10

Required Time: 30 minutes

Restrictions and Precautions: Do not show as examples pictures of graffiti lettering that is obviously the work of vandals. Take marker precautions.

Materials:

☐ Pictures of graffiti lettering downloaded from the Internet

☐ Pencil

☐ Paper

☐ Poster board

☐ Markers

Process

1. Most urban children are familiar with graffiti, but for those who are not, or need a visual reminder, show pictures of different styles of graffiti lettering.

2. Ask the children to identify the characteristics typical of graffiti lettering; for example, block letters with a three-dimensional appearance, stylized lettering where each letter touches or slightly overlaps, bright colors, and bold design.

3. Provide the children with paper and pencil and encourage them to experiment with different ways to write their names in block letters. They can vary the letters by making them rounded or with sharp angles, all large letters or a combination of large and small, slanted or straight up and down, and so on. Encourage them to personalize their style by dotting their "i's" in unusual ways (e.g., using lightning bolts, hearts, or stars) and adding images to rounded letters like "O," "Q," and "R" (e.g., eyes peering out, or smiley faces).

4. When the children are satisfied with the way their names look, demonstrate how to transfer their designs to the poster board, using light pencil marks.

5. Let them choose a marker to outline the letters.

6. Suggest using the markers to fill in each letter, by shading them or using graduating shades of color and/or bold designs (Figure Activity 3.7-1).

Figure Activity 3.7-1. Graffiti Name Sign

7. Encourage the children to hang up their name sign in their rooms or on the door.

ACTIVITY 3.8.   IN GOOD HANDS

Most children are enthusiastic about working in three-dimensional media, making this a very appealing activity to many. The activity has two distinct components: visual art and writing. The components should be done in two or more sessions, allowing for each to build on the preceding. Therefore, this activity is best suited for long-term patients or those who are seen regularly for treatment.

Therapeutic Goal: To foster self-esteem by focusing on personal strengths.

Age Group: School-age/adolescent

Adult/Child Ratio: 1:8

Required Time: Extensive advance preparation, which must be done at least five days prior to conducting the activity. Divide the time with the children into at least two sessions. Tip: Make extra hands for future use.

Restrictions and Precautions: Wear gloves, and prepare the plaster in a well-ventilated area. Take scissors, glue, and paint precautions.

Materials:

☐ One large mixing container, such as a 2-gallon pitcher

☐ Measuring cups
☐ Sifter
☐ Water
☐ Plaster of paris (available at most art supply stores and hardware stores)
☐ Paddle (to stir the plaster mixture)
☐ Latex gloves
☐ Acrylic paint
☐ Paintbrushes
☐ Magazines
☐ Scissors
☐ Glue

Process

1. Fill the container with 30 ounces of water.

2. Holding the sifter very close to the surface of the water, slowly sift the plaster into the water, until small "islands" form at the top and don't immediately dissolve. Avoid lumps forming.

3. Allow the solution to sit for several minutes.

4. Slowly mix the plaster, using your gloved hand or a large paddle.

5. Stretch the glove to be filled across your forefinger and thumb; or, if you have someone to assist you, let the assistant hold the glove open as wide as possible.

6. Pour the plaster mixture into the glove, taking care not to overfill it, as this will make it impossible to tie.

7. Tie the glove as you would a balloon.

8. Place the filled glove on a flat surface where it can remain for a few hours undisturbed. At this point, you can position the hand so that it hardens in a particular pose. Note, however, doing so will make it more difficult to remove the latex glove and might cause the finger to fall off.

9. Leave the hand undisturbed for approximately 12 hours and then carefully remove the glove.

10. Allow the hand to cure for five days. If the hand is not cured for an adequate amount of time, the paint will not absorb properly.

11. Introduce the activity by explaining that hands are often considered a symbol of strength. Discuss what is meant by "personal strengths."

12. Instruct the children to look through the magazines and cut out 10 words that describe some of their own personal strengths. If they cannot find a particular word they are looking for, print it from a computer.

13. Let the children paint their hands; allow the paint to dry.

14. Have the children glue the words they selected to the hands. Images and/or colorful papers may also be glued on for decoration (Figure Activity 3.8-1).

Figure Activity 3.8-1. **In Good Hands**

15. Invite the children to write poems about themselves, incorporating each of the 10 words they chose.

Variation

For younger children, help them trace their hands on construction paper and cut them out. Ask them to write or dictate important or fun things they can do with their hands.

For more ideas, see Bright Ideas Hand-i-Craft: Things to Make with Hand-Tracing Cutouts (Box Activity 3.8-1).

BOX ACTIVITY 3.8-1. BRIGHT IDEAS HAND-I-CRAFT: THINGS TO MAKE WITH HAND-TRACING CUTOUTS

- *Bookmark*: Write the child's name on the tracing. Cut the tracing out, punch a hole near the wrist, and thread a piece of ribbon or yarn through it and knot.

- *Turkey*: Cut the tracing out of brown paper. Use the thumb as the head and the fingers as feathers. Let the child color the "feathers" with crayons, and glue on eyes, feet, and a waddle cut from colored paper.

- *Wreath*: Cut multiple tracings out of green paper. Arrange in a circle and add a red bow.

- *Tree*: Cut multiple tracings out of green paper. Make a trunk and branches from brown construction paper and arrange the hands as leaves. This is an excellent long-term project to do with the family and friends of a child who is hospitalized or bedridden for an extended period of time. To make a Christmas tree, arrange the tracings in a triangular formation and put a star on top.

- *Rudolph the Reindeer*: Use a paper plate for the head. Make the antlers with two tracings cut from brown paper, and attach to the paper plate. Cut out a red circle for the nose, and smaller black circles for the eyes.

- *Dog head profile*: To make the tracing, invite the child to spread his or her fingers, with the third and fourth fingers touching and the first and second fingers touching. This creates an open mouth, with the child's thumb serving as the ear.

- *Flying bird*: Overlap the thumbs to create the bird's body, with the fingers and palms forming the wings.

- *Sun*: Paint the back of a paper plate yellow and attach eight yellow hand tracings to make the rays.

- *Duck*: For the duck's body, fold a paper plate in half and paint it yellow. Staple two tracings cut from yellow paper next to the fold on one side of the paper plate, to form tail feathers. Cut a yellow circle for the head. Cut three ovals out of orange paper. For the bill, cut the end off one oval. For the feet, cut zigzags on one end of each of the two remaining ovals. Assemble the duck with staples or glue.

ACTIVITY 3.9.   MAGAZINE NAME COLLAGES

The collages can be enhanced by encouraging the children to include pictures that represent aspects of their personality, interests, or activities.

Therapeutic Goal: To foster positive self-esteem by emphasizing uniqueness and individuality.	**Materials:**
Age Group: Primary/school-age	☐ Magazines
Adult/Child Ratio: 1:10	☐ Scissors
Required Time: 30 minutes	☐ Glue
Restrictions and Precautions: Take scissors and glue precautions.	☐ Construction paper

Process

1. Have the children look through magazines to locate and then cut out the letters in their name—enough copies to spell it out five or more times. Encourage the children to find letters that are at least 1/2 inch in height.

2. Instruct the children to arrange the letters on a piece of construction paper, spelling out their names multiple times. Encourage them to vary the angles of the letters so that they intersect, to create visual interest.

3. When the children are satisfied with the arrangement, have them glue the letters in place.

4. Encourage the children to display the collages in their rooms.

ACTIVITY 3.10.   MINI-ME PAPER DOLLS

Assess children carefully for participation in this activity. It is not appropriate for children from cultures that prohibit photographed images or find it objectionable for male children to play with dolls.

Therapeutic Goal: To foster self-esteem by emphasizing uniqueness and encouraging individuality.

Age Group: Preschool/primary

Adult/Child Ratio: 1:1

Required Time: 45 minutes advance preparation

Restrictions and Precautions: Do not allow children to handle the craft knife. Take marker precautions.

Materials:

- ☐ Digital camera
- ☐ Photo paper
- ☐ Foam board
- ☐ Craft glue
- ☐ Knife with disposable blade
- ☐ Cardstock
- ☐ Scissors
- ☐ Markers
- ☐ Tongue depressor (optional)
- ☐ Velcro dots

Process

1. Photograph the child wearing a bathing suit or in undergarments, with his or her arms slightly extended.
2. Enlarge the photo to 8 inches × 12 inches and print it.
3. Mount the photo onto the foam board and cut the image out with the knife.
4. Use the doll as a template to draw different outfits or costumes on cardstock. Include a hospital gown or pajamas.
5. Use markers to color and add details to the clothing (or let the child do this as part of the activity).
6. Attach a Velcro dot to each shoulder and the lower abdomen of the doll.
7. Attach corresponding dots to each item of clothing.
8. Give the child the doll to play with and help him or her make additional outfits for the doll, if desired.
9. Display the doll on a miniature easel; or attach a tongue depressor so that the doll can be used as a puppet.

Note: Adapted from an idea submitted by Shari Callaway to *Family Fun Magazine*, May 2005.

ACTIVITY 3.11.   NAME BRACELETS

These sparkly bracelets, personalized with the children's names and birthstones make little girls feel grown-up and special.

Therapeutic Goal: To foster self esteem by emphasizing uniqueness and individuality.

Age Group: Primary

Adult/Child Ratio: 1:4

Required Time: 30 minutes

Restrictions and Precautions: Take glue and glitter precautions. Use fixative in a well-ventilated area and away from children.

Materials:

- ☐ Cardboard tube (empty paper towel rolls work well), cut into rings 1/2 to 3/4 inches wide (one ring per child)
- ☐ Paint
- ☐ Paintbrushes
- ☐ Glue
- ☐ Glitter and/or sequins
- ☐ Self-adhesive craft jewels in birthstone colors
- ☐ Clear spray-on fixative

1. Provide each child with a cardboard ring. If the ring does not fit over the child's hand, cut out **Process**
   a small section so that it will easily slip on.
2. Let the children paint their bracelets with their favorite colors.
3. Help the children use glue to write their names on their bracelets.
4. Encourage the children to cover the glue with sequins or glitter.
5. Provide each child with craft jewels in the color of their birthstones so they can adhere them
   to their bracelets in a decorative fashion.

ACTIVITY 3.12.   PERSONALIZED PENNANTS

Sports enthusiasts will especially appreciate having a pennant for cheering them on, just like their
favorite team does.

Therapeutic Goal: To foster self-esteem by identifying personal space and emphasizing uniqueness and individuality.

Age Group: School-age/adolescent

Adult/Child Ratio: 1:10

Required Time: 30–45 minutes

Restrictions and Precautions: Advise children to handle the pennant stick safely. Take scissors, glue, and paint precautions.

Materials:

☐ Yardstick or ruler

☐ Felt
☐ Scissors
☐ Pencil
☐ Stencils
☐ Glue
☐ Fabric paint and/or decorative trims (e.g., lace, yarn, sequins, etc.)
☐ Hole punch
☐ Jumbo yarn
☐ Dowel rod (one per child)

1. To create the pennants, demonstrate for the children how to draw an isosceles triangle, at **Process**
   a height of 18 inches and a base of 8 inches, onto a piece of felt, and cut it out.
2. Give the children stencils to trace their names onto a contrasting colored piece of felt.
3. Have the children cut out each letter and then glue them to the pennant.
4. Let the children decorate the pennants using fabric paint and/or decorative trims (Figure
   Activity 3.12-1).
5. Show the children how to use the hole punch to make eight holes equidistant apart along the
   base of the triangle.
6. Demonstrate how to thread the yarn loosely through the holes in the pennant then ask the
   children to do the same.
7. Have the children slide the dowel rod through the loops of the yarn and pull the yarn so that
   it tightens around the rod.
8. Ask the children to cut the yarn and knot it at both ends.

Figure Activity 3.12-1. **Personalized Pennants**

9.   Encourage the children to display the pennant on the wall in their room, or to hang from their IV poles or on the back of their wheelchairs.

Variation

An easier method is to make the flag out of construction paper and use tape to attach it to a cardboard tube.

ACTIVITY 3.13.   UNO, DOSE

This activity can be successfully modified in many different ways, contingent on the size of the group, abilities of the participants, and their attention span. For example, a standard deck of cards can be made (as opposed to a larger Uno, Dose deck); or one child or family can make a complete deck of cards themselves. The theme of the deck can also be changed to something that more specifically targets the needs of the participants. Playing games with the cards is not even necessary; the therapeutic value is in the discussion preceding the activity and having the children create, then talk about, artistic expressions of themselves.

Therapeutic Goal: To foster self-esteem by emphasizing uniqueness and individuality and focusing
on personal strengths.

Age Group: School-age/adolescent

Adult/Child Ratio: Varies

Required Time: This is a progressive activity, best
suited for long-term patients or in areas where
groups of children are together regularly, such as
infusion clinics or support groups.

Restrictions and Precautions: Take marker, scissors,
and glue precautions.

Materials:

☐ Deck of blank playing cards (available from many recreation supply companies)

☐ Peel-and-stick numbers, 1-inch, in three or four colors

☐ Markers (same colors as numbers)

☐ Scissors

☐ Magazines

☐ Photos (optional)

Process

1.   Begin the activity by engaging the children in a discussion about how everyone is unique, and has different abilities, strengths, and values. Ask the children to give examples of different positive personality attributes about themselves and/or other members of the group.

2.   Explain to the children that they will making a deck of playing cards, decorating the cards to represent positive attributes that relate to them, such as their skills, talents, interests, feelings, values, relationships, and so on. To do so, they can incorporate photos, images, drawings or designs, and words cut from magazines.

3.   Divide the responsibility for making the complete deck of cards among the participants. They will make a series of cards in each color, to include: two of each of the numbers 1 to 10, two wild cards, instructional cards that have two reverse cards, two "lose one turn" cards, and two extra-turn cards in each of the colors. If needed, the adult can create one color series, or one color series can be eliminated.

4.   Provide each child with a marker and peel-and-stick numbers in their assigned color.

5.   Have the children make one card for each of the numbers, 1 to 10, putting the same number in the upper left-hand corner and lower right-corner of each card.

6.   Explain to the children how to create the instructional cards.

7.   Allow the children to decorate their cards as they wish (Figure Activity 3.13-1).

8.   Encourage the children to talk about what they have represented on their cards.

9.   Use the cards to play as you would in Uno. Directions can be downloaded from the Internet, if needed.

Figure Activity 3.13-1. Uno, Dose Cards

ACTIVITY 3.14.   V.I.P. (VERY IMPORTANT PATIENT OR PERSON)

Night nurses appreciate when children make these posters because it helps them to better know the patients they are caring for. The information about the child's unique personality can also help those interacting with him or her to identify topics of conversation through which they can provide meaningful affirmations.

Therapeutic Goal: To foster self-esteem by emphasizing uniqueness and individuality and focusing on personal strengths.

Age Group: Primary/school-age

Adult/Child Ratio: 1:1

Required Time: 20–30 minutes

Restrictions and Precautions: Take glue and marker precautions.

Materials:

- ☐ Poster board
- ☐ Markers
- ☐ Photograph of the child
- ☐ Tape or glue

Process

1. Write "Very Important Patient" (or "Person") in large letters across the top of the poster board.

2. Tape or glue the photograph of the child beneath the lettering.

3. Discuss with the child the reasons he or she is special—a "V.I.P."—emphasizing the child's unique strengths, qualities, interests, and accomplishments.

4. Ask the child to dictate or write a paragraph about (or a list of) all the unique aspects of him- or herself that the two of you identified. Put it under the child's photograph.

5. Invite the child to decorate the poster by drawing pictures or a border on it.

6. With the child's permission, hang the poster on the door or wall of his or her room.

ACTIVITY 3.15.   VOTE FOR ME!

This is a good, multifaceted activity to help children recognize and verbalize their positive qualities. It can be done as a progressive activity with long-term patients or those having repeated admissions.

Therapeutic Goal: To foster self-esteem by focusing on personal strengths.

Age Group: School-age

Adult/Child Ratio: 1:4

Required Time: Varies

Restrictions and Precautions: Take marker precautions.

Materials:

- ☐ Pencils
- ☐ Paper

☐ Photo of each child (large headshot preferred)   ☐ Tape

☐ Poster board (one per child)   ☐ Button-maker (optional)

☐ Markers

Process

1. Introduce the activity by discussing a political campaign that the children are familiar with (e.g., the most recent presidential, mayoral, or gubernatorial campaign). Talk about different techniques and items candidates use, such as slogans, buttons, posters, and songs, to inform the public of their positive attributes and accomplishments.

2. Tell the children to pretend they are running for the office of their choice. It could be a real position, such as governor or president, or imaginary, such as the Director of the Patients, Friends, and Visitors Union (PFVU). Inform the children that the campaign should be based on their own actual strengths.

3. Help each of the children craft a campaign slogan.

4. Invite the children to design and make a campaign poster, incorporating their campaign slogan and a photo of themselves. Let them select a prominent place to display their poster.

5. Show the children how make "campaign" buttons, for family and staff to wear (optional).

6. If the children are still engaged, or during a follow-up session, ask them to write a campaign song or speech to further "sell" themselves. Encourage them to give their speeches or perform their songs for other members of the group, staff, family, and/or friends.

ACTIVITY 3.16.   WHAT'S-IN-A-NAME POEMS

This activity can be done effectively with the adult serving as the scribe when working with children who are unable to participate physically.

Therapeutic Goal: To foster self-esteem by emphasizing uniqueness and individuality and focusing on personal strengths.

Age Group: School-age/adolescent

Adult/Child Ratio: 1:10

Required Time: 30 minutes

Restrictions and Precautions: Take marker precautions.

Materials:

☐ Poster board or paper

☐ Markers

Process

1. Ask the children to write their first names in capital letters vertically on the poster board.

2. Instruct the children to use each letter of their name to begin a word or phrase that describes themselves. For example:

Cute and cool   **J**okester
Active in sports   **U**ninhibited
Rocking   **S**ports star and enthusiast
Loving to others   **T**errific throwing arm
Yummy   **I**nteresting
                          Nimble and quick

3. Encourage the children to give examples of how they demonstrate these traits in their lives.

Ask the children to write their names in large block letters on poster board or paper then cut out the **Variation** names without separating the letters. In each block letter, encourage the children to write a word that describes them beginning with that letter.

ACTIVITY 3.17. YOU'RE IN THE MONEY

By the time they are preschoolers, most children have already developed an awareness of the value of money through the subtle and less-than-subtle messages they receive from the media and adults around them.

Therapeutic Goal: To foster self-esteem by emphasizing uniqueness and self-worth.

Age Group: Preschool/primary

Adult/Child Ratio: 1:4

Required Time: 20 minutes

Restrictions and Precautions: None

Materials:

☐ Photos of children

☐ Computer, printer, and scanner

☐ Thousand-dollar bill template (Figure Activity 3.17-1)

☐ Paper

☐ Scissors

☐ Crayons

Figure Activity 3.17-1. You're in the Money Template

1. Scan the template into your computer and use Photoshop or similar software to insert each **Process** child's picture into the center of a "bill."

2. Print multiple copies of each child's bill and cut them out.

3. Show the children a dollar bill and ask them to tell you who is pictured on it.

4. When the correct answer is given, ask the children if they know any of the other famous people whose pictures are on bills or coins. Discuss why they were honored in this way.

5. Remind the children that everyone is special. Ask the children to name some of the attributes about themselves that make them uniquely special. Help any children who are experiencing difficulty doing so.

6. As each of the children names something special about him- or herself, give the child a bill with his or her picture on it.

7. Encourage the children to design and color all of their bills. Remind them to recognize and be proud of the qualities for which they were awarded bills.

For more ideas, see Bright Ideas for Self-Esteem (Box Activity 3.17-1).

**BOX
ACTIVITY 3.17-1.
BRIGHT IDEAS
FOR
SELF-ESTEEM**

- Help the children create personal web pages.
- Make buttons with the child's name and/or picture and ask caretakers to wear them.
- Encourage children to write their autobiographies. Children too young to write can dictate their stories or draw pictures.
- For prolific artists, have a "one-person show," displaying the child's creations in a prominent area.
- When possible, encourage children to wear their own clothes or pajamas. This can be particularly beneficial for adolescents to help them maintain their sense of personal identity.
- Give girls alphabet beads and the materials to make name bracelets.
- For newly diagnosed children or chronically ill children, search online for famous people with the same diagnosis. Such sites exist for diabetes, Crohn's disease, irritable bowel disease, asthma, and sickle cell, to name just a few. Often, these sites include inspirational stories and quotes from some of the well-known people listed.
- Inspire children to declare a new holiday in honor of themselves. Name the holiday, pick a day, make decorations, and celebrate!
- Let each of the children research his or her name to find out what it means, what the country of origin is, and why their family chose it.

Chapter 4

Body Image

Body image refers to a person's inner picture of his or her outward appearance. It has two components: perceptions of the appearance of one's body, and emotional responses to those perceptions (*Gale Encyclopedia of Medicine*, 2008). This subjective picture of one's physical appearance is established by both self-observation and by noting the reactions of others.

Illness, disability, and hospitalization can have profound effects on how children and adolescents view their bodies, making the task of forming an accurate and positive body image very difficult. Medical treatment implies some internal or external defect requiring evaluation, treatment, and/or correction. The outcome may produce changes in the body, either temporarily or permanently, that require adjustment at many levels—perceptual, emotional, and behavioral. One of the first indicators that a child is struggling with conflict concerning body image may be discovered in his or her artwork, in the form of omission, exaggeration, or addition of body parts.

The activities in this chapter are designed to help identify and reduce body image disturbances. The activities in other chapters address self-esteem (Chapter 3), self-expression (Chapter 2), and group interactions (Chapter 5), to supplement those in this one.

LIST OF ACTIVITIES

Activity 4.1 Beauty from the Inside Out	Activity 4.9 If I Could Be Someone Else
Activity 4.2 Body Awareness for Babies	Activity 4.10 Mad Hatters
Activity 4.3 Body Glitter	Activity 4.11 Makeup Makeover
Activity 4.4 Body Molds	Activity 4.12 Mirror Me
Activity 4.5 Body Perception Comparisons	Activity 4.13 My Body Book
Activity 4.6 Connect the Dots	Activity 4.14 Shadow Dancing
Activity 4.7 Divergent Views	Activity 4.15 Silhouettes
Activity 4.8 Face and Body Paint	Activity 4.16 Somatic Diary

Exploring the Concept of Body Image

A complex and multidimensional psychological construct, body image encompasses body-related self-perceptions and self-attitudes, including thoughts, beliefs, feelings, and behaviors (Cash, 2004). Although at times research in the medical field considers body image to be a rather coherent and invariable construct (Hammar, Ozolins, Idvall, & Rudebeck, 2009), body image is not static (Nurit Bird, 2004). A constant molding of what may be understood as multiple body images occurs through interactions with the world, mainly with other people. White (2000) reminds us that adaptation to body image change is a dynamic psychosocial process.

Development of Body Image

Body image develops over time. Until recently it was thought that adolescence was the critical phase during which negative and positive factors had their strongest influence on body image. Adolescence is a time of critical personal and physical development, yet more recent research indicates that body image formation begins at a much younger age (Birbeck & Drummond,

2003; Dohnt & Tiggemann, 2005; Ricciardelli & McCabe, 2001; Sands & Wardle, 2003). We know that children of preschool age are aware of the ideal body for their gender. Body esteem seems to improve during the early elementary school years (Davison, Markey, & Birch, 2000). Both boys and girls experience a decrease in body esteem during middle school, although the decrease may be less dramatic and may show a faster recovery for boys than for girls (Smolak, 2004). Girls by late childhood and boys by early adolescence learn the association between body dissatisfaction and high levels of negative affect or depression and low levels of self-esteem.

Although, currently, the common denominator is the thin body ideal, numerous factors influence the development of body image (see Box 4.1). By Western sociocultural standards of attractiveness for women and men, thinness is equated with beauty, a notion that is perpetuated through the mass media and that may reinforce peer and family expectation of physical appearance (McCabe, Ricciardelli, & Ridge, 2006). Nevertheless, body image dissatisfaction is not an automatic outcome. Paxton (2002) and others report that higher self-esteem, resilience, the ability to interpret media messages about physical attractiveness and weight, and positive and supportive feedback from peers and families about their health and appearance all protect against body dissatisfaction.

BOX 4.1.
FACTORS
ASSOCIATED WITH
BODY
DISSATISFACTION

Biological Factors

- *Neglect of a body part*: Some psychological disorders or perception that a surgically removed limb is still present

- *Epilepsy and migraines*: Possible confusion in distinguished right/left orientation; delusions about body size

- *Biologically determined characteristics*: When departing from that which the individual considers socially accepted (e.g., male pattern hair loss, height, skin characteristics, breast size, facial features, disfigurement); when causing discomfort or inconvenience (e.g., very large breasts, pregnant body, menstruation, specific physical disabilities)

- *Actual body size*: Large discrepancies between actual body size and individual's body ideal

- *Small size*: Greater likelihood to overestimate body size

Culture

- *Preferred body features*: Cultural and ethnic differences in body features, such as weight, shape, skin tone, breast size (e.g., African American women accept a wider range of body weights, including a larger body size as ideal, than white women).

- *Degree of cultural identity*: Early-age immigrants more likely to share similar perceptions of ideal body size as dominant culture (e.g., immigrating to a Western culture at an early age influences the idea of thinness for Hispanic American females).

- *Shifts in the beauty ideal over time* (e.g., "Rubenesque" to hourglass to curvaceous to slim, for women; muscular for men): Risk if body shape does not conform to the current ideal.

Parents

- *Parental concerns and behaviors about their own bodies*: Possible imitation of parents' attitudes and behaviors

- *Parental criticism of child's body*: More body concerns and dieting

Peers

- *Appearance norms and ideal dictated*: Those with less similar appearance punished; those whose appearance conforms most closely to the ideal rewarded

- *Individual's perception that peers consider weight and shape important*: Reassurance for some through affirmation; or insecurity and body image concerns for others

- *Promotion of a certain body type*: Thin for girls; athletic and muscular for boys

- *Within and without peer group teasing*: Contributor to body dissatisfaction independent of the child's actual size

- *Weight-related teasing*: Predictor of later general body dissatisfaction
- *Low peer group emphasis on body image*: Low levels of body dissatisfaction

Media

- *Unrealistic and unrepresentative images*: Thin glamorous women and muscular athletic men; images often product of a rare body shape, image manipulation, or combination of both
- *High media exposure*: Associated with poor body image or disturbed eating
- *Previous experience*: Previous body dissatisfaction associated with more negative impact when viewing idealized images.

Social/Cultural Environment

- *Special high-risk environment*: For example, ballet schools and modeling schools
- *Combination of relationships between media, family, and peers*: Body image concerns more likely in culture that is weight- and shape-conscious from childhood through maturity

Puberty

- *Different rates of development*: Early or late maturation associated with anxiety; early-onset menstruation associated with greater body dissatisfaction
- *Changes in girls*: Pubic hair distribution or breast development associated with "chubbiness"

Sexual Abuse

- *Body disturbances*: Altered meaning of body; bodily shame; attempt to control the body and make it less vulnerable
- *Weight preoccupation*: Eating disorders, compulsive exercising
- *Sexual harassment*: Related to poorer body esteem in elementary school girls

Gender and Sexual Orientation

- *Devaluation of body type*: Affects both girls and boys
- *Overweight*: Of greater concern for girls
- *Homosexuality*: Assumption that cultural emphasis on physical attractiveness causes greater pressure, anxiety, and body concerns for homosexual boys than for heterosexual boys; assumption of less emphasis on physical attractiveness in regard to lesbians
- *Body size*: Possibly more acceptance of higher weights, or less concern about body size for lesbians.

Psychological

- *Depression anxiety, low self-esteem, negative emotionality*: Associated with negative self-evaluations, leading to poor body image
- *Depression and self-esteem*: Associated with body dissatisfaction; yet little evidence of causal relationship

Note. Adapted from: Family and Community Development Committee. (2005). *Inquiry into issues relating to the development of body image among young people and associated effects on their health and well-being.* Melbourne, Australia: Author. Retrieved from www.parliament.vic.gov.au/fcdc/inquiries/body_image/FCDC-Report_BodyImage_2005-07.pdf, February 26, 2010. Murnen, S., & Smolak, L. (2000). The experience of sexual harassment among grade-school students: Early socialization of female subordination? *Sex Roles, 43*, 1–17. Smolak, L. (2004). Body image in children and adolescents: Where do we go from here? *Body Image, 1*, 15–28.

Visible Differences

Whether it is referred to as disfigurement, abnormality, deformity, or defect, an individual's appearance does play a part in first impressions, even if those impressions are modified through subsequent contact (Rumsey & Harcourt, 2007). Visual differences can result from congenital anomalies, illnesses, injuries, or surgical interventions. It is difficult to determine the prevalence of such differences because what constitutes a visible difference may mean different things to different people. For example, although wearing eyeglasses has been associated with negative attributes, such as disfigurement and less attractiveness, some children do not mind wearing spectacles.

Visible differences may be congenital or acquired (Rumsey & Harcourt, 2007). A congenital difference may be fully manifested at birth, such as cleft palate, or, like neurofibromatosis, become more evident over time. An acquired difference may be caused by trauma, surgical intervention, treatment, disease, genetic predispositions to conditions that manifest in later life, or the absence of normal developmental processes. The change of appearance may be sudden and unexpected, as would be the case with burns, or secondary to survival and life-saving treatment, such as hair loss from chemotherapy.

Age-Related Issues

Issues that surface because of visual differences vary with the age of the child. Differences affect not only how children view themselves, but also how they are viewed by others.

Early Childhood and School Age. Key developmental challenges in early childhood may present some particular hurdles for children with a visible difference (Rumsey & Harcourt, 2007). Regarding development of self-perception, body dissatisfaction within the general population is thought to develop from as early as 2 or 3 years of age (Gilbert & Thompson, 2002). The parents' feelings about the child's appearance may be transmitted to the child, and then assimilated, which can influence the child's developing perceptions of body image and self-worth (Kearney-Cooke, 2002). By the time children enter school, parental influence typically decreases, as children with a visible difference—as do all children at this age—increasingly compare themselves with their peers. Research suggests that children with a visible difference may be more at risk than children in the general population for developing negative self-perceptions and psychosocial difficulties, such as anxiety or depression, at this time (Chamlin, 2006). Social relationships are affected by body dissatisfaction and general psychological disturbance, which are thought to be linked to appearance-related teasing (Gilbert & Thompson, 2002).

Adolescence. Adolescence is a period of monumental developmental changes, which lead to an increased focus on appearance and body weight. The link between outward appearance and self-perception is particularly strong for many adolescents. Because this is a time when adolescents try to prove they are like everyone else, yet still individuals, having a visible difference can affect self-perceptions and present challenges. Teenagers may consider undergoing surgery to look more like their peers, even though they also may feel that the visible difference is part of their identity. Dilemmas are posed by young people questioning whether the reason they would have surgery would be for their benefit or for others, to improve the perceptions others have of them (Aspinall, 2006).

Some visible differences, such as acne, are so commonplace that they are often considered a normal part of development (Rumsey & Harcourt, 2007). Yet research indicates that acne can be a significant and distressing condition, exacerbated by its fluctuating nature and a perception that others do not consider it to be serious (Wallace, 2006). Depression, anxiety, shame, self-consciousness, and emotional and behavioral difficulties all have been associated with acne (Chamlin, 2006; Tan, 2004).

Adolescents with visible differences related to life-threatening situations often undergo a different experience. Wallace, Harcourt, and Rumsey (2007) report that adolescents with conditions such as cancer or meningococcal septicemia (blood poisoning) have used their experience to reevaluate their attitudes toward appearance. Having lived with hair loss, amputation, or other appearance changes, they often reassess the value attached to the way they look in comparison to other aspects of life, such as friendships and family support.

Peer relationships are extremely important during adolescence. The support of a peer can be a potent factor in positive adjustment for a young person with a visible difference. However, establishing supportive relationships with peers can be challenging. Some teens become defensive and avoid social situations, or may limit their social groups to one or two peers with whom they feel safe. Even when relationships have been established, other concerns may surface, such as developing intimate relationships. However, not all teens with a visible difference experience problems with relationships. Blakeney and colleagues (2005) found that extraversion and high social risk taking contribute positively to adjustment.

Certain conditions make it very difficult for children to blend in with their peers. A sampling of them is discussed next.

Sampling of Conditions That Affect Body Image

Cerebral Palsy. In discussing children with cerebral palsy, Mulderij (1996) identifies seven categories of body perception that can affect body image:

1. The rebellious body: Refuses to obey intentions

2. The unreliable body: Cannot be trusted (e.g., jerky limbs or uncontrollable speech)

3. The sensitive body: Comes to the fore in, for example, pain or fatigue

4. The body in therapy: Constantly in need of training

5. The dependent body: In need of assistance to an unacceptable extent

6. The conspicuous body: Catches the gaze of others, a reminder of being physically different

7. The vital body: Forgetful of itself in rewarding activities

Mulderij (2000) concludes that the relational aspects of body image must be emphasized when the main concern is to help young people feel good about their bodies. The challenge arises when individuals relate to their bodies with less trust and esteem than their nondisabled peers.

Open-Heart Surgery. Research with children post open-heart surgery suggests that accepting a body image change is a process. Lin and Tsai (2008, p. 84) found that school-age children following open-heart surgery undergo a four-stage adaptive process:

1. *Impact*: Questioning, perception of punishment for wrongdoing, loss, anger

2. *Retreat*: Denial, anxiety, withdrawal, escaping social contact, inferiority

3. *Acknowledgment*: Cognitive change, active participation, future-oriented concerns

4. *Reconstruction*: Positive self-image, reconstructing body image

During the final stage, children accepted their surgical wounds as a symbol of bravery. Lin and Tsai considered this a breakthrough likely to help with their reentrance to school and normalization of life.

Spinal Cord Injury. It is undeniable that a spinal cord injury is one of the most catastrophic events an individual can experience. The sudden change from independent, self-sufficient, contributing individual to a patient dependent on various mechanical devices and healthcare personnel would be difficult for anyone, but much more so for 15- to 29-year-olds, the age group primarily affected (Dewis, 1989). Not only may normal development be disrupted, individuals in this age group may typically lack the life experience required to cope with the enormity of the multiple sequelae of the injury. Dewis explored the meaning of body changes for 15 individuals with spinal cord injuries, ages 18 to 30 years. The participants reported concern with normalcy and being valued, and the use of deliberate strategies chosen and acted upon to maintain a sense of normalcy. They tended to suppress the physiological imperative and proceed with the activity imperative as if normal.

The participants also shared a number of negative feelings about particular aspects of body appearance and/or dysfunction. Normalization efforts were strongest in relation to impaired excretory function, loss of musculature and physique, deterioration in personal appearance and hygiene, and the intrusion of rehabilitation appliances and aids (Dewis, 1989).

Cancer. Children with cancer often face a great deal of distress associated with temporary or permanent changes to their appearance resulting from treatment—hair loss, weight changes, skin complaints, scarring, or amputation (Wallace et al., 2007). In some instances, children with cancer have reported that such changes have been the most stressful issues of their cancer experience (Rollins, 2005b). Research findings suggest that an altered appearance during treatment can result in a host of psychosocial consequences that affect quality of life, such as abuse, taunting, reduced self-esteem, increased self-consciousness, problems with social interactions and relationships with peers, body image concerns, and a sense of social isolation (Grinyer, 2007; Larouche & Chin-Peuckert, 2006; Reiter-Purtill & Noll, 2003).

Not surprisingly, research reveals that experiencing these changes during adolescence presents particular challenges, as the usual processes of physical, social, and sexual development at this time often result in individuals being acutely aware of their body (Holmbeck, 2002). Williamson, Harcourt, Halliwell, Frith, and Wallace (2010) recently focused specifically on the stress of an altered appearance during cancer treatment for adolescents. They reported that the adolescents in their study typically struggled to adapt to new experiences and concerns related to the highly sensitive issue of appearance. Many teens felt anxious and self-conscious and were reluctant to reveal appearance changes in public. Such feelings were compounded by the negative reactions of others, such as staring, teasing, and inappropriate questioning. In some instances these negative reactions lead to avoidance of social situations and/or treatment noncompliance.

Other Conditions. Many conditions and/or their treatments can potentially result in a change in appearance. Conditions such as arthritis, for example, can cause contractures and swollen joints, and medications used to treat arthritis can result in "moon face" and weight gain.

Less Visible Differences

It is commonly assumed that the more severe a disability or difference, the less favorable the individual's body image. However, often, a less visible condition results in greater concern. For example, a mild motor disability may be hardly recognizable, and in this situation, people are likely to be less considerate and more demanding. With nondisabled peers as social comparison groups, individuals with mild disabilities may encounter too many failures (Hammar et al., 2009).

Even when differences can be "hidden," studies reveal that body image can, nevertheless, be profoundly affected (Nicholas, Swan, Gerstle, Allan, & Griffiths, 2008). For example, with ostomies, post surgical challenges exist with respect to diminished self esteem, peer socialization, social stigma, sexual identity, independence, body image shifts, embarrassment, grief, and loss of control (Olsson et al., 2003). Daily care requires constantly viewing the ostomy, which children identify at least initially as self-repulsion. In one study with adolescents, one participant said, "It was this massive swollen thing. I was grossed out by it. But I eventually got used to looking at it" (Nicholas et al., p. 114). Others reported feeling self-conscious and worried that people would notice the ostomy, a concern they described as embarrassing and, in some cases, humiliating. For instance, one adolescent expressed fear that when dancing the dance partner would feel it and say, "What's that?" (p. 114).

Obesity

Although the physical health issues associated with being overweight are well established, Wardle and Cooke (2005) remind us that the psychological impact can be equally disturbing. Children who are overweight or obese often experience social stigma (Puhl & Latner, 2007), bullying (Janssen, Craig, Boyce, & Pickett, 2004), and social isolation (Strauss & Pollock, 2003), all factors that can affect body image and self-esteem (Puhl & Latner). Research reveals that even preschool-age children hold negative attitudes toward overweight peers (Holub, 2008). Other studies indicate that elementary school-age children display high levels of weight and muscle concern, including body dissatisfaction and problem eating (Holt & Ricciardelli, 2008). Unfortunately, there is limited evidence to show that prevention programs aimed at body dissatisfaction and problem eating reduce or prevent body image concerns and/or problem eating (Holt & Ricciardelli).

Distorted Body Image

The loss of a limb, breast, or tooth may cause psychological trauma because of unresolved conflict in the change of body image. A distorted body image may be a causal factor in disturbed eating behavior (DEB), which is commonly defined as dieting for weight control; binge eating; self-induced vomiting; or the use of diuretics, laxatives, insulin omission, or intense exercise for weight control (Olmsted, Colton, Daneman, Rydall, & Rodin, 2008). In a culture that promotes thinness to symbolize good health, control, liberation, assertiveness, and an affiliation with a higher socioeconomic class, individuals, especially girls entering puberty, are at risk of developing an eating disorder due to distorted body image issues resulting from these misconceptions. Dieting may become a preoccupation, and some children may even personally choose to develop bulimia, in an effort to control their weight and their lives. Although anyone can develop an eating disorder, the following individuals are at a higher risk (Eating Disorder Treatment Center, 2009):

- Individuals who work in an industry that demands thinness, like acting, modeling, or dancing;

- Athletes, especially those in wrestling, running, cycling, swimming, gymnastics, and cheerleading;

- Individuals with depression;

- Survivors of sexual abuse;

- Children of alcoholic parents;

- High-achievers;

- Girls with fathers who simultaneously avoid them and are critical of their weight; and

- Children of parents who diet or talk about dieting constantly.

During the 1980s, a self-esteem approach in the prevention of eating problems was adopted. Over the years, researchers using strong self-esteem components as part of their controlled prevention interventions have produced improvements in body dissatisfaction, dietary restraint, internalization of the thin ideal, and attitudes associated with the eating disorders (O'Dea, 2006).

Special Considerations

The developmental progression of body image is a consideration when selecting interventions for body image disturbances. Just as the young child learns about body parts, and then their functioning, healthcare professionals can offer sequential therapeutic play activities that promote this knowledge. If the child knows body parts, then activities enabling the child to learn more about body functions can be used. Misconceptions can be remediated during the process. Accepting the body is another experiential level that can then be promoted through therapeutic play activities.

Children and adolescents should always be allowed to choose whether to participate in body image activities because the activities may be threatening to them. When conducting activities in groups, it is important to assure that the group is sensitive to each individual.

Activity Goals

The objectives of the activities in this chapter are to identify body image distortions, foster a more positive body image, express and explore feelings related to the body, promote body image confrontation, and increase body awareness or increase body awareness through kinesthetic exploration. Some of the activities have only one objective; others, such as expressing and exploring feelings related to the body and identifying body image distortions, always occur together.

Fostering a More Positive Body Image

Activities that address this objective include Beauty from the Inside Out, Mad Hatters, and Makeup Makeover.

Expressing and Exploring Feelings Related to the Body

Activities that address this issue include Beauty from the Inside Out, Body Perception Comparisons, Divergent Views, and If I Could Be Someone Else.

Promoting Body Image Confrontation

Activities that address this objective include Body Glitter, Body Molds, Face and Body Paint, Makeup Makeover, Mirror Me, My Body Book, and Silhouettes.

Increasing Body Awareness

Activities that increase body awareness include Body Awareness for Babies, Body Molds, Mirror Me, My Body Book, Shadow Dancing, Silhouettes, and Somatic Diary.

ACTIVITY 4.1.   BEAUTY FROM THE INSIDE OUT

Blank muslin dolls are frequently donated to hospitals by charity organizations such as Project Sunshine, sewing circles, Girl Scouts, and other service groups. They are given to children to color and are sometimes used for procedural preparation. A pattern to make the dolls is included here for those who wish to do so.

Therapeutic Goal: To address body image issues by expressing and exploring feelings related to the body in order to foster a more positive body image.

Age Group: School-age/adolescent

Adult/Child Ratio: 1:6

Required Time: 45 minutes–1 hour

Restrictions and Precautions: Take markers, scissors, and glue precautions.

Materials:

- ☐ 12-inch blank muslin dolls (Figures Activity 4.1-1 and Activity 4.1-2)
- ☐ Fabric markers
- ☐ Yarn, fabric scraps, decorative trims (optional)
- ☐ Glue (optional)
- ☐ Scissors
- ☐ Paper

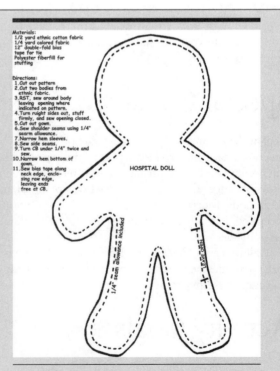

Figure Activity 4.1-1. Doll Pattern

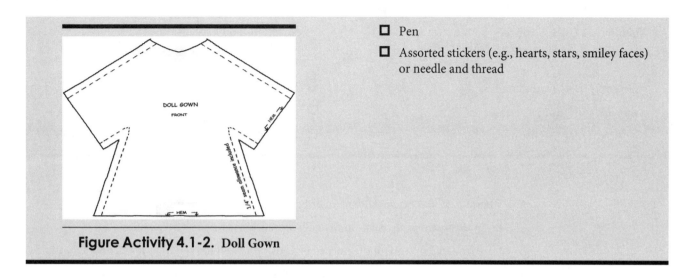

☐ Pen

☐ Assorted stickers (e.g., hearts, stars, smiley faces) or needle and thread

Figure Activity 4.1-2. Doll Gown

Process

1. Invite the children to color and decorate the dolls as representations of themselves, emphasizing what they especially like about how they look.

2. Engage the children in a discussion about how true beauty exists in one's heart or soul. Encourage the children to give examples of character traits that make people beautiful on the inside.

3. Ask the children to create an opening in their dolls, large enough to insert a small piece of folded paper, preferably in the chest area, as a metaphor for true beauty existing in our hearts.

4. Have the children write those character traits of inner beauty that they have or aspire to on tiny sheets of paper then tuck them into the doll.

5. Let the child choose a sticker to place over the opening, or sew it closed (Figure Activity 4.1-3).

Figure Activity 4.1-3. Sewn Doll

ACTIVITY 4.2.   BODY AWARENESS FOR BABIES

Body Awareness for Babies can help infants develop a more accurate perception of what is and isn't their bodies. This is especially beneficial for babies who are connected to medical equipment that may become incorporated into their body schema.

Therapeutic Goal: To address body image issues by increasing body awareness through kinesthetic exploration.	**Restrictions and Precautions:** None
	Materials:
Age Group: 9–36 months	☐ Doll
Adult/Child Ratio: 1:1	☐ Mirror
Required Time: 5–10 minutes	☐ Baby lotion

Process

1. Show the child the doll. Allow him or her to touch it for a few minutes.

2. Begin to identify body parts on the doll, repeating their names frequently.

3. Place the child in front of the mirror; or, if using a hand mirror, hold it in front of the child.

4. Identify each of the child's body parts. Gently rub and move each extremity when you name it to help the child integrate the words and sensations.

5. Repeat the process using baby lotion to provide additional tactile input and enhance awareness.

ACTIVITY 4.3.   BODY GLITTER

This is a quick activity that can make young girls feel glamorous.

Therapeutic Goal: To address body image issues by promoting body image confrontation.	☐ Tongue depressors
	☐ Fine polyester glitter
Age Group: Preschool/primary/school-age	☐ Measuring spoon
Adult/Child Ratio: 1:6	☐ White shipping labels
Required Time: 10 minutes	☐ Fine-lined markers
Restrictions and Precautions: Activity may be contraindicated for children with dermatologic or related problems. Avoid applying gel near the eyes.	☐ Mirror
Materials:	
☐ Aloe vera gel	
☐ Specimen cups	

Process

1. Give each child a specimen cup and tell them to fill it halfway with aloe vera gel.

2. Instruct the children to add about 1/2 teaspoon glitter to the gel and stir it in with a tongue depressor. Let them add more glitter if they wish.

3. Ask the children to screw the lid onto the cup.

4. Have the children write their name on a label, then decorate it and affix it to their cup.

5. Help the children apply the glitter-gel to their bodies, then give them a mirror to view themselves.

ACTIVITY 4.4. BODY MOLDS

Children who are fans of science fiction love these molds because they look like android versions of themselves.

Therapeutic Goal: To address body image issues by promoting body image confrontation and a more accurate body image, and increasing body awareness.

Age Group: Primary/school-age

Adult/Child Ratio: 1:4

Required Time: 20–30 minutes, depending on the number of children

Restrictions and Precautions: Take care when molding the aluminum foil around children's faces. If any children are reluctant to have their face covered, simply cut a hole in the foil through which they can insert their face. Follow scissors precautions.

Materials:

- ☐ Heavy-duty aluminum foil (wide)
- ☐ Clear packing tape
- ☐ Scissors
- ☐ Hole punch
- ☐ String or yarn

Process

1. Cut two sheets of foil for each child. The length of the foil should exceed the child's height of by at least 1 foot.

2. Lay the pieces of foil side by side vertically and tape them together.

3. Have the children, one at a time, lie down on the floor or a table.

4. Gently mold the foil to the children's faces and bodies, working outward down to the floor or table. With younger children, name each part of the body as you touch it (Figure Activity 4.4-1).

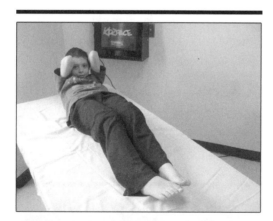

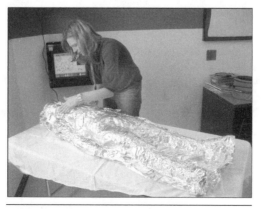

Figure Activity 4.4-1. Body Mold

5. Scrunch the excess foil together to make the mold thicker around the base.

6. Gently lift the foil off, taking care not to distort the mold.

7. Let the children cut away excess foil between the legs.

8. Punch holes near the top of each mold and affix a piece of tape across the top of the holes to reinforce them.

9. Thread yarn or string through the holes and tie the ends.

10. Hang the molds on a wall or from the ceiling.

ACTIVITY 4.5.   BODY PERCEPTION COMPARISONS

This activity is designed for use with eating disorder patients, and hence may elicit emotion-laden content. Therefore, it should be conducted only by a practitioner experienced in working with children, and who has an established therapeutic relationship with the patients.

Therapeutic Goal: To address body image issues by identifying body image distortions and expressing and exploring feelings related to the body.

Age Group: Preteen/adolescent

Adult/Child Ratio: 1:4

Required Time: Situational; allow ample time for processing and support

Restrictions and Precautions: Establish firm ground rules for dialogue when conducting this activity with a group. Take marker precautions.

Materials:

☐ Body outlines copied on transparencies (three per child)

☐ Permanent markers or china markers

Process

1. Let the children select three different colored markers.

2. Ask the children to choose one color of marker to represent how they perceive their body at present, and use it to draw that shape on a body outline (Figures Activity 4.5-1 and Activity 4.5-2).

3. Have the children select a different color marker to represent the body they desire, and use it to draw that shape on another body outline.

4. Finally, have the children select a color to represent how they will look when they reach their ideal/target weight, and draw that shape on a body outline.

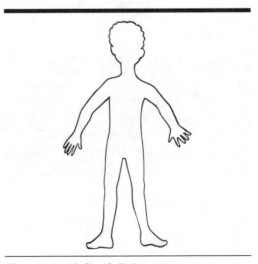

Figure Activity 4.5-1. Male Body Outline

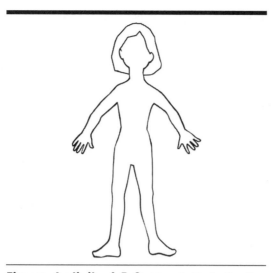

Figure Activity 4.5-2. Female Body Outline

5. Instruct the children to place their three body outlines in a stack so that they can easily see the differences between them.

6. Encourage the children to talk about the differences between the three body shapes they drew and help them explore the significance of these discrepancies.

Adapt this activity for use with obese children by instructing the children to draw (1) how they look now, (2) how they think others see them, and (3) how they will look at a healthy weight.   **Variation**

Note. Adapted from: Breiner, S. (2003). An evidence-based eating disorder program. *Journal of Pediatric Nursing, 18*(1):75−80.

ACTIVITY 4.6.   CONNECT THE DOTS

This activity may be conducted with the patient lying down, although being in a prone position may increase the child's feelings of vulnerability.

Therapeutic Goal: To address body image issues by identifying body image distortions and expressing and exploring feelings related to the body.

Age Group: School-age/adolescent

Adult/Child Ratio: 1:1

Required Time: 45 minutes

Restrictions and Precautions: Do not conduct this activity with an eating disorder patient soon after a meal. Take care when tracing around the groin area, as this may make the child uncomfortable.

Materials:

☐ Sheet of butcher paper, cut 1 foot longer than the height of the child

☐ Tape

☐ Broad-tipped markers, three different colors

1. Tape the butcher paper to a wall in a private area, where it is unlikely that you and the child will be disturbed.   **Process**

2. Arrange for the child to wear a leotard or other close-fitting clothing.

3. Instruct the child to stand against the paper on the wall.

4. Use a marker to make dots around the perimeter of the child's body, to designate the key parts, including the top of the head, shoulders, elbows, fingertips, waist, groin, and bottom of feet.

5. Give the child a different-colored marker and ask him or her to "connect the dots," drawing an outline of how big his or her body is. Allow the child to evaluate the drawing and make any corrections he or she deems appropriate.

6. Help the child position him- or herself against the wall, centered in the body outline.

7. Use a third colored marker to trace the child's body outline. As you are doing so, gently grip the child's head and extremities to assure that the tracing is as accurate as possible.

8. Look at the tracings with the child and share his or her initial reaction.

9. Lead the child through a discussion of each area of the body while asking reflective questions to elicit his or her feelings and concerns. Acknowledge the child's feelings and provide emotional support, as necessary.

Note. Adapted from Breiner, S. (2003). An evidence-based eating disorder program. *Journal of Pediatric Nursing, 18*(1), 75–80.

ACTIVITY 4.7.   DIVERGENT VIEWS

This activity may elicit emotion-laden content, particularly if done with children who have eating disorders, obesity, burns, or who have been disfigured by illness or treatment. It should be used only with careful consideration by experienced practitioners who have an established therapeutic relationship with the children.

Therapeutic Goal: To address body image issues by expressing and exploring feelings related to the body and identifying body image distortions.

Age Group: Adolescent

Adult/Child Ratio: 1:4

Required Time: Variable; allow ample time for discussion and support

Restrictions and Precautions: Avoid touching the crotch area when tracing. Do not trace eating disorder patients immediately after a meal.

Materials:

☐ Butcher paper

☐ Markers

☐ Paints

☐ Paintbrushes

Process

1. Tape a large piece of butcher paper (one per child) to the wall.

2. Have the children stand against the wall then lightly trace their bodies on the paper.

3. Inside the body outlines, invite the children to paint realistic or abstract images representing their inner feelings about their bodies.

4. Outside the body outline, ask the children to illustrate how they think others view them physically.

5. Help the children to explore the relationship between their own perception of their body and those of others.

Variation

Ask the children to draw a vertical line dividing their body outline in half and label one side positive and the other negative. On the appropriate side of the paper, ask the children to circle those areas on their body outlines that they see as positive or negative, and write their thoughts and feelings regarding each area next to it.

ACTIVITY 4.8.   FACE AND BODY PAINT

Older children can use body paint to write funny messages on their stomach or another part of their body that is hidden by clothing prior to being examined by their doctor or nurse.

Therapeutic Goal: To address body image issues by promoting body image confrontation.

Age Group: Preschool/school-age

Adult/Child Ratio: 1:4

Required Time: 30 minutes

Restrictions and Precautions: Do not use this activity with children who have skin sensitivity or open wounds. Avoid the eye area. This activity may not be appropriate for children of certain cultures.

Materials:

☐ Bowl

☐ Mixing spoon

☐ Cornstarch or baby powder

☐ Cold cream

☐ Water

☐ Medicine cups or other small containers

☐ Tongue depressors (for mixing)

☐ Food coloring

☐ Cotton swabs or toothettes

☐ Mirrors

☐ Facial tissue

☐ Inexpensive hats or wigs (optional)

Process

1. Combine two parts cornstarch or baby powder and one part each of cold cream and flour in the bowl and mix well.

2. Add one part water and stir.

3. Divide the mixture into as many portions as colors you wish to make. Place each portion in a medicine cup.

4. Have the children add food coloring, one drop at a time, and mix with a tongue depressor until the desired shade is achieved.

5. Let the children decide what they would like painted on their face and/or bodies, and where.

6. Where necessary, use a hair clip or headband to keep long hair out of the children's faces.

7. Apply the paint sparingly, using cotton swabs or toothettes.

8. Let the children select a hat or wig to wear (optional).

9. Provide mirrors and invite the children to view themselves. Note: This may be threatening, so children should not be pushed to do so.

10. To remove the face paint, wipe the mixture off with a towel or tissue and wash the area with soap and water.

11. For storage, cover the cups with foil, and refrigerate.

Variation

For heavy clown makeup, combine 2 tablespoons shortening, 5 teaspoons cornstarch, and 1 teaspoon flour. Add petroleum jelly in small amounts until the mixture is the desired consistency; tint with food coloring.

ACTIVITY 4.9.   IF I COULD BE SOMEONE ELSE

This activity is a comparatively nonthreatening method for assessing children's body image concerns.

Therapeutic Goal: To address body image issues by expressing and exploring feelings related to the body.

Age Group: School-age/adolescent

Adult/Child Ratio: 1:6

Required Time: 30–45 minutes

Restrictions and Precautions: Take scissors, glue, and marker precautions.

Materials:

☐ Digital photo of each child's face

☐ Magazines (preferably an assortment of fashion, health and fitness, celebrity, and news magazines)

☐ Scissors

☐ Construction paper

☐ Glue stick

☐ Markers

Process

1. Invite the children to look through magazines and pick a person whose body they would like to have more than their own.

2. Instruct the children to cut out the desired body image from the magazine.

3. Have the children cut out and glue the photo of their own face to the construction paper then glue the body they have selected beneath it.

4. Ask the children to write on their paper why they chose the body they did and what it would mean to them if they had it. Discuss whether they believe this person to be a role model; ask what specific qualities or characteristics they attribute to this person that they find most appealing. Help the children explore the distinction between physical attributes, personality qualities, achievement, and character.

ACTIVITY 4.10.   MAD HATTERS

This activity is especially beneficial for children who have lost their hair due to chemotherapy, alopecia, surgery, burns, or other medical conditions or interventions. Wigs are expensive and often children find them to be hot and uncomfortable. Hats and head wraps can provide stylish and inexpensive alternatives.

Therapeutic Goal: To address body image issues by promoting body image confrontation and fostering a more positive body image.

Age Group: Primary/school-age/adolescent

Adult/Child Ratio: 1:6

Required Time: 30 minutes

Restrictions and Precautions: Take marker and glue precautions.

Materials:

☐ Unadorned white canvas hats, such as baseball, sailor, painter, and/or sun hats (one per child)

☐ Fabric markers

☐ Puffy paint

☐ Assorted trims such as ribbons, fabric flowers, buttons, buckles, appliqués, and feathers

☐ Fabric glue or hot glue

☐ Mirror

1. Allow each child to select a hat to decorate.

2. Provide the children with decorative materials and encourage them to decorate their hats creatively.

3. Encourage the children to try on their hats and look in the mirror.

To make head wraps, give children each a piece of cotton or cotton-blend fabric cut into a 26-inch or 28-inch square. Let the children decorate their scarves with fabric markers, if desired. Give the children instructions on how to tie a head wrap and help them practice the technique (Figure Activity 4.10-1).

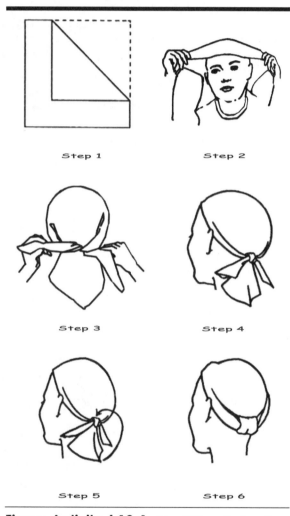

Figure Activity 4.10-1. Head Wrap Instructions

ACTIVITY 4.11.   MAKEUP MAKEOVER

Have a spa day. Create the appropriate atmosphere by lowering the lights and playing soothing music. Invite a professional cosmetologist, manicurist, massage therapist, and/or hair stylist to volunteer his or her time and talent to make the event a success. For refreshments, and to complete the effect, serve fresh fruit and cold water with lemon slices.

Therapeutic Goal: To address body image issues by fostering a more positive body image and promoting body image confrontation.

Age Group: Adolescent

Adult/Child Ratio: 1:5

Required Time: 1 hour

Restrictions and Precautions: Do not allow children to share cosmetics or applicators that come in direct contact with the skin. Obtain parental approval before planning the activity, as religious, cultural, or personal beliefs may prohibit the use of makeup. Check participants for history of allergies, facial skin irritation, or injury that would contraindicate the use of cosmetics.

Materials:

- ☐ Basins filled with water
- ☐ Specimen cups
- ☐ Washcloths
- ☐ Mild soap
- ☐ Towels
- ☐ Avocado
- ☐ Yogurt
- ☐ Honey
- ☐ Cucumber slices
- ☐ Fork
- ☐ Mirrors
- ☐ Cosmetics (preferably manufacturer's samples)
- ☐ Makeup applicators
- ☐ Cotton balls and swabs
- ☐ Tips for applying makeup (cut from fashion magazines or downloaded from the Internet)

Process

1. Provide each participant with a washcloth, mirror, towel, basin filled with water, specimen cup, and soap.

2. Ask the children to wash and dry their faces.

3. Instruct the children to combine 1/2 avocado, 1 tablespoon yogurt, and 1 tablespoon honey in a specimen cup then use a fork to mash the mixture well.

4. Help the children slather the mixture over their faces then ask them to sit in a comfortable position leaning backwards; place a cucumber slice over each eye.

5. After 20 minutes have elapsed, tell the children to rinse off their faces.

6. Encourage the children to study their reflections in the mirror and identify features they would like to enhance, such as skin tone, eyebrow fullness, lash length, or bone structure.

7. Invite the children to read makeup tips, or simply experiment with the cosmetics, to achieve their desired look.

ACTIVITY 4.12. MIRROR ME

This activity is particularly beneficial for children with anorexia, whose illness often causes them to feel so ineffective that it renders them unable to produce their own movements (Kaslow & Eicher, 1988).

Therapeutic Goal: To address body image issues by increasing body awareness and promoting kinesthetic exploration of the body.

Age Group: Preschool/primary/school-age

Adult/Child Ratio: 1:1

Required Time: 20–30 minutes

Restrictions and Precautions: To be determined on an individual basis.

Materials:

- ☐ CD player
- ☐ CDs
- ☐ Full-length mirror

1. Select a CD with a smooth rhythm and play it at low volume.

2. Instruct the child to follow your movements as closely as possible.

3. Begin by sitting on the floor (as this is less threatening than standing), face to face.

4. Progress slowly to doing movements while standing.

5. As the child becomes more fluid, have him or her take partial or complete leadership of the movement.

6. During subsequent sessions with the child, do the mirroring with the child parallel to you; eventually, the child can do this alone in front of a mirror.

ACTIVITY 4.13.   MY BODY BOOK

There are many commercially available children's books about the body. However, you can captivate children's interest and create a more meaningful learning tool by involving them in making their own personal books.

Therapeutic Goal: To address body image issues by promoting body image confrontation and increasing body awareness.

Age Group: Preschool/primary

Adult/Child Ratio: 1:1

Required Time: Some advanced preparation

Restrictions and Precautions: None

Materials:

☐ Digital camera
☐ Printer
☐ Photo paper
☐ Writing paper
☐ Glue stick
☐ Pen or thin marker
☐ Three-hole paper punch
☐ Cardboard binder
☐ Crayons

1. Take a full-length photograph of the child and close-up photographs of specific parts of the child's body.

2. Print the photos and mount them on paper.

3. Punch holes along the left-hand side of each page and put them into the binder.

4. Together with the child, write captions under each photo. Include the name of the body part, its function, and anything else the child wishes to say about that part of his or her body.

5. Invite the child to decorate the binder.

6. Look through the book with the child on multiple occasions to reinforce the information.

ACTIVITY 4.14.   SHADOW DANCING

Music can have a powerful effect on the emotions and affective state of children. The tempo, dynamic, and melody of a music composition can stimulate, calm, sooth, or rile the listener. Therefore, assess the children you will be working with to determine the best choice of music for this activity.

Therapeutic Goal: To address body image issues by increasing body awareness.

Age Group: Toddler/preschool

Adult/Child Ratio: 1:3–6 (depending on children's ages)

Required Time: 15 minutes

Restrictions and Precautions: None

Materials:

☐ Lamp or projector

☐ White sheet (if light-colored empty wall is not available)

☐ Tape

☐ CD player or radio

Process

1. If a plain, light-colored wall with sufficient space is unavailable, use a screen, or tape the sheet to the wall, low enough so the children can touch it.

2. Dim the room lights and shine the lamp or projector toward the screen; begin the music.

3. Demonstrate how to shadow-dance in the projector light. Encourage the children to imitate your movements. Name different body parts for the children to use in their dances (Figure Activity 4.14-1).

Figure Activity 4.14-1. Shadow Dancing
Courtesy of Snow City Arts.

4. As a fun follow-up, teach the children how to use their hands to create shadow animals; or do the perennial favorite, "Little Bunny Foo Foo Hopping Through the Forest."

5. If possible, videotape the activity to show children and parents at another time.

ACTIVITY 4.15.   SILHOUETTES

To help with separation, a silhouette of each family member can be made and hung together on the child's wall.

Therapeutic Goal: To address body image issues by promoting body image confrontation and a more accurate body image.

Age Group: School-age

Adult/Child Ratio: 1:1

Required Time: 30 minutes

Restrictions and Precautions: Take scissor precautions.

Materials:

☐ White construction paper

☐ Colored construction paper

☐ Tape

☐ Lamp

☐ Pencil

☐ Scissors

☐ Glue

☐ Mat for framing art (optional)

1. Have the child sit in a chair placed parallel to the wall.   Process

2. Tape white construction paper to the wall at the same level as the child's head.

3. Position the light source so that it shines directly on the paper, casting a shadow profile of the child's head.

4. Carefully trace his or her silhouette with a pencil. Be sure to include as much detail as possible (e.g., eyelashes, hair wisps).

5. Instruct the child to carefully cut out the silhouette.

6. Allow the child to select a contrasting color of construction paper and glue the silhouette on it.

7. If desired, mat the silhouette to create a finished appearance.

To do a more sophisticated version of a silhouette with older children, take a close-up photograph of   **Variation**
their profiles. Enlarge the images to the desired size on your computer and print. Let the children cut
out their profile and trace it on the back of wrapping paper or scrapbooking paper. Tell them to use
glue sparingly to adhere the image to another piece of decorative paper.

ACTIVITY 4.16.   SOMATIC DIARY

As a result of illness and its treatment, children frequently are subjected to a barrage of unpleasant, sometimes frightening, physical sensations. The nature and intensity of pain, nausea, burning sensations, and gasping for air—just to name a few—can be difficult for some children to identify and articulate. Somatic diaries can serve as valuable tools, both to help children express their physical experiences and chronicle them over time (especially nonwriters) and to serve as a record of these experiences, which may be helpful to those who care for them.

Therapeutic Goal: To address body image issues by increasing body awareness.	**Materials:**
Age Group: School-age/adolescent	☐ Journals with blank pages and covers
Adult/Child Ratio: 1:6	☐ Pencils or markers in a wide variety of colors and thicknesses
Required Time: Ongoing	
Restrictions and Precautions: Take marker precautions.	

1. Provide each child with a journal and a wide variety of coloring implements to use during the   **Process**
   initial activity and to keep for later use.

2. Ask the children to close their eyes and think about the physical sensations they have experienced as a result of their illness and/or its treatment.

3. Invite the children to explore and discuss what these sensations might look like visually in terms of color, size, shape, intensity, and texture.

4. Ask the children to think about what they are feeling physically at this moment. Encourage them, first, to picture where in their body the feeling is strongest, then draw a representative image of the feeling on the first page of their journal. Suggest that they date the image and add descriptive words or phrases, if they wish.

5. Encourage the children to personalize the cover of the journal and to continue to use it as a visual diary of the physical feelings they experience over time.

Variation

Provide the children with body templates to fill in by illustrating any tension, pain, weakness, or other sensations they are experiencing. Encourage the children to continue this project over time and keep the images they have created in a loose-leaf notebook.

For more ideas, see Bright Ideas for Body Image (Box Activity 4.16-1).

BOX ACTIVITY 4.16-1. BRIGHT IDEAS FOR BODY IMAGE

- Provide massage to help children, such as those with eating disorders, feel physically connected to their bodies.

- Trace children's bodies on large pieces of butcher paper and let the children color them in.

- If children require external corrective or postoperative devices temporarily, suggest they make or use calendars to track the time until their removal.

- Play the "hokey-pokey" naming all the different body parts.

- Provide video cameras to children as a flexible tool to promote body image confrontation and adaptation.

- Purchase commercial body puzzles.

- Place Plexiglas mirrors in infants' cribs to encourage self-discovery.

- Take digital pictures of girls and scan them into a computer so they can download their images into web sites that allow them to see how they look in different hairstyles or fashions.

- Help children write and rehearse responses to others who may tease them, act as bullies, or say hurtful things about their appearance.

- Encourage children to keep body image journals, creating drawings to chronicle the body changes they are experiencing over time.

CHAPTER 5

GROUP INTERACTION AND SOCIALIZATION

Illness can separate children from their friends and normal support systems. Group activities with pediatric patients promote new friendships and decrease feelings of isolation. Through activities that involve group interaction, children and adolescents can gain new insights and coping strategies from connecting with peers who are going through the same or similar experiences. Effective peer interaction is a major developmental task of childhood and adolescence; therefore, opportunities for group activities are an important part of a psychosocial treatment plan for pediatric patients. The activities in this chapter will help meet this objective.

Courtesy of Snow City Arts

LIST OF ACTIVITIES

Activity 5.1 Holding Hands	Activity 5.11 Group Mural
Activity 5.2 A View from All Sides	Activity 5.12 Group Tile Project
Activity 5.3 ABCs of Disease	Activity 5.13 Paper Bag Puppet Show
Activity 5.4 Autograph Books	Activity 5.14 Paper Quilt
Activity 5.5 Collaborative Proclamations	Activity 5.15 Progressive Story Writing
Activity 5.6 Finding Friends to Treasure	Activity 5.16 Puzzled
Activity 5.7 Friendly Face Banner	Activity 5.17 Sweet Meets
Activity 5.8 Tic-Tac-Know	Activity 5.18 The Truth-Be-Told Game
Activity 5.9 Group Mandala	Activity 5.19 The Web We Weave
Activity 5.10 Group Montage	

Benefits of Group Interaction/Socialization

Peer interactions are essential to growth during certain stages of childhood. This is reflected in the psychosocial needs of sick and hospitalized children. As discussed earlier, infants and children ages 2 to 4 years are most susceptible to separation anxiety, so interventions with this age group focus on parent involvement with children. Children ages 4 to 7 years are more active with other children, but they are still attached to the significant adults in their lives. Interventions with these children may involve both adults and peers. For the school-age child, interactions with peers may be even more important than interactions with adults because this age group is most concerned with mastery in peer relationships. Adolescents mature by way of their relationships outside the home, so peers take on even greater importance in the process of finding identity and learning how to relate to the opposite sex. For the school-age and adolescent patient, peer group activities are essential therapeutic experiences.

A critical factor in helping children cope with hospitalization is maintaining links to familiar environments, routines, and activities (Joseph, Keller, & Kronick 2008). Devoting appropriate group space and providing opportunities for children to interact with peers who are hospitalized is one way to help achieve this goal (Rollins, 2009). Research tells us that contact with peers can result in significant benefits in social and communication skills and the development of greater self-confidence and independence among pediatric patients (Fels, Waalen, Zhai, & Weiss, 2001;

Said, Salleh, Abu Bakar, & Mohamad, 2005). Interaction among peers is particularly important for hospitalized adolescents (Hutton, 2002, 2003). In some instances children may be unable to participate fully in a particular group activity. Nevertheless, being part of the group encourages socialization and allows these children to benefit vicariously from the play of other patients.

The provision of peer-to-peer support can positively influence children's coping, as well as healthcare outcomes during hospitalization (Rollins, 2009; Shepley, 2005). Through mutually enjoyed activities, children interact, share experiences, and help each other through difficult times. Although not intended to replace professionally mediated support, peer-to-peer support is a unique resource that promotes individual and family strengths through shared experience.

Skill-Building Groups

Group training has proven successful in increasing interaction, communication, and problem-solving skills in children with autism spectrum disorders (Herbrecht & Poustka, 2007). The research findings of Kashani, Nair, Rao, Nair, and Reid (1996) on hopelessness suggest that group interventions that encourage interaction with others and concern about the feelings of others might help reduce hopelessness for adolescents.

Hicks and Davitt (2009) remind us that due to changes in cognitive or physical performance, as well as specific cognitive deficits, many children with chronic illness have difficulty making and keeping friends. Also, due to misconceptions about illness, peers may retreat from the child with a chronic illness. Participating in activities in a group setting provides an opportunity for them to practice skills with peers.

In a study with children with special needs, group activities helped the children to express their views and opinions (Burke, 2005). What makes children different in other settings is what makes them the same in an issue-specific group. The young people said that participating in group activities developed their self-confidence and advocacy skills, which led them to be more confident in expressing their needs at school and in the community.

A task for children with chronic illnesses is assuming a leading role in the management of their health. Children with asthma or epilepsy who participated in five weekly group sessions that featured such activities as games, drawings, stories, videos, and role-playing showed significant improvements in knowledge, beliefs, attitudes, and behaviors compared to controls (Tieffenberg, Wood, Alonso, Tossutti, & Vicente, 2000).

Support Groups

An informal resource that attempts to offer healing components to a variety of problems and challenges, support groups outside of family, friends, or professionals often provide greater understanding, more similarity (for individuals experiencing similar life events), an opportunity to discuss things that they would not want to with family or friends, an opportunity for empathy and altruism, and a sense of identity for participants. Important aspects of the support group experience are learning new ways to handle challenges, cope with changes, and maintain new behaviors.

Healthcare professionals are increasingly recognizing the efficacy of peer support groups in helping children cope with difficult issues. For example, as bone marrow transplantation (BMT) has assumed a growing role in the treatment of a range of pediatric malignancies, hematologic diseases, and metabolic conditions, healthcare professionals have become aware of the adverse changes in quality of life (QOL) (Cella & Tulsky, 1995) and psychosocial adjustment experienced by many pediatric transplant recipients, both during active treatment (Barrera, Pringle, Sumbler, & Saunders, 2000; Sherman, Simonton, & Latif, 2004) and long-term recovery (Phipps, Dunavant, Srivastava, Bowman, & Mulhern, 2000). In a survey of 65 pediatric BMT centers, 60% reported having support groups for these patients (Sherman, Simonton, Lafit et al., 2004).

Support groups are helpful in a variety of ways. For example, Weber and colleagues (2008) reported that children with atopic dermatitis who attended support groups showed improvement of pruritus and quality of life. Adolescent mothers identify peer support as very important (Stiles, 2005). Participating with other teen mothers in a support group provided an opportunity to share their daily problems and concerns with peers who had similar problems, and helped them to realize that they were "not the only ones going through this" (p. 332).

Also, support groups are helpful for siblings of children who are ill or disabled. Siblings of children with cancer, for example, must cope with myriad emotions, isolation from the family, and many changes in daily life. In fact, Spinetta (1981) concluded that siblings of patients with cancer at times experience more stress than either their parents or their sick brother or sister. A sibling support group gives them the opportunity to alleviate their sense of isolation, ventilate negative feelings, and learn from each other.

Online Support. Technology has afforded an additional avenue for peer-to-peer support. Online support networks exist for hospitalized children, as well as for children with a vast array of health conditions. Computers have become commonplace in many pediatric hospitals, enabling children to access these networks while hospitalized; often, they continue participating upon discharge. Nicholas et al. (2007) found that participation in a pediatric online support network provided a means for seriously ill children to foster enjoyment, educate themselves, connect with peers, and cope. Information, social connection, and distraction served as catalysts for positive outcomes for children.

Barriers to network participation include inaccessibility and limited availability of computers, issues with technology, and discomfort with online interaction. Although there may be greater risk of people being dishonest online than in a face-to-face interaction, some individuals are actually more comfortable participating in online support groups due to the greater anonymity they offer (Pledge, n.d.).

The Environment

Children need space for socializing. In addition to playrooms and activity rooms, making space for small groups in other areas can encourage interactions among children, family members, and staff. Areas can be created in corridors and open spaces by providing comfortable seating, a pleasant view, and interesting activities.

If space permits, a separate room should be made available to adolescents. When this is not possible, a section of the playroom can be designated the teen area. Also, referring to this room as an "activity" room rather than a "play" room will seem more welcoming to teens.

Furniture placement can be important. In clinic waiting areas, for example, interaction is discouraged when chairs are aligned side-by-side (*sociofugal* seating arrangement), but encouraged with clustered L- or U-shaped seating (*sociopetal* seating arrangement), as illustrated in Figure 5.1.

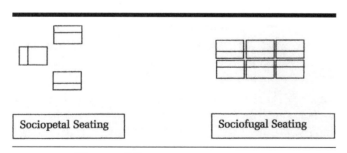

Figure 5.1. Seating Arrangements

Special Considerations

The first consideration when planning group activities is to determine how structured the group will be. The age group and goals of the group are important determinants of this decision. With young children, unstructured play experiences are often more desirable. With older age groups, the needs and abilities of the group's members can determine whether it is an informal recreational group or a more structured experience, such as a discussion and/or educational group on coping strategies.

Planning is essential for effective structured group activities. Howe and Schwartzberg (2001) describe five considerations in planning and reviewing group interventions:

1. *Maximum involvement through group-centered actions.* The group planner must consider the group members' levels of functioning and maturity.

2. *Maximum sense of individual and group identity.* Activities that enable the participants to be successful should be used. The leader should also present group goals, rules, and expectations. This structure and organization promote group identity.

3. *A "flow" experience.* The group activity should occur in a safe environment, where members feel in control of the process. A "flow" experience occurs when group members are functioning effectively at their levels of capability.

4. *Spontaneous involvement.* When the group leader models appropriate skills, subsequently, the members of the group will be able to exhibit these behaviors spontaneously when they are ready.

5. *Member support and feedback.* Member feedback and support for one another and the group offer opportunities for informal support, learning, and growth.

Starting a Support Group

Support groups for children can be held in a variety of settings, such as hospitals and medical centers, clinics, community agencies or centers, schools, churches, daycare centers, and community meetings rooms of local businesses. The following tips are recommended for starting a group:

1. *Do your homework.* Find out what groups may already exist. Contact organizations that serve the population of children you intend to address; they may have resources you can use, such as information about starting a support group, or suggestions for group activities or meeting topics.

2. *Determine interest.* Take a variety of communication routes, such as distributing flyers, posting notices in clinics, and the like, to generate awareness. You may want to hold an information meeting for children and their families. Healthcare professionals could be invited as well, especially if they are to be the source of referrals for the group.

3. *Decide on the structure of the group.* What ages of children will be included? Groups are most successful when composed of children close in age and who are experiencing similar life challenges. This does not mean that if the group is for children with chronic illnesses that all the children need to have the same condition. Actually, although every condition is unique, many of the challenges children face are the same, regardless of their illness. Frequency and length of meetings are other considerations.

4. *Set norms and expectations.* With the children, discuss expectations for group participation, such as respecting others' feelings and opinions, maintaining confidentiality, listening without interrupting, and so on.

5. *Assure participation for all.* Make certain that everyone has an opportunity to express their feelings and opinions, by offering a variety of expressive means, such as drawing a picture, writing a poem, singing a song, or performing a scene or dance about their experiences.

Activity Goals

The activities in this chapter each focus on a specific task. They provide some structure and parameters yet can be modified to allow more individual or group freedom. All the activities have the goal of fostering socialization; in addition, some also have the specific objective of facilitating the sharing of feelings and concerns, or establishing a sense of community.

Facilitating the Sharing of Feelings and Concerns

Activities that address this objective include Group Mandala, A View from All Sides, Group Mural, and Collaborative Proclamations.

Activities that target this objective are those that produce tangible finished products, which can be displayed and shown to others. Group Mandala, Group Mural, Holding Hands, Collaborative Proclamations, and Progressive Story Writing all meet this standard.

Establishing a Sense of Community

ACTIVITY 5.1. HOLDING HANDS

This activity highlights each child's uniqueness while simultaneously symbolizing the connectedness of the group. It is a good choice for a dialysis unit or specialty clinic.

Therapeutic Goal: To provide a group activity that will establish a sense of community.

Age Group: Primary/school-age

Adult/Child Ratio: 1:10

Required Time: 30 minutes, or can be done as a progressive activity

Restrictions and Precautions: Take scissors, marker, and glue precautions.

Materials:

☐ Manila file folders

☐ Pencils
☐ Multicultural Markers
☐ Bandages
☐ Hospital identification bracelets
☐ Straws or IV tubing
☐ Markers, assorted colors
☐ Scissors
☐ Glue

Process

1. Instruct each child to place one arm on a closed file folder, with his or her elbow toward the crease.

2. Ask another child or adult to trace the hand and forearm.

3. Give the children multicultural markers to color the hands and forearms, if they wish.

4. Let the children use other markers to draw clothing and accessories (e.g., ring, watch, nail polish).

5. Provide the children with bandages, hospital identification bracelets, and IV tubing (or straws) to add hospital-related details.

6. Help the children cut out the hands from both halves of the folder, without cutting them apart.

7. Invite the children to write their name, or a word describing how they can help others, on the hands.

8. Create a banner with the hands by interspersing the fingers of each hand with those of another; glue them together to create a chain (Figure Activity 5.1-1).

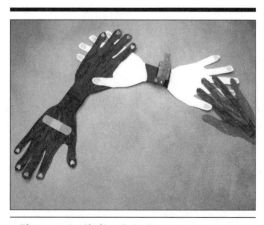

Figure Activity 5.1-1. Holding Hands

ACTIVITY 5.2.   A VIEW FROM ALL SIDES

This activity is for developing the skills necessary to evaluate complex interpersonal issues.

Therapeutic Goal: To provide a group activity that will foster socialization and facilitate the sharing of feelings and concerns.

Age Group: School-age/adolescents

Adult/Child Ratio: 1:5

Required Time: 30–45 minutes

Restrictions and Precautions: None

Materials:

☐ Pen

☐ Paper

Process

1. Based on the focus of the group, create one or more scenarios for the children to develop and explore. For example:

   • A girl returns to school after having her leg amputated and losing her hair. She feels that her friends and classmates are uncomfortable in her presence, and some are making fun of her.

   • Christmas day a child had to be rushed to the hospital before the family could open their presents.

   • After a lengthy hospitalization, a boy spiked a fever on the day he was scheduled to be discharged in time to attend an important school event.

2. Explain to the group that they will be choosing (or given) a scenario of a difficult event that happened to a sick child and that each member of the group will be writing and/or acting out a different perspective of the same scenario.

3. Assign each member of the group to act as one of the participants whose perspective they will develop. For example:

   Participant 1: A newsperson giving a factual accounting of the event

   Participant 2: The child who is the central character in the event

   Participant 3: The child's healthcare provider or teacher

   Participant 4: The child's parent

   Participant 5: The child's sibling or friend

4. Allow time for the children to think through and craft their responses.

5. Have the children take turns reading or acting out their responses to the group.

6. Encourage the children to discuss the different perspectives presented. Ask what they have gleaned from the activity and how they might apply that knowledge to their own lives.

ACTIVITY 5.3.   ABCs OF DISEASE

The object of this game can be to identify and define any words related to healthcare; or, when working with a group of children who have the same illness, to narrow the focus to that specific disease and its treatment.

Therapeutic Goal: To provide a group activity that will facilitate the sharing of feelings and concerns and establish a sense of community.

Age Group: School-age/adolescent

Adult/Child Ratio: 1:10

Required Time: 15 minutes

Restrictions and Precautions: None

Materials:

☐ Peel and Stick Letters

☐ Index cards

☐ A bag, to hold precut letters of the alphabet

Process

1. Adhere one letter of the alphabet on each index card.

2. Place all of the index cards in a bag.

3. Explain to children the type of words they will be asked to name (e.g., healthcare in general, or disease-specific, such as asthma, cancer, or hemophilia).

4. Have the children take turns picking a letter out of the bag then thinking of a word that begins with the letter they selected.

5. Discuss each word after the child says it, and encourage all the children to share any thoughts that come to mind when they hear it.

6. If a child can't think of a word, ask the group to provide one. For example:

   A—aspirin, abdomen, albuterol, alcohol, Ace Bandage, asthma, anesthesia

   B—blood, bone, barium, brace, Bethesda units, Broviac, breathing, bandage

   C—clot, crutches, clinic, carrier, chest compression, catheter, calcium, chemo

   D—drugs, dentist, disinfect, dialysis, dressing, doctor, diarrhea, deep breathing

   E—Emla, elbow, elevate, EEG, erythrocytes, edema, electrolyte, epinephrine

   F—factor, fingerstick, fibrin, fistula, fluid, fever, flushing

   G—gloves, gauze, genetics, germ, germ cell, gene, graft, guided imagery

   H—hemodialysis, heparin, Hickman, hemoglobin, hemorrhage, hospital

   I—IV, immune system, inhibitor, infection, immunization, inflammation, injection

   J—joint, jaundice, jelly

   K—kidney, kilogram, knee, ketones

   L—lymph node, laboratory, lipids, lidocaine, leukocytes, lumbar puncture

   M—muscle, mutation, movement, medicine, monitor, morphine

   N—node, nausea, needle, nerve, nurse, neutropenic, nebulizer

   O—orthopedic, oncology, operation, OR, oxygen

   P—port, platelets, potassium, pain, physical therapy, peritoneum, plasma, peak flow

   Q—quadriceps

   R—range of motion, radiation, red blood cell, reflex, relaxation

   S—swelling, syringe, serum, saline, stoma

   T—tourniquet, trauma, target joints, tape, trigger, tongue depressor

   U—urine, ultrasound, units, upper airway, urea

   V—vein, virus, vasoconstriction, vomit, vaccine, ventilation, vital signs, venipuncture

   W—weight, wig, white blood cell, wheezing

   X—X-ray, X chromosome

   Y—Y-chromosome, yellow fever

   Z—zero inhibitor, z-pack, zinc

ACTIVITY 5.4.   AUTOGRAPH BOOKS

Children may decide to use their autograph books to also record phone numbers and email addresses of new friends. To maintain appropriate professional boundaries, alert staff to have a response ready so they can tactfully decline children's requests for the inclusion of personal contact information with their autographs.

Therapeutic Goal: To provide a group activity that will foster socialization.

Age Group: Preteen/adolescent

Adult/Child Ratio: 1:10

Required Time: 30–45 minutes.

Restrictions and Precautions: Take scissors, glue, and marker precautions.

Materials:

☐ Decorative computer paper (five sheets)

☐ Cardboard

☐ Scissors

☐ Yarn

☐ Markers

☐ Fabric scraps (optional)

☐ Wrapping paper (optional)

☐ 3-hole paper punch

☐ Glue

Process

1. Provide each child with two pieces of cardboard, approximately 1/2 inch larger in width and length than the paper.

2. Instruct the children to punch three holes on the left-hand side of the papers and both pieces of cardboard then place the typing paper between the two pieces of cardboard.

3. Show the children how to thread a piece of yarn through each of the three holes and tie the ends in a bow.

4. Let the children decorate the cardboard cover of the book with wrapping paper, markers, and/or fabric scraps.

5. Encourage the children to invite staff, visitors, and other children to sign their books and perhaps write a message.

Variation

Give the children a blank muslin doll (the type often used for procedural preparation) that others can autograph (see Activity 4.1).

ACTIVITY 5.5.   COLLABORATIVE PROCLAMATIONS

This activity is a quick and easy way to initiate a discussion about almost any topic. It is a good choice for busy clinic waiting areas or where groups of children are receiving treatment, such as dialysis or chemotherapy facilities.

Therapeutic Goal: To provide a group activity that will facilitate the sharing of feelings and concerns and establish a sense of community.

Age Group: School-age/adolescent

Adult/Child Ratio: 1:10

Required Time: 30 minutes

Restrictions and Precautions: None

Materials:

☐ Post-it Easel Pads or easel paper and tape

☐ Markers in assorted colors

1. Attach a sheet of paper to the wall.

2. Select a theme for the proclamation, or engage the group in a discussion to select a topic of mutual interest on which they would like to share their views. Note: They might need help getting started, so offer some suggestions, such as school, friendship, hospitalization, illness, emotions, or coping strategies.

3. Once the topic has been selected, ask a group member to write an open-ended sentence about the topic in large letters across the top of a sheet of paper. For example:

   Being in the hospital is like . . .

   Friendship is . . .

   The worst thing about living with my illness is . . .

   My family is important to me because . . .

   The thing I find incredibly annoying is . . .

   When I have to do something I don't like I . . .

4. Ask each member of the group to complete the sentence and write it below the heading. Children who are unable to write can dictate their thoughts to someone else, who will write down their words. If the group is small, give the children the opportunity to offer several statements.

5. Invite one child to read the entire proclamation back to the children. Encourage discussion and comments.

6. Hang the proclamation in a prominent place.

Process

ACTIVITY 5.6.   FINDING FRIENDS TO TREASURE

This activity is a variation on a traditional treasure or egg hunt. Hide some of the containers in obvious places to assure that all of the children find a treasure.

Therapeutic Goal: To provide a group activity that will foster socialization and establish a sense of community.	**Materials:**
	☐ Small plastic eggs or plastic balls that can be opened to place something inside (at least five per child)
Age Group: Primary	
Adult/Child Ratio: 1:6	☐ Small pieces of paper
Required Time: 15 minutes	☐ Pens
Restrictions and Precautions: Children may need help reading the questions. Do not use this activity with children who become easily over-stimulated.	☐ Baskets or bags

1. Write simply worded, nonintrusive personal questions about interests and preferences on each piece of paper. For example:

   What is your favorite television show?

   What is your favorite board game?

   What is your favorite dessert?

   What is your favorite outdoor activity?

Process

2. Place each question in a ball or egg container and hide them around the room.

3. Give the children a basket or bag and challenge them to find as many containers as they can in a set amount of time.

4. When the hunt is over, ask the children to take turns saying their name, reading the questions they collected aloud, and answering them.

5. After each child has answered, ask everyone else who would have given the same answer to that question to raise their hands or stand up, so that the children can see who shares their interests and preferences.

ACTIVITY 5.7.   FRIENDLY FACE BANNER

This activity is particularly beneficial for use with culturally diverse groups. Most children are aware of skin color and other physical differences by age three (Drewes, 2005). Encouraging them to recognize and incorporate their skin color as one of their unique physical features is one strategy we can use to help them embrace their cultural identity.

Therapeutic Goal: To provide a group activity that will establish a sense of community.

Age Group: Preschool/primary

Adult/Child Ratio: 1:12

Required Time: 45 minutes–1 hour advance preparation, if the banner is sewn rather than glued; activity: 20–30 minutes

Restrictions and Precautions: Consider the ethnic makeup of the group when purchasing felt. Take glue, scissors, and marker precautions.

Materials:

☐ Felt, approximately 23 inches × 38 inches, for background

☐ Three to four pieces of felt (approximately 1–1/2 yards total), in a variety of skin-tone shades

☐ Pins

☐ 1–1/2 yards of grosgrain ribbon

☐ Needle and thread or fabric glue

☐ 8- or 10-inch paper plate

☐ Permanent markers

☐ Dimensional fabric paint

☐ Yarn, pom-poms, feathers, and other decorative materials

☐ Dowel or curtain rod

Process

1. Press under the edges of the cloth being used for the background 1/2 inch, folding the corners neatly; pin them in place.

2. Cut seven 8-inch pieces of ribbon to make loops through which to insert the dowel rod for hanging the banner.

3. Fold the pieces of ribbon in half and pin 1/2 inch of both ends of each piece, evenly spaced, to the top of the banner.

4. Topstitch or glue around the banner about 1/8 inch from the edges; remove all the pins.

5. Use the paper plate as a template to trace circles on the opposite sides of the felt and cut out *at least* as many circles as there are children in the group (ideally, give children several color options to choose from). You may wish to vary the size of the circles, depending on the number of children in the group.

6. Let the children pick a felt circle, then give them the paint and decorative materials to make faces on them.

7. Glue or stitch the faces to the banner.

8. Insert the dowel rod through the loops and let the children choose a place to display their banner.

ACTIVITY 5.8.   TIC-TAC-KNOW

This game can be used solely to promote socialization, or it can be developed using a theme relevant to the group.

Therapeutic Goal: To provide a group activity that will foster socialization. **Age Group:** School-age/adolescent **Adult/Child Ratio:** 1:15 **Required Time:** 20 minutes **Restrictions and Precautions:** None	**Materials:** ☐ Writing paper ☐ Marker ☐ Pen or pencil

Process

1. Make Tic-Tac-Know sheets by drawing two vertical lines and two horizontal lines on a sheet of paper, dividing it into nine boxes.

2. In each box write a potential commonality that the children share, which will require them to converse with one another. Instruct them to find someone who, for example:

   • Has undergone the same test or procedure as you

   • Was born in the same month as you

   • Feels the same as you do about being in the hospital

   • Has the same number of people in his or her family

   • Has the same favorite dessert as you

   • Wears the same size shoe as you

   • Has the same favorite singing group as you

   • Has the same doctor as you

3. Make a copy of the Tic-Tac-Know sheet for each participant and explain the rules of the game:

   a. Find a person who matches the statement in each box and ask him or her to sign his or her name in the box.

   b. Ask only one question of each person until you have interacted once with each member of the group.

   c. The child with the most signatures when the time runs out wins.

ACTIVITY 5.9.   GROUP MANDALA

The enclosed circular form of a mandala can become a safe space in which the children can connect and be a part of the whole group while maintaining their separate and distinct spaces. Select a theme that will be meaningful to the group with which you are working. For example, if the group consists of children with the same disease, the theme can be related to their common emotional and physical experiences. Or, children who have lost a loved one could have their mandala represent their fears and hopes for the future.

Therapeutic Goal: To provide a group activity that will establish a sense of community and facilitate the sharing of feelings and concerns. **Age Group:** Preteen/adolescent	**Adult/Child Ratio:** 1:6 **Required Time:** 30 minutes **Restrictions and Precautions:** Take scissor and glue precautions.

Materials:

- [ ] 2 large pieces of cardboard, cut into circles of the same size
- [ ] Yardstick
- [ ] Pencil

- [ ] Scissors
- [ ] Velcro circles
- [ ] Precut pictures and words from magazines
- [ ] Glue sticks

Process

1. Divide each cardboard circle into as many wedge-shaped segments as there are participants in the group.

2. Cut out the segments from one circle and attach a piece of Velcro to each, placing the dot at the same location on each of the segments. Place a corresponding Velcro dot in the same location on each segment of the uncut cardboard circle.

3. Give each child a segment.

4. Have the children either make a drawing or create a collage from the magazine cutouts in their segment of the circle, representing the selected theme.

5. When they have completed their segments, show the children how to attach them to a corresponding segment of the uncut circle to create a mandala.

6. As a group, discuss similarities and differences in the representations; or invite each child to talk about his or her own piece.

7. Display the finished work, or give each child his or her segment to keep.

ACTIVITY 5.10.   GROUP MONTAGE

The completed montages are usually quite large and visually striking, instilling a sense of pride and accomplishment among the children in the group. Vary the number of picture segments in accordance with the number of children in the group.

Therapeutic Goal: To provide a group activity that will foster socialization and establish a sense of community.

Age Group: School age/adolescent

Adult/Child Ratio: 1:16

Required Time: 45 minutes–1 hour

Restrictions and Precautions: Take paint, marker, and scissors precautions.

Materials:

- [ ] 8-inch × 10-inch photograph or picture
- [ ] Ruler

- [ ] Pencil
- [ ] Scissors
- [ ] Sixteen 1–foot × 1–foot cardboard pieces
- [ ] Paint and paintbrushes, markers, colored pencils, paper for collage
- [ ] Glue

Process

1. Have the group select a photograph or picture for the project, preferably one without too many details, which would make it difficult to draw.

2. On the back of the picture, draw a grid of 16 squares.

3. Number the squares 1 to 16 and cut them apart.

4. Number the cardboard pieces 1 to 16, as well.

5. Pair the cardboard pieces with the photo square having the corresponding number.

6. Distribute the squares among the children in the group.

7. Ask the children to draw an enlarged version of the photo square on the cardboard.

8. Give the children paint and paintbrushes, colored pencils, and/or collage paper to complete their segments.

9. When their artwork is completed, assemble the picture by placing the squares in a grid according to the numbers on the back of each square; then display it.

ACTIVITY 5.11.   GROUP MURAL

Creating a mural is an excellent activity for almost any group with a commonality, be it having a serious illness, losing a loved one, being the sibling of a sick child, or experiencing a disaster. In fact, for certain populations, such as those who have experienced the impact of a disaster, a group activity such as this is less threatening and may be preferable to individual interventions.

Therapeutic Goal: To provide a group activity that will facilitate the sharing of feelings and concerns and establish a sense of community.

Age Group: School-age/adolescent

Adult/Child Ratio: 1:8

Required Time: 1 hour

Restrictions and Precautions: Take paint and marker precautions.

Materials:

☐ Roll of butcher paper

☐ Pencil

☐ Paint and/or markers

☐ Paintbrushes

☐ Water

Process

1. Lead a discussion to select a theme for the mural, one that relates to the commonality shared by the group.

2. Once the theme has been selected, encourage the children to brainstorm how they wish to execute the theme. Allow ample time for this process, as this preplanning phase is the main focus of the activity. If necessary, help the group reach consensus.

3. After they have agreed on the approach, instruct the children to sketch the mural on the butcher paper in pencil first. This not only promotes continued discussion but also allows for changes, if desired.

4. When the group is satisfied with the sketch, let them paint or color the mural with markers.

5. Upon completion of the mural, invite the group to discuss and critique their work.

6. Allow the children to select where they wish to display their finished mural.

ACTIVITY 5.12.   GROUP TILE PROJECT

This activity is equally appealing to all ages, and can be added to over time.

Therapeutic Goal: To provide a group activity that will establish a sense of community.

Age Group: Preschool and up

Adult/Child Ratio: Varies, depending on the ages of the children

Required Time: 15–20 minutes, to paint the tiles; the time required to mount the tiles will vary depending on the number of tiles used.

Restrictions and Precautions: Wear gloves and a mask when applying silicone. Apply the silicone in a well-ventilated area, away from the children.

Materials:

- Ceramic tiles, 4 or 6 inches square (available from hardware and building supply stores)
- Acrylic or craft paint for tile work
- Paintbrushes
- Water
- Silicone caulk
- Masonite, 1/4 to 1/2 inch thick (large enough to accommodate the number of tiles being made)

Process

1. Have the group choose a theme for the project; or ask each child to create a representation of him- or herself.

2. Give the children paint and brushes to decorate their own tile(s). Encourage them to sign their tile(s).

3. When the tiles are complete, apply silicone caulk generously to the back of each tile and mount them in a grid formation on the Masonite base (Figure Activity 5.12-1).

Figure Activity 5.12-1. Group Tile Project

4. Allow the silicone to dry for at least 24 hours before standing the piece up or hanging it.

ACTIVITY 5.13. PAPER BAG PUPPET SHOW

The most important aspect of this activity is the interaction that occurs when the children plan and rehearse their puppet show. As such, there are many wonderfully creative techniques for making puppets, but we chose the paper bag version for this activity because of its simplicity.

Therapeutic Goal: To provide a group activity that will foster socialization.

Age Group: Primary/school-age

Adult/Child Ratio: 1:6

Required Time: 45 minutes

Restrictions and Precautions: Take scissors and glue precautions.

Materials:

- [ ] Paper
- [ ] Pen
- [ ] Small paper bags (assorted colors preferred)
- [ ] Construction paper
- [ ] Scissors
- [ ] White glue or glue stick

Process

1. Help the group select a theme or write a story, related to the purpose of the group, on which to base their puppet show.

2. Discuss the characters needed and divide responsibility for creating them among the children. Note: Limit the number of characters in accordance with the size of the group.

3. Have the children cut out the puppets' features, clothing, and extremities from construction paper then glue them on.

4. Allow the group ample time to discuss and rehearse their puppet show.

5. Invite the group to perform the puppet show for the staff or other children and families. Offer the group positive feedback, and applaud their efforts.

Variation

Make puppets from a multitude of items easily acquired in healthcare facilities, such as tongue depressors, hospital booties, spoons, and empty IV bags.

ACTIVITY 5.14.   PAPER QUILT

The bigger the quilt, the better it looks. This is an excellent activity in which to involve friends, family, and staff. Compared to fabric quilts, a paper quilt can be finished and displayed relatively quickly.

Therapeutic Goal: To provide a group activity that will foster socialization and establish a sense of community.

Age Group: Preschool/primary

Adult/Child Ratio: 1:10

Required Time: 20–30 minutes for children to prepare their individual squares; the time required to sew the quilt is contingent on the number of squares made

Restrictions and Precautions: Take scissors, markers, and glue precautions.

Materials:

- [ ] Heavy construction paper
- [ ] Scissors
- [ ] Crayons or markers
- [ ] Miscellaneous decorative craft materials
- [ ] Glue
- [ ] Hole punch
- [ ] Yarn
- [ ] Needlepoint needle

Process

1. Cut the construction paper into 8-inch × 8-inch squares.

2. Give each child a square on which to draw a picture or make a decorative collage.

3. Arrange the squares as desired.

4. Punch the same number of holes equidistant around the sides of each square, except for those on the ends where the square will not be sewn to another piece.

5. Thread the needle and sew the papers together as you would a fabric quilt. Allow those children who are able to assist with this.

6. Display the quilt where it can be seen by all the contributors.

ACTIVITY 5.15.   PROGRESSIVE STORY WRITING

This activity typically generates a great deal of laughter, which makes it an excellent choice for defusing tension.

Therapeutic Goal: To provide a group activity that will establish a sense of community and foster socialization.

Age Group: School-age/adolescent

Adult/Child Ratio: 1:10

Required Time: 30 minutes

Restrictions and Precautions: None

Materials:

☐ Colored paper

☐ Pens

Process

1. If desired, choose a theme for the story, or have the group select one. The theme can be medical or nonmedical; or the activity can be carried out with no theme at all.

2. Seat the group in a circle.

3. Give each child a different-color piece of paper and ask them to write one phrase or sentence to serve as the beginning of a story.

4. Have the children pass their piece of paper to the child on their left.

5. Ask the children, in turn, to read the first line of the story passed to them then write a second line.

6. Tell the children to fold over the paper so that only the last lines written are visible, and pass it to their left.

7. Repeat steps 5 and 6 until everyone has had a turn.

8. Continue until the stories have ample content; then ask the children to write a sentence to end the story they currently hold.

9. Give each child a turn reading aloud the story that he or she is holding.

Variation

Make a collaborative proclamation by writing an open-ended sentence on a large piece of butcher paper that is taped to the wall. Ask each child to complete the sentence then choose a different-color marker to write his or her ending below the heading. For example:

What helps me when I feel sad is . . .

Being in the hospital is like . . .

ACTIVITY 5.16.   PUZZLED

Children find it very satisfying to see the finished puzzle they have created together. Adapt the activity for younger children simply by giving each child a puzzle piece to paint or decorate as they wish, then ask them to help you assemble the puzzle.

Therapeutic Goal: To provide a group activity that fosters socialization and establishes a sense of community.

Age Group: School-age/adolescent

Adult/Child Ratio: 1:12

Required Time: 1 hour

Restrictions and Precautions: Take glue precautions.

Materials:

☐ Paper

☐ Pencils

☐ Large Styrofoam board (available from most home-improvement stores)	☐ Paintbrushes
	☐ Water
☐ Craft knife	☐ Decorative trims (e.g., feathers, beads, yarn)
☐ Paint	☐ Glue

Process

1. Invite the children to plan a picture and/or choose a message they would like to convey that is related to the group's focus (e.g., grief, hospitalization, sibling experience, chronic illness).

2. Help the children sketch the picture or message on the Styrofoam board, making sure to use the entire surface area in the drawing.

3. Use the craft knife to cut the Styrofoam into as many irregularly shaped pieces as there are members of the group.

4. Give each of the children a piece, along with the paint and trim items, and ask them to decorate it.

5. Reassemble the puzzle and let the children choose where to display it.

Variation

In advance of doing the activity with the group, sketch a picture or write a message on the Styrofoam board and cut it out. Without letting the participants know what the picture or message is, give each member of the group a piece of the puzzle and ask them to paint/decorate it. That way, the finished puzzle will be a surprise to them.

ACTIVITY 5.17.   SWEET MEETS

The themes for the questions comprising this activity can be easily adapted to meet a special goal established for each group. Children enjoy the added bonus of being allowed to eat their candy.

Therapeutic Goal: To provide a group activity that will foster socialization and facilitate the sharing of feelings and concerns.	**Materials:**
	☐ Poster board
Age Group: School-age/adolescent	☐ Marker
Adult/Child Ratio: 1:12	☐ Small bags of multicolored candy (e.g., M&Ms, jelly beans, Skittles, gummi bears)
Required Time: 45 minutes	
Restrictions and Precautions: Check for sugar sensitivity or special diets (see the Variation, below).	☐ Small paper plates or napkins

Process

1. Create a chart that lists a different type of personal information for each color of candy you are using. For example:

    Red: Something that makes you mad

    Green: Something you've always wanted

    Blue: Something you find soothing

    Yellow: Something you find scary

    Brown: Something you find funny

2. Tell the children to empty their bag of candy onto a paper plate or napkin.

3. Have the children take turns choosing one of their candies then answering the question that corresponds to the color.

4. Allow the children to eat that piece of candy after answering the question.

Variation   Substitute large colored beads for candy when conducting this activity with children on special diets or for whom candy is prohibited.

ACTIVITY 5.18.   THE TRUTH-BE-TOLD GAME

This activity is best used with children who already know each other.

Therapeutic Goal: To provide a group activity that will foster socialization.	**Restrictions and Precautions:** None
Age Group: Adolescents	**Materials:**
Adult/Child Ratio: Unlimited	☐ Paper
Required Time: Situational	☐ Pen

Process

1. Ask the participants to think of unusual or silly facts about themselves that others may be surprised to learn. Some examples include things they love or hate, places they have been, experiences they have had or things they have done, people they know, awards they have received, or childhood misconceptions.

2. Ask them to write down two true statements and then one that is not true.

3. Have each player, in turn, read aloud the three statements written on his or her paper.

4. Challenge the other players to guess which one of the statements is untrue.

ACTIVITY 5.19.   THE WEB WE WEAVE

This activity can easily be adapted to meet a multitude of treatment goals. It can be used simply to help children get to know one another, by asking them to use their turns to introduce and tell something about themselves. If children already know each other well, or if issue-specific goals have been set for the session, you can make the question more focused. For example, ask the children to use their turns to share a coping strategy for a common challenge the group shares, or to name an emotion and an experience in their lives that make them feel that way.

Therapeutic Goal: To provide a group activity that will foster socialization, facilitate the sharing of feelings and concerns, and establish a sense of community.	**Restrictions and Precautions:** None
	Materials:
Age Group: School-age/adolescent	☐ Ball of yarn
Adult/Child Ratio: 1:12	☐ Tape
Required Time: 30 minutes	

Process

1. Sit together with the children in a circle on the floor then, based on the commonality among the children and the goal of the activity, pose one or more questions to the children.

2. Tape the end of the yarn to the floor in front of you.

3. Explain to the children that in this activity it will be their turn when the ball of yarn is thrown to them. Inform them of what you would like them to tell the group when it is their turn. Assure the children that they don't have to answer the question if they prefer not to.

4. To begin play, throw the ball of yarn to someone in the circle. Ask that child to respond to the question chosen and tape the yarn to the floor in front of him or her.

5. Have the child throw the ball of yarn to someone else in the circle; repeat the process of asking a question and taping the yarn to the floor.

6. Continue until everyone has had a turn.

7. Ask each of the children what they think the design looks like.

For more ideas, see Bright Ideas for Group Activities (Box Activity 5.19-1).

• Give children plain T-shirts and fabric pens so they can autograph each other's shirts.

• Using a marker, write a "get to know you" question on each block of a Jenga game. Play as you would in regular Jenga, adding that each child must answer the question on the block they choose.

• Seat the children in a circle and pass around a roll of toilet paper. Without explaining what the game is, let each child take as many squares of the toilet paper as they think they will need to play. After everyone has taken some, ask each child to tell one thing about him- or herself for each square they have.

• Invite participants to describe three objects that are most important to them. Encourage them to explain why, and what the object might indicate about them as a person.

• Pair up the children with someone in the group they do not know; give the pairs five minutes to get to know one another. Ask each of the children to tell the group what he or she has learned about his or her "partner."

• Fold a brightly colored piece of paper into a "fortune teller"—otherwise known as a "cootie catcher." Instead of fortunes, write in questions for the children to answer.

• Organize game tournaments. Perennial favorites include cards, Scrabble, Monopoly, pool, and Ping-Pong. If you use a video game, children on bed rest or in isolation can participate by playing in their room and calling in their score to the activity room.

• For a progressive group activity, give children the opportunity to make a video. Divide the responsibilities for writing, set decoration, acting, directing, and filming among the children.

• Create a question box where group members can put questions in writing that they feel uncomfortable speaking about.

• Appoint a youth advisory board to promote group interaction and problem solving, as well as to validate for children that their input is important.

CHAPTER 6

DESENSITIZATION TO MEDICAL IMPLEMENTS

Many children experience unpredictable and severe procedure-related pain that can be associated with negative emotional and psychological implications. However, children also respond with fear even when the use of a medical implement, such as a stethoscope, typically has little association with pain. As mentioned previously, anything can be frightening when a child doesn't understand what it is.

This chapter offers expressive art activities that incorporate medical equipment as the medium for expression. The activities can be used when children are too anxious or afraid to engage in more formal types of medical play or preparation. Expressive art activities also are useful when children feel they are "too old" for medical play. The activities involve indirect and sometimes humorous ways to expose children to medical equipment. This form of medical play is a useful supplement to other medical play and preparation activities.

LIST OF ACTIVITIES

Activity 6.1 Bandage Prints	Activity 6.11 Medical Object Guessing Game
Activity 6.2 Doctor-Bag Collages	Activity 6.12 Parachute Jumpers
Activity 6.3 Five-Finger Puppets	Activity 6.13 Sunprints
Activity 6.4 Found Object Assemblage	Activity 6.14 Spatter Painting
Activity 6.5 Gauze Soft Sculpture	Activity 6.15 Syringe Butterflies
Activity 6.6 Hairy Hands	Activity 6.16 Syringe Spin-Art
Activity 6.7 Isolation Gown Wind Sock	Activity 6.17 Test Tube Glitter Wands
Activity 6.8 IV Tubing Necklaces	Activity 6.18 Tongue Depressor Puzzles
Activity 6.9 Medical Faux-Finishing	Activity 6.19 What Is It?
Activity 6.10 Medical Mobiles	

Procedures

Children undergo a variety of procedures in their encounters with the healthcare system. Whether in the hospital, a pediatrician's office, same-day surgery center, specialty clinic, or school nurse's office, all sites typically may involve contact with medical implements. Medical procedures cause anxiety, fear, and behavioral distress for children and their families, which may intensify their pain and interfere with the procedure.

A child's distress during painful medical procedures is strongly influenced by adult behaviors. Of interest is the notion that adult reassurance (e.g., "it's okay") is associated with increased child distress, whereas distraction is associated with increased child coping. Little is known about why reassurance shows this counterintuitive relationship with child distress. However, a recent study provided some insight into the complexity of adult reassurance, highlighting the important role of parental facial expression, tone, and verbal content during the procedure in conveying fear to children (McMurtry, Chambers, McGrath, & Asp, 2010). Further research is needed regarding the common, but apparently unhelpful, parental reassurance

111

behavior, for even when parents are trained to engage in more helpful behaviors, they still may reassure (Manimala, Blount, & Cohen, 2009).

Repeated invasive medical procedures may be common, which can be aversive despite pharmacological interventions for pain management. With recurring procedures, the child quickly sees the aversive stimulation as intermittent, unpredictable, and uncontrollable. A variety of negative behavioral sequelae can develop, including conditioned anxiety, emotional withdrawal, attempts to avoid or escape treatment, and, for some children, severe tantrums or aggression.

An awareness of the procedures children typically experience, and the medical equipment used to conduct them, can provide guidance for selecting the medical implements and supplies to use in medical art. Following is information about the procedures most common for children in outpatient and inpatient healthcare settings.

Procedures During Ambulatory Care

Common procedures that take place in ambulatory settings include immunizations, chemotherapy, diagnostic testing such as MRIs or CT scans, sutures for minor injuries, and minor procedures that require sedation. Increasingly, procedures that in the past required hospitalization are now being performed on an outpatient basis. For example, the rate of visits to freestanding ambulatory surgery centers increased about 300% from 1996 to 2006 (Cullen, Hall, & Golosinskly, 2009).

Procedures During Hospitalization

Children undergo a variety of procedures during hospitalization (see Table 6.1). The Agency for Healthcare Research and Quality (AHRQ) (2009) tracks procedures through discharge data for infants and for children 1 to 17 years.

Table 6.1 Number of Discharges, Percent Distribution, and Growth for the Most Frequent All-listed Inpatient Hospital Procedures by Age Group for Children, 1997 and 2007

Age Group and All-Listed CCS* Procedures	Number of Discharges in Thousands		Percent of Age-Specific Total Discharges		Cumulative Growth
	1997	2007	1997	2007	1997–2007
<1 year, total discharges	4,426	5,125	100%	100%	16
Prophylactic vaccinations and inoculations	549	1,461	12.4	28.5	166
Circumcision	1,159	1,299[†]	26.2	25.3	12
Vision and hearing diagnosis and treatment	‡	532	‡	10.4	‡
Respiratory intubation and mechanical ventilation	163	202	3.7	3.9	24
Enteral and parenteral nutrition	39	124	0.9	2.4	219
1–17 years, total discharges	1,821	1,658	100%	100%	−9
Appendectomy	74	82[†]	4.1	4.9	10
Repair of obstetric laceration	58	60[†]	3.2	3.6	3
Blood transfusion	26	45	1.4	2.7	72
Cancer chemotherapy	43	44[†]	2.4	2.7	3
Artificial rupture of membranes to assist delivery	40	44[†]	2.2	2.7	10

*Clinical Classifications Software
[†]2007 discharges are not statistically different from 1997 discharges at $p < 0.05$.
‡Statistics based on estimates with a relative standard error (standard error/weighted estimate) greater than 0.30 or with standard error equal to 0 in the nationwide statistics are not reliable.
Note. From Agency for Healthcare Research and Quality. (2009). *Facts and Figures 2007. Healthcare Cost and Utilization Project (HCUP).* Rockville, MD: Author. Retrieved March 13, 2010 from www.hcup-us.ahrq.gov/reports /factsandfigures/2007/exhibit3_2.jsp.

Infants. According to the Agency for Healthcare Research and Quality (2009), most common procedures performed on infants were routine, such as circumcision (performed in 25.3% of infant stays), vaccinations (performed in 28.5% of infant stays), and vision and hearing diagnosis and treatment (performed in 10.4% of infant stays). Procedures on infants also included those done for complex conditions affecting severely ill babies, such as enteral/parenteral nutrition, or tube feeding (performed during 124,000 infant stays in 2007). The use of tube feeding during infant hospitalizations increased 219% compared with a 16% growth in all infant discharges. Procedures for respiratory intubation/mechanical ventilation were common for infants, representing 4 to 5% of the discharges for this age group. Respiratory intubation grew rapidly from 1997 to 2007, up 24% for infants.

Children 1 to 17 Years. Overall, hospitalizations for children declined 9% between 1997 and 2007 (AHRQ, 2009). Appendectomy was the most common procedure for children 1 to 17 years old, accounting for 4.9% of hospitalizations in this age group. Other top procedures common in stays for children included repair of obstetric laceration in teen deliveries, cancer chemotherapy, and artificial rupture of membranes to assist in teen delivery. Blood transfusion was the third most common procedure for 1 to 17 year olds. With a 72% increase from 1997 to 2007, blood transfusion was one of the fastest-growing procedures for this age group.

Needles

Procedures involving needles are among the medical procedures most feared by children (Broome et al., 1990). To some extent, many people fear needles (Muscari, 2007). Once that fear becomes persistent, excessive, and unreasonable, it becomes a phobia (American Psychiatric Association, 2000). Needle phobia affects 3.5 to 10% of the population, with 5.5 years the median age of onset (Duff, 2003).

Confronted with a needle, individuals with needle phobia feel anxiety almost immediately, but the level of anxiety usually varies, with both the degree of proximity to the needle and the degree to which escape from the stimulus is limited. The intensity of the reaction is not always predictable. The individual can react differently to the same needle procedure on different occasions (Duff, 2003).

Possible somatic responses include rapid heart rate, rise in blood pressure, tremor, feeling faint or actually fainting, nausea, excessive sweating, and feelings of panic. When the individual believes that escape is impossible, a full-blown panic attach may occur (Friedman, Munir, & Erickson, 2006). Although fears of objects or situations are common during childhood, a distinction must be made for those that interfere with the child's daily functioning (Muscari, 2007). Children's symptoms may be similar to those of adults, or the child may cry, have tantrums, cling, freeze, or become physically agitated or immobilized (Duff, 2003; Friedman et al., 2006; Yim, 2006).

Some individuals react to needles with autonomic vasovagal reflex responses, which may include pallor, clamminess, excessive sweating, nausea, respiratory distress, loss of bladder and bowel control, and various levels of unresponsiveness (Hamilton, 1995). Evidence exists to support a hypothesis of a hereditary component to needle phobia. The vasovagal reflex and needle phobia strongly tend to run in families (Hamilton, 1995). This inherited vasovagal reflex of shock, triggered by successive needle puncture, is believed to be the etiology of needle phobia.

A genetic trait's presence among a species automatically indicates that the trait must have been selected for during the evolution of that species. The needle phobia trait in humans probably evolved in response to piercing, stabbing, and cutting injuries (Ellinwood & Hamilton, 1991). Most violent deaths in our species' evolutionary history have been caused by skin penetration from teeth, claws, fangs, and tusks; and from sticks, stone axes, knives, spears, swords, and arrows (Hamilton, 1995). Deaths resulted from direct trauma, hemorrhage, or infections secondary to skin penetration. Proposes Hamilton:

> A reflex that promoted the learning of a strong fear of skin puncture had clear
> selective value in teaching humans to avoid such injuries. Over the 4 million
> years of human evolution, surely many genes controlling blood pressure, pulse,

cardiac rhythm, and stress hormone release were selected for to create the vasovagal reflex. (p. 6)

Assessing for needle phobia can be an important first step. Suspect needle phobia in children who report needle fear, have anxiety responses when exposed to or in anticipation of a needle procedure, and who try to avoid a needle procedure. In individuals with needle phobia, needle fear and avoidance may interfere not only with healthcare but also with occupational, academic, or social activities, or cause marked distress. Children with a family history of needle phobia in a first-degree relative are at increased risk. Needle phobia also may result in clinical symptoms, such as decreased blood pressure, pulse, or both, with or without an initial rise in blood pressure, pulse, or both. Individuals may experience symptoms of syncope, light-headedness, or vertigo, along with other autonomic symptoms, and their electrocardiogram findings may be abnormal (Hamilton, 1995).

Medical Art

When individuals become sensitized to certain physical and psychological stimuli, their bodies and minds are conditioned to react to those stimuli with extreme hypersensitivity. Desensitization is a psychological process that gradually introduces the feared object to the child in a nonthreatening way. Even children who have not been sensitized to particular stimuli can benefit from exposure to medical equipment.

Medical art can be used in desensitization. For example, to address needle phobia, Kettwich and colleagues (2007) used the simple process of putting colorful images of flowers, music notes, and the like, on syringes and butterfly needles commonly used to draw blood for testing. Using them with children who had cancer, they found the "stress-reducing medical devices" were 76% effective in preventing overt needle phobia in the children. About two thirds of children in the general population are needle-phobic, the impact of which might be merely an inconvenience or life-threatening. Thus, it is very exciting to discover that a simple, inexpensive medical art intervention can make such a dramatic difference.

Medical play, which can be used to help familiarize children with medical implements and supplies, is a distinct concept within the phenomenon of play. It is a form of play that always involves medical themes or medical equipment. An adult or child can initiate medical play, but the child chooses to maintain it voluntarily. This type of play often is accompanied by laughter and relaxation, but also may be intense and aggressive. Medical play is of fundamental therapeutic value because it allows a child a change of roles, from persecuted to persecutor, from passivity to activity, while providing an opportunity for the child to regain a sense of control over reality (Favara-Scacco, Smirne, Schilirò, & DiCataldo, 2001). Medical play is not synonymous with preparation, because it does not involve an adult demonstrating a procedure or familiarizing a child in a formal educational manner.

A form of therapeutic play, medical play includes four basic types (McCue, 1988):

- *Role rehearsal/role reversal*. Children have the opportunity to take the role of the healthcare professional.
- *Medical fantasy play*. Children engage in role-play and fantasy with medical themes, but not real medical equipment.
- *Indirect medical play*. Children engage in play with medical themes and use medical equipment in a nonmedical way.
- *Medically related art*. Children use art activities to express their understanding of and reaction to a medical experience.

The activities in this chapter address the fourth type of medical play—medically related art.

Some purists may not consider medically related art as play; however, the opportunities for expression, creativity, and control are limitless (McCue, 1988). From direct painting and drawing to collage to three-dimensional creations, art activities take many forms. Although some art is precise and descriptive, other forms will be nonrepresentational or use medical equipment in its creation, but all medical art gives children the opportunity to express their understanding of and psychosocial reactions to their medical experiences.

Although McCue (1988) believes that either the process or the product of the activity can be important for the child, art therapists emphasize the process or the experience. A mental health profession, art therapy uses the creative process of art making to improve and enhance the physical, mental, and emotional well-being of individuals. Its objective is to use the creative process involved in artistic self-expression to help people to resolve conflicts and problems, develop interpersonal skills, manage behavior, reduce stress, increase self-esteem and self-awareness, and achieve insight (American Art Therapy Association, 2010). Art therapists use various media, such as painting, drawing, collage, or sculpting, to enable individuals to understand themselves, their feelings, and their relationships. Children can express themselves kinesthetically, affectively, cognitively, symbolically, and/or creatively.

Medical objects may always be available for children's spontaneous play in hospitals, clinics, or other healthcare settings. However, children obtain helpful exposure to medical equipment when it is used in expressive arts activities. Their knowledge and understanding of medical equipment increases with age in a manner best described by the Piagetian theoretical framework. Age-appropriate opportunities to manipulate and use medical equipment in a nonstressful situation, such as creating medical art, can assist in this learning process.

Research also indicates that children who have higher anxiety levels have less knowledge about equipment and procedures (Melamed, 1982; Siaw, Stephens, & Holmes 1986; Thompson, 1985). Studies suggest that medically related therapeutic play can be more effective in alleviating stress than unrelated play (Koller, 2008b). Fortunately most children need very little encouragement to participate in dramatic medical play (Jessee, Wilson, & Morgan, 2000).

Previous experience influences children's knowledge and the ways in which they interact with medical equipment. In a study that compared the responses of children that had not been exposed to intensive hospital treatment with those of children that had, McGrath & Huff (2001) found that children without exposure had a naïve, joyous curiosity about medical equipment and a very unsophisticated understanding of its purpose. This group of children integrated medical equipment into their play without hesitation, and were confident and interested in their exploration of the purpose of the equipment. In contrast, even with only secondary personal experience with hospitals (not hospitalized themselves but had a close relative with such medical experience), children's readiness to spontaneously play with medical equipment was limited and the naïve confidence was replaced by more fearful descriptions.

Other relevant research reveals that children who are chronically ill are able to use medical equipment to express their concerns about intrusive procedures (Ellerton, Caty, & Ritchie, 1985). Injection play was the most common type of intrusive procedure acted out in this study. An important part of this play was exploratory. Children first picked up the needle and syringe, examined them, and worked the plunger back and forth before acting out the intrusive procedure. Less intrusive and anxiety-provoking equipment produced fewer exploratory activities. These findings indicate that exploratory opportunities via medical art can help children familiarize themselves with medical equipment before or after role rehearsal/role reversal medical play and medical fantasy play occur.

Special Considerations

One of the first considerations when doing medical art with children is the role of the adult. Should the adult be actively involved in the project or a passive observer? Bolig, Fernie, and Klein (1986) believe that unstructured play without adult guidance offers the greatest opportunities for children to gain skills and achieve mastery. When play is inhibited because of immobility, dull or repetitious environments, overstimulating environments, or fear, then adults may need to take on a more active role in the medical play of the child (Crocker, 1978). The level of involvement and control of the adult should be carefully considered when conducting medical play (McCue, 1988). Children should be encouraged, but never forced, to handle medical equipment.

A second consideration in medical play is the type of equipment selected. Commercial equipment can be costly, but McCue (1988) notes that effective medical play also can occur with simple materials that are readily available in healthcare settings (e.g., cotton, bandage strips, syringes).

During medical art play, the activities of the child may not be directly interpretable. McCue (1988) suggests that the child be asked, "Were you thinking of anything special while you were . . . ?" rather than, "What is it?" The child is more likely to respond and provide meaningful information to the professional when asked a question in this form.

Activity Goals

All of the activities in this chapter have the same goal: to enable children to explore informally and use medical equipment to express themselves artistically. The activities use a variety of materials, which we hope will inspire you to create your own variations, as well as develop new activities.

ACTIVITY 6.1.   BANDAGE PRINTS

Substitute large stamp pads for paint to do this activity in a waiting room or other space where using messy paints would not be advisable.

Therapeutic Goal: To promote coping with medical experiences through familiarization with and desensitization to medical equipment/supplies.

Age Group: Preschool/primary

Adult/Child Ratio: 1:3

Required Time: 15 minutes

Restrictions and Precautions: Take paint precautions.

Materials:

- ☐ Shallow containers (wide enough to put brayers in)
- ☐ Tempera paint
- ☐ Adhesive bandages, assorted sizes and shapes
- ☐ Cardboard
- ☐ Brayers
- ☐ Paper

Process

1. Pour each color of paint into a shallow container.
2. Invite the children to create pictures or designs on the cardboard by adhering bandages.
3. Demonstrate how to use the brayers, then help the children roll paint onto their pictures.
4. Place a sheet of paper over the cardboard and gently rub over the surface to produce a print.

Variation

Use other disposable medical supplies dipped in paint and applied to paper to make prints.

ACTIVITY 6.2.   DOCTOR-BAG COLLAGES

By substituting tape for glue, this activity can be used successfully in such venues as health fairs and busy clinics, where time is limited and easy cleanup is required. Laminate the precut medical bags to allow for use during role-playing.

Therapeutic Goal: To promote coping with medical experiences through familiarization with and desensitization to medical equipment/supplies.

Age Group: Preschool/primary

Adult/Child Ratio: 1:5

Required Time: 15 minutes

Restrictions and Precautions: Take glue precautions, and limit the choice of objects for very young children

Materials:

☐ Doctor bag template (Figure Activity 6.2-1)

☐ Pencil

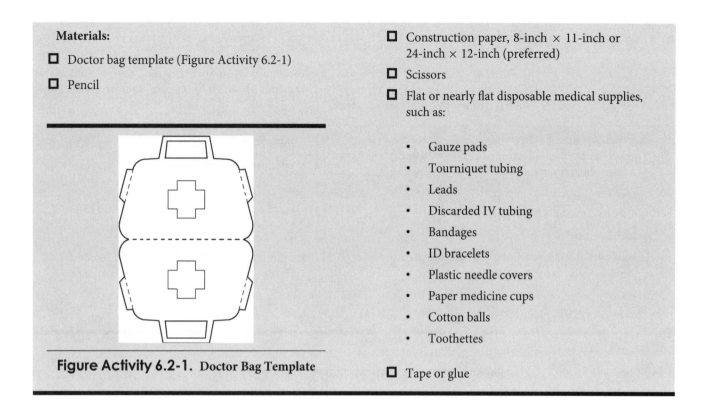

Figure Activity 6.2-1. Doctor Bag Template

☐ Construction paper, 8-inch × 11-inch or 24-inch × 12-inch (preferred)

☐ Scissors

☐ Flat or nearly flat disposable medical supplies, such as:

- Gauze pads
- Tourniquet tubing
- Leads
- Discarded IV tubing
- Bandages
- ID bracelets
- Plastic needle covers
- Paper medicine cups
- Cotton balls
- Toothettes

☐ Tape or glue

Process

1. Enlarge the template to fit the paper you are using.

2. Using the template, trace the doctor bag pattern onto colored paper and cut it out. Make a medical cross from two bandages.

3. Introduce the activity by telling the children that they are the doctors and can choose which supplies they need to put in their bags to take care of their patients.

4. Lay the paper cross-side down in front of the children.

5. Let the children arrange the materials on the construction paper in a decorative fashion and tape or glue them in place (Figure Activity 6.2-2).

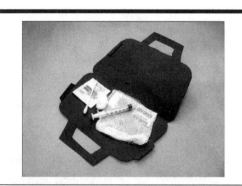

Figure Activity 6.2-2. Doctor Bag Collage

Variation

Older children can make more sophisticated collages using medical supplies on poster board. In addition to the materials listed above, provide pictures with medical themes cut from magazines, old menus, EEG tests, syringes without needles, and so on.

ACTIVITY 6.3.   FIVE-FINGER PUPPETS

Children often are able to express feelings through puppets that they may not be comfortable verbalizing otherwise. Providing five puppet characters with which to interact simultaneously allows the child to create more elaborate scenarios.

Therapeutic Goal: To promote coping with medical experiences through familiarization with and desensitization to medical equipment/supplies.

Age Group: Preschool/primary

Adult/Child Ratio: 1:1

Required Time: 10 minutes

Restrictions and Precautions: Take marker precautions.

Materials:

☐ Small examining glove

☐ Cotton balls

☐ Permanent markers

☐ Yarn

☐ Scissors

☐ Glue

☐ Rectangular facial tissue box, bottom removed, and painted or covered with decorative paper

Process

1. Stuff each finger of the examining glove with a cotton ball.

2. Place the glove on the child's nondominant hand.

3. Have the child use his or her dominant hand to draw a figure on each finger of the glove.

4. If desired, help the child cut yarn and glue it onto each fingertip, for hair.

5. Encourage the child to make up a story about the five figures he or she has created.

6. Help the child place the puppet on his or her dominant hand.

7. Demonstrate how to use the tissue box as a puppet stage by pushing your hand up from where the bottom of the box was and through the opening.

8. Encourage the child to do the same and tell the story he or she made up; or simply engage the child and the five puppet characters in a conversation.

ACTIVITY 6.4.   FOUND OBJECT ASSEMBLAGE

A found object assemblage is simply a three-dimensional collage. Like a collage, it is an excellent therapeutic art activity for children who do not enjoy or physically cannot partake in painting or drawing. Those children who are unable to actively engage in this activity can passively participate by selecting the objects they want to include from those available and giving an adult specific direction regarding assembling and gluing the objects together as the child wants. Often, even children who insist they do not like art can be enticed to do this activity by presenting it as a "building project."

Therapeutic Goal: To promote coping with medical experiences through familiarization with and desensitization to medical equipment/supplies.

Age Group: Adolescent

Adult/Child Ratio: 1:8

Required Time: 1 hour or more (may be done over two sessions)

Restrictions and Precautions: Take glue and paint precautions. Use spray paint in a well-ventilated area.

Materials:

☐ Pictures of assemblage art, downloaded from the Internet

☐ Medical and nonmedical objects found in the environment, such as:

- Packing material
- Syringes
- Specimen cups
- Plastic utensils
- Urinals/bedpans
- Old game pieces
- Tubing
- Bottle caps
- Old toy parts
- CDs
- Empty Jell-O cups

- Tongue depressors
- Wire
- Leads
- Computer parts
- Test tubes

☐ Rigid base for sculpture (e.g., Masonite, tile, canvas panel, heavy cardboard)

☐ Strong adhesive or low-temperature glue gun

☐ Paper clips or spring-release clothespins

☐ Nontoxic acrylic artist gesso (available from art supply stores)

☐ Foam paintbrushes, 1 inch wide

☐ Spray paint (optional)

Process

1. Show children images of assemblage art. Discuss how various artists used arrangement, texture, metaphor, and other techniques to transform found objects into art.

2. Lay out the objects you've assembled for the children to work with.

3. Provide the children with a base for their sculptures.

4. Invite the children to select objects for their sculptures; then give them time to experiment with different arrangements.

5. Instruct the children to glue the objects in place; allow to dry. Note: Paper clips or clothespins may be needed to stabilize the construction until the glue has thoroughly dried.

6. To produce a unified appearance, encourage the children to use the foam brush to apply acrylic gesso to the finished assemblage (optional). Gesso may be tinted with acrylic paint, if desired.

7. If desired, spray-paint the assemblage after the gesso has dried.

8. Encourage the children to give their finished creations a name.

For more ideas, see Bright Ideas for Medical Art (Box Activity 6.4-1).

- Finger-paint with ultrasound gel.
- Put leads on a Styrofoam head.
- Make a collage using old EEGs, leads, and colored wire.
- Turn empty IV bags into puppet bodies.
- Make snowmen out of cotton balls.
- Decorate disposable goggles to make cool "shades."
- Make bookmarks using large beads threaded on IV tubing.
- Cover medicine cups with foil to make little bells.

**BOX
ACTIVITY 6.4-1.
BRIGHT IDEAS
FOR MEDICAL ART**

ACTIVITY 6.5.   GAUZE SOFT SCULPTURE

For burn patients and many others, the application and removal of gauze can be part of a very painful process.

Therapeutic Goal: To promote coping with medical experiences through familiarization with and desensitization to medical equipment/supplies.

Age Group: School-age/adolescent

Adult/Child Ratio: 1:8

Required Time: 45 minutes

Restrictions and Precautions: Closely supervise the use of straight pins, and be sure to dispose of the pins when the activity is completed. Take glue and scissors precautions.

Materials:

☐ Pencil

☐ Paper, cut to size of gauze pads

☐ Large gauze pads (two per child)

☐ Straight pins

☐ Large plastic darning needle

☐ Fabric scraps

☐ Scissors

☐ Fabric glue

☐ Yarn

☐ Cotton balls

Process

1. Instruct the children to make a pattern by drawing an outline of an object, person, or shape on a piece of paper.

2. Have them cut out the outline to make a pattern.

3. Give each child two gauze pads, and tell them to place the pads together, matching all four corners.

4. Demonstrate for the children how to pin the pattern to the gauze pads and then cut it out.

5. Let the children decorate their form with fabric scraps and yarn. Decorations may be sewn or glued to the gauze.

6. Show the children how to thread the darning needle with yarn and sew their two pieces of gauze together, leaving a 2-inch opening.

7. Tell the children to push cotton balls through the opening, making sure they extend to all the corners.

8. Sew the opening closed.

Variations

Make bean bags by substituting dried beans for cotton balls.

Cut ice-skate shapes from large gauze pads. Attach paper clips for the blades, decorate with glitter, and use as ornaments.

During Halloween season, let the children make gauze ghosts.

ACTIVITY 6.6.   HAIRY HANDS

Children can wear these "hands" or place them strategically to look as if there's a monster under their sheet or inside a closet.

Therapeutic Goal: To promote coping with medical experiences through familiarization with and desensitization to medical equipment/supplies.

Age Group: School-age

Adult/Child Ratio: 1:8

Required Time: 30 minutes

Restrictions and Precautions: Take glue precautions.

Materials:

- [ ] Medium exam gloves (one pair per child)
- [ ] Scissors
- [ ] Fake fur
- [ ] Glue
- [ ] Craft-foam peel-and-stick precut ovals

Process

1. Give each child a pair of gloves.
2. Instruct the children to use one glove as a template to draw and cut two pieces of fur for the back of their hands, and then glue each piece to the back of a glove.
3. Cut small rectangles of fur to glue to the base of each finger, extending to the middle joint.
4. Place a heavy object on each glove while the glue dries.
5. After the glue has dried completely, tell the children to place one glove on their hand and press a foam oval onto each fingertip to make the nails. Remove the glove and repeat with the other glove (Figure Activity 6.6-1).

Figure Activity 6.6-1. Hairy Hands

Variation

Make Glamorous Gloves instead of Hairy Hands by substituting costume jewelry for the fur.

ACTIVITY 6.7.   ISOLATION GOWN WIND SOCK

These socks are great to hang on IV poles to make them look less mechanical and threatening. Just be careful to hang them in a way that won't interfere with the safe operation of the IV.

Therapeutic Goal: To promote coping with medical experiences through familiarization with and desensitization to medical equipment/supplies.

Age Group: School-age

Adult/Child Ratio: 1:12

Required Time: 45 minutes

Restrictions and Precautions: Take glue and scissors precautions.

Materials:

- [ ] Isolation gowns
- [ ] Scissors
- [ ] Rulers
- [ ] Yarn, cut into 18-inch pieces
- [ ] Hole punch
- [ ] Cloth scraps
- [ ] Fabric glue
- [ ] Fabric paint
- [ ] Crepe paper streamers, cut into 24-inch strips

Process

1. Cut the sleeves off the isolation gowns and give one to each child, along with three pieces of yarn

2. Have the children measure 12 inches down from the first cut, and cut it again.

3. Instruct the children to punch three equidistant holes at one end of their sleeve segment.

4. To make the hanger, tell the children to thread one end of a piece of yarn through each of the three holes and knot the ends around the edge of the gown sleeve so that the yarn won't slip through.

5. Show the children how to bring the untied ends of the three pieces of yarn together at the top and knot the ends together.

6. Have the children decorate the wind socks with cloth, fabric paint, and glue.

7. When the glue and paint are dry, instruct the children to glue five strips of crepe paper to their windsock on the end opposite the yarn.

8. Encourage the children to hang their windsock on their IV pole, traction apparatus, or near their window.

ACTIVITY 6.8.   IV TUBING NECKLACES

These colored "beads" can also be strung and used to decorate rooms or holiday trees, or be hung from IV poles.

Therapeutic Goal: To promote coping with medical experiences through familiarization with and desensitization to medical equipment/supplies.	**Materials:** ☐ IV tubing
	☐ Scissors
Age Group: Preschool/primary	☐ Cord
Adult/Child Ratio: 1:6	☐ Cup or bowl (one per child)
Required Time: 30 minutes	☐ Acrylic paints
Restrictions and Precautions: Take scissors and paint precautions. Not recommended for children who have fine-motor difficulties or limited use of their hands.	☐ Paintbrushes

Process

1. Cut the IV tubing into 1/2-inch pieces to make the "beads" (older children may be able to do this themselves).

2. Give each child a piece of cord that has been cut to a length that, when knotted, can easily slip over his or her head.

3. Give each of the children a cup with enough IV tubing segments to fill the length of cord they have. Let the children paint the "beads" in their choice of colors.

4. Encourage the children to string the "beads" in a pattern of their own design.

5. Knot the end of the cord so the children can wear their necklaces.

ACTIVITY 6.9.   MEDICAL FAUX-FINISHING

We have done this project on temporary construction walls in our hospital and received rave reviews. In fact, the walls looked so good that several people requested that we faux-finish their offices. The participants took great pride in the outcome and felt empowered by the opportunity to improve the hospital environment.

Therapeutic Goal: To promote coping with medical experiences through familiarization with and desensitization to medical equipment/supplies.

Age Group: Adolescents

Adult/Child Ratio: Contingent on the size of the object or area being painted

Required Time: Variable

Restrictions and Precautions: Take paint precautions—and note this can be a very messy activity. Assess children carefully to determine whether this activity is appropriate for them.

Materials:

☐ Heavy cardboard box (at least 2 feet × 2 feet), old wooden chair, file cabinet, or any flat surface suitable for latex paint

☐ Shallow containers (pie tins work well)

☐ Paintbrushes

☐ White eggshell or satin-finish latex paint

☐ Artist's acrylic paints (to tint latex)

☐ Paint stirrer

☐ Water

☐ 4 × 4 gauze pads, in large quantities, and/or nonlatex surgical gloves, to paint with

☐ Nonlatex surgical gloves, to wear

☐ Roller pan

Process

1. Pour some latex paint into three pie tins and help the children tint each with acrylic paint to create three harmonious colors; or choose a single color as a base.

2. Divide the base color into three portions; tint one with some white for a lighter hue and another with some black to create a darker hue.

3. Let the children paint the wall or object with the desired base coat; allow it to dry.

4. Instruct the children to pour the darker of the two remaining colors into the roller pan then thin with water until the paint is the consistency of milk.

5. Tell the children to put on a pair of gloves then immerse the gauze pad (or another glove) into the paint, remove it, and wring.

6. Show the children how to bunch up the gauze (or glove), to produce as many ridges as possible, and hold the gauze lightly—with just enough pressure to retain the shape.

7. Demonstrate how to use the gauze to dab lightly over the surface being painted, changing wrist position frequently so the pattern varies. Then invite the children to follow suit, covering the entire wall.

8. Repeat steps 4 to 8 using the remaining shade of paint.

Variation

Young children can don gloves and paint the glove (while their hand is inside). Then they can press their hand (or hands) across the surface to be painted.

Activity 6.10.   Medical Mobiles

Studies have shown that the use of "stress-reducing syringes" (e.g., conventional syringes decorated simply with stickers) resulted in diminished aversion, fear, and anxiety, and inhibited the typical needle-phobic responses in both children and adults (Kettwich et al., 2007). This activity uses syringes and an assortment of other commonly used medical supplies, and you may want to consider including others (e.g., gloves, respiratory treatment parts) that are unique to a child's situation.

Therapeutic Goal: To promote coping with medical experiences through familiarization with and desensitization to medical equipment/supplies.

Age Group: School-age

Adult/Child Ratio: 1:5

Required Time: 1 hour or more; can divide into two sessions

Restrictions and Precautions: Take glue, paint, glitter, and scissors precautions. Not appropriate for children with limited attention spans or poor motor coordination.

Materials:

☐ Tongue depressors (five per child)

☐ Tempera paint

☐ Paintbrushes

☐ Water

☐ Assorted disposable medical implements (e.g., medicine cups, needleless syringes, toothettes, gauze, cotton balls)

☐ Glue

☐ Decorative trims, small candies, food coloring, glitter, foil paper, cloth scraps, stickers

☐ Pushpins

☐ Hot glue

☐ Fishing line, cut into six 1-foot pieces and three 2-foot pieces

Process

1. Have the children paint the tongue depressors; allow them to dry.

2. Invite the children to decorate the medical implements, as desired. Some great ideas we have seen from children include:

   • Turn syringes into butterflies, using painted coffee filters for wings.

   • Put colored water into syringes.

   • Glue small candies into medicine cups.

   • Cover medicine cups with foil to make bells, with crumpled balls of foil for clappers.

   • Paint flattened paper medicine cups to make daffodils.

   • Construct people and animals from cotton balls and tongue depressors.

3. Use a pushpin to poke holes 1 inch from the end of each tongue depressor.

4. Ask the children to stack the tongue depressors then fan them out like the spokes on a bicycle, setting the ends with the holes farthest from the center.

5. Help the children use the hot glue to adhere the tongue depressors together in that formation.

6. Show the children how to insert one piece of fishing line through the holes on the end of each tongue depressor and tie a knot at the top of the hole.

7. Attach the implements by punching a hole in each, inserting one end of the fishing line through the hole, and tying a knot; or simply tie the item to the loose end of the fishing line.

8. To hang the mobile, thread three 2-foot pieces of fishing line under the crossed tongue depressors.

9. Gather the ends above the tongue depressors and knot.

10. Hang the mobile from the ceiling, a traction bar, or other apparatus that will allow the mobile to extend vertically.

ACTIVITY 6.11.   MEDICAL OBJECT GUESSING GAME

Medical Object Guessing Game is a good activity for children with poor motor control or paralysis or who require total care. It can be easily adapted to visually impaired children by letting them touch the objects to identify them.

Therapeutic Goal: To promote coping with medical experiences through familiarization with and desensitization to medical equipment/supplies.

Age Group: Preschool, primary, school-age

Adult/Child Ratio: 1:8

Required Time: 10 minutes

Restrictions and Precautions: Do not use sharp or breakable objects.

Materials:

- ☐ Pillow case
- ☐ Medical objects (e.g. syringe, reflex hammer, tourniquet, otoscope)
- ☐ Large box

Process

1. Place medical objects in the pillow case.
2. To make a partition in the room, place the box on its side on top of a table.
3. Stand one child behind the partition, along with the pillow case filled with medical objects.
4. Seat the other children in front of the partition.
5. Have the child behind the partition reach into the pillow case and remove one object without allowing the other children to see what it is.
6. Ask the child who selected the object to give clues to help the others identify what it is, such as the material it is made of, what it is used for, and what it looks like.
7. Encourage the other children to guess what the object is, based on the clues.
8. Once it has been identified, invite the children to talk about their experiences with the medical object.
9. Repeat the process until each child has had a turn behind the partition giving clues.

ACTIVITY 6.12.   PARACHUTE JUMPERS

Children who suffer the additional stress of having a loved one in the armed forces may use these parachute jumpers to act out some of their fears.

Therapeutic Goal: To promote coping with medical experiences through familiarization with and desensitization to medical equipment/supplies.

Age Group: Primary/school-age

Adult/Child Ratio: 1:10

Required Time: 30 minutes

Restrictions and Precautions: Take marker and glue precautions.

Materials:

- ☐ Isolation masks
- ☐ Wooden clothespin (not the spring-release type)
- ☐ Permanent markers
- ☐ Fabric scraps
- ☐ Glue
- ☐ Yarn or string

Process

1. To make the jumper, give the children markers to draw facial features on the rounded part of the clothespin.
2. Have the children use fabric scraps and glue (or, to save time, markers) to make the jumper's clothing.
3. If desired, let the children use markers to decorate the mask (parachute).
4. Show the children how to knot the four ties on the masks together.

5. Help the children use the yarn or string to tie the jumper to the ties, slightly above the knot.

6. To use, instruct the children to fold the corners of the parachute into the middle then roll it up and toss it into the air.

ACTIVITY 6.13.   SUNPRINTS

This project is quick and easy. It is, however, imperative to have access to a room with a sunny window that can be darkened, or the activity will not work.

Therapeutic Goal: To promote coping with medical experiences through familiarization with and desensitization to medical equipment/supplies.

Age Group: School-age

Adult/Child Ratio: 1:8

Required Time: 30 minutes

Restrictions and Precautions: Can only be done on a sunny day, and requires a room that can be darkened.

Materials:

☐ Assorted hospital implements and supplies that will cast interesting shadows (e.g., gauze, tubing, toothettes, bandages, swabs, syringes)

☐ Sunprint (light-sensitive) paper

☐ Cardboard

☐ Basin filled with water

☐ Paper towels

Process

1. Explain that sunprints are photographs made from materials that create shadows on light-sensitive paper.

2. Let the children select objects they wish to use, then experiment arranging them together on a flat surface to make an artistic composition.

3. When they are satisfied with their arrangement, darken the room and give the children a sheet of sunpaper to place, blue side up, atop a piece of cardboard.

4. Tell the children to re-create their arrangement of objects on top of the sunprint paper.

5. Instruct the children to place their sunprint paper in direct sunlight; wait three minutes.

6. When the time has elapsed, tell the children to remove the objects quickly.

7. Tell the children to immediately place the sunprint paper into water and gently swish it around for about a minute.

8. When the time has elapsed, tell the children to remove the paper from the water and place it on a flat surface to dry.

9. Encourage the children to hang their sunprints where visitors can see them.

ACTIVITY 6.14.   SPATTER PAINTING

Provide the children with some sort of smock to wear, as this activity can get quite messy.

Therapeutic Goal: To promote coping with medical experiences through familiarization with and desensitization to medical equipment/supplies.

Age Group: Primary/school-age

Adult/Child Ratio: 1:5

Required Time: 30 minutes

Restrictions and Precautions: Take paint precautions; and assure there are no broken wires on the screen that could scratch the children.

Materials:

☐ Paper or cardstock

☐ Assorted disposable medical implements

- ☐ Tape
- ☐ Tempera paints (diluted)
- ☐ Small containers
- ☐ Firm piece of wire screen affixed to a frame of heavy cardboard or wood
- ☐ Toothbrushes
- ☐ Colored construction paper
- ☐ Masking tape

Process

1. Cover the area where the children will be painting with newspaper.
2. Have the children select implements they wish to use, arrange them on a sheet of paper or cardstock, and secure each with a small piece of tape.
3. Instruct the children to dip a toothbrush into the thinned tempera paint, tapping off any extra paint.
4. Tell the children to hold the screen 3 to 5 inches from the paper and quickly rub the paint-soaked brush back and forth over the screen.
5. When the paint has dried, ask the children to remove the implements from the paper and mount the art on a piece of contrasting construction paper.

ACTIVITY 6.15. SYRINGE BUTTERFLIES

These colorful butterflies, when hung from the ceiling, can really cheer up a dreary hospital room.

Therapeutic Goal: To promote coping with medical experiences through familiarization with and desensitization to medical equipment/supplies.

Age Group: Preschool

Adult/Child Ratio: 1:6

Required Time: 15 minutes

Restrictions and Precautions: None

Materials:

- ☐ Medicine cups or other small containers for colorant
- ☐ Diluted tempera paint or food coloring and water
- ☐ Needleless syringes, bulb syringes, and/or eye-droppers
- ☐ Round paper coffee filters
- ☐ Clothespins
- ☐ Pipe cleaners, cut in 3-inch lengths (for antennae)

Process

1. Place the paint or colored water into the medicine cups.
2. Fill the syringes and/or eyedroppers with paint or food coloring.
3. Give the children the implements for dribbling colorant on the coffee filters, to create designs.
4. Allow the filters to dry.
5. Pinch the filters together in the center (like a bow tie) and clip them in the middle with a clothespin.
6. Fan each side of the filter to look like a butterfly's wings.
7. Twist the ends of two pipe cleaners around each clothespin to make antennae.

Variation

Use syringes instead of clothespins to make the butterfly bodies. Hot glue or pipe cleaners can be used to attach the filters.

For more ideas, see Bright Ideas: Top 10 Things to Do with Syringes (Box Activity 6.15-1).

BOX
ACTIVITY 6.15-1.
BRIGHT IDEAS:
TOP 10 THINGS
TO DO WITH
SYRINGES

1. Fill syringes with thin tempera paint and create art a là Jackson Pollack (see Figure Box Activity 6.15-1). Or use syringes filled with fabric paint to decorate T-shirts.

Figure Box Activity 6.15-1. **Top 10 Things to Do with Syringes**
Courtesy of Steven Koress Photography

2. Fill a syringe with water and use as a squirt gun.

3. Decorate cakes and cookies with syringes filled with frosting or decorator's icing (use 50cc syringe or smaller with tip cut off).

4. Use a syringe to decoratively drizzle syrup on plates around ice cream or other desserts (think fancy restaurant).

5. Make popping noises by moving the syringe plunger in and out.

6. Fill a syringe with layers of different-colored sand and use a long narrow stick to poke along the inner side of the syringe to create designs. Hot-glue the tips.

7. Cut tips off syringes and stuff with clay to use as a tool to write words, make hair, or form a mound of spaghetti.

8. Water small plants using a syringe.

9. Pour pancake batter through a syringe onto a griddle; make alphabet pancakes or spell out the child's name.

10. Make a rocket ship.

ACTIVITY 6.16.   SYRINGE SPIN-ART

This activity is good for children with low energy or short attention spans or who are non-English speaking.

Therapeutic Goal: To promote coping with medical experiences through familiarization with and desensitization to medical equipment/supplies.

Age Group: Preschool/primary

Adult/Child Ratio: 1:5

Required Time: 10–15 minutes

Restrictions and Precautions: Take paint precautions.

Materials:

☐ Salad spinner

☐ Paper plates

☐ Needleless syringes or eyedroppers

☐ Medicine cups

☐ Tempera paint

1. Lay a paper plate at the bottom of the spinner.
2. Have one of the children squirt or drop paint onto the paper plate.
3. Place the top on the spinner and ask the child to turn the handle to spin the plate.
4. Carefully remove the plate and allow the paint to dry.
5. Continue until each child has had a turn.

ACTIVITY 6.17.   TEST TUBE GLITTER WANDS

These wands make excellent distraction devices.

Therapeutic Goal: To promote coping with medical experiences through familiarization with and desensitization to medical equipment/supplies.

Age Group: Preschool/primary/school-age

Adult/Child Ratio: Varies, depending on children's capabilities and the level of adult assistance required.

Required Time: 15 minutes

Restrictions and Precautions: Take glitter precautions; and avoid using too many sparkles, as they expand and clog the tube.

Materials:

☐ Bowls
☐ Mineral oil or corn syrup
☐ Food coloring
☐ Test tubes 1/2 inch to 1 inch in diameter, or spinal-tap tubes
☐ Small plastic spoons (if possible, get the tiny spoons used at ice cream shops for giving samples)
☐ Glitter, sequins, and metallic stars
☐ Water
☐ Syringes
☐ Hot glue gun or duct tape

Process

1. Place the oil or corn syrup into a separate bowl for each child.
2. Have the children add a few drops of the food coloring of their choice; give them a tongue depressor to stir it.
3. Provide each child with a tube and help them use a spoon to put a small amount of glitter and/or sequins into it.
4. Show the children how to use a syringe to draw up the liquid from their bowl and squirt it into their tube, filling the tube to approximately 1/2 inch from the top.
5. Place the top on the tubes and secure tightly with hot glue or tape.
6. Encourage the children to gently rotate the tubes and watch the sparkles move about slowly.

ACTIVITY 6.18.   TONGUE DEPRESSOR PUZZLES

Children enjoy challenging friends and staff to assemble the puzzles they have made.

Therapeutic Goal: To promote coping with medical experiences through familiarization with and desensitization to medical equipment/supplies

Age Group: School-age

Adult/Child Ratio: 1:6

Required Time: 10–15 minutes

Restrictions and Precautions: Take marker precautions.

Materials:

☐ Tongue depressors
☐ Tape
☐ Markers
☐ Plastic sandwich bags

Process

1. Instruct the children to line up five or more tongue depressors, with the sides touching and the ends evenly aligned.

2. Help the children tape the tongue depressors together using two or three long pieces of tape.

3. Instruct the children to turn the tongue depressors over so that the side with the tape is facing down.

4. Invite the children to draw a picture on the tongue depressors, encouraging them to cover the entire space.

5. Ask the children to remove the tape and place the puzzle pieces in a plastic bag for storage and use later.

For more ideas, see Bright Ideas: Top 10 Things to Make with Tongue Depressors (Box Activity 6.18-1).

BOX ACTIVITY 6.18-1. BRIGHT IDEAS: TOP 10 THINGS TO MAKE WITH TONGUE DEPRESSORS	1. Bookmarks 2. Puppets 3. Sleds 4. God's eyes 5. Dominoes 6. Tic-tac-toe boards. Use circular bandages for the "O's" and small strip bandages for the "X's" 7. Picture frames 8. Snowflakes 9. Keepsake boxes 10. Totem poles

---

ACTIVITY 6.19.   WHAT IS IT?

This activity can serve as an innovative method for desensitizing children to medical equipment. But, as with any arts activity, the choice of subject matter should always be left to the children.

Therapeutic Goal: To promote coping with medical experiences through familiarization with and desensitization to medical equipment/supplies.

Age Group: School-age

Adult/Child Ratio: 1:1

Required Time: Can be broken into segments

Restrictions and Precautions: None

Materials:

☐ Digital camera

☐ Laptop computer with Photoshop or other computer program for viewing and printing images

☐ Computer printer

☐ Plain 8–1/2 × 11 inch paper

☐ Thin foam board or cardboard cut to 8–1/2 × 11 inches

☐ Hole punch (either one-, two-, or three-hole)

☐ Two or three binder rings

☐ Spray adhesive or rubber cement

Process

1. Take several ultra-close-up photographs of items found in a healthcare setting. Some suggestions include a bandage, a lead, or the drip chamber of an IV bag. Then photograph the items at a distance, to show the object in a recognizable format. Print out each image on a separate sheet of paper.

2. Show the children the close-up photographs and explain that they are images of items that can be found in a healthcare setting; ask them to guess what the items are.

3. Explain to the children that sometimes it is difficult to see the big picture, and that a single image may tell only part of the story.

4. After the children have guessed, correctly or incorrectly, what the item is, show them the image of it photographed from a distance.

5. Ask the children to identify other items in their environment that might be interesting to photograph close-up.

6. For each item identified, discuss different ways to position the camera to create visual interest.

7. Demonstrate how to use the camera.

8. Allow each child to take a series of photographs of the items, from distances of about 3 inches, 6 inches, and 12 inches. Children who are unable to take photographs themselves, or who can take only some of them, can give an adult specific directions regarding angle, distance, and so on, so that the adult can take the photographs as the child wants. A digital camera makes it possible for the adult to verify whether the child's intention was captured.

9. Once shooting is complete, download the photographs to the computer.

10. Using Photoshop or another similar computer program, print each image on a separate sheet of paper.

11. Go to an area with adequate ventilation and use spray adhesive or rubber cement to adhere each photograph to a piece of foam or cardboard.

12. Upon your return, help the children punch at least two holes, spaced at least 4 inches apart, at the top of each mounted photograph.

13. Help the children arrange their series of photographs in sequence, from the closest up to the farthest away; insert binder rings to hold them together.

14. View the finished book together, and encourage the children to share it with staff, family, and friends.

Note. Adapted from: Rollins, J. (2004). *Arts activities for children at bedside.* Washington, DC: WVSA arts connection.

CHAPTER 7

TENSION RELEASE

Injury, illness, and pain are major stressors for children, and medical treatments produce even greater stress. Play is one of the most powerful and effective means of reducing stress for children. It is a natural activity that connotes normalization for the pediatric patient and, thus, makes learning and adaptation possible. Play can be a diversion for distancing from a stressful event. It also can be an outlet for expressing emotions and an opportunity for processing and dealing with stressful events. All of these aspects of play activities make them valuable tools for tension release.

The activities in this chapter are designed to reduce tension by providing acceptable outlets for anger and aggression. Supplemental activities for self-expression and pain management may be found in Chapters 2 and 12, respectively.

Courtesy of Steven Koress Photography

LIST OF ACTIVITIES

Activity 7.1 Aggression Play with Blocks	Activity 7.9 Quiet-the-Scream Machine
Activity 7.2 Baby Rhythm Band	Activity 7.10 Snowball Fight
Activity 7.3 Battling Bad Cells	Activity 7.11 Target Practice
Activity 7.4 Bread Dough Magnets	Activity 7.12 Tear Away Tension
Activity 7.5 Butter Me Up	Activity 7.13 Tennis Anyone?
Activity 7.6 Foil Sculpture	Activity 7.14 That's the Way the Ball Bounces
Activity 7.7 Mad About Medicine	Activity 7.15 Tin Can Drums
Activity 7.8 Punch Pillows	Activity 7.16 Volcanic Eruption

Coping with the Stress of Illness

It is important to look at how children cope with illness, for several reasons (Ryan-Wenger, 1996). First, there is a positive relationship between coping processes and illness outcomes. Second, empirical evidence shows that coping strategies are learned and, therefore, are amenable to change. Finally, if coping strategies are learned (unlike coping *styles*, which are fairly stable personality traits), ineffective coping may be considered a risk factor, and thus preventative as well as palliative interventions can be implemented.

Ryan-Wenger's (1996) research synthesis found that social support was the most commonly reported coping strategy for children dealing with the stress of illness. Stressor modification was the second most commonly identified coping strategy, which included taking control or direct action against the stressor. In some instances, taking control was not associated with a positive outcome. Regarding age, cognitive strategies such as distraction, negative thinking, and problem solving, as well as social support, passive adherence, and relaxation, increased with age. As might be expected in the context of cognitive development theory, young children used primarily behavioral strategies, behavioral distraction, and ventilating feelings, as opposed to cognitive strategies.

Research with primarily healthy children indicates that boys tend to use aggressive behavior and physical activity more often than girls, and girls use social support and emotional expression more often than boys (Sharrer & Ryan-Wenger, 1991). In regard to children coping with illness-related stressors, findings show that boys more frequently than girls use cognitive restructuring and self-blame (Spirito, Stark, Gil, & Tyc, 1995), attempts to control (Savedra & Tesler, 1981), distraction, and food or drink (Tesler, Wegner, Savedra, Gibbons, & Ward, 1981). On the other hand, girls more frequently than boys use emotional regulation and social support (Spirito et al., 1995), information seeking (Savedra & Tesler, 1981), and the application of heat or cold as coping strategies (Tesler et al.). In five of the studies in Ryan-Wenger's synthesis of coping strategies of children with acute or chronic illness, no gender differences in the use of coping strategies were reported (1996).

Aggressive behavior was number 12 of 15 in the order of frequency of use (Ryan-Wenger, 1996). Of the 32 studies examined, 4 studies indicated aggressive activities as a coping strategy. Asarnow, Carlson, and Guthrie (1987) reported that depressed children with conduct disorders used physical aggression more often than nondepressed children. Not surprisingly, hospitalized children were reported to use resistive behaviors, hostility, and protest (Barnes, Bandak, & Beardslee, 1990). Blount et al. (1989) identified demonstrative distress (e.g., screaming, verbal resistance) in children with cancer during bone marrow aspiration. As mentioned in the Introduction, coping strategies may not always produce positive results. For example, Grey, Cameron, and Thurber (1991) found that yelling by children with diabetes was associated with poor adaptation.

Aggression

Aggressive behavior is a symptom of stress. Children's aggression is associated with many factors, among them poor parental practices, low socioeconomic status, and those of neurological, physiological, and genetic origin, which can be traced back to infancy, and even earlier. Maternal stress and tobacco use during pregnancy, and medical complications at birth, for example, are associated with a heightened risk of exhibiting above-average aggressive behaviors (World Health Organization, 2002). Others argue that aggression is a behavior learned from the environment, especially the family (Onyskiw & Hayduk, 2004), or from TV, movies, music, video games, or other media (American Academy of Pediatrics, 2000b). The frequency of physical aggression decreases from early childhood to adulthood, with the development of physical aggression peaking between 2 and 4 years of age (Tremblay, 2008). By the end of middle childhood, most children have learned to regulate their use of physical aggression. Girls tend to learn to use alternatives to physical aggression more quickly than boys.

In terms of children facing healthcare encounters, aggression is best defined as hostile, injurious, or destructive behavior or outlook, especially when caused by frustration (Merriam-Webster, n.d.). Vitiello, Behar, Hunt, Stoff, and Ricciuti (1990) explain that there are two types of aggression: *predatory* and *affective*. Each type has its own behavioral characteristics and outcomes, whose theoretical roots lie in neurobiological research in animals. Predatory aggression, for example, is a motivated, goal-oriented behavior that is executed with planning by the animal, with good motor control and with low autonomic nervous system (ANS) arousal. Possible behavioral characteristics of predatory aggression that the child might exhibit include (a) hiding aggressive acts, (b) having the ability to control own behaviors when aggressive, (c) being very careful to protect self from injury when aggressive, (d) planning of aggressive acts, and (e) stealing. Affective aggression, in contrast, is defensive in reaction to a threat. Characteristics of affective aggression are an unplanned attack, poor modulation of motor control, and high ANS arousal. Behavioral characteristics children with affective aggression may exhibit include (a) damaging their own property, (b) being completely out of control when aggressive, and (c) exposing themselves to injury and physical harm when aggressive. Affective aggression does not seem to have a purpose, is unplanned, and seemingly comes from out of nowhere.

The type of aggression more commonly seen in healthcare settings is affective. Children, especially young ones without the verbal skills to communicate what they are feeling, act out suddenly and aggressively when faced with frustration and situations beyond their control. Hospitalized children, therefore, need opportunities to ventilate and gain a better understanding of their feelings. Unfortunately, learning other methods of coping is frequently impeded by the hospital environment, with its often-rigid routines, the imbalance of power between children and healthcare professionals, and—with short lengths of stay—the lack of prolonged contacts needed to develop a trusting relationship with hospital personnel.

Although aggression is typically related to psychosocial issues, Turgay (2004) reminds us that at times the roots of aggression may be related to the child's condition. For example, aggression is sometimes seen in children with epilepsy. Problems may have several causes, such as fear, stress, or embarrassment about having epilepsy; or frustration with learning, and language difficulties. More complex factors include (a) malfunctions in areas of the brain that monitor and help control emotions and behavior, (b) an abnormality in those areas of the brain, (c) abnormal brain wave (epileptic) activity that disrupts normal brain function, or (d) antiepileptic drug therapy that alters the balance of chemical (neurotransmitters) in the brain that regulate behavior. Aggression in some children is also associated with endocrine diseases, such as diabetes or hyperthyroidism.

Hospitalized Children and Physical Release of Tension

The physical aspect of distress often surfaces as tension in the body. Distress may register as aggression, tight shoulders, stomach cramps, or cold, clammy palms. Heart and breathing rate increase and muscles are tense. Physically releasing pent-up tension is a method to restore a level of calm.

Children need safe ways to release tension. Combining the emotional with the physical is a powerful tool to break up the raw emotion in the child. This process can be profoundly cathartic.

Research by Ritchie, Caty, and Ellerton (1984) indicates that direct action is one of the most frequently used coping responses for hospitalized preschoolers during both low-stress and high-stress events. Study findings reveal that direct action behaviors for preschoolers include controlling, tension-reducing, and "attempting-to-protect-self-from-harm" behaviors. These behaviors reflect developmental concerns about autonomy and intrusion.

School-aged children are able to identify stressful events and their reactions to them. In a study by Ryan (1989), elementary school and junior high school students listed coping strategies that were analyzed by type, gender, and ages of the children. Physical exercise and aggressive motor activities were identified as common coping strategies of the children. Boys cited physical exercise activities more often than girls. Analyses of case studies of hospitalized children reveal that sick children also use active methods to reduce tension (Caty, Ellerton, & Ritchie, 1984). Clatworthy (1981) reported that interventions that allowed aggressive as well as other forms of play were therapeutic for school-aged children.

Research with adolescents also indicates that this age group uses physical activity as a means of coping with hospitalization and chronic illness (Patton, Ventura, & Savedra, 1986; Stevens, 1989). The amount of activity depended on illness limitations on this form of coping.

Special Considerations

Individual differences in coping strategies will be reflected in the type of activity a child chooses. Aggressive tension-reducing activities are not for every child. Other options may include activities in Chapter 2, for dealing with self-expression, and Chapter 12, for managing pain.

Adults need to feel comfortable with noise and aggressive acts directed at the materials used in these activities. Often, healthcare institutions are not responsive to such active means of children expressing themselves; therefore, an appropriate location for these activities within a healthcare setting should be considered. In addition, some activities involve messy play, so the setting should be appropriate in that regard as well.

These activities allow for active physical means for reducing tension, rather than taking a problem-solving approach to work toward solutions—that is, they offer outlets rather than solutions.

Activity Goals

All of the activities in this chapter provide the means for safe and acceptable opportunities for children to express anger and frustration, thereby allowing them to work off tension and stress. The activities also allow the children to regress in an acceptable way. This process, in turn, will promote the physical release of tension. The activities involve various materials, and all meet these same goals.

ACTIVITY 7.1.   AGGRESSION PLAY WITH BLOCKS

This activity is a simple, quick, and effective way to provide a physical outlet for children who are unwilling or cognitively unable to express their anger.

Therapeutic Goal: To promote the release of tension by providing an acceptable outlet for anger and frustration.

Age Group: Toddler/preschool/primary

Adult/Child Ratio: 1:1

Required Time: 10 minutes

Restrictions and Precautions: Avoid wooden blocks.

Materials:

☐ Lightweight blocks (cardboard, plastic, or foam)

☐ Ball

Process

1. Demonstrate how to build a tower with the blocks, stacking them one on top of another.

2. Share with the child something that makes you mad, such as, "I don't like it when I have to take medicine that tastes bad."

3. Immediately knock down the tower with your hand or by throwing the ball at it.

4. Encourage the child to rebuild the tower, assisting if necessary.

5. Ask the child what makes him or her angry.

6. When the child responds, immediately urge him or her to use the ball or his or her hand to knock the tower down. You may need to reinforce that this is acceptable and provide encouragement.

7. Repeat the activity, each time asking the child to name something else that evokes anger.

Variation

Let older children select an object, or draw something, to symbolize what makes them angry, and place it on top of the block tower before knocking it down.

ACTIVITY 7.2.   BABY RHYTHM BAND

The combination of hitting something and creating loud noise can be very satisfying for young children under stress.

Therapeutic Goal: To promote the release of tension by providing an acceptable outlet for anger and frustration.

Age Group: Toddler/preschool

Adult/Child Ratio: 1:3

Required Time: 10 minutes

Restrictions and Precautions: Stop the activity if children appear to become overstimulated. Do not conduct this activity with children who are hypersensitive to sound or touch.

Materials:

☐ CD player

☐ CDs with lively music	☐ Children's percussion instruments or items that can be used to make sounds (e.g., pie tins, heavy plastic spoons, rattles, bells)
☐ High chairs	

Process

1. If using high-chairs, arrange them in an arc, leaving enough space between each so that the children cannot accidentally strike another child sitting near them.

2. Seat the children in the high chairs or on the floor.

3. Start the music and give each child an instrument or noise-making object.

4. Demonstrate how to make noise with each instrument.

5. Use an instrument to follow the rhythm of the music, encouraging the children to use their instruments to play along with you.

6. Continue, changing the music and tempo to maintain interest; encourage body movement, clapping, and babbling or singing.

Variation

If the children are ambulatory, create a "marching band" to increase the physicality of the activity.

ACTIVITY 7.3.   BATTLING BAD CELLS

In this activity, a metaphor is created whereby germ cells or cancer cells are killed with medicine. The children design symbolic representations of "bad cells" and then shoot them down using syringes full of medicine (water), "melting" their images.

Therapeutic Goal: To promote the release of tension by providing an acceptable outlet for anger and frustration.	**Materials:**
	☐ 50ml syringes, or squirt guns
Age Group: Preschool/primary/school-age	☐ Water
Adult/Child Ratio: 1:8	☐ Plastic bottles with small necks (1-liter soda bottles work well)
Required Time: Varies according to the number of children playing	☐ Ping-Pong balls or similarly sized Styrofoam balls
Restrictions and Precautions: Set explicit limits regarding where children may squirt water, and supervise closely. Be sure to clean up any water on the floor.	☐ Water-soluble markers
	☐ Masking tape

Process

1. Fill the bottles with enough water to weight them.

2. Discuss how germs and/or cancer cells make our bodies sick and how medicine kills them and makes us better.

3. Ask children to draw representations on the balls of what they think germs or cancer cells look like.

4. Line up the bottles on a table and place a ball on the neck of each.

5. Use masking tape to draw a line on the floor, in front of the table, to indicate where children should stand. Make it close enough so that they can successfully squirt the balls with water.

6. With the children standing at the designated line, give them syringes or other squirting device to shoot water at the balls, until they knock them off the bottles.

7. Allow the children to continue squirting the "germs" until the images drawn on them begin to "melt" away.

8. If conducting the activity with an even number of children (four or more), divide the group into teams and play as a relay race.

Variation

Help younger children identify things that "bug" them. Place small, inexpensive plastic insects (bugs) on a large rimmed baking sheet and let children shoot at them with syringes or a squirt gun. Let the children keep any insects they move with their water stream (as long as they're not at risk of choking).

ACTIVITY 7.4.   BREAD DOUGH MAGNETS

Anyone who has baked bread from scratch will attest to the therapeutic benefits of kneading and pounding the dough. The aroma of freshly baked bread is an added bonus.

Therapeutic Goal: To promote the release of tension by providing an acceptable outlet for anger and frustration.

Age Group: Pre-teen/adolescent

Adult/Child Ratio: 1:10

Required Time: Two 30-minute sessions

Restrictions and Precautions: Take glue precautions.

Materials:

☐ Measuring cups
☐ Bowls
☐ Salt
☐ Water
☐ Flour
☐ Paintbrushes
☐ Cookie sheet, covered with tin foil
☐ Acrylic paints (optional)
☐ Acrylic polymer or other sealer
☐ Scissors
☐ Magnetic tape
☐ Glue

Process

1. Provide each child with a bowl containing 1 part salt, 1–1/2 parts water, and 4 parts flour.

2. Show the children how to knead the dough until it is firm and smooth.

3. Have the children mold the dough into any form they desire. Explain how to attach one piece of dough to another by brushing a small amount of water over the areas to be adhered and pressing the pieces together.

4. Give the children tools to create designs in the dough.

5. Place the dough forms on the cookie sheet and bake in a 350-degree oven until brown; or allow to air-dry for at least two days.

6. Let the children paint their forms, if desired.

7. After the paint has dried, apply sealer.

8. Instruct the children to cut a strip of magnetic tape to fit the back of their forms, and glue them in place.

Variation

Bake bread to eat. In addition to the therapeutic benefit of pounding the dough, the enticing aroma of freshly baked bread will create a more homelike atmosphere.

ACTIVITY 7.5.   BUTTER ME UP

Some baseball players, golfers, skiers, and other athletes shake their hands as a method to reduce tension before they play.

Therapeutic Goal: To promote the release of tension by providing an acceptable outlet for anger and frustration.

Age Group: Preschool/primary

Adult/Child Ratio: 1:6

Required Time: 15 minutes

Restrictions and Precautions: Check for dietary restrictions.

Materials:

☐ Small, clear, empty plastic container, with lid

☐ Heavy whipping cream

☐ Small paper cups.

☐ Plastic or paper plates

☐ Muffins, toast, crackers, or similar foodstuffs

☐ Plastic knives or tongue depressors

Process

1. Pour the cream into the container, leaving some space at the top.

2. Have the children take turns holding the container with both hands, and shaking it vigorously.

3. Encourage the children to continue until chunks of butter form, approximately 15 to 20 minutes.

4. Provide each of the children with a paper cup, and help them spoon some butter into it.

5. Allow the children to pick a foodstuff and help them spread it with butter.

6. Invite the children to eat and enjoy.

ACTIVITY 7.6. FOIL SCULPTURE

This activity can be enhanced by asking the children to sculpt a representation of something or someone that makes them feel angry and frustrated. Invite them to tell about what they have made and allow them to pound or crush it at the end of the activity, if they wish. Foil sculpture can also be used as a metaphor for things in life that change.

Therapeutic Goal: To promote the release of tension by providing an acceptable outlet for anger and frustration.

Age Group: School-age/adolescent

Adult/Child Ratio: 1:8

Required Time: 30 minutes

Restrictions and Precautions: None

Materials:

☐ Heavy aluminum foil

☐ Scissors

☐ Pictures of sculpture

Process

1. Provide each child with a large piece of foil.

2. To introduce the activity, show the children pictures of various sculptures, including a person, an animal, and an object.

3. Demonstrate how to mold a piece of foil into the shape of a person by making three cuts in a square of foil. Crumple some foil into a ball for the head. Crumple more foil for the arms and legs; twist the trunk slightly.

4. Then show the children how you can smooth out the creases in the foil and reshape it into something entirely different.

5. Invite the children to make their own creations with their pieces of foil (Figure Activity 7.6-1). Encourage them to experiment with different forms, poses, and positions so that they have more opportunities to reshape the foil.

Figure Activity 7.6-1. **Foil Sculpture**
Courtesy of Steven Koress Photography.

ACTIVITY 7.7.   MAD ABOUT MEDICINE

This is a cardboard variation of an old-fashioned slingshot. Using medicine cups as a symbolic representation of medical treatment can serve as a springboard for a discussion about feelings related to illness and hospitalization.

Therapeutic goal: To promote the release of tension by providing an acceptable outlet for anger and frustration.

Age Group: School-age

Adult/Child Ratio: 1:8

Required Time: 30 minutes

Restrictions and Precautions: Closely supervise children when engaging in this activity. Discontinue if children become overstimulated.

Materials:

☐ Two empty toilet paper rolls (per child), or cardboard tubes of similar size

☐ Scissors
☐ Mailing tape
☐ Plastic wrap
☐ Rubber band
☐ Paper clip
☐ Markers
☐ Ping-Pong balls or large marshmallows
☐ Medicine cups

Process

1. Give each child two toilet paper rolls and show them how to cut one in half lengthwise.

2. Help the children tape the tube back together again, making it just narrow enough to fit into the other tube.

3. Give the children crayons or markers to decorate tubes their tubes, if they wish.

4. Show the children how to tape plastic wrap to one end of the narrow tube, covering the opening completely.

5. Tell the children to insert the narrow tube into the larger one.

6. Tell the children to place two paper clips on one end of each of the tubes, across from each other (Figure Activity 7.7-1).

7. Partially insert the narrow tube into the larger one, with the paper clips of each tube on the opposite ends.

8. Attach one end of the rubber band to the paper clip on the larger tube; attach the second end to the opposing paper clip on the smaller tube.

9. To make a target, stack the medicine cups in a pyramid shape.

10. Place a Ping-Pong ball or marshmallow inside the tube.

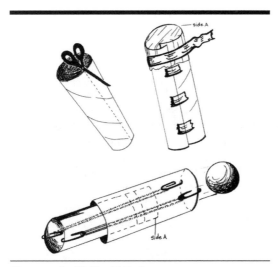

Figure Activity 7.7-1. Mad About Medicine

11. Demonstrate how to pull back the inner tube then release it to launch the ball or marshmallow toward the pyramid of medicine cups, trying to knock it down.

12. Have the children take turns building and knocking down medicine cup pyramids or other targets.

Note. Adapted from Thomas, J., & Thomas, D. (2002). *Kid concoctions and contraptions.* Strongsville, OH: Kid Concoctions Company.

ACTIVITY 7.8.   PUNCH PILLOWS

This activity is best used to redirect the behavior of children who, when angry, are destructive or physically aggressive to other people.

Therapeutic Goal: To promote the release of tension by providing an acceptable outlet for anger and frustration.	**Restrictions and Precautions:** Take marker precautions.
Age Group: Preschool/primary/school-age	**Materials:**
Adult/Child Ratio: 1:8	☐ White pillowcases (one per child)
	☐ Fabric paint, fabric markers, or fabric crayons
Required Time: 45 minutes	☐ Pillow (one per child)

Process

1. Discuss the emotion of anger with the children. Ask them to think of the types of events connected with being sick that make them angry (e.g., shots, pain, bad-tasting medications, loss of control).

2. Encourage the children to identify how they personally react when angry. Help them explore which responses are acceptable and which are inappropriate.

3. Have the children draw or paint on their pillowcase a representation of what angers them the most.

4. Provide each of the children with a pillow to put in their case.

5. Encourage the children to punch or hit the pillow when they are angry and/or feeling out of control.

ACTIVITY 7.9.   QUIET-THE-SCREAM MACHINE

Screaming at others is not a behavior that one would suggest to children as a healthy means to release anger; it is, nevertheless, what many do—even some adults scream to vent their anger and frustration. We endeavor to assist children in learning more positive ways than screaming at others to express anger, and the Quiet-the-Scream Machine can serve as an intermediary step toward achieving that goal. Giving children the opportunity to purposefully choose, construct, and take an alternate approach by screaming into the "machine" to modulate their anger may help them gain a sense of control and move toward even more socially acceptable behaviors.

Therapeutic Goal: To promote the release of tension by providing an acceptable outlet for anger and frustration.

Age Group: Preschool/primary/school-age

Adult/Child Ratio: 1:1

Required Time: To make: 15 minutes

Restrictions and Precautions: Encourage those involved in the care of the child to support the use of the "machine" when indicated.

Materials:

☐ Cardboard shoebox, with a hole the size of a toilet paper roll cut in the top

☐ Cotton, tissue, or other sound-absorbent materials

☐ Empty toilet paper roll or cardboard tube of similar size

☐ Scissors

☐ Duct tape

☐ Stickers

Process

1. Ask the child to stuff the box with the sound-absorbing material.

2. Have the child partially insert the empty toilet paper roll into the hole.

3. Assist the child, as needed, to cover the entire box with several layers of duct tape, making sure that the toilet paper roll is well secured.

4. Let the child decorate the box with stickers.

5. Encourage the child to scream into the box whenever he or she feels like doing so.

ACTIVITY 7.10.   SNOWBALL FIGHT

Even adults enjoy taking part in this activity. It is an excellent way to simultaneously relieve tension while sharing laughter.

Therapeutic Goal: To promote the release of tension by providing an acceptable outlet for anger and frustration.

Age Group: School-age/adolescent

Adult/Child Ratio: 1:12

Required Time: 20 minutes

Restrictions and Precautions: Set explicit limitations with aggressive children and stop the "fight" sooner, if necessary.

Materials:

☐ White paper

☐ Pen

Process

1. Give the children each two pieces of paper and ask them to write down something that makes them frustrated or angry on each.

2. Have the children crumple the paper into "snowballs."

3. Explain to the children that they are going to have a snowball fight, and explain the safety rules.

4. Call out, "snowball fight!" and allow the children to throw the paper balls at each other. Tell them they can pick snowballs off the floor and continue throwing them until the time is up.

5. When one to two minutes have elapsed, ask each child pick up the two snowballs closest to them and take turns reading aloud what is written on them.

6. As each snowball is read, ask the children whether they, too, have felt frustrated or angered by what was described on the paper and, if so, how they coped with it. Help the children identify more positive coping strategies, where indicated.

ACTIVITY 7.11. TARGET PRACTICE

This is simply a safe version of the traditional dart game.

Therapeutic Goal: To promote the release of tension by providing an acceptable outlet for anger and frustration.	**Materials:**
	☐ Scissors
	☐ Self-adhesive fastener tape
Age Group: School-age	☐ Ping-Pong balls
Adult/Child Ratio: 1:4	☐ Round objects in various sizes (e.g., plates, bowls)
Required Time: 1 hour	☐ Pencil and markers
Restrictions and Precautions: Take scissors and marker precautions.	☐ Poster board

Process

1. Cut thin strips out of one side of the fastener tape and adhere it to the balls, covering them generously.

2. Engage the children in a discussion about things that make them angry or frustrated.

3. Ask them to identify three to five things about their illness or care that anger or frustrate them, or cause them to feel stressed, and to rank them according to degree of emotion.

4. Give the children the round objects to serve as templates. Tell them to draw on the poster board the same number of concentric circles as anger-inducing things they have identified.

5. Ask the children to cut small squares out of the remaining side of the self-adhesive fastener tape and affix them to the target, covering it generously.

6. Instruct the children to write or draw in each of the circles a representation of one of the things that makes them angry, frustrated, or stressed. Tell them it is okay to draw over the fastener tape.

7. Suggest to the children that they color the remaining space in the bands around each picture, including the tape in it, each a different color.

8. Write a numerical value in each band, with the highest number in the center circle.

9. Lean the targets against a wall and have the children throw the balls, aiming at the circle with the greatest point value, which symbolizes what bothers them most.

Variation

Omit the fastener tape and laminate the target and let the children throw wads of wet toilet paper at it.

ACTIVITY 7.12. TEAR AWAY TENSION

There is something very satisfying about ripping things up into little pieces. Children engage in this activity with surprising vigor, and are quite gleeful at the end when they get to throw the paper in the air.

Therapeutic Goal: To promote the release of tension by providing an acceptable outlet for anger and frustration.

Age Group: Preschool/primary/school-age

Adult/Child Ratio: 1:10

Required Time: 20 minutes

Restrictions and Precautions: Limit the size of the group when engaging in this activity with children who have poor impulse control or become overstimulated easily.

Materials:

☐ Newspaper, old phone books, and/or paper of all kinds—ideally, reclaimed from the recycle bin

Process

1. Have the children sit in a circle on the floor.
2. Obtain a commitment from the children to help clean up when the activity is completed.
3. Lead a discussion about feelings, specifically the types of things that make them feel frustrated, sad, or angry.
4. Explain that the activity is a good way to release negative feelings.
5. Provide each child with paper and encourage them to think of the things that make them feel bad while they tear the paper into small pieces. When they are finished, ask them to pile the pieces in the center of the circle.
6. Once a substantial pile of paper has accumulated, lead the group in throwing the paper in the air.
7. Allow play to continue as long as the children remain interested.
8. Work as a group to pick up all of the torn paper and throw it into the trash container.

ACTIVITY 7.13.   TENNIS ANYONE?

This is a good choice for children who need to get out of bed and moving. If there is only one child participating, an adult will need to play.

Therapeutic Goal: To promote the release of tension by providing an acceptable outlet for anger and frustration.

Age Group: School-age

Adult/Child Ratio: 1:2

Required Time: 30 minutes

Restrictions and Precautions: Take balloon precautions. Monitor children for signs of over-stimulation.

Materials:

☐ Plastic can lids, 4–5 inches in diameter (one per player)

☐ Tongue depressors (one per player)

☐ Duct tape

☐ Long strip of gauze bandage (3 to 5 feet long)

☐ Balloon

Process

1. Make the "racquets" by taping each plastic can lid to a tongue depressor, leaving enough of the tongue depressor exposed so the children can grasp it while they are playing.
2. Make the net by tying or taping each end of the gauze to one of the chairs. Blow up the balloon.
3. Spread the chairs apart as far as possible.
4. Position the players on opposite sides of the net. The adult can play if there is only one child.
5. Play the game the same as in tennis. Players use their racquets to hit the balloon over the "net" to the other player, who must hit it back. If the balloon hits the floor when it is in play, the other player gets the point.
6. Continue play until one player earns 11 to 15 points.

ACTIVITY 7.14.   THAT'S THE WAY THE BALL BOUNCES

This mixture uses the same ingredients as the classic recipe for flubber (also known as gluep), but in different proportions that yield a less malleable consistency. The classic recipe for flubber (provided below under "Additional Recipes for Messy Mixtures") is better suited when the goal of the activity is to simply manipulate the mixture.

Therapeutic Goal: To promote the release of tension by providing an acceptable outlet for anger and frustration.

Age Group: School-age

Adult/Child Ratio: 1:4

Required Time: 30 minutes

Restrictions and Precautions: Set explicit limitations for the children—in particular, to bounce rather than throw the ball. Remove all breakables from the area where children will be playing. Dispose of the mixture in the trash, not down a sink.

Materials:

- ☐ Large pitcher
- ☐ 1 quart water
- ☐ 1 tablespoon Borax
- ☐ Large wooden spoon
- ☐ Plastic basin
- ☐ Food coloring
- ☐ Plastic spoon
- ☐ White glue
- ☐ Basin of cold water
- ☐ Plastic bag with zipper-lock closure

Process

1. Stir the water and Borax together in the pitcher; allow the mixture to sit for several minutes.

2. Fill the bowl 3/4 of the way with the Borax mixture and add a few drops of food coloring.

3. Have the children take turns stirring the mixture as you add the white glue in a thin, steady stream.

4. When a large stringy mass forms on the spoon, help the children remove the mass and drop it into the container of cold water.

5. Remove the mass from the water and divide it between the children.

6. Tell the children to dry their hands thoroughly before squeezing the mass for several minutes to remove any air bubbles.

7. Instruct the children to roll the mixture into a ball and then bounce it, to see how high it can go. Allow the children to continue to play as long as they remain interested.

8. Store the balls in the plastic bag.

Flubber

Additional Recipes for Messy Mixtures

2/3 cup warm water in a 1 cup measuring cup

1–1/2 teaspoon powdered Borax

4 drops food coloring

3/4 cup warm water

1 cup white glue

Mixing bowl

Wooden spoons

1. Add the Borax and food coloring to the water in the measuring cup and stir.

2. Combine the remaining water and glue in the bowl and stir. Pour the Borax mixture into the glue mixture.

3. Instruct the children to gently blend and turn the mixture with their hands, until a tablespoon or less of water remains.

Oobleck

1–1/2 cups cornstarch

Food coloring

1/2 cup water or more

1. Place the cornstarch in a bowl.

2. Mix the food coloring into the water.

3. Gradually stir the liquid into the cornstarch. Stir well, adding additional small amounts of water or cornstarch as needed, until the mixture separates when you move your finger through it and then melds together again.

Glarch

1 cup white school glue

Food coloring

1/2 cup Sta-Flo liquid laundry starch

1. Stir the food coloring into the glue.

2. Place the starch in a mixing bowl, slowly pour in the glue mixture, and stir with a wooden spoon.

3. Allow the mixture to set for approximately five minutes, or until the liquid starch is absorbed.

4. Remove the mixture from the bowl and knead.

ACTIVITY 7.15.   TIN CAN DRUMS

Banging on percussion instruments is an excellent way to release physical tension. In addition to giving the child an opportunity to pound on something, the "drums" constructed for this activity also provide the added gratification of making noise.

Therapeutic Goal: To promote the release of tension by providing an acceptable outlet for anger and frustration.

Age Group: Preschool (with assistance)/primary

Adult/Child Ratio: 1:4

Required Time: 30 minutes, plus advanced preparation

Restrictions and Precautions: None

Materials:

- ☐ Large 5-pound (preferred) cans with plastic lids (1 per child)
- ☐ Construction paper
- ☐ Additional 2-inch wide strips of construction paper (one per child), cut 1 inch longer than the length of the circumference of the can
- ☐ Scissors
- ☐ Tape or glue
- ☐ Cotton
- ☐ Dowel rods, 8 inches long (two per child)
- ☐ Cloth, cut into two 3-inch squares per child
- ☐ Rubber bands
- ☐ Markers (optional)

Process

1. For each can, cut a piece of construction paper 2 inches wider than its circumference.

2. Give each child a can and a piece of construction paper cut to fit it.

3. Instruct the children to wrap their cans in construction paper and secure it using tape or glue.

4. Ask the children to place the lids on their cans.

5. Demonstrate how to fringe a strip of paper, while the children follow along.

6. Show the children how to glue the fringed strip of paper around the top of their cans.

7. Help the children place a wad of cotton on one end of each of the dowel rods. Cover the cotton with a cloth and secure it to the dowel rods using rubber bands.

8. Allow the children to decorate the drums with markers, if they wish.

9. Encourage the children to play their "drums" either to accompany music or develop their own rhythms; or suggest they simply pound on them when they need a release.

Variation

Older children may make more substantial drums using small barrels and a rubber chamois for the drum head.

ACTIVITY 7.16.   VOLCANIC ERUPTION

A common classroom science experiment is to demonstrate how volcanic eruptions occur. This messy form of play is just as effective to facilitate the release of tension and destructive urges in a constructive manner. If desired, you can also use this activity as a springboard for discussing feelings that make children so angry that they feel as if they could "explode."

Therapeutic Goal: To promote the release of tension by providing an acceptable outlet for anger and frustration.

Age Group: School-age

Adult/Child Ratio: 1:1

Required Time: 45 minutes

Restrictions and Precautions: The chemical reaction in this activity is not dangerous; nevertheless, closely supervise the child in case of spillage.

Materials:

☐ Red food coloring

☐ Vinegar

☐ Measuring cup for liquids

☐ Small plastic soda bottle

☐ Funnel

☐ Baking soda

☐ Corn meal or clean sand

☐ Large platter or tray

☐ Paintbrush

☐ White glue

Process

1. In the measuring cup, combine 1 cup of vinegar with a few drops of red food coloring; set aside.

2. Using the funnel, place 1 tablespoon of baking soda into the soda bottle.

3. Help the child mound cornmeal in the center of the platter.

4. To make the volcano, have the child paint the sides of the soda bottle with glue, avoiding the mouth of the bottle, which will serve as the "crater."

5. Instruct the child to place the bottle into the center of the cornmeal mound.

6. Have the child make the mountain by packing the cornmeal around the bottle, so that only the bottle opening shows. Be sure no cornmeal gets into the bottle.

7. Give the child the sugar cubes to build small houses or igloos at the base of the volcano.

8. To make the volcano erupt, help the child pour (using the funnel, if needed) the vinegar into the bottle opening. A red foam will appear and eventually overflow and run down the mountain, destroying the sugar-cube houses in its path.

Variation

A satisfying "explosion" can be produced by letting children drop a Mento candy into a small bottle of Coke. The instantaneous eruption of foam can serve as a metaphor for a surge of emotion.

For more ideas, see Bright Ideas: Quick Kinesthetic Outlets for Anger and Aggression (Box Activity 7.16-1).

BOX ACTIVITY 7.16-1. BRIGHT IDEAS: QUICK KINESTHETIC OUTLETS FOR ANGER AND AGGRESSION	• Fill a surgical glove with prepared gelatin, Play-Doh, or flubber (see Activity 7.14) and tie the opening securely. Give to children to squeeze and manipulate during times of stress. • After removing their shoes or slippers, encourage children to stomp on large sheets of bubble wrap. • Provide gross-motor activities for younger ambulatory children. • Play the Don't Break the Ice game. • Purchase Bop Bags and give to children to punch. • Blow bubbles using purchased bubble solution; let the children pop the bubbles by shooting them with rubber bands. Children unable to shoot rubber bands can pop the bubbles by stomping on them. • Make stress balls using a funnel to fill a balloon with birdseed or salt; tie the opening securely closed. • Give children golf tees and a toy hammer or mallet to pound them into Styrofoam; or purchase toy pounding benches for them to use. • Allow children to throw wads of wet tissue at targets such as a picture of something they don't like. When outdoors, they can use balloons filled with water. • Make "aggression cookies" using homemade or store-bought oatmeal cookie mix. As children beat the batter, ask them to name everything that frustrates them or makes them angry.

CHAPTER 8

HUMOR

Children experience a variety of stressors when faced with illness, disability, or hospitalization, and the child who possesses a variety of coping strategies will be the most successful in adapting to these stressors. There is growing recognition among healthcare professionals that humor may be one of those strategies (Christie & Moore, 2005).

Buxman (1991) describes humor as an esthetic means of expression that increases a person's well-being, both physically and psychologically. Therapeutic humor, according to the Association for Applied and Therapeutic Humor (AATH, 2000), is

Courtesy of Steven Koress Photography

> any intervention that promotes health and wellness by stimulating a playful discovery, expression, or appreciation of the absurdity or incongruity of life's situations. This intervention may enhance health or be used as a complementary treatment of illness to facilitate healing or coping, whether physical, emotional, cognitive, social, or spiritual. (p. 1)

LIST OF ACTIVITIES

Activity 8.1 A Mona Lisa Smile	Activity 8.13 Leafy-Locks Pots (Chia Pet Wannabes)
Activity 8.2 Blister Blooper*	Activity 8.14 Leaking Bottle Trick
Activity 8.3 Bodacious Bookends	Activity 8.15 License Plate
Activity 8.4 Bogus Baby Burgers	Activity 8.16 Magic Realism à la Magritte
Activity 8.5 Crack-Up Collages	Activity 8.17 Master of Disguise
Activity 8.6 Dancing Raisins	Activity 8.18 Med Libs*
Activity 8.7 Don't Cry Over Spilled . . .	Activity 8.19 Mirth Mobiles
Activity 8.8 Flamboyant Flamingos and Other IV Pump Pals	Activity 8.20 Mirth-Aid Kit
Activity 8.9 Funglasses*	Activity 8.21 Pop-Up Card Critters*
Activity 8.10 Goofy Gadget Game	Activity 8.22 Puke Cookies*
Activity 8.11 Hilarious Headbands*	Activity 8.23 Steve Martin Meets Healthcare
Activity 8.12 Kooky Cookie Puppets*	Activity 8.24 Stick a Smile on Your Face

Note: Asterisk (*) denotes that the activity is available on the CD that accompanies this book.

Benefits of Humor

Research supports the use of humor for patients ranging from pediatric to geriatric, and as a tool to help healthcare providers cope in stressful surroundings. Extensive theoretical, anecdotal, and scientific literature has addressed the benefits of humor in the psychological and physiological healing process (Franzini, 2002; Klein, 2003). Benefits include reduced tension; improved circulation; muscle relaxation; and increased release of endorphins, T-cells, natural killer cells, and immunoglobulin (Berk, Felten, Tan, Bittman, & Westengard, 2001; Dowling, Hockenberry, & Gregory, 2003). Berk (2008) summarizes the benefits of humor, mirth, and laughter in Table 8.1.

Humor is classified as a nursing intervention to help children and others cope with illness and hospitalization (Frankenfield, 1996). Dowling's (2002) summary of the nursing research suggests that humor can be used as a complement to other strategies within a plan of care, to (a) establish warm, interpersonal relationships; (b) relieve anxiety, stress, and tension; (c) release

Table 8.1 Summary of the Effects of Humor, Mirth, and Laughter

Term	Definition	Findings
Humor	Cognitive perception of playful incongruity	• Reduces stress, anxiety and tension • Promotes psychological well-being • Raises self-esteem • Improves interpersonal interactions and relationships • Builds group identity, solidarity, and cohesiveness • Enhances memory (for humorous information)
Mirth	Positive emotion that accompanies humor	• Increases pain tolerance • Elevates mood • Increases hope, energy, and vigor • Counteracts depression and anxiety • Enhances creative thinking and problem solving • Increases friendliness and helpfulness
Laughter	Respiratory-vocal behavior that communicates mirth to others	• Intensifies mirth • Is contagious (induces mirth in others) • Increases interpersonal attraction and closeness • Exercises respiratory muscles

Note. Adapted from Berk, R. (2008). *What everyone should know about humor & laughter.* Retrieved from www.aath .org/documents/AATH-WhatWeKnowREVISED.pdf.

anger, hostility, and aggression in a socially acceptable manner; (d) allow the child or family to momentarily avoid or deny painful or frightening feelings; (e) manage shame and embarrassment; (f) facilitate learning; and (g) enhance immune function (p. 127).

Developmental Aspects of Humor

McGhee (1979) proposed developmental stages of humor, which he linked to Piagetian stages of cognitive development (see Table 8.2. Stages of Children's Humor Development in Relation to Piaget's Cognitive Stages). Although chronological ages may vary among individuals from one stage to another, the sequence is thought to be identical for all. Most researchers agree that humor is related to comprehending (humor reaction) or producing (humor creation) an "incongruity." The term *incongruity* refers to the simultaneous, or almost simultaneous, occurrence of normally incompatible elements (i.e., elements that are not ordinarily associated with each other in a given context (Bariaud, 1989).

In the sensorimotor stage objects do not fit the schema into which they are being assimilated; thus, they are temporarily used in a way that differs from an ordinary one, such as in a game of peekaboo. A baby looks for the puppet on one side of the crib and then erupts in laughter when it unexpectedly shows up on the other side. The young toddler often finds humor in observing the incongruous actions of objects, people, and animals, such as a talking telephone, a whimsical mime, or a dancing purple dinosaur (Dowling, 2002). During the preoperational stage, the child's ability to represent objects and events invokes new and broader uses of humor. Although the presence of objects may continue to play an important role, the verbal statement alone can create humor. After mastering a new word or object, children play with it, assign it new meaning, and often derive enjoyment from incongruous labeling (Bariaud, 1989). A pot may become a funny hat, for example. At about age 3, children begin to develop conceptual categories and take delight in distorting a familiar concept, and humor is centered on violations of conceptual representations. "Thus, a picture of a bicycle with square wheels, or an elephant sitting on a tree limb, may be humorous to a child" (Dowling, 2002, p. 126). The humor found in the Doctor Seuss books is very popular at this stage.

Children during the stage of concrete operations can consider logical relationships between events and solve problems from their experiences. Changes in humor during this stage are marked by the mastery of humor conventions and the search for an underlying meaning—with

Table 8.2 Stages of Children's Humor Development in Relation to Piaget's Cognitive Stages

Stage of Cognitive Development	Characteristics of Stage	Proposed Stage of Humor Development
Sensorimotor 0–2 years	• Object perception • Object permanence • Relationships between object and self	• Uses incongruity in play behaviors • Uses incongruous actions of objects, people, and animals
Preoperational Thought: Egocentric 2–4 years	• Views life from own perspective • Conversations with self • Perceptual problem solving	• Verbalizes incongruities • Creates incongruous labels for objects and events • Makes incongruous actions toward objects
Preoperational Thought: Intuitive 4–7 years	• Social/communicative conversations • Conceptual problem solving • Semilogical thinking	• Appreciates incongruities related to appearance and verbal expressions • Appreciates and creates nonsense words and pictures, rhymed sequences, and unexpected pronunciations of words
Concrete Operations 7–11 years	• Logical reasoning of concrete problems • More objective view of life • Emergence of cooperation and mutual respect	• Understands more abstract and implied incongruities • Searches for multiple meanings • Able to explain the reason for their amusement
Formal Operations 11–15 years	• Hypothetical and abstract reasoning • Transition from idealism to realism	• Appreciates the complex structure of humor and the motivations behind its use

Note. Adapted from McGhee, P. (1979). *Humor: Its origin and development.* San Francisco: W.H. Freeman.

that meaning often being somewhat shocking. Children in this stage may respond seriously to riddles, tell jokes without a punch line, or reject the intentional distortion of objects and events in cartoons (Bergen 1998). Children acquire deductive and inductive reasoning during the formal operations stage, which enhances their ability to understand, create, and explain the complexities of humor. They enjoy anecdotes and spontaneous wit. Although more sophisticated types of humor develop, characteristics of earlier stages of humor, such as an especially clever pun, remain to some extent into adulthood.

Selected Methods of Implementing Humor in Hospitals

In addition to incorporating humor into interactions with children, hospitals have developed special programs that feature humor to help children cope with the stresses of hospitalization and illness. Magic and clown-doctor programs are two such programs.

Hart and Walton (2010) describe magicians' integration of humor into a hospital magician-in-residence program. Magicians use tricks that incorporate two of the fundamental principles of comedy: surprise and humorous self-deprecation on the part of the comedian:

Magic

> From red balls popping out of the patient's hand to a vanishing silk appearing in the sleeve of a nurse, unexpected occurrences evoke surprise and laughter. The comedic situation is enhanced when the magician denies that any of this will work because he is not particularly good at magic. (p. 12)

Benefits of Magic. Magic can be used as a vehicle to motivate patients and reduce the frustration they often experience due to the repetitive nature of rehabilitation exercises (Healing of Magic, 2008; Kaufman, 2002). After evaluation by an occupational therapist to determine their rehabilitation needs, patients work with a specially trained magician to learn simple magic tricks that will help them achieve their motor, cognitive, perceptual, and/or mental health goals. Outcomes include increased concentration and improved motor, cognitive, and perceptual capabilities (Healing of Magic, 2008); and decreased recovery time, and increased enjoyment of the rehabilitative process (Fisher & Fisher, 2007). The American Occupational Therapy Association (AOTA) now endorses the use of magic as an authentic method of achieving therapeutic goals (Healing of Magic, 2008). Counselors, psychologists, and clinical social workers use magic to gain trust, ease tension, and establish rapport when working with children and adolescents (Gilroy, 2001) and to help resistant children become engaged in the therapeutic process (Bow, 1988).

Clown Doctors

Clown doctors are specially trained professional artists who work in a therapeutic program within a hospital or other healthcare facility. Clown doctors interact with patients, families, and healthcare staff in hospital rooms and hallways, and visit patients and their families at their bedside. They engage in play with children and adults, and try to introduce humor to what is often a sad situation. Unlike clowns, professional entertainers who make occasional visits to hospital bedsides for the sole purpose of entertaining and distracting patients, clown doctors are professionals of a very different sort, and their selection and training process is quite rigorous. Always working in pairs, they employ music, improvised play, and the artistry of traditional clowns (e.g., mime, dance, juggling, magic, pratfalls, set gags, and routines), and engage patients with short, improvised stories and scenes to assist them with personal coping mechanisms and to help them and their families develop positive attitudes and resilience in the face of illness, tragedy, and adversity. Unlike many traditional clowns, who paint their faces in a manner that may frighten children, clown doctors wear a red nose, which can be removed if they need to break character.

Benefits of Clown Doctors in Hospitals. Although the research on the benefits of clown doctors is in its infancy, the information that is available is positive. For example, in a study that investigated the effects of the presence of clown doctors on children's preoperative anxiety during the induction of anesthesia, children who were accompanied by a clown doctor and a parent were significantly less anxious during induction compared with the control group, who were accompanied only by a parent (Vagnoli, Caprilli, Robiglio, & Messeri, 2005). Results of a similar study found that clown doctors reduced the preoperative worries and emotional responses of parents as well (Fernandes & Arriaga, 2010).

Research also indicates that children appreciate the beneficial effects of a clown visit to them during their hospital stay. Data suggest that clown humor can mitigate some of the negative effects of hospitalization for sick children. Weaver, Prudhoe, Battrick, and Glasper (2007) found that after a clown doctor visit children's comments had a much more positive theme than before the visit. Perhaps the largest study of clown doctors to date was conducted by Dr. Bernie Warren of the University of Windsor, on the work of clown doctors at five Windsor hospitals over a three-year period (Warren, 2007). Results suggest that clown doctors (a) are effective in changing mood, (b) help change perceptions of time, (d) reframe perceptions of the hospital environment for patients, (c) help ease procedures for both patients and staff, (e) help reduce staff stress, (f) reduce the need for pain, anxiety, and antidepressant medications, (g) aid in the building of communitas, (h) help humanize the healthcare experience, and (i) enhance perception of healthcare delivery.

Special Considerations

In Buxman's words, humor is like a scalpel: "Wielded carelessly, it can do tremendous damage" (Buxman, 1991, p. 46). Although laughter is universal, what people think is funny is not. Humor should be seen as a complement to other coping strategies, not a substitute for them:

> Like denial, humor may be adaptive when it helps children get through a
> stressful situation, or maladaptive when children persistently use humor to

avoid acknowledging the existence of a stressor and other coping strategies (i.e., verbalizing feelings, seeking information, problem solving). (Dowling, 2002, p. 127)

Dowling (2002) suggests conducting a humor assessment to help determine a child's values and practices of humor (see the questions in Box 8.1). In general, there are three considerations for determining the appropriate and inappropriate use of humor:

1. *Timing.* Humor is inappropriate during a crisis; once the crisis subsides, humor can relieve anxiety and help the child and family adjust to the crisis.

2. *Receptiveness.* Assessment can occur while performing other tasks. Observations of interactions between the child and family provide helpful clues.

3. *Context.* It is important to remember that the purpose of using humor as an intervention is to laugh with one another, not *at* one another. Laughing with others stimulates acceptance, trust, commitment, and a positive sense of working together, which is therapeutic to healthcare professionals, patients, and families.

BOX 8.1. ASSESSING CHILDREN'S VALUES AND PRACTICES OF HUMOR

1. What makes you laugh?

2. What is your favorite funny TV show?

   • Why is it funny?

   • Can you give me an example of one of the funny things that happened in the show?

3. What is your favorite funny book?

   • Why is it funny?

   • Can you give me an example of one of the funny things that happened in the book?

4. What is the funniest event that happened at home this year?

5. What is the funniest event that happened in daycare/school this year?

6. Do you enjoy telling jokes, riddles, or humorous stories to others?

   • Can you tell me a joke, riddle, or story that you think is funny?

   • What makes that joke, riddle, or story funny?

7. With whom do you laugh the most?

8. How do you feel after a good belly (hard) laugh?

9. Can you tell me about a time when jokes and laughter have made you feel better?

10. Has there been a time when jokes and laughter have made you feel worse?

11. Is there anything else about your family's, your friends', or your own humor that you want to tell me?

Note. Adapted and reprinted from Dowling, J. (2002). Humor: A coping strategy for pediatric patients. *Pediatric Nursing, 28*(2), 123–131. Reprinted with permission.

There are other considerations. First, it goes without saying that ethnic, racist, sexist, religious, and ridiculing humor should be prohibited. Second, it is typically safer to allow children to be the first to joke about their circumstances. When children choose to use humor regarding their situation (e.g., surgical stitches, multiple needle sticks, hair loss), the subject is then open for discussion and therapeutic care (i.e., listening, counseling, teaching). Third, it is important to be considerate of other patients and families nearby, who might easily interpret humor as laughing at their expense. Finally, care must be taken to avoid minimizing the painfulness and seriousness of stressful situations.

As with all activities in this book, an important consideration in choosing which to use is the child's developmental stage. Table 8.3 provides guidance in this regard.

Table 8.3 Type of Humor and Suggested Interventions by Developmental Stage

Age	Type of Humor That Evokes Responses	Specific Interventions
0–4 months	Smiling, singing, gentle motions	Stimulation in environment Musical light-up toys Voices with varied inflections Patty cake
4–8 months	Surprises Toys that move and make noise	Peekaboo Bubbles ''I'm gonna getcha…'' and other physical contact games
8–18 months	Simple songs and finger plays Incongruities Gentle surprises	''Little Bunny Foo Foo'' Incorporating child's name into songs Making funny noises and faces Playing with toys in unexpected ways Behavior that deliberately contradicts norms Jack-in-the-box
18 months–3 years	Incongruities Exaggeration Repetition in song, verse, or activity	Oversized items, like giant toothbrush Mislabeling objects Giving a known object an untypical function (e.g., a pacifier as an airplane) ''Ring Around the Rosie''
3–5 years	Language play Motor activity Expectancy violations Fantasy	Dr. Seuss Cartoons Silly songs, like ''On Top of Spaghetti'' Face painting Knock-knock jokes Mr. Potato Head
5–12 years	Jokes and riddles Gross and crude things Puns Physical humor Slapstick	Slime and other gooey materials Comic books Mad Libs Silly String Pranks
Adolescent	Sophisticated jokes Wit Satire Sexual content irony	Bloopers Practical jokes Learning how to perform a magic trick Taboo topics Movies, stories, books featuring irony

Patient-Initiated Humor

When we think of humor in a healthcare setting, our first thoughts are likely to about caregiver-initiated humor. However, there is another important aspect of humor: that which is initiated by patients. When patients use humor to relieve feelings of stress, uncertainty, or embarrassment, they are trying to communicate with their caregivers (Adamie & Turkoski, 2006). Humor initiated by patients is not done to make light of their situation, but rather a way to allay feelings of dehumanization. Supporting the child's use of humor will (a) help to reinforce the child's control of his or her situation, (b) establish open communication lines, and (c) strengthen the therapeutic relationship between the child and the healthcare professional.

Although healthcare professionals can model healthy, appropriate humor, children are known for using ridiculing humor as a way to cope with their own anxieties and fears, as well as a means of gaining mastery over a situation. In such situations, healthcare professionals can ask children in a gentle, nonthreatening manner to explain what is funny to them. When children think and talk about the context of the humor interaction, they may better understand their feelings and recognize the inappropriateness of using ridiculing humor (Dowling, 2002).

Activity Goals

The activities in this chapter all share the goal of using humor to promote positive affect and laughter. Within the activities are additional objectives: fostering coping, enhancing personal relationships, and empowering children.

Activities that poke fun at something related to illness or its treatment are designed to foster coping. These activities include License Plate, Flamboyant Flamingos and Other IV Pump Pals, Puke Cookies, and Don't Cry Over Spilled . . . . **Fostering Coping**

These activities are conducted in a group setting and, therefore, have the additional objective of enhancing relationships between children. Activities with this objective include A Mona Lisa Smile, Goofy Gadget Game, Med Libs, and Mirth Mobiles. **Enhancing Interpersonal Relationships**

Activities with this objective involve playing a joke on someone. Blister Blooper, Bogus Baby Burgers, and Don't Cry Over Spilled . . . share this objective. **Empowering Children**

ACTIVITY 8.1.   A MONA LISA SMILE

This is a variation of the perennial children's party game, Pin the Tail on the Donkey.

Therapeutic Goal: To use humor to promote positive affect and laughter and enhance interpersonal relationships.

Age Group: Preschool/primary

Adult/Child Ratio: 1:10

Required Time: To make: 30 minutes; to play: situational

Restrictions and Precautions: Use care if children are tethered to IVs or other equipment. Do not spin children who have vestibular problems. Clear the area where children are playing of obstructions.

Materials:

- ☐ 8-inch × 11-inch prints of Leonardo da Vinci's *Mona Lisa*, downloaded from a computer
- ☐ Rubber cement
- ☐ Scissors
- ☐ Colored cardstock
- ☐ Laminator or clear contact paper
- ☐ Poster board
- ☐ Double-stick adhesive tape
- ☐ Erasable marker

Process

1. To make the playing pieces, enlarge Mona Lisa's smile on a copy machine or computer and make one copy for every player.

2. Cut the smiles out, glue them to cardstock, and laminate them.

3. Cut out the smiles from the cardstock, conforming to the shape of the smile, leaving a 1/2-inch border around each.

4. To make the game board, use the erase function of a photo-editing software program to remove Mona Lisa's smile from her image on your computer and print one copy. Or, if you don't have photo-editing capability, simply glue a small piece of colored paper over the smile. If possible, enlarge the image to poster size.

5. Glue the image onto poster board and laminate or cover with clear contact paper.

6. Place a piece of double-stick tape on the back of each playing piece.

7. To play, tape the game board to a wall.

8. Write each player's name on his or her playing piece.

9. One at a time, blindfold the players, spin them around once or twice, and tell them, without looking, to place their piece on the poster. The child who places the smile closest to where it belongs on the face wins.

Variations

Replace the image of Mona Lisa with a large yellow smiley face, cartoon character, or a singer or actor popular among children.

Children also find Pin the Band-Aid on the Doctor's Boo-boo quite amusing to play.

⊙ ACTIVITY 8.2.   BLISTER BLOOPER

Blister Blooper is located on the CD that accompanies this book.

ACTIVITY 8.3.   BODACIOUS BOOKENDS

These bookends are both funny and utilitarian. Like bronzed baby shoes popular in decades past, these bookends make very special keepsakes.

Therapeutic Goal: To use humor to promote positive affect and laughter.

Age Group: School-age/adolescent

Adult/Child Ratio: 1:5

Required Time: Two sessions: 10 minutes to fill shoes and 30 minutes to decorate

Restrictions and Precautions: Mix plaster in a well-ventilated area. Take glitter and marker precautions.

Materials:
- ☐ Pair of athletic shoes no longer worn by the children
- ☐ Large bowl
- ☐ Water
- ☐ Plaster of paris
- ☐ Scissors
- ☐ Assorted ribbon or yarn
- ☐ Fabric paint or permanent makers
- ☐ Glitter pens

Process

1. Mix the plaster of paris according to package directions.
2. Instruct the children to fill their shoes with the plaster, leaving enough room to allow the shoes to be laced.
3. Allow the plaster to dry completely.
4. Let the children select ribbon or yarn to use as shoelaces and lace the shoes in the traditional manner or in a more creative fashion.
5. Encourage the children to decorate the shoes using glitter pens, fabric paint, and/or markers.

ACTIVITY 8.4.   BOGUS BABY BURGERS

These "burgers" look amazingly real, and children love fooling staff with them.

Therapeutic Goal: To use humor to promote positive affect and laughter and empower children.

Age Group: Preschool/primary

Adult/Child Ratio: 1:4 (higher with older children)

Required Time: 20 minutes

Restrictions and Precautions: Check for dietary restrictions and food allergies. Make sure children wear gloves when preparing food.

Materials
- ☐ Specimen cup or small plastic food container with lid
- ☐ Water
- ☐ Measuring spoon
- ☐ Food coloring (red, yellow, and green)
- ☐ 1/4 cup flaked coconut
- ☐ 2 small bowls
- ☐ Canned vanilla frosting
- ☐ Spoon
- ☐ Tongue depressors
- ☐ 24 chocolate-covered mint cookies (the "burgers")
- ☐ 48 vanilla wafers (the "buns")
- ☐ Corn syrup
- ☐ Pastry brush

1. In the specimen cup or container, combine one or two drops of green food coloring with 1/3 teaspoon of water.

2. Add the coconut; cover and shake until the coconut is uniformly tinted.

3. Divide the frosting into two small bowls.

4. Give the children the food coloring to tint one dish red (for the ketchup) and one dish yellow (for the mustard).

5. Help the children, as needed, to use a tongue depressor to lightly spread the flat side of 24 vanilla wafers with red frosting and another 24 vanilla wafers with yellow frosting.

6. Have the children sprinkle a 1/2 teaspoon of coconut over the red frosting on each cookie.

7. Demonstrate how to place a mint cookie on top of the coconut, top with a vanilla wafer, and spread with yellow frosting, frosting side down.

8. Instruct the children to repeat step 7 until all the cookies have been used.

9. To "seed" the buns, show the children how to brush a small amount of corn syrup on the top of each "burger" and sprinkle with sesame or poppy seeds.

10. Let the children "fool" family and staff by offering them a hamburger.

ACTIVITY 8.5. CRACK-UP COLLAGES

The humor in this activity is visual, making it a good choice for children who do not speak English. Pictures may be cut out prior to beginning the activity when working with children who are unable to do so themselves, or if you need to complete the activity in a short amount of time.

Therapeutic Goal: To use humor to promote positive affect and laughter.

Age Group: School-age

Adult/Child Ratio: 1:10

Required Time: 30 minutes

Restrictions and Precautions: Take glue and scissors precautions.

Materials:

☐ Pictures of people cut from magazines, greeting cards, photographs, or images downloaded from a computer. (Note that children find it especially amusing when you include images of staff members.)
☐ Scissors
☐ Glue stick
☐ Paper or cardstock

1. Have the children cut off the heads, trunks, and limbs of the people in the pictures then mix them up in separate piles.

2. Give each child a piece of paper or cardstock.

3. Invite the children to combine, at random, a body component from each of the piles to make outlandish composites.

4. When they are satisfied with their creations, tell the children to glue their assemblages onto paper or cardstock.

5. Encourage the children to give their characters suitable names and write a few sentences about them.

Create tongue-twister collages by letting the children select pictures of words that all begin with the same sound, like puppy, popcorn, pig, and pie.

Encourage the children to make up a silly tongue twister using all the words pictured in the collage, such as, "The playful puppy and the perky pig ate popcorn and pie." The children can challenge the adults around them to try to say the tongue twister quickly, over and over again. Children experience great pleasure watching adults fumble over the words.

ACTIVITY 8.6.   DANCING RAISINS

Although this activity is actually a classic primary-grade science experiment, it rarely fails to make young children giggle. It is quick and easy to do, making it a good choice to diffuse tension in a busy clinic.

Therapeutic Goal: To use humor to promote positive affect and laughter.

Age Group: Preschool/primary

Adult/Child Ratio: 1:6

Required Time: 5 minutes

Restrictions and Precautions: None

Materials:

☐ Specimen cup or other clear cup
☐ Clear carbonated beverage
☐ Raisins
☐ 1 teaspoon baking soda
☐ Spoon

Process

1. Ask the children if they have ever seen raisins dance. They will say no, and possibly begin laughing just thinking about the absurdity of the notion.

2. Assure the children that you know a way to make raisins dance.

3. Slowly fill the cup with the carbonated beverage, minimizing the fizzing as much as possible.

4. Mix in the baking soda.

5. Drop several raisins into the soda pop and watch them go!

Variation

Racing Raisins: Fill 2 cups with equal amounts of soda, as described above. Select two players. On cue, each player drops a raisin into one of the cups. After first sinking to the bottom, carbon dioxide bubbles will gather on the raisin, causing it to quickly rise to the surface. The player whose raisin reaches the top first wins.

ACTIVITY 8.7.   DON'T CRY OVER SPILLED . . .

Children at that stage in the development of humor when they appreciate "grossness" will think it hilarious to use these specimen cup "sculptures" that have been "spilled," to fool families, friends, and staff.

Therapeutic Goal: To use humor to empower children, foster coping, and promote positive affect and laughter.

Age Group: School-age/adolescent

Adult/Child Ratio: 1:10

Required Time: 15 minutes, plus drying time

Restrictions and Precautions: Take glue precautions.

Materials:

☐ Specimen cups or other empty, clean liquid containers (one per child)
☐ Glue
☐ Yellow tempera paint or other color appropriate to container used
☐ Tongue depressors
☐ Small cookie sheets, covered with foil or waxed paper
☐ Spatula

Process

1. Instruct each of the children to place 1–2 tablespoons glue, 1–2 teaspoons water, and a few drops of tempera paint (or more until desired shade is achieved) in a specimen cup or other container, and stir the mixture with a tongue depressor.

2. Have the children lay their specimen cup on its side atop the cookie sheet, carefully allowing the glue mixture to spill out.

3. Allow the "spill" to set until completely dry (1–2 days).

4. Demonstrate for the children how to gently peel the spill and specimen cup from the foil. A spatula may be used if necessary.

5. Encourage the children to place their "spill sculpture" on a table or tray and watch how people react (Figure Activity 8.7-1).

Figure Activity 8.7-1. Don't Cry Over Spilled . . .

For more ideas, see Bright Ideas: More Medically Related Practical Jokes for Older Children (Box Activity 8.7-1).

- Fill a specimen cup with apple juice and drink in front of the person being "targeted."

- Attach a long piece of black string licorice to IV tubing, extending from the IV site to the bag and ask a caregiver to check it.

- Attach small plastic or paper fish to an IV bag.

- Use thin medical tape to attach small plastic insects around a port or IV site just before a staff member is about to check it.

- Inject a used IV bag and tubing with food coloring to make the liquid an unusual color (how about purple?). Hang it next to the real IV bag, carefully positioning it to obscure the bag with the real medicine.

- Hide realistic-looking scary toy animals under a gown in the area of the body that will be examined by a staff member.

- Place fake appendages and vomit in creative places.

- Make very realistic-looking fake "poop" by mixing green and red food coloring into store-bought sugar cookie dough until the right shade of brown is achieved. Mold into the "appropriate shape" and bake. Eat in front of the person being "targeted."

- Paint bull's-eyes on emesis basins or bedpans.

*Practical jokes allow older children and teenagers to release anger and aggression in a socially acceptable way.

ACTIVITY 8.8.   FLAMBOYANT FLAMINGOS AND OTHER IV PUMP PALS

Preschool children will enjoy transforming their IV poles into an "animal friend," but they will need precut shapes and considerable adult assistance to complete the project.

Therapeutic Goal: To use humor to foster coping and promote positive affect and laughter.

Age Group: Preschool/primary

Adult/Child Ratio: 1:1

Required Time: 30–45 minutes

Restrictions and Precautions: Take scissors and glue precautions. Avoid putting anything on the front of the IV pump.

Materials:

- ☐ Colored construction paper
- ☐ Fabric
- ☐ Large, black mailing labels
- ☐ Feathers
- ☐ Crepe-paper streamers
- ☐ Other found objects
- ☐ Scissors
- ☐ Masking tape
- ☐ String or yarn
- ☐ Glue

Process

1. Explain that it is easy and fun to turn an IV pump into an "animal friend."

2. Show the child pictures of animals and ask him or her to select one to disguise his or her IV pole.

3. Choosing from available materials, help the child to decorate portions of his or her IV pole, using the pump itself as the trunk of the animal. For example, a flamingo's head and large beak can be fashioned from construction paper and hung from the top of the pole with string. The upper portion of the pole can be made into the flamingo's long neck by wrapping it with crepe paper streamers. Feathers can be glued to construction paper and taped to the side of the pump, for wings. The flamingo's long legs can be fashioned out of crepe-paper streamers and then attached to the lower segment of the pole.

Variation

Children with low energy levels can easily add some whimsy to their IV poles by attaching mobiles, silly toys, or stuffed animals. School-age children can add personal humor to their IV poles in the form of a funny bumper sticker, or by making a "street sign" with their name (e.g., Stephanie Street, Lilly Lane) or a road sign, such as "Stop" or "Men Working."

Note. Adapted from Rollins, J. (2004). *Arts activities for children at bedside.* Washington, DC: WVSA arts connection.

⊙ ACTIVITY 8.9.   FUNGLASSES

Funglasses is located on the CD that accompanies this book.

ACTIVITY 8.10.   GOOFY GADGET GAME

This game encourages children to "think outside the box," frequently with hilarious results. It is a perfect choice for groups of children sitting in waiting areas, infusion clinics, and dialysis units.

Therapeutic Goal: To use humor to promote positive affect and laughter and enhance interpersonal relationships.

Age Group: Primary/school-age/adolescent

Adult/Child Ratio: 1:10

Required Time: Varies

Restrictions and Precautions: None

Materials:

- ☐ Assorted hospital-related objects (e.g., a tongue depressor, needle-less syringe, bedpan)
- ☐ Egg timer
- ☐ Paper
- ☐ Pens

Process

1. The object of the game is for players to use their imaginations to come up with unusual ways to use the object(s) *other* than that for which it is intended.

2. To play, set the timer for 3 minutes, and tell players to begin writing down all the ideas they can think of in the time allotted.

3. When time runs out, give players a turn reading their lists out loud. If anyone else has the same idea for using the object as on the current player's list, then everyone must cross it off.

4. The person with the most ideas that no one else has wins the round.

5. Continue play with different objects as long as the players remain interested.

ACTIVITY 8.11.   HILARIOUS HEADBANDS

Hilarious Headbands is located on the CD that accompanies this book.

ACTIVITY 8.12.   KOOKY COOKIE PUPPETS

Kooky Cookie Puppets is located on the CD that accompanies this book.

ACTIVITY 8.13.   LEAFY-LOCKS POTS (CHIA PET WANNABES)

Therapeutic horticulture, the goal-oriented use of plants and plant-related activities, has been shown to be an effective intervention in healthcare settings for sick children. This activity incorporates the benefits of therapeutic horticulture with those of therapeutic humor. It is especially good for patients who are long-term or receiving treatments that require regular visits to the hospital or clinic.

Therapeutic Goal: To use humor to promote positive affect and laughter.

Age Group: School-age

Adult/Child Ratio: 1:8

Required Time: 40 minutes

Restrictions and Precautions: Take glue, scissors, and paint precautions. Make sure that children with open wounds on their hands wear gloves while working with soil. Live plants may be contraindicated for some children.

Materials:
- ☐ Small terra-cotta plant containers
- ☐ Primer
- ☐ Paintbrush
- ☐ Acrylic paint
- ☐ Craft foam
- ☐ Scissors
- ☐ Craft glue
- ☐ Potting soil
- ☐ Grass or other plants

Process

1. Prime the terra-cotta containers and allow them to dry.

2. Explain to the children that the containers will become the head of a person or animal, and the leaves of the plant will serve as the hair.

3. Have the children paint their containers a bright color.

4. After the base paint has dried, instruct the children to paint facial features on the containers.

5. If they wish, let the children cut out shapes from craft foam to create dimensional details such as ears, a visor, earrings, nose, and/or a moustache, then glue them to their pots.

6. Help the children fill the containers with soil and pot the plant(s) they select (Figure Activity 8.13-1).

7. Explain how to care for the plants by providing water and sunlight.

Figure Activity 8.13-1. Leafy-Locks Pot

Variation

Give the children permanent markers to draw faces on large potatoes. Slice the top off the potatoes and bore a small hole in each one. Insert a ball of cotton moistened with water into the hole. Set the potatoes in a shallow cup to hold it upright. In about a week the potato heads will sprout "buzz cuts."

ACTIVITY 8.14.   LEAKING BOTTLE TRICK

Be sure to use only water as the liquid because the people who are the "targets" of this trick will certainly get a little water sprinkled on them.

Therapeutic Goal: To use humor to empower children and promote positive affect and laughter.	**Materials:**
	☐ Syringe, with a thick needle or tapestry needle
Age Group: Primary/school-age	☐ Empty plastic bottle, with screw-on cap
Adult/Child Ratio: 1:1	☐ Plastic basin filled with water (large enough to submerge the bottle in an upright position)
Required Time: 10 minutes	
Restrictions and Precautions: Closely supervise the use of the needle.	

Process

1. Show the child how to use the needle to make five small holes in the bottom of the bottle, assisting if needed.
2. Ask the child to remove the cap from the bottle and submerge the bottle in the basin of water until no more air bubbles come out.
3. With the bottle still submerged, have the child screw the cap on tightly.
4. Ask the child to remove the bottle from the water and dry it off.
5. Tell the child to select a target and ask that person to help unscrew the cap. When the cap is removed water will sprinkle on the target's feet or lap.

ACTIVITY 8.15.   LICENSE PLATE

Having their movement encumbered by medical equipment, such as IV poles and wheelchairs, is one of the many frustrations sick children may endure. These clever license plates help them use humor to cope with this challenge while expressing their individuality.

Therapeutic Goal: To use humor to promote positive affect and laughter and foster coping.

Age Group: School-age/adolescent

Adult/Child Ratio: Any size group

Required Time: 30 minutes

Precautions and Restrictions: Take scissors precautions.

Materials:
- ☐ Poster board, cut into 8-inch × 5-inch rectangles
- ☐ Ruler
- ☐ Pencil
- ☐ Scissors
- ☐ Peel-and-stick letters or stencils
- ☐ Clear contact paper or laminating machine (optional)

Process

1. Describe to the children different types of vanity license plates, (e.g., using one's own name, spelling one's name using an unusual combination of letters and/or numbers, spelling out a word or message with a creative mix of numbers and letters). For example:

IMLN (I am Ellen)	BNIS2ME (Be nice to me)
AWSUM (awesome)	IFELGR8 (I feel great)
2KUL (too cool)	IH8SHOTZ (I hate shots)
GWIZ (gee whiz)	EXSITZ (excites)
RUHAPE (Are you happy)	NOMORPILZ (no more pills)
ILUVU (I love you)	SIRJUN (surgeon)
1DER (wonder)	GUTZ (gutsy)
PDATRX (pediatrics)	IMBRAV (I am brave)
4MOST (foremost)	YMIHER (Why am I here)
PTUR (Peter)	IMKWIK (I am quick)
THANX (thanks)	YMEBCUZ (Why me, because)
ULISU (Alissa)	THUFUDSTNX (The food stinks)

2. Invite the children to describe vanity plates they have seen.

3. Ask the children to decide what they would like their license plates to say.

4. Have the children use a pencil to draw a faint line across the length of the license plate, to assist in aligning letters.

5. Give the children peel-and-stick letters to spell out the name or phrase they selected. Alternatively, let them stencil letters and numbers on the plates.

6. Cover the license plates with clear contact paper; or laminate, if desired.

7. Help the children tape or tie their license plates to their wheelchairs or IV poles.

ACTIVITY 8.16.   MAGIC REALISM À LA MAGRITTE

The works of surrealist painters such as Salvador Dali, René Magritte, and Joan Miró are bizarre, and often quite humorous. This simple activity captures a bit of the wit and whimsy of this revolutionary style of art. Pictures of objects may be cut out in advance for children who are unable to do so physically, or when time is limited.

Therapeutic Goal: To use humor to promote positive affect and laughter.

Age Group: School-age/adolescent

Adult/Child Ratio: 1:10

Required Time: 30 minutes

Restrictions and Precautions: Take glue and scissors
   precautions.

Materials:

- ☐ Several examples of surrealist art that juxtapose
   unrelated objects, such as "Why Not Sneeze
   Rose Selavy?" by Marcel Duchamp or "Time
   Transfixed," by René Magritte

- ☐ Magazines
- ☐ Scissors
- ☐ Lightweight cardboard or construction
   paper
- ☐ Glue

Process

1. Show the children examples of surrealist art. Explain how some of these artists juxtaposed completely unrelated objects in strange, sometimes absurd ways in a style of painting known as "magic realism."

2. Have the children cut out photographs of unrelated images of people and objects from magazines.

3. Tell the children to lay the photographs on the cardboard or construction paper, then experiment combining the images in nonsensical, amusing ways (Figure Activity 8.16-1).

Figure Activity 8.16-1. Magic Realism à la Magritte

4. When they are satisfied with their arrangements, let the children glue the pictures in place.

5. Encourage the children to write a poem about their creations.

Variation

Make "magic realism sculpture" by hot-gluing unrelated, everyday objects together with disposable medical materials.

ACTIVITY 8.17.   MASTER OF DISGUISE

Loss of control is a common issue for many hospitalized children. The closed system of authority in healthcare facilities has been likened by some to being in prison. Making funny faces on a picture of one of the "omnipotent" staff members may offer children a playful means of diffusing some of the tension and frustration they so often experience as a patient.

Therapeutic Goal: To use humor to promote positive affect and laughter and empower children.

Age Group: School-age/adolescent

Adult/Child Ratio: 1:10

Required Time: 15 minutes

Restrictions and Precautions: Take marker precautions.

Materials:

- ☐ 5-inch × 7-inch or 8-inch × 10-inch photograph (head and shoulder shots works best)
- ☐ Acrylic tabletop photo frame, sized to fit photo (one per child)
- ☐ Crayola Washable Window Markers
- ☐ Paper towels
- ☐ Water

Process

1. Have the children insert a photo of themselves or someone else they know into their frame.

2. Let the children disguise the person in their photo by using markers to draw directly on the frame. Inspire them to be imaginative and silly, drawing such things as goofy glasses, dramatic eyelashes, freckles, outrageous hair in not-found-in-nature colors, clownish clothing, and tacky jewelry. They can be creative with the background of the photos, as well.

3. Encourage the children to display their photos where others can see them and share the humor (Figure Activity 8.17-1).

Figure Activity 8.17-1. Master of Disguise

4. Inform the children that all they need to do to change their design is to wipe it off with a damp paper towel and start over as soon as it's dry.

Note. "Silly Faces" craft instruction provided courtesy of Crayola.com, © 2002–2010. Adapted with permission. Visit Crayola.com for other interesting ideas that can be adapted for therapeutic use.

 ## ACTIVITY 8.18.   MED LIBS

Med Libs is located on the CD that accompanies this book.

ACTIVITY 8.19.   MIRTH MOBILES

This is a good activity for entire families to participate in together. A well-stocked cart should contain items that appeal to every age group. Even parents appreciate the opportunity to let go and be silly—and you can often see them visibly relax when they do so.

Therapeutic Goal: To use humor to promote positive affect and laughter, empower children, and enhance interpersonal relationships.

Adult/Child Ratio: Varies

Age Group: All

Required Time: Varies

Precautions and Restrictions: Carefully assess the children and their families to ascertain whether any items on the cart may be offensive or inappropriate, and if so, remove them. Monitor practical jokes and the use of Silly String, to assure that appropriate targets are chosen.

Materials:

☐ Cart, custom made or purchased (Figure Activity 8.19-1)

☐ Brightly colored bins of assorted sizes

☐ Large computer labels

☐ Any or all of the following:

- DVD player (if cart will be used where none is available)
- Comedy DVDs and sports bloopers
- Comic books and joke books
- Wind-up toys that flip, twirl, jump, or chatter
- Funny hats, animal noses, glasses
- Silly String, squirting pens and flowers
- Can of "snakes"
- Oversized items (e.g., giant combs, toothbrushes, eating utensils)
- Gross things (e.g., body organ stress balls, fake vomit or poop)
- Rubber chickens, snakes, and insects
- Practical joke props

Figure Activity 8.19-1. Mirth Mobiles

Process

1. If you are having the cart made, you may wish to consider having it constructed in an unusual shape, such as a house or castle. If you are using a commercially made cart, paint or decorate it to make it colorful and fun. Be sure not to make it look too childish, or it may not appeal to adolescents.

2. Organize the materials by age group or type of humor.

3. Label the bins so that specific items can be easily located, either to give to the children or to remove prior to introducing the cart if certain items might be inappropriate. Use colorful word-art to make the labels, and be creative in naming the bins. Some ideas include:

   Wind-up toys: "All Wound Up"
   Practical joke items: "The Joke's on You"
   Oversized items: "Think Big"
   Gross items: "Gross Me Out!"

4. Introduce the cart to the children. Set a playful tone by wearing a silly hat or other goofy attire.

5. Encourage the children to explore the options and choose movies, books, and/or humorous toys that appeal to them.

6. If the children are selecting props to play jokes on others, help them devise a plan.

Variation If a cart is not practical, use an appropriately decorated "humor basket" to bring an assortment of items to the children.

ACTIVITY 8.20. MIRTH-AID KIT

Like a first-aid kit, a mirth-aid kit is designed to be compact and contain the necessary basic items to provide quick medical care when needed. With mirth-aid kits, the care provided is in the form of laughter, which many say is the best medicine.

Therapeutic Goal: To use humor to promote positive affect and laughter and enhance coping.

Age Group: School-age

Adult/Child Ratio: 1:8

Required Time: 30 minutes

Restrictions and Precautions: Take scissors and glue precautions.

Materials:

☐ Boxes with covers, shoebox size or larger (one per child)

☐ Comic sections from newspaper

☐ Smiles cut out from magazines

☐ Scissors

☐ Glue

☐ Mod Podge (optional)

☐ Brush (optional)

☐ Joke books, small toys, or other items that children may find amusing

Process

1. Explain to the children that a mirth-aid kit is a personal collection of funny objects, jokes, and sayings they can use when their spirits are down.

2. Ask the children to describe things that make them smile or laugh.

3. Let the children decorate their boxes by gluing comic strips and/or pictures of smiles to both the tops and bottoms, covering them completely.

4. If they wish to seal their boxes, give the children brushes to apply the Mod Podge; allow it to dry.

5. Invite the children to select some funny items to get their boxes started.

6. Encourage the children to collect jokes, comic strips, humorous greeting cards they have received, toys, and other small items that they find amusing, to keep in their boxes.

7. Urge the children to use their boxes when they "need a good laugh."

ACTIVITY 8.21. POP-UP CARD CRITTERS

Pop-Up Card Critters is located on the CD that accompanies this book.

ACTIVITY 8.22. PUKE COOKIES

Puke Cookies is located on the CD that accompanies this book.

ACTIVITY 8.23. STEVE MARTIN MEETS HEALTHCARE

Comedian Steve Martin often performed his stand-up routines while acting as if he was unaware that that there was an arrow going through his head. This activity is the healthcare version.

Therapeutic Goal: To use humor to promote positive affect and laughter and foster coping.	Materials:
Age Group: School-age/adolescent	☐ Plastic headbands, at least 1 inch wide (one per child)
Adult/Child Ratio: 1:4	☐ Serrated knife
Required Time: 10–15 minutes	☐ Pen or marker
Restrictions and Precautions: Take care when using the glue gun and knife.	☐ 30cc syringes (one per child)
	☐ Glue gun
	☐ Foil (optional)

Process

1. Remove and discard the rubber tips from the plungers.
2. Create a smooth surface where the rubber tips were by using the serrated knife to remove any protruding plastic.
3. Ask the children to don headbands.
4. Position the plunger and barrel on either side of the headbands so that they are aligned. Use a pen or marker to indicate the correct placement.
5. Use hot glue to secure the barrel of the syringes to one side of the headbands, and the plungers on the other.
6. Encourage the children to wear their special headband while having solemn conversations with others or making silly faces.

ACTIVITY 8.24.   STICK A SMILE ON YOUR FACE

These "smiles" can be used as a means of self-expression, especially for children who are unable to speak; or they can serve as a solution for children who are sick of being told to smile by the adults around them. Stick a Smile on Your Face can also be used by children to give a smile to someone who really needs one. And to cheer up a hospital room, make a "happy" bouquet by mixing several of these sticky smiles with flowers (real or child-made) in a vase.

Therapeutic Goal: To use humor to promote positive affect and laughter.	Materials:
Age Group: Preschool/school-age	☐ Photocopies or drawings of smiles
Adult/Child Ratio: 1:5	☐ Crayons or markers with an assortment of skin-tone shades
Required Time: 10 minutes	☐ Scissors
Restrictions and Precautions: Take scissors precautions.	☐ Tongue depressors
	☐ Tape

Process

1. Ask the children to select a smile and color it.
2. Have the children cut out their smiles (younger children will require assistance).
3. Tape each smile to a tongue depressor.

Variation

Instead of using a template, photograph the children's smiles and print them out in actual size or a bit larger. Then follow the instructions above.

For more ideas, see Bright Ideas: Creative Costumes for Bald Children (Box Activity 8.24-1), and Bright Ideas: Silly Celebrations, Kooky Contests, and Other Fun Stuff to Do (Box Activity 8.24-2).

BOX
ACTIVITY 8.24-1.
BRIGHT IDEAS:
CREATIVE
COSTUMES FOR
BALD CHILDREN

Six Flag Man
Punk rocker with a Mohawk
Lord Voldermort (from *Harry Potter*)
Professor Xavier (from *X-men*)
Ilia (from *Star Trek*)
Captain Jean Luc Picard (also from *Star Trek*)
Uncle Fester (from the *Addams Family*)

Gandhi
Telly Savalas (from *Kojak*)
Charlie Brown (from *Peanuts*)
Lex Luthor (from *Superman*)
Dr. Evil (from *Austin Powers*)
Mr. Clean
Curly (from the *Three Stooges*)

BOX
ACTIVITY 8.24-2.
BRIGHT IDEAS:
SILLY
CELEBRATIONS,
KOOKY
CONTESTS, AND
OTHER FUN
STUFF TO DO

- Celebrate Backwards Day: Wear clothing backwards, eat dessert first, and the like.
- Have Fools Day—but not as expected in April!
- List as many creative nonmedical uses for tongue depressors or bedpans as you can.
- Hold bubblegum-blowing contests (use surgical bonnets to protect hair).
- Create funny Top 10 Lists, like the top 10 reasons kids should run the hospital.
- Make up hospital-themed jokes, by coming up with answers to questions such as: "Why did the nurse cross the road?" Or, "How many doctors does it take to change a light bulb?" Or the classic preschool favorite, "Knock knock. Who's there?"
- Customize wheelchairs by folding playing cards in half and sliding them down in the spokes close to the center of the wheel; weaving colorful crepe paper in between the spokes; attaching a funny bumper sticker (use removable adhesive only); or cutting straws in half, slitting them lengthwise, and wrapping them around the spokes.
- Create a "laugh-aid" by writing a joke or riddle on a brightly colored card, putting it in an envelope, and sealing it with a Band-aid. Instruct the child to open it when he or she needs a laugh.
- Write happy thoughts on pieces of paper. Fold them in half, place them in a container, and allow the child to take one when needed.
- Try to talk in tongue twisters. Twice.
- Perform Karaoke.
- Take photographs with fish-eye lenses (if you don't have a fish-eye lens, stand very close to the subject so that the image distorts).
- Do magic tricks (no cutting people in half or other potentially threatening tricks).
- Have a caricature artists draw the children.
- Juggle scarves.
- Wear wax lips.
- Hold a staring contest. Players take turns making faces and noises to try to make the other person laugh.
- Rewrite familiar songs, using funny hospital themes.
- Fill flat-bottomed ice cream cones with cake batter, then bake, to make ice cream cones with no drip!

CHAPTER 9

DEATH AND BEREAVEMENT

Death is a significant and, at times, life-altering event in the life of a child. The activities in this chapter are designed to help children cope with their own dying or the death of a loved one.

LIST OF ACTIVITIES

Activity 9.1 Crayon Candles and Candle Lighting Ceremony	Activity 9.9 Moment Boards
	Activity 9.10 Mosaic Flower Pots
Activity 9.2 Fabric Hand Wall Hanging	Activity 9.11 Timeline
Activity 9.3 Friendship Bracelets	Activity 9.12 Remembrance Rocks
Activity 9.4 Keepsake Caches	
Activity 9.5 Life Necklace	Activity 9.13 Shadow Boxes
Activity 9.6 Memorabilia Frame	Activity 9.14 Stepping Stones
Activity 9.7 Memory Quilts	Activity 9.15 Time Capsules
	Activity 9.16 T-Shirt Pillows
Activity 9.8 Memory Box	Activity 9.17 Waving Good-bye

A Child's Response to Death

The ways a child responds to death depends on several factors, which include (a) the child's developmental level and temperament, (b) the child's relationship with the person who died, (c) how the person died—sudden or expected, (d) the age of the person who died, (e) whether the child witnessed the death, (f) how the child was told about the death, (g) the child's past experience with loss and death, (h) the child's culture, (g) the child's belief systems, and (h) the support available to the child. Children's understanding of death generally seems to follow their cognitive development. See Table 9.1 for children's age-related understanding of death, characteristic behaviors, language to use to describe death to children, and helpful interventions.

Children Who Are Dying

Until Bluebond-Langner's groundbreaking research in the late 1970s, it was common practice to withhold information from children about their fatal prognoses to protect them from the emotions this harsh reality might provoke and to maintain optimism and happiness for as long as possible. We now know that children discover the prognosis whether adults reveal it or not (Bluebond-Langner, 1978). In fact, Doka (1995) points out that keeping information from children is actually harmful; it inhibits the child from seeking support, causes additional anxiety, impairs trust, and complicates the child's response to crisis.

For a variety of reasons, children who are dying often conceal their knowledge of the prognosis from adults. However, examining their behavior can provide clues that they are, indeed, aware (Bluebond-Langner, 1978, 2000). For example, children who are dying may

- use distancing strategies such as anger or silence as rehearsal for final separation;
- ask the same questions of many people;
- donate their toys;

Table 9.1 Children's Understanding of Death by Age

Age	Understanding of Death	Characteristic Behaviors	Language	Interventions
Newborn–3 Years	• Does not comprehend death. • Aware of constant buzz of activity in the house. • Aware of Mom and Dad looking sad and teary-eyed. • Aware that someone in the home is missing.	• Has altered eating and sleeping patterns. • Is irritable. • Clings.	• Use "D-words": dying, death, dead. • Avoid euphemisms like "lost," "passed away," and "gone to sleep," which confuse young children. • Explain in physiologic terms; e.g., the dead person does not eat or drink, or have sensations, such as feeling cold after burial in the ground. • Expect questions to change. • Expect repeated questioning and testing to confirm information.	• Maintain routines, but allow for flexibility. • Choose familiar and supportive caregivers. • Assign a support person for each child during funeral, burial, and other rituals. • Acknowledge all feelings of child and adult by naming feelings and giving permission to express anger and sadness in developmentally appropriate ways. • Give extra hugs when needed to help child feel secure.
3–5-Year-Olds	• Sees death as temporary and reversible; child continually asks if person will return. • May feel ambivalent. • Through magical thinking, may assume responsibility for the death.	• Is concerned about own well-being. • Feels confused and guilty. • May use imaginative play, reenacting scene of CPR, etc. • Withdraws. • Is irritable. • Regresses.	• Explain cause of death factually; that which is mentionable is manageable. • Answer questions honestly; e.g., clarify wellness of sibling, unlike that of dying child. • Avoid abstracts. • Diffuse magical thinking. • Be consistent and persistent.	• Reinforce that when people are sad, they cry; crying is natural. • Read stories. • Provide art materials and encourage child to draw pictures. • Encourage dialogue/family meetings. • Expect misbehavior as child struggles with confusing feelings and issues. • Offer play with themes of death, while providing supportive guidance.
6–9-Year-Olds	• Begins to understand concept of death. • Feels it happens to others. • May be superstitious about death. • May be uncomfortable in expressing feelings. • Worries that other important people will die.	• May seem outwardly uncaring, inwardly upset. • May use denial to cope. • May attempt to "parent" parent. • May act out in school or home. • May play death games.	• Look for questions within questions. • Expect a more global view. • Encourage child to answer own questions. • Explore feelings by questions such as, "What do you think?"	• Listen carefully, to determine what kind of information the child is seeking. • Increase physical activity while role-modeling stress-reducing behaviors. • Work on identifying feelings, which are becoming more sophisticated, e.g., frustration, confusion. • Encourage creative outlets for feelings, e.g., drawing, painting, clay, blank books.

Table 9.1 (*continued*)

Age	Understanding of Death	Characteristic Behaviors	Language	Interventions
9–12-Year-Olds	• Accepts death as final. • Has personal fear of death. • May be morbidly interested in skeletons, gruesome details of violent deaths. • Concerned with practical matters about child's lifestyle.	• May act tough, or be funny. • May express and demonstrate anger or sadness. • May act like adult, but regress to earlier stage of emotional response.	• Provide more detail, as needed, especially to explain cause of death in physiologic context. • Probe for thoughts and feelings. • Allow for spiritual development. • Answer questions about an afterlife by, for example, stating, ''We don't really know but we believe that...''	• Encourage creative expressions of feelings. • Explore support group/peer-to-peer connection. • Establish family traditions and memorials. • Incorporate children into rituals, not just at time of death but at important anniversaries (e.g., taking balloons to the cemetery; creating a special ornament for the Christmas tree, which is always hung first; celebrating birthday dinners and memory nights).
Adolescents	• Has adult concept of death, but ability to deal with loss is based on experience and developmental factors. • Experiences thrill of recklessness. • Focuses on present. • Is developing strong philosophical view. • Questions existence of an afterlife.	• Relies increasingly on peers instead of family. • Has more episodes of moodiness and irritability. • May engage in risk-taking behaviors. • Appears rebellious, and tests limits. • May act impulsively or without common sense.	• Treat as an adult; give information and respect, and assign responsibility. • Role-model adult behaviors. • Allow to make informed choices.	• Allow for informed participation. • Encourage peer support. • Suggest individualized and group expressions of grief, e.g., school memorials. • Support group advocacy for causes; e.g., Students Against Drunk Driving (SADD). • Recommend creative outlets; e.g., writing, art, and music.

Note. Adapted from Pearson, L. (1999). Separation, loss, and bereavement. In M. Broome, & J. Rollins (Eds.), *Core curriculum for the nursing care of children and their families* (pp. 77–92). Pitman, NJ: Anthony J. Jannetti Publications, Inc. Reprinted with permission.

- be demanding because they know their time is short;
- lack interest in nondisease-related conversation and play;
- be preoccupied with death and disease imagery in play, art, and literature;
- have constant images of death;
- engage selected individuals in either disclosure conversations or disclosure speeches;
- avoid talking about the future; and
- refuse to cooperate with relatively simple, painless procedures.

Children who are dying want their parents near, but they would often like to share their knowledge about their prognosis with someone else, as well. Other caring individuals can listen to what children say, take cues from them, answer only what they ask, and on their terms. According to Bluebond-Langner (1978, p. 235): "The issue then is not whether to tell but how to tell, in a way that respects the children and all of their many, often conflicting needs."

When speaking with a child who is at end-of-life, it is important to not underestimate the child's capacity to understand. Open communication should be encouraged, but not forced. Wolfelt (1996) recommends using the following guidelines:

- Listen first, then offer support.

- Provide honest information.

- Remember that it is okay to say, "I don't know."

- Answer only what the child wants to know.

Often, children reveal their hopes and fears through play. By being attuned to symbols and themes in play, caring adults can better interpret the dying child's journey (van Breemen, 2009).

Children who are dying have reported death-related sensory experiences (DRSE), spiritually transforming events that are marked by the appearance of a messenger beyond the visible, observable universe to guide the dying person through the death process (Ethier, 2005). Most commonly seen are dead family members; next most common are religious beings. The dying individual and the apparition communicate, and the majority of individuals experiencing DRSEs report feelings of peace and comfort. Also referred to as veridical hallucinations, visions of the dying, deathbed visions, and predeath visions, DRSEs are common among people of all cultures, religions, races, ages, genders, socioeconomic statuses, and educational levels. Validating this intense spiritual experience provides a way to start a dialogue with a child regarding death.

Death of a Child

Nearly 40,000 children die each year in the United States (Centers for Disease Control and Prevention/National Center for Health Statistics, 2009a). Causes of death vary by age (see Table 9.2. Leading Causes of Death by Age). A family-centered approach to care considers the impact of the child's death on all members of the family, for because the family is a system, each member's response will resonate with others.

Parents

Universally recognized as perhaps the most deeply painful and stressful experience a parent will ever face, the death of a child results in parental grief that is unlikely to completely resolve across a parent's lifetime. Parental grief is complex; reactions may include frequent illness, overeating or undereating, insomnia, antisocial behavior, depression, and compulsions (Gilmer, 2010). Factors that may influence parental grief response include (a) social support, (b) prior positive coping skills, (c) family communication style, (d) gender, (e) cultural orientation, (f) spiritual and religious beliefs, (g) anticipatory grief, (h) location of child's death, and (i) opportunities to participate in child's care near the end of life (Aho, Tarkka, Astedt-Kurki, & Kaunonen, 2006; Hass & Walter, 2006).

Siblings

It is estimated that 22% of the adult population has experienced the death of a sibling (The Compassionate Friends [TCF], 2006). The death of a brother or sister is a unique experience:

> When your parents die, it is said you lose your past; when your spouse dies, you lose your present; and when your child dies, you lose your future. However, when your sibling dies, you lose a part of your past, your present, and your future. (TCF, 2009a, sec. 8)

Research on the effects of sibling death reveals four sources of stress: (a) the way in which the child died, (b) parental reactions to the death, (c) parental feelings toward the surviving youngsters, and (d) children's relationships with their sibling prior to and after the loss (Brenner, 1984). Siblings have a variety of experiences (TCF, 2009b). They may feel tired or restless and have difficulty paying attention and remembering. Some siblings feel anger toward themselves, other people, God, or even their brother or sister who died. They sometimes fear for their own safety and the safety of those they care about. They may feel guilty about what they did or did not do for their brother or sister, for enjoying themselves, or simply just for surviving. Some siblings feel rejected by parents who are distracted, irritable, or inattentive.

Table 9.2 Leading Causes of Death by Age

Age	Cause of Death
Birth–1 year	1. Congenital malformations, deformations, and chromosomal abnormalities 2. Disorders related to short gestation and low birth weight, not elsewhere classified 3. Sudden infant death syndrome (SIDS) 4. Newborn affected by maternal complications of pregnancy 5. Accidents (unintentional injuries) 6. Newborn affected by complications of placenta, cord, and membranes 7. Respiratory distress of newborn 8. Bacterial sepsis of newborn 9. Neonatal hemorrhage 10. Diseases of the circulatory system
1–4 years	1. Accidents (unintentional injuries) 2. Congenital malformations, deformations, and chromosomal abnormalities 3. Malignant neoplasms 4. Assault (homicide) 5. Diseases of heart 6. Influenza and pneumonia 7. Septicemia 8. Certain conditions originating in the perinatal period 9. In situ neoplasms, benign neoplasms, and neoplasms of uncertain or unknown behavior 10. Cerebrovascular diseases
5–14 years	1. Accidents (unintentional injuries) 2. Malignant neoplasms 3. Assault (homicide) 4. Congenital malformations, deformations, and chromosomal abnormalities 5. Diseases of heart 6. Intentional self-harm (suicide) 7. Chronic lower respiratory diseases 8. Cerebrovascular diseases 9. Septicemia 10. In situ neoplasms, benign neoplasms, and neoplasms of uncertain or unknown behavior
14–24 years	1. Accidents (unintentional injuries) 2. Assault (homicide) 3. Intentional self-harm (suicide) 4. Malignant neoplasms 5. Diseases of heart 6. Congenital malformations, deformations, and chromosomal abnormalities 7. Cerebrovascular diseases 8. Human immunodeficiency virus (HIV) disease 9. Influenza and pneumonia 10. Pregnancy, childbirth, and the time immediately after birth

Note: From Centers for Disease Control and Prevention/National Center for Health Statistics [CDC/NCHS]. (2009b). *Infant, neonatal, and postneonatal deaths, percent of total deaths, and mortality rates for the 15 leading causes of infant death by race and sex: United States, 2006.* Retrieved April 23, 2010, from http://www.cdc.gov/nchs/data/dvs/LCWK7_2006.pdf CDC/NCHS. (2009c). *Deaths, percent of total deaths, and death rates for the 15 leading causes of death in selected age groups, by race and sex: United States, 2006.* Retrieved April 23, 2010, from http://www.cdc.gov/nchs/data/dvs/LCWK3_2006.pdf.

Because most children believe that only old people die, the death of a sibling may be more difficult for children to understand and accept than the loss of a parent. Thus, a child's demise shakes other children's faith in their own immortality. Most children cope effectively if they are supported through an appropriate mourning period. Unfortunately, institutions and individuals often focus on supporting the bereaved parents, and often ignore or fail to recognize the suffering of the siblings (Brenner, 1984).

Grandparents

Each year, approximately 160,000 grandparents experience the death of a grandchild (Youngblut, Brooten, Blais, Hannon, & Niyonsenga, 2009). It is sometimes assumed that because grandparents are older than the parents of the deceased child, they will have had more experience with death and will know how to cope with the death of their grandchild, when in fact the loss of a grandchild is unlike any other. Grandparents experience a dual loss: mourning the death of their grandchild while also grieving for their adult child's suffering. They typically feel helpless; they cannot protect their adult child from, nor take away, the pain.

We know that common emotional reactions among grandparents include sadness, anger, denial, intense depression, and numbness. Some grandparents may experience increased alcohol and drug use and thoughts of suicide (Youngblut et al., 2009). Considerations include supportive resources available to grieving grandparents, the effects of the grandchild's death on the grandparent-parent relationship, and the influence of race and ethnicity on grandparent.

Most grandparents recognize the importance of being available to their other grandchildren—the brothers and sisters of the deceased child—to help them cope with this experience. The best situation in which to provide support is one where grandparents perceive they are adequately supported. Thus, appropriate support for grandparents can help them to be more effective in the role of supporting the remaining grandchildren.

Death of a Parent

An estimated 3.5% of children under age 18 in the United States have experienced the death of a parent (Social Security Administration, 2000). To heal from this family tragedy involves helping the child to adapt and integrate to the new reality through continuous interactions with family and supportive others throughout the process of the parent's illness, death, and reconstitution. According to Christ (2000), the characteristics of helpful interventions include interactions that

- inform, prepare, and guide children;
- resonate with children's feelings; and
- encourage, support, and give solace, meaning, and value to children's experiences.

Although some researchers today have questioned a stage model for the grieving process, such a model is helpful as a framework in timing the possible strategies to implement in order to help children cope with loss. Table 9.3 outlines strategies that clinicians and religious counselors agree can be helpful for parents and other caring adults to use with bereaved youngsters (Brenner, 1984). These experts caution, however, that any activity be limited to brief sessions, repeated only when a child seems ready for more. Refer to Table 9.1 for guidance about the ages when particular behaviors are likely to occur.

Special Considerations

An extremely important point to remember is that people—adults and children—grieve differently. Some individuals are *instrumental grievers*. Instrumental grievers are doers: To help them get through their grief, they want tasks to complete, tangible things to do. In contrast, *intuitive grievers* find it easier to talk about their emotions; they want to explore why they are feeling certain ways. They generally tend to lean more toward group support than do instrumental grievers.

Table 9.3 Stage-Related Strategies for Helping Children Cope with Death

Stage	Children's Behaviors	Helpful Adult Responses
Protest	Apparently not hearing or not understanding the news of the death; acting dazed.	Repeat the news later in the day or the next morning. Answer questions clearly and honestly. Wait for awareness to occur.
	Panic and fear of being alone; nightmares.	Maintain usual routines as much as possible. Be sure children know who will take care of them in the coming weeks. At night, keep a radio playing or leave a door open so the child can hear sounds of life. Be sure someone is near to comfort the child after a nightmare.
	Grabbing the limelight to tell about the death.	Allow this behavior. It won't last long.
	Denying that the death has occurred; becoming unusually active and boisterous, to keep from thinking about it.	Accept this behavior. If it persists more than three to six months, consult a therapist.
Grief	Sadness and tears; yearning; acute loneliness.	Share adult sadness and tears with children. Support crying; join in yearning. Hold, cuddle, touch. Review pleasant and unpleasant memories of the dead person. Together, make a memory book of photos, captioned by the child. Collect home movies, videotapes, and tape recordings for the memory file.
	Regression to earlier, more infantile behavior.	Accept and facilitate (e.g., if wanted, give a toddler a bottle), yet support attempts to regain mature skills.
	Searching for the dead person.	Allow this stage to continue until the child feels he or she had made a thorough search. Help the child to talk about repeated disappointments.
	Difficulty in school, inability to concentrate, onset of learning problems.	School problems may last as long as two years. Teachers can work with the class to address death issues; enlist the school counselor to work regularly with the child on personal problems, so that he or she can concentrate during class. Help children focus on their studies, but do not allow schoolwork to cut into their playtime.
	Anger and guilt. Anger may be misplaced and directed toward siblings, caretakers, or other adults.	Accept anger, understanding that it is misplaced. Empathize with the respective feelings. Reassure the child that hurting is part of grieving, and eventually will subside. Find physical outlets for the child's rage. Put aside adult activities when possible to emphasize the value of conversations about guilty or angry feelings. Encourage drawing, writing, and playing out feelings. Where possible, meet periodically with the siblings, as a group, to explore feelings of guilt and anger, and work out solutions to common problems with their new living situation.
	Hopelessness and despair.	Validate such feelings as legitimate and painful. Reassure child that these feelings are temporary. Use books and stories to show how others coped with death. Reading fairy tales where a child conquers adversity is a way to help restore meaning and hope.
Acknowledgment	Acknowledging loss; seeking closer bonds with new caretaker; strengthening relationships with siblings.	Allow memory of dead person to be a part of the child's present life, by remembering anniversaries and recalling feelings.

Note. Adapted from Brenner, A. (1984). *Helping children cope with stress.* San Francisco: Jossey-Bass, pp. 51–52. Reprinted with permission.

During the past century, the most widely accepted view of grief holds that for successful mourning to take place the mourner must disengage from the deceased and let go of the past. Only within the past 100 years have continuing bonds been denied as a normal part of bereavement behavior. Klass, Silverman, and Nickman (1996) believe it is time that we reconsider bereavement as a cognitive as well as an emotional process that takes place in a social context, of which the deceased is a part. The process does not end; bereavement affects mourners in different ways for the rest of their lives. Individuals do not "get over" the experience; rather, they are changed by it, and part of the change is a transformed but continuing relationship with the deceased. According to Klass and colleagues (1996), the person who has died becomes part of the child's inner world. Children continue the relationship by dreaming, by talking to the deceased, by believing that the deceased is watching them, by keeping things that belonged to the deceased, by visiting the grave, and by frequently thinking about the deceased. These connections are not static, but are developmentally appropriate to the child and to the child's present circumstances.

The process is similar for bereaved parents. They, too, develop a set of memories, feelings, and actions to keep them connected to the deceased child (Klass et al., 1996). Research with a self-help group of bereaved parents revealed that the processes by which parents resolved their grief involved intense interaction with their dead children, which they sustained by using similar means to those of the bereaved children.

Therefore, we may want to rethink the way we talk about the resolution of grief. The concept of a continuing relationship challenges the idea that the purpose of grief is to sever the bonds with the deceased in order for survivors to be free to make new attachments and to construct a new identity. According to Klass and colleagues (1996), these bonds do not end, they simply change.

Activity Goals

All of the activities in this chapter are designed to help children cope with grief, primarily through helping children and families preserve and create memories. No one wants to be forgotten. Children who are dying sometimes worry that, in time, people will forget them as if they never existed. Conversely, children who have lost a parent or other significant person in their lives sometimes worry that they will forget the person who died, especially if they were quite young at the time of the death.

A physical reminder of the person can be very helpful in relieving this worry. Children like carrying with them a picture or object that reminds them of their family member, or having a special place to store such keepsakes. Several of the activities in this chapter provide opportunities to create such legacy items to keep the memory of that person alive.

ACTIVITY 9.1.   CRAYON CANDLES AND CANDLE LIGHTING CEREMONY

Candle lighting ceremonies are a part of many traditions and cultures around the world. The warmth, light, and ultimate extinguishment of the flame are often used as metaphors for hope, death, and the human spirit. The creation of candles from crayons can also serve as a metaphor for how something can change but continue to exist in a different and meaningful way.

Therapeutic Goal: To promote coping with grief by creating a ritual to commemorate the person who died.

Age Group: Preteen/adolescent

Adult/Child Ratio: 1:4

Required Time: 2 sessions, 45 minutes each

Restrictions and Precautions: Be sure that participants wear oven mitts when working with hot wax. Advise children on the safe use of candles.

Materials:

☐ Crayons

☐ Wax melter or pot and stove

- ☐ Large jar
- ☐ Oven mitts
- ☐ Scented oil or perfume
- ☐ Wooden spoon or other stirrer
- ☐ Small jars (one per child)

- ☐ Wicks (one per child)
- ☐ Glue
- ☐ Large pillar candle
- ☐ Tray

Process

1. To introduce the activity, talk to children about funerals, memorials, and other rituals people use to say good-bye to someone they love. Discuss different ways candle lighting is used in the rituals of other cultures. Explain that they will be making special candles to remember their loved one who has died.

2. Let the children select the color(s) they would like for their candles, which may be the favorite color of the person who has died or represent an emotion they are feeling.

3. If using scent, let the children choose from the selection available. It is especially nice if there is a special scent that the children associate with the person who has died.

4. Ask the children to glue the metal portion of the wick onto the center of the bottom of their small jar.

5. Melt the crayons in the melter—in batches, if using more than one color. If using a double boiler, pour water into the bottom pot, filling it no more than halfway, and bring it to a boil on a stove or hot plate. Place the crayons into the jar then set the jar into the boiling water; leave until the crayons melt. (Note: The boiling water should reach no more than halfway up the side of the jar.)

6. After the crayons have melted, have the children stir in enough scented oil or perfume to achieve the desired intensity.

7. Help the children pour the melted wax into the small jar, until it reaches the top, leaving at 2 two inches of wick sticking out.

8. Allow the candles to harden; trim the wick, if needed.

9. During another session, sit the children in a circle, around a tray with the large, lit pillar candle in the center and the smaller candles they have made around it.

10. Ask each child to pick up the candle he or she has made and light it from the flame of the center candle. Then encourage them each to share the name of the person for whom the candle was made, and a special memory of that person.

11. After each child has spoken, allow a few moments of silence, or read a meaningful passage or poem.

Variation

For a simpler version of this activity suitable for younger children, or when time is limited, let the children personalize small, store-bought pillar candles by decorating near the base of the candles using fabric paints and craft gems with prongs.

Activity 9.2.   Fabric Hand Wall Hanging

These wall hangings carry great meaning for families, and look best when made from rich fabrics of different textures. High-quality, discontinued fabric samples can often be obtained from upholstery companies, furniture stores, designers, and factory sales representatives.

Therapeutic Goal: To promote coping with grief by creating a memorial.

Age Group: All

Adult/Child Ratio: 1:1

Required Time: Hand tracings may need to be acquired over a period of time; 30 minutes for advance preparation and assemblage

Restrictions and Precautions: Take scissors, glue, and staple precautions.

Materials:

- ☐ Glue or staple gun
- ☐ Artist canvas board
- ☐ Fabric, cut into pieces 2 inches larger than the canvas
- ☐ Assorted color-coordinated fabric squares, large enough to encompass an adult hand
- ☐ Paper-baked fusible web
- ☐ Iron
- ☐ Pencil or pen
- ☐ Sharp scissors

Process

1. Center the canvas board on top of the fabric.

2. Fold the cloth edges behind the board, pulling to make the fabric taut, and affix using the glue or staple gun.

3. Iron the fusible web to the back of the fabric squares.

4. Ask the child or a family member to identify the person they wish to include in the wall hanging.

5. Have the child or family member trace each person's hand on a fabric square they have selected and then cut them out.

6. Arrange the hands decoratively on the board, with fingers intertwined; iron in place.

7. Frame, if desired (Figure Activity 9.2-1).

Figure Activity 9.2-1. Fabric Hand Wall Hanging

ACTIVITY 9.3.   FRIENDSHIP BRACELETS

Children facing the death of a loved one may find comfort in making a friendship bracelet to symbolize the special bond between them. The bracelets can serve as a reminder that even when they are not together, there will always be a connection. Friendship bracelets can also be made by groups of children, such as school classes, in memory of a student who has died.

Therapeutic Goal: To promote coping with grief by creating a keepsake of a loved one.

Age Group: Primary school-age/adolescent

Adult/Child Ratio: 1:8

Required Time: 1 hour

Restrictions and Precautions: Take scissors precautions.

Materials:
- ☐ Yarn, in assorted colors
- ☐ Measuring tape
- ☐ Scissors
- ☐ Binder clip

Process

1. Explain the symbolic meaning of friendship bracelets to the children.

2. Ask the children to each select three colors of yarn and to cut their strands into 24-inch pieces.

3. Demonstrate for the children how to hold their three strands together at one end, make a loop around their finger, and tie a square knot (while maintaining the loop) at the end.

4. Have the children clip that end to a book or other stationary object.

5. Show the children how to braid the strands, as they would braid hair (bringing the outer string across the middle string, pulling tightly, and repeating, until the braid is long enough to fit comfortably around the wrist of the person who will be wearing it).

6. When the braid reaches the desired length, have the children tie the loose ends in a knot.

7. Instruct the children to repeat the process to make another identical bracelet for their loved one.

8. When they are ready to tie the bracelets around their wrists, illustrate for the children how to pull the knotted end through the loop and tie a square knot.

Variation

Matching bracelets can be made using elastic string, colored beads, and letter beads that spell out both the child's and the loved one's name.

Young children or those with short attention spans can instead, quickly and simply, make "friendship pins" by threading an identical pattern of small beads onto safety pins.

Activity 9.4. Keepsake Caches

These small pouches are for those who wish to keep a cherished memento of their loved one always close at hand to remind them of the special relationship they shared. Caches can be made small enough fit into a pocket or purse.

Therapeutic Goal: To promote coping with grief by creating a keepsake and encouraging identification and verbalization of feelings.

Age Group: School-age/adolescent

Adult/Child Ratio: 1:8

Required Time: 1 hour

Restrictions and Precautions: Exercise caution when using needles; and dispose of them properly.

Materials:
- ☐ Fabric pieces in assorted colors and patterns
- ☐ Measuring tape
- ☐ Thread
- ☐ Sewing needles (one per child)
- ☐ Yarn, cord, or string

Process

1. Cut the fabric into pieces with a length-to-width ratio of 1:3 (e.g., 4 inches × 12 inches, 3 inches × 9 inches, 5 inches × 15 inches).

2. Let the children each select the piece of fabric they want to use.

3. To make a space to insert the drawstring, ask the children to fold the width of one end of the fabric down 1 inch, creating a flap.

4. Help the children thread needles and show them how to sew the flap to the fabric, about 1/4 inch from the edge.

5. Instruct the children to repeat steps 1 and 2 on the opposite end of the fabric.

6. Ask the children to fold the fabric in half. If the fabric has a pattern, show them how to fold it so that the pattern is on the outside of the flap.

7. Demonstrate for the children how to sew the sides of the fabric together, approximately 1/4 inch from the edge, stopping at the point where the fold begins.

8. Have the children turn their bags inside out.

9. To create a drawstring, ask the children to thread a piece of yarn, cord, or string through both folds and tie the ends together.

10. Encourage the children to use their keepsake cache to hold a small memento of their loved one or of an experience they shared.

11. Allow each of the children who wish to do so time to share the meaning attached to the memento they have chosen to keep in their pouch.

ACTIVITY 9.5.   LIFE NECKLACE

Creating life necklaces gives children a visual representation of their personal journey through illness and treatment, one they may share with others.

Therapeutic Goal: To promote coping with grief by creating a legacy.

Age Group: Primary/school-age/adolescent

Adult/Child Ratio: 1:1

Required Time: Progressive; each session, 15–20 minutes, plus baking time

Restrictions and Precautions: Bake beads in a well-ventilated area. Watch closely to prevent scorching.

Materials:

☐ Polymer clay, in an assortment of colors

☐ Plastic knife
☐ Toothpicks
☐ Coffee stirrers
☐ Cookie sheets covered with aluminum foil
☐ Toaster oven (or use of a regular oven)
☐ Potholders
☐ Ribbon or cord
☐ Scissors

Process

1. Cut blocks of clay into smaller pieces.

2. Introduce the activity to the children after a procedure or other event, by explaining that they will be creating a special bead or group of beads to represent their experience.

3. Show the children how new colors of clay can be created through mixing those on hand.

4. Give the children different-colored pieces of clay to roll into a "snake" and then twist.

5. Demonstrate how to shape round beads, by taking a piece of clay from the "snake" and rolling it between your hands or on a tabletop.

6. Explain that beads need not be round; show how to make square, flat, and other-shape beads.

7. Demonstrate how to use toothpicks to produce texture, carve images, or write words.

8. Invite the children to select the colors they want to use.

9. Provide children with ample time for experimentation; when they are ready, ask them to give you their finished beads for baking.

10. Use a coffee stirrer to punch a hole all the way through the bead.

11. Place beads on the cookie sheet and bake in a 275-degree oven — 10 minutes for small beads, 15 minutes for larger ones.

12. Remove beads from oven and allow to cool.

13. Encourage the children to share the story behind their unique beads with you. Keep a written record of the children's descriptions.

14. To make an individual necklace, cut a piece of cord or ribbon to a size long enough to pass easily over the child's head. To make a life necklace, add beads to a long piece of ribbon or cord and tie a knot on either side of the beads, to prevent sliding.

15. Allow the child to make additional beads over time to chronicle new experiences.

16. At the termination of treatment, or in the event of the child's death, present the child or family with the narrative you transcribed, describing the symbolic meaning of each bead on the necklace.

Note. Adapted from a project begun by Lacretia Johnson, which was included in Rollins, J. (2004). *Arts activities for children at bedside.* Washington, DC: WVSA arts connection.

ACTIVITY 9.6.   MEMORABILIA FRAME

These visually rich frames offer a glimpse into the life of the person whose portrait they hold.

Therapeutic Goal: To promote coping with grief by creating legacies or memorials and encouraging identification and verbalization of feelings.

Age Group: Primary/school-age/adolescent

Adult/Child Ratio: Significant variation, depending on the ages of the participants

Required Time: 30 minutes with children; additional time to paint the frames and attach photos

Restrictions and Precautions: Take glue or glue gun precautions.

Materials:

☐ Photograph, 5-inch × 7-inch, or larger

☐ Frame or photo mount, size appropriate to photo (one per child)

☐ Assorted objects of meaning to the child (e.g., small toys, game pieces, barrettes, buttons, keys, inexpensive costume jewelry)

☐ White glue or glue gun

☐ Tongue depressor

☐ Letter stickers or alphabet macaroni

☐ Cardstock

☐ Tape (optional)

☐ Picture hanger

Process

1. Give the children time to experiment with different ways to decoratively arrange the objects on their frame or photo mount.

2. When the children are satisfied with their arrangements, show them how to affix the items with the glue gun, or how to use a tongue depressor to spread a thick layer of glue over the frame and then press the object into position.

3. If white glue is used, allow the frame to dry overnight.

4. Position the photo in the frame, and back with a piece of cardstock and glue or tape it in place.

5. Give the children letter stickers or alphabet macaroni to spell out the name of the person in the photograph, a meaningful quote, or random words that describe the person.

6. If needed, glue a picture hanger to the reverse side of the frame.

7. Allow time for the children to talk about the person who died, and the significance of the objects they have included on their frames (Figure Activity 9.6-1).

Figure Activity 9.6-1. Memorabilia Frame

Variation   Make simple frames out of tongue depressors, glued together, or CD jewel boxes.

ACTIVITY 9.7.   MEMORY QUILTS

Quilts memorializing a loved one can be made from fabric squares painted with representative images or quotes, fabric with patterns reflecting the interests of the loved one (e.g., favorite sports or television shows), and fabric squares cut from T-shirts or jerseys worn by the loved one during meaningful events or activities in his or her life. Portions of this activity can be carried out in a variety of settings—including clinics, hospitals, support groups, and classrooms—and be sewn together later.

Therapeutic Goal: To promote coping with grief by creating a memorial.

Age Group: Adolescent

Adult/Child Ratio: Squares can be made or provided by many different people. Assembling the quilt is done most effectively by one or two children or a skilled adult.

Required Time: A time-consuming activity requiring multiple sessions

Restrictions and Precautions: Have children exercise caution when using needles; and dispose of them properly.

Materials:

☐ Fabric squares (8 inches each), cut from plain white cotton; fabrics with patterns; and/or fabric squares cut from T-shirts representative of a meaningful event or activity in the loved one's life

☐ Fabric paint

☐ Quilt batting

☐ Yarn

☐ Thread

☐ Sewing needles

☐ Scissors

Process

1. If the children wish, have them invite family and friends to contribute to the quilt. Provide them with fabric paint to create an image or write an inspirational quote that reminds them of the person being memorialized (Figure Activity 9.7-1, step 1).

2. Show the children how to combine the squares decorated by family and friends with those cut from T-shirts or other decorative fabric. Encourage the children to talk about the meaning they attach to each square throughout the process of assembling the quilt.

3. Let the children choose a coordinated color backing for each square, and then pin the right sides of each pair of fabric squares together (Figure Activity 9.7-1, step 2).

Figure Activity 9.7-1. Memory Quilt Making

4. For each square, tell the children to remove the pins and stitch the decorated fabric square to the undecorated square, leaving an area of about 2 inches unstitched (Figure Activity 9.7-1, step 3).

5. Instruct the children to turn the fabric squares inside out, so the right sides are showing, and stuff them lightly with quilt batting (Figure Activity 9.7-1, step 4).

6. Demonstrate for the children how to slip-stitch the 2-inch opening closed (Figure Activity 9.7-1, step 5).

7. Show the children how to use yarn to make a knot in the middle of each square, by bringing the yarn down through the front and up through the back. Cut the ends about 1 inch from the quilt.

8. Let the children decide how to arrange the fabric squares.

9. Help the children sew the squares together to finish the quilt.

ACTIVITY 9.8. MEMORY BOX

Many children keep letters, cards, photos, and other reminders of the person in their life who has died. These items may be considered private by some, who prefer to keep them in a safe place where others can't see them. For these children, a memory box can serve as a special container in which to store, preserve, and revisit cherished items of their loved ones.

Therapeutic Goal: To promote coping with grief by preserving memories.

Age Group: School-age/adolescent

Adult/Child Ratio: 1:10

Required Time: 45 minutes

Restrictions and Precautions: Take glue and scissors precautions.

Materials:

☐ Sturdy decorative or plain box with lid (heart or oval shapes are nice, if available)

☐ Photo of the person who has died (optional)

☐ Craft glue

☐ Decorative flat or semiflat trims (e.g., wrapping   ☐ Marble, piece of driftwood, or small ball
   paper scraps, ribbons, craft jewels yarn, pictures   (optional)
   cut from magazines)   ☐ Mementos

☐ Scissors

☐ Hot glue

Process

1. If children are using a photograph, have them glue it to the box. Advise them not to center the picture if they plan to add a handle to the box.

2. Let the children embellish the box by gluing on decorative trims, both on the outside and inside of the box.

3. Help the children use hot glue to attach the handle, if they choose to have one.

4. Encourage the children to place their mementos in the box and find a special place to keep it.

Variation

Many different techniques can be used to decorate a memory box, including collage, paint, stencil, and mosaics.

For more ideas, see Bright Ideas for Memory Making (Box Activity 9.8-1).

BOX ACTIVITY 9.8-1. BRIGHT IDEAS FOR MEMORY MAKING

- Give the child or family a disposable camera to take pictures; or offer to take pictures for them.

- Help the child create a video self-portrait.

- Enlist the aid of a hospital photographer, or a professional photographer in the community, to take portraits of the child and his or her family together.

- Provide the materials for scrapbooking. Encourage siblings or the children of adult patients to collaborate with their loved one to create a scrapbook that celebrates their lives together.

- Encourage families to create a photo-memory collage on poster board in the child's favorite color. Suggest that they use images that represent the child's favorite activities, foods, vacations, pets, toys/games, holidays, and so on.

- Position a photograph of the child near the top of a large piece of foam board and write the child's name below it. Provide colored markers, and invite classmates, visitors, staff, and others to write a message or memory on the board.

- Provide a log for visitors to sign and share a message or memory.

- Organize a joyful activity for the families, which can become a meaningful tradition after their loved one dies. If the loved one has already died, make the activity one that the entire family enjoyed together in the past.

- Create "memory bags" for grieving children. Include in the bags items for memorializing, expressing feelings, and reducing stress, such as a photo frame, clay, markers, art pad, journal, comfort item, stress ball, or a yo-yo (to symbolize the ups and downs in life). Place all the items in a light-colored canvas tote bag that can be decorated with markers, and give to siblings or the children of adult patients.

ACTIVITY 9.9.   MOMENT BOARDS

Children are fascinated with these boards, on which they paint with water, only to see the images disappear within about 10 minutes. The fleeting image can provide a symbolic segue into a discussion of how important it is to savor each moment in life, because the image—as with all things in life—is only temporary. Children with life-threatening conditions, or those coping with the death of a loved one, seem to connect with this metaphor and gain comfort from the concept of appreciating the moment.

Therapeutic Goal: To promote coping with grief by encouraging the expression of feelings.

Age Group: Preschool/primary

Adult/Child Ratio: 1:1

Required Time: 20 minutes preparation

Restrictions and Precautions: Use rubber cement in a well-ventilated area.

Materials:

☐ Rigid corrugated cardboard, 11 inches × 14 inches

☐ Precut mat, 11 inches × 14 inches, with a 7–1/2 × 9–1/2-inch opening

☐ Brush-Up paper (available at many art supply sources)

☐ Scissors

☐ Rubber cement

☐ Bamboo brush

☐ Container for water

Process

1. With the Brush-Up paper right side up, put a dab of rubber cement on each corner.
2. Center the mat board over the Brush-Up paper and press to adhere.
3. Turn over and apply more rubber cement in the area backed by the mat board, being careful to avoid getting any on the Brush-Up paper.
4. Press mat board (with attached Brush-Up paper) to corrugated cardboard to form a solid bond.
5. Provide a container of water and bamboo brush and invite the child to make a brushstroke.
6. Explain that only clean water and a clean brush may be used on the board, and to avoid oversaturation. Let the water dry naturally.
7. Encourage the child to create an image using the bamboo brush and water, explaining that the image will only be temporary.
8. Ask the child to tell you about his or her creation, and how it felt to make something that would not last forever.

Note. Adapted from Valerie Conzett, artist, Omaha, NE, in Rollins, J. (2004). *Arts activities for children at bedside.* Washington, DC: WVSA arts connection.

ACTIVITY 9.10. MOSAIC FLOWER POTS

Many people find it meaningful to plant a living thing in memory of someone they love who has died. These pretty flower pots make a memorial planting uniquely personal by incorporating into the mosaic design symbols and keepsakes of the person who died.

Therapeutic Goal: To promote coping with grief through creating a memorial.

Age Group: School-age/adolescent

Adult/Child Ratio: 1:8

Required Time: 45 minutes–1 hour

Restrictions and Precautions: None

Materials:

☐ Plastic plant pot (one per child)

☐ Nontoxic acrylic latex grout

☐ Tongue depressor (one per child)

☐ Small tiles

☐ Small trinkets and/or keepsake objects

☐ Dirt

☐ Flowering plants or seeds

Process

1. Spread newspaper over table.

2. Ask the children to envision the design of their pot and decide which objects they would like to use. Lay out a design on a flat surface (Figure Activity 9.10-1).

Figure Activity 9.10-1. Mosaic Flower Pot Design

3. Give the children a tongue depressor to spread a small amount of grout onto the outside of the pot. Emphasize that it is best to work on one small area of the pot at a time, as the grout dries quickly.

4. Invite the children to press tiles and/or objects into the grout.

5. Repeat steps 3 and 4 until the entire outside of the pot is covered.

6. Allow the pot to dry overnight.

7. Give the children soil to add to the pot, along with either seeds or a plant.

Variation

Young children, children with low energy, or those with short attention spans can simply paint clean, small, plastic plant pots or yogurt containers, using acrylic paints; or glue on paper.

ACTIVITY 9.11.   TIMELINE

Constructing a timeline involves the child and family in reminiscing and reflecting about meaningful events in the life of the child.

Therapeutic Goal: To promote coping with grief by creating a legacy.	**Materials:**
Age Group: School-age/adolescent	☐ Butcher paper or poster board
Adult/Child Ratio: 1:1	☐ Marker
Required Time: Varies	☐ Yardstick
Restrictions and Precautions: Take marker precautions.	☐ Photographs (optional)

Process

1. Lay the butcher paper or poster board horizontally on a flat surface.

2. Using the yardstick as a guide, draw a horizontal line across the paper, several inches down from the top.

3. Write the child's birth date below the line, at the extreme left of the paper or board.

4. Draw a short vertical line from the birth date to intersect with the horizontal line directly above.

5. Ask the child and/or family members to generate a list of significant events in the child's life, along with the approximate dates they occurred. (Jot this information down on a piece of paper.) Encourage them to talk about what they were feeling at those times. If needed, facilitate the process by asking questions about such things as:

> Developmental milestones (e.g., first words, first steps, first day at school)
>
> Graduations
>
> Religious rites
>
> Birthdays
>
> Marriages
>
> Reunions
>
> Vacations
>
> Music recitals
>
> Important family occasions

6. When the child or family is satisfied with the list, number each event chronologically.

7. Have the child or family member divide the timeline into numbered segments corresponding to the child's age, assisting as needed. If certain years were more eventful than others, make those segments proportionately larger.

8. Ask the child or family member to write down the dates and events from the list in chronological order, below the line, going from left to right. Encourage them to write a sentence or more about the emotions they felt at the time. Children too young to write can draw pictures.

9. Draw a perpendicular line from the event to intersect the timeline.

10. Invite those involved to display the timeline and share their memories with others.

ACTIVITY 9.12.   REMEMBRANCE ROCKS

In some cultures, rocks are symbolic of strength. And because it is often the love and comfort of family and friends that bolster grieving children and give them the strength they need to endure, Remembrance Rocks can serve as a metaphor for that strength. They can be used by those visiting a hospital, hospice, or attending a memorial service.

Therapeutic Goal: To promote coping with grief by creating a memorial token and promoting the expression of feelings.

Age Group: School-age/adolescent

Adult/Child Ratio: Not applicable

Required Time: Ongoing

Restrictions and Precautions: None

Materials:

☐ Sheet of stationery

☐ Inexpensive frame

☐ Smooth river rocks, approximately 2–3 inches in diameter

☐ Decorative tray or plate

☐ Permanent metallic paint markers

☐ Large glass bowl

Process

1. Using a computer, make a sign that thanks visitors for coming and asks them to help create a special remembrance by writing their name and a personal message on a rock. Print the sign out on pretty paper, frame it.

2. Arrange the rocks in a pile on a tray or plate (Figure Activity 9.12-1).

Figure Activity 9.12-1. Remembrance Rocks

3. Position the markers, sign, bowl, and tray of rocks on a table near the entrance of the room.

4. After visitors write their message on a rock, ask them to place it in the bowl.

5. Display the rocks in the bowl; or arrange them in a memorial garden.

ACTIVITY 9.13.   SHADOW BOXES

Shadow boxes are a wonderful way to keep and display mementos. Rather than stashed away somewhere in a box or drawer, cherished items can be shared with others, and serve as a frequent reminder of fond memories.

Therapeutic Goal: To promote coping with grief by preserving memories and encouraging the expression of feelings.

Age Group: School-age/adolescent

Adult/Child Ratio: 1:8

Required Time: 1 hour or more

Restrictions and Precautions: Take sharps, glue, and paint precautions.

Materials:

☐ Cardboard box with dividers (one per child)

☐ Acrylic paint

☐ Paintbrushes

☐ Two-dimensional mementos (e.g., photos, invitations, greeting cards, comics, artwork, letters, stickers, menus, maps of special places)

☐ Three-dimensional mementos (e.g., shells, keys, jewelry, hospital bracelets, dried flowers, buttons, small toys, pieces from a favorite game, gym shoe laces, vacation souvenirs)

☐ Hot or craft glue

Process

1. Have the children paint the box and dividers; allow to dry.

2. When the paint is dry, invite the children to begin by arranging the two-dimensional mementos in the box sections. When they are pleased with the arrangement, tell them to affix the items with hot or craft glue.

3. Instruct the children to position the three-dimensional objects in each of the sections and glue them in place (Figure Activity 9.13-1).

4. Let the children decorate the outside of the box, if they wish.

5. Encourage the children to tell the story behind each item in the box.

Figure Activity 9.13-1. Shadow Box

ACTIVITY 9.14.   STEPPING STONES

The creation of an enduring object that can be placed outdoors in the splendor of nature makes this type of legacy or memorial activity especially appealing to children. Stepping stones can also be made from clay and then fired in a kiln, making them extremely hard and long-lasting.

Therapeutic Goal: To promote coping with grief by preserving memories.

Age Group: Preschool/school-age/adolescent

Adult/Child Ratio: 1:1 or with a small group

Required Time: 30 minutes, plus hardening time

Restrictions and Precautions: Wear gloves when working with concrete. Mix the concrete in a well-ventilated area, away from children with respiratory disorders. If the concrete comes in contact with skin, wash it off immediately with soap and water.

Materials:

☐ Paper

☐ Pencil

☐ Plastic basin

☐ Stepping stone concrete (available at many craft stores)

☐ Measuring cup

☐ Water

☐ Mixing stick

☐ Shallow box, approximately 12 × 18 inches, or a store-bought mold

☐ Tongue depressors

☐ Memorabilia (e.g., old jewelry, keys, coins, seashells, pebbles, marbles)

Process

1. Explain what stepping stones are and how they can be personalized to preserve a memory or memorialize an individual and then be placed in a garden or yard.

2. Help the children plan and sketch a special stepping stone that represents their loved one or symbolizes a special memory. Explain that they can incorporate pictures, patterns, writing, and/or memorabilia made of hard substances into the design.

3. In the plastic basin, prepare the stepping stone concrete according to package directions.

4. Pour the mixture into the cardboard box or mold.

5. Shake the box or mold gently to remove any air bubbles.

6. Wait five minutes for the mixture to set before allowing the children to press desired objects gently into the concrete.

7. After 20 to 30 minutes, give the children tongue depressors to draw a picture or write names, dates, and/or meaningful words in the concrete.

8. Allow the concrete to dry according to package directions.

9. Remove the cardboard mold and encourage the children to place the stepping stone in their yard or a garden (Figure Activity 9.14-1).

Figure Activity 9.14-1. Stepping Stone

ACTIVITY 9.15.   TIME CAPSULES

Time capsules can be created to commemorate a special day, period of time, or person. They can be made by a dying child to leave as a legacy for family and friends, or by a family to memorialize a lost loved one. Some people choose to bury their time capsules with the person who has died, or at a place that holds special meaning to them. Others prefer to tuck them away safely, to bring out at some meaningful date in the future.

Therapeutic Goal: To promote coping with grief by creating a legacy or memorial.

Age Group: Preschool and up

Adult/Child Ratio: Situational

Required Time: Requires multiple sessions

Restrictions and Precautions: Apply sealant in a well-ventilated area. Take paint precautions.

Materials:

☐ 3-foot length of PVC sewer and drainpipe, 4 inches in diameter

☐ 2–4-inch sewer and drainpipe end caps (available from home improvement stores)

☐ Paint for metals

☐ Paintbrushes

☐ Outdoor number and letter stickers (used on mailboxes)

☐ Waterproof, 100 percent silicone sealant

Process

1. Have the child or a family member paint a base coat on the pipe and caps, making sure to cover them completely. Allow the paint to dry thoroughly.

2. Let the child or family paint designs or pictures on the capsule for decoration.

3. Suggest using number and letter stickers to spell out the child's and/or family name and the date and year.

4. Place one end cap on the pipe.

5. Let the child or family member select and put keepsakes and mementos in the capsule. Some ideas include:

   • Tape recording of the child

   • Photographs

   • Letter or story written by the child

   • Lock(s) of hair

   • Drawing made by the child

   • Hand- or footprints

   • Newspaper from significant day

6. Place the remaining end cap on and apply sealant according to package directions.

Variation

Make time capsule decorations using clear plastic ornaments that can be opened. Fill them with small pictures, notes written on strips of pretty paper, rolled up and tied with tiny ribbon, and small mementos. Put the ball back together and add a ribbon, with the year written on it, and a bow.

ACTIVITY 9.16. T-SHIRT PILLOWS

Children often acquire T-shirts emblazoned with words and/or graphic designs on them as souvenirs of experiences they've had, places they've visited, schools they attended, teams they played on, or teams they've rooted for. T-shirts such as these, which often hold special meaning for the children who wore them, can be turned into soft, comforting keepsakes for their loved ones.

Therapeutic Goal: To promote coping with grief by creating a memorial.	**Materials:**
	☐ T-shirt or infant "onesies"
Age Group: School-age/adolescent	☐ Fabric scissors
Adult/Child Ratio: 1:8	☐ Needle
Required Time: 1 hour	☐ Thread
Restrictions and Precautions: Have children exercise caution when using needles; and dispose of them properly. Take precautions when using scissors.	☐ Cotton or polyester stuffing (one to two 12-ounce bags per pillow)

Process

1. If the length of the T-shirt exceeds that desired for the pillow, have the children cut off the excess fabric from the bottom of the shirt, leaving an inch of fabric for the seam.

2. Tell the child to turn the T-shirt inside out and sew the armholes and bottom of the shirt closed, leaving only the neck opening unsewn.

3. Now tell the children to turn the T-shirt right side out and begin inserting the cotton stuffing through the neck hole.

4. When they have achieved the desired fullness for their pillows, show the children how to sew the neck opening closed (Figure Activity 9.16-1).

Figure Activity 9.16-1. T-Shirt Pillow

ACTIVITY 9.17.   WAVING GOOD-BYE

This is a good activity to use with classmates or support-group participants.

Therapeutic Goal: To promote coping with grief by creating a memorial and encouraging the expression of feelings.

Age Group: Preschool/primary

Adult/Child Ratio: 1:10

Required Time: 30 minutes

Restrictions and Precautions: Take marker, scissors, and glue precautions.

Materials:

☐ Large piece of poster board or butcher paper

☐ Markers

☐ Construction paper

☐ Scissors (one per child)

☐ Glue

Process

1. Help the children write the word "Good-bye" in the center of the poster board or piece of butcher paper.

2. Trace each of the children's hands on construction paper.

3. Have the children cut out their paper hands.

4. Ask each child to write his or her name on their hand cutouts, along with something they will miss about the person who has died.

5. Give each child the opportunity to share with the group what he or she will miss about the person who has died.

6. Invite the children to glue their hands to the poster. Alternatively, suggest that they attach their hand cutouts to a tongue depressor and use them to wave good-bye symbolically to the person who has died.

7. Allow the children to choose where they would like to display the poster.

Variation

Make hand-prints by coating children's hands with finger paint or tempera paint and pressing them onto paper.

CHAPTER 10

CULTURE

Culture can be defined as the shared values, norms, traditions, customs, arts, history, and institutions shared by a group of people (Johnson, 2005). Issues of multicultural differences are encountered on a regular basis. Because play is considered the universal language of children, the literature suggests that play is the developmentally appropriate form of therapy for children regardless of cultural background (Ritter & Chang, 2002). Yet, to understand the play of a child, one needs to observe how cultural differences can assume a role in implementation of activities, play themes, and other activity outcomes.

LIST OF ACTIVITIES

Activity 10.1 African Wrap Dolls	Activity 10.11 Milagros
Activity 10.2 Carp Paper Sculpture	Activity 10.12 Native American Dream Catcher
Activity 10.3 Chamsa, or Hand of Fatima, Symbol	Activity 10.13 Native American Sand Painting
Activity 10.4 Chinese Good Luck Envelopes	Activity 10.14 Origami Cranes
Activity 10.5 God's Eyes	Activity 10.15 Prayer or Meditation Rugs
Activity 10.6 Hispanic Paper Flowers	Activity 10.16 Rice-a-Rainbow
Activity 10.7 Japanese Garden Theater	Activity 10.17 Tree of Life
Activity 10.8 Japanese Zen Garden	Activity 10.18 Ukrainian Eggs
Activity 10.9 Kachina Dolls	Activity 10.19 Worry Dolls
Activity 10.10 Mandalas	

Cultural Differences

Cultures differ in many ways (Carmichael, 2001). When people from one cultural group move to a place dominated by another cultural group, one of three styles of reconciling differences are evidenced (O'Connor, 1997). Some families may work to preserve differences. For example, their children may be taught the language of their culture of origin. Other families may attempt to acculturate, in other words, strive to reach a compromise between their own and the surrounding cultures. The third style of reconciling differences is assimilation, or being like the surrounding culture, as they adopt the region's style of dress, for example. Establishing how traditional children and their families are is important. As mentioned in the Introduction, children and families may be at different levels, and even members of the same family may not share the same views.

According to Le Vine (1988, cited in Okagaki & Divecha, 1993), across cultural groups parents hold common general goals for their children, such as survival and health, skill development, and societal acceptance. It is the specific parenting strategies for meeting these objectives that vary between cultural groups, and this variation is a function of the environmental context of the family. Contrasting with this view, Hoffman (1988, cited in Okagaki & Divecha, 1993) suggests that children satisfy different parental needs, and that these differ between cultures. Therefore, cultural values influence parental attitudes toward their goals for their children, thus leading to very diverse approaches to parenting in a multicultural society. Variations between cultural group expectations and practices may result in reduced early detection of children with developmental delay or behavioral problems (Williams & Holmes, 2004).

Triandis (1987) focuses on differences based on whether a culture defines people according to what they do or who they are. He gives the example of a mother spanking her child. If the focus is on what people do, then an observer from the culture may be horrified that one person is striking another. However, if the cultural emphasis is on who people are, then the observer might say that a mother has a right to spank her child.

The notion of trust is sacred for all cultures (Carmichael, 2001). Cultures differ, however, regarding their perception of whom to trust, and how. Some cultures only trust people inside their family, or those above a certain maturity level. Many cultures do not trust people of a specific racial origin. Trust is something that is won; in children, earning their trust is experiential.

Perceptions regarding age and gender differ among cultures, as well. Age may be equated with the gaining of wisdom, or of being "out of step." Eastern cultures are inclined to be age dominated. In some cultures, males are considered superior to females, whereas in other cultures, females dominate. Other cultures, such as African-American and Jewish cultures in the United States, tend to be matriarchal, while European cultures tend to be patriarchal. Middle Eastern cultures typically are male-dominated societies (Carmichael, 2001).

Children who come from a traditional tribal background, such as Native Americans and many Southeast Asians, are more responsive in groups (Carmichael, 2001). Tribal groups see the individual's problems as group problems. Children from cultures that value extended families may have grandparents or other relatives, rather than their parents, as their primary caregivers. Children from a tribe or extended family may be acculturated to a different norm.

Status, who it is given to and how, varies with culture. For example, status may be based on age or gender or be earned (Carmichael, 2001). In many traditional Asian cultures, teachers, therapists, or doctors are afforded status; therefore, members of such cultures may not question what practitioners of these professions tell them. In cultures where females have no status, suggestions from women are likely to be ignored.

Certain cultures focus on self-concept and individualism, and will protect what is good for the individual. Other cultures that have a people's identity or collectivist orientation will not be concerned about the individual, but what is best for the whole (Carmichael, 2001). Western cultures tend to be self-concept/individualist orientated; Eastern/South American cultures are inclined to be collectivist/people identity orientated.

Communication Styles and Values

A study of the collaboration styles of African-American, Asian-American, Native American, Hispanic-American, and Anglo-American communities revealed some similarities across communities in styles and markers of success, yet a great chasm separated each minority community from the Anglo-American communities (Elliott, Adams, & Sockalingam, 1999). This chasm was created by differences in expectations, styles, assumptions, values, body language, and privilege. The researchers concluded that although each minority community understands that great differences separate them from the Anglo-American mainstream cultures, Anglo-American communities do not have much awareness of the magnitude of these differences. Sometimes events open a small portal to this awareness, but Anglo-Americans do not experience cultural differences as a central concern in their lives. These differences are not only central but also vast and inescapable for minority communities.

A summary of normative communication styles and values identifies arenas of difference between ethnic groups that can destroy trust and respect when the differences are unknown to one or both parties in a communication (see Table 10.1.). Such unknown or invisible differences in communication style and values also can present difficulties because they may be presumed to be individual personality or ethical issues. Comparisons are not meant to stereotype individuals but rather to provide generalizations and valid observations about a group of people to highlight possible areas of miscommunication.

Differences in Play Styles

Play styles may vary across cultures (Drewes, 2005; Glover, 1999). For example, African-American children are more sensitive to verbal and nonverbal communications. They prefer hands-on experiences, and are persistent in completing a task. They may be louder than their peers in verbal interactions. Hispanic-American children are inclined to move about more and may take breaks from their play. Asian American children have a tendency to be quiet and to play in a more self-contained mode, rather than be interactive. In play, Native American children

Table 10.1 Normative Communication Styles and Values for Cross-Cultural Collaboration

Communication Style (Review of Literature)	Very little	Little	Medium	Much	Very Much
1. Animation/emotional expression	Asian,* Native*	Hispanic*	Anglo*		African*
2. Gestures	Asian, Native		Anglo	Hispanic	African
3. Range of pitch between words	Hispanic, Native	Asian	Anglo		African
4. Volume of speech	Asian	Hispanic	Native	Anglo	African
5. Directness of questions	Native, Asian	Hispanic			African, Anglo
6. Directness of answers	Native, Asian	Hispanic			African, Anglo
7. Directness of rhetorical style—"getting to the point"	Asian	Hispanic, Native			African, Anglo
8. Accusations require a direct response	Native, African, Asian	Anglo		Hispanic	
9. Directness of eye contact	Native, Asian	Hispanic			Anglo, African,
10. Firm, long handshaking	Native, Asian		Hispanic	African	Anglo
11. Touching	Native, Asian		Anglo		African, Hispanic
12. Concern with clock time	Native, Hispanic	African		Asian	Anglo
13. Hierarchical membership in group	Native, African	Anglo			Asian, Hispanic
14. Individualism more than lineal identity	Native	Hispanic, Asian, African			Anglo
15. Individualism more than collateral group identity	Asian	Hispanic, African	Native		Anglo
16. Awareness of unearned "white" privilege	Anglo				Native, African, Asian, Hispanic
17. Closeness when standing	Native, Asian	Anglo	African		Hispanic

*Asian-American, African-American, Anglo- or European-American, Native American, Hispanic-American, or Latino.
Note. From Elliott, C., Adams, R. J., & Sockalingam, S. (1999). *Summary of normative communication styles and values. Multicultural toolkit.* Retrieved from www.awesomelibrary.org/multiculturaltoolkit-styleschart.html. Reprinted with permission.

are not prevented from making mistakes, unless results are life-threatening. They are taught to be aware of nonverbal communications and to learn by watching; thus, long pauses and silence during play can be expected.

Healthcare Culture

The dominant culture of the healthcare community is rooted in Anglo-European beliefs, values, and practices, which are reflected in following cultural courtesies and customs:

1. The notion that all people are more or less equal:
   - Females and males are treated with equal respect.
   - People providing daily services (e.g., cabdrivers, waitresses, secretaries, sales clerks) are treated courteously.

2. People freely express their opinions:
   - Freedom of speech is a major characteristic of the culture.
   - However, some topics (e.g., sex, politics, religion, personal characteristics such as body odors) typically are not openly discussed, particularly with strangers.

3. Persons are greeted openly, directly, and warmly:

  - Not many rituals are associated with greetings; maybe a handshake, particularly among males.
  - People usually greet each other then quickly get to the point of the interaction.
  - Eye contact is maintained throughout the interaction.
  - It is considered impolite not to look at the person to whom you are speaking.

4. Social distance of about an arm's length is typically maintained in interactions:

  - People (males, in particular) do not expect to be touched except for greetings such as shaking hands.
  - People walking down the street together typically do not hold hands or put their arms around one another unless they are involved in a more intimate relationship.

5. Punctuality in and responsibility for keeping appointments are valued behaviors:

  - Time is valued, and most people expect punctuality.
  - It is considered rude to accept an invitation to someone's home and not show up, or to make an appointment with someone and not keep it.

The dominant culture in North America is centered primarily on the individual, as opposed to many other cultures that place much higher value on family or community, which leads people to see themselves as lacking a context of a tradition-bearing community (Lee, Menkart, & Okazawa-Rey, 1998). For a review of a comparison of other Anglo-American beliefs, values, and practices with contrasting ones from other cultures, see Table 10.2.

All components of the healthcare system are making great strides in encouraging and developing systems that are culturally sensitive. According to Pachter (1994), a culturally sensitive healthcare system

  - is accessible;
  - respects the beliefs, attitudes, and cultural lifestyles of its patients;
  - is flexible;

Table 10.2 Contrasting Beliefs, Values, and Practices

Anglo-American Values	Some Other Cultures' Values
Personal control over environment	Fate
Change	Tradition
Time dominates	Human interaction dominates
Human equality	Hierarchy/rank/status
Individualism/privacy	Group welfare
Self-help	Birthright inheritance
Competition	Cooperation
Future orientation	Past or present orientation
Action/goal/work orientation	"Being" orientation
Informality	Formality
Directness/openness/honesty	Indirectness/ritual/"face"
Practicality/efficiency	Idealism/theory
Materialism	Spiritualism/detachment

Note. From United States Department of Agriculture & United States Department of Health and Human Services. (1986). *Cross-cultural counseling: A guide for nutrition and health counselors.* Washington, DC: Author.

- acknowledges that health and illness are in large part molded by variables such as ethnic values, cultural orientation, religious beliefs, and linguistic considerations;

- acknowledges the culturally constructed meaning of illness as a valid concern of clinical care; and

- is sensitive to intragroup variations in beliefs and behaviors, and avoids labeling and stereotyping.

Special Considerations

Although it is important to gain knowledge about the most prevalent cultural groups in the community being served, it would be impossible to learn everything there is to know about the multiple cultures with which healthcare professionals might come in contact (Hinman, 2003), given the changing nature of cultures and the individual expressions of a culture's members. McGoldrick, Giordano, and Garcia-Presto (2005) recommend becoming aware of personal limitations, and communicating these limitations to children and their families by exhibiting an open-hearted curiosity and willingness to learn. This approach encourages the adult and child to collaborate in developing the adult's understanding, while also paving a pathway for mutual learning.

Gil (2005) outlines three important levels of response that are needed to become cross-culturally competent. The first step involves developing personal sensitivity, which entails introspection and a focus on the interactions between self and others. This process begins by becoming aware of one's own biases and values. Although there are numerous ways to develop sensitivity, the most obvious approach is to empathize with individuals by trying to understand their experiences, struggles, resources, and motivations. This requires slowing down, observing, listening, and tuning in to a child's experience of the world.

The second level involves obtaining knowledge responsibly. This can be done in many ways, such as reading, attending lectures, watching DVDs, taking classes, and so on. Gil (2005) suggests that probably the most powerful way to learn is to "practice with accountability"—that is, to allow experienced colleagues to watch you work: "Allowing exposure and inviting commentary on one's work are humbling and powerful experiences that usually yield valuable feedback and direction" (pp. (9–10).

The third level is the development of active competence, which can only be attained after introspection, which leads to heightened sensitivity and awareness, which in turn elicits the desire to learn. After obtaining the necessary knowledge and skills, the task becomes to change one's behavior, followed by development of an action plan. This allows an interactive, circular pattern of thought and response to take place. It is important to pay attention to internal experiences, the responses to those experiences, followed by behavioral attempts to address them, and the reshaping of the attempts based on external feedback (Gil, 2005).

Gil (2005) provides an example to illustrate how this process works. The play therapist thinks,

> "Oh, this kid is painfully shy. He won't make eye contact with me. Maybe he doesn't like me. My best joke fell flat. He looks terrified" (internal thought). Next, the therapist checks on his or her own feeling state: "My hands are sweating. I feel uncomfortable and anxious. I knew I shouldn't have taken this case. I'm better with outgoing hyperactive kids" (introspection). Then the therapist tries to empathize with the child: "Wow, he must be feeling really uncomfortable, even scared . . . wow, his little hands are shaking . . . poor guy. . . . I've got to help him relax" (sensitivity and a desire to help). "Okay, I am going to tell him that I'm a little nervous in new situations myself, and then I'm going to show him around. I remember Dr. Polland did that in the videotape" (accessing knowledge). Next the therapist takes action, and says, "You know, I hate going new places for the first time. Sometimes I get a little worried when I don't know what's going to happen. Let me show you the playroom and what's in here" (action). (pp. 10–11)

This circular process of converting knowledge into action continues, with the therapist remaining aware of self, behavior, and the child's response to each behavior. By continuing with those behaviors that elicit positive responses, the therapist will develop a unique pattern of interactions with the child, based on this interactive, circular pattern of thought and response (Gil, 2005).

The following tips are offered for working in a culturally diverse setting (Carmichael, 2001; Rollins & Mahan, 2010):

1. Have on hand a range of culturally diverse toys and other items (see Box 10.1).

2. View each child as an individual, with unique characteristics, strengths, and needs.

3. Bear in mind that because a child has a particular racial appearance, it does not mean that he or she is culturally different, as race is a poor indicator of culture difference.

4. When communicating:

   - Speak slowly and clearly.
   - Use simple sentences.
   - Use active verbs.
   - Pause more frequently.
   - Repeat each important idea.
   - Keep communication congruent; children may focus more on tone or intention than content.
   - Use visual means, such as illustrations or photographs.
   - Act out and demonstrate.
   - Focus on nonverbal behavior.
   - Remember that silence is communication, too. Listen.
   - Check comprehension.
   - Avoid using jargon and slang unless you are sure their meanings will be understood.

5. Ask children how they know they can trust someone; this is a good introduction when trying to establish trust.

6. Ask children how they celebrate events in their lives, to help identify customs.

7. Remember that some languages do not have words to describe subtle feelings or experiences; thus, avoid perceiving children as having a limited realm of feelings simply because their native vocabulary is limited in describing them.

BOX 10.1. ITEMS FOR THE PLAYROOM

- Ethnic dolls, sand-tray items, and puppets
- Crayons, markers, Play-Doh, in a variety of skin colors suitable to prevalent cultures
- Play food, dress-up clothes, and miniatures representative of various cultures
- Mirrors
- Toys with different environmental elements (e.g., jungle, dessert, mountains)
- Water and sand
- Different types of toy homes, transportation vehicles, cooking utensils, religious objects, and communication devices
- Different types and sizes of toy animal families
- A variety of cultural icons (e.g., photographs of leaders, Japanese kites)

Note. Adapted from Chang, C., Ritter, K., & Hays, D. (2005). Multicultural trends and toys in play therapy. *International Journal of Play Therapy, 14*(2), 69–85.

Activity Goals

Many of the activities in this chapter have several goals, among them: creating a culturally relevant symbol, modifying the environment with a culturally familiar aesthetic, encouraging self-expression, and recognizing and maintaining familiar beliefs and rituals.

ACTIVITY 10.1.   AFRICAN WRAP DOLLS

In Africa, dolls are more than children's playthings. They are considered an art form, and have both ritual and religious associations within the various folklores and cultures. As with knitting, many people find the repetitive hand movements involved in making these dolls relaxing.

Therapeutic Goal: To support cultural diversity by creating a culturally relevant symbol of spirituality and modifying the environment to include a culturally familiar aesthetic.

Age Group: School-age, adolescent

Adult/Child Ratio: 1:5

Required Time: 1 hour

Restrictions and Precautions: None

Materials:

☐ Cotton clothesline

☐ Fabric glue

☐ Fabric squares

☐ Paper towels

☐ Yarn

☐ Beads, feathers, and other adornments

Process

1. Form the head first. Have the children wad several paper towels into balls and place them in the center of the fabric square.

2. Show them how to gather the fabric around the balls and tie it with the clothesline. (Figure Activity 10.1-1, step 1). The ends of the clothesline will become the arms of the doll.

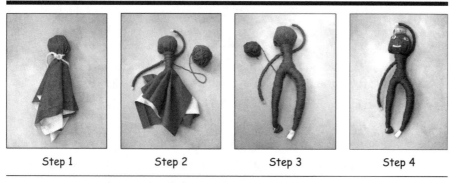

| Step 1 | Step 2 | Step 3 | Step 4 |

Figure Activity 10.1-1. African Wrap Doll

3. Tell the children wrap the yarn around the neck.

4. Demonstrate how to wrap the yarn first down then back up the length of one clothesline arm, leaving a small amount of fabric at the end to form the hands (Figure Activity 10.1-1, step 2).

5. Explain to the children how to wrap the yarn once around the neck, then cross over and repeat step 4 to make the other arm.

6. When the arms are complete, demonstrate how to wrap the yarn around the fabric to form the torso. About midway through, show how to separate the remaining fabric into two sections, to create the legs (Figure Activity 10.1-1, step 3).

7. Instruct the children to wrap the yarn up and down each leg.

8. To finish, tell the children to wrap the yarn up to the neck, tie a knot, and cut off any remaining yarn.

9. Encourage the children to make clothing, faces, and/or hair using fabric scraps, beads, feathers, and other adornments, and glue them in place (Figure Activity 10.1-1, step 4).

ACTIVITY 10.2.   CARP PAPER SCULPTURE

Unlike most other fish, carp swim upstream against the current. Because this is the case, the Chinese and Japanese view carp as a symbol of strength, courage, and determination.

Therapeutic Goal: To support cultural diversity by creating culturally relevant symbols and incorporating a culturally familiar aesthetic.

Age Group: School-age

Adult/Child Ratio: 1:10

Required Time: 45 minutes

Restrictions and Precautions: Take scissors and glue precautions.

Materials:

☐ Picture of a carp (can be downloaded from the Internet)

☐ Butcher paper or large sheet of construction paper (one sheet per child)

☐ Markers

☐ Scissors

☐ Glue

☐ Glue sticks

☐ Tissue paper, cut into pie-shaped wedges

☐ Shredded paper or toilet tissue

Process

1. Show the children the picture of a carp and explain it's symbolic meaning in Chinese and Japanese cultures.

2. Fold one sheet of paper in half, or stack two sheets together.

3. Ask the children to draw a large fish on one side of the folded paper or on the top piece of the stacked paper.

4. Instruct the children to cut out the fish shape from both layers of paper.

5. Demonstrate for the children how to apply a thin line of glue around the perimeter of the fish (except for the mouth) and glue both layers together. Allow to dry.

6. Let the children use markers to create eyes on both sides of the fish.

7. To make the scales, show the children how to place overlapping rows of tissue paper on one side of the fish, and use a glue stick to affix them. Repeat on the other side.

8. Have the children gently stuff their fish with the shredded paper or tissue, and then glue the mouth shut.

9. Invite the children to attach a ribbon loop so they can hang the carp in their rooms.

ACTIVITY 10.3.   CHAMSA, OR HAND OF FATIMA, SYMBOL

The Chamsa, or Hand of Fatima, is a symbol found in Jewish and Arab cultures. It is in the shape of a hand, typically with an eye at the center of the palm. Some people believe Chamsa, or Hand of Fatima, to be symbolic of good fortune, as protection from the "evil eye" and other sources of harm.

Therapeutic Goal: To support cultural diversity by creating a relevant symbol and modifying the environment to include culturally familiar art.

Age Group: Preschool/school-age

Adult/Child Ratio: 1:4

Required Time: 15 minutes

Restrictions and Precautions: Take scissors, markers, glitter, and glue precautions.

Materials:

☐ Wrapping paper, silver-colored (preferred), or heavy-duty aluminum foil, one 8-inch square per child

☐ Pencils

☐ Scissors

☐ Art materials (e.g., craft gems, glitter)

☐ Glue

☐ Hole punch

☐ Markers or crayons

☐ Tape

☐ Yarn

Process

1. Explain the symbolism of a chamsa, emphasizing that it is believed to have the power to bring good luck and keep people safe.

2. Help the children trace another person's hand onto the wrapping paper or foil.

3. Tell them to cut out the hand.

4. Allow the children to use the art materials to decorate their chamsas.

5. Illustrate for the children how to punch a hole in their chamsas and thread them with yarn.

6. Tell them to knot the ends of the yarn.

7. Invite the children to talk about the good luck they have had in their lives, and what they wish for in the future.

8. Encourage the children to follow the tradition of hanging their chamsas over their beds.

ACTIVITY 10.4. CHINESE GOOD LUCK ENVELOPES

A Chinese tradition is to give people they care about a red envelope with money, candy, or a special message for good luck. This activity is good for children who are the friends, classmates, siblings, or offspring of someone who is sick.

Therapeutic Goal: To support cultural diversity by creating a culturally relevant symbol of life and health and incorporating familiar rituals.

Age Group: Primary/school-age

Adult/Child Ratio: 1:20

Required Time: 20 minutes

Restrictions and Precautions: Take glue and marker precautions.

Materials:

☐ Red construction paper, origami paper, or copy paper, cut into 6-inch squares (at least one per child)

☐ Pencils

☐ Glue sticks

☐ Gold paint pen or gold marker

☐ Plain writing paper, stationery, or large scraps of wrapping paper

☐ Stickers (gold seals and others)

Process

1. Have children place their squares of paper in front of them and rotate them to be positioned in a diamond shape.

2. Ask the children to number each corner, going clockwise, penciling the numerals in lightly.

3. Demonstrate, with the children following along, how to fold corner 3 up about 1 inch, and then fold it up again 1 inch.

4. Tell the children to fold corners 2 and 4 toward the middle, so that they overlap (demonstrate if needed), and glue in place (Figure Activity 10.4-1).

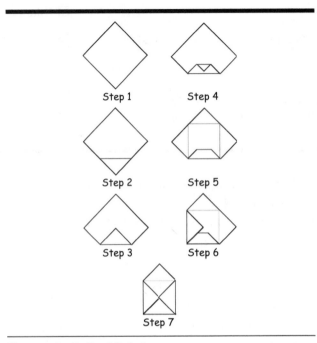

Figure Activity 10.4-1. Chinese Good Luck Envelope

5. Ask the children to write good luck messages or messages of affirmation on paper and place them in their envelopes.

6. Give the children stickers to seal the envelope; invite them to present it to their loved one.

ACTIVITY 10.5.   GOD'S EYES

In Mexican culture, the *Ojo de Dios* or Eye of God is a symbol of the belief that God will watch over us and grant us health, fortune, and a long life.

Therapeutic Goal: To support cultural diversity by creating a culturally relevant symbol.	**Materials:**
Age Group: School-age, adolescent	☐ Tongue depressors
Adult/Child Ratio: 1:5	☐ Yarn
Required Time: 1 hour	☐ Tape
Restrictions and Precautions: Ensure that children's attention span is adequate for following instructions.	☐ Scissors

Process

1. Instruct the children to tape two tongue depressors together to make a cross.

2. Let the children choose a color for the center of their "eye."

3. Have the children hold the yarn against the back center of the cross with their index finger while weaving the yarn through the frame of the sticks.

4. Demonstrate how to cross the yarn diagonally through the center of the sticks, passing over one stick and wrapping around the back of the stick (Figure Activity 10.5-1).

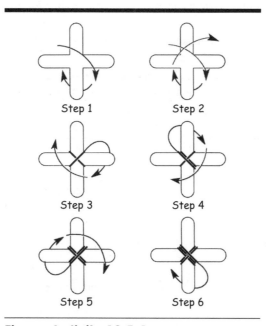

Step 1   Step 2

Step 3   Step 4

Step 5   Step 6

Figure Activity 10.5-1. Making God's Eyes

5. Tell the children to continue to work on a diagonal, passing over each stick then wrapping the yarn around it. The color of the yarn may be changed by tying a different color to the first color. Note: Tell the children to tie the knot at the back of the frame, so it cannot be seen on the front of the design.

6. When the God's Eye is completed, tell the children to cut the yarn and secure the end.

Make several God's Eyes and hang them from a coat hanger to form a mobile.   **Variation**

ACTIVITY 10.6.   HISPANIC PAPER FLOWERS

Large, colorful paper flowers are a traditional craft of Mexico and Central America. They are sold on street corners and used for decoration and in ceremonies.

Therapeutic Goal: To support cultural diversity by modifying the environment with a culturally familiar aesthetic.	**Materials:**
	☐ Crepe paper (preferred) or tissue paper
Age Group: School-age/adolescent	☐ Green florist's tape
Adult/Child Ratio: 1:10	☐ Pencils
Required Time: Varies	☐ Scissors with pointed edges
Restrictions and Precautions: Take scissors precautions.	☐ Wire, cut into 1-foot lengths (one per flower)

1. To make the center of the flower, tell the children to form a 1- to 2-inch ball out of crushed crepe or tissue paper then wrap the ball in another piece of paper, twisting the ends together and securing with tape.   **Process**

2. Illustrate for the children how to twist one end of wire around the base of the ball and then wrap tape over it.

3. For the petals, have the children draw and cut out at least four concentric circles, with the largest at least 12 inches in diameter. Show the children how to scallop the edges.

4. Tell the children to layer the paper petals together according to size, arranging them from largest to smallest.

5. Give the children scissors to make a hole in the middle of each layer, just large enough to pull the base of the center of the flower through.

6. Explain how to thread the wire through each hole, pulling it through until the base of the center is inserted in the hole, then wrap with floral tape, to the end of the wire.

7. Encourage the children to decorate their rooms with the flowers they made.

ACTIVITY 10.7. JAPANESE GARDEN THEATER

Nature plays a central role in Japanese culture, and gardening is a highly valued art form. In Garden Theater, children can create their own soil-less environment as a "stage" for play and interaction.

Therapeutic Goal: To support cultural diversity by incorporating familiar activities and encouraging self-expression.

Age Group: Preschool/school-age

Adult/Child Ratio: 1:1

Required Time: 30 minutes

Restrictions and Precautions: This activity may not be appropriate for children who are immune compromised.

Materials:

- ☐ Flat-bottomed shallow tray, bowl, or pie tin
- ☐ Pebbles and small rocks
- ☐ Water
- ☐ Bamboo
- ☐ Other plants, as desired
- ☐ Small figures

Process

1. Have the child place two or three layers of rocks on the bottom the container.
2. Pour in enough water until it is just visible through the rocks.
3. Let the child place the bamboo and other plants where he or she desires.
4. Invite the child to place the small figures in the garden and make up a story about them.

Note. Adapted from Hiromi Moriguchi in Rollins, J. (2004). *Arts activities for children at bedside*. Washington, DC: WVSA arts connection.

ACTIVITY 10.8. JAPANESE ZEN GARDEN

Zen gardens represent peace and tranquility in the Japanese culture, and are intended to be places of contemplation and meditation. Zen gardens traditionally consist simply of rocks and sand. Patterns are often made in the sand to represent rippling water. A Zen garden may be used to promote a sense of serenity in the often overwhelming life of a sick child.

Therapeutic Goal: To support cultural diversity by creating a culturally relevant symbol and incorporating a culturally familiar aesthetic.

Age Group: Preschool/school-age/adolescent

Adult/Child Ratio: Varies according to children's ages

Required Time: 30 minutes

Restrictions and Precautions: None

Materials:

- ☐ Shallow, rimmed container (e.g., tray)
- ☐ Clean sand or fine gravel
- ☐ Rocks and pebbles
- ☐ Miniature rakes or plastic forks
- ☐ CDs of tranquil music or meditation exercises (optional)

1. Introduce the activity by discussing the symbolism of, and purpose behind, Zen gardens in **Process**
the Japanese culture.

2. Have the children fill the container halfway to the rim with sand.

3. Ask the children to arrange the rocks and pebbles on the sand, as desired, and partially
submerge them in place (Figure Activity 10.8-1).

Figure Activity 10.8-1. Japanese Zen Garden

4. Invite the children to select and play a CD while they use a rake or fork to create wavy patterns
in the sand.

5. Encourage the children to use their Zen garden to help them relax during times of stress.

Make a "moonscape" using rocks and fine gravel to erect mountains, hills, and "meteor piles." The **Variation**
idea of weightlessness may be incorporated into progressive relaxation suggestions being used to
reduce anxiety or pain.

ACTIVITY 10.9.   KACHINA DOLLS

Kachina dolls represent a spirit of life in the Hopi Indian culture. Traditionally, they are hand-
crafted from wood. To make this activity easier for children with limited coordination or short
attention spans, eliminate steps 4 and 5, instead gluing on the head in advance.

Therapeutic Goal: To support cultural diversity
by creating a culturally relevant symbol and
encouraging self-expression.

Age Group: School-age

Adult/Child Ratio: 1:5

Required Time: 30–45 minutes

Restrictions and Precautions: Follow scissors and
glue gun precautions.

Materials:

☐ Cardboard toilet paper rolls (one per child)

☐ Scissors

☐ Tape

☐ Glue gun

☐ Styrofoam balls or Ping-Pong balls (1 per child)

☐ Acrylic or tempera paint, or markers (be sure to
include turquoise and salmon, traditional colors
of the Southwest)

☐ Fabric scraps, feathers, buttons, and/or other
decorative trims

☐ Piece of thick cardboard (to form a base)

1. Discuss how, in the Hopi Indian culture, Kachina dolls are figural representations of spirits **Process**
in life.

2. Let the children select something in life for their doll to represent.

3. To make the legs of the doll, show the children how to cut two narrow panels, opposite each other on the same end of the tube, extending about one third of the way up.

4. Tell the children to make two short cuts at the end of each slit, to form a "T."

5. Demonstrate for the children how to bend each flap into a small cylinder, making sure the edges meet. Secure with tape.

6. To make the doll's head, give the children the glue gun to attach the ball to the top of the tube.

7. Invite the children to add facial features and create clothing, using paints and/or decorative trims (Figure Activity 10.9-1).

Figure Activity 10.9-1. Kachina and Kokeshi Dolls

8. Help the children attach their dolls to the cardboard bases using a glue gun.

Variation   Kokeshi dolls are simple, wooden Japanese dolls with a trunk, an enlarged head, and no extremities. They can be made by simply eliminating steps 3 to 5 and using paint to create facial features and clothing.

ACTIVITY 10.10.   MANDALAS

The mandala is a sacred circle symbolic of healing and wholeness in the spiritual traditions of many cultures worldwide, including Hindu, Buddhist, and Native American. It exemplifies containment and can serve as an outlet for self-expression. The creation of mandalas is believed to promote relaxation, release tension, and invoke a sense of unity and a feeling of safety. A growing number of Western physicians now incorporate mandalas and other holistic techniques into their medical practices.

Therapeutic Goal: To support cultural diversity by creating a culturally relevant symbol of healing.

Age Group: School-age/adolescent

Adult/Child Ratio: 1:8

Required Time: 30 minutes–1 hour

Restrictions and Precautions: Take scissors and marker precautions.

Materials:

☐ Compass or circular template (a 10-inch paper plate works well)

☐ Drawing paper or thin cardboard, 12 inches × 18 inches

☐ Scissors

☐ Pencils

☐ Markers or oil pastels

1. To introduce the activity, explain the spiritual symbolism of mandalas.

2. Provide each child with a compass or template for drawing a circle in the center of the paper. Tell them to mark the center of the circle.

3. Encourage the children to make designs, symbols, and/or images in the circles, to create mandalas.

4. When they have finished, ask the children to indicate the top of the mandala with a tiny penciled "x."

5. Invite the children to talk about their mandalas, if they wish.

6. Encourage the children to display their mandalas where they can see them and contemplate their colors and designs.

ACTIVITY 10.11.   MILAGROS

Milagros are small, metal charms used in many Hispanic and Mediterranean cultures. Some people use them to ask for help, or to give thanks for favors. Others believe milagros to be good-luck charms.

Therapeutic Goal: To support cultural diversity by creating a culturally and situationally relevant symbol.	**Materials:**
	☐ Gel markers
Age Group: School-age	☐ Self-hardening clay
Adult/Child Ratio: 1:10	☐ White glue
Required Time: 30 minutes	☐ Aluminum foil
Restrictions and Precautions: Follow glue and marker precautions.	

1. Explain the cultural significance of milagros.

2. Ask the children to think of something special they wish for.

3. Give the children the clay to mold into a small shape that symbolizes their wish or has special meaning for them.

4. Give the children small pieces of foil, telling them to wrap their milagros tightly, while taking care to maintain the shape of the clay.

5. If needed, have the children glue the ends of the foil together.

6. Let the children decorate their milagros with gel markers.

7. Encourage the children to carry their milagros with them or to tuck them away in a safe place.

ACTIVITY 10.12.   NATIVE AMERICAN DREAM CATCHER

According to Native American folklore, dream catchers are believed to trap bad dreams in their web. As the legend goes, the bad dreams caught in the web burn away when the sun rises, while the good dreams pass through the center opening and slide down the feathers to reach the sleeping child. This is an excellent activity to help children express their fears and concerns.

Therapeutic Goal: To support cultural diversity by creating a culturally relevant symbol, and to promote coping.	Materials:
Age Group: School-age	☐ Embroidery hoop or 1-foot piece of bendable twig (1 per child)
Adult/Child Ratio: 1:5	☐ Thin wire (needed only if using twig)
Required Time: 30 minutes	☐ Twine
Restrictions and Precautions: Take scissors precautions.	☐ Scissors
	☐ Tapestry needle
	☐ Beads
	☐ Feathers

Process

1. If using twigs to make the hoops, bend each twig into a circular shape and tie the overlapping ends together with wire.

2. Before beginning the activity, discuss the legends about dream catchers. Engage the children in a discussion about good and bad dreams they have had. Encourage them to explore what they might like to dream about.

3. To start the web, have the children tie one end of the twine to the hoop, and string on one or two beads.

4. Tell the children to push the beads toward the tied end and then wrap the twine once around the hoop on the opposite side.

5. Encourage the children to repeat steps 2 and 3 until the piece resembles a spider's web.

6. Show the children how to tie three pieces of twine to the bottom third of their hoops.

7. Have the children thread two beads on each of the three pieces of twine, and tie on feathers.

8. Encourage the children to hang their dream catchers near their beds.

Variation

To help inspire good dreams, help the children find pictures or small objects that symbolize dreams they would enjoy having, and tie them to the ends of the twine in place of the feathers.

ACTIVITY 10.13.   NATIVE AMERICAN SAND PAINTING

Some Native American tribes, as part of their healing rituals, use sand to create paintings that feature symbols from their religion.

Therapeutic Goal: To support cultural diversity by modifying the environment to include culturally familiar art and color and creating a culturally relevant symbol of health.	Materials:
	☐ Clean sand
Age Group: School-age	☐ Specimen cups or other small containers
Adult/Child Ratio: 1:8	☐ Colored powders (e.g., ground spices, powdered paints, cornmeal, crushed charcoal)
Required Time: 45 minutes	
Restrictions and Precautions: To avoid inhalation when working with finely ground spices and powdered paints, make sure children with respiratory problems wear masks. Follow glue precautions.	☐ Tongue depressors
	☐ Sandpaper
	☐ Glue
	☐ Paint brushes
	☐ Matte fixative or hairspray

1. Introduce the activity by explaining the history behind sand paintings. If possible, show examples, pointing out the symbols they contain.

2. Place a portion of sand into as many specimen cups as different-colored powders you are using.

3. Give the children tongue depressors to stir one of the colored powders into the sand in each specimen cup, until the desired shades are achieved.

4. Illustrate for the children how to use the glue to "paint" designs directly onto the sandpaper. For thin lines, squirt the glue directly from the bottle. To fill larger areas, have children use a paintbrush to apply the glue.

5. Using one color at a time, show the children how to sprinkle sand where they have applied glue, working quickly to avoid the glue drying out.

6. In a well-ventilated area, spray matte fixative or hairspray on the painting.

7. Invite the children to talk about their sand paintings and what symbolism they may portray.

For toddlers or children with coordination difficulties, tape a piece of clear contact paper (sticky side up) to a piece of cardboard, cut slightly larger in size. Pour the sand into small salt shakers and let the children sprinkle it on the sticky surface. Shake off excess sand and place another sheet of clear contact paper over the sand to preserve the image.

ACTIVITY 10.14. ORIGAMI CRANES

Cranes, the Japanese symbol for good health, long life, and prosperity, are used in traditional art, rituals, and ceremonies. Many people throughout Asia believe that making 1,000 origami cranes will make a person's wishes come true. The traditional method of folding cranes is, however, complex and requires much practice. This is a simplified version, more suitable for young children who lack fine-motor coordination and/or have a low tolerance for frustration.

Therapeutic Goal: To support cultural diversity by creating a culturally relevant symbol of health.	**Restrictions and Precautions:** Requires the ability to follow directions, and patience and dexterity.
Age Group: School-age/adolescent.	**Materials:**
Adult/Child Ratio: 1:8	☐ Origami paper
Required Time: Varies; can be done over multiple sessions	☐ String
	☐ Scissors

1. Discuss the symbolic meaning of cranes in Asian culture.

2. Provide each of the children with a piece of origami paper and tell them to place it, colored side down, on a hard surface.

3. Demonstrate each of the following steps, and ask the children to follow along (Figure Activity 10.14-1a and b):

    a. Fold the paper in half, from the top pointed edge to the bottom pointed edge. Crease well.

    b. Fold the triangle in half to create a smaller triangle.

    c. Fold only the top two layers down, until they almost meet the left edge.

    d. To make the neck, take the left point of the triangle and fold it on an angle toward the right, creating a V-shape. Crease well.

    e. To make the head, take the point of the neck and fold it at an angle, back toward the left. Crease well.

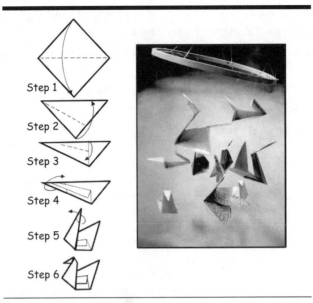

Figure Activity 10.14-1a and 1b. Origami Cranes

    f.   Encourage the children to make a multitude of cranes. Then help them make small holes in each one and string them together like garland; or create a mobile. (Figure Activity 14.1b).

4.   Invite the children to talk about what they wish for, and hang the cranes up in their room.

ACTIVITY 10.15.   PRAYER OR MEDITATION RUGS

Many peoples, including those of Islamic, Christian, and Buddhist cultures, kneel on special rugs or mats to protect their knees when they meditate or pray. Recent studies of the practice of both meditation and prayer have shown that it reduces stress, promotes coping, and improves physiological responses. Ask children to tell you about their daily routines at home to help identify those for whom this activity would be appropriate and meaningful.

Therapeutic Goal: To support cultural diversity by recognizing and maintaining familiar beliefs and rituals.

Age Group: School-age

Adult/Child Ratio: 1:8

Required Time: 1 hour

Restrictions and Precautions: Secure parental approval before initiating the activity to assure that it comports with their beliefs. Take scissors, paint, and glue precautions.

Materials:

☐ Canvas, 1 foot × 2 feet or larger, coated with artist's gesso and allowed to dry

☐ Pictures of prayer rugs downloaded from Internet (optional)

☐ Pencil

☐ Stencils (optional)

☐ Fabric or acrylic paints

☐ Paintbrushes

☐ Fabric

☐ Scissors

☐ Fabric glue

☐ Fringe

1. Explain to the children how special rugs are used for prayer or meditation.

2. Tell them that they will be designing their own prayer rugs. Display pictures of prayer rugs to the children, if they appear to need artistic inspiration.

3. Have the children first sketch the design for their rugs on paper. Note that Muslim prayer rugs typically have a "point" incorporated into their design, positioned to face toward Mecca when they are used.

4. When the children are satisfied with their designs, give them acrylic paints, fabric paints, and/or pieces of fabric to transfer their designs onto the rug.

5. If using canvas, fold over an inch or more around the edges and glue in place.

6. Give the children fabric glue to attach the fringe, if desired.

ACTIVITY 10.16.   RICE-A-RAINBOW

Just about everyone has seen St. Patrick's Day decorations that show a lucky pot of gold at the end of a rainbow. Rainbows are also considered symbolic of hope and good fortune by many other peoples and cultures, such as the Polynesians and Filipinos.

Therapeutic Goal: To support cultural diversity by creating a relevant symbol and modifying the environment to include culturally relevant art.

Age Group: Preschool/primary

Adult/Child Ratio: 1:4

Required Time: 15 minutes advanced preparation, 1-hour drying time, 20 minutes for activity

Restrictions and Precautions: Supervise the children closely to assure they do not ingest the rice. Take glue and marker precautions.

Materials:

☐ 3 cups rice

☐ 1 teaspoon each of red, blue, yellow, green, and orange food coloring

☐ 5 teaspoons rubbing alcohol

☐ 5 small containers with lids, or small plastic bags with zipper closures

☐ Cookie sheets or newspaper

☐ Paper plate cut in half, or cardstock

☐ Marker

☐ Glue

1. Divide the rice into five containers or plastic bags.

2. Place 1 teaspoon of alcohol and a different food coloring in each of the containers or bags.

3. Shake each until the colors are evenly dispersed.

4. Spread the rice on cookie sheets or newspaper, and allow the mixture to dry for approximately one hour.

5. Using a marker, draw a rainbow of five arcs on the paper plate or cardstock.

6. Talk to children about the symbolism of rainbows in different cultures. Encourage them to share some of their hopes and dreams.

7. Help the children fill in one arc with glue then sprinkle it with one color of rice until it is completely covered.

8. Repeat step 7 until all the colors have been used.

ACTIVITY 10.17.   TREE OF LIFE

The Tree of Life is featured prominently in many cultures and countries of the world. It is written about in literature, Hindu scripture, and the Judeo-Christian bible. In Muslim culture, Tree of Life motifs can be found in art and architecture and are woven into prayer rugs. Both India and Siberia have religious customs that include tying narrow bands of fabric or silk scarves to the branches of trees. Because of the prevalence of Tree of Life images across cultures, this activity is well suited for many different cultural groups.

Therapeutic Goal: To support cultural diversity by creating a culturally relevant symbol and incorporating familiar rituals.

Age Group: School-age

Adult/Child Ratio: 1:8

Required Time: 20 minutes

Restrictions and Precautions: Take scissors precautions. Mix plaster of paris in a well-ventilated area, away from the children.

Materials:

- ☐ 8-inch terra-cotta plant pot or 5-pound coffee can
- ☐ Plaster of paris, mixed according to package directions
- ☐ Tree branch, about 2 feet high
- ☐ Colored paper or pieces of gold and saffron fabric (for Buddhists)
- ☐ Scissors
- ☐ Fabric pens or permanent-ink markers
- ☐ Hole punch
- ☐ Ribbon

Process

1. Prior to the activity, mix the plaster of paris according to package directions.
2. Place the tree branch into the plaster and allow to dry.
3. To introduce the activity, discuss the symbolic meaning of the Tree of Life with the children.
4. Encourage the children to think of things they wish for, or, if appropriate, pray for. Explain that they will write each one of their wishes on a leaf or a piece of fabric.
5. If using leaves, have the children draw them and cut them out of colored paper. Those children using fabric should cut pieces large enough for them to write on.
6. Encourage the children to write each of their wishes on a separate leaf or piece of fabric.
7. Show the children how to punch a hole in the corner of each leaf or piece of fabric.
8. Ask the children to thread a piece of ribbon through the holes and tie their wishes to the tree.
9. Allow the children time to share their wishes, if they choose.

ACTIVITY 10.18. UKRAINIAN EGGS

Traditional Ukrainian eggs are called "pysanky." These hand-painted eggs incorporate intricate designs and symbols that have special meaning to many native Ukrainians. Painted eggs are found in Chinese folk art, as well.

Therapeutic Goal: To support cultural diversity by modifying the environment to include culturally familiar art and creating a culturally relevant symbol of health.

Age Group: School-age/adolescent

Adult/Child Ratio: 1:10

Required Time: 10–15 minutes advance preparation; 30 minutes–1 hour for the activity

Restrictions and Precautions: Take paint precautions.

Materials:

- ☐ Eggs (fresh or plastic)
- ☐ Needleless syringe
- ☐ Pencil
- ☐ Acrylic or tempera paints
- ☐ Small paintbrushes and/or cotton swabs
- ☐ Cardboard toilet paper rolls, cut into 1-inch rings

1. If using fresh eggs, remove the whites and yolks by piercing two small holes in either end of Process
the eggs using the syringe tip or pencil tip; then use the syringe to force air into them, or
simply blow into one end. Dry the eggs by placing them in a microwave for 15 to 25 seconds.

2. Discuss with the children the meaning of various symbols and colors used to decorate
Ukrainian eggs, particularly those that may have special significance to sick children. For
example, blue is the color of health, and waves and ribbons symbolize life without end.

3. Give the children a pencil to lightly sketch patterns and designs on their eggs. Encourage
them to include traditional symbolism, or invite them to create their own.

4. Let the children use the paintbrushes or cotton swabs dipped in paint to color in their designs.
Give them the cardboard rings to use as stands for the eggs while they are being painted; later,
the eggs can be displayed on them.

ACTIVITY 10.19.   WORRY DOLLS

In some Central American cultures, these little dolls are given to children who are having difficulty
sleeping because of their worries. According to the folklore, children can tell their worries to the dolls
then tuck them under their pillows at night. The dolls worry on behalf of the children, allowing the
children to sleep peacefully throughout the night and wake up worry-free. This project is appropriate
for any child experiencing a disaster, their own illness, or that of a loved one.

Therapeutic Goal: To support cultural diversity by
incorporating familiar rituals into the healthcare
plan.

Age Group: School-age

Adult/Child Ratio: 1:8

Required Time: 30 minutes

Restrictions and Precautions: Follow precautions
for using markers and glue guns. This activity is not appropriate for children lacking good
fine-motor coordination.

Materials:

☐ Flat, slotted clothespins with ball tops

☐ Tongue depressors
☐ Craft knife
☐ Paper
☐ Pens
☐ Glue gun
☐ Yarn or embroidery thread
☐ Markers
☐ Fabric scraps
☐ Wire or metallic pipe cleaners

1. Prior to beginning the activity, use a craft knife to score the tongue depressors 1–1/2 inches Process
from each end. Press the tongue depressor against a countertop edge and snap off both ends.

2. Explain the legend of worry dolls to the children, emphasizing the value of expressing one's
fears and concerns.

3. Ask the children to create a list of things they worry about, and discuss them.

4. Begin making the dolls: To fashion the arms, help the children glue, at an angle, the flat end
of a tongue depressor segment to each side of their clothespin.

5. Have the children place a dollop of glue just below the "neck," and affix the end of the yarn or
thread, and allow it to dry. Wrap the thread or yarn tightly around the arms, legs, and torso.

6. Give the children markers to make facial features and hair.

7. Invite the children to use fabric scraps, wire, and pipe cleaners to fashion clothing and jewelry
for their dolls.

Younger children can participate in this activity simply by using markers to make facial features and Variation
clothing.

For more ideas, see Bright Ideas: Embracing Cultural Diversity (Box Activity 10.19-1), and Bright
Ideas: Providing Culturally Appropriate Care (Box Activity 10.19-2).

Box **Activity 10.19-1.** **Bright Ideas:** **Embracing** **Cultural** **Diversity**	• Cook ethnic foods. • Invite children to make flags from their country of origin. • Celebrate holidays and special occasions of various cultures. • Provide books, toys, and music that reflect different cultures. • Have game boards and rules translated into various languages. • Fill a mobile "art cart" with posters representing a variety of cultural preferences for patients to choose from, to hang in their room and personalize their space. • Encourage families to scent their children's hospital rooms with familiar cultural fragrances used in their homes, such as patchouli in India, incense in Vietnam, and cooked basil in Italy. • Provide chopsticks for people who use them.

Box **Activity 10.19-2.** **Bright Ideas:** **Providing** **Culturally** **Appropriate** **Care**	• Have teaching materials available in different languages. • Incorporate different customs into routines. • Invite community groups of different cultures to visit the sick. • Educate all staff on each family's culture, and its implications in healthcare. • Understand and accommodate dietary laws of different religions. • Demonstrate routine procedures and the use of equipment to families that are newly arrived in the United States. • Offer a lending library with information about cross-cultural issues in healthcare. • Make translators routinely available. • Provide culture "kits." • Create a series of audio and audiovisual CDs in different languages to greet families and familiarize them with the hospital. • Learn to say some common phrases in different languages. The following list shows how to say "Welcome" in 22 different languages:

Afrikaans	Welkom
Arabic	Salaam
Bosnian	Dobrodošli
Chinese (Cantonese)	Foonying
Chinese (Mandarin)	Huanying
Danish	Velkommen
Dutch	Welkom
French	Bienvenue
German	Willkommen/Guten tag (good day)
Greek	Kalōs orisate
Hawaiian	Aloha
Hebrew	Shalom
Hindi	Swaagatam
Italian	Benvenuto
Japanese	Yōkoso
Korean	Hwangyong-hamnida
Polish	Serdecznie witamy
Russian	Dobro pozhalovet
Swahili	Umenikaribisha mimi
Tagalog	Mabuhay
Turkish	Merhaba
Vietnamese	Kinh chao qul khach

CHAPTER 11

ISOLATION AND IMMOBILIZATION

The restrictions imposed by immobilization and isolation place all children at risk for both physical and psychological problems, caused by loss of normal movement opportunities, sensory deprivation, and social isolation. All of the stressors associated with hospitalization are increased for children who are immobilized or isolated; this fact is especially troublesome, as children in these confined circumstances may have fewer coping strategies available to deal with these stressors.

Age influences children's reactions to immobilization or isolation. Regarding infants, professionals believe that infants under 6 months of age are unable to distinguish immobilization from normal life and quickly adapt, *as long as their physical and emotional needs are met*. Thus, in infants less than 6 months old, there is less observable reaction to immobilization. From 6 to 18 months, separation anxiety becomes a major factor influencing children's reactions to immobilization and isolation. For age-relevant issues and anticipated children's responses, see Table 11.1.

Regardless of age, children are at risk when immobilized or isolated due to restrictions in movement, space, and contact with the environment. Orientation to time and place is affected. Loss of bodily control and environmental control also are major challenges. Reduced interactions with the environment and the people in it can result in depersonalization. All of these factors threaten children's self-image and self-esteem. High levels of anxiety can result in restlessness, depression, egocentricity, difficulty with problem solving, and inability to concentrate on activities. Hallucinations, disorientation, dependence, depression, acting-out behavior, increased fantasizing, sluggish intellectual responses, sluggish psychomotor responses, or decreased communication skills are all possible outcomes related to the monotony a child may experience (Hockenberry & Wilson, 2007).

LIST OF ACTIVITIES

Activity 11.1 Air Freshener	Activity 11.10 Planetarium
Activity 11.2 Cardboard Dashboard	Activity 11.11 Silly Bedside Scavenger Hunt
Activity 11.3 Clean Mud	Activity 11.12 Special Place Collages
Activity 11.4 Fragrant Winter Wonderland	Activity 11.13 Sun Catchers
Activity 11.5 Gone Fishing	Activity 11.14 Tin Can Walkie-Talkies
Activity 11.6 Indoor Garden	Activity 11.15 Twirling Spirals
Activity 11.7 It's in the Bag Sculpture	Activity 11.16 Window Cling-ons
Activity 11.8 Newspaper Scavenger Hunt	Activity 11.17 Window Painting
Activity 11.9 Pillow Sachets	

Immobilization

Children immobilized by disease or as a part of a treatment regimen experience diminished environmental stimuli, with a loss of tactile, vestibular, and proprioceptive input, and an altered perception of themselves and their environment (Wilson, Curry, & DeBoer, 2007). In some instances, such as the need to remain in the hospital room attached to monitoring equipment, immobilization dramatically decreases social interaction with peers. Depending on their conditions, their fellow patients may be able to visit and provide some socialization. Other circumstances, such as being in traction for a fractured leg, may not restrict children to their

Table 11.1 Age-Related Responses to Isolation and Immobilization

	Issues	**Responses**
Infants	Separation anxiety	Become visibly upset when parents and significant others leave the room or bedside
Toddlers	Difficulty understanding the reason for their restraint or isolation	Regression and restlessness
	Limited opportunities for sensory motor exploration	Increased frustration (tantrums)
Preschoolers	Guilt	Less exploration of environment
School-agers	Loss of control	Initially, angry and hostile; later, usually one of three behavior patterns: responsibly independent, passively dependent, or manipulative
Adolescents	Body image perception, and fear of being different from peers	Initially, acting out, regression, anger, denial, and hostility; later, possibly boredom and apathy
	Developing independence challenges	

hospital room. Playroom doors typically are designed to allow children to enter in their beds; children also can be transported in their beds to other areas of the hospital (e.g., the hospital lobby) for entertainment and other special activities.

Regression is expected for hospitalized children, especially for those who are immobilized. Further, the circumstances preceding immobilization, such as an accident or other traumatic event, may result in fears, fantasies, or nightmares. Play has proven helpful for children dealing with these circumstances. For example, Gillis (1989) found that immobilized children ages 7 to 12 years who were exposed to planned creative play periods expressed more positive feelings toward themselves and significant others than those who did not participate in play sessions.

Isolation

The classic research of John Bowlby (1960) and James Robertson (1958) conducted in the middle of the last century provided evidence of the harmful effects of social isolation on developing children. Behavioral responses of children in isolation range from agitation to behavioral depression. The length of time a child is isolated can be associated with more serious side effects such as depression (Koller, Nicholas, Goldie, Gearing, & Selkirk, 2006). In a landmark study of the emotional reactions of 123 isolated children with cancer and of their mothers allowed only limited visitation revealed higher than normal levels of anxiety and depression, particularly in preschool children (Powazek, Goff, Schyving, & Paulson, 1978). In a study during the following decade, Casey (1989) reported that preschool children in respiratory isolation demonstrated irritability, sadness, and withdrawn behaviors, in addition to seeking human contact. Children were described as very demanding of parents' and nurses' time. More recently, Campbell (1999) studied five children with cancer, who were receiving chemotherapy in protective isolation. Through interviews, children revealed feelings of being "shut in," the need to cope with the experience, and the importance of knowing what to expect, maintaining contact with the outside world, and developing relationships with healthcare professionals. Maintaining contact with the outside world was a key coping strategy.

In a study conducted with hospitalized children isolated because of the 2003 outbreak of severe acute respiratory syndrome (SARS) in Canada, the emotional aspects reported were extensive and difficult (Koller et al., 2006). Children felt sad, which they attributed to feeling alone, and missed and/or worried about family members who, in some cases, were hospitalized elsewhere. Echoing older studies in which children perceived their isolation as a form of punishment or being trapped or confined (Casey, 1989; Kristensen, 1995), some children felt they were being punished "even though I didn't do anything" or "being in jail and you can't get out."

Although there is limited research on children's understanding of isolation, we know that many misconceptions exist. In a study of 54 isolated children's understanding of isolation procedures, Pidgeon (1966) reported that a total of 71% of children ages 3 to 7 years gave incorrect responses, and 25% of children ages 7 to 17 years gave incorrect responses to the reasons for isolation. In other research, children described feeling sad and scared in their rooms, and anticipating invasive medical procedures whenever a nurse came into the room with protective clothing (Broeder, 1985).

Regarding infection control, children are placed in isolation to protect others from their **Masks** infection, or to protect themselves from dangerous organisms that staff, family members, and visitors may bring in that could threaten an already compromised immune system. Being in isolation typically means that healthcare staff, family members, and sometimes the children themselves (when leaving their rooms for other areas of the hospital) must wear protective attire, including masks. Limited research has been conducted on the psychosocial impact of wearing masks while working with children and families (Beck et al., 2004). There is, however, the perception that surgical masks are frightening to children (Koller et al., 2006). One of the first child life specialists, Emma Plank, stated that for some children the masked adult "is often taken for a villain who hides his face to cover up his evil intentions" (Plank, 1971, p. 21).

However, children's fear of adults in masks may not be as prevalent as healthcare providers and parents believe. In an emergency department at a children's hospital, Forgie, Reitsma, Spacy, Wright, and Stobart (2009) showed 80 children, ages 4 to 10 years, photographs of physicians wearing surgical masks and face shields. They asked the children which set of physicians they would prefer to take care of them, and why. They also asked whether they found any of the physicians frightening and, if so, why. Of the 80 children, 59% stated that neither the physicians in the surgical masks nor the physicians in the face shields were frightening. However, 23% ($n = 18$) of the children said that the physicians in the surgical masks were more frightening, and 12 of those 18 children stated that it was because they could not fully see the faces of the physicians. Regarding the physicians in the face shields, 18% of the children found them more frightening. Today, many children have seen physicians with surgical masks on television, or have experienced surgery or previous hospital visits, at which time they have seen physicians and other healthcare workers wearing masks or face shields (Stewart, Algren, & Arnold, 1994). The researchers believe this may account for some of the comments in their study, in which 8% of the children thought that surgical masks or face shields were normal (Forgie et al., 2009).

Nevertheless, Forgie and colleagues' study (2009), as well as others (e.g., Maunder et al., 2003), indicate that many children find masks frightening. Beck et al. (2004) ask us to consider the impact of a hospital filled with "faceless" people on a young child: "Who is smiling? Who is frowning? How do I recognize my doctor? How does my nurse recognize me? Why is everyone so scared of me and my germs?" (p. 256).

Forgie et al. (2009) remind us that nonverbal communication is impaired when masks are worn: Subtle facial cues are absent or can be misread; lip-reading is impossible. For individuals for whom English is a second language, or individuals with hearing disabilities, this is particularly significant. Additionally, masks may be experienced as especially threatening for children who have been physically and/or sexually traumatized.

Communication is a necessary component in building an effective relationship with children, which can be negatively affected by the challenge of communicating while wearing a mask. Children may even be afraid of healthcare providers they know well when those individuals are wearing masks. For suggestions on ways to help decrease fright and misunderstanding, see Box 11.1.

---

1. If possible, allow children to see your face at the door or window to their room before donning the mask.

2. Reintroduce yourself to children and parents each time you see them.

3. Wear a picture ID where children can see it.

4. Exaggerate nodding your head, and eyebrow and eye movements.

5. Ask children and parents to repeat what you have said and describe what they understand.

6. Ask children and parents how they are coping, and let them know that you appreciate (and perhaps share) their frustrations.

BOX 11.1. SUGGESTIONS FOR HEALTHCARE PROVIDERS WHEN MASKS ARE REQUIRED

7. Offer children incentives and rewards (e.g., stickers or hand stamps) for wearing masks.

Note. Adapted in part from Beck, M., Antle, B., Berlin, D., Granger, M., Meighan, K., Neilson, B., ... Kaufman, M. (2004). Wearing masks in a pediatric hospital: Developing practical guidelines. *Canadian Journal of Public Health, 95*(4), 256–257.

Special Considerations

Immobilization and isolation both involve forced restricted activity, which deprives children of one of their most valuable means for dealing with stress. Assessment factors should include the ways limitations affect children's ability to deal with stress and their activities of daily living. Results can help guide the selection of appropriate activities to meet children's individual needs.

Regarding the activities in this chapter, with the exception of those listed as 1:1, adult/child ratios may vary significantly from those cited, depending on the age of the children, degree of immobilization, and location where the activity is conducted.

Activity Goals

The activities in this chapter are grouped into five purposes: providing sensory stimulation, stimulating kinesthesia, promoting orientation to time and place, encouraging social interactions, and reducing depersonalization. Some activities have dual purposes.

Providing Sensory Stimulation

Sensory stimulation involves offering activities that stimulate the five senses. Activities such as Air Freshener, Clean Mud, Fragrant Winter Wonderland, It's in the Bag Sculpture, Sun Catchers, and Twirling Spirals can achieve this goal.

Stimulating Kinesthesia

Kinesthesia, or a sense of movement, can be real or perceived. Perceived or real movement beyond the area of confinement is particularly helpful for children who are immobilized or isolated. Real movement experiences are provided in Gone Fishing. To simulate movement beyond the area of confinement, use activities such as Cardboard Dashboard, Planetarium, and Special Place Collages.

Promoting Orientation to Time and Place

Activities that help the child remain oriented to current time and place are especially helpful during prolonged immobilization or isolation. Activities such as Indoor Garden, as well as providing a calendar and a daily schedule, can accomplish this goal.

Encouraging Social Interactions

Interventions that reduce social isolation, such as Newspaper Scavenger Hunt, Silly Bedside Scavenger Hunt, and Tin Can Walkie-Talkies are important for restricted children.

Reducing Depersonalization

Children need to maintain a sense of self and their relationship to others outside the hospital. Activities addressing this goal include Pillow Sachets, Window Cling-ons, and Window Painting. Bringing in family photos, toys, a pillow or bedspread from home, and a favorite home-cooked meal, if permitted, can also accomplish this goal.

ACTIVITY 11.1.   AIR FRESHENER

The odors in hospitals typically range from just monotonous to really bad. This activity allows children the opportunity to choose how their room smells.

Therapeutic Goal: To facilitate coping with isolation and immobilization by providing sensory stimulation.

Age Group: School-age/adolescent

Adult/Child Ratio: 1:4

Required Time: 30 minutes, plus setting time

Restrictions and Precautions: None

Materials:

☐ 2 tablespoons unflavored gelatin

☐ 5–20 drops of cologne, perfume, or other fragrances (ideally, provide several options for the children to choose from)

☐ 1/2 cup hot water

☐ 1/2 cup ice-cold water

☐ Food coloring

☐ Specimen cup, with lid (or other small container, with lid)

☐ Bowl

☐ Spoon

☐ Various decorations (e.g., ribbon, yarn, glitter) (optional)

☐ Glue (optional)

Process

1. Have the children combine the gelatin and hot water in the bowl, and stir until the gelatin is completely dissolved.

2. Invite the children to smell the different fragrance options and then stir in the fragrance of their choice, along with the food coloring.

3. Tell the children to add the cold water and stir.

4. Let the children pour the mixture into the specimen cup, and cover with the lid.

5. Allow the mixture to set overnight.

6. Encourage the children decorate their containers, if they wish.

7. To use, tell the children to simply remove the lid to release the fragrance.

ACTIVITY 11.2.   CARDBOARD DASHBOARD

The rich imaginations of preschoolers make them very responsive to even a suggestion of movement.

Therapeutic Goal: To facilitate coping with isolation and immobilization by simulating movement beyond the area of confinement.

Age Group: Preschool

Adult/Child Ratio: 1:1

Required Time: 30 minutes advance preparation; usage time varies

Restrictions and Precautions: None

Materials:

☐ Copy-paper box or box similarly sized, top discarded

☐ Brads

☐ Pizza cardboard or paper plate

☐ Bottle caps

☐ Round plastic containers and lids

☐ Cardboard mailing tube or gift-wrap tube

☐ Markers

☐ Glue gun

☐ Key (optional)

Process

1. Cut off the bottom and one side of the box.

2. Use a brad to affix the pizza cardboard or paper plate to the box, to serve as the steering wheel.

3. Use the plastic containers, lids, and bottle caps to create the speedometer, tachometer, light switch, and other gauges and switches. Secure with brads or glue gun. Brads are preferable because they permit the parts to move.

4. Using markers, add numbers and other details to the speedometer and tachometer.

5. Use a brad to affix the cardboard tube to the side of the dashboard, to serve as the gearshift.

6. Create a slot for inserting the key (optional).

7. Facilitate the child taking an imaginary driving trip in his or her car by asking him or her to describe the destination and what he or she sees, smells, feels, and hears along the way.

Variation

For children who are not confined to their beds, make a car out of a cardboard box large enough for the child to sit it in. Slit then bend one of the sides to create a door, and make the dashboard as directed above. Just getting into the box can allow children to erect a barrier between themselves and the hospital.

ACTIVITY 11.3.   CLEAN MUD

Sick children frequently miss the opportunity to play outside, in mud and snow. This mud-without-the-mess activity helps children capture some of the fun inherent in sticking their hands in wet, moldable substances. The activity is also good for children who are tactile-defensive and can't tolerate touching actual snow or mud, but long to experiment with it.

Therapeutic Goal: To facilitate coping with isolation and immobilization by providing sensory input.	**Materials:**
Age Group: Preschool/primary	☐ Basin
Adult/Child Ratio: 1:5	☐ 1 cup water
Required Time: 15 minutes	☐ Red and green food coloring (optional)
Restrictions and Precautions: None	☐ 3 cups cornstarch
	☐ Tongue depressor or spoon, to stir with

Process

1. Place the cornstarch into the basin.

2. To tint the mixture to resemble mud, stir food coloring into the water.

3. Slowly stir approximately 1 cup of water into the cornstarch, until the mixture tears when you run your finger through it and "melts" when you squeeze it in your hand.

4. Give the mixture to the child play with.

Variation

Leave the mixture white, to simulate snow.

ACTIVITY 11.4.   FRAGRANT WINTER WONDERLAND

Children will enjoy looking at this winter scene and smelling its enticing aroma even if, because of their developmental or situational limitations, they are unable to do the project themselves.

Therapeutic Goal: To facilitate coping with isolation and immobilization by providing sensory input.	**Materials:**
Age Group: Preschool/primary	☐ Clean sand
Adult/Child Ratio: 1:1	☐ Allspice
Required Time: 20 minutes	☐ Tongue depressor
Restrictions and Precautions: This activity may not be appropriate for children who are immune suppressed.	☐ White modeling clay
	☐ Cloves
	☐ Cinnamon sticks

- ☐ Tiny branches from an evergreen or other fragrant winter tree (plastic can be used if fresh is contraindicated or unavailable)
- ☐ Glue or string
- ☐ Shallow pan with 2-inch-high sides
- ☐ Salt

Process

1. Spread a 1-inch layer of sand in the pan.
2. Have the child use the tongue depressor to manipulate the sand to form small mounds, to represent hills.
3. Let the child sprinkle allspice generously over the top of the sand.
4. Invite the child make a snowman out of modeling clay, using cloves for the eyes and a small piece of cinnamon stick for the nose.
5. Press some of the small sprigs into the sand to represent bushes.
6. Help the child make trees by gluing tiny branches to cinnamon sticks and pressing them into the sand.
7. Place the snowman atop the sand and pour salt over everything to create a snow scene.

ACTIVITY 11.5. GONE FISHING

Although it takes some time to make this game, it is very appealing and can be used over and over again.

Therapeutic Goal: To facilitate coping with immobilization by providing an opportunity to play beyond the area of confinement.

Age Group: Preschool/primary

Adult/Child Ratio: 1:4

Required Time: 40 minutes to make the game; 20 minutes to play

Restrictions and Precautions: Assure that the child does not lean over the side of the bed.

Materials:

- ☐ Fish template (Figure Activity 11.5-1)
- ☐ Construction paper
- ☐ Scissors
- ☐ Markers
- ☐ Clear contact paper or laminator
- ☐ Large paper clips
- ☐ Dowel rod
- ☐ String
- ☐ Tape
- ☐ Magnet
- ☐ Blue plastic tablecloth (available from party stores)

Figure Activity 11.5-1. Gone Fishing

Process

1. Use the template to trace fish shapes onto construction paper. You will need to make quite a few.
2. Cover each fish on both sides with contact paper, or laminate them. Cut out the fish.
3. Attach a paper clip to each fish.
4. Make a fishing pole by taping one end of the string to the dowel rod and the other end to the magnet.

5. To make the pond, cut the tablecloth into a large, irregular circular shape.

6. Place the "pond" on the floor and scatter the fish on top of it.

7. Give the child the fishing pole to catch all of the fish in the pond.

Variation   To add interest, write different numeric values on each fish, and make the activity into a game with the object being to catch the fish with the highest point value.

ACTIVITY 11.6.   INDOOR GARDEN

Horticulture therapy is recognized as an effective means of alleviating stress, promoting relaxation, and increasing an overall sense of well-being. In addition, it allows sick children, who are constantly surrounded by people taking care of them, the opportunity to reverse roles, becoming the caretaker in charge.

Therapeutic Goal: To facilitate coping with isolation or immobilization by providing a long-term, progressive project and reducing depersonalization.

Age Group: Primary/school-age/adolescent

Adult/Child Ratio: 1:1

Required Time: 45 minutes

Restrictions and Precautions: Make sure children wear disposable gloves and wash their hands immediately after removing them. This activity may not be appropriate for children who are immuno-compromised.

Materials:

☐ Glass jar with top, at least 8 inches in height, with an opening wide enough to fit your hand through

☐ Aquarium gravel or pebbles
☐ Activated charcoal
☐ Potting soil mix
☐ Small houseplants (e.g., Chinese elm, prayer plant, button fern, aluminum plant, sweet flag, African violet)
☐ Tongue depressor
☐ Syringe
☐ Water
☐ Small plastic wild animals (optional)
☐ Long cotton swabs
☐ Plant mister or spray bottle, filled with water

Process

1. Have the children cover the bottom of their jar with 1 inch of gravel or pebbles and 1/4 inch of activated charcoal.

2. Ask the children to top the mixture with potting soil, up to 1/4 of the height of the jar, and press down gently.

3. Give the children the tongue depressor to dig small holes for planting.

4. Instruct the children to remove the plants from their pots and place each in a hole, gently packing the soil around them with the tongue depressor.

5. Show the children how to fill a syringe with water and squirt a small amount of water on the soil at the base of each plant to moisten it.

6. Invite younger children to create a jungle scene by positioning small plastic animals and/or stones around the plants.

7. Use a cotton swab to clean the inside of the jar of any soil that has clung to it.

8. Lightly mist the plants with water and replace the lid on the jar.

9. Place the jar in a bright area, away from direct sunlight.

10. Tell the children that if heavy condensation forms inside the glass, they should temporarily remove the cover to let some of the moisture evaporate.

ACTIVITY 11.7. IT'S IN THE BAG SCULPTURE

This is a "simulated" messy activity for those children for whom a truly sloppy activity would be inappropriate. Working with the plaster while it is in a bag allows children to manipulate a wet, moldable substance without danger of it getting into open wounds, IV sites, or on a clean bed.

Therapeutic Goal: To facilitate coping with isolation and immobilization by providing sensory stimulation.

Age Group: School-age

Adult/Child Ratio: 1:1

Required Time: 15 minutes

Restrictions and Precautions: Combine the plaster of paris and powdered tempera paint in a well-ventilated area, outside the child's room.

Materials:

- ☐ Plaster of paris
- ☐ Powdered tempera paint
- ☐ Water
- ☐ Plastic freezer food storage bag with zipper closure (quart-size)
- ☐ Duct tape
- ☐ Glue gun (optional)
- ☐ Piece of wood or granite for base (small pieces usually available from companies that make granite countertops)
- ☐ Paint (optional)

Process

1. Pour the desired amount of plaster of paris into the freezer bag.
2. Add 1 to 2 tablespoons powdered paint to tint the mixture.
3. Add water according to package directions. Zip the bag closed and secure with duct tape.
4. Invite the child to squeeze the bag to combine the mixture.
5. Immediately after mixing (plaster sets quickly), encourage the child to mold the mixture into a desired shape *while it is still in the bag.*
6. Remove the sculpture from the bag after it has hardened.
7. Use a glue gun to attach the sculpture to a base and let the child paint it (optional).

ACTIVITY 11.8. NEWSPAPER SCAVENGER HUNT

This is a fun race that doesn't require the players to be able to move. It also allows children in isolation to participate with players elsewhere. In addition to all that, it's a great learning activity!

Therapeutic Goal: To facilitate coping with isolation and immobilization by reducing feelings of social isolation.

Age Group: School-age/adolescent

Adult/Child Ratio: Varies

Required Time: Contingent on how many items must be found

Restrictions and Precautions: Take scissors and glue precautions.

Materials:

- ☐ Newspapers (one per player)
- ☐ Scissors
- ☐ Glue sticks
- ☐ Large pieces of paper

Process

1. Create a list of items for children to look for in the newspaper. Examples include:
   - The price of a pound of grapes
   - The weather forecast for tomorrow

- A G-rated movie
- A number greater than a million
- A TV show that will air at 9:00 P.M.
- A store having a sale
- A used car in good condition
- The score from a game played yesterday

2. Provide each child with a newspaper, a copy of the list of things to find, scissors, a glue stick, and a large piece of paper.

3. Explain that they're in a race to find an example of each of the items on the list. When they find items, tell the children to cut them out and glue them to the paper.

4. The winner of the game can be either the first child who finds all the items on the list, or the child who finds the most items in a set amount time.

ACTIVITY 11.9. PILLOW SACHETS

Teens really enjoy the opportunity to combine individual ingredients to create their own unique scent.

Therapeutic Goal: To facilitate coping with isolation and immobilization by providing sensory stimulation and reducing depersonalization.

Age Group: Adolescent

Adult/Child Ratio: 1:8

Required Time: 45 minutes

Restrictions and Precautions: Be sure children are not sensitive to odors or allergic to plant materials. Have children exercise caution when using and disposing of needles.

Materials:

☐ Organza, moiré, or similar fabric

☐ Ruler

☐ Pencil

☐ Scissors

☐ Pins

☐ Sewing needles

☐ Thread

☐ Potpourri (premixed or ingredients to make custom combinations)

☐ Small scoop

☐ Ribbons, buttons, and/or silk flowers (optional)

☐ Fabric glue

Process

1. Show the children how to measure and cut the fabric into two 6-inch squares.
2. Tell the children to put the two pieces of fabric together, lining them up, right sides facing in, and insert pins around the perimeter.
3. Give the children the ruler to draw a line 1/2 inch from the edge of each side of the fabric squares.
4. Have the children thread their needles and then stitch along the lines, sewing together three sides.
5. Instruct the children to turn the fabric right side out.
6. Give the children the scoop to fill the pillow with potpourri, and then tell them to stitch the opening closed.
7. Invite the children to decorate the sachet by gluing on ribbon and other decorative trims.

ACTIVITY 11.10. PLANETARIUM

Gazing at the "stars" in a darkened room can have a very calming effect on an anxious child. Extend the activity by taking turns "writing" on the ceiling with the flashlight and guessing what was written.

Therapeutic Goal: To facilitate coping with isolation and immobilization by providing an opportunity for play that transcends the area of confinement.

Age Group: Primary/school-age

Adult/Child Ratio: 1:1

Required Time: 30–40 minutes

Restrictions and Precautions: Do not allow children to handle craft knives. Make sure there are no jagged edges on the can.

Materials:

- ☐ Flashlight
- ☐ Large tin can (approximately 5 inches in diameter), ends removed
- ☐ Tracing paper
- ☐ Craft knife with removable blade
- ☐ 7-inch squares of paper
- ☐ Constellation map (downloadable from the Internet)
- ☐ Rubber band

Process

1. Have the child use the tracing paper to mark the outlines of various constellations on the center of the paper squares.

2. Use the craft knife to cut out the stars.

3. Instruct the child to place a paper square at one end of the juice can, and secure it with a rubber band.

4. Darken the room and let the child shine the flashlight through the open end of the can toward the ceiling then rotate the image around the room. Encourage the child to identify the different constellations, or help him or her to learn their names.

Variation

Using a pointed tool, poke holes in the bottom of several paper cups to create different designs. Let the child shine a flashlight through each cup to project the images onto the ceiling. Insert different-colored pieces of cellophane into the bottom of the cups, and rotate the position of the cups to produce varied effects.

ACTIVITY 11.11.   SILLY BEDSIDE SCAVENGER HUNT

Too often, people entering a child's room are there to examine them or provide care; there is no meaningful interaction for the child. This activity helps to engage those entering a child's room in a playful social exchange.

Therapeutic Goal: To facilitate coping with isolation and immobilization by alleviating feelings of social isolation and engaging in a long-term project.

Age Group: School-age

Adult/Child Ratio: N/A

Required Time: Ongoing

Restrictions and Precautions: None

Materials:

- ☐ Pen
- ☐ Paper
- ☐ Digital camera
- ☐ Photo album, purchased or hand-made, or cardboard for mounting photos
- ☐ Glue

Process

1. Give the child a list of simple, silly things to ask staff or visitors to do for them, such as:
   - Try to touch your nose with your tongue.
   - Cross your eyes.
   - Stick your tongue out as far as you can and say, "Aaagh."
   - Draw a moustache on your ID photo (with water-soluble marker, of course).
   - Sing a silly song, accompanied by exaggerated gestures.
   - Wear something silly.

2. Have the child ask permission to photograph each staff member or visitor who performs one of the tasks. Stipulate that each person can do only one of the required tasks.

3. Encourage the child to place the photos into an album or mount them on cardboard.

ACTIVITY 11.12.   SPECIAL PLACE COLLAGES

The pictures that children choose to put in their collages can provide important information for the adult engaging the child in guided imagery sessions.

Therapeutic Goal: To facilitate coping with isolation and immobilization by simulating a movement experience.	**Materials:**
Age Group: School-age/adolescent	☐ Pictures cut from magazines, travel brochures, and the like, or downloaded from the Internet
Adult/Child Ratio: 1:2	☐ Scissors
Required Time: Multiple sessions	☐ Glue
Restrictions and Precautions: Take scissors and glue precautions.	☐ Digital camera
	☐ Poster board

Process

1. Encourage the children to think about a special place they would like to go. It could be a setting of fond memories, or a real or imaginary place they would like to visit. Examples might include the beach, on a sailboat, in the mountains, at an amusement park, their bedroom at home, and so on.

2. Have the children cut pictures from magazines that represent their "special place" or download them from the Internet.

3. When the children are satisfied with the number of pictures they have selected, describe to them how to create a collage. Once they like the arrangement, tell them to glue it in place.

4. Take a photo of each child; cut away the background.

5. Have the children glue their photos where they would like to appear in the collage.

6. Encourage the children to explain the significance of their special place; if a child has never been there, ask him or her describe why it is so appealing.

7. Use guided imagery to help children make imaginary visits to their special places.

Variation

Take the children on virtual field trips. Travel online to exotic lands—cruise down the Amazon, explore interesting museums, or visit historic sites. Although all web sites now contain text, many can still be enjoyed by low-level and nonreaders.

ACTIVITY 11.13.   SUN CATCHERS

Sun catchers are easy and quick to make. So, make a bunch and let the child put a different one in the window each day! This is a good project for siblings to do, as well.

Therapeutic Goal: To promote coping with isolation and immobilization by reducing depersonalization and providing sensory stimulation.	**Required Time:** 30 minutes
Age Group: Preschool/primary	**Precautions and Restrictions:** Do not allow children to use the iron. Keep the iron on the low-heat setting, and follow hospital policy for small appliance usage.
Adult/Child Ratio: 1:1	

Materials:

☐ Crayon shavings (either removed from a crayon sharpener or made with a cheese grater or vegetable parer)

☐ Ribbon, yarn, cutout letters, and/or other flat or semiflat decorations (optional)

☐ Waxed paper (sheets or bags)

☐ Clothes iron

Process

1. Have the child arrange the crayon shavings on a sheet of waxed paper.

2. If using additional decorations, let the child arrange them amid the shavings.

3. Place another sheet of wax paper atop the first.

4. With the iron on its lowest setting, briefly press the papers together until the shavings melt (about 5 to 10 seconds).

5. Let the child cut the sun catchers into any desired shape and hang them in the window.

ACTIVITY 11.14. TIN CAN WALKIE-TALKIES

Children have been playing with tin can walkie-talkies for many generations. Now there are sophisticated battery-operated walkie-talkies available for purchase that can be effectively used for this purpose. However, the therapeutic benefit of the activity increases when children make their own walkie-talkies, because it gives them a sense of accomplishment they won't get when using store-bought ones.

Therapeutic Goal: To facilitate coping with isolation and immobilization by alleviating feelings of social isolation.

Age Group: Preschool

Adult/Child Ratio: 1:2

Required Time: 20 minutes

Restrictions and Precautions: Be sure the cans have no sharp edges. Supervise the area when the walkie-talkies are in use, to ensure that no one trips over the string.

Materials:

☐ Two empty cans, each open at one end

☐ Spool of string or wire

☐ Yarn

☐ Glue

Process

1. Punch a small hole in the bottom-center of each can.

2. Encourage the children to decorate the cans by covering them with construction paper and then adding designs made with yarn and glue.

3. Thread the loose end of the string through the hole in one can and make several knots.

4. Unroll enough string or wire to extend from the bed of the isolated or immobilized child to the area where the other participant will be.

5. Cut the string or wire and thread that end through the hole in the second can; knot it securely.

6. Show the children how to communicate with the walkie-talkies by pulling the string taut and taking turns holding one can to their ear while the second child speaks into the other can.

ACTIVITY 11.15. TWIRLING SPIRALS

Staring at these gently twirling spirals can be mesmerizing.

Therapeutic Goal: To facilitate coping with isolation or immobilization by providing sensory stimulation.	**Materials:**
Age Group: Primary/school-age	☐ Plastic coffee can lids, with a small hole poked in the center (one per child)
Adult/Child Ratio: 1:4	☐ Permanent markers
Required Time: 10 minutes	☐ Scissors
Precautions and Restrictions: Take scissors, glue, and glitter precautions.	☐ Glitter
	☐ Glue
	☐ String

Process

1. Pass out markers to children and instruct them to draw a spiral on their lids, starting 1/2 inch from the hole in the center and gradually extending to the rim.
2. Tell children to cut along the line with the scissors.
3. Invite children to use glitter and glue to decorate the spiral.
4. Cut string to the desired length for hanging.
5. Knot one end of the string and then thread the other end through the hole in the center of the spirals.
6. If desired, glue two spirals together at their widest end to make a longer one.
7. Hang the spirals from the ceiling and, if possible, near an air vent to increase the motion.

ACTIVITY 11.16.   WINDOW CLING-ONS

Window cling-ons don't require tape and are easy to remove. Children can take them home and reuse them.

Therapeutic Goal: To facilitate coping with isolation and immobilization by reducing depersonalization.	**Materials:**
Age Group: School-age	☐ Large, clear, resealable plastic food storage bag
Adult/Child Ratio: 1:6	☐ Paper
Required Time: 30 minutes to make, plus drying time	☐ Marker
Restrictions and Precautions: Take glue, paint, and marker precautions.	☐ Dimensional fabric paint (also referred to as "puffy paint")
	☐ Paintbrush

Process

1. Have the children draw a shape (e.g., star, balloon, flower, heart) on a piece of paper, cut small enough to lie flat in the bag.
2. Tell the children to insert the shape into the bag and seal it.
3. On the outside of the bag, give the children the marker to trace the shape inside.
4. Have the children fill in the shape with fabric paint, urging them to apply it thickly and not leave any blank spots.
5. Allow the paint to dry thoroughly.
6. Help the child to carefully peel the design off the bag and then apply it to a clean, dry window.

Variation

For an easier version, let the children cut out shapes from static-cling black window film (used to tint automobile glass) and put them on the window.

ACTIVITY 11.17.   WINDOW PAINTING

These paints can also be used to write messages on the window to people "on the outside." Remind the children that they will need to write the letters in reverse.

Therapeutic Goal: To facilitate coping with isolation or immobilization by providing sensory stimulation.

Age Group: School-age/adolescent

Adult/Child Ratio: 1:1

Required Time: 30 minutes–1 hour

Precautions and Restrictions: The adult will need to do the painting for immobilized or very young children.

Materials:

☐ 1 tablespoon each of assorted colors of powdered tempera paint

☐ 2 tablespoons of clear dishwashing liquid for each color of tempera paint

☐ Containers for mixing pain (muffin pans work well)

☐ Bar of soap

☐ Paintbrushes

☐ Stencils (optional)

☐ Newspaper

☐ Masking tape

Process

1. In separate containers, mix 1 tablespoon of each color of tempera powder with 2 tablespoons of dishwashing liquid.

2. Use tape and newspaper to protect the window ledge and other adjacent areas from paint splashes.

3. Give the child the bar of soap to sketch the outline of the design or picture directly on the window, assisting as needed.

4. Help the child paint the window.

5. Remove dried paint by rubbing with a dry paper towel.

For more ideas, see Bright Ideas: Play Opportunities to Promote Large Muscle Movement (Box Activity 11.17-1).

BOX ACTIVITY 11.17-1. BRIGHT IDEAS: PLAY OPPORTUNITIES TO PROMOTE LARGE MUSCLE MOVEMENT

- Stationary bike or rocking horse
- Velcro darts: Attach string to the darts if the child can't get out of bed.
- Hopscotch: Use removable tape to create the board on the floor.
- Bottle bowling: Use empty 1- or 2-liter soda bottles for pins, and a lightweight ball. Children confined to their beds can throw the ball overhand.
- Basketball: Purchase a Nerf or Little Tykes basketball hoop—or just use a wastebasket!
- Spin art: Place paper plates in the bottom of a salad spinner and let the child squirt in paint (you can use a syringe for this). Put the cover back on and let the child turn the crank.

CHAPTER 12

PAIN

Research into the nature, assessment, and treatment of children's pain has grown exponentially over the last two decades (McGrath, 2005). Although in the past there was a relative lack of accountability for providing pain relief, the major focus today is on how to properly assess pain. Regulations developed by the Joint Commission (formerly called the Joint Commission on Accreditation of Healthcare Organizations [JCAHO]), consider pain "the fifth vital sign," and require caregivers to regularly assess and address pain (JCAHO, 2001). Nevertheless, pain remains one of the most misunderstood, underdiagnosed, and undertreated/untreated medical problems, particularly in children (Gerik, 2005).

The difficulty in accurately assessing pain in children may contribute to the use of pain reduction strategies when the actual problem is fear or anxiety. Conversely, fear- and anxiety-reducing strategies may be used when the major problem is pain. In this chapter, information is provided to enable individuals involved in planning therapeutic activities to develop a more individualized and effective plan for managing the pain children and adolescents experience.

Courtesy of Rush University Medical Center

LIST OF ACTIVITIES

What Is Pain?

According to the International Association for the Study of Pain, pain may be defined as "an unpleasant sensory and emotional experience associated with actual or potential damage, or described in terms of such damage" (Merskey & Bogduk, 1994, p. 209). That being said, pain is a unique personal experience, with individuals varying widely in their perception and tolerance of pain (Gerik, 2005). What may be perceived as a little nagging pain to one individual may be excruciating to another.

Pain is categorized in many ways. Perhaps the most common distinction is duration of pain—acute pain or chronic pain. Pain may also be classified by type.

Categories of Pain

Pain Duration. *Acute pain* is pain of brief duration, which goes away with treatment or healing, usually in six months or less. Onset may be sudden or slow. Acute pain is caused by injury (e.g., a broken bone), surgery, illness (e.g., strep throat), trauma, or painful medical procedures, and serves as a warning of disease or a threat to the body. *Chronic pain* exists beyond an expected time for healing, usually defined as three to six months. This category is further divided into *chronic malignant pain* and *chronic nonmalignant pain*. Chronic malignant pain is associated with a malignant disease such as leukemia. Pain in children with cancer may be caused by the disease itself, its treatment (e.g., surgery and radiotherapy), or may be completely unrelated (e.g., arthritis, migraine). Chronic malignant pain is expected to have an end, either by cure or death. Chronic nonmalignant pain, on the other hand, has no predictable ending.

Pain Type. A second method for classifying pain is by type—somatic, visceral, bone pain, and neuropathic. Sources of *somatic pain* are the skin, muscle, and connective tissues. Example causes include sprains, headaches, and arthritis. Somatic pain is localized, sharp or dull, and worsens with movement or touch. Internal organs are the source of *visceral pain*. Example causes include tumor growth, gastritis, and chest pain. In this type, pain is nonlocalized, but referred; it is dull and less affected by movement than somatic pain. Sensitive nerve fibers on the outer surface of bone are the sources of *bone pain*. Example causes of bone pain include cancer and fractures. This type of pain tends to be constant, and worsens with movement. Sources of *neuropathic pain* are nerves. Example causes include diabetic neuropathy, phantom limb pain, and cancer that has metastasized to the nerve plexus. Neuropathic pain is described as burning, stabbing, pins-and-needles, shock-like, and shooting.

Outcomes of Unrelieved Pain

Although pain assists us in avoiding physical harm, unrelieved pain may be inherently harmful, both psychologically and physiologically. Without intervention, impairment in functioning and disruption in families may result (Scanlon, 1991). Children's fear and anxiety are heightened, which in turn, increase perception of pain.

Neonates are especially at risk. According to Anand (1998), neonates experience increased sensitivity to pain as compared to children in older age groups. Even though physically they may not demonstrate a vigorous response, their hormonal, metabolic, and cardiovascular responses are greater (Johnston, Stevens, Yang, & Horton, 1995). Further, because the neonatal brain is so plastic, the neonate's vulnerability to early adverse experiences increases, which may lead to abnormal behavior and development. Neonates repeatedly exposed to pain may develop altered pain sensitivity, anxiety, stress disorders, hyperactivity and attention deficit disorder, impaired social skills, and patterns of self-destructive behavior (Anand & Scalzo, 2000).

In recent years sedation has been one method used to help children cope with painful procedures. However, sedation tends to cloud thinking and understanding, and so may actually heighten a child's sense of helplessness during procedures, further exacerbating the problem (Gerik, 2005).

Assessing Children's Pain

Considerable research has examined children's concepts of general illness from a developmental perspective. Far less research has examined the developmental course of children's understanding of pain (Gibson & Chambers, 2004). Nevertheless, a developmental approach remains the best method to accurately assess pain in children. Other factors to consider are the child's personality style and the situation. Factors that modify pain perceptions include age, cognition, gender, previous pain experience, temperament, cultural and family factors, and situational factors.

Three categories of behavioral indicators are widely used to assess children's pain (Gerik, 2005):

1. *Global rating scales*, which rely on assessment of predictable behavioral indicators of pain such as crying, wincing, or screaming.

2. *Indirect measures of pain*, such as requests for medication, or "well" behavior such as playing. However, requests for pain medication are not reliably linked to pain intensity; children in pain may actually be using play as a means to distract themselves from pain.

3. *Behavioral observation scales*, which focus on documentation of specific behaviors indicative of pain.

Helpful adjuncts to self-report and behavioral observation are physiologic measures, such as heart rate and blood pressure. However, there is only limited evidence to support clinicians' use of the practice (Foster, Yucha, Zuck, & Vojir, 2003).

Infants

Assessing pain in infants is challenging. One infant may manifest pain by crying; another may be silent. Some infants may wiggle and fidget, while others will be still. Infants in pain may not eat or sleep well, may have no interest in their surroundings, or may look pale and sweaty. In contrast, the cry of pain in the infant is very distinctive, and primary caregivers can easily distinguish and interpret cries (Gerik, 2005). Morison, Grunau, Oberlander, and Whitfield (2001) found that the most helpful pain indicators in neonates of more than 28 weeks' gestation are behavioral observations such as changes in facial expression and sleep/wake cycles, together with physiologic indexes of heart rate and oxygen saturation.

Toddlers

As their language skills develop, toddlers often can begin to talk about their pain. When asked with words they already know, they may be able to point to where it hurts, or may hold a body part that is hurting. Eating and sleeping difficulties may be apparent. For toddlers, medical procedures are perceived as pain, fear, and separation. Thus, interpreting their behavior may be difficult due to exacerbating factors such as separation anxiety, memory of previous painful experiences, and physical restraint. The fear factor is important with this age group, as well as with school-age children. When experiencing pain, some toddlers may become very quiet and inactive, while others may become very active. Pain may be manifest by angry outbursts. Caregiver report can be invaluable when assessing pain in the toddler.

School-Age Children

School-age children have a growing capacity to communicate accurately about their pain. Children 8 years and older can very reliably describe location of pain, and it is vital to take their report of pain seriously (Gerik, 2005). Other contributors should be examined, such as recurrent abdominal pain, headache, and absence from school. The school-age child in pain may have a "pained" face, hold a body part that is hurting, or not be able to pay attention. Again, behavioral observations can be misleading. For example, playing with a handheld video game may be a means of distraction. Some school-age children can exhibit great self-control when they are experiencing pain, and they may not report pain in an attempt to show bravery.

Most children ages 4 years and older can use symptom scales and self-report tools. Children who understand the concept of order or number (typically by age 8) can use a numeric rating scale or horizontal word-graphic rating scales. Older school-age children also can use word-graphic rating scales. Having school-age children keep a pain diary may be helpful in assessing and monitoring pain.

Adolescents

Teenagers can characterize and accurately describe pain, its intensity, and location. Psychological factors also may be important. Because they understand words and concepts that younger children do not, adolescents can explain pain more clearly. They may exhibit a high degree of control in their response to pain. In fact, the adolescent's greatest concern may be about maintaining a sense of control (Gerik, 2005). Thus, a trusting relationship is necessary to obtain an accurate appraisal of pain in this age group.

Other Influences on Children's Response to Pain

In addition to a child's age, other factors may influence his or her response to painful situations. Perhaps four of the most significant ones are the child's coping style, past experience with pain, family and cultural styles, and situational factors.

Child's Coping Style

Knowledge of a child's coping style is important in planning interventions to prepare or help him or her to cope with pain. As detailed in the Introduction, there are two basic types of coping styles: *attenders* or *monitors*, who are information seeking; and *distracters* or *blunters*, who are information avoiding. Thus, when having blood drawn, a monitor would likely cope more effectively when provided with detailed information before and throughout the procedure and perhaps would want to watch. In contrast, a blunter, would likely fare better when provided with distraction and minimal information.

Past Experience with Pain

Understanding a child's previous experience with pain can enhance pain assessment. For example, a child experiencing a lumbar puncture or a bone marrow aspiration without adequate pain management is likely to have difficulty undergoing the next invasive procedure. Weisman, Bernstein, and Shechter (1998) found that inadequate pain control during oncology procedures leads to significantly increased pain scores for subsequent painful procedures. Even neonates "remember" the experience of undergoing procedures with inadequate analgesia; research has found that they retain long-standing alterations in their response to and perceptions of painful experiences (Zempsky, Cravero, & the Committee on Pediatric Emergency Medicine, 2004). Lack of appropriate pain control or sedation for procedures or stressful medical experiences may even lead to posttraumatic stress disorder (Kain, Mayes, Wang, & Hofstadter, 1999; Wintgens, Boileau, & Robaey, 1997).

Family and Cultural Styles

Family beliefs, attitudes, and parental pain history influence how children learn about pain, its impact, and how to cope with different types of pain. Although little research has focused on these issues, factors that have been identified include the meaning of pain; cultural background; health and illness of family members; socioeconomic situation; and experience with and expectations of illness, hospitalization, and death. We have all witnessed simple evidence of this concept: We see a child fall down and immediately look at a parent for cues on how to react. But the concept might also have more complex expression. For example, a child aware of his or her family's poor financial situation may be concerned about the cost of pain medications and thus be reluctant to report or admit the presence of pain.

Regarding culture, some cultural groups value a stoic response to pain or uncomfortable situations. Thus, stoic children with severe pain may not report or show expected behavioral evidence of the severity of the pain. When language differences between the child and the healthcare professional erect a barrier to pain assessment, a parent or another adult who knows the child well can usually give a fairly credible assessment. That said, research indicates that there is a relatively pervasive and systematic tendency for proxy judgments to underestimate the pain experience of others (American Academy of Pediatrics/American Pain Society, 2001).

Situational Factors

McGrath (2005) cites three specific situation-specific factors related to how children experience pain: (1) what children and parents understand; (2) what they (and healthcare staff) do; and (3) how children and parents feel. Some situational factors can intensify pain and distress, while others can eventually trigger pain episodes, prolong pain-related disability, or maintain the cycle of repeated pain episodes in recurrent pain syndrome (McGrath & Hillier, 2001). These situational factors may affect children even more than adults because, unlike adults, children typically have not yet experienced the wide variety of pains of diverse etiology, intensity, and quality to provide them with a broad base of knowledge and coping behaviors. Adults who encounter new pains can evaluate them primarily within the context of their cumulative life experiences. Children, in contrast, must evaluate new pains primarily within the context of the immediate situation (McGrath).

Chronic Pain

Children with chronic pain are a particular concern. According to Lynch, Kashikar-Zuck, Goldschneider, and Jones (2007), children with chronic pain tend to have more anxious, internalizing characteristics than externalizing behavior problems:

> They frequently present as sensitive, conscientious children who are overwhelmed by the intensity and duration of their symptoms, worry about the impact of pain on their school performance, and are avoidant of physical and social activities that might exacerbate their pain. (pp. 212–213)

Biological and psychosocial characteristics are believed to play an interactive role in the experience and expression of pain (Fillingim, 2000), and also are likely to contribute to gender differences in adjustment and coping responses. Some research indicates that girls (ages 4 to 18 years) are more likely than boys to experience chronic pain, greater pain intensity, and multiple pain locations (Perquin et al., 2000). However, Lynch and colleagues (2007) found no gender differences for average pain intensity, a finding they believe may be attributed to the use of a clinical rather than a community sample: Boys with pain extreme enough to use healthcare services may be less reluctant to communicate their discomfort (Robinson et al., 2003).

Coping Strategies

The ways children cope with chronic pain is believed to play an important role in health-related outcomes such as pain intensity and functional disability (Varni et al., 1996). Even though earlier studies found no gender differences in the use of specific coping strategies among children with chronic pain (Sallfors, Hallberg, & Fasth, 2003), a more recent study by Lynch and colleagues (2007) found that girls used social support seeking more than boys, while boys used more behavioral distraction techniques. Regarding age, adolescents engaged in more positive self-statements (a cognitive strategy) than did younger children. Coping style preferences also might be considered traitlike characteristics that are unlikely to change regardless of the length of pain problems—in other words, "Once a worrier, always a worrier" (Lynch et al., 2007).

Special Considerations

Medications are available to help manage children's pain; however, children are frequently undermedicated (Helgadottir & Wilson, 2004). Although it is critically important that children in pain receive appropriate medication, other pain-management strategies are available in circumstances where pain medication is not enough or is contraindicated. Behavioral techniques can be used to distract children during painful procedures and to alleviate their fear and anxiety. Children, more so than adults, seem quite adept at using psychological therapies, presumably because they are generally less biased than adults about their potential efficacy (McGrath, 2005). Children particularly respond to pain-control strategies that involve their imaginations and senses of play (Gerik, 2005).

A Developmental Approach

Although each child is, of course, an individual, and each situation is different, a developmental approach can provide a starting point for suggestions for interventions to help manage pain. Interventions by developmental stage can be found in Table 12.1.

An interesting note from a study on the effects of various methods of distraction on pain relief in an emergency department setting found that children preferred music to toys (Tanabe, Ferket, Thomas, Paice, & Marcantonio, 2002). Perhaps, in this instance, a situational factor—namely, being in a noisy, bustling emergency department—carried heavier weight than other factors. Thus, while developmental recommendations are important, they are but one guide to helping children establish a sense of control in the journey to become victors rather than victims of pain.

Hypnosis

Under hypnosis, the child experiences an altered state of consciousness, in which concentration is focused, narrowed, and absorbed. Although techniques are similar to relaxation and guided

Table 12.1 Suggested Interventions for Managing Children's Pain by Developmental Stage

Stage	Suggested Interventions
Infant	Presence of parents Soothing verbal reassurance Rocking and holding Pacifier, for sucking Providing a familiar object to cuddle
Toddler	Presence of parents Distraction by talking, listening to music, blowing bubbles Video cartoons Active play, allowing child to act out the events being experienced
Preschool	Presence of parents Slow, rhythmic breathing, or touch in the form of rubbing Role-play of painful experience Distraction, by singing a favorite song, retelling a story, creating art Repetitive verbalizations
School-age	Distraction, by talking, listing to music, playing games, creating art Relaxation techniques Preparation and rehearsal of painful experience Reading books about similar situations
Adolescents	Verbalization Imagery Relaxation techniques Preprocedural preparation and practice Distraction, by playing CDs, reading books, creating art

imagery exercises, with hypnosis specific suggestions are made during the deepest relaxation phase of the exercise, which are designed to train the unconscious mind to promote pain relief, healing, or some other desired outcome (Gerik, 2005). Conducting hypnotherapy requires specialized training and certification.

Biofeedback

This approach uses instruments to detect and amplify specific physical states in the body and help bring them under one's voluntary control. The pain-relief mechanism is based on specific physiologic changes caused by the biofeedback. At times, very elegant systems are used to provide immediate positive feedback to children, and thus reinforce their ability to elicit relaxation and thereby reduce pain and anxiety (Gerik, 2005):

> . . . a child may sit in front of a computer monitor that displays a clown that may juggle or a flower that may open. Frequently, music accompanies the video display. Selected physiologic functions are measured, such as heart rate, skin temperature, galvanic skin response, electromyogram, or even electroencephalogram waves. The child applies relaxation techniques to bring those physiologic functions into some desired range and is promptly rewarded with a pleasing graphical display (clown juggling, flower opening) and pleasing music. When the physiologic functions are out of range, suggesting a stress response, the music and display cease. (p. 299)

Research is promising for the use of biofeedback to help children cope with pain. Powers and colleagues (2001), along with several other researchers, have reported the effectiveness of the use of biofeedback for pediatric headaches. Facilitating biofeedback requires specialized training and certification.

Activity Goals

All of the activities in this chapter have the goal of reducing pain and/or anxiety. The activities are listed under five common techniques used to help children cope with pain.

A form of relaxed, focused concentration, guided imagery leads the child to imagine and explore a favorite place or activity. This mind/body technique not only produces distraction, but also enhances relaxation. Research has demonstrated its effectiveness in studies with children, for instance, those experiencing abdominal pain (Ball, Shapiro, Monheim, & Weydert, 2003; Youssef et al., 2004). Activities in this chapter that use this technique include Beach in a Bottle, Imagination Vacation Scrapbooks, Magic Wands, and Ocean Motion.

Guided Imagery

When in pain, individuals frequently take very shallow breaths or hold their breath. Deep breathing can effectively induce a relaxation response. Rhythmic, deep-chest breathing or patterned, shallow breathing can be used to ease pain, stress, anxiety, and even panic (Gerik, 2005). The well-known Lamaze technique used during childbirth also can be implemented with children. We have known for a number of years the effectiveness of breathing techniques for a variety of painful procedures in children. For example, in a study of children undergoing bone-marrow aspiration, Jay, Elliot, Ozlins, Olson, and Pruitt (1985) found breathing exercises to be helpful in reducing behavioral distress. Activities in this chapter that use breathing techniques include Personal Comfort Kits and Tornado Twister.

Breathing Techniques

This technique helps children to recognize and relax body tension associated with pain, which in turn can decrease anxiety and discomfort and increase body awareness (Rusy & Weisman, 2000). Empirical evidence supports the use of PMR to alleviate tension headaches and insomnia, as an adjunct treatment in cancer, and for chronic pain management in inflammatory arthritis and irritable bowel syndrome (McCallie, Blum, & Hood, 2006). The Muscle Relaxation Exercise activity uses this technique.

Progressive Muscle Relaxation (PMR)

Children can develop new coping strategies and learn to distance and distract themselves from pain through the use of music, drawing, painting, storytelling, poetry, dance, and other art forms (Rollins, 2005a; 2008). Research suggests a relationship between arts experiences and the release of endorphins—the body's own pain reliever (Goldstein, 1980). Other research reports significant increases in oxygen saturation levels, an indicator of respiratory regularity directly affected by the individual's behavioral state and degree of pain (Collins & Kuck, 1991). Activities that use the arts in this chapter include Personal Comfort Kits, Manipulative Pain Thermometer, and Toasty Turtles.

The Arts

Attention is a key factor in the perception of painful stimuli. Pain is a subjective experience that requires a person to attend to and process painful sensory inputs (McCaul & Malott, 1984). A body of research documents the effectiveness of a variety of methods of distraction, especially for young children (Pira, Hayes, Goodenough, & Von Baeyer, 2006). Although many of the strategies mentioned previously for managing children's pain include the element of distraction, looking at distraction as a method within itself is useful when planning simple interventions to help children cope with procedures. Children can be distracted with "magic wands" that contain interesting floating objects; cylinders filled with beads and "seek-and-find" toys; bubbles; a cartoon; or something more sophisticated, such as virtual reality (VR), which demands substantial attentional resources (Hoffman et al., 2000). Research has found VR to be an effective distraction in several situations, such as with children undergoing IV placement (Gold, Kim, Kant, Joseph, & Rizzo, 2006), and as an adjunctive pain control during burn wound care (Hoffman et al., 2000).

Distraction

Activities here that use distraction include Bottled Bling, Bubbly Bags, Colorscope, Hide-and-Seek Bottles, Fish Squish, Iceboats, Last Night, for Dinner, I Had…, Magic Wands, Mini-Aquariums, Moving Paintings, Ocean Motion, Personal Comfort Kits, Rainbow Dough, Tornado Twister, and Twirl and Swirl.

ACTIVITY 12.1. BEACH IN A BOTTLE

Hockenberry and Wilson (2007) recommend activating as many senses as possible in guided imagery sessions. Thus, playing an audiotape of repetitive ocean sounds, accompanied by the fragrant aroma and silky feel of sunscreen lotion spread on children's skin, can enhance the effectiveness of Beach in a Bottle, by incorporating three additional sensory modalities—tactile, auditory, and olfactory—into the experience. Enriching the activity in this way is especially beneficial for children who are visually impaired, and who may have enjoyed a visit to the beach but are unable to recall visual images.

Therapeutic Goal: To reduce pain and/or anxiety by using guided imagery.

Age Group: School-age

Adult/Child Ratio: 1:5, making the bottles; 1:1, using the bottles

Required Time: 15 minutes to make the bottles; situational for use

Restrictions and Precautions: Exercise caution when using the glue gun.

Materials:

☐ Glass jar with lid

☐ Thick craft glue or low-temperature glue gun

☐ Funnel

☐ New sand (available from home and gardening stores)

☐ Small scoop

☐ Any or all of the following: clean shells, pebbles, sea glass, sea sponge, and driftwood

☐ Low-temperature glue gun

☐ Sunscreen lotion (optional)

☐ CD with sounds of the ocean

☐ CD player

Process

1. Have the children glue shells onto the lid of the jar; allow to dry.

2. Instruct the children to insert the funnel into the mouth of their jar.

3. Tell the children to scoop enough sand into their jars to cover the bottom.

4. Have the children place shells, pebbles, sea glass, and/or driftwood into their jars.

5. When the lids have completely dried, help the children screw them on tightly and secure with hot glue (Figure Activity 12.1-1).

Figure Activity 12.1-1. Beach in a Bottle

6. To initiate guided imagery, play the CD with sounds of the ocean.

7. Rub a small amount of sunscreen lotion onto the child's skin.

8. Use the jar as a prop to help the child visualize playing or relaxing on the beach. Encourage him or her to tell you exactly what he or she is doing, and about the sights, sounds, smells, and tastes he or she is experiencing.

ACTIVITY 12.2. BOTTLED BLING

These bottles generally work well with young children of any age. Toddlers will need to have the bottles made for them, but most preschoolers will enjoy making their own, with adult assistance. This is a good choice for use in clinics where time for activities such as this may be limited.

Therapeutic Goal: To reduce pain and/or anxiety by using visual distraction.

Age Group: Toddler/preschool/early school-age

Adult/Child Ratio: 1:1

Required Time: 10 minutes to make the bottle; situational for use

Restrictions and Precautions: Take glitter and glue gun precautions.

Materials:

☐ Clear plastic bottle (clean, old baby bottles are ideal)

☐ Corn syrup

☐ Water

☐ Variety of small, shiny objects (e.g., discarded costume jewelry, beads, pennies, metallic stars)

☐ Teaspoon

☐ Glitter

☐ Low-temperature glue gun

Process

1. Mix 3 parts corn syrup to 1 part water (amount contingent on the size of the bottle).

2. Ask the child to select and place the desired objects into the bottle.

3. Have the child add about 1 teaspoon of glitter to the bottle.

4. Fill the bottle with the corn syrup and water mixture, to within 1/2 inch from the top.

5. Cap the bottle tightly and secure it with hot glue.

6. To use as a visual distraction, shake the bottle gently while encouraging the child to focus on the moving objects.

ACTIVITY 12.3. BUBBLY BAGS

This manipulative technique offers the intrigue of bubbles and is suitable for use in waiting rooms and other areas where blowing bubbles might be undesirable.

Therapeutic Goal: To alleviate children's pain and/or anxiety by using visual distraction and providing an object to manipulate.

Age Group: Toddler/preschool

Adult/Child Ratio: 1:1

Required Time: 10 minutes advance preparation; situational for use

Restrictions and Precautions: Supervise the children closely to prevent them from mouthing or biting the bag.

Materials:

☐ Vacuum food-sealing machine with specially made bags

☐ Pieces of sponge, cut in interesting shapes

☐ Liquid dish soap

☐ Water

☐ Food coloring

☐ Duct tape

Process

1. Ask the child to help you saturate the sponges with liquid soap.

2. Have the child place the sponges into the bags.

3. Fill the bags about half full with water and add a drop of food coloring.

4. Seal the bags according to machine instructions.

5. To use during a painful experience, encourage the child to manipulate the bag to create bubbles.

ACTIVITY 12.4. HIDE-AND-SEEK BOTTLES

Similar toys are available commercially, but they are very expensive. And by making these bottles yourself, you can personalize them by selecting items that may be of particular interest or meaning to the individual children for whom you are making them.

Therapeutic Goal: To reduce pain and/or anxiety by using cognitive games as distraction.

Age Group: School-age

Adult/Child Ratio: 1:8

Required Time: 10 minutes to make; situational for use

Restrictions and Precautions: Exercise caution when using the glue gun.

Materials:

☐ Clear, plastic cylindrical containers with lids (The container should be narrow enough so that the children can comfortably hold and turn it.)

☐ White rice or birdseed

☐ Assortment of various small items (e.g., a penny, paper clip, dice, game pieces, button, jelly bean, shell, or safety pin)

☐ Paper

☐ Pencil

☐ Low-temperature glue gun

Process

1. Fill the containers with rice or birdseed and five or more small items, leaving enough space for them to shift when the containers are turned.

2. Make a checklist of all of the objects in the containers.

3. Secure the lids using the glue gun (Figure Activity 12.4-1).

Figure Activity 12.4-1. Hide-and-Seek Bottle

4. Give the children the hide-and-seek bottles and have them find each of the objects on the list, crossing them off as they are located. The children will need to shake and turn the containers frequently to do so.

For visually impaired children, put enough rice in a basin to fill it halfway. Add the small objects to the rice and let children search for them using their hands. **Variation**

ACTIVITY 12.5. FISH SQUISH

This is a quick and easy activity that is well-suited for use in a clinic or other setting where activity time is limited.

Therapeutic Goal: To reduce pain and/or anxiety by using visual distraction and providing an object to manipulate.	**Materials:**
	☐ Plastic, 1-cup food freezer bags with zipper closure
Age Group: Preschool	☐ Small plastic fish
Adult/Child Ratio: 1:1	☐ Blue hair-styling gel in squeezable bottle
Required Time: 10 minutes	☐ Duct tape
Restrictions and Precautions: Supervise children closely to prevent them from mouthing or biting the bag.	

1. Have the child place the plastic fish in the bag. **Process**
2. Help the child fill the bag with styling gel, to 1/4 inch from the top, and zip closed (Figure Activity 12.5-1).

Figure Activity 12.5-1. Fish Squish

3. Secure the bag with duct tape.
4. Encourage the child to manipulate the bag to "make the fish swim."

ACTIVITY 12.6. ICEBOATS

Under certain circumstances, children may be required to keep their hands or feet in ice water for an uncomfortably long period of time, as a result of burn injuries, certain chemotherapy drugs, or in an effort to minimize swelling of the extremities. Although purchased small plastic boats can be used, making these iceboats is often worth the extra effort, as most children enjoy being able to use something they have made.

Therapeutic Goal: To reduce pain and/or anxiety by encouraging the child's cooperation with pain treatment regimes.

Age Group: Preschool

Adult/Child Ratio: 1:1

Required Time: 5 minutes advance preparation, plus time for the liquid to freeze

Restrictions and Precautions: Closely supervise use of the stapler.

Materials:

☐ Empty, clean 1-cup milk or juice cartons

☐ Water

☐ Food coloring

☐ Duct tape

☐ Sharp knife

☐ Straw or wooden dowel

☐ Cellophane triangle, 3 × 4 × 5 inches

☐ Small stickers

☐ Basin

☐ Cold water

Process

1. Fill cartons with 3/4 cup of water and add several drops of food coloring.

2. Seal the top with duct tape and shake gently.

3. Lay the sealed cartons on one side and then use the knife to cut a small "X" through the center on the side facing up.

4. Push the straws or dowels through the openings and place the cartons in the freezer until frozen solid.

5. To make the sail, help the child fold the cellophane triangle along the 4-inch side, 1/2 inch in from the edge; staple to hold.

6. Let the child decorate the sails with stickers.

7. Help the child peel the carton away from the frozen "boat" and slip the sail onto the mast.

8. Launch the boats in the basin in which the child is soaking.

9. Encourage the child to use his or her hands or feet to create gentle waves, to move the boats around in the basin.

For more ideas, see Bright Ideas: More Ideas for Cold Cutaneous Stimulation (Box Activity 12.6-1).

BOX ACTIVITY 12.6-1. BRIGHT IDEAS: MORE IDEAS FOR COLD CUTANEOUS STIMULATION

• Freeze small plastic objects in ice cubes then let the child go on a treasure hunt to locate the objects and free them from the ice.

• Float ice cubes and small plastic fish in a bucket or basin of water and have child "ice fish" with his or her hands to find them.

• Place arctic animal toys, such as penguins and polar bears, into a shallow basin filled with ice cubes and water, and use to stimulate imaginative play on the "polar ice caps."

• Create scenarios of adventure heroes on an icy planet or in the icy ocean depths. Fill basins of water with ice cubes and plastic toys appropriate to the chosen theme and ask the child to "play out" the stories.

• Set foam blocks made for use during bath time into a basin of water and ice, and build with them.

• For an icy manipulative, fill a surgical glove with a mixture of 2/3 cup water and 1/3 cup alcohol, and freeze. The alcohol will prevent the liquid from freezing completely.

• Sprinkle dry tempera paint onto finger paint paper then rub ice cubes over the paint.

ACTIVITY 12.7. IMAGINATION VACATION SCRAPBOOKS

This is a good activity for long-term patients. Depending on how computer-savvy the child (or adult who is assisting) is, photo-manipulation software can be used to add the children's images to photographs of any location that appeals to them, including outer space or imaginary scenes. The possibilities are endless!

Therapeutic Goal: To reduce pain and/or anxiety by using guided imagery.

Age Group: School-age/adolescent

Adult/Child Ratio: 1:8

Required Time: 1 hour or more

Restrictions and Precautions: Take glue and scissors precautions.

Materials:

☐ Computer

☐ Magazines, travel brochures, or downloaded photos

☐ Scissors

☐ Markers

☐ Glue

☐ Scrapbooks

Process

1. Using the computer, make colorful word art cutouts of the following headings:

   - Where I Would Like to Go
   - What I Will See When There
   - What I Will Be Doing
   - Who Will Be There with Me
   - What It Will Smell Like

2. Glue each heading to a different scrapbook page.

3. Begin the activity by encouraging the children to visualize a place, real or imaginary, where they would like to go on vacation. It could be a place of adventure, or very relaxing—wherever would make them happy at that moment. Invite children who are having difficulty envisioning or selecting a dream destination to tour potential choices by visiting travel web sites on the Internet.

4. When the children have selected their destinations, have them fill in the scrapbook pages, using words, drawings, and pictures printed from the computer or cut from magazines or travel brochures, to create a vivid depiction of the place they envision.

5. Encourage the children to look at the scrapbook when they are anxious or in pain, and imagine they are in that special place. Ask them to think about everything they would be experiencing through their senses—smells, tastes, temperature, sounds, and sights.

ACTIVITY 12.8.   LAST NIGHT, FOR DINNER, I HAD . . .

This activity requires neither materials nor movement, making it possible to do regardless of the children's ability to see or use their hands, or their positioning. It can be done anywhere there is an anxious child or a child in pain—such as a waiting room in a clinic or in an ambulance on the way to the hospital. The theme can be easily varied to capture or sustain children's interest.

Therapeutic Goal: To reduce pain and/or anxiety by using cognitive games as distractions.

Age Group: School-age/adolescent

Adult/Child Ratio: 1:10

Required Time: Situational

Restrictions and Precautions: None

Materials: None

Process   1. Begin the game by having the first player state, "Last night, for dinner, I had . . . (player must name something beginning with the letter "A," such as avocado, apple pie, or artichokes).

                        2. The second player repeats the phrase, "Last night, for dinner, I had . . ." then restates the foods named by the previous player(s) before adding a food beginning with the next consecutive letter of the alphabet.

                        3. Play continues through each letter of the alphabet in this manner. (The letter "X" may need to be omitted because of a lack of food items beginning with this letter.)

Variation   Play this game with younger children by substituting food with a category familiar to them, such as "animals at the zoo" or "things that are red." Then have the children take turns naming something from that category that hasn't yet been mentioned by another player.

                        For more ideas, see Bright Ideas: Additional Ideas for Cognitive Challenges (Box Activity 12.8-1).

BOX ACTIVITY 12.8-1. BRIGHT IDEAS: ADDITIONAL IDEAS FOR COGNITIVE CHALLENGES

- Using fishing wire and paper clips, hang lightweight plastic or acrylic toys and/or figural Christmas tree ornaments from the frames of drop ceilings. Make a list of all of the objects used and challenge children to try and find everything on the list.

- Mount pages from the I Spy or Where's Waldo book series on foam board then laminate or cover them with clear contact paper. Use during procedures.

- Count backwards from 100.

ACTIVITY 12.9.   MAGIC WANDS

This is an excellent activity to use with guided imagery. For those not familiar with the process, many excellent resources are available by Leora Kuttner and others on how to do guided imagery.

Therapeutic Goal: To reduce pain and/or anxiety by using visual distraction and guided imagery.

Age Group: Preschool/young school-age

Adult/Child Ratio: 1:3

Required Time: 15 minutes (to make the wands)

Restrictions and Precautions: Take glitter, scissors, and glue precautions. Do not use the suggestion of magic with a child whose family might find it objectionable for religious, cultural, or other reasons.

Materials:

☐ Rigid tube approximately 1/4 – 1/2 inch in diameter (e.g., cardboard tube from coat hanger or colored plastic tube from craft store, one per child)

☐ Aluminum foil

☐ Tape

☐ Pencil

☐ Colored cardboard or cardstock

☐ Star-shaped cookie cutter or stencil, approximately 2 to 3 inches at its widest point (or purchase precut stars)

☐ Scissors

☐ Glitter

☐ Glue

☐ Tape

☐ Curling ribbon, cut to the length of the tube, and curled

Process   1. Wrap the tube tightly with foil and secure it with tape.

                        2. Trace stars onto the cardstock and cut them out.

                        3. Have the children decorate the stars with glitter.

4. Sandwich the tube between the two stars and tape or glue it in place.

5. Help the children tape curled ribbons to the tubes, at the base of the stars.

6. Use the wand simply as a sparkling visual distracter during a procedure, or as a "magic wand" during guided imagery to help children imagine their pain "magically floating away" as the wand moves slowly back and forth in front of them.

ACTIVITY 12.10.   MINI-AQUARIUMS

This is an undersea variation of the ever-popular winter-scene snow globes. Other outdoor scenes that appeal to the children may be substituted.

Therapeutic Goal: To reduce pain and/or anxiety by using visual distraction.

Age Group: School-age

Adult/Child Ratio: 1:8

Required Time: 20 minutes

Restrictions and Precautions: Take glitter and glue gun precautions.

Materials:

☐ Clear jar with screw-on lid

☐ Polymer clay

☐ Small plastic or rubber aquatic animals and plants

☐ Small shells

☐ Aquarium gravel

☐ Water

☐ Glycerin

☐ Blue glitter

☐ Low-temperature glue gun

Process

1. Have the children press a lump of clay into the inside of the jar lid, extending it close to the outer edge.

2. Ask the children to press the bottoms of the plastic animals and plants into the clay. Then have them completely cover the remaining surface of the clay with gravel and shells, pressing them in lightly so they will stay in place but still be visible.

3. Help the children fill their jars almost to the top with water.

4. Let the children add a few drops of glycerin and a small amount of glitter to the water.

5. Help the children screw the lids tightly onto their jars.

6. Secure the lids with hot glue.

7. To use, invite the children to invert their jars, shake them gently, and watch as the glitter slowly settles to the bottom.

ACTIVITY 12.11.   MUSCLE RELAXATION EXERCISE

Muscle Relaxation Exercise is located on the CD that accompanies this book.

ACTIVITY 12.12.   OCEAN MOTION

These bottles are similar to lava lamps. Watching them can have a calming and mesmerizing effect, which can be further enhanced by adding the soothing sounds of waves gently lapping the shore.

Therapeutic Goal: To reduce pain and/or anxiety by using visual distraction and guided imagery.

Age Group: School-age

Adult/Child Ratio: 1:5 to make; 1:1 when using imagery or distraction techniques

Required Time: 15 minutes to make; situational for use

Restrictions and Precautions: Be sure the child does not have an aversion to being on the water or a history of motion sickness. It may not be appropriate for children who feel nauseated from chemotherapy, or for other reasons. Exercise care when using a glue gun.

Materials:

☐ Large clear plastic bottles with a tight-fitting twist top (one per child)

☐ Funnel

☐ Mineral oil

☐ Water

☐ Blue food coloring

☐ Low-temperature glue gun

☐ CD of ocean sounds (optional)

☐ CD player (optional)

Process

1. Have the children insert the funnel into the bottle opening and pour water through it until it is half full.

2. Ask the children to tint the water with a few drops of blue food coloring and then swirl their bottles gently, to mix.

3. Instruct the children to fill the bottles to the top with mineral oil, leaving no space for air.

4. Help the children twist the bottle tops on tightly and secure with hot glue.

5. To use, lay a bottle on its side and gently rock it to simulate ocean waves, while playing the relaxation CD in the background.

6. Guide the child in imagining relaxing on a boat that is drifting on the ocean. Describe the positive sensory experiences he or she might be having, such as the warm feel of the sun on the skin, the gentle rocking of the boat, the fragrant smell of saltwater in the air, or the rhythmic sound of seagulls flapping their wings above.

ACTIVITY 12.13.   MANIPULATIVE PAIN THERMOMETER

This tool is an adaptation of two measures widely used with pediatric patients to determine their level of pain: the Wong-Baker FACES Pain Rating Scale (Wong & Baker, 1988) and a pain thermometer (developer unknown), described by Kuttner (1996) as "one of the most useful [pain measurement tools] for all ages." This variation may be particularly helpful for children with ADHD, autism spectrum disorders, and other cognitive impairments. These children are typically visual, kinesthetic, and tactile learners who may benefit from being able to both see and manipulate the thermometer.

Therapeutic Goal: To reduce pain and/or anxiety by providing a tool to help children self-report their pain.

Age Group: School-age

Adult/Child Ratio: 1:1

Required Time: 45 minutes

Restrictions and Precautions: Take glue and marker precautions. Exercise caution when using needles and the artist's utility knife.

Materials:

☐ Poster board

☐ Pencil

☐ Ruler

☐ Markers

☐ Artist's utility knife

☐ White ribbon, 2 inches wide, 13 inches long

☐ Red ribbon, 2 inches wide, 13 inches long

☐ Needle and thread or fabric glue

Process

1. Draw a thermometer measuring 1 foot in height on the poster board. Write the numbers 5 to 0, evenly spaced, down the left-hand side. **Process**

2. On the bottom right-hand side of the thermometer (corresponding to the 0), use a cool-colored marker to write "no hurt" next to a smiley face.

3. On the top right-hand side of the thermometer, corresponding to the number 5, use a red marker to write "most hurt" accompanied by a crying, grimacing face.

4. Continue with numbers 1 to 4, writing "hurts a little bit," "hurts a little more," "hurts even more," "hurts a lot," respectively.

5. Alongside each number draw faces representing the degree of pain described.

6. Use the utility knife to cut two 3-inch horizontal slits, one 2 inches from the top and the other 2 inches from the bottom of the thermometer.

7. Sew or glue one end of the red ribbon to one end of the white ribbon.

8. Insert one end of the ribbon through each slit and sew or knot the two ends together in back.

9. Show the child a real thermometer and demonstrate the way it is used to show what their body temperature is.

10. Now show the child the pain thermometer and explain that it can be used to help describe how much they hurt. Explain that the smiley face next to the 0 indicates they don't hurt at all, and the crying, grimacing face next to the 5 means they feel the worst hurt possible.

11. Demonstrate how to slide the ribbon along the thermometer to indicate different levels of pain.

12. Encourage the children to use the pain thermometer as a visual aid to describe their pain to adults.

Have the child identify a particular activity or distracter for each pain level. Help the child make a chart **Variation**
by writing the numbers 1 through 5 with corresponding coping strategies alongside each number
(e.g., 5: practice muscle relaxation; 4: squeeze a manipulative; 3: watch a movie).

ACTIVITY 12.14. PERSONAL COMFORT KITS

This activity is particularly beneficial for children who will have to endure many short, painful procedures over time. Encourage the children to bring their kit whenever they visit the hospital or clinic.

Therapeutic Goal: To reduce pain and/or anxiety by using visual distraction, providing an object to manipulate, and promoting slow, deep breathing.

Age Group: Preschool/school-age/adolescent

Adult/Child Ratio: Contingent on ages and abilities of participants

Required Time: Situational

Restrictions and Precautions: With repeated usage, items in the box may lose their interest to children and will need to be changed.

Materials:

☐ Plastic shoebox or other similarly sized box

☐ Scissors

☐ Pictures cut from magazines, stickers, and other collage materials

☐ Glue

☐ Paintbrush

☐ Mod Podge (optional)

☐ Permanent markers

☐ Age-appropriate objects that promote breathing:

- Kazoos
- Pinwheels
- Party blowers
- Whistles
- Incentive spirometers

- • Sing-along CDs
- • Bubbles
- ☐ Age-appropriate objects to manipulate:
  - • Play-Doh
  - • Soft doll or stuffed animal
  - • Stress balls
  - • Surgical glove filled with sand (Be sure to check for allergies before introducing products with latex.)
  - • Koosh balls
- ☐ Age-appropriate visual distracters:
  - • Pop-up books

- • Sand/water timers
- • Video games
- • Acrylic wands
- • Humorous videos
- • Laser pointers
- • Light-up toys
- • Kaleidoscopes
- • I Spy or Where's Waldo books

Process

1. Ask the children to cut out pictures of some of their favorite things, (e.g., foods, animals, toys, fictional characters, colors, flowers) and glue them to the outside of their boxes, in collage fashion.

2. Have the children brush on Mod Podge, covering the whole box.

3. After the boxes are completely dry, show the children the selection of objects available for inclusion in their comfort kits. Demonstrate the use of any objects the children may not be familiar with.

4. Let the children select one item from each category of objects to add to their boxes.

5. Encourage the children to use the objects in their comfort kits during painful and/or anxiety-producing procedures.

6. If children are having difficulty focusing on the items in the box, engage them in diversional talk about the images they chose to decorate their boxes with.

Variation

When time is an issue, forgo personalizing the box. Simply provide children with an attractive container and let them select distraction items to put in it.

For more ideas, see Bright Ideas: Additional Comfort Measures (Box Activity 12.14-1).

Box Activity 12.14-1. Bright Ideas: Additional Comfort Measures	Presence of caregiver	Dimming lights
	Soft touch or massage	Pacifier
	Decreasing external stimuli	Warm or cold compress
	iPods	Holding hands
	Playing soothing music	Supportive holding
	Metronomes	Introducing pleasant scents
	Transitional object (blanket or toy)	

 ACTIVITY 12.15.   RAINBOW DOUGH

Rainbow Dough is located on the CD that accompanies this book.

ACTIVITY 12.16.   TORNADO TWISTER

This activity, popular among elementary school science teachers, can, in healthcare settings, lend itself to images of a tornado "blowing away the pain."

Therapeutic Goal: To reduce pain and/or anxiety by using visual distraction and promoting slow, deep breathing.

Adult/Child Ratio: 1:5 to make; 1:1 to use

Age Group: School-age

Required Time: 30 minutes

Restrictions and Precautions: Take glitter precautions.

Materials:

- ☐ Two 2-liter clear plastic bottles (per child)
- ☐ Water
- ☐ Food coloring
- ☐ Glitter
- ☐ 1-inch metal washer
- ☐ Duct tape

Process

1. Have children pour water into one of the bottles until it is 3/4 full.

2. Ask them to add a few drops of food coloring and a small amount of glitter.

3. Show the children how to place the metal washer over the opening of the bottle.

4. Turn the second bottle upside down and position it on top of the metal washer.

5. Help the children fasten the two bottles and the metal washer together with duct tape. Be sure to tape tightly, so that no water will leak out when using the bottle.

6. To use, quickly and carefully turn the tornado twister so that the bottle with the water is on top. Move the bottle in a circular motion until a "tornado" forms in the top bottle as the water rushes into the bottom.

7. Urge the children to take a slow, very deep breath, sucking in their pain; then tell them to blow the pain out with the strength of a tornado.

ACTIVITY 12.17.   TWIRL AND SWIRL

The creation of different patterns in the liquid solution not only will hold children's interest but also can be made into a game by challenging children to describe what the patterns look like to them (like taking a Rorschach test).

Therapeutic Goal: To reduce pain and/or anxiety by using visual distraction, providing an object to manipulate, and using a cognitive distraction.

Age Group: School-age

Adult/Child Ratio: 1:8 to make; 1:1 to use

Required Time: 15 minutes to make; situational for use

Restrictions and Precautions: Take glue gun precautions.

Materials:

- ☐ 8- or 12-ounce clear plastic bottles, with screw-on caps (one per child)
- ☐ Liquid hand soap containing glycol stearate (Caution: Do *not* use soap with glycol distearate.)
- ☐ Food coloring
- ☐ Water
- ☐ Low-temperature glue gun or duct tape

Process

1. Have the children fill their bottles about 1/4 full of liquid soap.

2. Ask the children to add two drops of food coloring.

3. Tell the children to fill their bottles, very slowly, to the top with water. Caution them not to pour the water in too fast, or it will produce unwanted foam.

4. Tell the children to screw the caps on their bottles tightly.

5. Have the children turn their bottles upside down—slowly—a few times to mix the soap and water. (If foam emerges, remove the cap and trickle more water into the bottle so that the foam runs over the edge.)

6. Tell the children to recap their bottles then help them secure the tops with hot glue or duct tape.

7. To use the bottles, have the children twirl and shake them at different speeds and angles to see the different patterns created by the soap.

8. Encourage children to describe what the patterns look like to them.

ACTIVITY 12.18.   COLORSCOPE

Children enjoy making these "colorscopes" and creating their own light show. Although there are many steps to this activity, it is relatively easy to do and is excellent to use for distraction.

Therapeutic Goal: To reduce pain and/or anxiety through visual distraction and manipulating objects.

Age Group: School-age

Adult/Child Ratio: 1:6 to make; 1:1 to use

Required Time: 45 minutes–1 hour

Restrictions and Precautions: Take scissors, markers, and paint precautions. Exercise caution when using the utility knife.

Materials:

☐ Cardboard tubes, the size of paper towel roll (one per child)

☐ Aluminum foil

☐ Clear plastic report cover (one per child)

☐ Ruler

☐ Pen or marker

☐ Artist's utility knife

☐ 4-inch squares of black construction paper, plastic wrap, and waxed paper (one each per child)

☐ Hole punch

☐ Scissors

☐ Rubber band

☐ Clear tape

☐ Colored transparent beads, tiny sequins, bits of colored cellophane, and/or shiny confetti

☐ Acrylic paints and paintbrushes, colorful contact paper, and/or stickers

☐ Medical or masking tape

Process

1. Help the children measure and cut a piece of aluminum foil 1 inch longer than the length of their tube.

2. Have the children roll the foil loosely, with the shiny side facing inward.

3. Instruct the children to insert the rolled foil into their tube, leaving 1/2 inch extending from both ends of the tube.

4. Tell the children to carefully unfurl the roll in the tube then press the ends against the outside edges of the tube.

5. Instruct the children to draw an 8-inch × 4-inch rectangle on the report cover and cut it out using the utility knife.

6. Help the children draw three horizontal lines across the rectangle, dividing it into three 1–1/4-inch segments, plus one 1/4-inch segment.

7. Show the children how to fold the plastic along the lines, forming a triangular shape; tell them to leave the 1/4-inch strip on the outside and tape the triangle, so it remains closed.

8. Tell the children to slide the plastic triangle into the paper towel roll carefully, so as not to tear the aluminum foil.

9. Instruct the children to turn the tube on one end and trace a circle around it on the construction paper. Then, have them cut out the circle, poke a hole through the center, and tape it over one end of the tube.

10. Demonstrate how to place a square of plastic wrap on the other end of the tube then press down to create a pouch in the end of the plastic triangle. Ask the children to do the same and then add some beads, confetti, cellophane, and/or sequins to the pouch.

11. Have the children lay a square of waxed paper over the pouch and then stretch the rubber band over both the waxed paper and plastic wrap, making sure it is on securely.

12. Allow the children to decorate the tube with paint or stickers.

13. To use, show the children how to hold the tube up to one eye, point it toward light, and turn it.

ACTIVITY 12.19.   TOASTY TURTLES

The Toasty Turtle is a soft, whimsical, microwave heating bag that stays comfortably warm for about 20 minutes. Making it is an especially good activity for children from Costa Rica, where turtles are considered very lucky. Young children or children who are physically unable to do this project may still benefit using a Toasty Turtle that has been made for them, as a pain intervention

Therapeutic Goal: To reduce pain by applying heat.

Age Group: School-age/adolescent

Adult/Child Ratio: 1:8

Required Time: 1 hour

Restrictions and Precautions: Do not use with children who are unable to communicate if the turtle is too hot. Do not microwave the turtles for more than 2 minutes, or leave the oven unattended while in use. Test the temperature of the turtles before giving them to children. Use scissors and needle precautions.

Materials:

☐ Dried herbs, dried spices, dried flowers, or fragrant oils (optional)

☐ Rice (uncooked)

☐ Cotton fleece, cotton flannel, or cotton terrycloth pieces, cut into 12-inch squares (two per child)

☐ Pencil

☐ Scissors

☐ Needle and thread

☐ Template (Figure Activity 12.19-1)

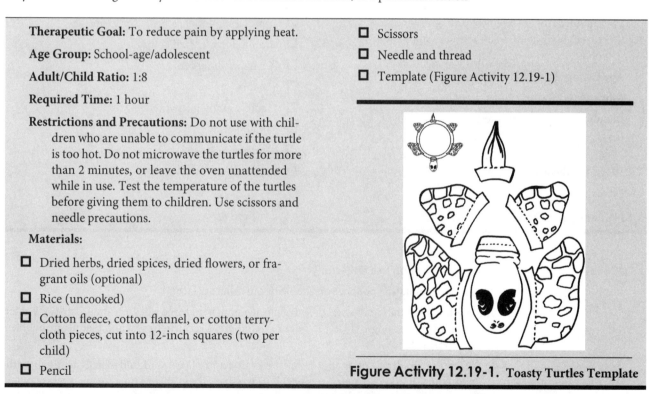

Figure Activity 12.19-1. Toasty Turtles Template

Process

1. Two days prior to the activity, mix the herbs, spices, and/or essential oil with the dried rice; allow it to sit in a sealed container, stirring occasionally (optional).

2. For the turtle shell, have the children trace an oval shape on two fabric squares and cut them out.

3. Show the children how to sew the pieces together, leaving a 1/2-inch border around the edges and a 2-inch opening.

4. Help the children fill the shells, approximately 3/4 full, with rice. Do not overfill them or they will be too rigid to mold around the children's bodies.

5. Once the turtle shell is filled, help the children sew the opening closed; make sure the rice is contained at the opposite side while doing so.

6. Using the template, have the children trace the turtle's head, feet, and tail onto the felt and cut each piece out.

7. Help the children sew the extremities to the appropriate areas on the shell.

8. To use, lay the Toasty Turtle flat in a *clean* microwave and heat for 1 to 2 minutes. (As when heating any food in a microwave, do not leave unattended.)

9. Carefully remove the turtle and gently shake it to distribute the heat. Test the temperature.

10. Give the Toasty Turtles to the children to apply to an area of their body that hurts.

Variation

For a quick no-sew microwave heating bag, make a Snuggly Snake by filling a clean tube sock with dried rice and tying the open end closed. Add facial features with a permanent marker.

ACTIVITY 12.20.   MOVING PAINTINGS

Although similar to other activities that incorporate oil and water to make distraction objects, this activity requires greater skill, hence allows for greater creativity, making it suitable for adolescents. The foam pieces inside the pouches allow the children to add their own design elements and erect obstacles around which the liquids flow, producing unique and interesting designs.

Therapeutic Goal: To reduce pain and/or anxiety through visual distraction and manipulating objects.

Age Group: Preteen/adolescent

Adult/Child Ratio: 1:6

Required Time: 45 minutes

Restrictions and Precautions: Take scissors and marker precautions. Supervise children closely when the iron is in use.

Materials:

☐ Clothes iron or flat iron for hair

☐ Laminating pouches, 8–1/2 × 11 inches
☐ Craft foam, assorted colors
☐ Permanent markers
☐ Scissors
☐ Liquid watercolor paints
☐ Mineral oil
☐ Measuring spoons
☐ Paper towels

Process

1. Preheat the iron to a low setting.

2. Lay the laminating pouches on a table or other flat surface.

3. Use the tip of the iron to seal the edge of each pouch on three sides, creating a strip 1/2-inch wide. Check the edges closely to be sure that there is an airtight seal and that no air bubbles have formed.

4. Have the children cut shapes from the craft foam sheets and add details to them with permanent markers. Suggest to the children to base these shapes on a theme, such as outer space, with stars, planets, and a crescent moon; or the sea, with fish, shells, and squid. Or they can simply make abstract shapes.

5. Ask the children to select three paint colors that are near one another on the color wheel. Explain that using complementary colors will result in brown when combined.

6. Help each child hold his or her pouch securely, with the unsealed side up, before opening it widely (or have children work in pairs).

7. Tell the children to pour in 2 tablespoons of oil and 3 tablespoons of paint *without* allowing the liquids to touch the open edge of the pouch. Explain that they must clean the top edge well with a paper towel, or the pouch will not seal properly.

8. Demonstrate how to press the open edges together to prevent the liquids from escaping, before placing the edge on a slightly raised surface, such as a box top, allowing the pouch containing the paint to rest on the table.

9. Show how to seal the pouch with the iron. Inspect the sealed edges on the children's pouches carefully to assure they are airtight and that no bubbles have formed.

10. When the children are having painful procedures, encourage them to use their pouch as a visual distraction. Show them how to use their fingers to swirl the colors gently around.

CHAPTER 13

BREATHING

Some of the most common health problems in the pediatric age group are related to disturbed respiratory function, with respiratory infections accounting for the majority of acute illnesses in children. Respiratory distress is the eighth leading cause of death in the newborn period, with pneumonia ranking in the top 10 causes of death for all ages of children (Xu, Kochanek, & Tejada-Vera, 2009).

Courtesy of Steven Koress Photography

Healthcare professionals designing play activities for pediatric patients with diminished lung expansion, impaired airflow, or other abnormalities that interfere with respiratory function need to understand that developmental differences exist between the child and adult respiratory systems. The size and position of a child's airway means that it can be easily obstructed with any respiratory disease. Even a minimal amount of swelling and inflammation along the airway can cause respiratory distress in a child. Airways of the infant and young child are less developed than in the adult; therefore, they are more easily obstructed by vomit, blood, or edema. In the young infant, too, the ribs are more pliable and thus more likely to fail to support the lungs, leading to retractions with respiratory problems. Respirations are further compromised when the chest cannot compensate, as in the child with asthma or abdominal distention.

A child has a higher metabolic rate in comparison to an adult; therefore, a pulmonary illness that compromises respiratory function can result in increased metabolic demands and oxygen consumption. For example, in a child with bronchiolitis, the illness may interfere with air exchange in the lungs.

LIST OF ACTIVITIES

Understanding Respiratory Problems

For any child with respiratory problems, having information about his or her present illness is important (e.g., Is this an acute illness? Is this a chronic illness? Does the child have recurrent upper or lower respiratory tract infections?). Respiratory problems in children can be caused by disease, trauma, and physical anomalies, or may be seen as a manifestation of a disturbance in another organ or system.

Asthma, a chronic disease characterized by recurrent attacks of breathlessness and wheezing, is the most common chronic disease among children (World Health Organization, 2010). Although the fundamental causes of asthma are not completely understood, the strongest risk factors are a combination of genetic predisposition with environmental exposure to inhaled substances and particles, which may provoke allergic reactions or irritate the airways. Asthma does not have the mortality rate of other chronic diseases, yet failure to use appropriate medications or adhere to treatment can lead to death. In addition to feelings of loneliness, because they are unable to keep up with their peers, children and adolescents with asthma often report living with fear, a fear of death, and a lack of self-confidence in handling asthma episodes efficiently (Rhee, Wenzel, & Steeves, 2007).

Most communicable diseases have respiratory system involvement. Some diseases of the lungs, such as cystic fibrosis, are inherited. Diseases, such as asthma or bronchitis, have both genetic and environmental causes. It is not uncommon to find that irritants in the environment may exacerbate asthmatic symptoms. Pets, vegetation, color dyes, toys, and secondary smoke also can be possible irritants.

Coughing is a protective reflex of the respiratory system. The child with asthma or cystic fibrosis typically coughs more in the early morning and upon awakening. A child with a respiratory infection is more likely to have a loose-sounding, productive cough rather than one that is dry and nonproductive.

Environmental Factors

In recent years, environmental factors have become a growing concern in regard to children's health, not only in respect to asthma, but to other conditions as well. Regarding secondhand smoke (SHS), infants and children who spend extended time in such an environment have been found to have adverse respiratory consequences, including more frequent occurrences and earlier onset of asthma (Bouzigon et al., 2008), as well as increases in coughing and wheezing (Annesi-Maesano, Agabiti, Pistelli, Couilliot, & Forastiere, 2003; Gibson et al., 2001), and airway obstruction, airway hyperreactivity, and bronchiolitis (Annesi-Maesano et al., 2003). Further, there is mounting evidence of an association of prenatal and postnatal exposure to SHS and increased risk of sudden infant death syndrome (SIDS) (Fleming & Blair, 2007; Pollack, 2001; Wisborg, Kesmodel, Henriksen, Olsen, & Secher, 2000).

Postoperative Respiratory Problems

Respiratory infections are a potential complication after surgery, attributed at least in part to anesthesia. Anesthesia can dry and thicken the mucous secretions in the respiratory tract. Mucous may then become difficult to dislodge, and tend to remain in the air passages. Mucous plugs may form, putting the bronchi or bronchioles in danger of becoming blocked. Although normally the child's cough reflex would be stimulated, this reflex may be depressed by pain medication. Also, the child may be reluctant to cough because it is painful.

Blockage of the bronchus or bronchioles may cause absorption collapse, or atelectasis, of a segment of a lobe of the lung. When the main bronchus is occluded, the entire lung may collapse.

When mucous secretions are not removed, there is danger of infection. Thus, pneumonia or bronchopneumonia are other possible complications. Finally, although not as frequent with the anesthesia used today, aspiration pneumonia may occur due to the inhalation of vomit.

Obesity

Fiorino and Brooks (2009) report that the impact of obesity on the growing individual, in particular the growing lung, may be unique and particularly detrimental. The impact of childhood obesity on respiratory disease can be categorized as (a) the impact on pulmonary mechanics, (b) its possible link with and impact on asthma, and (c) the risk factor it poses for sleep-disordered breathing. Increasingly, studies indicate a relationship between obesity and asthma (Rodriguez, Winkleby, Ahn, Sundquist, & Kraemer, 2002). The prevalence of both conditions has increased in children over the past several decades; however, the significance of the association is unclear (Fiorino & Brooks, 2009).

Research suggests that obese children may have more severe asthma than normal-weight children. Carroll, Bhandari, Zucker, and Schramm (2006) found that children with asthma and obesity who are admitted to the intensive care unit (ICU) during an exacerbation require more medication, supplemental oxygen for a longer period of time, and lengthier duration of care in the ICU. Another study found that obese children with asthma reported more medication use (Pianosi & Davis, 2004); and a third study linked more emergency department care for wheezing, as well as more medication for obese children with asthma, compared to children with asthma who were of normal weight (Belamarich et al., 2000).

Several factors are thought to be possible contributors to the association between obesity and asthma. Glazebrook and colleagues (2006) suggest that asthma may create a psychological barrier to exercise, rendering children more sedentary and thus at greater risk for obesity. Other issues include mechanical factors, gastroesophageal reflux (GER), and hormonal factors (Fiorino & Brooks, 2009).

Treating Respiratory Problems

Young children are unable to describe difficulty breathing (dyspnea); however, one can look for clues while observing the child's behavior during activity. The child may exhibit lower exercise tolerance or shortness of breath with activity. A child having some shortness of breath may be quiet, inactive, or lack interest and enthusiasm for play activities. Children with pulmonary edema or asthma may be uncomfortable except in a semisitting position, and may prop themselves up and rest their weight on their arms. Children with asthma and cystic fibrosis frequently exhibit retractions when they breathe. Grunting and nasal flaring are most often seen in young children in respiratory distress.

The child with chronic respiratory disease may have repeated hospital admissions, for a variety of reasons. These children often require numerous medications and therapies to control respiratory symptoms. Understanding the action and side effects of the medications and daily treatments is essential for individuals working with children who have chronic respiratory problems. Some of the treatments, such as chest physiotherapy, are time-consuming, whereas other treatments are expensive and unpleasant for the child. Any of these inconveniences may foster stress and anxiety in both the child and family.

Children with respiratory disease may require an additional source of oxygen, both in the hospital and at home. A nasal cannula, the most common method for administering the oxygen, can be irritating, because it is often held in place by tape applied to the face. If one is caring for a child requiring supplemental oxygen, understanding how to change and secure the cannula may be necessary.

Children with respiratory problems, whether acute or chronic, have altered nutritional requirements. Most children experiencing respiratory dysfunction have difficulty eating during acute episodes. Adequate hydration is essential for any child with an illness that causes mucous production, to prevent the mucous from becoming thick and tenacious. Thus, children are encouraged to drink their favorite fluids at frequent intervals.

During the acute phase of a respiratory disease process, a child may suffer sleep deprivation. Frequent coughing, which is most prevalent at night, may interrupt the child's sleep pattern. Thus, a child may require quiet times during the day to rest. Activities that conserve the child's energy may need to be planned.

The child with respiratory dysfunction may have pain from bronchospasms or as the result of injections for therapy. Each child's pain experience is unique. For further information about the assessment and management of pediatric pain, refer to Chapter 12, where distraction and other pain relief measures also are discussed.

Children with chronic respiratory problems undergo physical changes. For example, the child with cystic fibrosis may exhibit a barrel chest, pallor, short stature, and clubbing of fingernails and toenails. They may view their bodies as inferior because of the physical limitations. For instance, they may need to take breaks to rest or cough, and may be teased or overlooked in normal activities; peers may avoid them. Children need strategies to help cope with these difficult situations; role-playing and support groups can be helpful.

As with other children, those with respiratory dysfunction need to continue their normal developmental progress. To promote growth and development, diversionary activities should be provided that are appropriate to age, play ability, interest, and peer involvement. The activity may need to be started slowly, with the tempo gradually increased as tolerance improves. The ideal activity may be one at which the child can define the pace. Peer activity is important, too, because social skills—communication, interaction, and sharing—are best learned in a social situation.

Effectively designed play activities should be an integral part of a treatment plan for pediatric patients with respiratory dysfunction. Play activities can provide children with an incentive to comply with numerous medical treatments. Children also benefit psychologically from activities that help to relieve the stress and anxiety associated with an illness and give them a sense of control.

Special Considerations

Care must be taken to use appropriate activities with respiratory patients. It is important to consult with the child's physician to discuss any restrictions before beginning activities.

Most of the activities in this chapter require mild-to-moderate expenditure of energy. Children with cardiac or respiratory conditions should be monitored for any sign of difficult breathing or shortness of breath with exertion. If the child's breathing changes, he or she seems "out of breath," or activity level decreases, the activity should be discontinued. The child should be assisted to a resting position and evaluated by a physician.

The intensity of therapeutic activities with children who have had surgery depends on the type of surgery, the location and size of the incision, and the degree of mobility allowed during the recuperative process. Following any use of general anesthesia, respiratory exercises that promote alveolar expansion and exchange of oxygen and carbon dioxide are usually encouraged. Deep breathing and coughing help prevent pneumonia after surgery. Thus, every effort is taken to aerate the lungs and remove secretions. Children's lungs are auscultated regularly to identify abnormal sounds or any areas of diminished or absent breath sounds (Hockenberry & Wilson, 2007).

Children may be reluctant to do such exercises because of the fear of pain and concern about "opening" the surgical incision; they will need reassurance that the incision is secure. Deep breathing usually is painful postoperatively, but children can splint the operative site (depending on the location) by hugging a small pillow or a favorite stuffed animal.

Following certain neurologic and ophthalmologic surgeries, coughing may be contraindicated. It is important to check for restrictions before involving the child in any activities.

Activity Goals

The activities in this chapter can be grouped according to three major goals: promoting coughing, deep breathing, and pursed-lip breathing. Some of the activities involve the use of balloons, so please review the information about balloons in the Introduction before introducing them to children.

Promoting Coughing

Having children huff or exhale several breaths while successively increasing rapidity and force can encourage coughing. Children frequently feel and act on the urge to cough without ever being told to do so. Activities such as Balloon Football foster the use of breathing during play.

Promoting Deep Breathing

Activities to promote deep breathing require slow, deep inhalation, for best effect. This type of breathing promotes full expansion of the alveoli in both lobes of the lungs. The use of incentive inspirometers rewards the child for deep inhalation, and deemphasizes the exhalation phase of respiration. Activities such as Sailing Away, Super Bubbles, Ping-Pong Ball Magic Tricks, Airway Fairway, Blow Carts, Blowing Home, Bubble Printing, Cotton Ball Hockey, Just Suck It Up!, and Kazoos require moderate-to-deep breaths to implement.

Promoting Pursed-Lip Breathing

Children with asthma are often taught to use a pursed-lip breathing technique to help open and maintain a clear airway. To perform pursed-lip breathing, the child takes a slow, deep breath. During the slow exhalation through the mouth, the lips are pursed or puckered. Doing so increases the air resistance during the exhalation phase. This breathing method maintains some positive end-expiratory pressure within the alveoli, preventing complete collapse of these elastic air sacs and prolonging the air exchange portion of the respiratory sequence. Blown Tone, Straw Blow Painting, and Pinwheels are activities that promote pursed-lip breathing. Blowing pieces of paper with a straw along a tabletop racetrack also can encourage a child to use pursed-lip breathing techniques.

ACTIVITY 13.1.   AIRWAY FAIRWAY

As an incentive for participation, place small prizes in each "hole" and give them to the players when they "make a hole."

Therapeutic Goal: To improve respiratory function by encouraging deep breathing and lung expansion.

Age Group: Primary/school-age

Adult/Child Ratio: 1:3

Required Time: Contingent on needs of the children

Restrictions and Precautions: Paper towel tubes should be discarded after each use. Monitor children's respiratory status.

Materials:

- ☐ Ping-Pong ball
- ☐ Paper cups with large openings
- ☐ Tape
- ☐ Tongue depressors
- ☐ Small sticky notes
- ☐ Marker
- ☐ Paper towel tubes (one for each player)
- ☐ Small prizes (optional)

Process

1. Decide how many holes you want for the game. Tape that number of paper cups to one side of a table, making the cup openings level with the tabletop.

2. Create flags for each hole by numbering the sticky notes consecutively, then adhering them to one end of a tongue depressor.

3. Tape the opposite end of each tongue depressor to a corresponding cup at the point opposite the table edge. The flag should stand above the cup.

4. Remove any chairs so the players have unobstructed access on both sides of the table.

5. Provide each player with a paper towel tube.

6. Tell the children to take slow deep breaths then exhale through the tube to propel the ball into the paper cups.

7. Allow each player 15 seconds to direct the ball into a cup; if the ball falls to the floor, the player's turn ends.

ACTIVITY 13.2.   BALLOON FOOTBALL

This activity requires no advance preparation and only one piece of equipment, making it a quick and easy activity to do in almost any setting.

Therapeutic Goal: To improve respiratory function by promoting coughing to expand lungs, increase expiratory volume, and clear airways of mucous and secretions.

Age Group: Primary/school-age

Adult/Child Ratio: 1:6

Required Time: Situational, based on children's breathing status

Restrictions and Precautions: Collect balloons at the end of each activity session. Monitor children's respiratory status.

Materials:

- ☐ Balloon
- ☐ Table

Process

1. Divide the players into two evenly divided teams. The adult can play on one team if there is an odd number of players, or if there is only one child.

2. Have the players line up on opposite sides of the table.

3. Place the balloon in the center of the table.

4. Each team tries to make a goal by blowing the balloon off the opposing team's side of the table, *without* touching the balloon with any part of their body.

5. The first team to make a predetermined number of goals wins.

ACTIVITY 13.3.   BLOW CARTS

Most children enjoy the challenge of designing their own blow carts, but if time is short or a child is unwilling or unable to do so, make one for him or her and let the child blow it around the track.

Therapeutic Goal: To improve respiratory function by encouraging deep breathing and lung expansion.	**Materials:**
Age Group: School-age	☐ Nonbendable plastic drinking straws
	☐ Life Savers or other candy with the same shape and size
Adult/Child Ratio: 1:8	☐ Paper
Required Time: 1 hour	☐ Paper clips
Restrictions and Precautions: Monitor children's respiratory status.	☐ Tape
	☐ Scissors

Process

1. Give each child three straws, four Life Savers, one piece of paper, two paper clips, a pair of scissors, and tape (which children can share).

2. Have the children create a blow cart (a go-cart that must blown on to move) using the materials provided. If the children find this too challenging, help them attach the Life Savers for wheels; the straws, for axles; and the paper to make a sail and "chassis."

3. Attach tape to the floor to define a racecar track, or let the children just imagine one.

4. Instruct the children to blow on their sails to move the carts around the track (Figure Activity 13.3-1).

5. Invite the children to experiment with different designs for their blow carts, to see which will go fastest.

Figure Activity 13.3-1. Blow Carts

ACTIVITY 13.4.   BLOWING HOME

This activity requires substantial advance preparation time. However, because it is somewhat intellectually challenging, it may be worth the effort when working with school-agers who may find other blowing activities too childish. Also, if the maze is well-constructed, it can be used over and over.

Therapeutic Goal: To improve respiratory function by encouraging deep breathing and lung expansion.

Age Group: School-age

Adult/Child Ratio: 1:6

Required Time: 1 hour preparation time; activity time variable.

Restrictions and Precautions: Monitor children's respiratory status.

Materials:

- ☐ Tape or pencil
- ☐ Cardboard box lid (computer paper box works well)
- ☐ Large piece of green foam board, cut to fit inside the box top
- ☐ Medical tape, masking tape, or a pencil
- ☐ Corrugated cardboard, cut in long strips 2 inches wide, various lengths corresponding to the design of the maze
- ☐ Glue gun
- ☐ Cardboard box or large piece of heavy cardboard
- ☐ Scissors or box cutter
- ☐ Paints
- ☐ Paintbrush
- ☐ Ping-Pong ball
- ☐ Straw

Process

1. Use tape or a pencil to draw a maze on the foam board.
2. To erect the walls of the maze, spread glue on the bottom of the corrugated cardboard strips and, following the pattern, affix the cardboard perpendicular to the foam board base. Be sure that connecting cardboard strips butt up to the strips next to them.
3. Glue connecting strips together to stabilize them.
4. Turn the corrugated box or heavy cardboard into a house or other building. Use the box cutter or scissors to cut out a door, large enough for the Ping-Pong ball to pass through.
5. Add decorative details to the house with paint (optional).
6. Place the house at the end of the maze, aligning the door opening so that the ball can enter it from the maze.
7. To play, position the Ping-Pong ball at the beginning of the maze (Figure Activity 13.4-1).
8. Have the children take turns blowing through the straw to move the Ping-Pong ball through the maze and into the house.

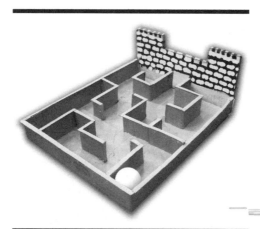

Figure Activity 13.4-1. Blowing Home

ACTIVITY 13.5. BLOWN TONE

You can encourage increased fluid intake by filling these bottles with a child's favorite beverage. Have the child experiment by drinking some of the beverage to see how having less fluid in the bottle changes the tone it makes when air is blown into it.

Therapeutic Goal: To improve respiratory function by promoting pursed-lip breathing.	**Restrictions and Precautions:** Use only clean bottles, which have never contained toxic substances. Monitor children's respiratory status.
Age Group: Preschool/primary	**Materials:**
Adult/Child Ratio: 1:1	☐ 8 narrow-mouthed empty bottles
Required Time: 20–30 minutes	☐ Water or beverage

Process

1. Fill all the bottles with liquid, varying the amounts in each. Bottles with more liquid will produce a higher pitch.
2. Align the bottles in a row, starting with the bottle with the least amount of liquid and ending with the bottle containing the most.
3. Let the child blow into the mouth of each bottle to create musical sounds. Add or remove water to achieve a different pitch.
4. Encourage the child to compose original tunes or try to duplicate simple, familiar ones.

For more ideas, see Bright Ideas for Breathing (Box Activity 13.5-1).

BOX ACTIVITY 13.5-1. BRIGHT IDEAS FOR BREATHING

- Offer breath-propelled items such as party blowers, marshmallow shooters, harmonicas, blow pens, slide flutes, bubbles, and whistles.
- Blow up paper bags and pop them.
- Hold a pretend birthday party. Sing and whistle party tunes, use noisemakers, and blow out candles on an imaginary cake.
- Tell the story of "The Three Little Pigs" and ask the children to join, exaggerating the "huffing, and puffing, and b-l-o-w-i-n-g the house down" part.
- Coordinate a bubblegum-blowing contest. (If the children are really good at it, surgical hats may be necessary!)
- Make an old-fashioned peashooter out of a drinking straw and let the children shoot small wads of paper at specified targets.
- Help the children make a simple whistle by cutting two 1/2-inch slits into one end of a paper drinking straw and flattening that end. Cut off the opposite end in short increments to produce progressively deeper sounds.
- Hold relay races in which the children form teams and use straws to blow small paper cups or feathers to a designated point, and back. Repeat play until all the players on each team have had their turns.

ACTIVITY 13.6.   BUBBLE PRINTING

The paper created in this activity makes a lovely cover for a special book or journal.

Therapeutic Goal: To improve respiratory function by encouraging deep breathing and lung expansion.	**Restrictions and Precautions:** Supervise children so that they do not aspirate or ingest the paint. If using tempera paint, let the children practice first, using a mixture of water and food coloring. Check the children's tongues for coloring to ensure that the activity is being done correctly. Monitor children's respiratory status.
Age Group: Primary/school-age	
Adult/Child Ratio: 1:8	
Required Time: 20–30 minutes	

Materials:

☐ Liquid dishwashing soap

☐ Emesis basins or other shallow containers

☐ Liquid tempera paint or food coloring

☐ Straw or 4-inch piece of IV tubing

☐ Finger-paint paper or construction paper

Process

1. To prepare the bubble mixture, combine 1 part tempera paint with 1 part soap in each basin.

2. Add a small amount of water to thin the mixture.

3. Have the children place one end of a straw in the paint mixture and blow through the other end. Make sure the children blow, rather than suck.

4. When the soap bubbles rise above the edge of the container, give the children a piece of paper to hold horizontally above the bubbles; tell them to slowly lower it until it touches the bubbles for a few seconds.

5. Repeat the process with several colors.

6. Suggest ways the paper can be used; or just display it on a wall.

ACTIVITY 13.7. COTTON BALL HOCKEY

Use the soccer variation below with children from South America, Europe, and other countries where hockey is not a popular sport.

Therapeutic Goal: To improve respiratory function by encouraging deep breathing

Age Group: Primary/school-age

Adult/Child Ratio: 1:2

Required Time: 30 minutes

Restrictions and Precautions: Monitor children's respiratory status.

Materials:

☐ Cardboard box lid (computer paper box lids work well)

☐ 2 plastic food tubs (small margarine tubs work well)

☐ Scissors

☐ Glue gun

☐ Marker

☐ Ruler

☐ Cotton balls (the pucks)

☐ 2 straws (the hockey sticks)

Process

1. Set the box lid on a flat surface, rim side up.

2. Cut a 2-inch section out of each margarine tub (Figure Activity 13.7-1).

3. To create the goals, glue one margarine tub to each end of the box top.

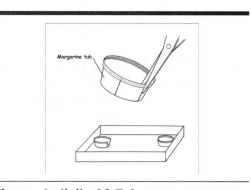

Figure Activity 13.7-1. Cottonball Hockey

4. Use the ruler to determine the center point in the box and draw a line through it, across the width, to create two team courts.

5. Give each player a straw to blow through.

6. Put the cotton ball on the center line and challenge the players try to blow it into their opponent's goal, while defending their own.

Variation

Make a "blow soccer" game by covering the inside bottom of a large shallow box with green felt, to simulate a grass field. Set up a goal on opposite ends of the box. After placing an equal number of Ping-Pong balls on each player's half of the field, give the children straws to blow as many balls as possible into their opponent's goal.

ACTIVITY 13.8.   JUST SUCK IT UP!

This activity requires little preparation, is portable, and requires only a small space in which to implement it.

Therapeutic Goal: To improve respiratory function by encouraging lung expansion.	**Materials:**
	☐ Marker
Age Group: Primary/school-age	☐ Egg carton, top removed (one for every player)
Adult/Child Ratio: 1:8	
Required Time: Variable	☐ Small shallow bowl (one for each player)
Restrictions and Precautions: Monitor children's breathing status.	☐ Dry lima beans
	☐ Straws

Process

1. Write a number, from 1 to 6 (not in consecutive order), in each cup on one side of each egg carton.

2. Repeat step 1 on the opposite side of each egg carton, varying the order of the numbers.

3. Fill the bowls with lima beans.

4. Explain that the object of the game is to be the first to match the number of beans in each cup to the number written on the cup.

5. Give each player a straw and an egg carton.

6. Show the players how to pick up the beans from the bowl by sucking through the straw and then dropping them into the cups on their side of the carton, until they have the appropriate number.

7. Play stops when one person has filled all of his or her cups. Count the beans: If not accurate, play resumes with the remaining players until someone wins.

ACTIVITY 13.9.   KAZOOS

Store-bought kazoos may be used, but making them adds incentive for children to use them.

Therapeutic Goal: To improve respiratory function by encouraging deep breathing and lung expansion.	**Restrictions and Precautions:** Take paint precautions. Keep scissors or other sharp instruments out of children's reach. Monitor children's respiratory status.
Age Group: Preschool/primary	
Adult/Child Ratio: 1:5	**Materials:**
Required Time: 30 minutes	☐ Tempera paint

☐ Paintbrushes

☐ Cardboard tube from toilet tissue roll

☐ Pointed scissors or other sharp instrument

☐ Wax paper, cut into circles 1 inch greater in diameter than the tubes

☐ Rubber band

Process

1. Have the children paint the tubes, leaving a 1-inch space at one end unpainted.

2. When the paint has dried, use the scissors or other sharp instrument to punch three holes 2 inches apart vertically along the tubes.

3. Help the children mold a wax paper circle to cover the opening of the painted end of the tube and secure it with a rubber band (Figure Activity 13.9-1).

4. Encourage the children to sing, whistle, or hum into the open end of the kazoo.

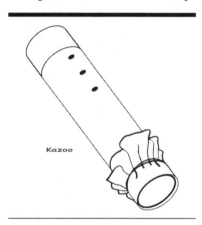

Kazoo

Figure Activity 13.9-1. Kazoo

Variation

Make a harmonica by folding waxed paper over a plastic comb. Tape the wax paper in place on the side opposite to the teeth. Show the children how to place the teeth side between their lips, and hum.

ACTIVITY 13.10. PING-PONG BALL MAGIC TRICKS

This activity combines a physics demonstration with the fun of a magic trick and the benefits of deep breathing. It works because fast-moving air has lower pressure than slow-moving air. When the child blows through the funnel, there is higher pressure upward, so the ball stays in the funnel.

Therapeutic Goal: To improve respiratory function by encouraging deep breathing and lung expansion.

Age Group: Primary/school-age

Adult/Child Ratio: 1:1

Required Time: Variable

Restrictions and Precautions: Monitor children's respiratory status.

Materials:

☐ Ping-Pong ball

☐ Bendable drinking straw

☐ Funnel

Process

1. Instruct the child to put one end of the straw in his or her mouth while holding the table-tennis ball above the other end of the straw.

2. Tell the child to take a deep breath, blow hard, and release the ball. The ball should stay in place.

3. Now have the child place the ball into the wide end of the funnel, and put the narrow end of the funnel into his or her mouth; tell him or her to tilt his or her head back, so that the top of the funnel points up.

4. Tell the child to blow hard, while keeping the funnel pointed up.

5. While still blowing, instruct the child to point the funnel down. The ball should stay in place.

6. When the child has mastered the trick, encourage him or her to perform it for others.

ACTIVITY 13.11.   PINWHEELS

Pinwheels can be purchased, but making them gives children an added incentive to use them.

Therapeutic Goal: To improve respiratory function by promoting pursed-lip breathing.

Age Group: Preschool/primary

Adult/Child Ratio: 1:3

Required Time: 30 minutes

Restrictions and Precautions: Monitor children's respiratory status.

Materials:

☐ Heavy construction paper

☐ Ruler

☐ Pencil

☐ Penny

☐ Scissors

☐ Markers or crayons

☐ Straws

☐ Brads

Process

1. Cut the construction paper into 1-foot squares.

2. Using the ruler, draw two lines: one from the upper right to the lower left corner, the second from the upper left to the lower right corner.

3. Use the penny to trace a circle around the point in the center where the two lines intersect.

4. Let children decorate the paper on the front and back.

5. Cut along the lines, inward to the edge of the circle. There will now be four connected sections.

6. Punch a hole in the straws.

7. Carefully bend (don't fold) the right corner of each section to the center and hold in place.

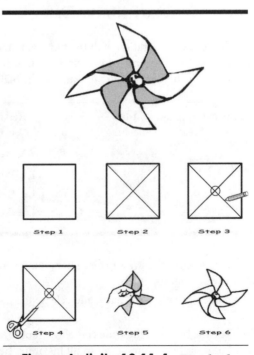

Figure Activity 13.11-1. Pinwheel

8. Push the brad through the four corners of the paper and through one end of the straw.

9. Fasten the brad by bending the tips (Figure Activity 13.11-1).

10. Encourage the children to blow on the pinwheel to make it spin.

ACTIVITY 13.12. SAILING AWAY

Hold an "America's Cup" event and, at the end, award each participant a small plastic trophy.

Therapeutic Goal: To improve respiratory function by encouraging deep breathing and lung expansion.	☐ Specimen cup lids or jar lids 2–3 inches in diameter
Age Group: Prechool/primary	☐ Scissors
Adult/Child Ratio: 1:6	☐ Construction paper
Required Time: 30 minutes	☐ Crayons
Restrictions and Precautions: Monitor children's respiratory status.	☐ Infant tongue depressor
	☐ Tape
Materials:	☐ Straw
☐ Clay	☐ Large, shallow container filled with water

Process

1. To form the sails, cut construction paper into triangles the width of the jar lids (the boats).

2. Place a wad of clay in the center of each jar lid.

3. Give each of the children a paper sail to decorate with crayons.

4. Help the children tape their sails to a tongue depressor, leaving 1 inch of the tongue depressor uncovered.

5. Insert the uncovered end of the tongue depressor into the clay, molding the clay around it.

6. Set the boats in the water and show the children how to move the boats by blowing on the sails through straws.

Variation

To make smaller boats, use corks and toothpicks instead of jars and tongue depressors.

ACTIVITY 13.13. STRAW BLOW PAINTING

This method of painting creates an interesting marbleized effect. Like bubble print painting, the finished product can be used as wrapping paper or to cover journals or books.

Therapeutic Goal: To improve respiratory function by promoting pursed-lip breathing.	coloring. Check children's tongues for coloring to ensure that they are doing the activity correctly. Monitor children's respiratory status.
Age Group: Preschool/primary	**Materials:**
Adult/Child Ratio: 1:3	
Required Time: 10–15 minutes	☐ Thin tempera paint or food coloring, in several colors
Restrictions and Precautions: Make sure young children understand how to blow through the straw, so they do not aspirate or ingest the paint. If in doubt, substitute the paint with food	☐ Heavyweight paper
	☐ Straws
	☐ Crayons or markers (optional)

Process

1. Drip the paint onto the paper.

2. Let the children blow the paint around the paper using a straw.

3. Repeat with one or more colors.

4. Allow the paint to dry.

5. Invite the children to use crayons or markers to add detail to the painting.

ACTIVITY 13.14.   SUPER BUBBLES

These huge bubbles are very appealing, but they can become quite messy and so should be used with discretion.

Therapeutic goal: To improve respiratory function by encouraging deep breathing and lung expansion.

Age Group: Toddler/preschool/primary

Adult/Child Ratio: 1:1

Required Time: Varies

Restrictions and Precautions: Be sure no sharp edges are exposed when forming the bubble wand. Monitor children's respiratory status.

Materials:

- ☐ Liquid dishwashing soap (Dawn works well)
- ☐ Glycerin (available from drug stores) or corn syrup
- ☐ Water (distilled water produces a longer-lasting bubble solution)
- ☐ Soft wire
- ☐ Shallow pan
- ☐ Bowl

Process

1. Prepare the bubble solution by combining 1 part dishwashing soap, 9 parts water, and 1/2 part glycerin or corn syrup.

2. Turn the wire into a wand; or use empty spools or paper cups with the bottom cut out.

3. Model optimal breathing technique by blowing bubbles using evenly paced slow, deep breaths.

4. Encourage the children to do the same.

CHAPTER 14

TEACHING

Information is a powerful tool. Knowledge can offer protection, promote adherence to treatment, instill confidence, and help to assure the best quality of life for children. In today's world of increased concern about infectious diseases, information regarding the prevention and spread of infection can provide protection against serious and even life-threatening conditions. Of special concern in healthcare settings is methicillin-resistant staphylococcus aureus (MRSA), which is common among people who have weak immune systems and are in hospitals, nursing homes, and other heathcare centers.

Courtesy of Steven Koress Photography

Although the rate of child abuse and neglect has been decreasing in recent years (Iannelli, 2010), approximately 1 in every 58 children in the United States is abused each year, and an average of 4 children die every day as a result of abuse or neglect. Educating children about their bodies, what constitutes child abuse, and how to respond, can arm them with the necessary tools to protect themselves should such issues arise.

For many children, information seeking is their most effective coping strategy. Children who are educated about their medical condition can be spared unnecessary worry, and through the empowerment information promotes, they learn to advocate for themselves early on and enjoy a higher quality of life. Furthermore, children who understand their condition and the purpose of therapeutic interventions are more likely to adhere to treatment.

Many opportunities exist within healthcare settings to provide children with knowledge to help them cope with illness and other health issues. Siblings, too, have a need for information about their brother or sister's condition and treatment. As mentioned in the Introduction, siblings frequently have many misconceptions and worries that can be allayed with age-appropriate information. As others often look upon siblings as "family informants," it is important that they not only have accurate information, but also learn how to express this information to peers, teachers, neighbors, and others.

Transitions are important times for children coping with healthcare issues. Healthcare professionals can help ease the transition of a child returning to the community by educating other children in the child's life (e.g., classmates, fellow youth group members, Scout troops, team members). Siblings also can derive great benefit when this same intervention is carried out with their peers.

A major transition for the child with a chronic illness or disability is moving from pediatric to adult-oriented care as an adolescent or young adult. Successful transition is the result of important groundwork that is laid when the child is young. A major component of this preparation is the child assuming increasing responsibility for his or her care, and self-advocacy. A critical piece in achieving the self-efficacy needed to accomplish these goals is education.

The activities in this chapter offer exciting, hands-on, developmentally appropriate methods to help children understand important health-related concepts. Also included are activities that help prepare both patients and their healthy siblings for important health-related transitions.

LIST OF ACTIVITIES

Activity 14.1 Peristaltic Waves: A Moving Experience*	Activity 14.7 Demonstrating Diabetes*
Activity 14.2 Be Safe Collages	Activity 14.8 The Digestion Question
Activity 14.3 Blood Components	Activity 14.9 Disease Transmission Through Droplets
Activity 14.4 Transmission of Bloodborne Pathogens	Activity 14.10 Excuse Yourself!*
Activity 14.5 Conceptualizing Bone Marrow	Activity 14.11 Learning the Food Groups
Activity 14.6 Cystic Fibrosis Demonstration	Activity 14.12 Heart Smart*

LIST OF ACTIVITIES (continued)

Note: Asterisk (*) denotes that the activity is available on the CD that accompanies this book.

Vygotsky's Social Development Theory

Vygotsky's theory of social development (Vygotsky, 1962, 1978) provides a model for education and preparation for children coping with healthcare issues. Basic principles of the theory are simple: (a) Cognitive development is limited to a certain range at any given age; and (b) full cognitive development requires social interaction. The framework incorporates three major themes:

1. *Social interaction.* In contrast to Piaget's understanding of child development, in which development necessarily precedes learning, Vygotsky believed that social learning precedes development. He theorized that every function in the child's cultural development appears twice: first, on the social level and, later, on the individual level; first, between people (interpsychological) and then inside the child (intrapsychological).

2. *More Knowledgeable Other (MKO).* Anyone who has a better understanding or a higher ability level than the learner, with respect to a particular task, process, or concept, is an MKO. Although normally thought of as being a teacher, coach, or older adult, the MKO may also be a peer, a younger person, or even a computer.

3. *Zone of Proximal Development (ZPD).* The distance between a child's ability to perform a task under adult guidance and/or with peer collaboration and the child's ability to solve the problem independently is called the ZPD. In Vygotsky's model, learning occurs in this zone.

Thus, with the assistance of a more knowledgeable other, children can be brought to a deeper level of understanding of concepts, exceeding what they would be able to attain on their own. What children can do on their own is referred to as their level of *actual development*; what they can do with guidance or collaboration is their level of *potential development*. The MKO uses *scaffolding*, continually adjusting the level of help in response to the child's level of performance. An effective form of teaching, scaffolding not only produces immediate results, but also instills the skills necessary for independent problem solving in the future.

Children's Understanding of Illness

Having an accurate sense of children's knowledge is helpful in predicting how they understand the information provided about illness and in interpreting their statements in this regard. Research of children's understanding of illness has generally supported one of two views: the *naive child* approach and the *sophisticated child* approach (Raman & Winer, 2002). More recent research also finds support for a coexistence model.

As briefly outlined in the Introduction, the most common theory is that children's understanding of illness follows a developmental course. A Piagetian approach argues that young children's understanding of illness is relatively unsophisticated and develops in stages. Some proponents of this approach have suggested that young children's conception of the origins of illness is often characterized by what Piaget has termed *immanent justice* (Piaget, 1965), the idea that illness is punishment for past misdeeds (Shweder, Much, Mahapatra, & Park, 1997). Researchers have reported preschool and elementary school children's belief in immanent justice as a cause of illness (Kister & Patterson, 1980; Perrin & Gerrity, 1981).

Bibace and Walsh's (1981) pioneering work in this field explored the relationship between the work of Piaget (Piaget & Inhelder, 1969) and Werner (Werner, 1948; Werner & Kaplan, 1963) and children's conceptions of illness. Their studies led to six qualitatively different categories of explanations of illness that are developmentally ordered (Bibace & Walsh, 1977, 1979, 1980): Phenomenism, Contagion, Contamination, Internalization, Physiological, and Psychophysiological.

Koopman, Baars, Chaplin, and Zwinderman (2004) considered the possibility that variables other than stress might be linked to the maturing cognitive development of children and their thoughts about illness. Their model, Through the Eyes of the Child (TEC), assigns perception a fundamental role in understanding how children develop their concept of illness. The model illustrates a progression in illness understanding that follows the perceptual development of the child from a personal causation, external view to a symptom-related internal view. This progression through the seven developmental phases—Invisible, Distance, Proximity, Contact, Internalization, Body Process or Body Inside, and Body and Mind—can be observed independently of disease and variations in personal development and situation.

The TEC model and how it relates to the models of cognitive and perceptual development is illustrated in Table 14.1. Koopman and colleagues (2004) conclude that, to assist the child in understanding illness, it is necessary to present information in relation to the perceptual level of the child. They also point out that more cross-cultural similarities than differences in children's causal attributions for health and illness may exist, increasing the model's likelihood of general validity.

As with the concept of illness, a more complete definition of the concept of "health" also follows a developmental course. Schmidt and Frohling (2000) explored the concepts of children, adolescents, and their mothers with regard to different aspects of health and illness, and found that although even children as young as 5 years of age could recognize health as the absence of illness, a greater number of older children and adolescents were able to identify health positively (well-being) and not merely as the absence of illness.

The Naive Child Approach

Studies suggest that children know more about the causes of illness than had been previously thought (Siegal, Patty, & Eiser, 1990; Springer & Ruckel, 1992). Kalish (1996) found that preschoolers' understanding of illness is not limited to symptoms or obvious features; the children identified a wide range of causes (from an adult perspective) as instances of illness. Kalish concluded that young children can benefit from information about causes of illnesses, and children will be less worried about catching an illness if told it is not caused by an infection. They also may be able to understand that not all germ-based illnesses are transmittable through casual contact (e.g., AIDS).

Siegal (1988) found that preschoolers used immanent justice reasoning only as a fallback position to explain an illness that was not within the range of their personal experience. This is consistent with the results of Rosen and Rozin's study (1993), where preschoolers recognized that certain physical problems caused by accident (e.g., scraped knees, bumps) are not contagious, and they generally accepted that contamination through contact with a dirty spoon could be prevented by washing.

The Sophisticated Child Approach

Most theories of development involve "replacement" concepts; that is, development is seen to occur in a linear stage-by-stage fashion, with a later step replacing, and not being able to coexist with, an earlier one (Siegler, 1994). Bibace, Dillon, and Sagarin (1999) argue that these

Coexistence Concept

Table 14.1 Cognitive and Perceptual Development of Children

Cognitive Development (Piaget, 1927)	Perceptual Development (Werner, 1948)	Illness Category System (Bibace & Walsh, 1978)	Through the Eyes of the Child TEC Model	Visualization TEC Model	Examples of Illness Interview Answers
1. Sensory-motor 0–2 years		1. Incomprehension	1. Invisible		"A cold is during vacation."
2. Preoperations 2–7 years	1. Global; whole qualities are dominant	2. Phenomenism	2. Distance		"When you leave the window open, your blankets get cold, which can make you a little bit sick."
		3. Contagion	3. Proximity		"Well, for example, when somebody else has a cold and you get close, and the next day she is better and you have a cold."
3. Concrete-operational 7–11 years	2. Analytical; perception is selectively directed toward parts	4. Contamination	4. Contact		"Well, when you cough really hard, then drops can land on your face; there are germs in there, and they make you ill."
		5. Internalization	5. Internalization		"When you cough, those germs go through the air and someone else can breathe them in, and then I think it gets in your blood. Then you also get a cold."
4. Formal-operational 11 years	3. Synthetic; parts become integrated with respect to the whole	6. Physiological	6. Body Inside		"Well the germs get into your blood, and the white blood cells will fight them, but if they lose you will get ill."
		7. Psycho-physiological	7. Body-Mind Inside		"This can happen in different ways. Sometimes a cold is not so bad. It depends on how you feel."

Note. From Koopman, H., Baars, R., Chaplin, J., & Zwinderman, K. (2004). Illness through the eyes of the child: The development of children's understanding of the causes of illness. *Patient Education and Counseling, 55(2),* pp. 367–368. Reprinted with permission.

theories lack the possibility of coexistence of *all* stages together within a single individual. With the coexistence concept of development, initial immature forms of thinking are not seen as supplanted with development, or as unfolding out of earlier forms, but as coming to coexist alongside later more mature forms. Bibace et al. (1999) propose that a coexistence concept of development is more comprehensive, because it accounts for group differences related to age, and encompasses individual and intraindividual differences, which they observed in their study.

Related research also supports the concept of coexistence. For example, Kushner (1983) provided many examples of adults who appeared to use immanent justice to explain why misfortune struck them or their loved ones. Gilovich (1991) found evidence that some people blame the sick and disabled for their misfortunes, and that some sick or disabled individuals blame themselves. Meyerowitz (1980) reports a high incidence of people who assumed that their cancer was God's will. Other researchers make reference to the just-world hypothesis. For example, Lerner (1971) reported that in the event of a serious accident, adults frequently search for an explanation in the previous bad behavior or bad personality of the accident victim, assuming that the victim got what he or she deserved.

Other Considerations

Research indicates that the child's mother's ideas about disease are not good indicators of the ideas the child will have. However, the literature suggests that as the child gets older, explanations of illness will look more and more like those of the mother (Campbell, 1978; Mechanic, 1979). Therefore, it is implied that children learn about illness in relation to their cognitive and social development (Carandang, Folkins, Hines, & Steward, 1979).

Lau, Bernard, and Hartman (1989) report that a higher education level of the parents stimulates the development of the child's understanding about illness. Other aspects of the child's environment influence the child's thinking about illness. For example, children from the higher social classes are less dependent and passive in their notion or view of the causes of illness (Shapiro, 1983). Also, research has determined that children who perceive greater personal control over their health demonstrate a more sophisticated conceptual understanding of disease than do children with a more external orientation (Shagena, Sandler, & Perrin, 1988).

Children's Understanding of Their Internal Bodies

Healthy children's conceptualizations of their internal bodies follow a well-established developmental progression. The preschool child's primitive view is often filled with fantasy. The school-ager can name several organs and their functions, but does not understand how organs are interrelated. Adolescents are able to construct an integrated view of organ systems (Badger & Jones, 1990).

Children tend to recognize some organs before others (Crider, 1981). For example, almost all 6-year-old children know about the heart, brain, and bones, but rarely understand what intestines are. In fact, most 10-year-olds would have difficulty explaining intestines. A young child first recognizes the more perceptually available organs: (a) the heart, which can be perceived when it beats; (b) the brain, which can be identified by the inner speech accompanying thought; and (c) bones, which can be felt through the skin.

We know less, however, about how children with chronic or disabling conditions view their body interior. Some research suggests that children with chronic conditions do not follow the normal developmental progression in formulating a schema of the internal body; they tend to focus on the organ or organ system affected by their disease, identify fewer organ functions than their healthy peers, and hold distorted views of affected parts (Neff & Beardslee, 1990). Badger's and Jones' study (1990) found that children who were deaf knew significantly fewer body parts than hearing children. However, a more recent study determined that children with congenital heart disease have the same level of knowledge about their internal bodies as children without it (Vessey & O'Sullivan, 2000). Further, a study that compared knowledge of body functions of children with cancer, children with orthopedic problems, and children with no serious health problem, reported that children with cancer had more knowledge than did the other groups (Neff & Beardslee, 1990). They attributed this finding to the specific cumulative experience of illness and hospitalization.

Medical Procedures

Medical procedures have many dimensions; some are "routine," and over quickly; others are quite complex and may last for an extended period of time. Some procedures are a one-time experience; others are repeated. Often, procedures require a special room or special equipment; others may use what may be considered familiar equipment. Certain procedures, such as the commonly performed radiologic procedure known as the voiding cystourethrography (VCUG), require children to be alert and cooperative (Butler, Symons, Henderson, Shortliffe, & Spiegel,

Table 14.2 Dimensions of Medical Procedures

1. Any Procedure—The body-instrument interaction
The specific interaction in which children perceive themselves being pressed or interrupted by the world

Level 1 Preoperational	Level 2 Transitional	Level 3 Concrete-Operational	Level 4 Transitional	Level 5 Formal-Operational
Magical thinking predominates Defined by perceptual cues (e.g., smell, touch, sound) Understood animistically (e.g., "The needle is mean to me.")	Defined by context (e.g., "One hospital you get babies, another, operations.") Defined by time of day (e.g., "The blood lady comes at 10 a.m.") Overdiscrimination more likely than overgeneralization Sees slight variations (e.g., new doctor can't find vein) as a whole new experience	Correctly identifies procedures Functions sometimes interpreted literally Understands sequence of multiple steps Following rules of procedure important May believe more is better ("I got three shots a day and other children got only one.")	Begins to abstract the essence and function of a procedure, even with variations (e.g., substitutions in equipment, personnel, sequence of administration) Begins to cope with an emergency and use what is at hand (a ski or tree limb to splint a leg)	Can conceptually coordinate multiple procedures to serve diagnostic or therapeutic functions Can explain the relative efficacy of different procedures proposed Can imagine a procedure that does not yet exist and describe how it would function

2. Conducted or Supervised by Medical Personnel
The social role relationships between the patient and the medical personnel, specifically characterized in terms of authority and control

Level 1 Preoperational	Level 2 Transitional	Level 3 Concrete-Operational	Level 4 Transitional	Level 5 Formal-Operational
Identifies medical personnel based on perceptual cues (e.g., clothing) or physical setting (e.g., clinic, hospital) Sees power of medical authority as absolute Sees source of power as magical (e.g., doctor perceived as powerful because has red hair, like child's father) Has sense of personal ownership (e.g., refers to "my doctor")	Often sees medical personnel as good guys and bad guys, based on painfulness of procedures they administer while the child is awake and alert	Respects authority of medical personnel, though not uniformly beloved Understands the hierarchy of command (e.g., doctor, nurse, patient) Understands that medical personnel can delegate authority to other persons Often delighted to accept supervision on self-administered procedures	Understands relative nature of authority Sometimes challenges medical personnel Has growing sense of responsibility of self-care Can perceive discrepancy between the feelings of medical authorities and patient rights or feelings	Understands that authority of medical personnel is relative to the patient's agreement to comply Can be emotionally and cognitively sensitive to the role of medical personnel Knows that he or she can choose another doctor, or choose not to be under doctor's care at all Can accept responsibility for self-care, using the doctor's expertise and supervision

Table 14.2 (*continued*)

3. To Evaluate or Modify Health Status The meaning of the procedure for the child as proposed by the medical personnel				
Level 1 Preoperational	**Level 2 Transitional**	**Level 3 Concrete-Operational**	**Level 4 Transitional**	**Level 5 Formal-Operational**
Sees the purpose of a procedure as independent of health status (e.g., ''to crush me,'' ''to steal my blood,'' ''to hurt me because I'm bad,'' ''so that I can get a dolly'') Cannot discriminate between evaluative and therapeutic procedures (e.g., all procedures should make you well or kill you) Becomes confused and frightened when a procedure causes sickness before resulting in feeling better Understands health status existentially as sick or okay in absolute and dual terms (e.g., symptom criteria unique to the child but primarily visible and on the other body)	Understands purpose for selected procedures May still believe procedures are personal assault (''She hurt me so I hurt her.'') Understands some gradation in health status (e.g., feeling better, feeling worse)	Can classify procedures according to evaluative or therapeutic functions Often has literal understanding of procedure (e.g., may refuse to cooperate with a CT scan of brain for fear it would read bad thoughts) Understands sequential changes in health status if explained beforehand (e.g., following chemotherapy comes hair loss) May need to test out explanations before believing them (e.g., postoperatively, expressing relief that didn't die under anesthesia)	Can correctly place new procedures in a diagnostic or therapeutic category Can coordinate the relationship of a procedure to health status (e.g., urine sample for checkup for well child; urine sample to monitor health status of ill child)	Understands the probable impact of various procedures on health status Can evaluate probable impact of procedures physically and psychologically on quality of life

Note. Adapted from Steward, M., & Steward, D. (1981). Children's conceptions of medical procedures. In R. Bibace & M. Walsh (Eds.), *New directions for child development: Children's conceptions of health, illness, and bodily function* no. 14 (pp. 67–83). San Francisco: Jossey-Bass. Reprinted with permission.

2005); for other procedures, such as a bone marrow aspiration, children may be sedated (Burkle et al., 2004). Procedures may be performed by strangers or by familiar persons, such as the family doctor, the primary nurse, a parent, or even children themselves.

Steward and Steward (1981) describe three dimensions of medical procedures: (a) any procedure; (b) a procedure conducted or supervised by medical personnel; and (c) a procedure for the purpose of evaluating or modifying health status. They have attempted to rate the structure of responses, drawn from the literature and verbatim from children, according to developmental levels (see Table 14.2). Note: There also is "Level 0: Lack of Comprehension," which has been omitted from the table.

Transition to Adult Care

One of the most challenging life events teenagers with chronic illness and families face is transitioning from a pediatric health setting to an adult health setting for care. The word *transition* implies a gradual process that takes place over time. In the case of a child transferring to adult care, transition may mean not only a transfer of medical records and care from one physician and medical setting to another, it also may refer to the transfer of the child's care from pediatric staff and family to self-care.

Another part of transitioning for the adolescent is preparing to move from the world of school to the world of adulthood. Although it is uncommon to identify health-related needs and goals when developing a statement of transition services within a student's Individual Education Program (IEP), lack of attention to health needs and health management can jeopardize goals for learning, working, and living safely in the community (Shapland, 2006). Thus, it is important that children learn how to manage their own healthcare, and work with appropriate professionals as partners in their care.

Preparing for Transition

Transition, as just noted, is a gradual process, where the leadership of a child's care, over the years, ideally and ultimately is transferred to the child. Figure 14.1 illustrates how this gradual transfer of leadership takes place (Kieckhefer & Trahms, 2000). The bold arrows in the figure show the need for the parent to guide this movement, along with the important idea that both parent and child have an active role to play. This relationship between the parent and child is dynamic in nature:

> Initially, the parent provides all of the necessary care to the child, regardless of the child's age. As the child grows in cognitive and physical skill development, experience with the condition, and management competence, the parent transfers some of the responsibility for self-care to the child. The parent becomes the "manager" and the child the "provider" for these carefully articulated, skill-appropriate responsibilities. The parent is available to support the child's provider skills and stands ready to re-assume some of these tasks for a short time if it is necessary because the child is ill or other life complications require additional parent support. As the child's becomes more confident and

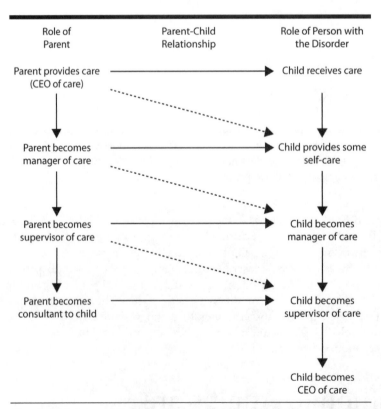

Figure 14.1. **Leadership Model for Systematic Transition of Care**

Note. From Kieckhefer, G., & Trahms, C. (2000). Supporting development of children with chronic conditions: From compliance toward shared management. *Pediatric Nursing, 26*(4), 354–363. Reprinted with permission.

competent in self-management, the parent and child negotiate the next step. The parent becomes the "supervisor" and the child becomes the manager of specific tasks. The parent is, again, poised to resume the managerial role or specific tasks for a short time, if necessary. However, the parent and child must both understand and agree that the child does not regress to a previous stage; the parent provides additional support during times of stress, and the child continues to progress in self-management skills and self-management responsibility development. Eventually, the parent assumes a "consultant" role in the child's management of the disorder, and the child becomes the "supervisor," manager, and provider of care. The parent supplies information, support, decision-making guidance, and resources, but the child assumes ultimate responsibility for his or her health care as the "CEO." (pp. 356–357)

Because children grow and develop at different rates, there is no specific age ascribed to the leadership stages, although CEO status often occurs in conjunction with emancipation from the family. However, the Leadership Model can be integrated with the development model for guidance. See Table 14.3, Pragmatic Actions That Support Leadership Skills, which outlines age-related capabilities and actions that form the basis for leadership skills, as well as actions parents can take to support these growing capacities.

Special Considerations

When teaching, it is important to remember that people have preferred modes of communication and learning styles. The best learning will occur when the method of teaching matches the child's preferred learning style. Learning styles fall into one of three categories: visual, auditory, or kinesthetic:

- *Visual learners learn best through seeing.* They need to see the teacher's body language and facial expressions to fully understand the content of education session. In a group session, visual learners tend to prefer sitting at the front, to avoid visual obstructions (e.g., other people's heads). Visual learners may think in pictures, hence learn best from visual displays, including diagrams, illustrated books, overhead transparencies, videos, DVDs, PowerPoint presentations, flipcharts, and handouts. They often need, and may prefer, to take detailed notes, to help them absorb the information.

- *Auditory learners learn best through listening.* Verbal lectures, discussions, talking things through, and listening to what others have to say are all good methods for auditory learners. They interpret the underlying meanings of speech through listening to tone of voice, pitch, speed, and other nuances. Written information may have little meaning until they hear it. Auditory learners often benefit from reading text aloud and using a tape recorder.

- *Tactile/kinesthetic learners* learn best through moving, doing, and touching—taking a hands-on approach and actively exploring the physical world around them. Tactile/kinesthetic learners may find it difficult to sit still for long periods of time, and may become distracted by their need for activity and exploration.

Listening to and observing children can provide clues to their learning style. For instance, children who respond with, "I see what you mean," "That looks good to me," "It looks like . . ." or "I can just picture that," may indicate visual learners. They like their own space and do not want people to intrude on it without asking permission. An auditory learner may use hearing and thinking terms such as, "I hear what you are saying," "I hear you loud and clear," or "Sounds good to me." They may not like to be touched without invitation, and displays of emotion may be uncomfortable for them. Children who are tactile/kinesthetic use feeling words freely, such as, "I am angry," "I am happy," or "It is exciting." Tactile/kinesthetic children like to be in the middle of the action. They enjoy learning in groups.

Table 14.3 Pragmatic Actions that Support Leadership Skills

Stage/Age	Child Capabilities/Actions that Form the Basis for Leadership Skills	Parents' Leadership Actions to Support the Child's Growing Capabilities
Infant (0–12 months)	Though dependent on parents for care it is helpful if the child gives clear cues of distress so parents can grow in the recognition of emergent needs and appropriate responses. For example, clear cues of hunger and satiety help the parent understand when to offer formula and when to withdraw it. Similarly, clear cues of increasing respiratory effort (e.g., grunting, use of accessory muscles) provide parents with a sign of respiratory distress in asthma. Clear cues of optimal health (e.g., adequate growth, development, social interaction) also enable parents to identify the positive impact of their actions to promote good management.	Learn ramifications of the condition and how/what resources can help. Learn how to ask questions that can assist managing the condition in the context of an overall healthy living pattern. Participate in support activities to increase knowledge of disorder and its management. Develop routine regarding daily treatment that fits with family life patterns. Recognize signs of immediate distress and seek emergency care. Recognize signs of early distress and seek evaluation. Learn to acknowledge those challenges that are developmentally typical for most children vs. challenges specific to the child's condition. Learn how to share information with extended family and daycare providers. See/acknowledge evidence that the child is thriving under attentive management. Assume the role of "repository for condition specific information" regarding the child's reaction to the treatment.
Toddler (1–3 years)*	Cooperate with routine treatments. Help hold equipment and work with parent to make equipment function as needed, e.g., use of blender to prepare formula for PKU or the nebulizer for asthma medication delivery. Develop a sense that parents are a source of help/comfort. Accept constraints of condition and treatment with limited behavioral acting out, e.g., "yes foods/no foods" for PKU or "trigger" avoidance with asthma. Understand firm limits of parents, e.g., "no."	Develop rituals regarding treatment so child knows what to expect and can begin to learn through repetition. Begin to recognize the child needs to have roles in the management of the condition. Identify possible roles the parents are willing to begin to share with the child. Change the established management routine based on the child's growing capabilities and areas of cooperation. Continue to build clinical and community support network.
Preschool (4–5 years)	Identify body parts important to early identification of a problem or treatment. Test limits of cooperation. Use magical thinking, which may lead to fears. Imitate adult's behaviors. Learn labels for condition specific "problems" so can communicate treatment needs. Learn labels for feelings associated with condition and its treatment so can communicate feelings.	Acknowledge regressions, allow very brief period of reorganization, and then resume and praise prior skill performance. Set fair and appropriate limits. Model acceptance of the management routines and limits. Encourage some flexibility in rituals of treatment so child begins to experience multiple ways to accomplish same goal. Develop relationships with school personnel re: specific needs.
Early School Age (6–9 years)	Recognize and act on 1–2 of major internal body cues of a problem. Participate actively in concrete monitoring of condition. Increase understanding of condition, cause and effect, concrete level of what's going on inside the body, to necessitate management.	Continue to label cues and give positive reward for child's recognition. Start negotiating with child for what each party will do regarding management and set criteria for forward movement that fits with family life. Be prepared to renegotiate for cause. Establish logical consequences for actions. Negotiate the "rules" for working together to get all necessary treatments completed. Be positive and reinforcing about what needs to get done. Avoid overemphasis on condition. Support normative activities and integrate treatment needs. Model telling others about the disorder for the child. Discuss the approach to telling teachers, friends, coaches, and others about the disorder and the amount of detail necessary to share.

Table 14.3 (*continued*)

Stage/Age	Child Capabilities/Actions that Form the Basis for Leadership Skills	Parents' Leadership Actions to Support the Child's Growing Capabilities
Late school age (10–12)	Increase level of understanding of condition; begin to understand long-term needs. Develop new labels that are medically articulate so can effectively discuss with providers. Learn how and when to respond to peer pressure yet still take care of self. Enact most psychomotor skills associated with treatment with parental support. Learn more sophisticated system for reporting symptoms, management steps, and outcomes. Develop specific set of self-management tasks that are completed independently.	Remain present for the child, that is, involved in care and monitoring decision making. Accept the manager vs. CEO role in much of treatment. Insure that child has told important others, e.g., friends, parents, coaches, of the condition and what assistance they could provide if needed. Be there in case of emergencies and/or new presentation, out of the routine needs both cognitive changes in treatment and maybe even the doing of some aspects. Provide the tools so the child can self-manage, e.g., get the formula, get the prescriptions. Support the child in actively communicating with their provider, encouraging discussion of the child's monitoring system so as to help the child grow in understanding.
Early adolescent	Become main manager of daily, routine care. Develop strategies to insure completion of all of the necessary routine management tasks. Know how to effectively ask for assistance in complex situations. Know where can be flexible vs. not flexible and be able to enact the flexibility when appropriate.	Shadow, or observe the performance closely so can offer immediate corrective feedback. Negotiate and renegotiate who does what. Become the consultant vs. remaining the manager. Discuss new issues, e.g., sex, drugs, alcohol, for their normative and any special condition effects.
Late adolescent	Make a commitment to lifetime treatment. Increase understanding of the disorder and its long term as well as short term consequences on other aspects of life, e.g., vocations, intellectual achievement, well being. Achieve sense of self as capable manager of disorder. Integrate the realities of the condition with the invincible nature of their years. Appreciate of benefits that the constraints of the management allow. Continue to develop more independent clinic and community support network as transition to adult-based care services.	Develop a flexible way of communicating with the child so can stay informed while not seen as interfering. Remain "present" for support and problem solving with the youth. Provide support and guidance as the youth transitions from pediatric to adult care services.

*If condition initially diagnosed at this age (e.g., asthma), the earlier child capabilities and parental support actions need to be addressed before attempting to accomplish/master those listed in this section.

Note. From Kieckhefer, G., & Trahms, C. (2000). Supporting development of children with chronic conditions: From compliance toward shared management. *Pediatric Nursing, 26*(4), 354–363. Reprinted with permission.

Language is another important consideration when teaching children. Using the child's age plus one is a good guide for the number of words to use in a sentence. Choice of words can also make a difference in understanding. For example, certain words that have different meanings, (e.g., *shot, stretcher, put to sleep*) can be very confusing or even frightening for children. Words also can be experienced as "hard" or "soft." For example, "The medicine will burn," sounds much harder than "Some children say they feel a very warm feeling." Unfamiliar terms, such as *anesthesia, incision,* or *electrodes,* may also confuse or frighten children. For an excellent discourse on choosing language, see *Psychosocial Care of Children in Hospitals: A Clinical Practice Manual from the ACCH Child Life Research Project* (1990), by Gaynard et al., which is available from the Child Life Council (see www.childlife.org for details).

Activity Goals

Helping children better understand their illness and treatment serves to (1) improve compliance; (2) provide a sense of control; (3) help peers understand the child's condition; and (4) assist with transition to adult care. All of the activities in this chapter promote understanding by demonstrating educational concepts and/or providing hands-on learning opportunities.

Activity 14.1. Peristaltic Waves: A Moving Experience

Peristaltic Waves: A Moving Experience is located on the CD that accompanies this book.

Activity 14.2. Be Safe Collages

This activity can be adapted to reinforce teaching about safe and unsafe practices for a variety of illnesses. For example, collages might illustrate an asthma trigger; safe and unsafe sports and other physical activities for bleeding-disorder patients; or foods that are allowed for, or to be avoided by, children on special diets, such as those with renal failure, diabetes, or Crohn's disease.

Therapeutic Goal: To promote understanding by reinforcing educational concepts and enhancing feelings of self-efficacy.

Age Group: Preschool/primary/school-age

Adult/Child Ratio: 1:6

Required Time: 30–45 minutes for older children; less for younger children

Restrictions and Precautions: Take scissors and glue precautions.

Materials:

☐ Poster board or paper

☐ Magazines that will yield relevant pictures for the children (e.g., sports or food publications)

☐ Scissors

☐ Glue sticks

Process

1. Discuss activities the children must avoid doing, or foods they must avoid eating, to stay healthy; then name foods and activities that *are* safe for them to eat and do.

2. Provide the children with an assortment of magazines and have them identify and cut out pictures of safe and unsafe activities and/or foods. (Cut out appropriate pictures in advance of the activity for preschoolers or children who are unable to use scissors.)

3. Give each child poster board or paper.

4. Ask the children to divide their paper in half vertically, horizontally, or in a ying-and-yang teardrop design.

5. Have the children glue pictures of items to avoid on one side, and those that are acceptable on the other.

Activity 14.3. Blood Components

This activity always captures children's interest; and the snack produced at the end is a tasty, fun way to reinforce the information.

Therapeutic Goal: To promote understanding by demonstrating educational concepts and providing a hands-on learning experience.

Age Group: School-age

Adult/Child Ratio: 1:20

Required Time: 30 minutes

Restrictions and Precautions: Handle the bags of "blood" carefully to avoid them opening and

creating a mess. Check diets when making the
blood "snack."

Materials:

- ☐ Cardboard tube from paper towels or wrapping paper, painted blue (for the vein)
- ☐ X-ACTO knife, or scissors with a sharp tip
- ☐ Red jelly beans or red-hot candies (for the red blood cells)
- ☐ White jelly beans or circular gummy candies (for the white blood cells)

- ☐ Minimarshmallows (for the platelets)
- ☐ Pretzel sticks (optional, for the fibrins)
- ☐ Elbow macaroni (for sickle cells)
- ☐ Small bowls
- ☐ Plastic quart-sized freezer bag with zip-lock closure.
- ☐ Plastic spoons
- ☐ Corn syrup (for the plasma)
- ☐ Vanilla ice cream

Process

1. Cut a 2-inch × 1-inch rectangle out of the paper towel tube to create a "window."

2. Place each of the foods representing the different blood components into separate small bowls; label each bowl.

3. Combine some of each of the blood components in three plastic bags. Vary the ratio of red to white blood cells in each, to represent a normal white count, low white count, and high white count. If desired, add elbow macaroni to illustrate sickle cell disease.

4. Show the children the contents of each bowl and explain, in an age-appropriate manner, the function of that particular blood component. Crush several mini marshmallows in your hand to reinforce the concept of platelets sticking together to form a plug.

5. Add corn syrup to one of the bags. Explain how plasma holds all of the blood cells together and helps transport them through the veins. Seal the bag well.

6. Insert the filled bag into the cardboard tube to illustrate blood flowing through the vein.

7. To reinforce the information and conclude the activity, give each child a scoop of ice cream in a paper cup and invite them to top their ice cream with a teaspoon of each of the edible "blood" components (excluding the elbow macaroni, of course) while you review the information discussed.

ACTIVITY 14.4.   TRANSMISSION OF BLOODBORNE PATHOGENS

The continuing threat of AIDS and drug use among children underscores the importance of ensuring that they understand this concept.

Therapeutic Goal: To promote understanding by demonstrating educational concepts.

Age Group: School-age

Adult/Child Ratio: Any size group

Required Time: 15 minutes

Restrictions and Precautions: None

Materials:

- ☐ Cornstarch
- ☐ Plastic snack bag with zip-lock closure
- ☐ Large sewing needle
- ☐ 2 large glass bowls, 3/4 filled with water
- ☐ Iodine

Process

1. Fill both snack bags with cornstarch and zip them closed.

2. Use the needle to puncture several holes in one of the bags.

3. Introduce the activity by explaining that some diseases, such as AIDS and hepatitis B, are spread through contaminated blood. Emphasize to the children that the only way they can "catch" a bloodborne illness is if the blood of a sick person enters their body through an opening.

4. Explain that in the demonstration the cornstarch-filled bags represent the body, and the iodine-tinted water represents contaminated blood.

5. Place each bag into a glass bowl.

6. Add several drops of iodine to the water in each bowl.

7. Remove the bags and point out that the iodine was only able to get into the bag that was punctured. Explain how this is analogous to the transmission of a bloodborne pathogen. Reinforce for the children that they cannot "catch" a bloodborne pathogen simply by being near or touching someone who is infected.

ACTIVITY 14.5. CONCEPTUALIZING BONE MARROW

This teaching aid can be adapted to provide schematic representations of leukemia, aplastic anemia, and other diseases of the bone marrow.

Therapeutic Goal: To promote understanding by illustrating educational concepts.

Age Group: Preschool/primary/school-age

Adult/Child Ratio: Any

Required Time: 15 minutes

Restrictions and Precautions: None

Materials:

☐ 2 hollow dog bones (available from pet stores)

☐ Newspaper

☐ Hot glue gun

☐ Red beads (with older children, use two sizes: larger beads represent healthy red blood cells; smaller beads represent immature cells)

☐ White beads (with older children, use two sizes: larger beads represent healthy white blood cells; smaller beads represent immature/blast cells)

Process

1. Stuff each end of the dog bones firmly with newspaper, to 1/2 inch from the top.

2. Spread a layer of hot glue over the newspaper on one end of one of the bones. To illustrate healthy marrow, combine a layer of red and white beads on the newspaper, making sure there are more of the larger red beads and fewer of the larger white beads (the normal ratio of red to white blood cells is about 600:1). Add another layer of hot glue followed by another one of beads, with the same ratio of red and white beads. Repeat if necessary, until the beads reach the end of the bone. Seal with a thin layer of hot glue (Figure Activity 14.5-1).

Figure Activity 14.5-1. Conceptualizing Bone Marrow

3. Repeat step 2 on the opposite end of the bone.

4. With the second bone, repeat steps 2 and 3, changing the ratio of red and white beads to illustrate a particular disease (e.g., more white blood cells for leukemia).

5. Explain the function of healthy white and red blood cells.

6. First show the children the bone with healthy marrow then the bone with diseased marrow. Point out how they are different.

7. Using developmentally appropriate language and detail, discuss how the variation in number, size, and function of the unhealthy blood cells affect the body of a person with a bone marrow disease.

Activity 14.6.   Cystic Fibrosis Demonstration

This demonstration can also be used for teaching about pneumonia, asthma, or the effects of smoking.

Therapeutic Goal: To promote understanding by demonstrating educational concepts and providing a hands-on learning experience.

Age Group: Primary

Adult/Child Ratio: Any

Required Time: 30 minutes

Restrictions and Precautions: None

Materials:

☐ Poster board

☐ Markers

☐ 2 plastic zip-lock style sandwich bags

☐ Cotton balls

☐ Tape

☐ 2 straws

☐ Liquid honey

☐ Glue dots

Process

1. Draw a life-size outline of a child's torso on the poster board.

2. Prepare two models of lungs, one healthy and one with cystic fibrosis, by placing several cotton balls in each sandwich bag.

3. For the healthy lung, insert a straw through the top of one of the bags and place tape around the hole to create an airtight seal. Zip the bag closed and reinforce with tape.

4. Repeat this process for the model with cystic fibrosis. But before closing and sealing the bag with the tape, carefully pour about 1/2 to 1 cup honey into the bag, making sure that some of the honey gets on the cotton balls, and dribble some into the straw.

5. Explain the function of the lungs, in an age-appropriate manner.

6. Show the children the healthy lung model. Explain that the cotton balls in the plastic bag represent the air sacs in our lungs, and the straw the windpipe (trachea).

7. Ask the children to watch what happens when you breath into the straw (i.e., the bag inflates). Squeeze the air out and call the children's attention to how the bag deflates. Explain that this is the way healthy lungs work.

8. Use the tape or glue dots to attach the healthy lung model to the torso in the appropriate area.

9. Show the children the model with cystic fibrosis. Try to inflate the lung by blowing into the straw. Discuss what happens. Attach the lung model to the torso.

10. Explain that children with cystic fibrosis have trouble breathing because of sticky mucous in their lungs. Provide additional information about the disease that is developmentally and situationally appropriate. Emphasize that cystic fibrosis is not a contagious disease.

11. Make green-tinted "mucous" with the children (use the recipe for flubber in Activity 7.14). Encourage the children to manipulate the mixture. Discuss the texture, likening it to the mucous that is produced in the lungs of someone who has cystic fibrosis.

Activity 14.7.   Demonstrating Diabetes

Demonstrating Diabetes is located on the CD that accompanies this book.

ACTIVITY 14.8.   THE DIGESTION QUESTION

This activity can be used to explain why children are not permitted to eat immediately after surgery, and what happens when someone vomits.

Therapeutic Goal: To promote understanding by demonstrating educational concepts and providing a hands-on learning experience.

Age Group: Preschool/primary

Adult/Child Ratio: 1:10

Required Time: 10 minutes

Restrictions and Precautions: None

Materials:

☐ Plastic tube, at least 2 inches wide (to represent the esophagus)

☐ Quart-size plastic bag (the stomach)

☐ Pint-sized plastic bags with zip-lock closures

☐ Medical tape

☐ Stethoscope

☐ Banana, thinly sliced

☐ Bread, cut into small cubes

☐ Small cups of juice

Process

1. Tape the large plastic bag (the stomach) around the opening of one end of the plastic tube.

2. Have the children take turns using the stethoscope to listen to their stomachs.

3. Explain that the sounds they hear are their stomachs at work digesting food.

4. Demonstrate the digestive process by dropping some banana, bread, and juice down the tube into the stomach

5. To show how the stomach breaks down foods, squeeze the food inside the bag until the individual foods are no longer discernable

6. Give each child a securely closed bag containing banana, bread, and juice, and encourage them to squeeze it themselves to replicate the breakdown of food.

7. Relate the activity to the child's relevant issue.

ACTIVITY 14.9.   DISEASE TRANSMISSION THROUGH DROPLETS

This activity demonstrates the abstract concept of how germs are transmitted by droplets, and can help children understand why, sometimes, it is necessary to be isolated in a healthcare facility.

Therapeutic Goal: To promote understanding by demonstrating educational concepts.

Age Group: Preschool/primary

Adult/Child Ratio: 1:6

Required Time: 10 minutes

Restrictions and Precautions: None

Materials:

☐ Plant misters or spray bottles

☐ Water

☐ Liquid watercolor paint or tempera paint thinned with water

☐ Construction paper, cut into 4- × 4-inch squares (1 per child)

☐ Tape

☐ White paper (1 sheet per child)

☐ Stencils and/or flat or nearly flat disposable objects

Process

1. Fill one mister or bottle with water and the others with paint.

2. Explain to the children that certain germs in our body may make us sick. Tell them that although germs are too tiny to see with the naked eye, they can be spread from one person

to another in various ways, one of which is via droplets that are expelled when coughing or sneezing.

3. Tape a piece of construction paper to each child's arm or chest.

4. Tell the children that you are going to pretend to sneeze.

5. Stand several feet away from the children and spray each one with water from the mister while saying loudly, "Ah-*choo!*"

6. Point out the water droplets that appear on the construction paper. Explain that they represent the germs that could spread from your sneeze and that they just caught a pretend cold.

7. Use the mister to spray some water directly into the light so that the children can see the fine mist suspended in the air.

8. Spray the water again toward the light while covering the nozzle with your elbow to show how covering your nose and mouth can prevent the spread of germs.

9. As a follow-up art activity, give each child a sheet of white paper.

10. Ask the children to arrange the stencils and/or flat objects on the white paper in a decorative fashion.

11. Have the children spray a fine mist of paint onto the paper.

12. Let the children reposition the objects to overlap previously covered areas before spraying again with a different color.

ACTIVITY 14.10.   EXCUSE YOURSELF!

Excuse Yourself! is located on the CD that accompanies this book.

ACTIVITY 14.11.   LEARNING THE FOOD GROUPS

Both sick and healthy children will benefit from understanding the food groups and how to balance meals.

Therapeutic Goal: To promote understanding by demonstrating educational concepts.	**Materials:**
Age Group: Preschool/primary	☐ Food magazines
Adult/Child Ratio: 1:6	☐ Scissors
Required Time: Varies	☐ Tape
Restrictions and Precautions: Take scissors precautions.	☐ Lunch or shoe boxes (5)

Process

1. Cut pictures representative of each of the food groups from the magazines.

2. On the inside of each lunch box lid, tape a picture representing one of the food groups:

   • Meats, poultry, fish, eggs poultry, nuts, beans

   • Grains, bread cereal, rice, pasta

   • Fruits

   • Vegetables

   • Milk, yogurt, cheese

3. After teaching them about the food groups, have the children sort through the cutout pictures and put them into the correct lunchboxes/food groups.

4. During mealtime, encourage the children to look at the food on their plates and try to find an item from each of the food groups.

Variation

Have the children create a balanced meal from the pictures and glue them to three-section paper plates.

 ACTIVITY 14.12.   HEART SMART

Heart Smart is located on the CD that accompanies this book.

ACTIVITY 14.13.   INFECTION DETECTION

This activity can help children better understand the need for taking contact precautions, as well as the importance of using a good hand-washing technique.

Therapeutic Goal: To promote understanding by demonstrating educational concepts and providing a hands-on learning experience.

Age Group: School-age

Adult/Child Ratio: 1:10

Required Time: 30 minutes

Restrictions and Precautions: Use balloons only for demonstration and under supervision.

Materials:

☐ Plate

☐ Flour or glitter

☐ Balloon

☐ Black construction paper (1 sheet per child)

Process

1. Explain to the children that certain germs in our body make us sick, and that though germs are too tiny to see with the naked eye, they can be spread from one person to another simply by touching the same object.

2. Sprinkle flour or glitter over the plate, covering it completely, explaining that the flour represents germs.

3. Have the children stand or sit in a circle.

4. Ask one child to place his or her hands into the flour or glitter, coating them well.

5. Ask that child to pass the balloon to the child on his or her right, without touching hands. Repeat until each child has handled the balloon.

6. Give each of the children a sheet of black paper and tell them to press their hands against it. Flour or glitter from their hands will be transferred to the paper.

7. Point out that all of them were "infected" with the germs, even though they never touched the "infected" child's hands.

8. Explain that hand washing is our best protection against the transmission of many types of disease.

ACTIVITY 14.14.   ORGANIZE YOUR ORGANS

As a follow-up activity, play a variation of Pin the Tail on the Donkey. Pin all of the organs but one on the body outline. Make multiple copies of the omitted organ and give one to each participant, along with a small piece of tape. Tape the body outline to a wall. One by one, blindfold each of the children and spin them around twice. Let them try to tape the organ as close as they can to where it belongs.

Therapeutic Goal: To promote understanding by providing a hands-on learning experience.

Age Group: Primary/school-age

Adult/Child Ratio: 1:10

Required Time: Significant preparation time, but can be used repeatedly

Restrictions and Precautions: None

Materials:

☐ Photocopy of organ templates (Figures Activity 14.14-1 – Actvity14.14-5)

☐ Pencil

☐ Colored paper

☐ Scissors

☐ Laminator

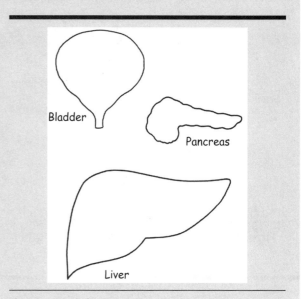

Figure Activity 14.14-3. Bladder, Pancreas, and Liver

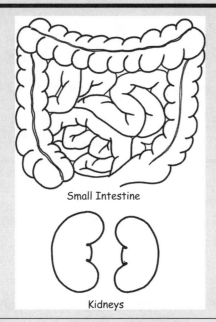

Figure Activity 14.14-1. Intestine and Kidney

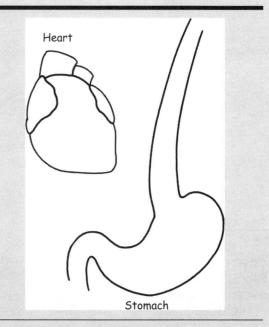

Figure Activity 14.14-4. Heart and Stomach

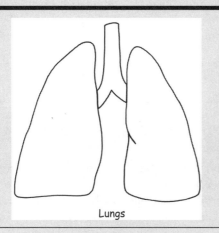

Figure Activity 14.14-2. Lungs

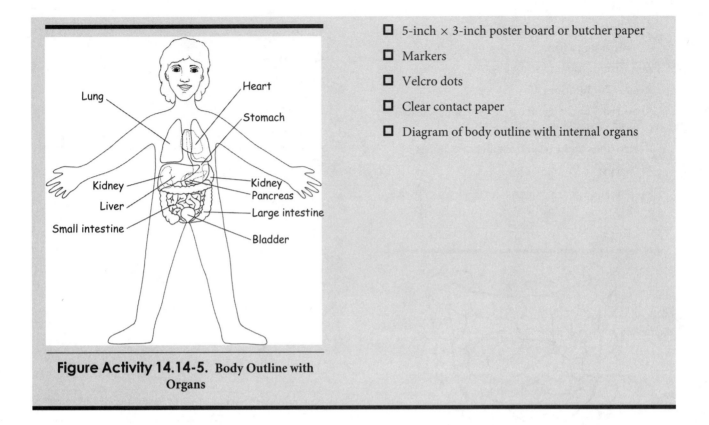

☐ 5-inch × 3-inch poster board or butcher paper

☐ Markers

☐ Velcro dots

☐ Clear contact paper

☐ Diagram of body outline with internal organs

Figure Activity 14.14-5. **Body Outline with Organs**

Process

1. Use the templates to trace each organ onto a different color of paper.

2. Laminate the sheets of colored paper then cut out the organs, leaving a 1/2-inch border around each.

3. Draw a body outline on the poster board and cover it entirely with clear contact paper.

4. Position the organs in their proper places on the body outline.

5. Tear the paper off the rough side of a Velcro dot and attach it to the back of one of the organs.

6. Tear the paper off the soft side of a Velcro dot and attach it to the body outline, centered in the area where that organ is located. Repeat steps 5 and 6 for each of the organs.

7. Show the children the diagram and review with them where the internal organs are located.

8. Put the diagram away then ask the children to take turns putting each organ in its correct location on the body outline.

For more ideas, see Bright Ideas: Conceptualizing the Body (Box Activity 14.14-1).

Box Activity 14.14-1. Bright Ideas: Conceptualizing the Body

• Use chicken legs and wings to illustrate bones, muscles, tendons, ligaments, and cartilage. Cut open a soup bone to show the bone marrow.

• Purchase animal parts such as lamb kidneys, beef tongues, brains, tripe (cow stomach lining), or intestinal lining (chitlins) from a butcher store to provide sensory experiences for children who are learning about the body. Avoid doing this with children who are squeamish or sensitive to smells. Kidneys smell of blood and urine, and other organs may also exude odors that children find unpleasant.

• Use a cardboard tube and red and white marbles to simulate blood flowing though a vein. Cut a square out of the tube to show what happens when there is a bleed.

• Let children weave paper to help them understand how fibrin works.

- Have older children blow into balloons to demonstrate lung capacity. Measure the circumference of each child's balloon to compare.

- Use a 24-foot tape measure or piece of rope to show how long the intestines are. Have children walk along it to understand how far their food travels after it leaves the stomach.

- Purchase a mold of the human brain and fill it with watermelon gelatin prepared according to package directions. Allow to set. Unmold and use to show children the appearance and texture of the brain.

- Use a balloon filled with water to demonstrate how the bladder expands when filled with urine, and how the sphincter, a contracting muscle, holds the liquid in. Release the opening of the balloon to illustrate how the bladder releases urine when the sphincter is released.

- Pour a mixture of ground-up chalk and water through a coffee filter to illustrate how the kidneys filter waste.

- Make a puzzle of the different parts of the brain, labeling each area with its name and function. Ask the children to put the puzzle together.

- To reinforce the names and locations of various bones in children's minds, do the Hokey Pokey, naming bones instead of extremities.

- Display fifteen 12-ounce cans of soda pop to show children how much blood is in an average adult's body. Hold up one can to compare how much blood is in a newborn baby's body.

- Use diagrams of the skeletal system, internal organs, brain, or a full-body outline and ask children to label what they see.

- To illustrate the interrelation of smell and taste, tell children to hold their noses and take a bite of an apple, and then a potato.

ACTIVITY 14.15.   PREPARATION FOR AN EEG

This activity can be done while you are explaining EEG placement to the child, or after explaining the procedure, as a means to reinforce the information.

Therapeutic Goal: To prepare a child for a procedure by demonstrating the process and familiarizing him or her with equipment that will be used.

Age Group: Preschool/primary/school-age

Adult/Child Ratio: 1:1

Required Time: 30 minutes

Restrictions and Precautions: Take marker precautions.

Materials:

☐ Photograph of EEG machine

☐ Styrofoam wig form

☐ Electrodes

☐ EEG sticky paste, or toothpaste

☐ Blow dryer

☐ EEG paper

☐ Completed EEG

☐ Crayons or markers

Process

1. Explain, or reinforce, the purpose of an EEG and the sequence of events that will occur during the test.

2. Demonstrate the placement of the electrodes on the wig form, using sticky paste or toothpaste to adhere them (Figure Activity 14.15-1).

3. Allow the child to place electrodes on the wig form also.

4. Use the blow dryer on the coolest setting to simulate the instrument used during an EEG to dry the paste. First, aim the blow dryer toward the electrodes that have been placed on the wig

form so the child can hear the sound. Then, to familiarize the child with how the streaming air feels, encourage the child to direct the air onto his or her hand, and then head.

Figure Activity 14.15-1. EEG Preparation

5. Show the child the photograph of the EEG machine and explain that the electrodes send signals from the brain to a computer to record the results, and which can then be printed out like a diagram on the EEG paper (with younger children, use the word *picture*).

6. Show the child some EEG paper before it has been used, and then show the child a completed test.

7. Elicit questions or concerns.

8. Conclude the activity by inviting the child to color or add designs to the EEG paper.

ACTIVITY 14.16.   PREPARATION FOR EYEDROPS

Therapeutic Goal: To prepare a child for a procedure by demonstrating the process and familiarizing him or her with equipment that will be used.

Age Group: Preschool/primary

Adult/Child Ratio: 1:1

Required Time: 20 minutes

Restrictions and Precautions: None

Materials:

- ☐ Eyedroppers
- ☐ Medicine cups or other small containers
- ☐ Water or saline solution
- ☐ Food coloring
- ☐ Construction paper
- ☐ Hole punch
- ☐ Paper clips
- ☐ Photographs of room where exam or treatment will take place, and other equipment, if indicated
- ☐ Baby doll with blinking eyes

Process

1. Mix food coloring and water or saline solution in medicine cups or other containers.

2. Place an eyedropper in each medicine cup or container.

3. Punch holes into a long strip of construction paper. Use paper clips to fasten the strip to another piece of construction paper of a different color.

4. Begin the preparation by explaining to the child that he or she will need to have drops put in his or her eyes, and why. Include as much detail about the procedure as is age-appropriate.

5. If indicated, show photographs of where the exam will take place, where the child will be sitting or lying down, and the equipment that will be used.

6. Demonstrate putting drops in the doll's eyes. Then allow the child to put drops in the doll's eyes, several times.

7. Wiggle the doll as the child continues to put more drops in the doll's eyes. Point out that, now, the drops are getting all over the doll's face, not in its eyes.

8. Lay the doll flat so that its eyes close then ask the child to try to put drops in its eyes again. Point out that the drops can't get in the doll's eye's when they are closed.

9. Explain to the child that the baby doll might need help to stay still and keep her eyes open during her eye exam, and that he or she might, as well.

10. Allow time for the child to think about what he or she has learned about the procedure before eliciting questions or concerns.

11. Give the child the two pieces of construction paper that were previously prepared.

12. Give the child the eyedroppers to drop tinted water or paint into the holes. Let dry.

13. Carefully lift the strip up and refasten it to an empty space on the construction paper and repeat the process. Allow to dry, then hang.

ACTIVITY 14.17. PREPARATION FOR SUTURE REMOVAL

This simple activity can be very reassuring to children who become frightened at the prospect of having their sutures or staples removed.

Therapeutic Goal: To prepare a child for a procedure by demonstrating the process familiarizing him or her with the equipment that will be used.

Age Group: Preschool/primary/school-age

Adult/Child Ratio: 1:1

Required Time: 10 minutes advance preparation; 10 minutes for activity

Restrictions and Precautions: Supervise the child closely while he or she is removing the sutures.

Materials:

☐ Stuffed animal made of cloth (not fake fur) of a light color

☐ Suture kit (or buttonhole thread and large-eye needle) or staple gun

☐ Scissors

☐ Sewing cards (store-bought or made with tag board and a hole punch)

☐ Yarn

☐ Yarn needle

Process

1. Select a shade of marker just dark enough to be visible when used on the stuffed animal.

2. Draw a line to represent an incision, making it similar in size and form to that of the child's.

3. Use the suturing kit, buttonhole thread, or staple gun to give the stuffed animal stitches.

4. If the child's incision is dressed, place the same type of dressing on the stuffed animal.

5. Explain to the child that his or her sutures are going to be taken out and that you are going to show how this will be done.

6. Let the child remove the dressing.

7. Demonstrate removing one or two sutures on the stuffed animal. Point out that the animal wasn't "stuck" in the process and that the healed wound remained closed.

8. Allow the child to remove the remaining sutures from the stuffed animal.

9. Elicit questions or concerns.

ACTIVITY 14.18.　PREPARATION FOR ULTRASOUND

This activity is particularly helpful for children with sensory issues.

Therapeutic Goal: To promote understanding by demonstrating educational concepts.

Age Group: Preschool/primary/school-age

Adult/Child Ratio: 1:1

Required Time: 15 minutes

Restrictions and Precautions: Adapt language to child's developmental level.

Materials:

☐ Photograph of room where the test will take place

☐ Photograph of ultrasound machine

☐ Hospital gown

☐ Ultrasound gel

☐ Discarded computer mouse or transducer

☐ Ultrasound image

☐ Finger-paint paper

Process

1. Squeeze some ultrasound gel into a shallow bowl.

2. Explain the purpose of the test to the child.

3. Show the child the hospital gown and explain that, upon arrival for the test, he or she will be asked to change into a gown like this to wear during the test.

4. Show the child the picture of the room where the test will take place, taking care to point out the exam table where he or she will lie down during the test. Describe the machine as being like a big computer.

5. Tell the child that gel will be applied to his or her abdomen, and that it feels somewhat cool. Encourage the child to spread some gel on his or her hand to see what it feels like.

6. While showing the child the mouse or transducer, explain that the technician will gently move a device like this, called a transducer, over the gel. Encourage the child to manipulate the device.

7. Show the child the ultrasound image and explain that a special picture like this is the result the technician gets after he or she uses the transducer.

8. Elicit questions or concerns.

9. If age-appropriate, invite the child to finger-paint with the ultrasound gel.

ACTIVITY 14.19.　SOCIAL STORY PREPARATION

Children with autism spectrum disorder, and others who have difficulty comprehending verbal instructions, find new situations difficult and experience transitions as stressful. Such children will benefit from the use of social stories. Coupled with standard sensory preparation, social stories can help them learn to follow instructions, cope with transitions, and actively participate in their own care.

Therapeutic Goal: To promote understanding by providing a hands-on learning experience.

Age Group: School-age/adolescent

Adult/Child Ratio: 1:1

Required Time: Varies

Restrictions and Precautions: None

Materials:

☐ Paper

☐ Colored pencils or thin-tipped markers

1. Make a series of comic strip frames.   Process

2. Incorporating simple illustrations and symbols, draw one step of a medical procedure in each comic strip frame. Choose logical colors to represent feelings, such as green for happy, blue for sad, red for pain, and black for angry.

3. Add thought bubbles and speech balloons, as appropriate, in which to convey the words, thoughts, and feelings of everyone involved. Be sure to suggest coping strategies when indicated.

4. After providing basic sensory preparation, use the social stories to reinforce the information already given, identify transitions and other stress points that will occur, and suggest coping strategies.

Hint: To enhance the effectiveness of this intervention, involve the child in its creation, and/or incorporate the child's favorite cartoon character into the illustrations.

ACTIVITY 14.20.   THEN WHAT? SEQUENCING CARDS

This activity is especially beneficial for children with autism spectrum disorder and other visual learners.

Therapeutic Goal: To promote understanding by providing a hands-on learning experience.

Age Group: Preschool/primary/school-age/children with special needs

Adult/Child Ratio: 1:1

Required Time: 10–15 minutes

Restrictions and Precautions: None

Materials:

☐ Digital camera

☐ Photographic printing paper

☐ Colored cardboard

☐ Glue sticks

1. Take step-by-step digital photographs depicting the sequence of events that will take place   Process during the procedure, surgery, or exam you wish to address.

2. Print the photos, mount them on the colored cardboard, laminate, and then cut out.

3. One by one, show the child the pictures as you describe what will occur during that step of the procedure.

4. Mix up the pictures and ask the child to try to arrange them in the sequence just explained in step 3. Detail the process again as the child goes along.

5. With autistic children, use the cards during the procedure to provide a greater sense of structure.

For children who need to receive immediate reinforcement for each task they finish, make "first-then"   Variation cards. Pair up each step of the process with a picture of a positive reinforcement that will occur after the step is completed. For example, *first* drink medicine, *then* play a video game. Use a minimum of words.

 ## ACTIVITY 14.21.   VASCULAR VISUALIZATION

Vascular Visualization is located on the CD that accompanies this book.

ACTIVITY 14.22.   WASHING WELL

With the threat of global pandemic ever present these days, this simple activity can help reinforce to children the importance of using a proper hand-washing technique to keeping them healthy.

Therapeutic Goal: To promote understanding by demonstrating educational concepts.

Age Group: Preschool/primary

Adult/Child Ratio: 1:10

Required Time: 10–15 minutes

Restrictions and Precautions: None

Materials:

☐ Petroleum jelly

☐ Cinnamon or glitter in shaker dispenser

☐ Access to a sink, or basins of cold and warm water

☐ Soap

☐ Paper towels

Process

1. Facilitate a discussion about the importance of thorough hand washing.

2. Have the children rub a thin layer of petroleum jelly on both their hands.

3. Sprinkle cinnamon or glitter generously on the children's hands. Be sure to include the areas between the fingers.

4. Explain to the children that the glitter or cinnamon represents germs on their hands.

5. Ask the children to wash their hands with just cold water.

6. Point out that they were unable to get their hands clean in this way.

7. Ask the children to now wash their hands with warm water and soap, encouraging them children to count aloud with you until their hands are completely clean.

8. Discuss how and why the soap and water is more effective for cleaning hands. Ask the children how long it took for them to wash with soap to get their hands really clean, then reinforce that they always take the necessary time to wash their hands thoroughly.

For more ideas, see Bright Ideas: Conceptualizing Illness (Box Activity 14.22-1); Bright Ideas: Conceptualizing Treatment (Box Activity 14.22-2); and Bright Ideas: Games and Activities Easy to Adapt for Teaching (Box Activity 14.22-3).

BOX ACTIVITY 14.22-1. BRIGHT IDEAS: CONCEPTUALIZING ILLNESS

- Grow germs in agar.

- Use "finger traps" to help illustrate anxiety-induced vasoconstriction, which makes blood draws and IV placement difficult, or to demonstrate the constriction children experience during an asthma attack.

- Make flubber (see Activity 7.14) to help children visualize lung secretions.

- To demonstrate the effect of clogged arteries on blood flow, pour orange juice through a clear drinking straw or tubing. Repeat with molasses.

- To simulate what breathing is like for someone with chronic lung disease, give children a thin straw and have them breath through it for 30 seconds. Caution: Do this *only* with children who have healthy lungs, and instruct them to stop immediately if breathing becomes difficult or they feel dizzy.

- To illustrate the concept of a ruptured appendix, combine baking soda and vinegar in a balloon.

- Set up dominoes to demonstrate chain reactions in the body, such as clotting. Remove a domino to illustrate how even one thing missing, such as a clotting factor or digestive enzyme, disrupts the chain.
- Analogize a football quarterback to explain the function of T-cells.

- Peel off layers of an onion to illustrate debridement.
- Use a Slinky to demonstrate how lying in a curled position opens the spine.
- Use a small doll and a segment of a paper towel or toilet paper roll to show children the positioning of the head/body in MRI or CT machines.
- Help children conceptualize chemotherapy using action figures to act as "chemo-warriors" attacking the evil cancer cells.
- Use Crayola Changeable Markers to demonstrate how chemotherapy alters body cells.
- Let children give injections to grapefruits, using blunt-tipped syringes and colored water, to help them understand how shots are given to them.
- Create an ostomy bag for a doll using a small plastic bag with a zip-lock closure, and a sticky pectin wafer with a scaled-to-size opening. Secure the bag to the doll using Stomahesive.

BOX ACTIVITY 14.22-2. BRIGHT IDEAS: CONCEPTUALIZING TREATMENT

Jeopardy	Family Feud
Scattergories	Word jumbles
Pictionary	Picture and word matching
Jenga	Bingo (use Boardmaker to make cards)
Word searches	Who Wants to Be a Millionaire
Crossword puzzles	

BOX ACTIVITY 14.22-3. BRIGHT IDEAS: GAMES AND ACTIVITIES EASY TO ADAPT FOR TEACHING

CHAPTER 15

ACTIVITIES OF DAILY LIVING

Medical advances in recent decades have shifted the focus in pediatric health care from tracking fatal outcomes to measuring nonfatal outcomes, such as morbidity, functional status, and health-related quality of life (Odetola, 2009). *Functional status* is defined as the level of activities performed by an individual to realize needs of daily living in many aspects of life including physical, psychological, social, spiritual, intellectual, and roles (Wang, 2004). Activities of daily living (ADLs) include self-care (feeding, bathing, dressing, and grooming oneself), school, work, leisure, and whatever else may be a part of the child's typical routine.

Illness, especially if accompanied by hospitalization, means a change from the usual state of health and daily routines for both the child and the family. This chapter focuses on the impact of an illness or hospitalization on the activities of daily living, the everyday activities that support health maintenance, such as nutrition, fluids, and daily hygiene. Therapeutic activities are suggested that promote the cooperation of the child in modifying the activities of daily living.

LIST OF ACTIVITIES

Activity 15.1 Aroma Jars	Activity 15.9 Juice Box Boat
Activity 15.2 Bath Fizzers	Activity 15.10 Magic Potion Punch
Activity 15.3 Chug-It Challenge	Activity 15.11 Soap Surprises
Activity 15.4 Clean Cream Finger Paint	Activity 15.12 Scented Soap
Activity 15.5 Daily Schedule	Activity 15.13 Sticker Chart
Activity 15.6 Flavored Lip Gloss	Activity 15.14 Toothsome Toothpaste
Activity 15.7 Food Paint	Activity 15.15 Yellow + Red = Orange
Activity 15.8 Foot Painting	

Changes in the Child's Daily Routine

The goals and nature of everyday activities typically change with illness or hospitalization. Mobility may be limited, feeding routines are changed, and medical procedures and therapies become a part of the daily routine. Such changes in children's daily living activities may result in their becoming uncooperative, and even refusing to accept the modification of their normal activities.

One factor influencing children's response to change in routine is the amount of control they feel they maintain. In the hospital, numerous situations exist that lower the degree of control allowed children. Children's responses to decreased control are greatly influenced by their developmental level.

Infants have an inner schedule that dictates when they are hungry, sleepy, or in need of stimulation. Having a consistent caregiver can help ensure prompt attention to meeting infants' needs. If parents have established a routine, such as singing at bedtime, attempting to maintain that routine as much as possible will help the infant feel more secure.

Toddlers strive for autonomy, and typically have definite rituals for eating, sleeping, bathing, toileting, and playing. When the toddler's routines are disrupted, negativism and regression are the most common responses. Normalizing as many of a toddler's routines as possible can help limit the negative effects of an illness. The preschooler's egocentric and magical thinking limits

299

his or her ability to understand events. Lack of information and unfamiliar settings and routines may contribute to a child in this age group exaggerating and/or fantasizing explanations for the illness or hospitalization. Clear, simple explanations and illustrations are important for the preschooler.

School-age children and adolescents are struggling for independence, self-assertion, and peer acceptance. Unfortunately, because of the nature of the patient role, many daily activities in a hospital usurp individual independence and identity. Both school-age children and adolescents may react with frustration and anger to enforced bed rest, use of bed pans, inability to choose favorite foods, assistance with bathing, and limited or assisted mobility. Providing opportunities to participate in planning care, promoting privacy, and facilitating some form of peer interaction are important coping strategies for these age groups.

Generally, when working with any age child to carry out daily living activities, the caregiver should strive to give the child a sense of control. Explanations for modification of daily activities can ease anxiety and allow the child to identify opportunities to cooperate. The explanations should include what is to be done, what the child can expect from the caregiver, and what the caregiver expects from the child. Cooperative behavior should be positively reinforced. If possible, the child should be allowed to participate in scheduling activities and making choices about the plan of care.

An important aspect of initial assessment is gaining some understanding of the child's normal routine. Incorporating as many of the familiar home routines as possible into the healthcare setting promotes a sense of normalcy in an otherwise stressful situation.

Issues for Parents

A child's hospitalization typically requires parents to make changes in their usual parenting role. Often, especially in tense situations such as emergency department visits or resuscitation, parents are separated from their children. In many cases, parents have reported the loss of their parenting role as more traumatic than their child's illness (Miles & Carter, 1982).

Hospitalization typically escalates fear in children, and parents, as their children's protectors, often feel helpless to do anything about it. Research findings imply that effective, efficient care depends on addressing parents' fears, being aware of their sensitivity to the suffering of their children, and supporting their desire to alleviate it (Koenig, Chesla, & Kennedy, 2003). Continuity is ensured when there is a single primary care provider on whom parents can rely throughout the hospital stay and in the primary care setting. Such continuity can provide the opportunity to address issues of concern in depth, such as the interpretation of crying, and allows for teaching to be adapted more appropriately to individual needs.

Involving the parent or primary caregiver in the child's care should be encouraged because their involvement not only can be a source of comfort to the child, but also has been shown to improve healthcare outcomes (Bell, Johnson, Desai, & McLeod, (2008). It is important, however, that the parent or other primary caregiver not feel required to participate in the care of the child, especially if he or she feels uncomfortable or anxious. In most cases, the parent wants to maintain some part of the primary caregiver role, even when the child is hospitalized. Parental involvement in procedures seems to counter the helplessness, distress, and anxiety that may come from observing one's child's discomfort and resistance (Bulter, Symons, Henderson, Shortliffe, & Spiegel, 2005). In a study of parents of hospitalized children with leukemia, Jones (1994) found a positive relationship between the number of activities a parent participated in and the child's behavior during hospitalization.

Special Considerations

Activities of daily living encompass various aspects. A sampling of significant ones related to children's illness and hospitalization include nutrition and hydration, daily routines, hygiene, and ambulation.

Good childhood nutrition promotes good health throughout the life span. Adequate nutrition and hydration are essential factors that influence optimal growth and development, as well as normal functioning of all organ systems. Sufficient calories and nutrients are essential to support growth and development. Inadequate nutrition or hydration has its greatest impact during fetal development and the first two years of life—critical periods of rapid cell division. A child grows faster during infancy than at any other time of life. From birth to adolescence, growth occurs in two distinct phases (The Merck Manual, 2009):

Nutrition and Fluids

- birth to about age 1 to 2 years—rate of growth decreases over that period; and

- 2 years to the onset of puberty—growth occurs in relatively constant annual increments.

At puberty, a second growth spurt occurs. This spurt affects boys and girls slightly differently, coming earlier for girls (The Merck Manual, 2009).

Adequate hydration also is important for maintenance and development of body systems. The fluid in the body is primarily water. Water is the medium within which electrolytes and other substances are distributed throughout the body. The body's ability to excrete wastes requires water. The movement of water into and out of cells is essential to cellular function and metabolism. Water assists in the maintenance of normal body temperature and provides a cushion for body structures. Body water is derived from oral fluids (50%); ingested food solids; and oxidation at the cellular level of proteins, fats, and carbohydrates. Water is lost from the body through the kidneys as urine, from the gastrointestinal tract in stool, from the lungs and skin, from the body in drainage from wounds and fistula, and with blood loss.

Good nutrition and adequate hydration have a positive effect on a child's ability to learn (Meyers & Cahwla, 2000). Studies of children with iron deficiency and anemia demonstrate that these deficiencies are associated with poor attention span and cognitive deficits (Halterman, Kaczorowski, Aligne, Auinger, & Szilagyi, 2001). Development of many diseases is related to nutrition and dietary habits. Food consumption patterns are partly the result of parental influence and the environment in which the child lives.

Most children find it difficult to accept a complete change in certain aspects of their lifestyles, particularly in relation to dietary habits. Patterns of food use are based on past experiences and a set of learned behaviors. Many eating behaviors are established early in life and are influenced by the family, the culture, and the social groups to which a person belongs. However, a recent study that examined the similarities between children's and their parents' dietary intakes found that child-parent dietary resemblance in the United States is relatively weak, and varies by nutrients and food groups and by the types of parent-child dyads and social demographic characteristics, such as age, gender, and family income (Beydoun & Wang, 2009). Other factors such as community and school, food environment, peer influence, television viewing, as well as individual factors such as self-image and self-esteem, seem to play an important role.

Biological influences predominate in infancy, with a preference for sweet over bitter or sour; this influence helps to ensure nutritional adequacy through the consumption of breast milk or formula. Thus, human food intake at the beginning of life is at least partially controlled by both biological systems and internal cues. However, as infants mature and begin to eat solid food, parental influence and society factors become increasingly important. Early on, learning processes modify these innate preferences, playing a major role in the development of food preferences and food rejections. Three major processes that modify food acceptance patterns of the child have been identified (Westenhoefer, 2001):

1. *Exposure to unknown food* (i.e., the repeated experience of tasting and eating it) reduces the tendency to reject the unknown food; thus the preference for initially novel food increases with exposure, in children as well as in college students.

2. *Social influences modify food acceptance.* Children learn to prefer food eaten by adults, by their peers, or by fictional heroes in a story. Especially in preschoolers, peer influence may be even more influential than parental influence.

3. *The child learns to associate the physiological consequences of food intake with taste cues from the food.* Eventually, these learning processes result in cognitive structures and processes, such as

attitudes and beliefs about food and eating, which play an important role in the control of food intake in adults.

As the infant matures, feeding becomes associated with human interaction and a means of finding security, comfort, and love. By the time the child reaches preschool age, he or she has developed definite food habits and has learned much about the role that food plays in the family's cultural and socioeconomic environment. School-aged children and adolescents experience increasing choices, pressures, physical changes, and nutritional demands. Some children may learn that food is a reward for good behavior, or that its loss is a consequence of bad behavior.

During adolescence, eating habits are influenced by developmental issues, increasing independence, decreasing acceptance of existing values, need for peer acceptance, and dissatisfaction with body image. Some of these issues contribute to serious eating disorders such as anorexia nervosa and obesity. The social stigma associated with obesity causes stress in many of those affected; but more important, obesity is a health risk.

A child's state of health influences nutritional status, just as nutritional status influences the state of health. For example, an acute, self-limiting illness temporarily increases nutritional requirements, whereas decreased appetite, nausea, or pain can interfere with the child's ability to increase food intake. Chronic diseases and disabilities can affect digestion, caloric requirements, and the destruction and excretion of nutrients. Special therapeutic diets are frequently part of the child's medical management, to prevent further deterioration of nutritional status and to provide energy for health restoration. Adjustments or restrictions of dietary intake are part of the management of several different clinical situations:

1. *Preparation for diagnostic tests.* Dietary restrictions may be necessary to prevent influencing test results.

2. *Presedation or anesthesia.* Food and fluids are restricted so that the stomach is empty. This prevents nausea and vomiting and reduces the risk of aspiration. The child is to receive nothing by mouth (NPO).

3. *Therapeutic diets.* The child who has type 1 diabetes requires insulin and a specifically prescribed diet to control the disease.

4. *Restricted diets.* Children may be restricted from eating certain foods (e.g., food allergy). Children with compromised immune systems (e.g., transplant patients) are restricted from eating certain fruits and vegetables because of possible harmful microorganisms.

5. *Fluid restriction.* In some instances, the child's illness or medication regime requires a limit on the amount of fluid intake. Children with renal or cardiac disease frequently have specific fluid intake and salt restrictions.

6. *Pushing fluids.* In cases of dehydration, where too much fluid is lost from the body (e.g., through vomiting or diarrhea), a child may be asked to drink (or receive through another method) extra fluids to replace those that were lost.

7. *Dietary supplements.* An impaired nutritional state in a child may necessitate supplemental meals or nutritional supplements by intravenous fluids. Children who have difficulty swallowing or absorbing nutrients may receive them by alternative routes (e.g., gastric feeding tubes, intravenous solutions).

When fluid or nutrition restrictions are necessary, it is important to understand the exact limitations for the child, as well as the rationale behind the special orders. In some cases, an exact record of all oral intake is necessary to monitor calories and fluids. Food restrictions are difficult for all ages of children. Diversionary activities are helpful, especially when others are eating. Close supervision is necessary to prevent the child from consuming restricted food and fluids.

Following a Daily Routine

Identifying a daily routine during illness gives the child a sense of consistency and predictability around the events of the day. This is especially true for children with long-term or chronic illnesses. It is important to explain to the child the need to have some flexibility in the schedule, to accommodate tests and procedures that may not be part of the original plan. Forewarning the child of schedule changes and providing adequate preparation promote cooperative behavior.

Hygiene

A clean and well-cared for child typically feels healthier and experiences greater self-esteem (Roberts, 2008). Attending to personal hygiene needs is as important in the hospital as it is at home—and considering infection control, perhaps even more so. Activities such as bathing are frequently part of a child's daily routine. Continuing this practice can help normalize the hospital experience for the child and provide a sense of control.

Good oral hygiene is needed for the development of strong, healthy teeth and to reduce the risk of infection (Johnstone, Spence, & Koziol-McClain, 2010). Oral care is one area of hygiene that frequently is neglected in hospitalized children. In one study, nearly 82% of the children reported no tooth-brushing while in the hospital. In some instances, for example, post bone marrow transplantation, adherence to good oral hygiene habits is a critical element of care, to minimize discomfort and maximize the chances for a successful transplant.

Ambulation

Ambulation is usually a common activity performed every day without much thought. For the sick child who may be weak from the disease process or from medications or surgery, assistance with ambulation may be needed until he or she regains muscle strength, balance, and coordination.

Understanding and using good body mechanics are important when assisting someone to ambulate; implementing an appropriate technique can prevent falls and potential muscle or back strain for the caregiver. That said, in 2009, the federal government passed the *Safe Patient Handling and Injury Prevention Standard*, which calls upon the use of lifting equipment (U.S. Congress, 2009). Safe lifting demonstrates that when a patient or patient limb is greater than 35 pounds, lifting equipment should be used (Waters, 2007). Thus, any child weighing over 35 pounds should be lifted using technology. Ceiling and floor-based lifts are available for healthcare institutions, schools, and homes (Motacki & Motacki, 2009). For children who become easily fatigued but who want and need to participate in diversionary activities, a wheelchair may be necessary.

Activity Goals

Learning About Fluid and Nutrition

Therapeutic play activities that involve learning about food, preparing food, or eating food are enjoyable for most children. Food Paint and ideas listed in the Bright Ideas Box Activity 15.7-1 offer suggestions for addressing this goal. Through such activities, children are given an opportunity to learn more about the nutritional aspects of their illness or disease. In some cases, a child's appetite may be stimulated through play activities involving food, and the opportunity for interaction with other children. Participating in a normal activity such as preparing food can be reassuring and comforting to an anxious, ill child.

A word of caution: Before initiating activities involving food, it is important to carefully check diet orders and inquire about any special precautions. Some medications may not be taken with certain foods, for example. Moreover, in hospital settings, dietary orders can change several times within a few hours.

Increasing Appetite

Aroma Jars is an activity that encourages interest in food through sensory stimulation. Other activities give the child the opportunity to try out new foods, with variations. Food Paint encourages food consumption by capturing the child's interest in an engaging activity.

Following a Daily Routine

Activities such as Daily Schedule and Sticker Chart help to give the child a sense of security and control by informing him or her about what will happen, what he or she is expected to do, and how long the activity will last.

Promoting Hygiene

Bath Fizzers and Clean Cream Finger Paint promote good hygiene.

Encouraging Ambulation

Ambulation requires muscle strength, balance, and coordination; therefore, activities should be selected based on the child's tolerance and energy reserve. Foot Painting can be a good starter activity, leaving others for when the child can be up for extended periods.

ACTIVITY 15.1.   AROMA JARS

Just the aroma of food wafting through the air can be enough to stimulate secretions from the salivary glands in anticipation of eating. Unfortunately, hospital patients rarely benefit from the enticing smells of food, since meals are not prepared in patient care areas. Even the odors of food delivered to patients are often masked by other strong medical smells common in patient care areas.

Therapeutic Goal: To promote activities of daily living by increasing food intake.

Age Group: Preschool/primary

Adult/Child Ratio: 1:1

Required Time: 5–10 minutes

Restrictions and Precautions: Do not use foods that may cause an allergic reaction. Do not conduct this activity with children who are experiencing nausea.

Materials:

☐ Specimen cups or baby food jars

☐ Foods with distinct, appetizing odors, such as:

- Cinnamon rolls
- Cocoa mix
- Mashed ripe bananas
- Bacon
- Orange segments
- Pizza
- Strawberries
- Popcorn

Process

1. Out of sight of the child, place a few tablespoons of each ingredient in a cup or jar.
2. Have the child close his or her eyes and smell each cup, inhaling deeply.
3. Ask the child to try to identify the food he or she smells.
4. Let the child taste the food to see if he or she guessed correctly.

Variation

Use scratch-and-sniff stickers with appealing food scents.

ACTIVITY 15.2.   BATH FIZZERS

Even though they may be too young to participate in making these fizzers, toddlers will be mesmerized when they see the effervescence in their bathwater.

Therapeutic Goal: To promote activities of daily living by encouraging cooperation in daily care routines.

Age Group: Preschool/primary/school-age

Adult/Child Ratio: 1:4

Required Time: 15 minutes, plus drying time

Restrictions and Precautions: None

Materials:

☐ Mixing bowl

☐ Measuring spoon

☐ Measuring cup

☐ Cornstarch

☐ Vitamin C crystals (available at health-food stores)

☐ Food coloring

☐ Fragrance oil, such as lavender or eucalyptus (optional)

☐ Olive or almond oil

☐ Candy molds or mini-ice cube trays, preferably in fun shapes

1. Help the children combine 2 tablespoons cornstarch, 2 tablespoons vitamin C crystals, and 1/4 cup baking soda in the bowl, then slowly pour in 2 tablespoons oil. If desired, let them add a few drops of food coloring and fragrance oil.

2. With either a spoon or their hands, have the children combine the mixture well.

3. Ask the children to press the mixture into the candy molds or ice-cube trays; allow to air-dry for two days.

4. Remove the fizzers from the molds or trays and let the children drop them into their bathwater.

Process

Help adolescents make bath salts by combining in a jar several cups of sea salt, a few drops of aromatic bath oil, and a spoonful or two of dried fragrant plants, such as rose or sage. Encourage the teens to add several tablespoons of the mixture to their bathwater and enjoy a relaxing soak.

Variation

ACTIVITY 15.3.   CHUG-IT CHALLENGE

This activity is very funny to both watch and do, making humor an additional potential benefit. An adult can play with the child if another child is not available to do so.

Therapeutic Goal: To promote activities of daily living by increasing fluid intake.	**Materials:**
Age Group: Primary/school-age	☐ Water or other clear liquid beverage such as 7-Up
Adult/Child Ratio: 1:2	☐ Plastic cups
Required Time: 5 minutes	☐ Basins
Restrictions and Precautions: None	

1. Position the basin on a table, to catch spills.

2. Fill two cups with equal amounts of the beverage.

3. Explain the rule first, that the water must be drunk from the edge of the cup furthest away from them; then challenge the children to see who can drink all of the fluid in their cup without spilling (or spilling the least).

4. Emphasize that this is not a race, but a competition based on skill.

Process

ACTIVITY 15.4.   CLEAN CREAM FINGER PAINT

This is an easy, fun, and effective way to entice children, who would benefit from an extended soak, to spend more time in the tub.

Therapeutic Goal: To promote activities of daily living by encouraging cooperation in daily care routines.	**Materials:**
Age Group: Preschool/primary	☐ Muffin tin
Adult/Child Ratio: 1:1	☐ Unscented shaving cream for sensitive skin
Required Time: 5 minutes, to prepare paint	☐ Food coloring
Restrictions and Precautions: Do not allow child to eat the "paint."	☐ Tongue depressors and/or small sponges

Process

1. Drop a dollop of shaving cream into the muffin tin, one for each color paint you wish to make.

2. Add two to three drops of food coloring to each dollop and stir with the tongue depressor.

3. Position the paint within easy reach of the bathtub and encourage the children to dip their hands, tongue depressors, or small sponges into the paints and create designs or pictures on the walls and tub.

4. Rinse away the paint when cleaning the tub.

ACTIVITY 15.5.   DAILY SCHEDULE

The structure and visual cues provided by daily schedules are especially beneficial to children with traumatic brain injuries and autism. Daily schedules are helpful to staff, as well, to remind them of each child's routine.

Therapeutic Goal: To promote activities of daily living by encouraging cooperation in daily care routines and providing predictability and structure.

Age Group: All ages, including infants

Adult/Child Ratio: 1:1

Required Time: 30–60 minutes

Restrictions and Precautions: None

Materials:

☐ Poster board

☐ Markers

☐ Boardmaker software (hand-drawn pictures or images cut from magazines are also fine)

☐ Scissors

☐ Glue stick

☐ Clock

☐ Post-It Notes (preferably in one of the fun shapes available)

Process

1. Confer with the child, nurse, family, and other members of the child's healthcare team to determine how the child's day will be structured.

2. Make two columns on the poster board and label them: Time (left-hand column) and Activity (right-hand column). For prereaders, leave space for clock templates and pictures.

3. Preferably together with the child or parent(s), in the Time column write down each time slot. For prereaders, draw a clock next to the written time to show the corresponding time. Use the moon and sun to indicate day or night.

4. In the Activity column, list the activity next to the corresponding time. If appropriate for the child, include breakfast, lunch, dinner, bathing, rest or nap, bedtime, therapies, medications, play time, visiting, homework, and any other predictable events that will occur.

5. Print from Boardmaker, cut from magazines, or simply draw a representative picture next to each activity (or let the child do so, if he or she is able).

6. Hang the schedule where the child can see it, and give him or her a clock.

7. Use Post-It notes to add or obscure an activity that causes a change in the schedule on a particular day.

For more ideas, see Bright Ideas for Activities of Daily Living (Box Activity 15.5-1).

BOX ACTIVITY 15.5-1. BRIGHT IDEAS FOR ACTIVITIES OF DAILY LIVING

- Give children plaque-disclosing tablets to determine how well they're brushing their teeth; encourage them to do a better job, if necessary.

- Make bathtime finger puppets by cutting the fingers off rubber gloves and using waterproof markers to add facial features and other details.

- Sew a simple puppet from two washcloths, to use while bathing (see Activity 2.6 for template).
- Encourage ambulation by using an electronic piano mat that plays different notes when the child steps on the various keys.
- Make a sampler of fun bandage choices and let children select which one they want.
- Use "twisty straws" to encourage increased fluid intake.
- Put "googly eyes" or stickers on breathing masks, flovent inhalers, and other equipment, to disguise their threatening appearance.
- Read stories to children during chest percussion, or while they are receiving nebulizer treatments.
- Create fun rituals for treatment times or immediately after, such as singing a song, giving a standing ovation, or slapping a "high five."
- Give flashlight puppets to children experiencing night terrors.
- Conduct a treasure hunt to increase ambulation.

ACTIVITY 15.6.   FLAVORED LIP GLOSS

Hospitals routinely use petroleum jelly to ease the discomfort of cracked, dry lips. Although lip gloss is widely available commercially, this activity gives children the opportunity to make their own, in many choices.

Therapeutic Goal: To promote activities of daily living by encouraging cooperation in daily care routines.

Age Group: Preschool/school-age/adolescent

Adult/Child Ratio: 1:1

Required Time: 5 minutes, plus cooling time

Restrictions and Precautions: None

Materials:

- ☐ Petroleum jelly
- ☐ Measuring spoons
- ☐ Microwave-safe measuring cup
- ☐ Tongue depressor
- ☐ Fruit-flavored powdered drink mix (avoid citrus flavors)
- ☐ Small, clean plastic container with lid, such as a pill bottle or 35mm film container

Process

1. Place 2 tablespoons petroleum jelly into the measuring cup and microwave until liquefied (1 to 2 minutes).

2. Allow to cool slightly, then use the tongue depressor to stir in the powdered drink mix.

3. Pour the mixture into the container and refrigerate for 30 minutes or until firm.

ACTIVITY 15.7.   FOOD PAINT

In addition to being creative and fun, this activity is successful with children because it gives them a sense of control, by allowing them to select and prepare their own food.

Therapeutic Goal: To promote activities of daily living by increasing food intake.

Age Group: Preschool/primary

Adult/Child Ratio: 1:10

Required Time: 20 minutes

Restrictions and Precautions: Screen children for lactose, gluten, or other food allergies.

Materials:

- ☐ Medicine cups or other small cups or shallow bowls

☐ Milk (1–2 tablespoons per child)		☐ Light-colored bread	
☐ Food coloring		☐ Toaster	
☐ New, clean, thin paintbrushes		☐ Assorted sandwich ingredients	

Process

1. Pour 1 to 2 tablespoons of milk into each of the medicine cups.

2. Add several drops of food coloring to each cup.

3. Let the children paint pictures or designs on the bread.

4. Toast the bread lightly.

5. Help the children prepare a sandwich of their liking using the special bread they made.

For more ideas, see Bright Ideas: Fun Things to Do with Foods That Just Might Get Children to Eat (Box Activity 15.7-1).

BOX ACTIVITY 15.7-1. BRIGHT IDEAS: FUN THINGS TO DO WITH FOODS THAT JUST MIGHT GET CHILDREN TO EAT (ESPECIALLY IF THEY HELP MAKE IT)

- Read Eric Carle's book, *The Hungry Caterpillar*. Then make a caterpillar by cutting a banana into 8 slices. Spread each slice with peanut butter sweetened with a drop of honey; press the slices together. Use thin pretzels to make the legs and antennae. For eyes, attach raisins with a dab of peanut butter.

- Send the children fishing in a pond (blue paper plate) of Goldfish crackers. For a fishing rod, place a dab of cream cheese on the end of a long, thin pretzel (Figure Box Activity 15.7-1).

Figure Box Activity 15.7-1. Fun Things to Do with Food

- Make a fruit pizza: First, add a small amount of honey and peanut butter to softened cream cheese, then spread the mixture onto small, pocketless pita bread rounds, and top with sliced fruit.

- Provide opportunities to make choices by setting up a taco bar, salad bar, or an ice cream bar, complete with fresh-fruit toppings.

- Make edible aquariums by placing grapes (for aquarium gravel) on the bottom of clear plastic cups or a small fish bowl. For water, add partially set blue gelatin to the cups or bowl. Add several gummy fish to the "water" to complete the creation (Figure Box Activity 15.7-1).

- Make "ants on a log" by spreading celery sticks with peanut butter, sprinkled with raisins.

- Create necklaces by stringing Cheerios or other ring-shaped cereal on clean IV tubing or licorice strings, then let the children eat them off.

- Turn popcorn balls into "baseballs" using licorice strings for lacing.

- Make a puppy's head: First cut a pear in half vertically then place it cut side down on a plate. For eyes, hollow out two holes and insert blueberries or raisins. Use a halved strawberry to make ears, and a slice of another strawberry to make a tongue.

- Make edible "dirt" by placing chocolate pudding in a clear bowl, clear plastic cup, or a small, new toy pail. Sprinkle with crumbled chocolate cookies, and add a few gummy worms. Complete the theme by serving the "dirt" using a new toy shovel. (Figure Box Activity 15.7-1).

ACTIVITY 15.8.   FOOT PAINTING

Lively music can be very effective in energizing children. However, it is not always the best choice. Music should be selected with consideration of children's mood, energy level, physical status, and treatment goals.

Therapeutic Goal: To promote activities of daily living by encouraging ambulation.

Age Group: Toddler/preschool/primary

Adult/Child Ratio: Varies with age, number, and physical status of participants.

Required Time: 30 minutes

Restrictions and Precautions: Assess children for fall risk and take appropriate precautions.

Materials:

- ☐ Large basins filled with 2-inches of water
- ☐ Tempera paint
- ☐ Paint stirrer or other mixing tool
- ☐ Roll of butcher paper
- ☐ Tape
- ☐ Brayer or clean, large paint brush (optional)
- ☐ CD player and assortment of music CDs
- ☐ Towels
- ☐ Soap
- ☐ Large basin filled with warm water

Process

1. Add tempera paint to each basin of water until it is the consistency of milk.
2. Tape one 8-foot long sheet of butcher paper to the floor for each child and place a basin of paint at one end.
3. Start the music and help the children place their feet in a basin of paint or use a clean, large paint brush or brayer to apply paint directly to the children's feet.
4. Encourage the children to create designs on the butcher paper by walking or dancing on it. (Figure Activity 15.8-1)

Figure Activity 15.8-1. Foot Painting

5. To extend the children's interest, repeat using different colored paint.

6. Wash the children's feet when the activity is finished.

Variations   If foot painting is not practicable, encourage ambulation by using purchased play materials such as pull toys or electronic piano keyboard mats. Make simple pull toys by decorating cardboard boxes as animals and attaching a string.

ACTIVITY 15.9.   JUICE BOX BOAT

The key here is to get the child curious and excited to see the toy you are going to make.

Therapeutic Goal: To promote activities of daily living by encouraging cooperation in daily care routines.

Age Group: Preschool/primary

Adult/Child Ratio: 1:1

Required Time: 20 minutes

Restrictions and Precautions: Take scissors precautions.

Materials:

☐ Juice, in unopened individual-size box containers (ideally, offer several flavors for the child to choose from)

☐ Scissors

☐ Straw

☐ Cardstock, cut into a 2-inch triangle

☐ Crayons

☐ Hole punch

Process

1. Explain to the child that you can help him or her make a fun toy from an empty juice box.

2. Tell the child that he or she will first need to drink all of the juice in a box so that you can use the empty container to make the toy.

3. Invite the child to select a juice and drink it, so that you can start the project.

4. When the juice has been consumed, rinse out the box and lay it flat on its widest plane.

5. Use the scissors to cut a small "X" in the center of the side facing up.

6. Ask the child decorate the triangle with crayons, explaining that it will be used to make a sail for a boat.

7. Punch a hole at the top and bottom of the triangle.

8. Thread the straw through the holes in the sail and insert it into the "X" you have cut.

9. Let the child use the boat during bathtime or water play.

ACTIVITY 15.10.   MAGIC POTION PUNCH

This beverage fizzes, and the melting ice creates pretty swirls of color, which may help entice even a reluctant child, especially one restricted to a clear liquid diet, to drink more.

Therapeutic Goal: To promote activities of daily living by increasing fluid intake.

Age Group: Preschool/primary

Adult/Child Ratio: 1:3

Required Time: 15 minutes, plus advance preparation

Restrictions and Precautions: None

Materials:

☐ Two 3-ounce envelopes unsweetened powdered drink mix (different colors)

☐ 3 cups

☐ Ice-cube trays (unusual shapes, if available)

☐ Clear plastic cups or plastic stemware

☐ Craft plastic jewels (peel-and-stick preferred)

☐ Clear carbonated soda (e.g., ginger ale, lemon-lime soda, tonic water)

Process

1. Well in advance of the activity, combine each envelope of drink mix with 1 – 1/2 cups of water.

2. Pour into ice-cube trays and freeze until solid.

3. Let the children decorate their cups with the craft jewels.

4. Invite the children to select the color ice cube they would like, and add it to their glass.

5. Pour in the carbonated soda — slowly — and encourage the children to drink up.

ACTIVITY 15.11.   SOAP SURPRISES

This is a fun, tactile activity that usually excites children. The toy inside provides an incentive for them to lather the soap vigorously — even those who are not especially fond of bathing. Children who are unable to participate in making the soap will still enjoy using the finished product.

Therapeutic Goal: To promote activities of daily living by encouraging good hygiene.

Age Group: Preschool/primary

Adult/Child Ratio: 1:4

Required Time: 30 minutes plus drying time

Restrictions and Precautions: With children under 4, only use toys they cannot choke on.

Materials:

☐ Food coloring

☐ Food extract (e.g., almond, vanilla, coconut) or perfume

☐ 1/2 cup water

☐ 4 small bowls

☐ 4 cups Ivory Soap flakes

☐ Tongue depressor

☐ Small rubber toys or animals (one per child)

Process

1. In individual bowls, combine the water with a drop each of food coloring and extract.

2. Help the children add 1 cup of soap flakes.

3. Have the children use their hands to mix the ingredients together until it stiffens.

4. Help the children shape the soap into balls large enough to encompass the rubber toys that will be added.

5. Explain to the children that the soap needs to dry overnight.

6. Out of sight of the children, use the tongue depressor to make a hole in the center of each ball and insert a toy.

7. Fill the hole with extra soap.

8. Let the soap to dry overnight.

9. When you are together again with the children, tell them that there is now a surprise inside their soap balls and that they will have to keep using it every day until the surprise is revealed. Give the children the soap to use for bathing.

ACTIVITY 15.12.   SCENTED SOAP

Although it is not necessary to use scent or other special ingredients to make this soap, they do add interest and enhance the sensory experience.

Therapeutic Goal: To promote activities of daily living by encouraging good hygiene and providing sensory stimulation.

Age Group: School-age/adolescent

Adult/Child Ratio: 1:2

Required Time: 20 minutes, plus cooling time

Restrictions and Precautions: Closely supervise the children when they are using the knife and handling hot melted soap. And, note, a loofah is a natural product that can scratch or irritate the skin, so omit it with children who have skin problems.

Materials:

☐ Clear, glycerin-based melt-and-pour soap base (available at craft stores)

☐ Microwave-safe liquid measuring cup

☐ Microwave

☐ Tongue depressor

☐ Scented oil, oatmeal, and/or flower petals (optional)

☐ Food coloring or colorants made specifically for soap making, available at craft stores (optional)

☐ Soap molds, or loaf pans lined with foil

☐ Loofah sponge, piece small enough to fit in mold (optional)

☐ Serrated knife

Process

1. Supervise the children as they place chunks of soap base into the microwave-safe container and heat for 40 seconds. Then have them stir it *gently* with a tongue depressor. If the soap has not completely melted, microwave again for 10-second intervals until it has.

2. Invite the children to stir in a few drops of color and/or fragrance, oatmeal, and/or flower petals, if desired.

3. Help the children fill each mold halfway with melted soap.

4. If using a loofah, have the children add it carefully to the molds. Immediately thereafter, help the children pour the remaining soap into the molds until it is fully absorbed by the loofah. (Note: The loofah will stick out slightly.)

5. Allow the soap to cool until it is set and dry (approximately 1 hour); gently remove it from the molds.

6. Help the children cut the soap into slices.

ACTIVITY 15.13.   STICKER CHART

For some children, the motivational power of a simple sticker can be significant. This is classic behavior modification and can be a very effective intervention to help young, short-term patients in a crisis situation. However, sticker charts and other similar reward systems are not recommended for long-term and chronic patients, as the motivational power of any reward will soon diminish. More importantly, these children need to develop intrinsic motivation, as the new behaviors they are learning may need to become part of daily routines for the rest of their lives.

Therapeutic Goal: To promote activities of daily living by encouraging cooperation in daily care routines.

Age Group: Preschool/young school age

Adult/Child Ratio: 1:1

Required Time: 30 minutes

Restrictions and Precautions: Make sure the chart is used consistently by all caretakers.

Materials:

☐ Large piece of white or light-colored poster board

☐ Pictures printed from the Boardmaker computer program, downloaded from the Internet, or cut from magazines

☐ Scissors

☐ Glue

☐ Markers

☐ Tape

☐ Assorted stickers or gummed stars

1. Assemble pictures that represent daily care activities or behaviors to be included on the chart (e.g., smiling face showing teeth; or a toothbrush, to illustrate brushing teeth). Try to find at least two pictures representing each activity so that children can choose the one they prefer.

2. Draw a grid comprising a row for each picture and a column for each day of the week. Write the corresponding day of the week above each column.

3. If possible, include the child at this point. Explain that he or she will be awarded a point or sticker for each accomplishment or positive behavior. Invite the child to participate in creating the chart.

4. Ask the child to select the pictures that will represent each activity or behavior to be included on the chart. While doing this, explain the rationale behind each behavior and identify something tangible that will occur when the goals are accomplished.

5. Help the child glue on the pictures, vertically down the left side of the poster board.

6. Write the child's name in bold letters across the top of the chart.

7. Display the chart in a prominent place.

8. Each time the child completes a daily care activity, give praise and allow him or her to select a sticker to place next to the appropriate picture on the chart.

9. As an added incentive, give a prize when the child has earned a previously determined number of stickers.

ACTIVITY 15.14.   TOOTHSOME TOOTHPASTE

Children love to use things they have made themselves. Making their own toothpaste allows children to experiment with different flavors and gives them a sense of control. This activity is especially helpful for those children who don't like the common mint flavor used in most commercial brands.

Therapeutic Goal: To promote activities of daily living by encouraging cooperation in daily care and routines.

Age Group: Preschool/primary

Adult/Child Ratio: 1:5

Required Time: 20 Minutes

Restrictions and Precautions: Supervise children to make sure they don't add too much water or extract, which will make the mixture runny and/or taste awful.

Materials:
- ☐ Small bowls (one per child)
- ☐ Tongue depressors (or spoons)
- ☐ 4 teaspoons baking soda
- ☐ 1 teaspoon salt
- ☐ Medicine dropper
- ☐ 1 drop food extract (mint, orange, lemon, vanilla, etc.)
- ☐ 1 teaspoon water (or less)
- ☐ Specimen cups or 1/2-pint plastic zip-lock bags

1. Divide the ingredients equally among the number of children participating in the activity and put them in a small bowl.

2. Help the children use the medicine dropper to add the extract. Avoid adding too much.

3. Give the children the tongue depressors to blend the mixture well.

4. Add enough water to make a thick paste.

5. Store the toothpaste in specimen cups or plastic bags and use as needed.

ACTIVITY 15.15.   YELLOW + RED = ORANGE

The visible change in this mixture is a helpful reinforcement for some learners.

Therapeutic Goal: To promote activities of daily living by encouraging self-efficacy in diabetic patients.

Age Group: School-age/adolescent

Adult/Child Ratio: 1:1

Required Time: 20 minutes per session; may require several sessions

Restrictions and Precautions: Do not leave needles or vials at the child's bedside unattended. Dispose of used needles properly.

Materials:

☐ Insulin syringe

☐ 2 vials sterile water

☐ Yellow and red food coloring

Process

1. Determine the amount of insulin to be drawn.

2. Using the syringe, inject a small amount of yellow food coloring into one vial of sterile water, and a small amount of red food coloring into the second vial.

3. Give the child the red and yellow vials of sterile water. Explain that they represent two types of insulin and that he or she is going to practice drawing insulin into the syringe.

4. Instruct the child to draw a specified amount of yellow water into the syringe, followed by a specified amount of red water into the same syringe.

5. Instruct the child to shake the syringe to mix the water, pointing out the change in color.

6. Explain that there are two types of insulin, just as there are two colors of water in the syringe. To achieve the color of orange needed, the correct amounts of red and yellow must be mixed.

For more ideas, see Bright Ideas: Just a Spoonful of Sugar (Box Activity 15.15-1).

BOX ACTIVITY 15.15-1. BRIGHT IDEAS: JUST A SPOONFUL OF SUGAR—HELPING CHILDREN TAKE MEDICINE

Always check dietary restrictions before using any of the food items suggested in this activity.

1. To disguise the taste of liquid medicine:

   - Numb children's taste buds by having them suck on their favorite-flavor Popsicle before giving the medicine.

   - Chill the medicine itself, to mask the taste.

   - Mix the medicine with a pleasant-tasting, concentrated flavor, such as a powdered drink mix, pancake syrup, honey, chocolate syrup, or syrups used to flavor coffees. Let the child choose which flavor to add.

   - Prior to giving the medicine, coat the child's tongue with peanut butter, flavored with a little honey or agave syrup.

   - Let the child select a juice to use as a "chaser" after swallowing the medicine.

   - Combine Crystal Light with barium.

2. To give crushed or powdered medicines:

   - Crush pills with a pill crusher or between two spoons, then mix it with a food the child likes and that doesn't require chewing (e.g., apple sauce, pudding, yogurt, or flavored oatmeal). Let the child practice swallowing the food without chewing prior to adding the medicine.

   - Mix the crushed pill with frozen juice concentrate, such as apple or raspberry. Both the cold temperature and the flavor will help mask the taste.

3. To overcome the challenge of swallowing pills and capsules:

- Chop the pills into halves or quarters.

- Press the pill into gelatin, ice cream, or a sliced canned peach, and encourage the child to let it slide down his or her throat.

- Microwave a Starburst Fruit Chews for about 10 seconds and roll it into a ball around the pill.

- Hide a pill inside a JELL-O JIGGLERS (recipe can be downloaded from the Internet).

- Allow children over 8 who are unable to swallow pills to practice with small candies such as M&M's, Skittles, or Tic Tacs.

- Insert a small pill into a soft chocolate-covered mint or truffle.

- Briefly dip a gel cap in ice water to make the coating slippery and easier to swallow.

- Freeze pills completely and coat them with Magic Shell, a syrup that hardens on contact with frozen foods, to form a candylike coating.

- Wet a small piece of a Fruit Roll-Up and wrap it around the pill prior to giving to the child to swallow.

Note. Adapted from: Pediatric Advisor. (2009). *Helping children swallow medicines.* Retrieved from www.med.umich.edu/1libr/pa/pa_swallmed_hhg.htm. Pediatric Oncology Resource Center. *How to get kids to take ....pills!* Retrieved from www.acor.org/ped-onc/treatment/pills/pills.html.

CHAPTER 16

PERCEPTUAL MOTOR

Regardless of the diagnosis, the presence of a perceptual-motor disability imposes additional challenges for the child and parents. The impact of a perceptual-motor dysfunction on a child's social, emotional, and cognitive development differs considerably, depending on the child's age at onset, the constraints imposed by the condition at each phase of the child's development, the child's psychological resiliency, the natural history and prognosis of the illness, the necessity for physical care, and the degree to which the illness or disability is visible.

LIST OF ACTIVITIES

This chapter provides information to enable individuals involved in planning therapeutic activities for children with perceptual-motor dysfunctions to develop effective plans for helping these children and their families. Children with perceptual-motor disabilities have the same needs and developmental concerns as other children. They have hobbies, favorite sports teams, classes, and friends. Activities suggested in this chapter support the individual child's level of perceptual-motor ability. Additionally, the activities can be used to challenge some children to develop or relearn a skill.

The Importance of Sensory Information

A child's brain needs sensory stimulation to function properly. As we know, children's typical growth and development follow a sequence of events. According to Piaget (1952), children's best learning occurs in conjunction with hands-on, interactive play and self-discovery, rather than when adults try to simply impart knowledge to them. Passing through each developmental stage, children interact with their environment, which provides the sensory stimulation to which they adapt and grow.

It is believed that humankind's natural curiosity is essential to the survival not only of the individual but also of the species (Reio, Petrosko, Wiswell, & Thongsukmag, 2006). Curiosity fosters cognitive, social, emotional, spiritual, and physical development over the life span by stimulating exploratory behavior. Curiosity can be broadly defined as a desire to acquire new knowledge and new sensory experiences, which motivates exploratory behavior (Litman & Spielberger, 2003). There are at least two distinct types of curiosity: (a) information seeking, or cognitive curiosity, which stimulates information-seeking, exploratory behavior; and (b) sensory curiosity, which stimulates sensation-seeking, exploratory behavior. Piaget (1952) believed that active curiosity is a prerequisite for the construction of knowledge because it motivates the acquisition of new information and the seeking of new stimuli, and referred to both the cognitive and sensory types of curiosity. He maintained that experiences gained through the information-seeking and sensory types of curiosity and exploratory behavior promoted cognitive development through the construction of new knowledge.

Learning is dependent on the ability of children to take in sensory information derived from the environment and from movement of their bodies, to process and integrate these sensory inputs within the central nervous system, and to use this sensory information to plan and produce organized behavior. Sensory integration refers to a neurological process that enables the individual to take in, interpret, integrate, and use the spatial-temporal aspects of sensory information from the body and the environment to plan and produce organized motor behavior (Bumin & Kayihan, 2001). As a theory of brain-behavior relationship, difficulties with this process may result in perceptual and motor-learning deficits.

Perceptual-Motor Delay or Disability

A cognitive-perceptual-motor dysfunction is the inability to adapt and to integrate environmental experiences (Gilfoyle & Grady, 1971). In children with this condition, the nervous system does not assimilate sensory stimuli, thus the body cannot direct or sustain appropriate and effective motor accommodations. This results, instead, with isolated schemas and insufficient sensory-motor integration, which, in turn leads to inaccurate adaptations and a failure to provide sound information for the formation of cognitive structures.

Children with perceptual-motor delay or disability demonstrate a deficit beyond normal variability for age and experience in coordination, movement patterns, quality, or range of motion or strength and endurance of gross (large muscle), fine (small muscle), or perceptual motor (integration of sensory and motor) abilities, which adversely affects their ability to learn or acquire skills relative to one or more of the following (New York State Education Department, 2003):

- Maintaining or controlling posture
- Functional mobility (e.g., walking, running)
- Sensory awareness of the body or movement
- Sensory-integration
- Reach and/or grasp of objects
- Tool use
- Perceptual motor abilities (e.g., eye-hand coordination for tracing)
- Sequencing motor components to achieve a functional goal

A variety of conditions place children at risk for perceptual motor dysfunction. Some of the more common conditions are described in the following sections.

Infants with Very Low Birthweight

Advanced technology and care has resulted in the survival of increasing numbers of infants with very low birthweight (VLBW = <1,500 grams); however, developmental morbidity associated with this trend persists (Campbell, Kolobe, Wright, & Linacre, 2002). Children especially likely to have poor motor outcomes that do not show recovery after infancy are infants with extremely low birthweight (McCormick, McCarton, Tonascia, & Brooks-Gunn, 1993), infants with chronic lung disease (Majnemer et al., 2000), and infants with central nervous system (CNS) insults (Pinto-Martin, Whitaker, Feldman, Van Rossem, & Paneth, 2000).

Developmental Motor Disorders

There are two major forms of developmental motor disorders: cerebral palsy (CP) and developmental coordination disorder (DCD). With both CP and DCD, children differ in the expression of their motor dysfunction, in comorbidity such as the presence of cognitive and behavioral disorders, and in etiology.

Children with Cerebral Palsy. CP, a disorder of movement and posture, results from an insult or anomaly to the immature central nervous system that affects about 1 in 500 live-born children (Hagberg, Hagberg, Olow, & Von Wendt, 1996). The disorder is commonly associated with a spectrum of developmental disabilities, including intellectual disabilities; epilepsy; and visual, hearing, speech, cognitive, and sensory-perceptual problems. Sensory integrative dysfunction may be the result of neurological dysfunction within the brainstem, or limited sensory experience from lack of normal motor control. Sensory-perceptual problems include

- impairment of body image,
- right-left discrimination,
- position in space,
- visual perception,
- finger agnosi (the inability to distinguish the fingers on the hand),
- astereognosis (the inability to identify an object by touch without visual input), and
- apraxia (loss of the ability to execute or carry out learned purposeful movements, despite having the desire and the physical ability to perform the movements).

Some children with cerebral palsy have abnormalities of the eye, such as cataracts, chorioretinitis, retinopathy, macular colobomata, or optic atrophy. These disorders may share the same etiological factors as the motor impairment itself (e.g., infection, congenital disorders), but are not frequent in cerebral palsy. Visual impairment in children with cerebral palsy more often is due to lesions in the retrochiasmatic visual pathway and other cerebral areas involved in perception and processing of visual stimuli (Guzzetta, Cioni, Cowan, & Mercuri, 2001). This condition, described as cerebral visual impairment, may include poor visual acuity, reduction in visual fields, disorders of eye movement, strabismus, and complex visual-perceptual defects.

Children with mild to moderate forms of CP often benefit from active practice. This is usually accompanied by a mixture of the application of handling techniques and an encouragement of active movement (Hadders-Algra, 2000).

Developmental Coordination Disorder (DCD). Previously referred to by the pejorative term "clumsy children," children who have such poor motor coordination that it affects their daily activities at home and at school, but with normal intelligence and without obvious neurological pathology, are said to have a developmental coordination disorder (American Psychiatric Association, 1994). The prevalence of DCD is reported to be about 10% of children (Hadders-Algra, 2000). Treatment typically includes perceptual-motor training, sensory integration, and kinesthetic training. Research reveals that DCD can have a negative impact on children's self-efficacy, and limit their performance and participation in school, as well as in leisure activities performed after school hours (Engel-Yeger & Kasis, 2010).

Children Treated for Cancer or Hematologic Disorders

Treatments such as pediatric blood transplant protocols are aggressive yet life-saving procedures for children diagnosed with some cancers, or blood or metabolic disorders, but may result in changes in cognitive, educational, and visual motor integration. Barrera, Atenafu, Andrews, and Saunders (2008) found that perceptual motor scores and arithmetic scores of children at two years post hematopoietic stem cell transplant were significantly below the population norms. They report this finding as consistent with previously reported deficits in arithmetic in survivors of leukemia or central nervous system tumors (Barrera, Shaw, Speechley, Maunsell, & Pogany, 2005; Kaemingk, Carey, Moore, Herzer, & Hutter, 2004). Because numerical operations and perceptual motor skills typically are learned in the first years of school, they form the basis for more complex learning of mathematics and writing.

Children Who Have Had Strokes

Although the incidence of stroke in childhood is relatively low—1.3 to 13 per 100,000 children per year—(Lynch, 2004), stroke is one of the top 10 causes of death in children (*Children and Stroke,* 2006). Slightly more common in children under 2 years, about one third of strokes occur in newborns. Stroke in childhood is typically caused by birth defects, infections (e.g., meningitis, encephalitis), trauma, and blood disorders such as sickle cell disease. After a stroke, children often have problems with speech and communication (aphasia and dysphagia), as well as visual problems such as trouble with visual perception. Further, there are stroke-related disabilities that are unique to children, such as cerebral palsy and epilepsy.

Children with Traumatic Brain Injury and Brain Lesions

Traumatic brain injury (TBI), described in the Introduction, is the most common cause of death and disability for children and adolescents in America (Centers for Disease Control and Prevention [CDC], 2000). Babikian and Asarnow (2009) conducted a meta-analysis on 28 carefully selected articles on TBI and found that the worse the injury, the worse the neurocognitive outcome, especially on measures of general intellectual functioning and processing speed. They reported that general intellectual functioning and attention/executive skills were similar for both the moderate and severe groups at 24 months postinjury. After two years, problems persisted for many children with moderate TBI despite previous improvement in intellectual functioning, attention, and weakness. The good news was that memory and visual-spatial skills seemed more or less normal by two-plus years, with even the moderately injured performing in the same range as controls.

However, children with severe TBI needed more help, showing robust and significant problems on IQ, executive functioning (processing speed, attention), and verbal memory (both immediate and delayed). The authors concluded that there are significant, persistent neurocognitive impairments in a subset of children with severe TBI. Children in this group not only failed to catch up to peers, but seemed to fall further behind over time, suggesting that severe traumatic brain injury may throw off children's normal developmental timetable. Babikian and Asarnow (2009) noted that severe brain injuries at younger ages poses a double hazard because younger children have more development ahead of them.

According to Guzzetta et al. (2001), visual abnormalities are frequent in children with brain lesions of antenatal and perinatal onset, but the association does not always follow the rules observed in adults. Visual abnormalities tend to be more frequent in full-term infants with hypoxic-ischemic encephalopathy than in preterm infants. Although lesions in preterm infants of the occipital visual cortex are generally associated with impaired visual function, in full-term infants both unilateral and bilateral occipital lesions are often associated with normal vision, probably explained by the difference in type and site of lesions.

Some infants show transient visual impairment, with gradual recovery, often within the first months after birth (Groenendaal & van Hof-van Duin, 1992). Even some infants with a normal ophthalmological examination may have abnormal visual function. Cioni, Fazzi, Ipata, Canapicchi, & van Hof-van Duin (1996) explain that visual attention, and more generally visual function, may also be disturbed by other clinical problems often occurring in children with brain lesions, such as severe oculomotor impairment or severe epilepsy.

Children Who Are Obese

Stable postural orientation is a requisite for many daily activities, including accurate upper-limb movements. Research indicates that being overweight or obese is detrimental for fine motor skill performance in two different postural conditions: sitting and standing in tandem stance on a balance beam (D'Hondt, Deforche, De Bourdeaudhuij, & Lenoir, 2008). Although investigators reasoned that this could result from the mechanical demands related to the movement of the arm itself, they believe that findings suggest that children who are obese might also have underlying perceptual-motor coordination difficulties.

Children with Hearing and Visual Disorders

The child's ability to process sensory input is influenced by the level of functioning of his or her sensory organs. Much of the sensory data a child uses to interpret the world is visual and auditory. Thus, it is not surprising that children with visual or hearing disorders may have perceptual motor difficulties. A child who is deaf or blind has an important avenue for receiving information blocked.

Ittyerah and Sharma (1997) reported that children with hearing loss were less coordinated and more accident prone than children without hearing loss. Their findings suggest that children with impaired hearing differ from those with normal hearing in the performance of tasks that are influenced by language processes and motor ability.

In a longitudinal study that followed 10 children who were blind from birth, 5 of the children at age 3 years showed major delays in all areas of gross-motor development that increased with age (Troster, 1994). However, even less severe conditions have serious implications. For example, strabismus (where the child's eyes are misaligned), one of the most common visual disorders in infancy, has been shown to affect perceptual-motor and motor function (Caputo et al., 2007).

Sensory Integration Dysfunction

Sensory integration dysfunction (SID) is a neurological disorder described by A. Jean Ayres, PhD, OTR, who developed the sensory integration theory to explain the relationship between behavior and brain functioning (Ayres, 1994). We commonly speak of five senses—touch, taste, smell, hearing, and vision—which respond to external stimuli from the environment. In sensory integration theory, we also speak of other senses, some internal and some external, such as the sense of well-being.

The feelings, thoughts, and actions children experience occur through the complex actions of their brains. How they process environmental and internal information has a major impact on their feelings, thoughts, and actions. The slightest change in their brain processes can influence how children manage daily living skills, academic progress, and social interaction.

Sensory integration dysfunction or disorder (SID) is but one example of what can go wrong in the processes of the brain (Ayres, 1994). Approximately 1 in 6 children experiences symptoms of sensory processing disorder that are significant enough to affect their ability to participate fully in everyday life (Sensory Processing Disorder Foundation, n.d.). Children may have difficulty with underprocessing, overprocessing, or processing with interference/"white noise." Although the cause of SID is unclear, it is believed to be likely the result of both genetics and environment (Miller, 2006).

Because of the complexity of the various areas that are dependent on and interact with each other, as well as the child's own personality and environment, it is impossible to produce a single list of symptoms that identify sensory integrative dysfunction. Nevertheless, Table 16.1 includes a sampling of some of the most commonly observed symptoms of sensory integration dysfunction.

Special Considerations

The nature of a child's perceptual motor and related disorders often requires the services of a physical or occupational therapist. The expertise of the physical or occupational therapist can be critical in developing and delivering an effective plan of care.

The child's developmental level is the starting point for selection of appropriate activities. Clear, simple directions and adequate supervision are necessary for activities involving the child with a developmental disability or delay.

A child with a deficit in motor skills may be at increased risk for accidental injury. Lack of motor control may make children unable to protect themselves against falling from a bed or chair. During activities, children must be positioned appropriately, and postural supports used to maintain body alignment. Safety restraints must always be used for children who use wheelchairs.

Activities may be limited for children with seizure disorders, or a protective helmet may be used. Sometimes, fear of falls can result in children being overprotected, and families and staff having low expectations. Children with atonic seizures, which involve a sudden loss of tone and consciousness, and last only a few seconds without respiratory compromise, are at extremely high risk for falls and resulting injury because of the clinical presentation of their seizure (Yamamoto, Olaes, & Lopez, 2004).

The inherent risk for falls is greater for children in the hospital environment than in the home, due to physiologic factors, medications, toileting needs, and use of equipment (Child Health Corporation of America Nursing Falls Study Task Force, 2009). The Joint Commission

Table 16.1 Sampling of Common Symptoms of Sensory Processing Disorder

Sensory	Symptoms
Auditory	Responds negatively to unexpected or loud noises. Holds hands over ears. Cannot filter out background noise. Seems oblivious within an active environment.
Visual	Prefers to be in the dark. Hesitates going up and down steps. Avoids bright lights. Stares intensely at people or objects. Avoids eye contact.
Taste/Smell	Avoids certain tastes/smells that are typically part of children's diets. Routinely smells nonfood objects. Seeks out certain tastes or smells. Does not seem to smell strong odors.
Body Position	Continually seeks out all kinds of movement activities. Hangs on other people, furniture, objects, even in familiar situations. Seems to have weak muscles; tires easily; has poor endurance. Walks on toes.
Movement	Becomes anxious or distressed when feet leave the ground. Avoids climbing or jumping. Avoids playground equipment. Seeks all kinds of movement, and this interferes with daily life. Takes excessive risks while playing; has no safety awareness.
Touch	Avoids getting messy in glue, sand, finger paint, tape. Is sensitive to certain fabrics (clothing, bedding). Touches people and objects at an irritating level. Avoids going barefoot, especially in grass or sand. Has decreased awareness of pain or temperature.
Attention, Behavior and Social	Jumps from one activity to another frequently, and it interferes with play. Has difficulty paying attention. Is overly affectionate with others. Seems anxious. Is accident prone. Has difficulty making friends; does not express emotions.

Note. From Center of Development. (n.d.). *Sensory integration.* Retrieved from http://developmental-delay.com/page.cfm/250. Reprinted with permission.

requires hospitals to assess and reassess patients' risk for falls, to develop and implement an action plan to address any identified risks and to evaluate the efficacy of the program (Joint Commission, 2007). The results of the task force's survey revealed several measures to prevent patient falls (see Box 16.1).

BOX 16.1.
SUGGESTED
MEASURES TO
PREVENT
PEDIATRIC FALLS

1. Complete fall risk screen; reassess if physiologic/motor/sensory/ cognitive status changes.

2. Identify at-risk patients with sticker, ID band, or symbol.

3. Adhere to institutional safety protocols:

   - Orient child/parent to room/bed.
   - Use assistive devices properly.
   - Maintain surveillance of floors and surfaces for fluids/objects.
   - Assist with ambulation, as needed.
   - Place call light, telephone, personal articles within reach.
   - Use cribs, high chairs, and infant seats properly.
   - Use side rails, protective devices (crib hood, gait belt, etc.) appropriately.
   - Keep beds/cribs/stretchers in the lowest, locked position.

- Use wheel locks when indicated.

- Keep environment uncluttered and free of obstacles.

- Provide adequate lighting.

4. Individualize standardized care plan.

5. Have child wear nonslip footwear when up.

6. Offer patient assistance to the bathroom; place commode at bedside.

7. Evaluate medication administration times.

8. Monitor frequently; keep door open.

9. Position caregiver/sitter at bedside.

10. Assign room that provides more direct observation.

11. Assess parents'/primary caregivers' ability to set appropriate behavioral/activity limits.

12. Educate parents/primary caregivers regarding:

- Fall risk factors

- Appropriate transfer/ambulation needs

- Appropriate use of side rails

Note. From Child Health Corporation of America Nursing Falls Study Task Force. (2009). Pediatric falls: State of the science. *Pediatric Nursing, 35*(4), p. 231. Reprinted with permission of the publisher, Jannetti Publications, Inc.

Modification of activities may be needed for children with disabilities; finger painting may become toe painting, for example. Visual cues and pictures may have to replace verbal communications. The child with a visual impairment may need to touch the physical boundaries of a room or play area to identify spatial relationships and points of reference.

Children's assistive devices may necessitate modifying activities. Toys can be adapted with special controls to allow children to operate them. Play materials, games, and books can be stabilized to allow the child more independent manipulation. Advances in electronic communication aids and computer-assisted educational equipment are providing new opportunities for children with perceptual-motor dysfunction to learn and be independent. It is important, however, that the electronic aids and computers be appropriate to the child's needs and capabilities, so as not to lead to frustration and failure for the child.

Many of the activities in this chapter are designed to provide sensory stimulation. As noted in Table 16.1, a child with sensory integration disorder may have difficulty with a variety of sensory stimuli. Thus, care should be taken to learn as much as possible about the nature of these issues before conducting these or any other activities with the child.

Activity Goals

Activities for children with perceptual-motor dysfunction are directed toward accomplishing the following: (1) maximizing the child's perceptual and motor abilities; (2) enabling the child to learn methods of enhancing movement, control, and sensation; and (3) preventing complications associated with immobility or sensory impairment. The goal of activities should be to maximize the child's independence and freedom while providing safeguards from accidents.

ACTIVITY 16.1.   BEDPAN TOSS

Bedpans are used in this activity rather than a more traditional receptacle because school-age children in that stage in the acquisition of humor when they find "gross" things amusing, think it is hilarious. If preferred, beanbags or balls can be used in place of the IV bags, and buckets or bowls substituted for the bedpans.

Therapeutic Goal: To improve motor skills by developing eye-hand coordination and promoting arm movement.	**Materials:**
Age Group: Primary/school-age	☐ IV bag filled with water, or beanbag or ball
Adult/Child Ratio: 1:6	☐ Masking tape
Required Time: Varies with number of participants	☐ Bedpans (5 or more)
Restrictions and Precautions: None	

Process

1. Lay a strip of masking tape on the floor to designate where the children should stand when throwing the bags.

2. Arrange the bedpans in a vertical line in front of the masking tape, leaving a 6-inch space between each.

3. Have the children stand behind the line and take turns throwing the IV bags or beanbags into the bedpans, starting with the closest bucket and proceeding outward. Let each child continue until he or she misses; play then goes to the next child. Small prizes can be awarded for each successful throw.

Variations

For older children, add more bedpans and arrange them in a triangular formation. Assign points to each bedpan based on its proximity to the thrower. Divide larger groups into teams to play.

For more ideas, see Bright Ideas to Improve Perceptual-Motor Capabilities (Box Activity 16.6-1).

BOX ACTIVITY 16.1-1. BRIGHT IDEAS TO IMPROVE PERCEPTUAL-MOTOR CAPABILITIES

- Hide objects in uncooked rice and challenge total-care patients, or those with other motor disabilities, to find them.

- Play hopscotch to improve eye-foot coordination. Use masking tape to make a removable hopscotch board on the floor.

- Hold relay races that meet specific movement needs of the children.

- Sponsor a carnival or Olympic-type tournament adapted to meet the movement treatment goals of the children participating.

- Design an obstacle course.

- Offer special aerobic classes. Exercise movements can even be adapted for children on bed rest, or those with paralysis.

- Produce a dramatic play called "A Visit to the Zoo," in which the children "star" as the animals. Start the children off by encouraging them to jump like a frog, hop like a kangaroo, glide like an inchworm, walk like a duck, crawl like a crab, and so on.

- Do basic yoga, at a level appropriate for children.

- Promote motor coordination by playing follow the leader.

ACTIVITY 16.2.   FEET FEAT CHALLENGE

Feet Feat Challenge is located on the CD that accompanies this book.

ACTIVITY 16.3.   ICE HOCKEY GAME

Therapeutic Goal: To improve motor skills by developing eye-hand coordination and fine-motor skills.

Age Group: Primary/school-age

Adult/Child Ratio: 1:2

Required Time: 15 minutes to make the "rink," plus time to freeze it

Restrictions and Precautions: None

Materials:
- ☐ Large cookie sheet with sides (the ice rink)
- ☐ Gimp
- ☐ Scissors
- ☐ Glue gun
- ☐ Plastic berry basket, cut in half (the goals)
- ☐ 2 tongue depressors (the hockey sticks)
- ☐ Checker (the puck)

Process

1. Cut a length of gimp to the width of the cookie sheet.

2. Center the gimp across the width of the pan and glue it in place.

3. To make the goals, position one of the basket halves in the center on each end of the cookie sheet, with the openings facing the middle. Glue in place.

4. Fill the "rink" with water and freeze until completely solid.

5. Give each player a tongue depressor to use as a hockey stick.

6. To play, instruct children to use their "hockey sticks" to get the "puck" into their opponent's goal.

ACTIVITY 16.4.   MEMORY GAME

This activity can be helpful for children with brain injuries.

Therapeutic Goal: To improve cognitive function by increasing concentration skills.

Age Group: Preschool/school-age/adolescent

Adult/Child Ratio: 1:10

Required Time: Varies

Restrictions and Precautions: None

Materials:
- ☐ Assortment of small objects the children are familiar with
- ☐ Towel
- ☐ Timer
- ☐ Paper
- ☐ Pen

Process

1. Make a list of all the objects.

2. Out of sight of the children, arrange the objects on a table or tray and cover them with a towel.

3. With the children, specify the amount of time they have to study the objects; set the timer accordingly.

4. Remove the towel and allow the children to study the objects until the timer rings.

5. Again cover the objects with the towel.

6. Challenge the children to write or dictate the names of all the objects they can remember.

7. Repeat using different objects.

Variation   After the children have studied the objects, remove one or two without letting them see. Ask the children to name the missing object(s).

ACTIVITY 16.5.   ODOR MATCH GAME

When they are done playing this game, allow the children to create pictures with the spices and other materials used in this activity. Give each child a piece of paper and glue that has been thinned with water, to spread over one area of the paper at a time, and then sprinkle it with a different material.

Therapeutic Goal: To improve cognitive function by increasing sensory input.

Age Group: Preschool/primary

Adult/Child Ratio: 1:2

Required Time: 30 minutes preparation; 10 minutes to play

Restrictions and Precautions: Do not use with children experiencing nausea.

Materials:

- ☐ 10–14 screw-on bottle caps, approximately 2 inches in diameter
- ☐ Glue
- ☐ Water
- ☐ Paintbrush
- ☐ Dried spices or other fragrant materials, such as:
  - Cinnamon
  - Cloves
  - Potpourri
  - Oregano
  - Coffee grounds
  - Garlic powder
  - Mint flakes
  - Wood shavings
- ☐ Scissors
- ☐ Magnetic strips with adhesive backing
- ☐ Cookie sheet
- ☐ Spray paint for metal surfaces (optional)

Process

1. Mix equal amounts of glue and water and spread the mixture on the inside of the bottle caps.
2. Sprinkle each of the dried materials being used into two of the bottle caps.
3. Allow the glue to dry.
4. For each bottle cap, cut a magnetic strip to the same width and adhere it to the back.
5. If desired, paint the cookie sheet a bright color and allow it to dry.
6. Arrange the bottle caps randomly on the cookie sheet.
7. Invite the children to smell each bottle cap; next, challenge them to find the matching ones; then, ask them to arrange the caps in the correct pairs on the cookie sheet.

Variation   Select four or more liquids with distinctive odors and saturate two cotton balls with each one. Cut index cards in half and glue one cotton ball on each piece. Have the children try to match the cotton balls by sniffing them.

ACTIVITY 16.6.   PICTURE WEAVING

The variation of photographs and colored construction paper captures children's interest and keeps them engaged.

Therapeutic Goal: To improve motor skills by developing hand-eye coordination.

Age Group: Primary/school-age

Adult/Child Ratio: 1:6

Required Time: 30 minutes

Restrictions and Precautions: Take scissors and glue precautions.

Materials:

- ☐ Selection of computer prints of photographs or artwork
- ☐ Construction paper, 8–1/2 × 11 inches
- ☐ Ruler
- ☐ Pencil
- ☐ Scissors
- ☐ Glue stick

Process

1. Fold the pictures in half vertically.
2. Using the ruler, draw a vertical line along the edge opposite the fold, to create a 1/2-inch margin.
3. Make cuts 3/4 inch apart, starting at the fold and ending at the margin.
4. Let the children choose a color of construction paper and cut it into strips lengthwise, 3/4 inch wide.
5. Demonstrate how to weave a strip through the picture going under, over, under over.
6. Have the children weave the next strip over, under, over.
7. Let the children continue weaving as described in steps 5 and 6 until all of the construction paper is used.
8. Glue the ends of each strip.

For more ideas, see Bright Ideas for the Sensory Stimulation of Infants and Toddlers (Box Activity 16.6-1).

BOX ACTIVITY 16.6-1. BRIGHT IDEAS FOR THE SENSORY STIMULATION OF INFANTS AND TODDLERS

- Blow bubbles for the babies to watch. Encourage them to try and catch the bubbles.
- Hang mobiles and objects over cribs, changing them regularly.
- Collect bells of different tones, then place them one by one into the baby's hands and help the infant shake them.
- Finger-paint with pudding or yogurt.
- Gather some specimen cups or other small plastic containers with lids. Place something different in each one, such as: 3 tablespoons of sand, 3 tablespoons of rice, 3 marbles, a few screws, a few small rocks, a few tablespoons of water, and the like. Attach the lids securely. Hold the baby's hands on the cup and help him or her shake them.
- Sing children's songs while moving the baby's hands to the rhythm.
- Provide toys that light up, move, and make sounds simultaneously.
- Collect a variety of textured materials (e.g., velvet, fun-fur, silk, corrugated cardboard, sandpaper, cotton ball). Rub the materials gently against the baby's skin.
- Play peekaboo with a soft blanket.
- Give the baby a wad of cellophane tape or masking tape and help him or her manipulate it.
- Bounce the baby on your lap in front of a mirror.
- Play pat-a-cake.

ACTIVITY 16.7.   PINCER PICKUP

This activity is easy to individualize by choosing objects that will appeal to each child's unique interests.

Therapeutic Goal: To improve motor skills by improving eye-hand coordination and pincer grasp.

Age Group: Toddler/preschool

Adult/Child Ratio: 1:1

Required Time: 5–10 minutes

Restrictions and Precautions: Supervise children closely to ensure they do not put small objects in their mouths.

Materials:

☐ Box with dividers 1 inch wide and no more than 2 inches tall; the height of the box should not exceed the length of the child's fingers (e.g., containers for bead storage, found in craft stores)

☐ Several high-interest objects, small enough to fit in the box compartments

Process

1. Place the objects into the compartments of the box.

2. Encourage the child to remove all of the objects from the compartments.

ACTIVITY 16.8.   PIQUANT POMANDERS

Because the pomanders need to dry for a week or two, this activity is most suitable for use in a clinic where children come weekly, or for children who will be hospitalized for at least 10 days.

Therapeutic Goal: To improve motor skills by providing olfactory and tactile stimulation and develop fine-motor coordination.

Age Group: Primary/school-age/adolescent

Adult/Child Ratio: 1:8

Required Time: 30 minutes, plus drying time

Restrictions and Precautions: None

Materials:

☐ Oranges (one per child)

☐ Cloves

☐ Paper bags (one per child)

☐ Cinnamon

☐ Nutmeg

☐ Allspice

☐ Ribbon or raffia

☐ Ribbon or picture frame wire

Process

1. Show the children how to push whole cloves into an orange, randomly or in patterns, until the fruit is completely covered. Caution them not to insert the cloves too far into the orange, or it will shrink as it dries out.

2. Place each orange in a paper bag and sprinkle it with spices.

3. Allow to dry for one to two weeks.

4. Let the children remove the oranges from their bags and shake off the excess spices.

5. Help the children wrap their pomanders completely around with ribbon or picture wire, to create a hanger.

6. Encourage the children to hang their pomanders somewhere they are able to enjoy the sweet fragrance.

ACTIVITY 16.9.   RAINSTICKS

Rainsticks were used in some traditional cultures during rainmaking ceremonies. Today, rainsticks are used as musical instruments, which create a soothing, rhythmic sound. They make excellent distraction devices for children experiencing anxiety or pain.

Therapeutic Goal: To improve motor skills by promoting movement, and cognitive function by providing sensory input through sound.

Age Group: School-age

Adult/Child Ratio: 1:8

Required Time: 45 minutes

Restrictions and Precautions: Do not do this activity with children who are hypersensitive to sound or touch. Assess participants to assure they have the strength and dexterity to help construct the rainstick. Take glue gun and sharps precautions.

Materials:

☐ Cardboard mailing tube, 2 inches in diameter, (preferably white), with plastic end pieces

☐ 1 to 1–1/2-inch nails

☐ Hammer (optional)

☐ Filler (e.g., dry rice, lentils, or uncooked popcorn)

☐ Measuring cup

☐ Acrylic paint or permanent markers

☐ Paintbrushes (if using paint)

☐ Colored paper/decorative trims (optional)

☐ Glue gun or tape

Process

1. Explain how rainsticks were used in ancient times and how they are used today, as musical instruments. Show the children a completed rainstick and upend it slowly to demonstrate the sound it makes.

2. Let the children assist with hammering or poking nails into the tube at 1/2-inch intervals, spiraling down the tube (Figure Activity 16.9-1), then push nails in as far as possible. (Note: Contact paper may be applied before this step, for decoration, rather than painting later).

Figure Activity 16.9-1. Rainstick

3. Ask the children to remove one of the plastic ends and pour approximately 1 cup of filler into the tube then reattach the plastic end securely with glue gun or tape.

4. Invite the children to paint and/or decorate their rainsticks.

5. To use their rainsticks, have the children turn them up and down very slowly, allowing the filler to slide from the top of the tube to the bottom.

Variation   A simpler version can be made using thin cardboard tubes and straight pins or toothpicks. The ends can be fashioned from discs of wax paper slightly larger than the diameter of the tube and secured to the tube with rubber bands.

ACTIVITY 16.10.   SCRATCH-AND-SNIFF ART

Scratch-and-sniff stickers are very popular among children. This activity expands the concept to painting.

Therapeutic Goal: To improve cognitive function by increasing sensory input.

Age Group Preschool/primary

Adult/Child Ratio: 1:6

Required Time: 15 minutes, plus preparation and drying time

Restrictions and Precautions: None

Materials:

☐ Unsweetened powdered drink mixes, assorted colors

☐ Water

☐ Medicine cups

☐ Paintbrushes

☐ Container of water for cleaning brushes

☐ Watercolor paper, coffee filters, paper towels, or other porous material

Process

1. Mix 1 part drink mix to 1 part water to achieve the desired amount of paint.

2. Place a different color of paint in each of the medicine cups.

3. Give the children brushes to apply the paint to the porous material being used.

4. Allow the paint to dry completely.

5. Have the children lightly scratch the different colors of paint and inhale the various smells.

Variation   Make edible finger paint by sprinkling different flavors of dry gelatin on wax paper or cooking parchment, and adding a small amount of water.

ACTIVITY 16.11.   SPAGHETTI SCULPTURE

Children delight in the slimy, slithery texture of cooked spaghetti. To add to the fun, lead them in a few rounds of the perennially favorite silly song, "On Top of Spaghetti."

Therapeutic Goal: To improve cognitive function by providing tactile stimulation.

Age Group: Preschool/primary

Adult/Child Ratio: 1: 6

Required Time: 20–30 minutes

Restrictions and Precautions: Supervise children closely to make sure they don't eat the spaghetti.

Materials:

☐ Spaghetti, cooked, drained, and cooled

☐ Cooking oil

☐ Liquid watercolor paints or food coloring

☐ Paper plates (one per child)

1. Add a small amount of cooking oil to the cooked spaghetti.

2. Give each child a plate with 1 – 1/2 cups of spaghetti on it.

3. Allow the children to select a color and add a small amount of it to their portion of spaghetti.

4. Have the children use their hands to mix the colorant into the spaghetti. Allow them to continue to manipulate and play with the mixture for a few minutes before asking them to mound it in the middle of their plates.

5. Drizzle a tablespoon (or more) of glue over each child's mound of spaghetti and challenge them to shape and sculpt it into a work of art.

6. Allow to dry completely.

ACTIVITY 16.12.   TACTILE COLLAGE

This activity is good for children with poor eye-hand coordination or experiencing fine-motor difficulties.

Therapeutic Goal: To improve cognitive function by providing tactile stimulation.

Age Group: Preschool/primary/school-age

Adult/Child Ratio: 1:5

Required Time: 20 – 30 minutes.

Restrictions and Precautions: None

Materials:

- ☐ Clear contact paper
- ☐ Scissors
- ☐ Construction paper or poster board
- ☐ Glue stick
- ☐ Tape
- ☐ Fabric scraps, assorted textures
- ☐ Sandpaper, cut in small pieces of varying shapes
- ☐ Cotton puffs
- ☐ Gauze
- ☐ Buttons
- ☐ Feathers

1. Cut the contact paper to the desired size(s). Vary the size in accordance with each child's needs and capabilities.

2. Cut pieces of construction paper or poster board to a size slightly larger than the contact paper.

3. Glue the contact paper to the construction paper or poster board, with the adhesive facing up.

4. Encourage the children to create collages by placing assorted materials on the adhesive.

5. Discuss their creations, emphasizing the different textures and shapes.

ACTIVITY 16.13.   TAG! YOU'RE LIT!

This is a good activity for postoperative scoliosis patients and others who must lie in a supine position for an extended period of time.

Therapeutic Goal: To improve motor skills and facilitate coping with immobilization by providing an opportunity to play beyond the area of confinement.

Age Group: Preschool/primary

Adult/Child Ratio: 1:2

Required Time: Varies with the child's degree of interest

Restrictions and Precautions: None

Materials:

- ☐ Flashlights (one per player)

Process

1. Darken the room.

2. Give each player a flashlight.

3. Allow the children time to experiment with their flashlights by shining it on the ceiling and drawing straight lines and different kinds of designs.

4. Initiate a game of flashlight tag by moving your light swiftly and smoothly across the ceiling, in a straight line.

5. Challenge the children to use their flashlights to "hop" across the ceiling and "land" somewhere along the path of light you created.

6. Make the game more challenging by "hopping" your light around the ceiling, while the children use theirs to try to catch it.

7. Let the children take turns moving their lights around while the others' lights attempt to catch it.

8. Vary the game by drawing designs, shapes, or letters on the ceiling. Start with simple patterns and then proceed to more intricate ones while the other players try to keep their light continuously on the path of the one that is moving.

Variation   Cover the flashlight head with pieces of various-colored cellophane to change the color of the light.

ACTIVITY 16.14.   TOUCH-AND-TELL GAME

This simple activity is loved by children who enjoy guessing games.

Therapeutic Goal: To improve cognitive function by increasing concentration and tactile input.	**Materials:**
Age Group: Preschool/primary/school-age	☐ Shoe box or similar-size box
Adult/Child Ratio: 1:1	☐ Scissors
Required Time: 20 minutes	☐ Assorted objects of various shapes and textures that are familiar to the child
Restrictions and Precautions: Do not use objects with sharp edges.	

Process

1. At one end of the box, cut a hole large enough for the child to insert his or her hands.

2. Cut a hole in the opposite and that is large enough to insert the selected objects.

3. Place one object in the box without letting the child see what it is.

4. Instruct the child to, with eyes closed, insert his or her hand in the box.

5. Challenge the child to describe the attributes of the object then try to identify it.

6. Repeat this activity using different objects.

ACTIVITY 16.15.   TUTTI-FRUTTI DOUGH

This is a classic play-dough recipe with a fragrant twist.

Therapeutic Goal: To improve cognitive function by providing olfactory and tactile stimulation.

Age Group: Preschool/primary

Adult/Child Ratio: 1:6

Required Time: 20–30 minutes

Restrictions and Precautions: Although the mixture is nontoxic, do not allow children to consume it.

Materials:

☐ Bowls

☐ Spoon

☐ 2 or more packages of powdered drink mixes, in different flavors

☐ 3 cups flour

☐ 1 cup salt

☐ 1 cup water (approximate)

☐ Tongue depressors

☐ Assorted cookie cutters

Process

1. Combine the flour, salt, and water in a bowl and mix well.

2. Divide the mixture into as many portions as drink mix flavors being used.

3. Add one package powdered drink mix to each portion and let the children take turns mixing it.

4. Tell the children to knead the mixture until it becomes soft and pliable.

5. Give the children the cookie cutters and tongue depressors to create various forms and shapes; or they can use their hands. While the children are working with the mixture, encourage them to smell the aromas and identify the fruit flavors.

ART MATERIALS AND PROJECTS FOR CHILDREN AND OTHER HIGH-RISK INDIVIDUALS

Children under age 12 or who are intellectually or physically disabled or chronically ill, older adults, and other individuals at elevated risk from exposure to toxic chemicals can replace toxic materials with safer ones.

Do Not Use Solvents and Solvent-Containing Products	Use Instead Water-Based and Solvent-Free Products
Alkyd, oil enamels, or other solvent-containing paints	Substitute acrylics, oil sticks, water-based paints, watercolors, or other water-based paints containing safe pigments.
Turpentine, paint thinners, citrus solvents, or other solvents for cleaning up or thinning oil paints	Mix oil-based, solvent-free paints with linseed oil only. Clean brushes with baby oil, followed by soap and water.
Solvent-based silkscreen inks and other printing inks containing solvents or requiring solvents for cleanup	Use water-based silkscreen, block printing, or stencil inks with safe pigments.
Solvent-containing varnishes, mediums, and alcohol-containing shellacs	Replace with acrylic emulsion coatings; or let the teacher apply it for children, under proper conditions.
Rubber cement and thinners for paste-up and mechanicals	Use low-temperature wax methods, double-sided tape, glue sticks, or other solvent-free materials.
Airplane glue and other solvent-containing glues	Substitute methyl cellulose glues, school paste, glue sticks, preservative-free wheat paste, and solvent-free glues.
Permanent felt-tip markers, whiteboard markers, and other solvent-containing markers	Use water-based markers or chalk.
Powdered Dusty Materials	**Dustless Products or Processes**
Clay from mixing dry clay, sanding greenware, and other dusty processes	Purchase talc-free, low-silica, premixed clay. Trim clay when leather-hard; clean up often during work. Practice good hygiene and dust control.
Ceramic glaze dust from mixing ingredients, applying, and other processes	Do not use even lead-free glazes with grade 6 children or under. Substitute with paints. The teacher can seal the paints with water-based acrylic varnish.
Metal enamel dust. Even lead-free enamels contain other toxic metals. Avoiding enamels altogether will eliminate the dangerous heat and acids involved in the enameling process.	Substitute with paints.
Powered tempera and other powdered paints	Purchase premixed paints, or have the teacher mix them.
Powered dyes for batik, tie-dying, and other textile processes.	Use vegetable and plant materials (e.g., onion skins, tea), FDA-approved food dyes, or unsweetened Kool-Aid.
Plaster dust. Do not sand plaster or perform other dusty work. To avoid burns, do not cast hands or other body parts in plaster.	Have teachers premix plaster outdoors or in local exhaust ventilation. Cut rather than tear plaster-impregnated casting cloth.
Instant papier-mache dust from finely ground magazines, newspapers, etc.	Replace with pieces of plain paper or black-and-white newspaper with methyl cellulose glues, paste, or other safe glues.
Pastels, chalks, or dry markers that create dust	Use oil pastels or sticks, crayons, and dustless chalks.

Aerosols and Spray Products	Liquid Materials
Spray paints, fixatives, etc.	Substitute water-based liquids that can be brushed, dripped, or splattered on; or have the teacher use sprays in local exhaust ventilation or outdoors.
Airbrushes	Replace with other paint methods. Do not inhale mist. Guard against misuse of airbrushes.
Miscellaneous Products	**Substitutes**
All types of professional artist's materials	Use products approved and recommended for children when teaching children or high-risk adults.
Toxic metals such as arsenic, lead, cadmium, lithium, barium, chrome, nickel, vanadium, manganese, antimony, etc. These are common ingredients in ceramic glazes, enamels, paints, and many art materials.	Use only materials free of highly toxic substances.
Epoxy resins, instant glues, or plastic resin adhesives	Replace with methyl cellulose, library paste, or glue sticks.
Plastic resin casting systems or preformed plastics	Use only preformed plastics, and in ways that do not involve heat, solvents, or any other method that will release vapors, gases, and/or odors.
Acid etches and pickling baths	Do not use.
Bleach for reverse dyeing of fabric or colored paper	Do not use. Thinned white paint can be substituted to simulate bleach on colored paper.
Photographic chemicals	Use blueprint paper to make sun-grams. Use digital or Polaroid cameras. Be sure students do not mishandle Polaroid film or pictures, which contain toxic chemicals.
Stained-glass projects using lead, solder, or glass cuttings	Replace with colored cellophane and black paper or tape to simulate stained glass. In the leading process, use plastic came rather than lead came to divide and set plastic pieces. Teachers can glue it in a ventilated area.
Industrial talcs contaminated with asbestos, or nonfibrous asbestos minerals contained in many white clays; slip-casting clays, glazes, French chalk, and parting powders	Replace with other, talc-free products.
Sculpture stones contaminated with asbestos, such as some soapstones, steatites, serpentines, etc.	Always use stones determined on analysis to be free of asbestos.
Face and skin painting/tattooing with art paints or markers that are not labeled and approved for this use	Always use products approved for use on the skin (e.g., cosmetics or colored sunscreen creams).
Random assortments of plants and seeds	Identify all plants to be sure no toxic or sensitizing plants are used (e.g., poison oak, castor).
Donated, found, or old materials whose ingredients are unknown	Use only clean, new materials. Products containing food or other animal or organic materials may harbor bacteria or other hazardous microbes (e.g., washed, plastic meat trays may harbor salmonella).

Note. Adapted from M. Rossol. (2001). *The artist's complete health and safety guide* (3rd ed.). New York: Allworth Press, pp. 366–369. Reprinted with permission.

Appendix B

Web Sites

Activities/Crafts

Activities for Kids: www.activitiesforkids.com

Activity Idea Place: www.123child.com

Amos Craft Publishing: www.craftideas.com

Artistic Flair Painting and Home Services: www.artisticflair.com

Aunt Annie's Crafts: www.auntannie.com

Cartoon Critters: www.cartooncritters.com

Crayola: www.crayola.com

Dolls Mania: www.dollzmania.com

EARLYCHILDHOOD.COM: www.earlychildhood.com

Elmers: www.elmers.com

Enchanted Learning: www.enchantedlearning.com

The Idea Box: www.theideabox.com

Kaboose: www.kaboose.com/index.html

Making Friends.com: www.makingfriends.com

Michaels: www.michaels.com

The Perpetual Preschool: www.perpetualpreschool.com

Puzzle Maker: www.puzzlemaker.com

Disease and Disability

Abilityonline: www.abilityonline.com

American Diabetes Association: www.diabetes.org

Cancer Source Kids: www.cancersourcekids.com

A Lion in the House (cancer): www.mylion.org

Medicine/Pill Taking

Baylor International Pediatric AIDS Initiative: www.bayloraids.org/resources/pillprimer/index

Kidsmeds: www.kidsmeds.org/tipsfortaking.html

Ped-Onc Resource Center: www.acor.org/ped-onc/treatment/Pills/pills.html

Eating Disorders

Eating Disorder Hope: www.eatingdisorderhope.com

Eating Disorders Publications and Resources: www.gurze.com

Massachusetts General Hospital Harris Center: www.massgeneral.org/harriscenter

National Association of Anorexia Nervosa and Associated Eating Disorders: www.anad.org

Siblings

Sibling Support Project: www.siblingsupport.org

Supersibs: www.supersibs.org

Virtual Tours

Kennedy Space Center: www.nasa.gov/centers/kennedy/home/index.html

Online Field Trips: www.thinkport.org/Classroom/trips.tp

Tramline: www.field-trips.org/trips.htm

Programming Resources

National Storytelling Network: www.storynet.org

Play Therapy United Kingdom: www.playtherapy.org.uk

REFERENCES

Adamie, K., & Turkoski B. (2006). Responding to patient-initiated humor: Guidelines for practice. *Home Healthcare Nurse*, *24*(10), 638–644.

Agency for Healthcare Research and Quality. (2009). *Facts and figures 2007. Healthcare Cost and Utilization Project (HCUP)*. Rockville, MD: Author. Retrieved from www.hcup-us .ahrq.gov/reports/factsandfigures/2007/exhibit3_2.jsp.

Aho, A. L., Tarkka, M. T., Astedt-Kurki, P., Kaunonen, M. (2006). Fathers' grief after the death of a child. *Issues in Mental Health Nursing*, *27*, 647–663.

American Academy of Pediatrics. (2000a). American Academy of Pediatrics Clinical Practice Guideline: Diagnosis and evaluation of the child with attention-deficit/hyperactivity disorder. *Pediatrics*, *105*, 1158–1170.

American Academy of Pediatrics. (2000b). *Joint statement on the impact of entertainment violence on children*. Congressional Public Health Summit, July 26, 2000. Retrieved from www.aap .org/advocacy/releases/jstmtevc.htm.

American Academy of Pediatrics/American Pain Society. (2001). The assessment and management of acute pain in infants, children and adolescents. *Pediatrics*, *108*(3), 793–797.

American Academy of Pediatrics Committee on Psychosocial Aspects of Child and Family Health. (1999). How pediatricians can respond to the psychosocial implications of disasters *Pediatrics*, *103*(2), 521–523.

American Academy of Pediatrics, Work Group on Disasters. (1995). *Psychosocial issues for children and families in disasters: A guide for the primary care physician* (Publication No. [SMA] 95–3022). Washington, DC: U.S. Department of Health and Human Services.

American Art Therapy Association. (2010). *About art therapy*. Retrieved from www .americanarttherapyassociation.org/aata-aboutarttherapy.html.

American Humane Association. (2008). *Guidelines for helping children experiencing abuse or neglect*. Retrieved from www.americanhumane.org/about-us/newsroom/fact-sheets/guidelines-for-helping-children.html.

American Psychiatric Association. (1994). *Diagnostic and statistical manual of mental disorders* (4th ed.). Washington, DC: American Psychiatric Association.

American Psychiatric Association. (2000). *Diagnostic and statistical manual of mental disorders* (4th ed., text rev.). Washington, DC: Author.

Anand, K. (1998). Clinical importance of pain and stress in preterm neonates. *Biology of the Neonate*, *73*, 1–9.

Anand, K., & Scalzo, F. (2000). Can adverse neonatal experiences alter brain development and subsequent behavior? *Biology of the Neonate*, *77*, 69–82.

Annesi-Maesano, I., Agabiti, N., Pistelli, R., Couilliot, M-F., & Forastiere, F. (2003). Subpopulations at increased risk of adverse health outcomes from air pollution. *European Respiratory Journal*, *40* (suppl.), 57s–63s.

Antle, B. J. (2004). Factors associated with self-worth in young people with physical disabilities. *Health & Social Work*, *29*, 167–175.

Arvidson, J., Larsson, B., & Lonnerholm, G. (1999). A long-term follow-up study of psychosocial functioning after autologous bone marrow transplantation in childhood. *Psycho-Oncology*, *8*, 123–134.

Asarnow, J. R., Carlson, G. A., & Guthrie, D. (1987). Coping strategies, self-perception, hopelessness, and perceived family environment in depressed and suicidal children. *Journal of Consulting and Clinical Psychology*, *55*, 361–366.

Aspinall, C. (2006). Do I make you uncomfortable? Reflections on using surgery to reduce the distress of others. In E. Parens (Ed.), *Surgically shaping children: Technology, ethics, and the pursuit of normality* (pp. 13–28). Baltimore, MD: Johns Hopkins University Press.

Association for Applied and Therapeutic Humor. (2000). *Official definition of 'therapeutic humor.'* Retrieved from www.aath.org.

Ayers, A. J. (1994). *Sensory integration and the child*. Los Angeles: Western Psychological Services.

Babikian, T., & Asarnow, R. (2009). Neurocognitive outcomes and recovery after pediatric TBI: Meta-analytic review of the literature. *Neuropsychology, 23*(3), 283–296.

Badger, T. A., & Jones, E. (1990). Deaf and hearing children's conceptions of the body interior. *Pediatric Nursing, 16*(2), 201–205.

Ball, T., Shapiro, D., Monheim, C., & Weydert, J. (2003). A pilot study of the use of guided imagery for the treatment of recurrent abdominal pain in children. *Clinical Pediatrics, 42*, 527–532.

Barber, S., Grubbs, L., & Cottrell, B. (2005). Self-perception in children with attention deficit/hyperactivity disorder. *Journal of Pediatric Nursing, 20*(4), 235–254.

Bariaud, F. (1989). Age differences in children's humor. In P. McGhee (Ed.), *Humor and children's development: A guide to practical applications* (pp. 15–45). New York: Haworth Press.

Barnes, C. M., Bandak, A. G., & Beardslee, C. I. (1990) Content analysis of 186 descriptive cases of hospitalized children. *Maternal-Child Nursing Journal, 19*, 281–296.

Barrera, M., Atenafu, E., Andrews, G., & Saunders, F. (2008). Factors related to changes in cognitive, educational and visual motor integration in children who undergo hematopoietic stem cell transplant. *Journal of Pediatric Psychology, 33*(5), 536–546.

Barrera, M., Pringle, L.-A. B., Sumbler, K., & Saunders, F. (2000). Quality of life and behavioral adjustment after pediatric bone marrow transplantation. *Bone Marrow Transplantation, 26*, 427–435.

Barrera, M., Shaw, A., Speechley, K., Maunsell, E., & Pogany, L. (2005). Educational and social late effects of childhood cancer and related clinical, personal, and familial characteristics. *Cancer, 104*(8), 1751–1760.

Beck, M., Antle, B., Berlin, D., Granger, M., Meighan, K., Neilson, B.,... Kaufman, M. (2004). Wearing masks in a pediatric hospital: Developing practical guidelines. *Canadian Journal of Public Health, 95*(4), 256–257.

Belamarich, F., Luder, E., Kattan, M., Mitchell, H., Islam, S., Lynn, H., & Crain, E. (2000). Do obese inner-city children with asthma have more symptoms than nonobese children with asthma? *Pediatrics, 106*, 1436–1441.

Bell, J., Johnson, B., Desai, P., & McLeod, S. (2008). Family-centered care and the implications for child life practice. In R. Thompson (Ed.), *The handbook of child life* (pp. 95–115). Springfield, IL: Charles C. Thomas.

Berenbaum, J., & Hatcher, J. (1992). Emotional distress of mothers of hospitalized children. *Journal of Pediatric Psychology, 17*(3), 359–372.

Bergen, D. (1998). Development of the sense of humor. In W. Ruch (Ed.), *The sense of humor: Explorations of a personality characteristic* (pp. 329–358). Berlin, Germany: Mouton de Gruyter.

Berk, L. (1997). *Child development* (4th ed.). Boston: Allyn & Bacon.

Berk, L., Felten, D. L., Tan, S. A., Bittman, B. B., & Westengard, J. (2001). Modulation of neuroimmune parameters during the eustress of humor-associated mirthful laughter. *Alternative Therapies, 7*(2), 62–76.

Berk, R. (2002). *Research critiques incite words of mass destruction*. Retrieved from www.aath.org/articles/art_berk.html.

Berk, R. (2008). *What everyone should know about humor & laughter*. Retrieved from www.aath.org/documents/AATH-WhatWeKnowREVISED.pdf.

Betancourt, J., Green, A., & Carrillo, J. (2002). *Cultural competence in health care: Emerging frameworks and practical approaches*. New York: The Commonwealth Fund.

Beydoun, M. A., & Wang, Y. (2009). Parent-child dietary intake and pattern resemblance in the United States: Evidence from a large representative survey. *Social Science and Medicine, 68*(12), 2137–2144.

Bibace, R., Dillon, J., & Sagarin, J. (1999). Toward a coexistence of causal reasoning about illness in children and adults. In I. Siegel (Ed.), *Advances in applied developmental psychology* (pp. 27–36). Westport, CT: Ablex.

Bibace, R., & Walsh, M. (1977, August). *The development of children's concepts of health, illness, and medical procedures*. Paper presented at the Annual Meeting of the American Psychological Association, San Francisco, CA.

Bibace, R., & Walsh, M. (1979). Developmental stages of children's conceptions of illness. In G. Stone, F. Cohen, & N. Adler (Eds.), *Health psychology: A handbook* (pp. 285–301). San Francisco: Jossey-Bass.

Bibace, R., & Walsh, M. (1980). Development of children's concepts of illness. *Pediatrics, 66*(6), 912–917.

Bibace, R., & Walsh, M. (1981). *Children's conceptions of illness. New directions for child development, no. 14* (pp. 31–48). San Francisco: Jossey-Bass.

Birbeck, D. J., & Drummond, M. J. N. (2003). Body image and the pre-pubescent child. *Journal of Educational Enquiry, 4*(1), 117–127.

Black, M., Papas, M., Hussey, J., Hunter, W., Dubowitz, H., Kotch, J., . . . Schneider, M. (2002). Behavior and development of preschool children born to adolescent mothers: Risk and 3-generation households. *Pediatrics, 109*(4), 573–580.

Blakeney, P., Thomas, C., Holzer, C., Rose, M., Berniger, F., & Meyer, W. (2005). Efficacy of a short-term, intensive social skills training program for burned adolescents. *Journal of Burn Care & Rehabilitation, 26*(6), 546–555.

Blount, R. L., Corbin, S. M., Sturges, J. W., Wolfe, V. V., Prater, J. M., & James, L. D. (1989). The relationship between adults behavior and child coping and distress during BMA/LP procedures: A sequential analysis. *Behavior Therapy, 20*, 585–601.

Bluebond-Langner, M. (1978). *The private worlds of dying children*. Princeton, NJ: Princeton University Press.

Bluebond-Langner, M. (2000). *In the shadow of illness*. Princeton, NJ: Princeton University Press.

Board, R. (2004) Father stress during a child's critical care hospitalization. *Journal of Pediatric Health Care, 18*, 244–249.

Board, R. (2005). School-age children's perceptions of their PICU hospitalization. *Pediatric Nursing, 31*(3), 166–175.

Bolig, R. (1990). Play in health care settings: A challenge for the 1990s. *Children's Health Care, 19*(4), 229–233.

Bolig, R. (2005). Play in children's health-care settings. In J. Rollins, R. Bolig, & C. Mahan (Eds.), *Meeting children's psychosocial needs across the health-care continuum* (pp. 77–117). Austin, TX: ProEd.

Bolig, R., Fernie, D., & Klein, E. (1986). Unstructured play in hospital settings: An internal locus of control rationale. *Children's Health Care, 15*, 101–107.

Bossert, E. (1994a). Factors influencing the coping of hospitalized school-age children. *Journal of Pediatric Nursing, 9*(5), 299–306.

Bossert E. (1994b). Stress appraisals of hospitalized school-age children. *Children's Health Care, 23*(1), 33–49.

Bouzigon, E., Corda, E., Aschard, H., Dizier, M., Boland, A., Bousquet, J., . . . Demenais, F. (2008). Effect of 17q21 variants and smoking exposure in early-onset asthma. *New England Journal of Medicine, 359*, 1985–1994.

Bow, J. (1988). Treating resistant children. *Child and Adolescent Social Work*, *5*(1), 3–15.

Bowlby, J. (1960). Separation anxiety. *The International Journal of Psychoanalysis*, *41*, 89–113.

Brantly, D. (1991). Conducting a psychosocial assessment of the child. In D. Smith (Ed.), *Comprehensive child and family nursing skills* (pp. 43–47). St. Louis, MO: Mosby Year Book.

Branzei, S. (1995). *Grossology*. Reading, MA: Planet Dexter/Addison Wesley.

Brehler, R., & Kutting, B. (2001). Natural rubber latex allergy: A problem of interdisciplinary concern in medicine. *Archives of Internal Medicine*, *161*(23), 1057–1064.

Breiner, S. (2003). An evidence-based eating disorder program. *Journal of Pediatric Nursing*, *18*(1):75–80.

Brenner, A. (1984). *Helping children cope with stress*. San Francisco: Jossey-Bass.

Broeder, J. L. (1985). School-age children's perceptions of isolation after hospital discharge. *MCN American Journal of Maternal Child Nursing*, *14*(3), 153–174.

Broome, M. E., Bates, T. A., Lillis, P. P., & McGahee, T. W. (1990). Children's medical fears, coping behaviors, and pain perceptions during a lumbar puncture. *Oncology Nursing Forum*, *17*(3), 361–367.

Bumin, G., & Kayihan, H. (2001). Effectiveness of two different sensory-integration programmes for children with spastic diplegic cerebral palsy. *Disability and Rehabilitation*, *23*(9), 394–399.

Burke, P. (2005). Listening to young people with special needs: The influence of group activities. *Journal of Intellectual Disabilities*, *9*(4), 359–376.

Burkle, C. M., Harrison, B. A., Koenig, L. F., Decker, P. A., Warner, D. O., & Gastineau, D. A. (2004). Morbidity and mortality of deep sedation in outpatient bone marrow biopsy. *American Journal of Hematology*, *77*(3), 250–256.

Butler, E. A., Egloff, B., Wilhelm, F. H., Smith N. C., Erikson, E. A., & Gross, J. J. (2003). The social consequences of expressive suppression. *Emotions*, *3*(1), 48–67.

Butler, L., Symons, B., Henderson, S., Shortliffe, L., & Spiegel, D. (2005). Hypnosis reduces distress and duration of an invasive medical procedure for children. *Pediatrics*, *115*(1), e77–e85.

Buxman, K. (1991). Make room for laughter. *American Journal of Nursing*, *91*(12), 46–51.

Cameron, M., Schleien, C., & Morris, M. (2009). Parental presence on pediatric intensive care unit rounds. *The Journal of Pediatrics*, *155*(4), 522–528.

Campbell, J. (1978). The child in the sick role: Contributions of age, sex, parental status and parental values. *Journal of Health and Social Behavior*, *9*, 35–51.

Campbell, S., Kolobe, T., Wright, B., & Linacre, J. (2002). Validity of the test of infant motor performance for prediction of 6-, 9- and 12-month scores on the Alberta Infant Motor Scale. *Developmental Medicine and Child Neurology*, *14*(4), 263–272.

Campbell, T. (1999). Feelings of oncology patients about being nursed in protective isolation as a consequence of cancer chemotherapy treatment. *Journal of Advanced Nursing*, *30*, 439–447.

Canning, E. H., Canning, R. D., & Boyce, W. T. (1992). Depressive symptoms and adaptive style in children with cancer. *Journal of the American Academy of Child and Adolescent Psychiatry*, *31*, 1120–1124.

Caputo, R., Tinelli, F., Bancale, A., Campa, L., Frosini, R., Guzzetta, A., . . . Cioni, G. (2007). Motor coordination in children with congenital strabismus: Effects of late surgery. *European Journal of Paediatric Neurology*, *11*(5), 285–291.

Carandang, M., Folkins, C., Hines, P., & Steward, M. (1979). The role of cognitive level and sibling illness in children's conceptualizations of illness. *American Journal of Orthopsychiatry*, *49*, 474–481.

Carmichael, K. D. (2001). Play therapy with special populations. *Georgia Association for Play Therapy Newsletter*, *6*(2), 2–4.

Carroll, C. L., Bhandari, A., Zucker, A. R., & Schramm, C. M. (2006). Childhood obesity increases duration of therapy during severe asthma exacerbations. *Pediatric Critical Care Medicine, 7*, 527–531.

Carroll, J. (2002). Play therapy: The children's views. *Child and Family Social Work, 7*, 177–187.

Casey, V. (1989). The child in isolation: Treatment or abuse? *Nursing Praxis in New Zealand, 5*, 19–22.

Cash, T. (2004). Body image: Past, present, and future. *Body Image, 1*, 1–5.

Caty, S., Ellerton, M., & Ritchie, J. (1984). Coping in hospitalized children: An analysis of published case studies. *Nursing Research, 33*, 277–282.

Cella, D. F., & Tulsky, D. S. (1995). Methods and problems in measuring quality of life. *Supportive Care in Cancer, 3*, 11–22.

Center of Development. (n.d.). *Sensory integration.* Retrieved from http://developmental-delay .com/page.cfm/250, April 15, 2010.

Centers for Disease Control and Prevention. (2000). *Injury prevention and control.* Retrieved from www.cdc.gov/traumaticbraininjury/assessing_outcomes_in_children.html.

Centers for Disease Control and Prevention/National Center for Health Statistics [CDC/ NCHS]. (2009a). *Deaths by 10-year age groups: United States and each state, 1999–2006.* Retrieved from http://www.cdc.gov/nchs/nvss/mortality/gmwk23f.htm.

Centers for Disease Control and Prevention/National Center for Health Statistics [CDC/ NCHS]. (2009b). *Infant, neonatal, and postneonatal deaths, percent of total deaths, and mortality rates for the 15 leading causes of infant death by race and sex: United States, 2006.* Retrieved from www.cdc.gov/nchs/data/dvs/LCWK7_2006.pdf.

Centers for Disease Control and Prevention/National Center for Health Statistics [CDC/ NCHS]. (2009c). *Deaths, percent of total deaths, and death rates for the 15 leading causes of death in selected age groups, by race and sex: United States, 2006.* Retrieved from www.cdc.gov/nchs/data/dvs/LCWK3_2006.pdf.

Chamlin, S. (2006). The psychosocial burden of childhood atopic dermatitis. *Dermatologic Therapy, 19*, 104–107.

Chang, C., Ritter, K., & Hays, D. (2005). Multicultural trends and toys in play therapy. *International Journal of Play Therapy, 14*(2), 69–85.

Child Health Corporation of America Nursing Falls Study Task Force. (2009). Pediatric falls: State of the science. *Pediatric Nursing, 35*(4), 227–231.

Children and Stroke. (2006). Retrieved from www.st-johns.org/services/stroke_center/Children .aspx.

Christ, G. (2000). *Healing children's grief: Surviving a parent's death from cancer.* New York: Oxford University Press.

Christie, W., & Moore, C. (2005). The impact of humor on patients with cancer. *Clinical Journal of Oncology Nursing, 9*(2), 211–218.

Chundamala, J., Wright, J., & Kemp, S. (2009). An evidence-based review of parental presence during anesthesia induction and parent/child anxiety. *Canadian Journal of Anaesthesia, 56*(1), 57–60.

Cioni, G., Fazzi, B., Ipata, A., Canapicchi, R., & van Hof-van Duin, J. (1996). Correlation between cerebral visual impairment and magnetic resonance imaging in children with neonatal encephalopathy. *Developmental Medicine & Child Neurology, 38*, 120–132.

Clatworthy, S. (1981). Therapeutic play: Effects on hospitalized children. *Children's Health Care, 9*(4), 108–113.

Collins, S., & Kuck, K. (1991). Music therapy in the neonatal intensive care unit. *Neonatal Network, 9*, 23–26.

The Compassionate Friends. (2006). *When a child dies: 2006 survey.* Retrieved from www .compassionatefriends.org/pdf/When_a_Child_Dies-2006_Final.pdf.

The Compassionate Friends. (2009a). *Adults grieving the death of a sibling*. Retrieved from www .compassionatefriends.org/Brochures/adults_grieving_the_death_of_a_sibling.aspx.

The Compassionate Friends. (2009b). *When a brother or sister dies*. Retrieved www .compassionatefriends.org/Brochures/when_a_brother_or_sister_dies.aspx.

Coyne, I. (2006). Children's experiences of hospitalization. *Journal of Child Health Care, 10*(4), 326–336.

Crider, C. (1981). Children's conceptions of the body interior. In R. Bibace & M. Walsh (Eds.), *New directions for child development. Children's conceptions of health, illness, and bodily functions, no. 14* (pp. 49–65). San Francisco: Jossey-Bass.

Crisis Prevention Institute (CPI). (2009). *The art of setting limits*. Brookfield, WI: CPI.

Crisp, J., Ungerer, J., & Goodnow, J. (1996). The impact of experience on children's understanding of illness. *Journal of Pediatric Psychology, 21*(1), 57–72.

Crocker, E., (1978). Play programs in pediatric settings. In E. Gellert (Ed.), *Psychosocial aspects of pediatric care* (pp. 95–110). New York: Grune & Stratton.

Cullen, K., Hall, M., & Golosinskly, A. (2009). *Ambulatory surgery in the United States, 2006*. National Health Statistics Reports, no. 11. Revised. Hyattsville, MD: National Center for Health Statistics.

Currier, J., Hermes, S., & Phipps, S. (2009). Brief report: Children's response to serious illness: Perceptions of benefit and burden in a pediatric cancer population. *Journal of Pediatric Psychology, 34*(10), 1129–1134.

Daboo, J. (2007). Michael Chekhov and the embodied imagination: Higher self and non-self. *Studies in Theatre and Performance, 27*(3), 261–273.

Darwin, C. (1872). *The expression of the emotions in man and animals*. New York: D. Appleton and Company.

Davalos, S. (1999). *Making sense of art: Sensory-based art activities for children with autism, Asperger syndrome, and other pervasive developmental disorders*. Shawnee Mission, KS: Autism Asperger Publishing Company.

Davison, K., Markey, C., & Birch, L. (2000). Etiology of body dissatisfaction and weight concerns among 5-year-old girls. *Appetite, 35*, 143–151.

Denham, S. A. (1998). Emotional development in young children. *The Guildford Series on Social and Emotional Development, 2*, 19–57.

Denholm, G. (1990). Memories of adolescent hospitalization: Results from a 4-year follow-up study. *Children's Health Care, 19*(2), 101–105.

Dewis, M. (1989). Spinal cored injured adolescents and young adults: The meaning of body changes. *Journal of Advanced Nursing, 14*, 389–396.

D'Hondt, E., Deforche, B., De Bourdeaudhuij, I., & Lenoir, M. (2008). Childhood obesity affects fine motor skill performance under different postural constraints. *Neuroscience Letters, 440*(1), 72–75.

Diaz-Caneja, A., Gledhill, J., Weaver, T., Nadel, S., & Garralds, E. (2005). A child's admission to hospital: A qualitative study examining the experiences of parents. *Intensive Care Medicine. 31*(9), 1248–1254.

Dickinson, H. O., Parkinson, K. N., Ravens-Sieberer, U., Schirripa, G., Thyen, U., Arnaud, C., . . . Colver, A. (2007). Self-reported quality of life of 8–12-year-old children with cerebral palsy: A cross-sectional European study. *Lancet, 369*, 2171–2178.

Dixon, S. D., & Stein, M. T. (2006). *Encounters with children: Pediatric behavior and development* (4th ed.). St. Louis, MO: Mosby.

Dohnt, H., & Tiggemann, M. (2005). Peer influences on body dissatisfaction and dieting awareness in young girls. *British Journal of Developmental Psychology, 23*, 103–116.

Doka, K. (1995). *Children mourning: Mourning children*. Washington, DC: Hospice Foundation of America.

Dowling, J. (2002). Humor: A coping strategy for pediatric patients. *Pediatric Nursing, 28*(2), 123–131.

Dowling, J., Hockenberry, M., & Gregory, R. (2003). Sense of humor, childhood cancer stressors, and outcomes of psychosocial adjustment, immune function, and infection. *Journal of Pediatric Oncology Nursing, 20*(6), 271–292.

Drewes, A. (2005). Play in selected cultures: Diversity and universality. In Gil, E., & Drewes, A. (Eds.), *Cultural issues in play therapy* (pp. 26–71). New York: Guilford Press.

Duff, A. (2003). Incorporating psychological approaches into routine paediatric venipuncture. *Archives of Disease in Childhood, 88*, 931–937.

Eating Disorder Treatment Center. (2009). *Distorted body image.* Retrieved from www.edtreatmentcenters.com/distorted-body-image.php.

Elkin, T. D., Phipps, S., Mulhern, R. K., & Fairclough, D. (1997). Psychological functioning of adolescent and young adult survivors of pediatric malignancy. *Medical and Pediatric Oncology, 29*, 582–588.

Ellerton, M., Caty, S., & Ritchie, J. (1985). Helping young children master intrusive procedures through play. *Children's Health Care, 13*, 167–173.

Ellinwood, E. H., & Hamilton, J. G. (1991). Case report of a needle phobia. *Journal of Family Practice, 32*, 420–423.

Elliott, C., Adams, R. J., & Sockalingam, S. (1999). *Summary of normative communication styles and values. Multicultural toolkit.* Retrieved from www.awesomelibrary.org/multiculturaltoolkit-styleschart.html.

Emshoff, J. G., & Anyan, L. L. (1991). From prevention to treatment. Issues for school-aged children of alcoholics. *Recent Developments in Alcoholism, 9*, 327–346.

Engel-Yeger, B., & Kasis, A. (2010). The relationship between developmental co-ordination disorders, child's perceived self-efficacy and preference to participate in daily activities. *Child: Care, Health and Development, Early view.* Retrieved from http://0-www3.interscience.wiley.com.library.lausys.georgetown.edu/cgi-bin/fulltext/123353973/PDFSTART.

Erikson, E. H. (1950). *Childhood and society.* New York: Norton.

Ethier, A. (2005). Death-related sensory experiences. *Journal of Pediatric Oncology Nursing, 22*(2), 104–111.

Family and Community Development Committee. (2005). *Inquiry into issues relating to the development of body image among young people and associated effects on their health and well-being.* Melbourne, Australia: Author. Retrieved from www.parliament.vic.gov.au/fcdc/inquiries/body_image/FCDC-Report_BodyImage_2005-07.pdf.

Farley, L., DeMaso, S., D'Angelo, E., Kinnamon, C., Bastardi, H., Hill, C., . . . Logan, D. (2007). Parenting stress and parental post-traumatic stress disorder in families after pediatric heart transplantation. *Journal of Heart and Lung Transplantation, 26*(2), 120–126.

Favara-Scacco, C., Smirne, G., Schilirò, G., & DiCataldo, A. (2001). Art therapy as support for children with leukemia during painful procedures. *Medical and Pediatric Oncology, 36*(4), 474–480.

Fels, D., Waalen, J. K., Zhai, S., & Weiss, P. (2001). Telepresence under exceptional circumstances: Enriching the connection to school for sick children. In *Proceedings of IFIP INTERACT01: Human-Computer Interaction 2001* (pp. 617–624). Tokyo, Japan: IFIP Technical Committee No. 13 on Human-Computer Interaction.

Fernandes, S., & Arriaga, P. (2010). The effects of clown intervention on worries and emotional responses in children undergoing surgery. *Journal of Health Psychology, 15*(3), 405–415.

Fillingim, R. (2000). Sex, gender, and pain: Women and men really are different. *Current Review of Pain, 4*(1), 24–30.

Findler, L. (2000). The role of grandparents in the social support system of mothers of children with a physical disability. *Families in Society, 81*(4), 370–381.

Fiorino, E., & Brooks, L. (2009). Obesity and respiratory diseases in childhood. *Clinics in Chest Medicine, 30*(3), 601–608.

Fisher, D., & Fisher, C. (2007, July 23). Magic touch: Rehabbracadabra. *ADVANCE for Occupational Therapy Practitioners, 23*(15), 14–18.

Fleitas, J. (2000). When Jack fell down . . . Jill came tumbling after: Siblings in the web of illness and disability. *MCN, The American Journal of Maternal/Child Nursing, 25*(5), 267–273.

Fleming, P., & Blair, P. (2007). Sudden infant death syndrome and parental smoking. *Early Human Development, 83*, 721–725.

Flores, G. (2000). Culture and the patient-physician relationship: Achieving cultural competency in health care. *Journal of Pediatrics, 136*(1), 14–23.

Forgie, S., Reitsma, J., Spady, D., Wright, B., & Stobart, K. (2009). The 'fear factor' for surgical masks and face shields, as perceived by children and their parents. *Pediatrics, 124*(4), e777–e781.

Foster, R. L., Yucha, C. B., Zuck, J., & Vojir, C. P. (2003). Physiologic correlates of comfort in healthy children. *Pain Management Nursing, 4*(10), 23–30.

Frankenfield, P. (1996). The power of humor and play as nursing interventions for a child with cancer: A case report. *Journal of Pediatric Oncology Nursing, 13*(1), 15–20.

Franzini, L. (2002). *Kids who laugh.* Garden City Park, NY: Square One Publishers.

Friedman, S., Munir, K., & Erickson, M. (2006). *Anxiety disorder: Specific phobia.* eMedicine from WebMD. Retrieved from www.emedicine.com/ped/topic2659.htm.

Gale Encyclopedia of Medicine. (2008). Farmington Hills, MI: The Gale Group.

Gaynard, L., Wolfer, J., Goldberger, J., Thompson, R., Redburn, L., & Laidley, L. (1990). *Psychosocial care of children in hospitals: A clinical practice manual from the ACCH Child Life Research Project.* Bethesda, MD: Association for the Care of Children's Health.

Gentschel, D., & McLaughlin, F. (2000). Attention deficit hyperactivity disorder as a social disability: Characteristics and suggested methods of treatment. *Journal of Developmental and Physical Disabilities, 12*, 333–347.

Gerik, S. (2005). Pain management in children: Developmental considerations and mind-body therapies. *Southern Medical Journal, 98*(3), 295–302.

Gibson, P. G., Simpson, J. L., Chalmers, A. C., Toneguzzi, R. C., Wark, P. A., Wilson, A. J., & Hensley, M. (2001). Airway eosinophilia is associated with wheeze but is uncommon in children with persistent cough and frequent chest colds. *American Journal of Respiratory and Critical Care Medicine, 164*, 977–981.

Gibson, S., & Chambers, C. (2004). Pain over the life span: A developmental perspective. In F. Hakjistavropoulos & K. Craig (Eds.), *Pain: Psychological perspectives* (pp. 113–154). Hillsdale, NJ: Erlbaum.

Gil, E. (2005). From sensitivity to competence in working across cultures. In E. Gil & A. Drewes (Eds.), *Cultural issues in play therapy* (pp. 1–25). New York: Guilford Press.

Gilbert, S., & Thompson, J. (2002). Body shame in childhood & adolescence. In P. Gilbert & J. Miles (Eds.), *Body shame.* Hove, UK: Brunner-Routledge.

Gilfoyle, E., & Grady, A.P. (1971). Cognitive-perceptual-motor behaviour. In S. Clare & S. Helen (Eds.), *Occupational therapy* (pp. 401–479). Philadelphia: JB Lippincott Company.

Gillis, A. (1989). The effect of play on immobilized children in hospital. *International Journal of Nursing Studies, 26*(3), 261–269.

Gilmer, M. (2010). Parental grief and mourning. In A. Ethier, J. Rollins, & J. Stewart (Eds.), *Pediatric oncology palliative and end-of-life care resource* (pp. 117–120). Glenview, IL: Association of Pediatric Hematology/Oncology Nurses.

Gilovich, T. (1991). *How we know what isn't so: The fallibility of human reason in everyday life.* New York: Free Press.

Gilroy, B. D. (2001). Using magic therapeutically with children. In H. Kaduson & C. E. Schaefer (Eds.), *101 more favorite play therapy techniques* (pp. 429–437). Northvale, NJ: Jason Aronson, Inc.

Glazebrook, C., McPherson, A. C., Macdonald, I. A., Swift, J., Ramsay, C., Newbould, R., & Smyth, A. (2006). Asthma as a barrier to children's physical activity: Implications for body mass index and mental health. *Pediatrics, 118,* 2443–2449.

Glover, G. (1999). Multicultural consideration in group play therapy. In D. S. Sweeney & L. E. Homeyer (Eds.), *The handbook of group play therapy* (pp. 278–295). San Francisco: Jossey-Bass.

Gold, J., Kim, S., Kant, A., Joseph, M., & Rizzo, A. (2006). Effectiveness of virtual reality for pediatric pain distraction during IV placement. *CyberPsychology & Behavior, 9*(2), 207–212.

Goldman, J., Salus, M., Wolcott, D., & Kennedy, K. (2003). *A coordinated response to child abuse and neglect: The foundation for practice.* Washington, DC: USDHHS, Office on Child Abuse and Neglect.

Goldstein, A. (1980). Thrills in response to music and other stimuli. *Physiological Psychology, 8,* 126–129.

Greaves, R. (1996). Visual expression for the child in hospital. *Children in Hospital, 22*(1), 9–11.

Green, M. (2007). *Self-expression.* Oxford, UK: Oxford University Press.

Grey, M., Cameron, M. E., & Thurber, F. W. (1991). Coping and adaptation in children with diabetes. *Nursing Research, 40,* 144–149.

Grinyer, A. (2007). *Young people living with cancer: Implications for policy and practice.* London: Open University Press.

Groenendaal, F., & van Hof-van Duin, J. (1992). Visual deficits and improvements in children after perinatal hypoxia. *Journal of Visual Impairment and Blindness, 86,* 215–218.

Guzzetta, A., Cioni, G., Cowan, F., & Mercuri, E. (2001). Visual disorders in children with brain lesions: Maturation of visual function in infants with neonatal brain lesions: Correlation with neuroimaging. *European Journal of Paediatric Neurology, 5,* 107–114.

Hadders-Algra, M. (2000). The neuronal group selection theory: Promising principles for understanding and treating developmental motor disorders. *Developmental Medicine & Child Neurology, 42,* 707–715.

Hagan, J. Jr., & the Committee on Psychosocial Aspects of Child and Family Health and the Task Force on Terrorism. (2005). Psychosocial implications of disaster or terrorism on children: A guide for the pediatrician. *Pediatrics, 116,* 787–795.

Hagberg, B., Hagberg, G., Olow, I., & Von Wendt, L. (1996). The changing panorama of cerebral palsy in Sweden. VII. Prevalence and origin in the birth year period 1987–1990. *Acta Paediatrica, 85,* 954–60.

Hall, E. (2004a). A double concern: Grandmothers' experiences when a small grandchild is critically ill. *Journal of Pediatric Nursing, 19*(1), 61–69.

Hall, E. (2004b). A double concern: Danish grandfathers' experiences when a small grandchild is critically ill. *Intensive and Critical Care Nursing, 20,* 14–21.

Halterman, J., Kaczorowski, J., Aligne, C., Auinger, P., & Szilagyi, P. (2001). Iron deficiency and cognitive achievement among school-aged children and adolescents in the United States. *Pediatrics, 107*(6) 1381–1386.

Hamilton, J. (1995). Needle phobia: A neglected diagnosis. *Journal of Family Practice, 2,* 169–175.

Hammar, G., Ozolins, A., Idvall, E., & Rudebeck, C. (2009). Body image in adolescents with cerebral palsy. *Journal of Child Health Care, 13*(1), 19–29.

Hart, D., & Bossert, E. (1994). Self-reported fears of hospitalized school-age children. *Journal of Pediatric Nursing, 9*(2), 83–90.

Hart, R., & Walton, M. (2010). Magic as a therapeutic intervention to promote coping in hospitalized pediatric patients. *Pediatric Nursing, 36*(1), 11–16.

Harter, S. (1983). The development of the self system. In M. Hetherington (Ed.), *Handbook of child psychology: Social and personality development: Vol. 4* (pp. 276–385). New York: Wiley.

Harter, S. (1988). *Manual for the self-perception profile for adolescents*. Denver, CO: University of Denver.

Harter S. (1993). Causes and consequences of low self-esteem in children and adolescents. In R. F. Baumeister (Ed.), *Self-esteem: The puzzle of low self-regard* (pp. 87–116). New York: Plenum Press.

Harter, S. (1999). *The construction of the self: A developmental perspective*. New York: Guilford Press.

Harter, S., & Pike, R. (1984). The pictorial scale of perceived competence and social acceptance for young children. *Child Development, 55*, 1969–1982.

Harvey, D. H. P., & Greenway, A. P. (1984). The self-concept of physically handicapped children and their non-handicapped siblings: An empirical investigation. *The Journal of Child Psychology and Psychiatry, 25*, 273–284.

Hass, J. K., & Walter, T. (2006). Parental grief in three societies: Networks and religion as social supports in mourning. *Omega-Journal of Death & Dying, 54*, 179–198.

Hayes, V., & Kjiox, J. (2006). The experience of stress in parents of children hospitalized with long-term disabilities. *Journal of Advanced Nursing, 9*(4), 333–341.

Healing of Magic. (2008). *Information for the therapists*. Retrieved from www.magictherapy.com/therapists.html.

Heimlich, T., Westbrook, L., Austin, J., Cramer, J., & Devinsky, O. (2000). Brief report. Adolescents' attitudes toward epilepsy: Further validation of the child attitude toward illness scale (CATIS). *Journal of Pediatric Psychology, 25*, 339–345.

Heiney, S. P., Dunaway, N. C., & Webster, J. (1995). Good grieving—an intervention program for grieving children. *Oncology Nursing Forum, 22*(4), 649–655.

Heiney, S. P., & Lesesne, C. A. (1996). Quest. An intervention program for children whose parent or grandparent has cancer. *Cancer Practice, 4*(6), 324–329.

Helgadottir, H., & Wilson, M., (2004). Temperament and pain in 3- to 7-year-old children undergoing tonsillectomy. *Journal of Pediatric Nursing, 19*(3), 204–213.

Helgeson, V. S., Reynolds, K. A., & Tomich, P. L. (2006). A meta-analytic review of benefit finding and growth. *Journal of Consulting and Clinical Psychology, 74*, 797–816.

Herbrecht, E., & Poustka, F. (2007). Frankfurt group social communication and interaction skills training for children and adolescents with autism spectrum disorders. *Zeitschrift fur Kinder-und Jugendpsychiatrie und Psychoteraple, 35*(1), 33–40.

Hicks, M., & Davitt, K. (2009). Chronic illness and rehabilitation. In R. Thompson (Ed.), *The handbook of child life: A guide for pediatric psychosocial care* (pp. 257–286). Springfield, IL: Charles C. Thomas.

Hinman, C. (2003). Multicultural considerations in the delivery of play therapy services. *International Journal of Play Therapy, 12*(2), 107–122.

Hockenberry, M., & Wilson, D. (2007). *Wong's nursing care of infants and children* (8th ed.). St Louis: Mosby Elsevier.

Hoffman, H., Patterson, D., Seibel, E., Soltani, M., Jewett-Leahy, L., & Sharar, S. (2000). Virtual reality as an adjunctive pain control during burn would care in adolescent patients. *Pain, 85*, 305–309.

Hoffman, L. (1998). Cross cultural differences in child rearing goals. *New Directions in Child Development, 40*, 99–102.

Holmbeck, G. (2002). A developmental perspective on adolescent health and illness: An introduction to the special issues. *Journal of Pediatric Psychology, 27*, 409–415.

Holt, K., & Ricciardelli, L. (2008). Weight concerns among elementary school children: A review of prevention programs. *Body Image, 5*(3), 233–243.

Holub, S. (2008). Individual differences in the anti-fat attitudes of preschool-children: The importance of perceived body size. *Body Image, 5*(3), 317–321.

Howe, M. C., & Schwartzberg, S. L. (2001). *A functional approach to group work in occupational therapy* (3rd ed.). Philadelphia: J.B. Lippincott/Williams.

Hudson, J. (2006). *Prescription for success: Supporting children with autism spectrum disorders in the medical environment*. Shawnee Mission, KS: Autism Asperger Publishing Company.

Huitt, W. (2009). *Self-concept and self-esteem. Educational Psychology Interactive.* Valdosta, GA: Valdosta State University. Retrieved from www.edpsycinteractive.org/topics/regsys/self.html.

Hutton, A. (2002). The private adolescent: Privacy needs of adolescents in hospitals. *Journal of Pediatric Nursing, 17*(1), 67–72.

Hutton, A. (2003). Activities in the adolescent ward environment. *Contemporary Nurse, 14,* 312–319.

Hyde, N. D. (1971). Play therapy—The troubled child's self encounter. *American Journal of Nursing, 71,* 1366–1370.

Hyson, M. C. (1994). *The emotional development of young children: Building an emotion-centered curriculum.* New York: Teachers College Press.

Iannelli, V. (2010). *Child abuse statistics.* Retrieved from http://pediatrics.about.com/od/childabuse/a/05_abuse_stats.htm.

Ittyerah, M., & Sharma, R. (1997). The performance of hearing-impaired on handedness and perceptual motor tasks. *Genetic, Social, and General Psychology Monographs, 123*(3), 285–302.

Janssen, I., Craig, W. M., Boyce, W. F., & Pickett, W. (2004). Associations between overweight and obesity with bullying behaviors in school-aged children. *Pediatrics, 113,* 1187–1194.

Jay, S., Elliott, C., Ozlins, M., Olson, R., & Pruitt, S. (1985). Behavioral management of children's distress during painful medical procedures. *Behavior Research and Therapy, 23,* 513–520.

Jee, S., Conn, K., Nilsen, W., Szilagyi, M., Forbes-Jones, E., & Halterman, J. (2008). Learning difficulties among children separated from a parent. *Ambulatory Pediatrics, 8*(3), 163–168.

Jemta, L., Dahl, M., Fugl-Meyer, K. S., & Stensman, R. (2005). Well-being among children and adolescents with mobility impairment in relation to demographic data and disability characteristics. *Acta Paediatra, 94,* 616–623.

Jemta, L., Fugl-Meyer, K., Oberg, K., & Dahl, M. (2009). Self-esteem in children and adolescents with mobility impairment: Impact on well-being and coping strategies. *Acta Paediatrica, 98,* 567–572.

Jessee, P., & Gaynard, L. (2009). Paradigms of play. In R. Thompson (Ed.), *The handbook of child life* (pp. 136–159). Springfield, IL: Charles C. Thomas and Sons.

Jessee, P., Wilson, H., & Morgan, D. (2000). Medical play for young children. *Childhood Education, 76,* 215–218.

Johnson, B. (Producer). (1975). *To prepare a child* [Film]. Washington, DC: Children's National Medical Center.

Johnson, L. (2005). Cultural influences in children's health care. In J. Rollins, R. Bolig, & C. Mahan (Eds.), *Meeting children's psychosocial needs across the health-care continuum* (pp. 421–453). Austin, TX: ProEd.

Johnston, C., Stevens, B., Yang, F., & Horton, L. (1995). Differential response to pain by very premature neonates. *Pain, 61*(3), 471–479.

Johnstone, L., Spence, D., & Koziol-McClain, J. (2010). Oral hygiene care in the pediatric intensive care unit: Practice recommendations. *Pediatric Nursing, 36*(2), 85–96.

Joint Commission. (2007). *The Joint Commission national patient safety goals.* Retrieved from www.jointcommission.org/PatientSafety/NationalPatientSafetyGoals/05_cah_npsgs.htm.

Joint Commission on Accreditation of Healthcare Organizations (JCAHO). (2001). *Comprehensive accreditation manual for hospitals* (CAMH). Oakbrook, IL: JCAHO.

Jones, D. (1994). Effect of parental participation on hospitalized child behavior. *Issues in Comprehensive Pediatric Nursing, 17*(2), 81–92.

Joseph, A., Keller, A., & Kronick, K. (2008). Transforming care in children's hospitals through environmental design: Literature review. In *Evidence for innovation: Transforming children's health through the physical environment* (pp. 18–95). Alexandria, VA: National Association of Children's Hospitals and Related Institutions.

Kaemingk, K., Carey, M., Moore, I., Herzer, M., & Hutter, J. (2004). Math weakness in survivors of acute lymphoblastic leukemia compared to healthy children. *Child Neuropsychology, 10*(1), 14–23.

Kain, Z., Caldwell-Andrews, A., Mayes, L., Wang, S., Krivutza, D., & LoDolce, M. (2003). Parental presence during induction of anesthesia: Physiological effects on parents. *Anesthesiology, 98*, 56–64.

Kain, Z., Mayes, L., Wang, S., & Hofstadter, M. (1999). Postoperative behavioral outcomes in children: Effects of sedative premedication. *Anesthesiology, 90*, 758–765.

Kalish, C. (1996). Causes and symptoms in preschoolers' conceptions of illness. *Child Development, 67*, 1647–1670.

Karling, M., Stenlund, H., & Hagglof, B. (2007). Child behaviour after anaesthesia: Associated risk factors. *Acta Paediatrica, 96*(5), 740–747.

Kashani, J., Nair, S., Rao, V., Nair, J., & Reid, J. (1996). Relationship of personality, environmental, and DICA variables to adolescent hopelessness: A neural network sensitivity approach. *Journal of the American Academy of Child and Adolescent Psychiatry, 35*(5), 640–645.

Kaslow, N., & Eicher, V. (1988). Body image therapy: A combined creative arts therapy and verbal psychotherapy approach. *Arts in Psychotherapy, 15*(3), 177–188.

Kaufman, R. (2002). *David Copperfield's Project Magic handbook*. Canada: David Copperfield's Project Magic Fund.

Kazak, A. E., Alderfer, M., Rourke, M. T., Simms, S., Streisand, R., & Grossman, J. R. (2004). Posttraumatic stress disorder (PTSD) and posttraumatic stress symptoms (PTSS) in families of adolescent childhood cancer survivors. *Journal of Pediatric Psychology, 29*, 211–219.

Kazak, A. E., Boeving, C. A., Alderfer, M. A., Hwang, W., & Reilly, A. (2005). Posttraumatic stress symptoms during treatment in parents of children with cancer. *Journal of Clinical Oncology, 23*, 7405–7410.

Kearney-Cooke, A. (2002). Familial influences on body image development. In T. Cash & T. Pruzinsky (Eds.), *Body image: A handbook of theory, research and clinical practice* (pp. 99–107). New York: Guilford Press.

Kellerman, J., Zeltzer, L., Ellenberg, L., Dash, J., & Rigler, D. (1980). Psychological effects of illness in adolescence. I. Anxiety, self-esteem, and perception of control. *Journal of Pediatrics, 97*, 126–131.

Kernic, M., Holt, V., Wolf, M., McKnight, B., Huebner, C., & Rivara, F. (2002). Academic and school health issues among children exposed to maternal intimate partner abuse. *Archives of Pediatrics & Adolescent Medicine, 156*(6), 549–555.

Kettwich, S., Sibbitt, W., Brandt, J., Johnson, C., Wong, C., & Bankhurst, A. (2007). Needle phobia and stress-reducing medical devices in pediatric and adult chemotherapy patients. *Journal of Pediatric Oncology Nursing, 24*(1), 20–28.

Kieckhefer, G., & Trahms, C. (2000). Supporting development of children with chronic conditions: From compliance toward shared management. *Pediatric Nursing, 26*(4). 354–363.

Kister, M. C., & Patterson, C. J. (1980). Children's conceptions of the causes of illness. Understanding contagion and the use of immanent justice. *Child Development, 51*, 839–846.

Klass, D., Silverman, P., & Nickman, S. (1996). *Continuing bonds: New understanding of grief*. Philadelphia: Taylor & Francis.

Klein, A. (Ed.). (2003). *Humor in children's lives: A guidebook for practitioners*. Westport, CT: Praeger.

Koenig, K., Chesla, C. A., & Kennedy, C. M. (2003). Parents' perspectives of asthma crisis hospital management in infants and toddlers: An interpretive view through the lens of attachment theory. *Journal of Pediatric Nursing. 18*(4), 233–243.

Koller, D. (2008a). *Child Life Council Evidence-based Practice Statement: Child life assessment: Variables associated with a child's ability to cope with hospitalization.* Retrieved from www.childlife.org/files/EBPAssessmentStatement-Complete.pdf.

Koller, D. (2008b). *Child Life Council Evidence-based Practice Statement: Therapeutic play in pediatric health care: The essence of child life practice.* Retrieved from www.childlife.org/files/EBPPlayStatement-Complete.pdf.

Koller, D., Nicholas, D., Goldie, R., Gearing, R., & Selkirk, E. (2006). Bowlby and Robertson revisited: The impact of isolation on hospitalized children during SARS. *Developmental and Behavioral Pediatrics, 27*(2), 134–140.

Koopman, H., Baars, R., Chaplin, J., & Zwinderman, K. (2004). Illness through the eyes of the child: The development of children's understanding of the causes of illness. *Patient Education and Counseling, 55*, 367–368.

Kristensen, K. L. (1995). The lived experience of childhood loneliness: A phenomenological study. *Issues in Comprehensive Pediatric Nursing, 18*, 125–137.

Kury, S., & Rodrigue, J. (1995). Concepts of illness causality in a pediatric sample. Relationship to illness duration, frequency of hospitalization, and degree of life-threat. *Clinical Pediatrics, 34*(4), 178–182.

Kushner, H. (1983). *When bad things happen to good people.* New York: Schocken Books.

Kuttner, L. (1996). *A child in pain.* Vancouver, Canada: Hartley & Marks.

Kyle, T. (2008). *Essentials of pediatric nursing.* Philadelphia: Lippincott Williams & Wilkins.

LaMontagne, L. L., Hepworth, J. T., Johnson, B. D., & Cohen, F. (1996). Children's preoperative coping and its effects on postoperative anxiety and return to normal activity. *Nursing Research, 45*(3), 141–147.

LaMontagne, L. L., Johnson, J. E., Hepworth, J. T., & Johnson, B. D. (1997). Attention, coping, and activity in children undergoing orthopaedic surgery. *Research in Nursing & Health, 20*, 487–494.

Langlois, J., Rutland-Brown, W., & Thomas, K. (2006). *Traumatic brain injury in the United States: Emergency department visits, hospitalization, and deaths.* Atlanta, GA: Centers for Disease Control and Prevention, National Center for Injury Prevention and Control.

Larouche, S., & Chin-Peuckert, L., (2006). Changes in body image experienced by adolescents with cancer. *Journal of Pediatric Oncology Nursing, 23*, 200–209.

Latimer, E. (1978). Play is everybody's business in the children's ward. *Nursing Mirror, 147*, 21–24.

Lau, R., Bernard, R., & Hartman, K. (1989). Further explorations of common-sense representations of common illnesses. *Health Psychology, 8*, 195–219.

Lazarus, R. S., & Folkman, S. (1984). *Stress, appraisal, and coping.* New York: Springer.

Lee, E., Menkart, D., & Okazawa-Rey, M. (1998). *Beyond heroes and holiday: A practical guide to K–12 anti-racist, multicultural education and staff development.* Washington, DC: Network of Educators on the Americas.

Lerner, M. (1971). The observer's evaluation of a victim: Justice, guilt and veridical perception. *Journal of Personality and Social Psychology, 20*, 127–135.

Lewis, P. (2007). Portrait of the patient as a young man: An exploration of the use of photographs in hospital. *Journal of Bioethical Enquiry, 4*(1), 51–55.

Lewis, P., Kerridge, I., & Jorden, C. (2009). Creating space: Hospital bedside displays as facilitators of communication between children and nurses. *Journal of Child Health Care, 13*(2), 93–100.

Lin, H., & Tsai, J. (2008). A study of the process by which a school-age child adapted to body image changes following open-heart surgery. *Hu Li Za Zhi*, *53*(5), 84–92.

Litman, J. A., & Spielberger, C. D. (2003). Measuring epistemic curiosity and its diversive and specific components. *Journal of Personality Assessment*, *80*, 75–86.

Lynch, A., Kashikar-Zuck, S., Goldschneider, K., & Jones, B. (2007). Sex and age differences in coping styles among children with chronic pain. *Journal of Pain and Symptom Management*, *33*(2), 208–216.

Lynch, J. (2004). Cerebrovascular disorders in children. *Current neurology and neuroscience reports*, *4*(2), 129–138.

Mabe, P. A., Treiber, F. A., & Riley, W. T. (1991). Examining emotional distress during pediatric hospitalization for school-aged children. *Children's Health Care*, *20*(3), 162–169.

MacLeod, K., Whitsett, S., Mash, E., & Pelletier, W. (2003). Pediatric sibling donors of successful and unsuccessful hematopoietic stem cell transplants (HSCT): A qualitative study of their psychosocial experience. *Journal of Pediatric Psychology*, *28*(4), 223–230.

Majnemer, A., Riley, P., Shevell, M., Birnbaum, R., Greenstone, H., & Coates, A. L. (2000). Severe bronchopulmonary dysplasia increases risk for later neurological and motor sequelae in preterm survivors. *Developmental Medicine & Child Neurology*, *42*, 53–60.

Manimala, M., Blount, R., & Cohen, L. (2009). The effects of parental reassurance versus distraction on child distress and coping during immunizations. *Child Health Care*, *29*, 161–177.

Maunder, R., Hunter, J., Vincent, I., Bennett, J., Peladeau, N., Leszcz, M.,... Mazzulli, T. (2003). SARS outbreak in a teaching hospital. *Canadian Medical Association Journal*, *168*(10), 1245–1251.

Mauro, T. (2009). *Autism spectrum disorders*. Retrieved from http://specialchildren.about.com/od/gettingadiagnosis/g/Autism.htm.

Mazurek Melnyk, B. M., & Feinstein, N. F. (2001). Mediating functions of maternal anxiety and participation in care on young children's posthospital adjustment. *Research in Nursing & Health*, *24*, 18–26.

McCabe, M., Ricciardelli, L., & Ridge, D. (2006). Who thinks I need a perfect body? Perceptions and internal dialogue among adolescents about their bodies, *Sex Roles*, *55*(5–6), 409–419.

McCallie, M., Blum, C., & Hood, C. (2006). Progressive muscle relaxation. *Journal of Human Behavior in the Social Environment*, *13*(3), 51–66.

McCaul, K., & Malott, J. (1984). Distraction and coping with pain. *Psychological Bulletin*, *95*, 516–533.

McClowry, S. (1990). The relationship of temperament to pre- and post-hospitalization behavioral responses of school-age children. *Nursing Research*, *39*(1), 30–35.

McClowry, S. (1991). Behavioral disturbances among medically hospitalized school-age children. *Journal of Child and Adolescent Psychiatric Nursing*, *4*(2), 62–67.

McCormick, M. C., McCarton, C., Tonascia, J., & Brooks-Gunn, J. (1993). Early educational intervention for very low birth weight infants: Results from the Infant Health and Development Program. *Journal of Pediatrics*, *123*, 527–533.

McCue, K. (1988). Medical play: An expanded perspective. *Children's Health Care*, *16*(3), 157–161.

McGhee, P. (1979). *Humor: Its origin and development*. San Francisco: W. H. Freeman.

McGhee, P., & Chapman, A. (Eds.). (1980). *Children's humor*. Chichester, UK: Wiley.

McGoldrick, M., Giordano, J., & Garcia-Presto, N. (2005). Overview: Ethnicity and family therapy. In M. McGoldrick, J. Giordano, & N. Garcia-Presto (Eds.), *Ethnicity and family therapy* (3rd ed.) (pp. 1–30). New York: Guilford Press.

McGrath, P. (2005). Children—not simply 'little adults.' In H. Merskey, J. Loeser, & R. Dubner (Eds.), *The paths of pain 1975–2005* (pp. 433–446). Seattle, WA: IASP Press.

McGrath, P., & Hillier, L. (Eds.). (2001). *The child with headache: Diagnosis and treatment (Progress in Pain Research and Management, Vol. 19)*. Seattle: IASP Press.

McGrath, P., & Huff, N. (2001). What is it?: Findings on preschoolers' responses to play with medical equipment. *Child: Care, Health & Development, 27*(50), 451–462.

McKay, K., & Halperin, J. (2001). ADHD, aggression, and antisocial behavior across the lifespan: Interactions with neurochemical and cognitive function. *Annals of the New York Academy of Sciences, 931*, 84–96.

McMurtry, C., Chambers, C., McGrath, P., & Asp, E. (2010). When 'don't worry' communicates fear: Children's perceptions of parental reassurance and distraction during a painful medical procedure. *Pain, 150*(1), 52–58.

Mechanic, D. (1979). The stability of health and illness behavior: Results from a 16-year follow-up. *American Journal of Public Health, 69*, 1142–1145.

Meeks, R. (2009). Parental presence in pediatric trauma resuscitation: One hospital's experience. *Pediatric Nursing, 35*(6), 376–380.

Melamed, B. (1982). Reeducation of medical fears: An information processing analysis. In J. Boulougouris (Ed.), *Learning theory approaches to psychiatry* (pp. 205–218). New York: Wiley.

The Merck Manual. (2009). *Physical growth*. Retrieved from www.merck.com/mmpe/sec19/ch269/ch269b.html, April 4, 2010.

Merriam-Webster. (n.d.). *Aggression*. Retrieved from www.merriam-webster.com/dictionary/aggression, March 20, 2010.

Merskey, H., & Bogduk, N. (Eds.). (1994). *IASP Task Force on Taxonomy classification of chronic pain* (2nd ed.). (pp. 209–214). Seattle, WA: International Association for the Study of Pain.

Meyerowitz, B. (1980). Psychological correlates of breast cancer and its treatments. *Psychological Bulletin, 87*, 108–131.

Meyers, A., & Cahwla, N. (2000). Nutrition and the social, emotional, and cognitive development of infants and young children. *Zero to Three, 21*(1), 5–12.

Miles, M., & Carter, M. (1982). Sources of parental stress in pediatric intensive care units. *Children's Health Care, 11*, 65–69.

Miller, L. (2005). International adoption, behavior, and mental health. *The Journal of the American Medical Association, 293*(20), 2533–2535.

Miller, L. (2006). *Sensational kids: Hope and help for children with sensory processing disorder*. New York: Putnam.

Miller, S. (1991). Monitoring and blunting in the face of threat: Implications for adaptation and health. In L. Montada, S. Filipp, & M. Lerner (Eds.), *Life crises and experiences of loss in adulthood* (pp. 255–273). Englewood Cliffs, NJ: Erlbaum.

Miller, S., Fang, C., Diefenbach, M., & Bales, C. (2001). Tailoring psychosocial interventions to the individual's health information-processing style. In A. Baum & B. Anderson (Eds.), *Psychosocial interventions for cancer* (pp. 343–362). Washington, DC: American Psychological Association.

Miyahara, M., & Piek, J. (2006). Self-esteem of children and adolescents with physical disabilities: Quantitative evidence from meta-analysis. *Journal of Developmental and Physical Disabilities, 18*, 219–234.

Morison, S., Grunau, R., Oberlander, T., & Whitfield, M. (2001). Relations between behavioral and cardiac autonomic reactivity to acute pain in preterm neonates. *Clinical Journal of Pain, 17*(4), 350–358.

Mossman, B. (2004). How I do it: Using walkie-talkies to overcome the fear of separation in children having surgery. *ORL—Head and Neck Nursing, 22*(2), 21–22.

Motacki, K., & Motacki, L. (2009). Safe patient handling and movement in a pediatric setting. *Pediatric Nursing, 35*(4), 221–225.

Mott, S. (1999). Chronic conditions: Intervention strategies. In M. Broome & J. Rollins (Eds.), *Core curriculum for the nursing care of children and their families* (pp. 305–317). Pitman, NJ: Jannetti Publications, Inc.

Mulderij, K. (1996). Research into the lifeworld of physically disabled children. *Child: Care, Health and Development*, *22*(5), 311–322.

Mulderij, K. (2000). Dualistic notions about children with motor disabilities. Hands to lean on or to reach out? *Qualitative Health Research 10*(1), 39–50.

Murnen, S., & Smolak, L. (2000). The experience of sexual harassment among grade-school students: Early socialization of female subordination? *Sex Roles*, *43*, 1–17.

Muscari, M. (2007). *What can I do to help patients with belonephobia (fear of needles)?* Retrieved from www.medscape.com/viewarticle/555513, March 13, 2010.

Musher-Eizenman, D., Holub, S., Miller, A., Goldstein, S., & Edwards-Leeper, L. (2004). Body size stigmatization in preschool children: The role of control attributions. *Journal of Pediatric Psychology*, *29*(8), 613–620.

National Center for Children Exposed to Violence. (2005). *Parents' guide in helping children in the wake of disaster*. New Haven, CT: Author.

National Center on Birth Defects and Developmental Disabilities. (2006). *Monitoring developmental disabilities*. Centers for Disease Control and Prevention. Retrieved from www.cdc.gov/ncbddd/dd/ddsurv.htm.

National Information Center for Children and Youth with Disabilities. (1997). *General information about emotional disturbance*. Retrieved from www.kidsource.com/NICHCY/emotional.disab .k12.2.html.

National Institute of Mental Health. (2008). *Helping children and adolescents cope with violence and disasters: What community members can do*. Bethesda, MD: Author.

National Institute of Neurological Disorders and Stroke. (2002). *Traumatic brain injury: Hope through research* (NIH Publication No. 02-158). Bethesda, MD: National Institutes of Health.

Neff, E. J., & Beardslee, C. I. (1990). Body knowledge and concerns of children with cancer as compared with the knowledge and concerns of other children. *Journal of Pediatric Nursing*, *5*(3), 179–189.

Nehring, W. (1999). Chronic conditions: The continuum of care. In M. Broome & J. Rollins (Eds.), *Core curriculum for the nursing care of children and their families* (pp. 331–341). Pitman, NJ: Jannetti Publications, Inc.

New York State Education Department. (2003). *Guide for determining eligibility and special education programs and/or services for preschool students with disabilities*. Retrieved from www.vesid.nysed .gov/specialed/publications/preschool/guide/eligibdeter.htm#motor.

Nicholas, D., Darch, J., McNeill, T., Brister, L., O'Leary, K., Berlin, D., & Koller, D. (2007). Perceptions of online support for hospitalized children and adolescents. *Social Work in Health Care*, *44*(3), 205–223.

Nicholas, D., Swan, S., Gerstle, T., Allan, T., & Griffiths, A. (2008). Struggles, strengths, and strategies: An ethnographic study exploring the experiences of adolescents living with an ostomy. *Health and Quality of Life Outcomes*, *6*, 114.

Nizam, M., & Norzila, M. Z. (2001). Stress among parents with acutely ill children. *Medical Journal of Malaysia*, *56*, 428–434.

Nurit Bird, D. (2004). Illness-images and joined being. A critical/Nayaka perspective on intercorporeality. *Social Anthropology*, *12*(3), 325–339.

Oatley, K. (1992). *Best laid schemes: The psychology of emotions*. Cambridge, UK: Cambridge University Press.

O'Connor, K. (1997). Ecosystemic play therapy. In K. O'Connor, & L. Braverman (Eds.), *Play therapy theory and practice: A comparative presentation*. (pp. 234–284). New York: Wiley.

O'Dea, J. A. (2006). Self-concept, self-esteem and body weight in adolescent females: A 3-year longitudinal study. *Journal of Health Psychology, 11*, 599–611.

Odetola, F. (2009). Assessing the functional status of hospitalized children. *Pediatrics, 124*, e163–e165.

Okagaki, L., & Divecha, D., (1993). Development of parent beliefs. In T. Luster & L. Okagaki (Eds.), *Parenting: An ecological perspective* (pp. 35–68). Mahwah, NJ: Erlbaum.

Olmsted, M., Colton, P., Daneman, D., Rydall, A., & Rodin, F. (2008). Prediction of the onset of disturbed eating behavior in adolescent girls with type 1 diabetes. *Diabetes Care, 31*(10), 1978–1982.

Olson, C. (1999). Acute conditions: The continuum of care. In M. Broome & J. Rollins (Eds.), *Core curriculum for the nursing care of children and their families* (pp. 215–221). Pitman, NJ: Jannetti Publications, Inc.

Olsson, C., Bond, L., Johnson, M., Forer, D., Boyce, M., & Sawyer S. (2003). Adolescent chronic illness: A qualitative study of psychosocial adjustment. *Annals, Academy of Medicine Singapore, 32*(1), 43–50.

Onyskiw, J., & Hayduk, L. (2004). Processes underlying children's adjustment in families characterized by physical aggression. *Family Relations, 50*(4), 376–385.

Oremland, E. K., & Oremland, J. D. (2000). *Protecting the emotional development of the ill child: The essence of the child life profession.* Madison, CT: Psychosocial Press.

Owen, P., Thompson, J., Elixhauser, A., & Ryan, J. (2003). *Care of children and adolescents in U.S. hospitals.* Rockville, MD: Agency for Healthcare Research and Quality.

Pachter, L. (1994). Culture and clinical care: Folk illness beliefs and behaviors and their implications for health care delivery. *Journal of the American Medical Association. 271*(9), 690–694.

Packman, W., Beck, V., VanZutphen, K., Long, J., & Spengler, G. (2003). The human figure drawing with donor and nondonor siblings of pediatric bone marrow transplant patients. *Art Therapy: Journal of the American Art Therapy Association, 20*(2), 83–91.

Pao, M., Ballard, E., & Rosenstein, D. (2007). Growing up in the hospital. *Journal of the American Medical Association, 297*(24), 2752–2755.

Patton, A., Ventura, J., & Savedra, M. (1986). Stress and coping responses of adolescents with cystic fibrosis. *Children's Health Care, 14*(3), 153–156.

Paxton, S. (2002). *An overview of body image dissatisfaction prevention interventions.* Retrieved from www.health.vic.gov.au/healthpromotion/downloads/research_review.pdf.

Pearson, L. (1999). Separation, loss, and bereavement. In M. Broome & J. Rollins (Eds.), *Core curriculum for the nursing care of children and their families* (pp. 77–92). Pitman, NJ: Jannetti Publications, Inc.

Pearson, L. (2005). Children's hospitalization and other health-care encounters. In J. Rollins, R. Bolig, & C. Mahan (Eds.), *Meeting children's psychosocial needs across the health-care continuum* (pp. 1–41). Austin, TX: ProEd.

Pearson, L. (2009). Child life interventions in critical care and at the end of life. In R. Thompson (Ed.), *The handbook of child life* (pp. 220–237). Springfield, IL: Charles C. Thomas.

Pediatric Advisor. (2009). *Helping children swallow medicines.* Retrieved from www.med.umich.edu/1libr/pa/pa_swallmed_hhg.htm.

Pediatric Oncology Resource Center. *How to get kids to take....pills!* Retrieved from www.acor.org/ped-onc/treatment/pills/pills.html.

Pennebaker, J. (1997). *Opening up: The healing power of expressing emotions.* New York: Guilford Press.

Perquin, C., Hazebroek-Kampschreur, A., Hunfeld, J., Bohnen, A., va Suijlekom-Smit, L., Passchier, J., & va der Wouden, J. (2000). Pain in children and adolescents: A common experience. *Pain, 87*(1), 51–58.

Perrin, E. C., & Gerrity, P. S. (1981). There's a demon in your belly: Children's understanding of illness. *Pediatrics, 67*, 841–849.

Peterson, L. (1989). Coping by children undergoing stressful medical procedures: Some conceptual, methodological, and therapeutic issues. *Journal of Consulting and Clinical Psychology, 57*, 380–387.

Phipps, S., Brenner, M., Heslop, H., Krance, R., Jayawardene, D., & Mulhern, R. (1995). Psychological effects of bone marrow transplantation on children and adolescents: Preliminary report of a longitudinal study. *Bone Marrow Transplant, 15*, 829–835.

Phipps, S., Dunavant, M., Srivastava, D. K., Bowman, L., & Mulhern, R. (2000). Cognitive and academic functioning in survivors of pediatric bone marrow transplantation. *Journal of Clinical Oncology, 18*, 1004–1011.

Phipps, S., & Srivastava, D. K. (1997). Repressive adaptation in children with cancer. *Health Psychology, 16*, 521–528.

Phipps, S., & Steele, R. (2002). Repressive adaptive style in children with chronic illness. *Psychosomatic Medicine, 64*, 34–42.

Piaget, J. (1952). *The origins of intelligence in children.* New York: International Universities Press.

Piaget, J. (1965). *The moral judgment of the child.* London: Kegan, Paul, Trench, Trubner. (Original work published 1932.)

Piaget, J., & Inhelder, B. (1969). *The psychology of the child.* New York: Basic Books.

Pianosi, P. T., & Davis, H. S. (2004). Determinants of physical fitness in children with asthma. *Pediatrics, 113*(3 Pt 1), e225–e229.

Pidgeon, V. A. (1966). Deprivation: Barriers to nurse-patient communication. Children's concepts of the rationale of isolation technique. In *ANA clinical sessions* (pp. 21–27). New York: Appleton-Century-Crofts.

Pine, D. S., & Cohen, J. A. (2002). Trauma in children and adolescents: Risk and treatment of psychiatric sequelae. *Biological Psychiatry, 51*, 519–531.

Pinto-Martin, J. A., Whitaker, A. H., Feldman, J. F., Van Rossem, R., & Paneth, N. (2000). Relation of cranial ultrasound abnormalities in low-birthweight infants to motor or cognitive performance at ages 2, 6, and 9 years. *Developmental Medicine & Child Neurology, 41*, 826–833.

Pira, T., Hayes, B., Goodenough, B., & Von Baeyer, C. (2006). Effects of attentional direction, age, and coping style on cold-pressor pain in children. *Behaviour Research and Therapy, 44*(6), 835–848.

Plank, E. (1971). *Working with children in hospitals: A guide for the professional team* (2nd ed.). Chicago: Year Book.

Pledge, D. (n.d.). *Support groups.* Retrieved from www.minddisorders.com/Py-Z/Support-groups.html.

Pollack, H. (2001). Sudden infant death syndrome, maternal smoking during pregnancy, and the cost-effectiveness of smoking cessation intervention. *American Journal of Public Health, 91*, 432–436.

Powazek, M., Goff, J., Schyving, J., & Paulson, M. (1978). Emotional reactions of children to isolation in a cancer hospital. *Journal of Pediatrics, 92*, 834–837.

Powers, S., Mitchell, M., Byars, K., Bentti, A., Lecates, S., & Hershey, A. (2001). A pilot study of one-session biofeedback training in pediatric headache. *Neurology, 56*, 133.

Prugh, D. (1955). Investigations dealing with reactions of children and families to hospitalization and illness: Problems and potentialities. In G. Caplan (Ed.), *Emotional problems of early childhood.* New York: Basic Books.

Puhl, R. M., & Latner, J. D. (2007). Stigma, obesity and the health of the nation's children. *Psychological Bulletin, 113*, 557–580.

Quinton, D., & Rutter, M. (1976). Early hospital admissions and later disturbances of behavior: An attempted replication of Douglas' findings. *Developmental Medicine and Child Neurology*, *18*, 447–459.

Raman, L., & Winer, G. (2002). Children's and adults' understanding of illness: Evidence in support of a coexistence model. *Genetic, Social, and General Psychology Monographs*, *128*, 325–355.

Rappaport, D., Cellucci, M., & Leffler, M. (2010). Implementing a family-centered rounds: Pediatric residents' perceptions. *Clinical Pediatrics*, *49*(3), 228–234.

Reasoner, R. (1983). Enhancement of self-esteem in children and adolescents. *Family & Community Health*, *6*, 51–64.

Reed, P., Smith, P., Fletcher, M., & Bradding, A. (2003). Promoting the dignity of the child in hospital. *Nursing Ethics*, *10*(1), 67–76.

Reio, T., Petrosko, J., Wiswell, A., & Thongsukmag, J. (2006). The measurement and conceptualization of curiosity. *The Journal of Genetic Psychology*, *167*(2), 117–135.

Reiter-Purtill, J., & Noll, R. (2003). Peer relationships of children with chronic illness. In M. Roberts (Ed.), *Handbook of pediatric psychology* (pp. 176–193). New York: Guilford Press.

Rennick, J., & Rashotte, J. (2009). Psychological outcomes in children following pediatric intensive care unit hospitalization: A systematic review of the research. *Journal of Child Health Care*, *13*(2), 128–149.

Rennick, J. E., Johnston, C. C., Dougherty, G., Platt, R., & Ritchie, J. A. (2002). Children's psychological responses after critical illness and exposure to invasive technology. *Developmental and Behavioral Pediatrics*, *23*(3), 133–144.

Rennick, J. E., Morin, I., Kim, D., Johnston, C. C., Dougherty, G., & Platt, R. (2004). Identifying children at high risk for psychological sequelae after pediatric intensive care unit hospitalization. *Pediatric Critical Care Medicine*, *5*(4), 358–363.

Rhee, H., Wenzel, J., & Steeves, R. (2007). Adolescents' psychosocial experiences living with asthma: A focus group study. *Journal of Pediatric Health Care*, *21*(2), 99–107.

Ricciardelli, L. A., & McCabe, M. P. (2001). Children's body image concerns and eating disturbance: A review of the literature. *Clinical Psychology Review*, *21*(3), 325–344.

Rice, C. (2009). Prevalence of autism spectrum disorders-Autism and developmental disabilities monitoring network, United States, 2006. *Morbidity and Mortality Weekly Report*, *58*(SS-10). Retrieved from http://www.cdc.gov/ncbddd/autism/data.html.

Ritchie, J., Caty, S., & Ellerton, M. (1984). Concerns of acutely ill, chronically ill, and healthy preschool children. *Research in Nursing and Health*, *7*, 265–274.

Ritter, K., & Chang, C. (2002). Play therapists' self-perceived multicultural competence and adequacy of training. *International Journal of Play Therapy*, *11*(1), 103–113.

Roberts, C. (2010). Unaccompanied hospitalized children: A review of the literature and incidence study. *Journal of Pediatric Nursing* *25*(6), 470–476.

Roberts, S. (2008). Meeting the personal hygiene needs of a hospitalized child. *British Journal of Healthcare Assistants*, *2*(5), 214–216.

Robertson, I. (1999). *Mind sculpture: Your brain's untapped potential*. London: Bantam Press.

Robertson, J. (1958). *Young children in hospitals*. New York: Basic Books.

Robinson, J. R., Rankin, J. L., & Drotar, D. (1996). Quality of attachment as a predictor of maternal visitation to young hospitalized children. *Journal of Pediatric Psychology*, *21*, 401–417.

Robinson, M., Gangon, C., Dannecker, R., Brown, J., Jump, R., & Price, D. (2003). Sex differences in common pain events: Expectations and anchors. *Journal of Pain*, *4*(1), 40–45.

Rodriguez, M. A., Winkleby, M. A., Ahn, D., Sundquist, J., & Kraemer, H. C. (2002). Identification of population subgroups of children and adolescents with high asthma prevalence: Findings from the Third National Health and Nutrition Examination Survey. *Archives of Pediatric and Adolescent Medicine*, *156*, 269–275.

Rodriguez, S. (1992). *The special artist's handbook: Art activities and adaptive aids for handicapped students.* Palo Alto, CA: Dale Seymour Publications.

Roesch, S., Weiner, B., & Vaughn, A. (2002). Cognitive approaches to stress and coping. *Current Opinion in Psychiatry, 15*(6), 627–632.

Rollins, J. (1990). Childhood cancer: Siblings draw and tell. *Pediatric Nursing, 16*(1), 21–27.

Rollins, J. (1991). Assisting with therapeutic play. In D. Smith (Ed.), *Comprehensive child and family nursing skills* (pp. 70–77). St. Louis, MO: Mosby Year Book.

Rollins, J. (1997). Minimizing the impact of community violence on child witnesses. *Critical Care Nursing Clinics of North America, 9*(2), 211–219.

Rollins, J. (2005a). The arts in children's health-care settings. In J. Rollins, R. Bolig, & C. Mahan (Eds.), *Meeting children's psychosocial needs across the health-care continuum* (pp. 119–174). Austin, TX: ProEd.

Rollins, J. (2005b). Tell me about it: Drawing as a communication tool for children with cancer. *Journal of Pediatric Oncology Nursing, 22*(4), 2005, 203–221.

Rollins, J. (2008). Arts for children in hospitals: Helping put the 'art' back in medicine. In B. Warren (Ed.), *Using the creative arts in therapy and healthcare* (3rd ed.) (pp. 181–195). East Sussex, UK: Routledge.

Rollins, J. (2009). The influence of two hospitals' designs and policies on social interaction and privacy as coping factors for children with cancer and their families. *Journal of Pediatric Oncology Nursing, 26*(6), 340–353.

Rollins, J., & Mahan, C. (2010). *From artist to artist-in-residence: Preparing artists to work in pediatric healthcare settings* (2nd ed.). Washington, DC: Rollins & Associates.

Rosen, A. B., & Rozin, P. (1993). Now you see it . . . now you don't: The preschool child's conception of invisible particles in the context of dissolving. *Developmental Psychology, 29*, 300–311.

Rossol, M. (2001). *The artist's complete health and safety guide.* New York: Allworth Press.

Rumsey, N., & Harcourt, D. (2007). Visible difference amongst children and adolescents: Issues and interventions. *Developmental Neurorehabilitation, 10*(2), 113–123.

Russo, R. N., Miller, M. D., Haan, E., Cameron, I. D., & Crotty, M. (2008). Pain characteristics and their association with quality of life and self-concept in children with hemiplegic cerebral palsy identified from a population register. *Clinical Journal of Pain, 24*, 335–342.

Rusy, L., & Weisman, S. (2000). Complementary therapies for acute pediatric pain management. *Pediatric Clinics of North American, 47*, 589–599.

Ryan, N. (1989). Stress-coping strategies identified from school-age children's perspective. *Research in Nursing & Health, 12*, 111–122.

Ryan-Wenger, N. (1992). A taxonomy of children's coping strategies: A step toward theory development. *American Journal of Orthopsychiatry, 62*(2), 256–263.

Ryan-Wenger, N. A. (1996). Children, coping, and the stress of illness: A synthesis of the research. *Journal of the Society of Pediatric Nursing, 1*(3), 126–138.

Rylance, G. (1999). Privacy, dignity and confidentiality: Interview study with structured questionnaire. *British Medical Journal, 318*(7179), 301.

Said, I., Salleh, S., Abu Bakar, M., & Mohamad, I. (2005). Caregivers' evaluation on hospitalized children's preferences concerning garden and ward. *Journal of Asian Architecture and Building Engineering, 4*, 331–338.

Sallfors, C., Hallberg, L., & Fasth, A. (2003). Gender and age differences in pain, coping and health status among children with chronic arthritis. *Clinical and Experimental Rheumatology, 21*(6), 785–793.

Salmela, M., Salanterä, S., & Aronen, E. (2009). Child-reported hospital fears in 4- to 6-year-old children. *Pediatric Nursing, 35*(5), 269–276, 303.

Savedra, M., & Tesler, M. (1981). Coping strategies of hospitalized school-age children. *Western Journal of Nursing Research*, *3*, 371–384.

Sands, E. R., & Wardle, J. (2003). Internalization of ideal body shapes in 9-12-year-old girls. *International Journal of Eating Disorders*, *33*(2), 193–204.

Saylor, C. F. (1993). Introduction: Children and disasters: Clinical and research issues. In C.F. Saylor (Ed.), *Children and disasters* (pp. 1–10). New York: Plenum Press.

Scanlon, J. (1991). Appreciating neonatal pain. *Advances in Pediatrics*, *38*, 317–331.

Schmidt, L., & Frohling, H. (2000). Lay concepts of health and illness from a developmental perspective. *Psychology and Health*, *15*, 229–238.

Sensory Processing Disorder Foundation. (n.d.). *About SPD*. Retrieved from www.spdfoundation .net/about-sensory-processing-disorder.html.

Shagena, M., Sandler, H., & Perrin, E. (1988). Concepts of illness and perception of control in healthy children and in children with chronic illness. *Journal of Developmental and Behavioral Pediatrics*, *9*, 252–256.

Shapiro, J. (1983). Family reactions and coping strategies in response to the physically ill or handicapped child: A review. *Social Science and Medicine*, *7*, 913–931.

Shapland, D. (2006). What does health have to do with transition? Everything! *Parent Brief*, 1–5. Retrieved from http://www.ncset.org/publications/parent/NCSETParent_May06 .pdf.

Sharrer, V., & Ryan-Wenger, N. (1991). Measurements of stress and coping among school-aged children with and without recurrent abdominal pain. *Journal of School Health*, *61*, 86–91.

Shaw, E. G., & Routh, D. K. (1982). Effect of mother presence on children's reaction to aversive procedures. *Journal of Pediatric Psychology*, *7*(1), 33–42.

Shepley, M. (2005). The healthcare environment. In J. Rollins, R. Bolig, & C. Mahan (Eds.), *Meeting children's psychosocial needs across the health-care continuum* (pp. 313–349). Austin, TX: ProEd.

Sherman, A., Simonton, S., Latif, U., Nieder, M., Adams, R., & Mehta, P. (2004). Psychosocial supportive care for children receiving stem cell transplantation: Practice patterns across centers. *Bone Marrow Transplantation*, *34*, 169–174.

Sherman, A. C., Simonton, S., & Latif, U. (2004). Quality of life outcomes and psychosocial adjustment following pediatric stem cell transplantation. In P. Mehta (Ed.), *Pediatric stem cell transplantation* (pp 99–115). Boston: Jones & Bartlett.

Shields, N., Loy, Y., Murdoch, A., Taylor, N. F., & Dodd, K. J. (2007). Self-concept of children with cerebral palsy compared with that of children without impairment. *Developmental Medicine & Child Neurology*, *49*, 350–354.

Shipman, K., & Taussig, H. (2009). Mental health treatment of child abuse and neglect: The promise of evidence-based practice. *Pediatric Clinics of North America*, *56*, 417–428.

Shweder, R. A., Much, N. C., Mahapatra, M., & Park, L. (1997). The 'big three' of morality (autonomy, community, divinity) and the 'big three' explanations of suffering. In A. Brand & P. Rozin (Eds.), *Morality and health* (pp. 119–169). New York: Routledge.

Siaw, S., Stephens, L., & Holmes, S. (1986). Knowledge about medical instruments and reported anxiety in pediatric surgery patients. *Children's Health Care*, *14*(3), 134–141.

Siegal, M. (1988). Children's knowledge of contagion and contamination as causes of illness. *Child Development*, *59*, 1353–1359.

Siegal, M., Patty, J., & Eiser, C. (1990). A re-examination of children's conceptions of contagion. *Psychology and Health*, *4*, 159–165.

Siegler, R. (1994). Cognitive variability: A key to understanding cognitive development. *Current Directions in Psychological Science*, *3*(1), 1–5.

Sieving, R., & Zirbel-Donisch, S. (1990). Development and enhancement of self-esteem in children. *Journal of Pediatric Health Care*, *4*, 290–296.

Simons, R. (1987). *After the tears: Parents talk about raising a child with a disability*. Orlando, FL: Harcourt Brace & Company.

Small, L., & Melnyk, B. M. (2006). Early predictors of post-hospital adjustment problems in critically ill young children. *Research in Nursing & Health, 29,* 622–635.

Smolak, L. (2004). Body image in children and adolescents: Where do we go from here? *Body Image, 1,* 15–28.

Social Security Administration. (2000). *Intermediate assumptions of the 2000 trustees report*. Washington, DC: Office of the Chief Actuary of the Social Security Administration.

Spinetta, J. (1981). The sibling of the child with cancer. In J. Spinetta & P. Deasy-Spinetta (Eds.), *Living with childhood cancer* (pp. 133–142). St Louis, MO: Mosby.

Spirito, A., Stark, L., Gil, K., & Tyc, V. (1995). Coping with everyday and disease-related stressors by chronically ill children and adolescents. *Journal of the American Academy of Child and Adolescent Psychiatry, 34,* 283–290.

Spirito, A., Stark, L., & Tyc, V. (1994). Stressor and coping strategies described during hospitalization by chronically ill children. *Journal of Clinical Child Psychology, 23*(3), 314–322.

Springer, K., & Ruckel, J. (1992). Early beliefs about the cause of illness: Evidence against immanent justice. *Cognitive Development, 7,* 429–443.

State of the Field Committee. (2009). *State of the field report: Arts in healthcare*. Washington, DC: Society for the Arts in Healthcare.

Stevens, M. (1989). Coping strategies of hospitalized adolescents. *Children's Health Care, 18*(3), 163–169.

Steward, M., & Steward, D. (1981). Children's conceptions of medical procedures. In R. Bibace & M. Walsh (Eds.), *New directions for child development: Children's conceptions of health, illness, and bodily function, no. 14* (pp. 67–83). San Francisco: Jossey-Bass.

Stewart, E. J., Algren, C., & Arnold, S. (1994). Preparing children for a surgical experience. *Today's OR Nurse, 16*(2), 9–14.

Stiles, A. (2005). Parenting needs, goals, & strategies of adolescent mothers. *MCN, American Journal of Maternal Child Nursing, 30*(5), 327–333.

Straus, M. (1995). Corporal punishment of children and adult depression and suicide ideation. In J. McCord (Ed.), *Coercion and punishment in long-term perspectives* (pp. 59–77). New York: Cambridge University Press.

Strauss, R. S., & Pollock, H. A. (2003). Social marginalization of overweight children. *Archives of Pediatric and Adolescent Medicine, 157,* 746–752.

Tan, J. (2004). Psychosocial impact of acne vulgaris: Evaluation of the evidence. *Skin Therapy, 9,* 7.

Tanabe, P., Ferket, K., Thomas, R., Paice, J., & Marcantonio, R. (2002). The effect of standard care, ibuprofen, and distraction on pain relief and patient satisfaction in children with musculoskeletal trauma. *Journal of Emergency Nursing, 28*(2), 118–125.

Taussig, H. N., & Culhane, S. E. (2005). *Foster care as an intervention for abused and neglected children*. Kingston, NJ: Civic Research Institute.

Tedeschi, R. G., & Calhoun, L. G. (2004). Post-traumatic growth: Conceptual foundations and empirical evidence. *Psychological Inquiry, 15,* 1–18.

Tesler, M., Wegner, C., Savedra, M., Gibbons, P., & Ward, J. (1981). Coping strategies of children in pain. *Issues in Comprehensive Pediatric Nursing, 5,* 351–359.

Thomas, D., & Gaslin, T. (2001). 'Camping up' self-esteem in children with hemophilia. *Issues in Comprehensive Pediatric Nursing, 24,* 253–263.

Thomas, J., & Thomas, D. (2002). *Kid concoctions and contraptions*. Strongsville, OH: Kid Concoctions Company.

Thompson, R. (1985). *Psychosocial research on pediatric hospitalization and health care: A review of the literature.* Springfield, IL: Charles C. Thomas.

Thompson, R. H., & Vernon, D. T. (1993). Research on children's behavior after hospitalization: A review and synthesis. *Journal of Developmental & Behavioral Pediatrics, 14,* 28–35.

Thurber, C., Patterson, D., & Mount, K. (2007). Homesickness and children's adjustment to hospitalization: Toward a preliminary model. *Children's Healthcare, 36*(1), 1–28.

Thurber, C. A. (1995). The experience and expression of homesickness in preadolescent and adolescent boys. *Child Development, 66,* 1162–1178.

Thurber, C. A. (1999). The phenomenology of homesickness in boys. *Journal of Abnormal Child Psychology, 27,* 125–139.

Thurber, C. A. (2005). Multimodal homesickness prevention in boys spending two weeks at a residential summer camp. *Journal of Consulting and Clinical Psychology, 73,* 555–560.

Thurber, C. A., & Sigman, M. D. (1998). Preliminary models of risk and protective factors for childhood homesickness: Review and empirical synthesis. *Child Development, 69,* 903–934.

Thurber, C. A., Sigman, M. D., Weisz, J. R., & Schmidt, C. K. (1999). Homesickness in preadolescent and adolescent girls: Risk factors, behavioral correlates, and sequelae. *Journal of Clinical Child and Adolescent Psychology, 28,* 185–196.

Thurber, D., Walton, E., & Council on School Health. (2007). Preventing and treating homesickness. *Pediatrics, 119,* 192–201.

Tiedeman, M. E., & Clatworthy, S. (1990). Anxiety responses of 5- to 11-year-old children during and after hospitalization. *Journal of Pediatric Nursing, 5*(5), 334–343.

Tieffenberg, J., Wood, E., Alonso, A., Tossutti, M., & Vicente, M. (2000). A randomized field trial of ACINDES: A child-centered training model for children with chronic illness. *Journal of Urban Health, 77*(2), 280–297.

Tremblay, R. E. (2008). Understanding development and prevention of chronic physical aggression: Towards experimental epigenetic studies. *Philosophical Transactions of the Royal Society of London, Series B: Biological Sciences, 363*(1503), 2613–2622.

Triandis, H. (1987). Collectivism vs. individualism: A reconceptualization of a basic concept in cross-cultural social psychology. In D. C. Bagley & G. K. Verma (Eds.), *Personality, cognition and values: Cross-cultural perspectives of childhood and adolescence.* London: Macmillan.

Troster, H. (1994). Longitudinal study of gross-motor development in blind infants and preschoolers. *Early Child Development and Care, 104,* 61–78.

Turgay, A. (2004). Aggression and disruptive behavior disorders in children and adolescents. *Expert Review of Neurotherapeutics, 4*(4), 623–632.

Twyman, K., Saylor, C., Saia, D., Macias, M., Taylor, L., & Spratt, E. (2010). Bullying and ostracism experiences in children with special health care needs. *Journal of Developmental and Behavioral Pediatrics, 31,* 1–8.

U.S. Census Bureau. (2003). *Grandparents living with grandchildren.* Retrieved from www.census.gov/prod/2003pubs/c2kbr-31.pdf.

U.S. Census Bureau. (2008). *America's families and living arrangements.* Retrieved from www.census.gov/population/www/socdemo/hh-fam/cps2008.html.

U.S. Congress. (2009). *H.R. 2381.* Retrieved from www.govtrack.us/congress/bill.xpd?bill=h111-2381.

U.S. Department of Health and Human Services, Administration for Children & Families. (2000). *The Developmental Disabilities Assistance and Bill of Rights Act of 2000.* Retrieved from http://www.acf.hhs.gov/programs/add/ddact/DDACT2.html.

U.S. Department of Health and Human Services, Administration on Children, Youth and Families [USDHHS, ACYF]. (2009). *Child maltreatment 2007.* Washington, DC: U.S. Government Printing Office.

U.S. Department of Health and Human Services, Substance Abuse and Mental Health Services Administration [USDHHS, SAMHSA]. (2003). *Children's mental health facts: Children and adolescents with mental, emotional, and behavioral disorders.* Retrieved from http://mentalhealth.samhsa.gov/publications/allpubs/CA-0006/default.asp.

United States Department of Agriculture & United States Department of Health and Human Services (1986). *Cross-cultural counseling: A guide for nutrition and health counselors.* Washington, DC: Author.

Urquiza, A., & Winn, C. (1994). *Treatment for abused and neglected children: Infancy to age 18.* Washington, DC: USDHHS.

Vagnoli, L., Caprilli, S., Robiglio, A., & Messeri, A. (2005). Clown doctors as a treatment for preoperative anxiety in children: A randomized, prospective study. *Pediatrics, 116*(4), e563–567.

van Breemen, C. (2009). Using play therapy in paediatric palliative care: Listening to the story and caring for the body. *International Journal of Palliative Nursing, 15*(10), 510–514.

Varni, J., Waldron, S., Gragg, R., Rapoff, M., Bernstein, B., Lindsley, C., & Newcomb, M. (1996). Development of the Waldron/Varni pediatric pain coping inventory. *Pain, 67*(1), 141–150.

Vernon, D., Schulman, J., & Foley, J. (1966). Changes in children's behavior after hospitalization. *American Journal of Diseases of Children, 111*, 581–593.

Verschuur, M. J., Eurelings-Bontekoe, E. H. M., Spinhoven, P., & Duijsens, I. J. (2003). Homesickness, temperament and character. *Personality and Individual Difference, 35*, 757–770.

Vessey, J., & O'Sullivan, P. (2000). A study of children's concepts of their internal bodies: A comparison of children with and without congenital heart disease. *Journal of Pediatric Nursing, 15*(5), 292–298.

Vitiello, B., Behar, D., Hunt, J., Stoff, D., & Ricciuti, A. (1990). Subtyping aggression in children and adolescents. *Journal of Neuropsychiatry & Clinical Neurosciences, 2*, 189–192.

Vize, A. (2010). *Making adaptive equipment the easy way.* Retrieved from www.brighthub.com/education/special/articles/61848.aspx, January 24, 2010.

Vygotsky, L. S. (1962). *Thought and language.* Cambridge, MA: MIT Press.

Vygotsky, L. S. (1978). *Mind in society.* Cambridge, MA: Harvard University Press.

Wallace, M. (2006). *The psychological impact of conditions altering appearance during adolescence.* (Unpublished doctoral dissertation). University of West of England, Bristol, England.

Wallace, M., Harcourt, D., & Rumsey, N. (2007). Adjustment to appearance changes resulting from meningococcal septicaemia during adolescence: A qualitative study. *Development neurorehabilitation, 10*(2), 125–132.

Wang, F., Wild, T., Kipp, W., Kuhle, S., & Veugelers, P. (2009). The influence of childhood obesity on the development of self-esteem. *Health Reports, 20*(2), 21–27.

Wang, T. (2004). Concept analysis of functional status. *International Journal of Nursing Studies, 41*(4), 457–462.

Wardle, J., & Cooke, L. (2005). The impact of obesity on psychological well-being. *Best Practice and Research Clinical Endocrinology and Metabolism, 19*(3), 421–440.

Warren, B. (2007). The fools are come hither: A personal reflection on the work of Fools for Health. *Research in Drama Education, 12*(3), 364–369.

Waters, T. (2007). When is it safe to manually lift a patient? The revised NIOSH Lifting Equation provides support for recommended weight limits. *American Journal of Nursing, 107*(8), 53–58.

Weaver, K., Prudhoe, G., Battrick, C., & Glasper, E. (2007). Sick children's perceptions of clown doctor humour. *Journal of Children's and Young People's Nursing, 1*(8), 359–365.

Weber, M., Fontes Neto, P., Prati, C., Soirefman, M., Mazzotti, N., Barzenski, B., . . . Cestari, T. (2008). Improvement of pruritus and quality of life of children with atopic dermatitis and their families after joining support groups. *Journal of the European Academy of Dermatology & Venereology, 22*(8), 992–997.

Weisman, S., Bernstein, B., & Shechter, N. (1998). Consequences of inadequate analgesia during painful procedures in children. *Archives of Pediatric Adolescent Medicine, 152*, 147–149.

Werner, H. (1948). *Comparative psychology of mental development*. Chicago: Follett Publishing Company.

Werner, H., & Kaplan, B. (1963). *Symbolic formation*. New York: Wiley.

Westenhoefer, J. (2001). Establishing good dietary habits—capturing the minds of children. *Public Health Nutrition, 4*, 125–129.

White, C. (2000). Body image dimensions and cancer: A heuristic cognitive behavioural model. *Psycho-oncology, 9*, 183–192.

Williams, J., & Holmes, C. (2004). Children of the 21st century: Slipping through the net. *Contemporary Nurse, 18*(1–2), 57–66.

Williams, K., & Nida, S. (2009). Is ostracism worse than bullying? In M. J. Harris (Ed), *Bullying, rejection, and peer victimization: A social cognitive neuroscience perspective* (pp. 279–296). New York: Springer.

Williamson, H., Harcourt, D., Halliwell, E., Frith, H., & Wallace, M. (2010). Adolescents' and parents' experiences of managing the psychosocial impact of appearance change during cancer treatment. *Journal of Pediatric Oncology Nursing, 27*(3), 168–175.

Wilson, D., Curry, M., & DeBoer, S. (2007). The child with musculoskeletal or articular dysfunction. In M. Hockenberry & D. Wilson (Eds.), *Wong's nursing care of infants and children* (pp. 1730–1842). St Louis, MO: Mosby.

Wintgens, A., Boileau, B., & Robaey, P. (1997). Posttraumatic stress symptoms and medical procedures in children. *Canadian Journal of Psychiatry, 42*, 611–616.

Wisborg, K., Kesmodel, U., Henriksen, T. B., Olsen, S. F., & Secher, N. J. (2000). A prospective study of smoking during pregnancy and SIDS. *Archives of Disease of Childhood, 83*, 203–206.

Wistrom, B. (2005). Communicating via expressive arts: The natural medium of self-expression for hospitalized children. *Pediatric Nursing, 12*(6), 480–485.

Wolfram, R. W., Turner, E. D., & Philput, C. (1997). Effects of parental presence during young children's venipuncture. *Pediatric Emergency Care, 3*(5), 325–328.

Wong, D., & Baker, C. (1988). Pain in childern: Comparison of assessment scales. *Pediatric Nursing, 14*(1), 9–17.

Woodbridge, S., Buys, L., & Miller, E. (2009). Grandparenting a child with a disability: An emotional rollercoaster. *Australas Journal of Ageing, 28*(1), 37–40.

World Health Organization. (2002). *World report on violence and health*. Geneva: World Health Organization.

World Health Organization. (2010). *Asthma*. Retrieved from www.who.int/mediacentre/factsheets/fs307/en/index.html, March 30, 2010.

Xu, J., Kochanek, K. D., & Tejada-Vera, B. (2009). Deaths: Preliminary data for 2007. *National Vital Statistics Reports, 58*(1). Hyattsville, MD: National Center for Health Statistics.

Yamamoto, L., Olaes, E., & Lopez, A. (2004). Challenges in seizure management: Neurologic versus cardiac emergencies. *Topics in Emergency Medicine, 26*(3), 212–224.

Yim, L. (2006). Belonephobia: A fear of needles. *Australian Family Physician, 25*, 623–624.

Yoos, H., & McMullen, A. (1996). Illness narratives of children with asthma. *Pediatric Nursing, 22*(4), 285–290.

Youngblut, J., Brooten, D., & Kuluz, J. (2005). Parent reactions at 24–48 hrs after a preschool child's head injury. *Pediatric Critical Care Medicine, 6*(5), 550–556.

Youngblut, J., Brooten, D., Blais, K., Hannon, J., Niyonsenga, T. (2009). Grandparent's health and functioning after a grandchild's death. *Journal of Pediatric Nursing.* doi:10.1016/j.pedn.2009.02.021.

Youssef, N., Rosh, J., Loughran, M., Schuckalo, S., Cotter, A., Verga, B., & Mones, R. (2004). Treatment of functional abdominal pain in children with cognitive-behavioral strategies. *Journal of Pediatric Gastroenterology and Nutrition, 39*, 192–196.

Zempsky, W., Cravero, J., & The Committee on Pediatric Emergency Medicine and Section on Anesthesiology and Pain Medicine. (2004). Relief of pain and anxiety in pediatric patients in emergency medical systems. *Pediatrics, 114*(5), 1348–1356.

AUTHOR INDEX

SUBJECT INDEX

Page numbers in *italics* indicate diagrams or illustrations. Page numbers followed by *t* indicate tables.

Author Biographies

Robyn Hart is the Director of Child Life Services at Rush University Medical Center, Chicago, where she has served for more than 20 years. In addition to published articles, she coauthored *Therapeutic Play Activities for Hospitalized Children*, which received 1992 Book-of-the-Year Awards from both *Pediatric Nursing* and the *American Journal of Nursing*. She is a frequent lecturer on pediatric palliative care, therapeutic humor, and other topics related to the psychosocial needs of children and families in healthcare settings.

Ms. Hart has been instrumental in establishing two unique programs that help children cope better with illness and treatment. The first, Snow City Arts, is an internationally recognized artists-in-residence program that uses the arts as a vehicle for self-expression and educational and cultural enrichment. Snow City Arts was a recipient of the President's Coming Up Taller Award in 2006. The second program, Open Heart Magic, is a therapeutic program for sick children designed to enhance self-esteem, provide opportunities for control, and increase socialization. She has served as a board member of both organizations, and continues to participate in the training of all their staff. Ms. Hart was also on the board of directors of the Midwest chapter of the Starlight Foundation.

To improve the hospital experience for adults with intellectual and developmental disabilities, Ms. Hart also designed a multifaceted program that was recognized for its innovation by the Agency for Healthcare Research and Quality. As a result of this work, Ms. Hart received the 2009 Eugene Thonar, PhD Award for diversity leadership. She both writes and lectures on this topic.

Judy Rollins, PhD, RN, researcher and consultant with Rollins & Associates, Inc., is adjunct assistant professor in the Department of Family Medicine, with a secondary appointment in the Department of Pediatrics at Georgetown University School of Medicine, Washington, DC. Also a visual artist and an Ambassador of the Society for the Arts in Healthcare, she has developed arts in healthcare programming for children and families in hospitals, hospice care, and the community; coordinates the Studio G Artists-in-Residence program in Pediatrics at Georgetown; and developed the Allies in the Arts program for Wounded Warriors at Walter Reed Army Medical Center. She also serves on the Wellness Committee for the National Intrepid Center of Excellence, an advanced facility dedicated to the research, diagnosis, and treatment of military personnel and veterans suffering from traumatic brain injury and psychological health issues.

Author of nearly 100 publications, Dr. Rollins is editor for *Pediatric Nursing* and North America regional editor for the Society for the Arts in Healthcare's *Arts & Health: An International Journal for Research, Policy and Practice*. She consults, writes, and researches on children's issues nationally and internationally, with a special interest in the psychosocial needs of children and families in healthcare settings, and the use of the arts in research to allow children's voices to be heard.

In addition to Book of the Year awards from the *American Journal of Nursing* and *Pediatric Nursing*, Dr. Rollins is a recipient of the International Society of Nurses in Cancer Care Research Award, Johnson & Johnson/Society for the Arts in Healthcare Partnership to Promote Arts and Healing Award, National Science Foundation Scholarship, and the Japan Foundation Center for Global Partnership Travel Award.

STUDY PACKAGE
CONTINUING EDUCATION
CREDIT INFORMATION
Therapeutic Activities for Children and Teens Coping with Health Issues

Our goal is to provide you with current, accurate and practical information from the most experienced and knowledgeable speakers and authors.

Listed below are the continuing education credit(s) currently available for this self-study package. *Please note: Your state licensing board dictates whether self study is an acceptable form of continuing education. Please refer to your state rules and regulations.*

COUNSELORS: PESI, LLC is recognized by the National Board for Certified Counselors to offer continuing education for National Certified Counselors. Provider #: 5896. We adhere to NBCC Continuing Education Guidelines. This self-study package qualifies for **3.0** contact hours.

SOCIAL WORKERS: PESI, LLC, 1030, is approved as a provider for continuing education by the Association of Social Work Boards, 400 South Ridge Parkway, Suite B, Culpeper, VA 22701. www.aswb.org. Social workers should contact their regulatory board to determine course approval. Course Level: All Levels. Social Workers will receive **3.0** (Clinical) continuing education clock hours for completing this self-study package.

ADDICTION COUNSELORS: PESI, LLC is a Provider approved by NAADAC Approved Education Provider Program. Provider #: 366. This self-study package qualifies for **3.5** contact hours.

Procedures:

1. Review the material and read the book.

2. If seeking credit, complete the posttest/evaluation form:

   -Complete posttest/evaluation in entirety, including your email address to receive your certificate much faster versus by mail.

   -Upon completion, mail to the address listed on the form along with the CE fee stated on the test. Tests will not be processed without the CE fee included.

   -Completed posttests must be received 6 months from the date printed on the packing slip.

Your completed posttest/evaluation will be graded. If you receive a passing score (70% and above), you will be emailed/faxed/mailed a certificate of successful completion with earned continuing education credits. (Please write your email address on the posttest/evaluation form for fastest response.) If you do not pass the posttest, you will be sent a letter indicating areas of deficiency, and another posttest to complete. The posttest must be resubmitted and receive a passing grade before credit can be awarded. We will allow you to re-take as many times as necessary to receive a certificate.

If you have any questions, please feel free to contact our customer service department at 1.800.844.8260.

PESI LLC
PO BOX 1000
Eau Claire, WI 54702-1000

PO BOX 1000
Eau Claire, WI 54702
800-844-8260

Therapeutic Activities for Children and Teens Coping with Health Issues

Any persons interested in receiving credit may photocopy this form, complete and return with a payment of $15.00 per person CE fee. A certificate of successful completion will be sent to you. To receive your certificate sooner than two weeks, rush processing is available for a fee of $10. Please attach check or include credit card information below.

Mail to: PESI, PO BOX 1000, Eau Claire, WI 54702 or fax to PESI (800) 554-9775 (both sides)

CE Fee: $15: (Rush processing fee: $10)   **Total to be charged** _____

Credit Card #: _____ **Exp Date:** _____ **V-Code*:** _____
(*MC/VISA/Discover: last 3-digit # on signature panel on back of card.) (*American Express: 4-digit # above account # on face of card.)

	LAST	FIRST	M.I.

Name (please print): _____ _____ _____

Address: _____ Daytime Phone: _____

City: _____ State: _____ Zip Code: _____

Signature: _____ Email: _____

Date Completed: _____ Actual time (# of hours) taken to complete this offering: _____hours

Program Objectives After completing this publication, I have been able to achieve these objectives:

1. Discuss the continuum of care.	1. Yes	No
2. Describe children's responses to illness and hospitalization.	2. Yes	No
3. Identify factors that may influence family members' reactions to a child's illness or hospitalization.	3. Yes	No
4. List seven general guidelines for working with children.	4. Yes	No
5. Demonstrate three methods for adapting activities for special populations of children.	5. Yes	No
6. Discuss safety considerations when facilitating activities with children.	6. Yes	No

PESI LLC
PO BOX 1000
Eau Claire, WI 54702-1000

Participant Profile:

1. Job Title: _____ Employment setting: _____

POST-SEMINAR QUESTIONS – Periodically reviewed to assure learner outcomes.

1. In what age group is separation anxiety the primary source of stress?
a. 0 to 6 months.
b. 6 months to 3 years.
c. 3 to 5 years.
d. 5 to 9 years.

2. When talking to children about their creative endeavors, which of the following statements can undermine the joy of the experience?
a. "Would you like to tell me about your drawing?"
b. "What is it?"
c. "What an interesting way you are using your crayons."
d. "I like that you are not afraid to try new things."

3. Which of the following are risk factors for low self-esteem?
a. Being chronically ill.
b. Abuse and neglect.
c. Being bullied or ostracized.
d. Corporal punishment.
e. All of the above.

4. Children of what age become aware of the ideal body for their gender?
a. Toddlers.
b. Preschool.
c. School-age.
d. Adolescents.

5. Group interaction and socialization is especially important for which age group?
a. Toddlers.
b. Preschool.
c. School-age.
d. Adolescence.

6. Medial play includes which of the following types?
a. Role rehearsal/role reversal.
b. Medical fantasy play.
c. Indirect medical play.
d. Medically related art.
e. All of the above.

7. When considering aggressive tension releasing activities, which of the following statements are true?
a. Aggressive tension-reducing activities are appropriate for all children.
b. Adults need to feel comfortable with noise and aggressive acts directed at the materials used in the activities.
c. An appropriate location for aggressive tension releasing activities must be identified.
d. a and b.
e. b and c.

8. Children in which of the following stages of cognitive development tend to respond best to riddles?
a. Sensorimotor.
b. Preoperational.
c. Concrete operations.
d. Formal operations.

9. At what age do children begin to understand the concept of death?
a. 3 to 5 years.
b. 6 to 9 years.
c. 10 to 12 years.
d. Adolescents.

10. Children from which culture have a tendency to be quiet and play in a more self-contained mode, rather than be interactive?
a. African American.
b. Hispanic American.
c. Asian American.
d. Native American.

PESI LLC
PO BOX 1000
Eau Claire, WI 54702-1000

About the CD-ROM

Introduction

This appendix provides you with information on the contents of the CD that accompanies this book. For the latest information, please refer to the ReadMe file located at the root of the CD.

System Requirements

A computer with a processor running at 120 Mhz or faster

- At least 32 MB of total RAM installed on your computer; for best performance, we recommend at least 64 MB
- A CD-ROM drive

Note: Many popular word processing programs are capable of reading Microsoft Word files. However, users should be aware that a slight amount of formatting might be lost when using a program other than Microsoft Word.

Using the CD with Windows

To install the items from the CD to your hard drive, follow these steps:

1. Insert the CD into your computer's CD-ROM drive.
2. The CD-ROM interface will appear. The interface provides a simple point-and-click way to explore the contents of the CD.

If the opening screen of the CD-ROM does not appear automatically, follow these steps to access the CD:

1. Click the Start button on the left end of the taskbar and then choose Run from the menu that pops up.
2. In the dialog box that appears, type **d:\start.exe**. (If your CD-ROM drive is not drive d, fill in the appropriate letter in place of *d*.) This brings up the CD Interface described in the preceding set of steps.

Using the CD With a MAC

Insert the CD into your computer's CD-ROM drive.

The CD-ROM icon appears on your desktop, double-click the icon.

Double-click the Start icon.

The CD-ROM interface will appear. The interface provides a simple point-and-click way to explore the contents of the CD.

Note for Mac users: the content menus may not function as expected in newer versions of Safari and Firefox; however, the documents are available by navigating to the Contents folder.

What's on the CD

The following sections provide a summary of the software and other materials you'll find on the CD.

Content

This book's accompanying CD contains tables that expand upon introductory material as well as nearly 300 activities and activity templates in Word format so that users can easily customize and reproduce them as needed. These evidence-based, age-appropriate activities provide useful ideas for interventions that promote coping, and are specifically designed for working with children within the healthcare system. These activities are organized to correspond to the book's chapters, which target specific topics for children in healthcare situations, such as separation anxiety, self-esteem issues, body image, death, isolation, and pain. The activities can be quickly read and readily implemented in a variety of settings such as hospitals, ambulatory clinics, homes, schools, community agencies, and camps.

Applications

The following applications are on the CD:

OpenOffice.org. OpenOffice.org is a free multi-platform office productivity suite. It is similar to Microsoft Office or Lotus SmartSuite, but OpenOffice.org is absolutely free. It includes word processing, spreadsheet, presentation, and drawing applications that enable you to create professional documents, newsletters, reports, and presentations. It supports most file formats of other office software. You should be able to edit and view any files created with other office solutions.

Shareware programs are fully functional, trial versions of copyrighted programs. If you like particular programs, register with their authors for a nominal fee and receive licenses, enhanced versions, and technical support.

Freeware programs are copyrighted games, applications, and utilities that are free for personal use. Unlike shareware, these programs do not require a fee or provide technical support.

GNU software is governed by its own license, which is included inside the folder of the GNU product. See the GNU license for more details.

Trial, demo, or evaluation versions are usually limited either by time or functionality (such as being unable to save projects). Some trial versions are very sensitive to system date changes. If you alter your computer's date, the programs will "time out" and no longer be functional.

Customer Care

If you have trouble with the CD-ROM, please call the Wiley Product Technical Support phone number at (800) 762-2974. Outside the United States, call 1(317) 572-3994. You can also contact Wiley Product Technical Support at http://support.wiley.com. John Wiley & Sons will provide technical support only for installation and other general quality control items. For technical support on the applications themselves, consult the program's vendor or author.

To place additional orders or to request information about other Wiley products, please call (877) 762-2974.